A PLUME

THE ORGANIZ

Daniel J. Levitin, PhD, is the James McGill Professor of Psychology and Behavioral Neuroscience at McGill University—where he also teaches in the graduate school of business—and dean of the College of Arts and Humanities at the Minerva Schools at KGI. The author of two previous *New York Times* bestselling books, *This Is Your Brain on Music* and *The World in Six Songs*, he divides his time between Montreal, Quebec, and the San Francisco Bay Area.

Praise for *The Organized Mind*

"Levitin is about as knowledgeable a guide to neuroscience as one might hope for."

—*The New York Times Book Review*

"[An] impressively wide-ranging and thoughtful work . . . *The Organized Mind* is an organized book, but it also rewards dipping in at any point, for there are fascinating facts and examples throughout."

—*The Wall Street Journal*

"From how not to lose your keys to how to decide when the risks of surgery are worth it, Levitin focuses on smart ways to process the constant flow of information the brain must deal with."

—*The Washington Post*

"More than a self-help book . . . Levitin's insights into sleep, time, socializing, and decision making are profound."

—*San Jose Mercury News*

"*The Organized Mind* is a lot more than a self-help book with an uncommonly solid scientific underpinning. It's a book that, if you let it, might just change the way you live."

—*The Gazette* (Montreal)

"[An] ingenious combination of neuroscience and self-help."

—*Kirkus Reviews*

"By learning about how the mind processes information, readers with an interest in the brain will come away with insight into how they can better organize their lengthy lists, overflowing junk drawers, and cluttered schedules."

—*Library Journal*

"Levitin is a beautifully clear writer when it comes to science: the long section on using statistical analysis to parse medical advice is worth the price of admission on its own. . . . You can flip open *The Organized Mind* to nearly any page and find some fascinating aperçu."

—Clive Thompson, *Literary Review of Canada*

"An eloquent spokesperson for our field. Levitin writes about the brain with an ease and familiarity that is captivating."

—The late David Hubel, Nobel Laureate in honor of discoveries concerning information processing in the human visual system

"Fascinating . . . Combing neuroscience and cognitive psychology, *The Organized Mind* underscores the critical importance of individuals taking charge of their own attentional and memory systems so they can lead optimally productive and satisfying lives. Invaluable insights are offered with regard to organizing our homes, social world, time, decision making, and business world."

—Nadine J. Kaslow, PhD, president of the American Psychological Association and professor and vice chair, Emory University School of Medicine

"This book is far more than tips on how to think clearly and manage information overload. It is also a tour through some of the most exciting aspects of contemporary neuroscience and cognitive science, with a specific emphasis on implications for everyday life. Anyone who has ever wondered about the mind will find much that is fascinating and useful in these pages."

—Stephen Kosslyn, dean of Minerva Schools of Arts and Sciences at the Keck Graduate Institute, former chair of the department of psychology, Harvard University

"*The Organized Mind* is the perfect antidote to the effects of information overload. Loved it."

—Scott Turow, *New York Times* bestselling author of *Identical* and *Innocent*

"Running a major PBS television series on tight budgets and turnarounds requires organization and efficiency and sometimes a little magic too. Levitin's behind the curtain peek at the brain's inner workings of decision making provides that extra bit of magic—and would make a fascinating documentary in and of itself!"

—Pamela Hogan, Emmy award–winning producer for PBS

"A how-to book on how to stay sane—how to tamp down on that fire-hose of information and choices that we face each day, and direct it all toward our own goals and purposes. It's an owner's manual for your mind."

—Congressman Alan Grayson, U.S. House of Representatives

"In the age of TMI, we all need better organized minds. With characteristically clear prose and scientific insight, Dan Levitin gives us tips on how to get our mental closets in order. I really enjoyed this book."

—Joseph LeDoux, Center for Neural Science, New York University

"Dan Levitin has done it again. Having explained music and the brain, now he shows us the best, most effective ways to organize the rest of our life by giving us key insights into how the brain works. His style is so appealing, his knowledge so deep and practical, that we learn, from *The Organized Mind*, not only why we do what we do, but how, potentially, we can run our lives more smoothly, efficiently, and even happily."

—Cathy N. Davidson, director of The Futures Initiative, City University of New York, and author of *Now You See It*

"Using the latest information on the brain and how it works, Levitin presents a series of ideas on how to organize one's life and business. Essential reading for anyone who aspires to be highly effective. Or even find their keys!"

—David Eidelman, MD, dean of the McGill University Medical School

"*The Organized Mind* is for anyone interested in how the human mind organizes, and on occasion disorganizes, the world around us. Move over, *Freakonomics*, there's a new kid on the bookcase."

—Gerry Altmann, professor of psychology at the University of Connecticut, and author of *The Ascent of Babel*

"An extraordinary work from one of our most gifted writers."

—The late Phil Ramone, producer for Bob Dylan, Aretha Franklin, Elton John, and Luciano Pavarotti

"Levitin is funny, informative, and insightful. It's like having a friend who's a neuroscientist showing you how creating a little order in your brain can unlock so much creativity."

—Len Blum, screenwriter of *The Pink Panther, Meatballs*

"A great book for making you think about things you think you know, and then thinking harder about them. Levitin is brilliant."

—Tom Tombrello, Robert H. Goddard Professor of Physics at Caltech

"I have been savoring this book—I didn't want it to end. A beautifully crafted and poetic book."

—Ben Sidran, jazz pianist, original member of the Steve Miller Band

"From my time as a Navy Seal to serving as governor and senator for Nebraska to running a university, I've found that the most challenging part of my life has been managing the constant wash of conflicting and often distracting information. This has never been truer than now. Dan is the perfect guide to how to use the newest findings in neuroscience to become more productive and creative. This book will change your life for the better."

—Bob Kerrey, former U.S. senator, former president of the New School

"Any CEO or individual who seriously cares about understanding his or her customer will have a desire to better understand the complexity of the human brain. Levitin's intellectual curiosity and sharp mind come through with new and additional insights in *The Organized Mind*."

—John Venhuizen, president and CEO of
Ace Hardware Corporation

"A profound piece of work. Levitin documents the mismatch between our narrow bandwidth hunter-gatherer minds and the multitasking chaos of today's world. He even shows us how to stay sane in environments that are constantly tempting us to stretch ourselves hopelessly thin."

—Philip E. Tetlock, Wharton School,
University of Pennsylvania

"An erudite synthesis of Levitin's own contributions, recent advances in our understanding of attention and memory, and a deep perspective on the ways the human mind works."

—Stanley Prusiner, MD, Nobel Laureate, director of the
Institute for Neurodegenerative Diseases,
University of California, San Francisco

"Daniel Levitin's book follows in the ancient tradition of knowledge as a guide to a better life. Discover the creative power of organized thought, whether you are a writer or a scientist, a disorganized mess or a super robot seeking new frontiers of effectiveness."

—Eric Kaplan, coexecutive producer and writer, *The Big Bang Theory*; writer, *The Simpsons* and *Flight of the Conchords*

"The time is rapidly approaching when insights driven by Big Data will dominate not only most business decisions but also many choices we make in our personal lives. So when I read a review of Levitin's book, I sat up and took notice because I'm bombarded by information every hour of every day. Levitin does an excellent job in discussing the science of thinking in language that's not only clear and informative but also entertaining. Readers of this book will get a better understanding of the mind along with some valuable guidance on how to exploit the emerging world of Big Data."

—Mark Hurd, co-CEO of Oracle Corp, *Bloomberg*

ALSO BY DANIEL J. LEVITIN

This Is Your Brain on Music: The Science of a Human Obsession

The World in Six Songs: How the Musical Brain Created Human Nature

THE ORGANIZED MIND

Thinking Straight in the Age of Information Overload

Daniel J. Levitin

A PLUME BOOK

PLUME
Published by the Penguin Group
Penguin Group (USA) LLC
375 Hudson Street
New York, New York 10014

USA | Canada | UK | Ireland | Australia | New Zealand | India | South Africa | China
penguin.com
A Penguin Random House Company

First published in the United States of America by Dutton, a member of
Penguin Group (USA) LLC, 2014
First Plume Printing 2015

THE LIBRARY OF CONGRESS HAS CATALOGED THE DUTTON EDITION AS FOLLOWS:
Levitin, Daniel J.
The organized mind : thinking straight in the age of information overload / Daniel J. Levitin.
pages cm
Includes bibliographical references and index.
ISBN 978-0-525-95418-7 (hc.)
ISBN 978-0-14-751631-2 (pbk.)
ISBN 978-0-14-751721-0 (pbk. internat'l)
1. Distraction (Psychology) 2. Attention. 3. Time management. 4. Tidiness. I. Title.
BF323.D5L49 2014
153.4'2—dc23
2014011046

Printed in the United States of America
1 3 5 7 9 10 8 6 4 2

Set in Minion Pro with Gill Sans
Original hardcover design by Daniel Lagin

To my mother and father
for all they taught me

CONTENTS

PART THREE

INTRODUCTION

Information and Conscientious Organization

We humans have a long history of pursuing neural enhancement—ways to improve the brains that evolution gave us. We train them to become more dependable and efficient allies in helping us to achieve our goals. Law schools, business schools, and medical schools, music conservatories and athletic programs, all strive to harness the latent power of the human brain to deliver ever higher levels of achievement, to provide an edge in a world that is increasingly competitive. Through the sheer force of human ingenuity, we have devised systems to free our brains of clutter, to help us keep track of details that we can't trust ourselves to remember. All of these and other innovations are designed either to improve the brain we have, or to off-load some of its functions to external sources.

One of the biggest advances in neural enhancement occurred only 5,000 years ago, when humans discovered a game-changing way to increase the capacity of the brain's memory and indexing system. The invention of written language has long been celebrated as a breakthrough, but relatively little has been made of what exactly were the first things humans wrote—simple recipes, sales receipts, and business inventories mostly. It was around 3000 BCE that our ancestors began to trade nomadic lifestyles for urban ones, setting up increasingly large cities and centers of commerce. The increased trade in these cities put a strain on individual merchants' memories and so early writing became an important component of recording business transactions. Poetry, histories, war tactics, and instructions for building complex construction projects came later.

Prior to the invention of writing, our ancestors had to rely on memory, sketches, or music to encode and preserve important information. Memory is fallible, of course, but not because of storage limitations so much as *retrieval* limitations. Some neuroscientists believe that nearly every conscious experience is stored somewhere in your brain; the hard part is finding it and pulling it out again. Sometimes the information that comes out is incomplete, distorted, or misleading. Vivid stories that address a very limited and unlikely set of circumstances often pop to mind and overwhelm statistical information based on a large number of observations that would be far more accurate in helping us to make sound decisions about medical treatments, investments, or the trustworthiness of people in our social world. This fondness for stories is just one of many artifacts, side effects of the way our brains work.

It's helpful to understand that our modes of thinking and decision-making evolved over the tens of thousands of years that humans lived as hunter-gatherers. Our genes haven't fully caught up with the demands of modern civilization, but fortunately human knowledge has—we now better understand how to overcome evolutionary limitations. This is the story of how humans have coped with information and organization from the beginning of civilization. It's also the story of how the most successful members of society—from successful artists, athletes, and warriors, to business executives and highly credentialed professionals—have learned to maximize their creativity, and efficiency, by organizing their lives so that they spend less time on the mundane, and more time on the inspiring, comforting, and rewarding things in life.

Cognitive psychologists have provided mountains of evidence over the last twenty years that memory is unreliable. And to make matters worse, we show staggering overconfidence in many recollections that are false. It's not just that we remember things wrongly (which would be bad enough), but we don't even *know* we're remembering them wrongly, doggedly insisting that the inaccuracies are in fact true.

The first humans who figured out how to write things down around 5,000 years ago were in essence trying to increase the capacity of their hippocampus, part of the brain's memory system. They effectively extended the natural limits of human memory by preserving some of their memories on clay tablets and cave walls, and later, papyrus and parchment. Later, we developed other mechanisms—such as calendars, filing cabinets, computers, and smartphones—to help us organize and store the information we've written down. When our computer or smartphone starts to run slowly, we might buy a larger memory card. That memory is both a metaphor and a physical reality. We are off-loading a great deal of the processing that our neurons would normally do to an external device that then becomes an extension of our own brains, a neural enhancer.

These external memory mechanisms are generally of two types, either following the brain's own organizational system or reinventing it, sometimes overcoming its limitations. Knowing which is which can enhance the way we use these systems, and so improve our ability to cope with information overload.

Once memories became externalized with written language, the writer's brain and attentional system were freed up to focus on something else. But immediately with those first written words came the problems of *storage, indexing*, and *accessing*: Where should the writing be stored so that it (and the information it contains) won't get lost? If the written message is itself a reminder, a kind of Stone Age "To Do" list, the writer needs to remember to look at it and where she put it.

Suppose the writing contains information about edible plants. Maybe it was written at the morbid scene of watching a favorite uncle die from eating a poisonous berry—wanting to preserve information about what that plant looks like and how to distinguish it from a nutritious plant that is similar in appearance. The indexing problem is that there are several possibilities about where you store this report, based on your needs: It could be stored with other writings about plants, or with writings about family history, or with writings about cooking, or with writings about how to poison an enemy.

Here we come upon two of the most compelling properties of the human brain and its design: *richness* and *associative access. Richness* refers to the theory that a large number of the things you've ever thought or experienced are still in there, somewhere. *Associative access* means that your thoughts can be accessed in a number of different ways by semantic or perceptual associations—memories can be triggered by related words, by category names, by a smell, an old song or photograph, or even seemingly random neural firings that bring them up to consciousness.

Being able to access any memory regardless of where it is stored is what computer scientists call *random access.* DVDs and hard drives work this way; videotapes do not. You can jump to any spot in a movie on a DVD or hard drive by "pointing" at it. But to get to a particular point in a videotape, you need to go through every previous point first (*sequential access*). Our ability to randomly access our memory from multiple cues is especially powerful. Computer scientists call it *relational memory.* You may have heard of relational databases—that's effectively what human memory is. (This is revisited in Chapter 3.)

Having relational memory means that if I want to get you to think of a fire truck, I can induce the memory in many different ways. I might make the sound of a siren, or give you a verbal description ("a large red truck with ladders on the side that typically responds to a certain kind of emergency"). I might try to trigger the concept by an association game, by asking you to name as many *red* things as you can in one minute (most people come to "fire truck" in this game), or to name as many emergency vehicles as you can. All of these things and more are *attributes* of the fire truck: its redness, its emergency vehicle-ness, its siren, its size and shape, the fact that uniformed men and women are usually found riding both in and on it, that it is one of only a small subset of motor vehicles that carries a ladder around.

If you just started thinking, at the end of that last sentence, what *other* vehicles carry ladders (for example, telephone company repair trucks or the vans belonging to window installers, roofers, and chimney sweeps), then you have come upon an important point: We can categorize objects in many, and often seemingly infinite, ways. And any one of those cues has its own route to the neural node that represents *fire truck* in your brain.

The concept of *fire truck* is represented in the picture (opposite) by a circle in the center—a node corresponding to a cluster of neurons in the brain. That neuronal cluster is connected to other neuronal clusters that represent the different features or properties of *fire truck.* In the drawing, other concepts that are most closely associated with a fire truck, and are retrieved from memory more quickly, are shown closer to the fire truck node. (In the brain, they may not actually be physically closer, but the neural connections are stronger, allowing for easier retrieval.) Thus, the node containing the fact that a fire truck is red is closer than the one that says it sometimes has a separate steering wheel in the back.

In addition to neural networks in the brain that represent attributes of things, those attributes are also connected associatively to other things. A

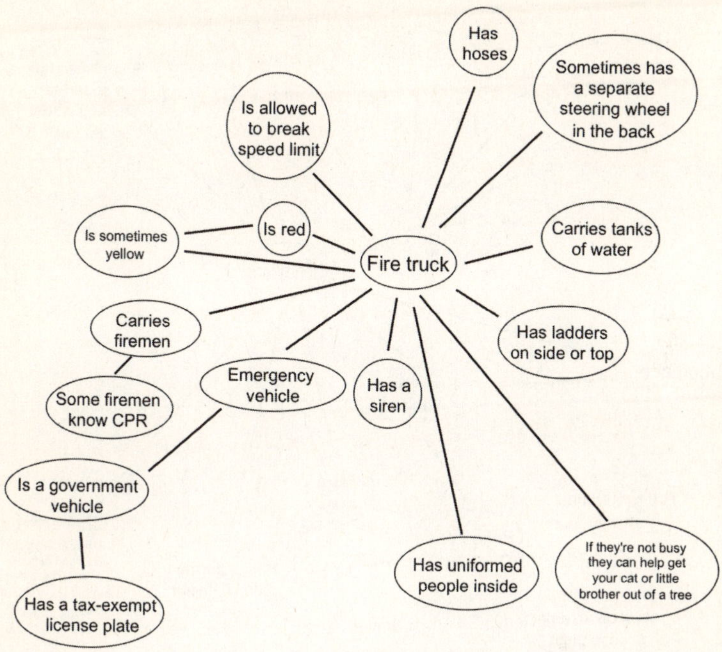

fire truck is red, but we can think of many other things that are: cherries, tomatoes, apples, blood, roses, parts of the American flag, and Sun-Maid raisin boxes, for example. Did you ever wonder why, if someone asks you to name a bunch of red things, you can do it so quickly? It's because by concentrating on the thought *red*, represented here by a neural node, you're sending electrochemical activation through the network and down the branches to everything else in your brain that connects to it. Below, I've overlaid additional information that resides in a typical neural network that begins with *fire truck*—nodes for other things that are red, for other things that have a siren, and so forth.

Thinking about one memory tends to activate other memories. This can be both an advantage and a disadvantage. If you are trying to retrieve a particular memory, the flood of activations can cause competition among different nodes, leaving you with a traffic jam of neural nodes trying to get through to consciousness, and you end up with nothing.

The ancient Greeks sought to improve memory through brain training methods such as memory palaces and the method of loci. At the same time,

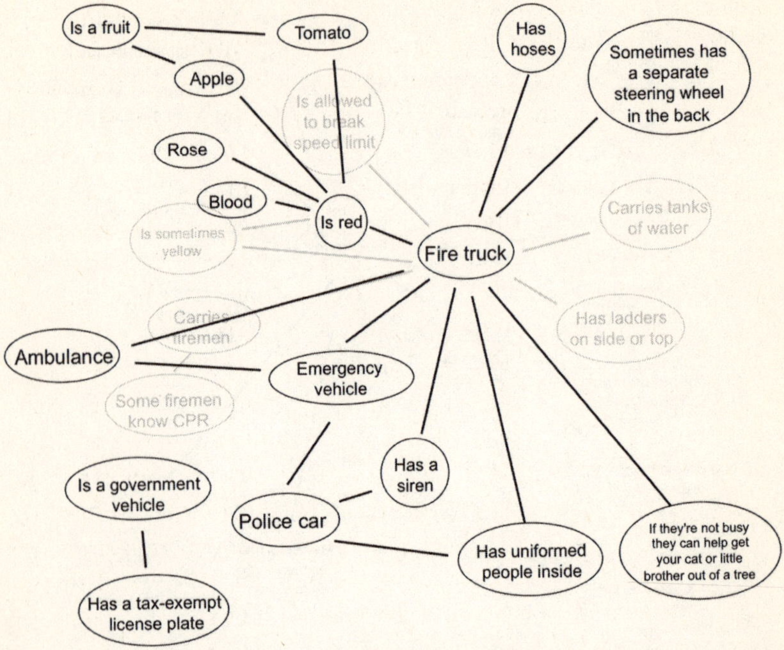

they and the Egyptians became experts at externalizing information, inventing the modern library, a grand repository for externalized knowledge. We don't know why these simultaneous explosions of intellectual activity occurred when they did (perhaps daily human experience had hit a certain level of complexity). But the human need to organize our lives, our environment, even our thoughts, remains strong. This need isn't simply learned, it is a biological imperative—animals organize their environments instinctively. Most mammals are biologically programmed to put their digestive waste away from where they eat and sleep. Dogs have been known to collect their toys and put them in baskets; ants carry off dead members of the colony to burial grounds; certain birds and rodents create symmetrically organized barriers around their nests in order to more easily detect intruders.

A key to understanding the organized mind is to recognize that on its own, it doesn't organize things the way you might want it to. It comes preconfigured, and although it has enormous flexibility, it is built on a system that evolved over hundreds of thousands of years to deal with different kinds and different amounts of information than we have today. To be more specific: The brain isn't organized the way you might set up your home office or bathroom medicine cabinet. You can't just put things anywhere you want to. The evolved architecture of the brain is haphazard and disjointed, and incorporates multiple systems, each of which has a mind of its own (so to speak). Evolution doesn't *design* things and it doesn't build systems—it *settles on* systems that, historically, conveyed a survival benefit (and if a better way comes along, it will adopt that). There is no overarching, grand planner engineering the systems so that they work harmoniously together. The brain is more like a big, old house with piecemeal renovations done on every floor, and less like new construction.

Consider this, then, as an analogy: You have an old house and everything is a bit outdated, but you're satisfied. You add a room air conditioner during one particularly hot summer. A few years later, when you have more money, you decide to add a central air-conditioning system. But you don't remove that room unit in the bedroom—why would you? It might come in handy and it's already there, bolted to the wall. Then a few years later, you have a catastrophic plumbing problem—pipes burst in the walls. The plumbers need to break open the walls and run new pipes, but your central air-conditioning system is now in the way, where some of their pipes would ideally go. So they run the pipes through the attic, the long way around. This works fine until one particularly cold winter when your uninsulated attic causes your pipes to freeze. These pipes wouldn't have frozen if you had run them through the walls, which you couldn't do because of the central air-conditioning. If you had planned all this from the start, you would have done things differently, but you didn't—you added things one thing at a time, as and when you needed them.

Evolution has built our brain in much the same way. Of course, evolution has no will, no plan. Evolution didn't *decide* to give you memory for where you put things. Your *place memory* system came about gradually, through the processes of descent with modification and natural selection, and it evolved separately from your memory for facts and figures. The two systems might come to work together through further evolutionary processes, but they are not necessarily going to do so, and in some cases, they may be in conflict with each other.

It might be helpful to learn *how* our brain organizes information so that we can use what we have, rather than fight against it. It is built as a hodgepodge of different systems, each one solving a particular adaptive problem. Occasionally they work together, occasionally they're in conflict, and occasionally they aren't even talking to one another. Two of the key ways that we can control and improve the process are to pay special attention to the way we enter information into our memory—*encoding*—and the way we pull it out—*retrieval*. This will be unpacked in Chapters 2 and 3.

The need for taking charge of our attentional and memory systems has never been greater. Our brains are busier than ever before. We're assaulted with facts, pseudo facts, jibber-jabber, and rumor, all posing as information. Trying to figure out what you need to know and what you can ignore is exhausting, and at the same time, we are all doing more. Consequently, trying to find the time to schedule all our various activities has become a tremendous challenge. Thirty years ago, travel agents made our airline and rail reservations, salesclerks helped us find what we were looking for in stores, and professional typists or secretaries helped busy people with their correspondence. Now we do most of those things ourselves. The information age has off-loaded a great deal of the work previously done by people we could call information specialists onto all of the rest of us. We are doing the jobs of ten different people while still trying to keep up with our lives, our children and parents, our friends, our careers, our hobbies, and our favorite TV shows. It's no wonder that sometimes one memory gets confounded with another, leading us to show up in the right place but on the wrong day, or to forget something as simple as where we last put our glasses or the remote.

Every day, millions of us lose our keys, driver's licenses, wallets, or scraps of paper with important phone numbers. And we don't just lose physical objects, but we also forget things we were supposed to remember, important things like the password to our e-mail or a website, the PIN for our cash cards—the cognitive equivalent of losing our keys. These are not trivial things; it's not as if people are losing things that are relatively easy to replace, like bars of soap or some grapes from the fruit bowl. We don't tend to have general memory failures; we have specific, temporary memory failures for one or two things. During those frantic few minutes when you're searching for your lost keys, you (probably) still remember your name and address, where your television set is, and what you had for breakfast—it's just this one memory that has been aggravatingly lost. There is evidence that some things are typically lost far more often than others: We tend to lose our car keys but not our car, we lose our wallet or cell phone more often than the stapler on our desk or soup spoons in the kitchen, we lose track of coats and sweaters and shoes more often than pants. Understanding how the brain's attentional and memory systems interact can go a long way toward minimizing memory lapses.

These simple facts about the kinds of things we tend to lose and those that we don't can tell us a lot about how our brains work, and a lot about why things go wrong. This book is about both of those ideas, and I hope it will be a useful guide to preventing such losses. There are things that anyone can do to minimize the chances of losing things, and to quickly recover when things do get lost. We are better able to follow instructions and plans the more thoroughly we understand them (as any cognitive psychologist would say), so this book discusses a number of different aspects of our organizing mind. We'll review the history of organizational systems that humans have tried over many centuries, so that we can see which systems succeeded and which failed, and why. I will explain why we lose things in the first place and what clever, organized people do so they don't. Part of the story involves how we learned things as children, and the good news is that certain aspects of childhood thinking can be revisited to help us as adults. Perhaps the heart of the story is about organizing our time better, not just so we can be more efficient but so we can find more time for fun, for play, for meaningful relationships, and for creativity.

I'm also going to talk about business organizations, which are called organizations for a reason. Companies are like expanded brains, with individual workers functioning something like neurons. Companies tend to be collections of individuals united to a common set of goals, with each worker performing a specialized function. Businesses typically do better than individuals at day-to-day tasks because of distributed processing. In a large business, there is a department for paying bills on time (accounts payable), and another for keeping track of keys (physical plant or security). Although the individual workers are fallible, systems and redundancies are usually in place, or should be, to ensure that no one person's momentary distraction or lack of organization brings everything to a grinding halt. Of course, business organizations are not always prefectly organized, and occasionally, through the same cognitive blocks that cause us to lose our car keys, businesses lose things, too—profits, clients, competitive positions in the marketplace. In my sideline as a management consultant, I've seen tremendous inefficiencies and lack of oversight causing different kinds of problems. I've learned a lot from having this fly-on-the-wall view of companies in prosperity and companies in crisis.

An organized mind leads effortlessly to good decision-making. As an undergraduate, I had two brilliant professors, Amos Tversky and Lee Ross, both of whom were pioneers in the science of social judgments and decision-making. They sparked a fascination for how we assess others in our social world and how we interact with them, the various biases and *mis*information we bring to those relationships, along with how to overcome them. Amos, with his colleague Daniel Kahneman (who won the Nobel Prize for their work together a few years after Amos passed away), uncovered a host of systematic errors in the way the human brain evaluates evidence and processes information. I've been teaching these to university undergraduates for twenty years, and my students have helped me to come up with ways to explain these errors so that all of us can easily improve our decision-making. The stakes are particularly high in medical decision-making, where the wrong decision has immediate and very serious consequences. It is now well documented that most MDs don't encounter these simple rules as a part of their training, don't understand statistical reasoning. The result can be muddled advice. Such advice could lead you to take medications or undergo surgeries that have a very small statistical chance of making you any better, and a relatively large statistical chance of making you worse. (Chapter 6 is devoted to this topic.)

We are all faced with an unprecedented amount of information to remember, and small objects to keep track of. In this age of iPods and thumb drives, when your smartphone can record video, browse 200 million websites, and tell you how many calories are in that cranberry scone, most of us still try to keep track of things using the systems that were put in place in a precomputerized era. There is definitely room for improvement. The dominant metaphor for the computer is based on a 1950s *Mad Men*–era strategy for organization: a desktop with folders on it, and files inside of those. Even the word *computer* is outdated now that most people don't use their computer to compute anything at all—rather, it has become just like that big disorganized drawer everyone has in their kitchen, what in my family we called the junk drawer. I went to a friend's house the other day, and here is what I found in *his* junk drawer (all I had to do was ask, "Do you have a drawer that you just throw things in when you don't know where else to put them?"):

batteries

rubber bands

shish kebab skewers

string

twist ties

photos

thirty-seven cents in change

an empty DVD case

a DVD without a case (unfortunately, not the same one)

orange plastic covers to put over his smoke detector if he ever decides to paint the kitchen, because the paint fumes can set off the detector

matches

three wood screws of various sizes, one with stripped threads

a plastic fork

a special wrench that came with the garbage disposal; he isn't sure what it is for

two ticket stubs from a Dave Matthews Band concert last summer

two keys that have been around for at least ten years, and no one in the house knows what they are for (but they are afraid to throw them away)

two pens, neither of which writes

a half dozen other things that he has no idea what they are for but is afraid to throw out

Our computers are *just like that* but thousands of times more disorganized. We have files we don't know about, others that appeared mysteriously by accident when we read an e-mail, and multiple versions of the same document; it's often difficult to tell which is the most current. Our "computing machine" has become a large, inglorious, and fantastically disorganized kitchen drawer full of electronic files, some of indeterminate origin or function. My assistant let me have a look at her computer, and a partial inventory revealed the following contents, typical, I've found, of what many people have on their computers:

photographs

videos

music

screen savers of cats wearing party hats, or smiling pigs with human mouths Photoshopped in

tax documents

travel arrangements

correspondence

checking account registers

games

appointment books

articles to read

various forms related to employment: request for time off, quarterly report, sick day accounting, request for retirement fund payroll deduction

an archived copy of this book (in case I lose mine)

dozens of lists—lists of area restaurants, university-approved hotels, office locations and phone numbers for members of the department, an emergency telephone tree, safety procedures in the event of various calamities, protocol for disposing of obsolete equipment, and so on

software updates

old versions of software that no longer work

dozens of files of foreign-language keyboard layouts and fonts in case she ever needs to type Romanian, Czech, Japanese, or ancient or modern Hebrew characters little electronic "Post-its" reminding her where important files are located, or how to do certain things (like create a new Post-it, delete a Post-it, or change the color of a Post-it)

It's a wonder we don't lose more.

Of course, some of us are more organized than others. From the many thousands of ways that individuals differ from one another, a mathematical model can be constructed that accounts for a great deal of variation, organizing human differences into five categories:

extroversion

agreeableness

neuroticism

openness to new experience

conscientiousness

Of these five, the conscientiousness trait of being organized is most highly associated with conscientiousness. Conscientiousness comprises industriousness, self-control, stick-to-itiveness, and a desire for order. And it, in turn, is the best predictor of many important human outcomes, including mortality, longevity, educational attainment, and a host of criteria related to career success. Conscientiousness is associated with better recovery outcomes following surgery and transplants. Conscientiousness in early childhood is associated with positive outcomes decades later. Taken together, the evidence suggests that as societies become more Westernized and complex, conscientiousness becomes more and more important.

The cognitive neuroscience of memory and attention—our improved understanding of the brain, its evolution and limitations—can help us to better cope with a world in which more and more of us feel we're running fast just to stand still. The average American is sleep-deprived, overstressed, and not making enough time for things she wants to do. I think we can do better. Some of us are doing better and I've had the opportunity to talk to them. Personal assistants to Fortune 500 CEOs and to other high achievers keep their bosses working at full capacity while still finding them time for fun and relaxation. They and their bosses don't get bogged down by information overload because they benefit from the technology of organization, some of it new, some of it quite old. Some of their systems will sound familiar, some may not, still others are incredibly nuanced and subtle; nevertheless, they all can make a profound difference.

There is no one system that will work for everyone—we are each unique—but in the following chapters are general principles that anyone can apply *in their own way* to recapture a sense of order, and to regain the hours of lost time spent trying to overcome the disorganized mind.

THE ORGANIZED MIND

PART ONE

1

TOO MUCH INFORMATION, TOO MANY DECISIONS

The Inside History of Cognitive Overload

One of the best students I ever had the privilege of meeting was born in communist Romania, under the repressive and brutal rule of Nicolae Ceauşescu. Although his regime collapsed when she was eleven, she remembered well the long lines for food, the shortages, and the economic destitution that lasted far beyond his overthrow. Ioana was bright and curious, and although still young, she had the colors of a true scholar: When she encountered a new scientific idea or problem, she would look at it from every angle, reading everything she could get her hands on. I met her during her first semester at university, newly arrived in North America, when she took my introductory course on the psychology of thinking and reasoning. Although the class had seven hundred students, she distinguished herself early on by thoughtfully answering questions posed in class, peppering me with questions during office hours, and constantly proposing new experiments.

I ran into her one day at the college bookstore, frozen in the aisle with all the pens and pencils. She was leaning limply against the shelf, clearly distraught.

"Is everything all right?" I asked.

"It can be really terrible living in America," Ioana said.

"Compared to Soviet Romania?!"

"Everything is so complicated. I looked for a student apartment. Rent or lease? Furnished or unfurnished? Top floor or ground floor? Carpet or hardwood floor . . ."

"Did you make a decision?"

"Yes, finally. But it's impossible to know which is best. Now . . ." her voice trailed off.

"Is there a problem with the apartment?"

"No, the apartment is fine. But today is my fourth time in the bookstore. Look! An entire *row* full of pens. In Romania, we had three kinds of pens. And many times there was a shortage—no pens at all. In America, there are more than fifty different kinds. Which one do I need for my biology class? Which one for poetry? Do I want felt tip, ink, gel, cartridge, erasable? Ballpoint, razor point, roller ball? One hour I am here reading labels."

Every day, we are confronted with dozens of decisions, most of which we would characterize as insignificant or unimportant—whether to put on our left sock first or our right, whether to take the bus or the subway to work, what to eat, where to shop. We get a taste of Ioana's disorientation when we travel, not only to other countries but even to other states. The stores are different, the products are different. Most of us have adopted a strategy to get along called *satisficing,* a term coined by the Nobel Prize winner Herbert Simon, one of the founders of the fields of organization theory and information processing. Simon wanted a word to describe not getting the very best option but one that was good enough. For things that don't matter critically, we make a choice that satisfies us and is deemed sufficient. You don't really know if your dry cleaner is *the best*—you only know that they're good enough. And that's what helps you get by. You don't have time to sample all the dry cleaners within a twenty-four-block radius of your home. Does Dean & DeLuca really have the best gourmet takeout? It doesn't matter—it's good enough. Satisficing is one of the foundations of productive human behavior; it prevails when we don't waste time on decisions that don't matter, or more accurately, when we don't waste time trying to find improvements that are not going to make a significant difference in our happiness or satisfaction.

All of us engage in satisficing every time we clean our homes. If we got down on the floor with a toothbrush every day to clean the grout, if we scrubbed the windows and walls every single day, the house would be spotless. But few of us go to this much trouble even on a weekly basis (and when we do, we're likely to be labeled obsessive-compulsive). For most of us, we clean our houses until they are clean enough, reaching a kind of equilibrium between effort and benefit. It is this cost-benefits analysis that is at the heart of satisficing (Simon was also a respected economist).

Recent research in social psychology has shown that happy people are not people who have more; rather, they are people who are happy with what they already have. Happy people engage in satisficing *all of the time*, even if they don't know it. Warren Buffett can be seen as embracing satisficing to an extreme—one of the richest men in the world, he lives in Omaha, a block from the highway, in the same modest home he has lived in for fifty years. He once told a radio interviewer that for breakfasts during his week-long visit to New York City, he'd bought himself a gallon of milk and a box of Oreo cookies. But Buffett does not satisfice with his investment strategies; satisficing is a tool for not wasting time on things that are not your highest priority. For your high-priority endeavors, the old-fashioned pursuit of excellence remains the right strategy. Do you want your surgeon or your airplane mechanic or the director of a $100 million feature film to do *just good enough* or do the best they possibly can? Sometimes you want more than Oreos and milk.

Part of my Romanian student's despondency could be chalked up to culture shock—to the loss of the familiar, and immersion in the unfamiliar. But she's not alone. The past generation has seen an explosion of choices facing consumers. In 1976, the average supermarket stocked 9,000 unique products; today that number has ballooned to 40,000 of them, yet the average person gets 80%–85% of their needs in only 150 different supermarket items. That means that we need to ignore 39,850 items in the store. And that's just supermarkets—it's been estimated that there are over one million products in the United States today (based on SKUs, or *stock-keeping units*, those little bar codes on things we buy).

All this ignoring and deciding comes with a cost. Neuroscientists have discovered that unproductivity and loss of drive can result from *decision overload*. Although most of us have no trouble ranking the importance of decisions if asked to do so, our brains don't automatically do this. Ioana knew that keeping up with her coursework was more important than what pen to buy, but the mere situation of facing so many trivial decisions in daily life created neural fatigue, leaving no energy for the important decisions. Recent research shows that people who were asked to make a series of meaningless decisions of just this type—for example, whether to write with a ballpoint pen or a felt-tip pen—showed poorer impulse control and lack of judgment about subsequent decisions. It's as though our brains are configured to make a certain number of decisions per day and once we reach that limit, we can't make any more, regardless of how important they are. One of the most useful findings in recent neuroscience could be summed up as: *The decision-making network in our brain doesn't prioritize.*

Today, we are confronted with an unprecedented amount of information, and each of us generates more information than ever before in human history. As former Boeing scientist and *New York Times* writer Dennis Overbye notes, this information stream contains "more and more information about our lives—where we shop and what we buy, indeed, where we are right now—the economy, the genomes of countless organisms we can't even name yet, galaxies full of stars we haven't counted, traffic jams in Singapore and the weather on Mars." That information "tumbles faster and faster through bigger and bigger computers down to everybody's fingertips, which are holding devices with more processing power than the Apollo mission control." Information scientists have quantified all this: In 2011, Americans took in five times as much information every day as they did in 1986—the equivalent of 175 newspapers. During our leisure time, not counting work, each of us processes 34 gigabytes or 100,000 words every day. The world's 21,274 television stations produce 85,000 hours of original programming every day as we watch an average of 5 hours of television each day, the equivalent of 20 gigabytes of audio-video images. That's not counting YouTube, which uploads 6,000 hours of video every hour. And computer gaming? It consumes more bytes than all other media put together, including DVDs, TV, books, magazines, and the Internet.

Just trying to keep our own media and electronic files organized can be overwhelming. Each of us has the equivalent of over half a million books stored on our computers, not to mention all the information stored in our cell phones or in the magnetic stripe on the back of our credit cards. We have created a world with 300 exabytes (300,000,000,000,000,000,000 pieces) of human-made information. If each of those pieces of information were written on a 3 x 5 index card and then spread out side by side, just one person's share—*your* share of this information—would cover every square inch of Massachusetts and Connecticut combined.

Our brains do have the ability to process the information we take in, but at a cost: We can have trouble separating the trivial from the important, and all this information processing makes us tired. Neurons are living cells with a metabolism; they need oxygen and glucose to survive and when they've been working hard, we experience fatigue. Every status update you read on Facebook, every tweet or text message you get from a friend, is competing for resources in your brain with important things like whether to put your savings in stocks or bonds, where you left your passport, or how best to reconcile with a close friend you just had an argument with.

The processing capacity of the conscious mind has been estimated at 120 bits per second. That bandwidth, or window, is the speed limit for the traffic of information we can pay conscious attention to at any one time. While a great deal occurs below the threshold of our awareness, and this has an impact on how we feel and what our life is going to be like, in order for something to become encoded as part of your experience, you need to have paid conscious attention to it.

What does this bandwidth restriction—this information speed limit—mean in terms of our interactions with others? In order to understand one person speaking to us, we need to process 60 bits of information per second. With a processing limit of 120 bits per second, this means you can barely understand two people talking to you at the same time. Under most circumstances, you will not be able to understand three people talking at the same time. We're surrounded on this planet by billions of other humans, but we can understand only two at a time at the most! It's no wonder that the world is filled with so much misunderstanding.

With such attentional restrictions, it's clear why many of us feel overwhelmed by managing some of the most basic aspects of life. Part of the reason is that our brains evolved to help us deal with life during the hunter-gatherer phase of human history, a time when we might encounter no more than a thousand people across the entire span of our lifetime. Walking around midtown Manhattan, you'll pass that number of people in half an hour.

Attention is the most essential mental resource for any organism. It determines which aspects of the environment we deal with, and most of the time, various automatic, subconscious processes make the correct choice about what gets passed through to our conscious awareness. For this to happen, millions of neurons are constantly monitoring the environment to select the most important things for us to focus on. These neurons are collectively the *attentional filter*. They work largely in the background, outside of our conscious awareness. This is why most of the perceptual detritus of our daily lives doesn't register, or why, when you've been driving on the freeway for several hours at a stretch, you don't remember much of the scenery that has whizzed by: Your attentional system "protects" you from registering it because it isn't deemed important. This unconscious filter follows certain principles about what it will let through to your conscious awareness.

The attentional filter is one of evolution's greatest achievements. In nonhumans, it ensures that they don't get distracted by irrelevancies. Squirrels are interested in nuts and predators, and not much else. Dogs, whose olfactory sense is one million times more sensitive than ours, use smell to gather information about the world more than they use sound, and their attentional filter has evolved to make that so. If you've ever tried to call your dog while he is smelling something interesting, you know that it is very difficult to grab his attention with sound—smell trumps sound in the dog brain. No one has yet worked out all of the hierarchies and trumping factors in the human attentional filter, but we've learned a great deal about it. When our protohuman ancestors left the cover of the trees to seek new sources of food, they simultaneously opened up a vast range of new possibilities for nourishment and exposed themselves to a wide range of new predators. Being alert and vigilant to threatening sounds and visual cues is what allowed them to survive; this meant allowing an increasing amount of information through the attentional filter.

Humans are, by most biological measures, the most successful species our planet has seen. We have managed to survive in nearly every climate our planet has offered (so far), and the rate of our population expansion exceeds that of any other known organism. Ten thousand years ago, humans plus their pets and livestock accounted for about 0.1% of the terrestrial vertebrate biomass inhabiting the earth; we now account for 98%. Our success owes in large part to our cognitive capacity, the ability of our brains to flexibly handle information. But our brains evolved in a much simpler world with far less information coming at us. Today, our attentional filters easily become overwhelmed. Successful people—or people who can afford it—employ layers of people whose job it is to *narrow the attentional filter*. That is, corporate heads, political leaders, spoiled movie stars, and others whose time and attention are especially valuable have a staff of people around them who are effectively extensions of their own brains, replicating and refining the functions of the prefrontal cortex's attentional filter.

These highly successful persons—let's call them HSPs—have many of the daily distractions of life handled for them, allowing them to devote all of their attention to whatever is immediately before them. They seem to live completely in the moment. Their staff handle correspondence, make appointments, interrupt those appointments when a more important one is waiting, and help to plan their days for maximum efficiency (including naps!). Their bills are paid on time, their car is serviced when required, they're given reminders of projects due, and their assistants send suitable gifts to the HSP's loved ones on birthdays and anniversaries. Their ultimate prize if it all works? A Zen-like focus.

In the course of my work as a scientific researcher, I've had the chance to meet governors, cabinet members, music celebrities, and the heads of Fortune 500 companies. Their skills and accomplishments vary, but as a group, one thing is remarkably constant. I've repeatedly been struck by how liberating it is for them not to have to worry about whether there is someplace else they need to be, or someone else they need to be talking to. They take their time, make eye contact, relax, and are *really there* with whomever they're talking to. They don't have to worry if there is someone more important they should be talking to at that moment because their staff—their external attentional filters—have already determined for them that this is the best way they should be using their time. And there is a great amount of infrastructure in place ensuring that they will get to their next appointment on time, so they can let go of that nagging concern as well.

The rest of us have a tendency during meetings to let our minds run wild and cycle through a plethora of thoughts about the past and the future, destroying any aspirations for Zen-like calm and preventing us from being in the here and now: Did I turn off the stove? What will I do for lunch? When do I need to leave here in order to get to where I need to be next?

What if you could rely on others in your life to handle these things and you could narrow your attentional filter to that which is right before you, happening right now? I met Jimmy Carter when he was campaigning for president and he spoke as though we had all the time in the world. At one point, an aide came to take him off to the next person he needed to meet. Free from having to decide when the meeting would end, or any other mundane care, really, President Carter could let go of those inner nagging voices and be *there*. A professional musician friend who headlines big stadiums constantly and has a phalanx of assistants describes this state as being "happily lost." He doesn't need to look at his calendar more than a day in advance, allowing each day to be filled with wonder and possibility.

If we organize our minds and our lives following the new neuroscience of attention and memory, we can all deal with the world in ways that provide the sense of freedom that these HSPs enjoy. How can we actually leverage this science in everyday life? To begin with, by understanding the architecture of our attentional system. To better organize our mind, we need to know how it has organized itself.

Two of the most crucial principles used by the attentional filter are *change* and *importance*. The brain is an exquisite change detector: If you're driving and suddenly the road feels bumpy, your brain notices this change immediately and signals your attentional system to focus on the change. How does this happen? Neural circuits are noticing the smoothness of the road, the way it sounds, the way it feels against your rear end, back, and feet, and other parts of your body that are in contact with the car, and the way your visual field is smooth and continuous. After a few minutes of the same sounds, feel, and overall look, your conscious brain relaxes and lets the attentional filter take over. This frees you up to do other things, such as carry on a conversation or listen to the radio, or both. But with the slightest change—a low tire, bumps in the road—your attentional system pushes the new information up to your consciousness so that you can focus on the change and take appropriate action. Your eyes may scan the road and discover drainage ridges in the asphalt that account for the rough ride. Having found a satisfactory explanation, you relax again, pushing this sensory decision-making back down to lower levels of consciousness. If the road seems visually smooth and you can't otherwise account for the rough ride, you might decide to pull over and examine your tires.

The brain's change detector is at work all the time, whether you know it or not. If a close friend or relative calls on the phone, you might detect that her voice sounds different and ask if she's congested or sick with the flu. When your brain detects the change, this information is sent to your consciousness, but your brain doesn't explicitly send a message when there is no change. If your friend calls and her voice sounds normal, you don't immediately think, "Oh, her voice is the same as always." Again, this is the attentional filter doing its job, detecting change, not constancy.

The second principle, importance, can also let information through.

Here, importance is not just something that is objectively important but something that is personally important to you. If you're driving, a billboard for your favorite music group might catch your eye (really, we should say catch your *mind*) while other billboards go ignored. If you're in a crowded room, at a party for instance, certain words to which you attach high importance might suddenly catch your attention, even if spoken from across the room. If someone says "fire" or "sex" or your own name, you'll find that you're suddenly following a conversation far away from where you're standing, with no awareness of what those people were talking about before your attention was captured. The attentional filter is thus fairly sophisticated. It is capable of monitoring lots of different conversations as well as their semantic content, letting through only those that it thinks you will want to know about.

Due to the attentional filter, we end up experiencing a great deal of the world on autopilot, not registering the complexities, nuances, and often the beauty of what is right in front of us. A great number of failures of attention occur because we are not using these two principles to our advantage.

A critical point that bears repeating is that attention is a limited-capacity resource—there are definite limits to the number of things we can attend to at once. We see this in everyday activities. If you're driving, under most circumstances, you can play the radio or carry on a conversation with someone else in the car. But if you're looking for a particular street to turn onto, you instinctively turn down the radio or ask your friend to hang on for a moment, to stop talking. This is because you've reached the limits of your attention in trying to do these three things. The limits show up whenever we try to do too many things at once. How many times has something like the following happened to you? You've just come home from grocery shopping, one bag in each hand. You've balanced them sufficiently to unlock the front door, and as you walk in, you hear the phone ringing. You need to put down the grocery bags in your hands, answer the phone, perhaps being careful not to let the dog or cat out the open door. When the phone call is over, you realize you don't know where your keys are. Why? Because keeping track of *them*, too, is more things than your attentional system could handle.

The human brain has evolved to hide from us those things we are not paying attention to. In other words, we often have a cognitive blind spot: We don't know what we're missing because our brain can completely ignore things that are not its priority at the moment—even if they are right in front of our eyes. Cognitive psychologists have called this blind spot various names, including *inattentional blindness.* One of the most amazing demonstrations of it is known as the basketball demo. If you haven't seen it, I urge you to put this book down and view it now before reading any further. The video can be seen here: http://www.youtube.com/watch?v=vJG698U2Mvo. Your job is to count how many times the players wearing the white T-shirts pass the basketball, while ignoring the players in the black T-shirts.

(Spoiler alert: If you haven't seen the video yet, reading the next paragraph will mean that the illusion won't work for you.) The video comes from a psychological study of attention by Christopher Chabris and Daniel Simons. Because of the processing limits of your attentional system that I've just described, following the basketball and the passing, and keeping a mental tally of the passes, takes up most of the attentional resources of the average person. The rest are taken up by trying to ignore the players in the black T-shirts and to ignore the basketball they are passing. At some point in the video, a man in a gorilla suit walks into the middle of things, bangs his chest, and then walks off. The majority of the people watching this video don't see the gorilla. The reason? The attentional system is simply overloaded. If I had *not* asked you to count the basketball passes, you would have seen the gorilla.

A lot of instances of losing things like car keys, passports, money, receipts, and so on occur because our attentional systems are overloaded and they simply *can't* keep track of everything. The average American owns thousands of times more possessions than the average hunter-gatherer. In a real biological sense, we have more things to keep track of than our brains were designed to handle. Even towering intellectuals such as Kant and Wordsworth complained of information excess and sheer mental exhaustion induced by too much sensory input or mental overload. This is no reason to lose hope, though! More than ever, effective *external* systems are available for organizing, categorizing, and keeping track of things. In the past, the only option was a string of human assistants. But now, in the age of automation, there are other options. The first part of this book is about the biology underlying the use of these external systems. The second and third parts show how we can all use them to better keep track of our lives, to be efficient, productive, happy, and less stressed in a wired world that is increasingly filled with distractions.

Productivity and efficiency depend on systems that help us organize through categorization. The drive to categorize developed in the prehistoric wiring of our brains, in specialized neural systems that create and maintain meaningful, coherent amalgamations of things—foods, animals, tools, tribe members—in coherent categories. Fundamentally, categorization reduces mental effort and streamlines the flow of information. We are not the first generation of humans to be complaining about too much information.

Information Overload, Then and Now

Humans have been around for 200,000 years. For the first 99% of our history, we didn't do much of anything but procreate and survive. This was largely due to harsh global climactic conditions, which stabilized sometime around 10,000 years ago. People soon thereafter discovered farming and irrigation, and they gave up their nomadic lifestyle in order to cultivate and tend stable crops. But not all farm plots are the same; regional variations in sunshine, soil, and other conditions meant that one farmer might grow particularly good onions while another grew especially good apples. This eventually led to specialization; instead of growing all the crops for his own family, a farmer might grow only what he was best at and trade some of it for things he wasn't growing. Because each farmer was producing only one crop, and more than he needed, marketplaces and trading emerged and grew, and with them came the establishment of cities.

The Sumerian city of Uruk (~5000 BCE) was one of the world's earliest large cities. Its active commercial trade created an unprecedented volume of business transactions, and Sumerian merchants required an accounting system for keeping track of the day's inventory and receipts; *this* was the birth of writing. Here, liberal arts majors may need to set their romantic notions aside. The first forms of writing emerged not for art, literature, or love, not for spiritual or liturgical purposes, but for business—all literature could be said to originate from sales receipts (sorry). With the growth of trade, cities, and writing, people soon discovered architecture, government, and the other refinements of being that collectively add up to what we think of as civilization.

The appearance of writing some 5,000 years ago was not met with unbridled enthusiasm; many contemporaries saw it as technology gone too far, a demonic invention that would rot the mind and needed to be stopped. Then, as now, printed words were promiscuous—it was impossible to control where they went or who would receive them, and they could circulate easily without the author's knowledge or control. Lacking the opportunity to hear information directly from a speaker's mouth, the antiwriting contingent complained that it would be impossible to verify the accuracy of the writer's claims, or to ask follow-up questions. Plato was among those who voiced these fears; his King Thamus decried that the dependence on written words would "weaken men's characters and create forgetfulness in their souls." Such externalization of facts and stories meant people would no longer need to mentally retain large quantities of information themselves and would come to rely on stories and facts as conveyed, in written form, by others. Thamus, king of Egypt, argued that the written word would infect the Egyptian people with fake knowledge. The Greek poet Callimachus said books are "a great evil." The Roman philosopher Seneca the Younger (tutor to Nero) complained that his peers were wasting time and money accumulating too many books, admonishing that "the abundance of books is a distraction." Instead, Seneca recommended focusing on a limited number of good books, to be read thoroughly and repeatedly. Too much information could be harmful to your mental health.

The printing press was introduced in the mid 1400s, allowing for the more rapid proliferation of writing, replacing laborious (and error-prone) hand copying. Yet again, many complained that intellectual life as we knew it was done for. Erasmus, in 1525, went on a tirade against the "swarms of new books," which he considered a serious impediment to learning. He blamed printers whose profit motive sought to fill the world with books that were "foolish, ignorant, malignant, libelous, mad, impious and subversive." Leibniz complained about "that horrible mass of books that keeps on growing" and that would ultimately end in nothing less than a "return to barbarism." Descartes famously recommended ignoring the accumulated stock of texts and instead relying on one's own observations. Presaging what many say today, Descartes complained that "even if all knowledge could be found in books, where it is mixed in with so many useless things and confusingly heaped in such large volumes, it would take longer to read those books than we have to live in this life and more effort to select the useful things than to find them oneself."

A steady flow of complaints about the proliferation of books reverberated into the late 1600s. Intellectuals warned that people would stop talking to each other, burying themselves in books, polluting their minds with useless, fatuous ideas.

And as we well know, these warnings were raised again in our lifetime, first with the invention of television, then with computers, iPods, iPads, e-mail, Twitter, and Facebook. Each was decried as an addiction, an unnecessary distraction, a sign of weak character, feeding an inability to engage with real people and the real-time exchange of ideas. Even the dial phone was met with opposition when it replaced operator-assisted calls, and people worried *How will I remember all those phone numbers? How will I sort through and keep track of all of them?* (As David Byrne sang with Talking Heads, "Same as it ever was.")

With the Industrial Revolution and the rise of science, new discoveries grew at an enormous clip. For example, in 1550, there were 500 known plant species in the world. By 1623, this number had increased to 6,000. Today, we know 9,000 species of grasses alone, 2,700 types of palm trees, 500,000 different plant species. And the numbers keep growing. The increase of scientific information alone is staggering. Just three hundred years ago, someone with a college degree in "science" knew about as much as any expert of the day. Today, someone with a PhD in biology can't even know all that is known about the nervous system of the squid! Google Scholar reports 30,000 research articles on that topic, with the number increasing exponentially. By the time you read this, the number will have increased by at least 3,000. The amount of scientific information we've discovered in the last twenty years is more than all the discoveries up to that point, from the beginning of language. Five exabytes (5×10^{18}) of *new* data were produced in January 2012 alone—that's 50,000 times the number of words in the entire Library of Congress.

This information explosion is taxing all of us, every day, as we struggle to come to grips with what we really need to know and what we don't. We take notes, make To Do lists, leave reminders for ourselves in e-mail and on cell phones, and we still end up feeling overwhelmed.

A large part of this feeling of being overwhelmed can be traced back to our evolutionarily outdated attentional system. I mentioned earlier the two principles of the attentional filter: change and importance. There is a third principle of attention—not specific to the attentional filter—that is relevant now more than ever. It has to do with the difficulty of *attentional switching.* We can state the principle this way: Switching attention comes with a high cost.

Our brains evolved to focus on one thing at a time. This enabled our ancestors to hunt animals, to create and fashion tools, to protect their clan from predators and invading neighbors. The attentional filter evolved to help us to stay on task, letting through only information that was important enough to deserve disrupting our train of thought. But a funny thing happened on the way to the twenty-first century: The plethora of information and the technologies that serve it changed the way we use our brains. Multitasking is the enemy of a focused attentional system. Increasingly, we demand that our attentional system try to focus on several things at once, something that it was not evolved to do. We talk on the phone while we're driving, listening to the radio, looking for a parking place, planning our mom's birthday party, trying to avoid the road construction signs, and thinking about what's for lunch. We can't truly think about or attend to all these things at once, so our brains flit from one to the other, each time with a neurobiological switching cost. The system does not function well that way. Once on a task, our brains function best if we stick to that task.

To pay attention to one thing means that we *don't* pay attention to something else. *Attention is a limited-capacity resource.* When you focused on the white T-shirts in the basketball video, you filtered out the black T-shirts and, in fact, most other things that were black, including the gorilla. When we focus on a conversation we're having, we tune out other conversations. When we're just walking in the front door, thinking about who might be on the other end of that ringing telephone line, we're not thinking about where we put our car keys.

Attention is created by networks of neurons in the prefrontal cortex (just behind your forehead) that are sensitive only to dopamine. When dopamine is released, it unlocks them, like a key in your front door, and they start firing tiny electrical impulses that stimulate other neurons in their network. But what causes that initial release of dopamine? Typically, one of two different triggers:

1. Something can grab your attention automatically, usually something that is salient to your survival, with evolutionary origins. This

vigilance system incorporating the attentional filter is always at work, even when you're asleep, monitoring the environment for important events. This can be a loud sound or bright light (the startle reflex), something moving quickly (that might indicate a predator), a beverage when you're thirsty, or an attractively shaped potential sexual partner.

2. You effectively *will* yourself to focus only on that which is relevant to a search or scan of the environment. This deliberate filtering has been shown in the laboratory to actually change the sensitivity of neurons in the brain. If you're trying to find your lost daughter at the state fair, your visual system reconfigures to look only for things of about her height, hair color, and body build, filtering everything else out. Simultaneously, your auditory system retunes itself to hear only frequencies in that band where her voice registers. You could call it the *Where's Waldo?* filtering network.

In the *Where's Waldo?* children's books, a boy named Waldo wears a red-and-white horizontally striped shirt, and he's typically placed in a crowded picture with many people and objects drawn in many colors. In the version for young children, Waldo might be the only red thing in the picture; the young child's attentional filter can quickly scan the picture and land on the red object—Waldo. Waldo puzzles for older age groups become increasingly difficult—the distractors are solid red and solid white T-shirts, or shirts with stripes in different colors, or red-and-white vertical stripes rather than horizontal.

Where's Waldo? puzzles exploit the neuroarchitecture of the primate visual system. Inside the occipital lobe, a region called the visual cortex contains populations of neurons that respond only to certain colors—one population fires an electrical signal in response to red objects, another to green, and so on. Then, a separate population of neurons is sensitive to horizontal stripes as distinct from vertical stripes, and within the horizontal stripes neurons, some are maximally responsive to wide stripes and some to narrow stripes.

If only you could send instructions to these different neuron populations, telling some of them when you need them to stand up straight and do your bidding, while telling the others to sit back and relax. Well, you can—this is what we do when we try to find Waldo, search for a missing scarf or wallet, or watch the basketball video. We bring to mind a mental image of what we're looking for, and neurons in the visual cortex help us to imagine in our mind's eye what the object looks like. If it has red in it, our red-sensitive neurons are involved in the imagining. They then automatically tune themselves, and inhibit other neurons (the ones for the colors you're not interested in) to facilitate the search. *Where's Waldo?* trains children to set and exercise their visual attentional filters to locate increasingly subtle cues in the environment, much as our ancestors might have trained their children to track animals through the forest, starting with easy-to-see and easy-to-differentiate animals and working up to camouflaging animals that are more difficult to pick out from the surrounding environment. The system also works for auditory filtering—if we are expecting a particular pitch or timbre in a sound, our auditory neurons become selectively tuned to those characteristics.

When we willfully retune sensory neurons in this way, our brains engage in top-down processing, originating in a higher, more advanced part of the brain than sensory processing.

It is this top-down system that allows experts to excel in their domains. It allows quarterbacks to see their open receivers and not be distracted by other players on the field. It allows sonar operators to maintain vigilance and to easily (with suitable training) distinguish an enemy submarine from a freighter ship or a whale, just by the sound of the *ping*. It's what allows conductors to listen to just one instrument at a time when sixty are playing. It's what allows you to pay attention to this book even though there are probably distractions around you right now: the sound of a fan, traffic, birds singing outdoors, distant conversations, not to mention the visual distractions in the periphery, outside the central visual focus of where you're holding your book or screen.

If we have such an effective attentional filter, why can't we filter out distractions better than we can? Why is information overload such a serious problem now?

For one thing, we're doing more work than ever before. The promise of a computerized society, we were told, was that it would relegate to machines all of the repetitive drudgery of work, allowing us humans to pursue loftier purposes and to have more leisure time. It didn't work out this way. Instead of more time, most of us have less. Companies large and small have off-loaded work onto the backs of consumers. Things that used to be done for us, as part of the value-added service of working with a company, we are now expected to do ourselves. With air travel, we're now expected to complete our own reservations and check-in, jobs that used to be done by airline employees or travel agents. At the grocery store, we're expected to bag our own groceries and, in some supermarkets, to scan our own purchases. We pump our own gas at filling stations. Telephone operators used to look up numbers for us. Some companies no longer send out bills for their services—we're expected to log in to their website, access our account, retrieve our bill, and initiate an electronic payment; in effect, do the job of the company for them. Collectively, this is known as *shadow work*—it represents a kind of parallel, shadow economy in which a lot of the service we expect from companies has been transferred to the customer. Each of us is doing the work of others and not getting paid for it. It is responsible for taking away a great deal of the leisure time we thought we would all have in the twenty-first century.

Beyond doing more work, we are dealing with more *changes* in information technology than our parents did, and more as adults than we did as children. The average American replaces her cell phone every two years, and that often means learning new software, new buttons, new menus. We change our computer operating systems every three years, and that requires learning new icons and procedures, and learning new locations for old menu items.

But overall, as Dennis Overbye put it, "from traffic jams in Singapore to the weather on Mars," we are just getting so much more information shot at us. The global economy means we are exposed to large amounts of information that our grandparents weren't. We hear about revolutions and economic problems in countries halfway around the world right as they're happening; we see images of places we've never visited and hear languages spoken that we've never heard before. Our brains are hungrily soaking all this in because that is what they're designed to do, but at the same time, all this *stuff* is competing for neuroattentional resources with the things we need to know to live our lives.

Emerging evidence suggests that embracing new ideas and learning is helping us to live longer and can stave off Alzheimer's disease—apart from the advantages traditionally associated with expanding one's knowledge. So it's not that we need to take in less information but that we need to have systems for organizing it.

Information has always been the key resource in our lives. It has allowed us to improve society, medical care, and decision-making, to enjoy personal and economic growth, and to better choose our elected officials. It is also a fairly costly resource to acquire and handle. As knowledge becomes more available—and decentralized through the Internet—the notions of accuracy and authoritativeness have become clouded. Conflicting viewpoints are more readily available than ever, and in many cases they are disseminated by people who have no regard for facts or truth. Many of us find we don't know whom to believe, what is true, what has been modified, and what has been vetted. We don't have the time or expertise to do research on every little decision. Instead, we rely on trusted authorities, newspapers, radio, TV, books, sometimes your brother-in-law, the neighbor with the perfect lawn, the cab driver who dropped you at the airport, your memory of a similar experience. . . . Sometimes these authorities are worthy of our trust, sometimes not.

My teacher, the Stanford cognitive psychologist Amos Tversky, encapsulates this in "the Volvo story." A colleague was shopping for a new car and had done a great deal of research. *Consumer Reports* showed through independent tests that Volvos were among the best built and most reliable cars in their class. Customer satisfaction surveys showed that Volvo owners were far happier with their purchase after several years. The surveys were based on tens of thousands of customers. The sheer number of people polled meant that any anomaly—like a specific vehicle that was either exceptionally good or exceptionally bad—would be drowned out by all the other reports. In other words, a survey such as this has statistical and scientific legitimacy and should be weighted accordingly when one makes a decision. It represents a stable summary of the average experience, and the most likely best guess as to what your own experience will be (if you've got nothing else to go on, your best guess is that your experience will be most like the average).

Amos ran into his colleague at a party and asked him how his automobile purchase was going. The colleague had decided against the Volvo in favor of a different, lower-rated car. Amos asked him what made him change his mind after all that research pointed to the Volvo. Was it that he didn't like the price? The color options? The styling? No, it was none of those reasons, the colleague said. Instead, the colleague said, he found out that his brother-in-law had owned a Volvo and that it was always in the shop.

From a strictly logical point of view, the colleague is being irrational. The brother-in-law's bad Volvo experience is a single data point swamped by tens of thousands of good experiences—it's an unusual outlier. But we are social creatures. We are easily swayed by first-person stories and vivid accounts of a single experience. Although this is statistically wrong and we should learn to overcome the bias, most of us don't. Advertisers know this, and this is why we see so many first-person testimonial advertisements on TV. "I lost twenty pounds in two weeks by eating this new yogurt—and it was delicious, too!" Or "I had a headache that wouldn't go away. I was barking at the dog and snapping at my loved ones. Then I took this new medication and I was back to my normal self." Our brains focus on vivid, social accounts more than dry, boring, statistical accounts.

We make a number of reasoning errors due to cognitive biases. Many of us are familiar with illusions such as these:

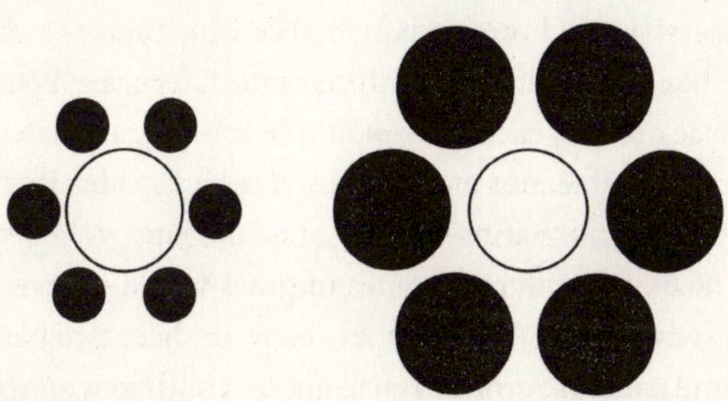

In Roger Shepard's version of the famous "Ponzo illusion," the monster at the top *seems* larger than the one at the bottom, but a ruler will show that they're the same size. In the Ebbinghaus illusion below it, the white circle on the left seems larger than the white circle on the right, but they're the same size. We say that our eyes are playing tricks on us, but in fact, our eyes aren't playing tricks on us, our brain is. The visual system uses heuristics or shortcuts to piece together an understanding of the world, and it sometimes gets things wrong.

By analogy to visual illusions, we are prone to cognitive illusions when we try to make decisions, and our brains take decision-making shortcuts. These are more likely to occur when we are faced with the kinds of Big Data that have become today's norm. We can learn to overcome them, but until we do, they profoundly affect what we pay attention to and how we process information.

The Prehistory of Mental Categorization

Cognitive psychology is the scientific study of how humans (and animals and, in some cases, computers) process information. Traditionally, cognitive psychologists have made a distinction among different areas of study: memory, attention, categorization, language acquisition and use, decision-making, and one or two other topics. Many believe that attention and memory are closely related, that you can't remember things that you didn't pay attention to in the first place. There has been relatively less attention paid to the important interrelationship among *categorization*, attention, and memory.

The act of categorizing helps us to organize the physical world-out-there but also organizes the mental world, the world-in-here, in our heads and thus what we can pay attention to and remember.

As an illustration of how fundamental categorization is, consider what life would be like if we failed to put things into categories. When we stared at a plate of black beans, each bean would be entirely unrelated to the others, not interchangeable, not of the same "kind." The idea that one bean is as good as any other for eating would not be obvious. When you went out to mow the lawn, the different blades of grass would be overwhelmingly distinct, not seen as part of a collective. Now, in these two cases, there are perceptual similarities from one bean to another and from one blade of grass to another. Your perceptual system can help you to create categories based on appearances. But we often categorize based on conceptual similarities rather than perceptual ones. If the phone rings in the kitchen and you need to take a message, you might walk over to the junk drawer and grab the first thing that looks like it will write. Even though you know that pens, pencils, and crayons are distinct and belong to different categories, for the moment they are functionally equivalent, members of a category of "things I can write on paper with." You might find only lipstick and decide to use that. So it's not your perceptual system grouping them together, but your cognitive system. Junk drawers reveal a great deal about category formation, and they serve an important and useful purpose by functioning as an escape valve when we encounter objects that just don't fit neatly anywhere else.

Our early ancestors did not have many personal possessions—an animal skin for clothing, a container for water, a sack for collecting fruit. In effect the entire natural world was their home. Keeping track of all the variety and variability of that natural world was essential, and also a daunting mental task. How did our ancestors make sense of the natural world? What kinds of distinctions were fundamental to them?

Because events during prehistory, by definition, left no historical record, we have to rely on indirect sources of evidence to answer these questions. One such source is contemporary preliterate hunter-gatherers who are cut off from industrial civilization. We can't know for sure, but our best guess is that they are living life very much as our own hunter-gatherer ancestors did. Researchers observe how they live, and interview them to find out what they know about how their own ancestors lived, through family histories and oral traditions. Languages are a related source of evidence. The "lexical hypothesis" assumes that the most important things humans need to talk about eventually become encoded in language.

One of the most important things that language does for us is help us make distinctions. When we call something edible, we distinguish it from—implicitly, automatically—all other things that are inedible. When we call something a fruit, we necessarily distinguish it from vegetables, meat, dairy, and so on. Even children intuitively understand the nature of words as restrictive. A child asking for a glass of water may complain, "I don't want *bathroom* water, I want *kitchen* water." The little munchkins are making subtle discriminations of the physical world, and exercising their categorization systems.

Early humans organized their minds and thoughts around basic distinctions that we still make and find useful. One of the earliest distinctions made was between now and not-now; *these* things are happening in the moment, these other things happened in the past and are now in my memory. No other species makes this self-conscious distinction among past, present, and future. No other species lives with regret over past events, or makes deliberate plans for future ones. Of course many species respond to time by building nests, flying south, hibernating, mating—but these are preprogrammed, instinctive behaviors and these actions are not the result of conscious decision, meditation, or planning.

Simultaneous with an understanding of *now* versus *before* is one of object permanence: Something may not be in my immediate view, but that does not mean it has ceased to exist. Human infants between four and nine months show object permanence, proving that this cognitive operation is innate. Our brains represent objects that are here-and-now as the information comes in from our sensory receptors. For example, we see a deer and we know through our eyes (and, downstream, a host of native, inborn cognitive modules) that the deer is standing right before us. When the deer is gone, we can remember its image and represent it in our mind's eye, or even represent it externally by drawing or painting or sculpting it.

This human capacity to distinguish the here-and-now from the here-and-not-now showed up at least 50,000 years ago in cave paintings. These constitute the first evidence of any species on earth being able to explicitly represent the distinction between what *is* here and what *was* here. In other words, those early cave-dwelling Picassos, through the very act of painting, were making a distinction about time and place and objects, an advanced cognitive operation we now call *mental representation*. And what they were demonstrating was an articulated sense of time: There was a deer *out there* (not here on the cave wall of course). He is not there now, but he was there before. Now and before are different; *here* (the cave wall) is merely representing *there* (the meadow in front of the cave). This prehistoric step in the organization of our minds mattered a great deal.

In making such distinctions, we are implicitly forming categories, something that is often overlooked. Category formation runs deep in the animal kingdom. Birds building a nest have an implicit category for materials that will create a good nest, including twigs, cotton, leaves, fabric, and mud, but not, say, nails, bits of wire, melon rinds, or shards of glass. The formation of categories in humans is guided by a cognitive principle of wanting to encode as much information as possible with the least possible effort. Categorization systems optimize the ease of conception and the importance of being able to communicate about those systems.

Categorization permeates social life as well. Across the 6,000 languages known to be spoken on the planet today, every culture marks, through language, who is linked to whom as "family." Kinship terms allow us to reduce an enormous set of possible relations into a more manageable, smaller set, a usable category. Kinship structure allows us to encode as much relevant information as possible with the least cognitive effort.

All languages encode the same set of core (biological) relations: mother, father, daughter, son, sister, brother, grandmother, grandfather, granddaughter, and grandson. From there, languages differ. In English, your mother's brother and your father's brother are both called uncles. The husbands of your mother's sister and of your father's sister are also called uncles. This is not true in many languages where "uncledom" follows only by marriage on the father's side (in patrilineal cultures) or only on the mother's side (in matrilineal cultures), and can spread over two or more generations. Another point in common is that all languages have a large collective category for relatives who are considered in that culture to be somewhat distant from you—similar to our English term *cousin*. Although theoretically, many billions of kinship systems are possible, research has shown that actual systems in existence in disparate parts of the world have formed to minimize complexity and maximize ease of communication.

Kinship categories tell us biologically adaptive things, things that improve the likelihood that we have healthy children, such as whom we can and cannot marry. They also are windows into the culture of a group, their attitudes about responsibility; they reveal pacts of mutual caring, and they carry norms such as where a young married couple will live. Here is a list, for example, that anthropologists use for just this purpose:

- Patrilocal: the couple lives with or near groom's kin
- Matrilocal: the couple lives with or near bride's kin
- Ambilocal: married couple can choose to live with or near kin of either groom or bride

- Neolocal: couple moves to a new household in a new location
- Natolocal: husband and wife remain with their own natal kin and do not live together
- Avunculocal: couple moves to or near residence of the groom's mother's brother(s) (or other uncles, by definition, depending on culture)

The two dominant models of kinship behavior in North America today are *neolocal* and *ambilocal:* Young married couples typically get their own residence, and they can choose to live wherever they want, even many hundreds or thousands of miles away from their respective parents; however, many choose to live either with or very near the family of the husband or wife. This latter, ambilocal choice offers important emotional (and sometimes financial) support, secondary child care, and a built-in network of friends and relatives to help the young couple get started in life. According to one study, couples (especially low-income ones) who stay near the kin of one or both partners fare better in their marriages and in child rearing.

Kinship beyond the core relations of son-daughter and mother-father might seem to be entirely arbitrary, merely a human invention. But it shows up in a number of animal species and we can quantify the relations in genetic terms to show their importance. From a strictly evolutionary standpoint, your job is to propagate as many of your genes as possible. You share 50% of your genes with your mother and father or with any offspring. You also share 50% with your siblings (unless you're a twin). If your sister has children, you will share 25% of your genes with them. If you don't have any children of your own, your best strategy for propagating your genes is to help care for your sister's children, your nieces and nephews.

Your direct cousins—the offspring of an aunt or uncle—share 12.5% of your genes. If you don't have nephews and nieces, any care you put into cousins helps to pass on part of the genetic material that is you. Richard Dawkins and others have thus made cogent arguments to counter the claim of religious fundamentalists and social conservatives that homosexuality is "an abomination" that goes against nature. A gay man or lesbian who helps in the raising and care of a family member's child is able to devote considerable time and financial resources to propagating the family's genes. This has no doubt been true throughout history. A natural consequence of this

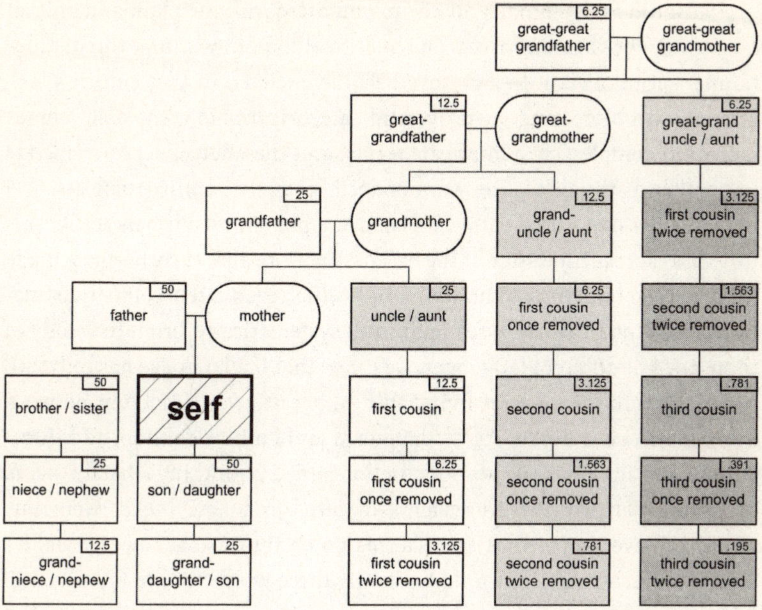

chart is that first cousins who have children together increase the number of genes they pass on. In fact, many cultures promote marriage between first cousins as a way to increase family unity, retain familial wealth, or to ensure similar cultural and religious views within the union.

The caring for one's nephews and nieces is not limited to humans. Mole rats will care for nieces and nephews but not for unrelated young, and Japanese quails show a clear preference for mating with first cousins—a way to increase the amount of their own genetic material that gets passed on (the offspring of first cousins will have 56.25% of their DNA in common with each parent rather than 50%—that is, the "family" genes have an edge of 6.25% in the offspring of first cousins than in the offspring of unrelated individuals).

Classifications such as kinship categories aid in the organization, encoding, and communication of complex knowledge. And the classifications have their roots in animal behavior, so they can be said to be precognitive. What humans did was to make these distinctions linguistic and thus explicitly communicable information.

How did early humans divide up and categorize the plant and animal kingdom? The data are based on the lexical hypothesis, that the distinctions most important to a culture become encoded in that culture's language. With increasing cognitive and categorizational complexity comes increased complexity in linguistic terms, and these terms serve to encode important distinctions. The work of sociobiologists, anthropologists, and linguists has uncovered patterns in naming plants and animals across cultures and across time. One of the first distinctions that early humans made was between humans and nonhumans—which makes sense. Finer distinctions crept into languages gradually and systematically. From the study of thousands of different languages, we know that if a language has only two nouns (naming words) for living things, it makes a distinction between human and nonhuman. As the language and culture develop, additional terms come into use. The next distinction added is for things that fly, swim, or crawl—roughly the equivalents of *bird, fish,* and *snake.* Generally speaking, two or three of these terms come into use at once. Thus, it's unlikely that a language would have only three words for life-forms, but if it has four, they will be *human, nonhuman,* and two of *bird, fish,* and *snake.* Which two of those nouns gets added depends, as you might imagine, on the environment where they live, and on which critters the people are most likely to encounter. If the language has four such animal nouns, it adds the missing one of these three. A language with five such animal terms adds either a general term for *mammal* or a term for smaller crawling things, combining into one category what we in English call *worms* and *bugs.* Because so many preliterate languages combine worms and bugs into a single category, ethnobiologists have made up a name for that category: *wugs.*

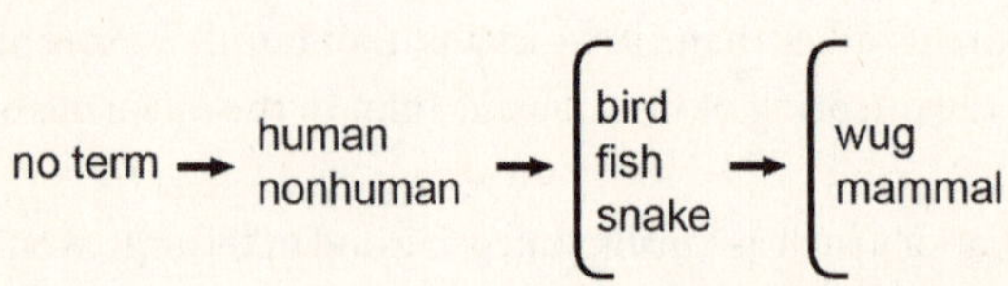

Most languages have a single folksy word for creepy-crawly things, and English is no exception. Our own term *bugs* is an informal and heterogeneous category combining ants, beetles, flies, spiders, aphids, caterpillars, grasshoppers, ticks, and a large number of living things that are biologically and taxonomically quite distinct. The fact that we still do this today, with all our advanced scientific knowledge, underscores the utility and innateness of *functional categories.* "Bug" promotes cognitive economy by combining into a single category things that most of the time we don't need to think about in great detail, apart from keeping them out of our food or from crawling on our skin. It is not the biology of these organisms that unites them, but their function in *our* lives—or our goal of trying to keep them on the outside of our bodies and not the inside.

The category names used by preliterate, tribal-based societies are similarly in contradiction to our modern scientific categories. In many languages, the word *bird* includes bats; *fish* can include whales, dolphins, and turtles; *snake* sometimes includes worms, lizards, and eels.

After these seven basic nouns, societies add other terms to their language in a less systematic fashion. Along the way, there are some societies that add an idiosyncratic term for a specific species that has great social, religious, or practical meaning. A language might have a single term for *eagle* in addition to its general term *bird* without having any other named birds. Or it might single out among the mammals a single term for *bear.*

A universal order of emergence for linguistic terms shows up in the plant world as well. Relatively undeveloped languages have no single word for plants. The lack of a term doesn't mean they don't perceive differences, and it doesn't mean they don't know the difference between spinach and skunk weed; they just lack an all-encompassing term with which to refer to plants. We see cases like this in our own language. For example, English lacks a single basic term to refer to edible mushrooms. We also lack a term for all the people you would have to notify if you were going into the hospital for three weeks. These might include close relatives, friends, your employer, the newspaper delivery person, and anyone you had appointments with during that period. The lack of a term doesn't mean you don't understand the concept; it simply means that the category isn't reflected in our language. This could be because a need for it hasn't been so pressing that a word needed to be coined.

If a language has only a single term for nonanimal living things, it is *not* the all-encompassing word *plant* that we have in English. Rather, it is a single word that maps to tall, woody growing things—what we call *trees.* When a language introduces a second term, it is either a catchall term for grasses and herbs—which researchers call *grerb*—or it is the general term for *grass* and grassy-like things. When a language grows to add a third term for plants and it already has *grerb*, the third, fourth, and fifth terms are *bush, grass,* and *vine* (not necessarily in that order; it depends on the environment). If the language already has *grass*, the third, fourth, and fifth terms added are *bush, herb,* and *vine.*

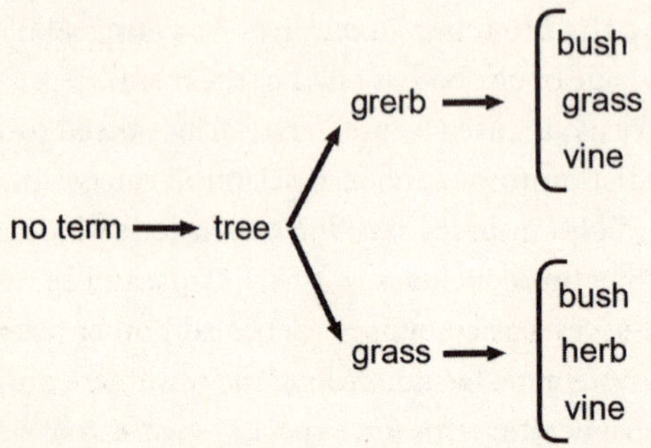

Grass is an interesting category because most of the members of the category are unnamed by most speakers of English. We can name dozens of vegetables and trees, but most of us just say "grass" to encompass the more than 9,000 different species. This is similar to the case with the term *bug*—most of the members of the category remain unnamed by most English speakers.

Orders of emergence in language exist for other concepts. Among the most well known was the discovery by UC Berkeley anthropologists Brent Berlin and Paul Kay of a universal order of emergence for color terms. Many of the world's preindustrial languages have only two terms for color, roughly dividing the world into *light* and *dark* colors. I've labeled them WHITE and BLACK in the figure, following the literature, but it doesn't mean that speakers of these languages are literally naming only white and black. Rather, it means that half the colors they see get mapped to a single "light colors" term and half to a single "dark colors" term.

Now here's the most interesting part: When a language advances and adds a third term to its lexicon for color, the third term is always *red.* Various theories have been proposed, the dominant one being that red is important because it is the color of blood. When a language adds a fourth

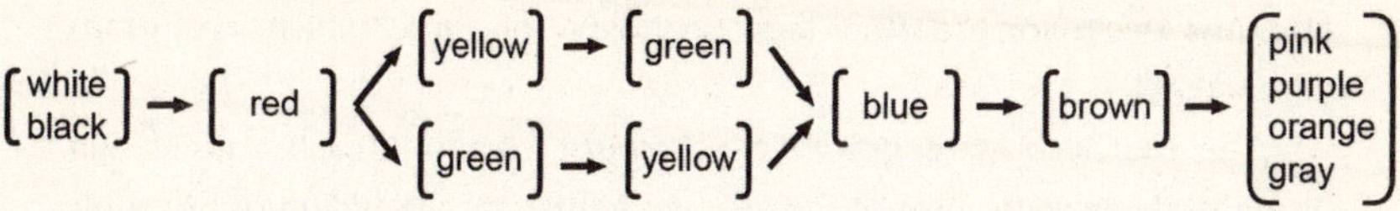

term, it is either *yellow* or *green*. The fifth term is either *green* or *yellow*, and the sixth term is *blue*.

These categories are not just academic or of anthropological interest. They are critical to one of the basic pursuits of cognitive science: to understand how information is organized. And this need to understand is a hardwired, innate trait that we humans share because knowledge is useful to us. When our early human ancestors left the cover of living in trees and ventured out onto the open savanna in search of new sources of food, they made themselves more vulnerable to predators and to nuisances like rats and snakes. Those who were interested in acquiring knowledge—whose brains enjoyed learning new things—would have been at an advantage for survival, and so this love of learning would eventually become encoded in their genes through natural selection. As the anthropologist Clifford Geertz noted, there is little doubt that preliterate, tribal-based subsistence humans "are interested in all kinds of things of use neither to their schemes [n]or to their stomachs. . . . They are not classifying all those plants, distinguishing all those snakes, or sorting out all those bats out of some overwhelming cognitive passion rising out of innate structures at the bottom of the mind. . . . In an environment populated with conifers, or snakes, or leaf-eating bats, it is practical to know a good deal about conifers, snakes, or leaf-eating bats, whether or not what one knows is in any strict sense materially useful."

An opposing view comes from the anthropologist Claude Lévi-Strauss, who felt that classification meets an innate need to classify the natural world because the human brain has a strong cognitive propensity toward order. This preference for order over disorder can be traced back through millions of years of evolution. As mentioned in the Introduction, some birds and rodents create boundaries around their nests, typically out of rocks or leaves, that are ordered; if the order is disturbed, they know that an intruder has come by. I've had several dogs who wandered through the house periodically to collect their toys and put them in a basket.

Humans' desire for order no doubt scaffolded on these ancient evolutionary systems.

The UC Berkeley cognitive psychologist Eleanor Rosch argued that human categorization is not the product of historical accident or arbitrary factors, but the result of psychological or innate principles of categorization. The views of Lévi-Strauss and Rosch suggest a disagreement with the dichotomy Geertz draws between cognitive passion and practical knowledge. My view is that the passion Geertz refers to is *part* of the practical benefit of knowledge—they are two sides of the same coin. It can be practical to know a great deal about the biological world, but the human brain has been configured—wired—to acquire this information and to *want* to acquire it. This innate passion for naming and categorizing can be brought into stark relief by the fact that *most* of the naming we do in the plant world might be considered strictly unnecessary. Out of 30,000 edible plants thought to exist on earth, just eleven account for 93% of all that humans eat: oats, corn, rice, wheat, potatoes, yucca (also called tapioca or cassava), sorghum, millet, beans, barley, and rye. Yet our brains evolved to receive a pleasant shot of dopamine when we learn something new and again when we can classify it systematically into an ordered structure.

In Pursuit of Excellent Categorization

We humans are hardwired to enjoy knowledge, in particular knowledge that comes through the senses. And we are hardwired to impose structure on this sensory knowledge, to turn it this way and that, to view it from different angles, and try to fit it into multiple neural frameworks. This is the essence of human learning.

We are hardwired to impose structure on the world. A further piece of evidence for the innateness of this structure is the extraordinary consistency of naming conventions for biological classification (plants and animals) across widely disparate cultures. All languages and cultures—independently—came up with naming principles so similar that they strongly suggest an innate predisposition toward classification. For example, every language contains primary and secondary plant and animal names. In English we have *fir trees* (in general) and *Douglas fir* (in particular). There are *apples* and then there are *Granny Smiths, golden delicious,* and *pippins.*

There are salmon and then sockeye salmon, woodpeckers and acorn woodpeckers. We look at the world and can perceive that there exists a category that includes a set of things more alike than they are unalike, and yet we recognize minor variations. This extends to man-made artifacts as well. We have chairs and easy chairs, knives and hunting knives, shoes and dancing shoes. And here's an interesting side note: Nearly every language also has some terms that mimic this structure linguistically but in fact don't refer to the same types of things. For example, in English, silverfish is an insect, not a type of fish; prairie dog is a rodent, not a dog; and a toadstool is neither a toad nor a stool that a toad might sit on.

Our hunger for knowledge can be at the roots of our failings or our successes. It can distract us or it can keep us engaged in a lifelong quest for deep learning and understanding. Some learning enhances our lives, some is irrelevant and simply distracts us—tabloid stories probably fall into this latter category (unless your profession is as a tabloid writer). Successful people are expert at categorizing useful versus distracting knowledge. How do they do it?

Of course some have that string of assistants who enable them to be in the moment, and that in turn makes them more successful. Smartphones and digital files are helpful in organizing information, but categorizing the information in a way that is helpful—and that harnesses the way our brains are organized—still requires a lot of fine-grained categorization by a human, by us.

One thing HSPs do over and over every day is *active sorting,* what emergency room nurses call *triage. Triage* comes from the French word *trier,* meaning "to sort, sift, or classify." You probably already do something like this without calling it active sorting. It simply means that you separate those things you need to deal with *right now* from those that you don't. This conscious active sorting takes many different forms in our lives, and there is no one right way. The number of categories varies and the number of times a day will vary, too—maybe you don't even need to do it every day. Nevertheless, one way or another, it is an essential part of being organized, efficient, and productive.

I worked as the personal assistant for several years for a successful businessman, Edmund W. Littlefield. He had been the CEO of Utah Construction (later Utah International), a company that built the Hoover Dam and many construction projects all over the world, including half the railroad tunnels and bridges west of the Mississippi. When I worked for him, he also served on the board of directors of General Electric, Chrysler, Wells Fargo, Del Monte, and Hewlett-Packard. He was remarkable for his intellect, business acumen, and above all, his genuine modesty and humility. He was a generous mentor. Our politics did not always agree, but he was respectful of opposing views, and tried to keep such discussions based on facts rather than speculation. One of the first things he taught me to do as his assistant was to sort his mail into four piles:

1. Things that need to be dealt with right away. This might include correspondence from his office or business associates, bills, legal documents, and the like. He subsequently performed a *fine sort* of things to be dealt with today versus in the next few days.
2. Things that are important but can wait. We called this the *abeyance pile.* This might include investment reports that needed to be reviewed, articles he might want to read, reminders for periodic service on an automobile, invitations to parties or functions that were some time off in the future, and so on.
3. Things that are *not* important and can wait, but should still be kept. This was mostly product catalogues, holiday cards, and magazines.
4. Things to be thrown out.

Ed would periodically go through the items in all these categories and re-sort. Other people have finer-grained and coarser-grained systems. One HSP has a two-category system: things to keep and things to throw away. Another HSP extends the system from correspondence to everything that comes across her desk, either electronically (such as e-mails and PDFs) or as paper copies. To the Littlefield categories one could add subcategories for the different things you are working on, for hobbies, home maintenance, and so on.

Some of the material in these categories ends up in piles on one's desk, some in folders in a filing cabinet or on a computer. Active sorting is a powerful way to prevent yourself from being distracted. It creates and fosters great efficiencies, not just practical efficiencies but intellectual ones. After you have prioritized and you start working, knowing that what you are doing is the most important thing for you *to* be doing at that moment is surprisingly powerful. Other things can wait—*this* is what you can focus on without worrying that you're forgetting something.

There is a deep and simple reason why active sorting facilitates this. The most fundamental principle of the organized mind, the one most critical to keeping us from forgetting or losing things, is to shift the burden of organizing from our brains to the external world. If we can remove some or all of the process from our brains and put it out into the physical world, we are less likely to make mistakes. This is not because of the limited capacity of our brains—rather, it's because of the nature of memory storage and retrieval in our brains: Memory processes can easily become distracted or confounded by other, similar items. Active sorting is just one of many ways of using the physical world to organize your mind. The information you need is in the physical pile *there*, not crowded in your head *up here*. Successful people have devised dozens of ways to do this, physical reminders in their homes, cars, offices, and throughout their lives to shift the burden of remembering from their brains to their environment. In a broad sense, these are related to what cognitive psychologists call *Gibsonian affordances* after the researcher J. J. Gibson.

A Gibsonian affordance describes an object whose design features tell you something about how to use it. An example made famous by another cognitive psychologist, Don Norman, is a door. When you approach a door, how do you know whether it is going to open in or out, whether to push it or pull it? With doors you use frequently, you could try to remember, but most of us don't. When subjects in an experiment were asked, "Does your bedroom door open *in* to the bedroom or *out* into the hall?" most couldn't remember. But certain features of doors encode this information for us. They *show* us how to use them, so we don't have to remember, cluttering up our brains with information that could be more durably and efficiently kept in the external world.

As you reach for the handle of a door in your home, you can see whether the jamb will block you if you try to pull the door toward you. You are probably not consciously aware of it, but your brain is registering this and guiding your actions automatically—and this is much more cognitively efficient than your memorizing the flow pattern of every door you encounter. Businesses, office buildings, and other public facilities make it even more obvious because there are so many more people using them: Doors that are meant to be *pushed* open tend to have a flat plate and no handle on one side, or a push bar across the door. Doors that are meant to be *pulled* open have a handle. Even with the extra guidance, sometimes the unfamiliarity of the door, or the fact that you are on your way to a job interview or some other distracting appointment, will make you balk for a moment, not knowing whether to push or pull. But most of the time, your brain recognizes how the door works because of its affordance, and in or out you go.

Similarly, the design of the telephone on your desk *shows* you which part you're meant to pick up. The handset is just the size and shape to *afford* your picking it up and not picking up a different part. Most scissors have two finger holes, one larger than the other, and so you know where to put your finger and where to put your thumb (usually to the annoyance of those who are left-handed). A tea kettle's handle tells you how to pick it up. The list of affordances goes on and on.

This is why key hooks work. Keeping track of things that you frequently lose, such as car keys, glasses, and even wallets involves creating affordances that reduce the burden on your conscious brain. In this age of information overload, it's important that we gain control of that environment, and leverage our knowledge of how the brain operates. The organized mind creates affordances and categories that allow for low-effort navigation through the world of car keys, cell phones, and hundreds of daily details, and it also will help us make our way through the twenty-first-century world of ideas.

2

THE FIRST THINGS TO GET STRAIGHT

How Attention and Memory Work

We live in a world of illusions. We think we're aware of everything going on around us. We look out and see an uninterrupted, complete picture of the visual world, composed of thousands of little detailed images. We may know that each of us has a blind spot, but we go on day to day blissfully unaware of where it actually is because our occipital cortex does such a good job of filling in the missing information and hence hiding it from us. Laboratory demonstrations of inattentional blindness (like the gorilla video of the last chapter) underscore how little of the world we actually perceive, in spite of the overwhelming feeling that we're getting it all.

We attend to objects in the environment partly based on our will (we choose to pay attention to some things), partly based on an alert system that monitors our world for danger, and partly based on our brains' own vagaries. Our brains come preconfigured to create categories and classifications of things automatically and without our conscious intervention. When the systems we're trying to set up are in collision with the way our brain automatically categorizes things, we end up losing things, missing appointments, or forgetting to do things we needed to do.

Have you ever sat in an airplane or train, just staring out the window with nothing to read, looking at nothing in particular? You might have found that the time passed very pleasantly, with no real memory of what exactly you were looking at, what you were thinking, or for that matter, how much time actually elapsed. You might have had a similar feeling the last time you sat by the ocean or a lake, letting your mind wander, and experiencing the relaxing feeling it induced. In this state, thoughts seem to move seamlessly from one to another, there's a merging of ideas, visual images, and sounds, of past, present, and future. Thoughts turn inward—loosely connected, stream-of-consciousness thoughts so much like the nighttime dream state that we call them daydreams.

This distinctive and special brain state is marked by the flow of connections among disparate ideas and thoughts, and a relative lack of barriers between senses and concepts. It also can lead to great creativity and solutions to problems that seemed unsolvable. Its discovery—a special brain network that supports a more fluid and nonlinear mode of thinking—was one of the biggest neuroscientific discoveries of the last twenty years. This network exerts a pull on consciousness; it eagerly shifts the brain into mind-wandering when you're not engaged in a task, and it hijacks your consciousness if the task you're doing gets boring. It has taken over when you find you've been reading several pages in a book without registering their content, or when you are driving on a long stretch of highway and suddenly realize you haven't been paying attention to where you are and you missed your exit. It's the same part that took over when you realized that you had your keys in your hand a minute ago but now you don't know where they are. Where *is* your brain when this happens?

Envisioning or planning one's future, projecting oneself into a situation (especially a social situation), feeling empathy, invoking autobiographical memories also involve this daydreaming or mind-wandering network. If you've ever stopped what you were doing to picture the consequence of some future action or to imagine yourself in a particular future encounter, maybe your eyes turned up or down in your head from a normal straight-ahead gaze, and you became preoccupied with thought: That's the daydreaming mode.

The discovery of this mind-wandering mode didn't receive big headlines in the popular press, but it has changed the way neuroscientists think about attention. Daydreaming and mind-wandering, we now know, are a natural state of the brain. This accounts for why we feel so refreshed after it, and why vacations and naps can be so restorative. The tendency for this system to take over is so powerful that its discoverer, Marcus Raichle, named it the *default mode*. This mode is a resting brain state, when your brain is not engaged in a purposeful task, when you're sitting on a sandy beach or relaxing in your easy chair with a single malt Scotch, and your mind wanders fluidly from topic to topic. It's not just that you *can't* hold on to any one thought from the rolling stream, it's that no single thought is demanding a response.

The mind-wandering mode stands in stark contrast to the state you're in when you're intensely focused on a task such as doing your taxes, writing a report, or navigating through an unfamiliar city. This stay-on-task mode is the other dominant mode of attention, and it is responsible for so many high-level things we do that researchers have named it "the central executive." These two brain states form a kind of yin-yang: When one is active, the other is not. During demanding tasks, the central executive kicks in. The more the mind-wandering network is suppressed, the greater the accuracy of performance on the task at hand.

The discovery of the mind-wandering mode also explains why paying attention to something takes effort. The phrase *paying attention* is well-worn figurative language, and there is some useful meaning in this cliché. Attention has a cost. It is a this-or-that, zero-sum game. We pay attention to one thing, either through conscious decision or because our attentional filter deemed it important enough to push it to the forefront of attentional focus. When we pay attention to one thing, we are necessarily taking attention away from something else.

My colleague Vinod Menon discovered that the mind-wandering mode is a network, because it is not localized to a specific region of the brain. Rather, it ties together distinct populations of neurons that are distributed in the brain and connected to one another to form the equivalent of an electrical circuit or network. Thinking about how the brain works in terms of networks is a profound development in recent neuroscience.

Beginning about twenty-five years ago, the fields of psychology and neuroscience underwent a revolution. Psychology was primarily using decades-old methods to understand human behavior through things that were objective and observable, such as learning lists of words or the ability to perform tasks while distracted. Neuroscience was primarily studying the communication among cells and the biological structure of the brain. The psychologists had difficulty studying the biological material, that is, the hardware, that gave rise to thought. The neuroscientists, being stuck down at the level of individual neurons, had difficulty studying actual behaviors. The revolution was the invention of noninvasive neuroimaging techniques, a set of tools analogous to an X-ray that showed not just the contours and structure of the brain but how parts of the brain behaved in real time during actual thought and behavior—pictures of the thinking brain at work. The technologies—positron emission tomography, functional magnetic resonance imaging, and magnetoencephalography—are now well known by their abbreviations PET, fMRI, and MEG.

The initial wave of studies focused primarily on localization of brain function, a kind of neural mapping. What part of the brain is active when you mentally practice your tennis serve, when you listen to music, or perform mathematical calculations? More recently, interest has shifted toward developing an understanding of how these regions work together. Neuroscientists have concluded that mental operations may not always be occurring in one specific brain region but, rather, are carried out by circuits, networks of related neuron groups. If someone asked, "Where is the electricity kept that makes it possible to operate your refrigerator?" where would you point? The outlet? It actually doesn't have current passing through it unless an appliance is plugged in. And once one is, it is no more the place of electricity than circuits throughout all the household appliances and, in a sense, throughout the house. Really, there is no single place where electricity is. It is a distributed network; it won't show up in a cell phone photo.

Similarly, cognitive neuroscientists are increasingly appreciating that mental function is often spread out. Language ability does not reside in a specific region of the brain; rather, it comprises a distributed network—like the electrical wires in your house—that draws on and engages regions throughout the brain. What led early researchers to think that language might be localized is that disruption to particular regions of the brain reliably caused loss of language functions. Think of the circuits in your home again. If your contractor accidentally cuts an electrical wire, you can lose electricity in an entire section of your home, but it doesn't mean that the electricity *source* was at the place that was cut—it simply means that a line necessary for transmission was disrupted. In fact, there is almost an infinity of places where cutting the wires in your house will cause a disruption to service, including cutting the wire at the source, the circuit breaker box. From where you stand in your kitchen with a blender that won't mix your smoothie, the effect is the same. It begins to look different only when you set out to repair it. This is how neuroscientists now think of the brain—as a set of intricate overlapping networks.

The mind-wandering mode works in opposition to the central executive mode: When one is activated, the other one is deactivated; if we're in one mode, we're not in the other. The job of the central executive network is to prevent you from being distracted when you're engaged in a task, limiting what will enter your consciousness so that you can focus on what you're doing uninterrupted. And again, whether you are in the mind-wandering or central executive mode, your attentional filter is almost always operating, quietly out of the way in your subconscious.

For our ancestors, staying on task typically meant hunting a large mammal, fleeing a predator, or fighting. A lapse of attention during these activities could spell disaster. Today, we're more likely to employ our central executive mode for writing reports, interacting with people and computers, driving, navigating, solving problems in our heads, or pursuing artistic projects such as painting and music. A lapse of attention in these activities isn't usually a matter of life or death, but it does interfere with our effectiveness when we're trying to accomplish something.

In the mind-wandering mode, our thoughts are mostly directed inward to our goals, desires, feelings, plans, and also our relationship with other people—the mind-wandering mode is active when people are feeling empathy toward one another. In the central executive mode, thoughts are directed both inward and outward. There is a clear evolutionary advantage to being able to stay on task and concentrate, but not to entering an irreversible state of hyperfocus that makes us oblivious to a predator or enemy lurking behind the bushes, or to a poisonous spider crawling up the back of our neck. This is where the attentional network comes in; the attentional filter is constantly monitoring the environment for anything that might be important.

In addition to the mind-wandering mode, the central executive, and the attentional filter, there's a fourth component of the attentional system that allows us to switch between the mind-wandering mode and the central executive mode. This switch enables shifts from one task to another, such as when you're talking to a friend at a party and your attention is suddenly shifted to that other conversation about the fire in the kitchen. It's a neural switchboard that directs your attention to that mosquito on your forehead and then allows you to go back to your post-lunchtime mind-wandering. In a 2010 paper, Vinod Menon and I showed that the switch is controlled in a part of the brain called the insula, an important structure about an inch or so beneath the surface of where temporal lobes and frontal lobes join. Switching between two external objects involves the temporal-parietal junction.

The insula has bidirectional connections to an important brain part called the anterior cingulate cortex. Put your finger on the top of your head, just above where you think the back of your nose is. About two inches farther back and two inches below that is the anterior cingulate. Below is a diagram showing where it is, relative to other brain structures.

The relationship between the central executive system and the mind-wandering system is like a see-saw, and the insula—the attentional switch—is like an adult holding one side down so that the other stays up in the air. This efficacy of the insula-cingulate network varies from person to person, in some functioning like a well-oiled switch, and in others like a rusty old

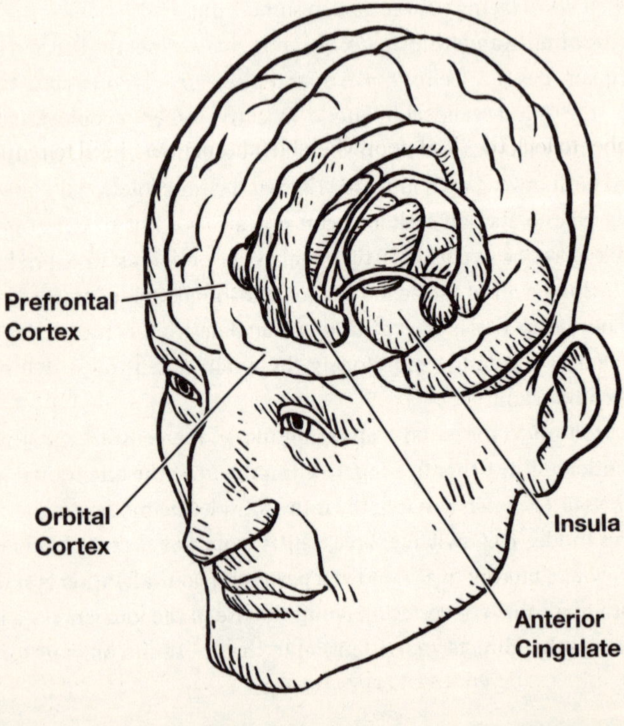

gate. But switch it does, and if it is called upon to switch too much or too often, we feel tired and a bit dizzy, as though we were see-sawing too rapidly.

Notice that the anterior cingulate extends from the orbital and prefrontal cortex in front (left on the drawing) to the supplementary motor area at the top. Its proximity to these areas is interesting because the orbital and prefrontal areas are responsible for things like planning, scheduling, and impulse control, and the supplementary motor area is responsible for initiating movement. In other words, the parts of your brain that remind you about a report you have due, or that move your fingers across the keyboard to type, are biologically linked to the parts of your brain that keep you on task, that help you to stay put in your chair and finish that report.

This four-circuit human attentional system evolved over tens of thousands of years—distinct brain networks that become more or less active depending on the situation—and it now lies at the center of our ability to organize information. We see it every day. You're sitting at your desk and there is a cacophony of sounds and visual distractions surrounding you: the fan of the ventilation unit, the hum of the fluorescent lights, traffic outside your window, the occasional glint of sunlight reflecting off a windshield outside and streaking across your face. Once you've settled into your work, you cease to notice these and can focus on your task. After about fifteen or twenty minutes, though, you find your mind wandering: Did I remember to lock the front door when I left home? Do I need to remind Jeff of our lunch meeting today? Is this project I'm working on right now going to get done on time? Most people have internal dialogues like this going on in their heads all the time. It might cause you to wonder who is asking the questions inside your head and—more intriguingly—who is answering them? There isn't a bunch of miniature you's inside your head, of course. Your brain, however, is a collection of semidistinct, special-purpose processing units. The inner dialogue is generated by the planning centers of your brain in the prefrontal cortex, and the questions are being answered by other parts of your brain that possess the information.

Distinct networks in your brain can thus harbor completely different thoughts and hold completely different agendas. One part of your brain is concerned with satisfying immediate hunger, another with planning and sticking to a diet; one part is paying attention to the road while you drive, another is bebopping along with the radio. The attentional network has to monitor all these activities and allocate resources to some and not to others.

If this seems far-fetched, it may be easier to visualize if you realize that the brain is already doing this all the time for cellular housekeeping purposes. For example, when you start to run, a part of your brain "asks" the question, "Do we have enough oxygen going to the leg muscles to support this activity?" while in tandem, another part sends down an order to increase respiration levels so that blood oxygenation is increased. A third part that is monitoring activity makes sure that the respiration increase was carried out per instructions and reports back if it wasn't. Most of the time, these exchanges occur below the level of consciousness, which is to say, we're not aware of the dialogue or signal-response mechanism. But neuroscientists are increasingly appreciating that consciousness is not an all-or-nothing state; rather, it is a continuum of different states. We say colloquially that this or that is happening in the subconscious mind as though it were a geographically separate part of the brain, somewhere down deep in a dank, dimly lit basement of the cranium. The more accurate neural description is that many networks of neurons are firing, much like the network of telephones simultaneously ringing in a busy office. When the activation of a neural network is sufficiently high, relative to *other* neural activity that's going on, it breaks into our attentional process, that is, it becomes captured by our conscious mind, our central executive, and we become aware of it.

Many of us hold a folk view of consciousness that is not true but is compelling because of how it feels—we feel as though there is a little version of ourselves inside our heads, telling us what is going on in the world and reminding us to take out the trash on Mondays. A more elaborated version of the myth goes something like this: There's a miniature version of us inside our heads, sitting in a comfortable chair, looking at multiple television screens. Projected on the screens are the contents of our consciousness—the external world that we see and hear, its tactile sensations, smells, and tastes—and the screens also report our internal mental and bodily states: I'm feeling hungry now, I'm too hot, I'm tired. We feel that there is an internal narrator of our lives up here in our heads, showing us what's going on in the outside world, telling us what it all means, and integrating this information with reports from inside our body about our internal emotional and physical states.

One problem with the account is that it leads to an infinite regress. Is there a miniature you sitting in a theater in your head? Does that miniature you have little eyes and ears for watching and listening to the TV screens? And a little brain of its own? If so, is there an even smaller miniature person inside *its* brain? And another miniature person inside the brain of *that* miniature person? The cycle never ends. (Daniel Dennett showed this explanation to be both logically and neurally implausible in *Consciousness Explained*.) The reality is more marvelous in its way.

Numerous special-purpose modules in your brain are at work, trying to sort out and make sense of experience. Most of them are running in the background. When that neural activity reaches a certain threshold, you become aware of it, and we call that consciousness. Consciousness itself is not a thing, and it is not localizable in the brain. Rather, it's simply the name we put to ideas and perceptions that enter the awareness of our central executive, a system of very limited capacity that can generally attend to a maximum of four or five things at a time.

To recap, there are four components in the human attentional system: the mind-wandering mode, the central executive mode, the attentional filter, and the attentional switch, which directs neural and metabolic resources among the mind-wandering, stay-on-task, or vigilance modes. The system is so effective that we rarely know what we're filtering out. In many cases, the attentional switch operates in the background of our awareness, carrying us between the mind-wandering mode and the central executive mode, while the attentional filter purrs along—we don't realize what is in operation until we're already in another mode. There are exceptions of course. We can *will* ourselves to switch modes, as when we look up from something we're reading to contemplate what is said. But the switching remains subtle: You don't say, "I'm switching modes now"; you (or your insula) just do it.

The Neurochemistry of Attention

The last twenty years in neuroscience have also revealed an enormous amount about how paying attention actually happens. The mind-wandering network recruits neurons within the prefrontal cortex (just behind your forehead and eyes) in addition to the cingulate (a couple of inches farther back), joining them to the hippocampus, the center of memory consolidation. It does this through the activity of noradrenaline neurons in the locus coeruleus, a tiny little hub near the brainstem, deep inside the skull, which has evolved a dense mass of fibers connected to the prefrontal cortex. Despite the similarity of names, noradrenaline and adrenaline are not the same chemical;

noradrenaline is most chemically similar to dopamine, from which it is synthesized by the brain. To stay in the mind-wandering mode, a precise balance must be maintained between the excitatory neurotransmitter glutamate and the inhibitory neurotransmitter GABA (gamma-Aminobutyric acid). We know dopamine and serotonin are components of this brain network, but their interactions are complex and not yet fully understood. There is tantalizing new evidence that a particular genetic variation (of a gene called COMT) causes the dopamine and serotonin balance to shift, and this shift is associated both with mood disorders and with responsiveness to antidepressants. The serotonin transporter gene SLC6A4 has been found to correlate with artistic behaviors as well as spirituality, both of which appear to favor the mind-wandering mode. Thus a connection among genetics, neurotransmitters, and artistic/spiritual thinking appears to exist. (Dopamine is no more important than glutamate and GABA and any number of other chemicals. We simply know more about dopamine because it's easier to study. In twenty years, we'll have a far more nuanced understanding of it and other chemicals.)

The central executive network recruits neurons in different parts of the prefrontal cortex and the cingulate, plus the basal ganglia deep inside the center of the brain—this executive network is not exclusively located in the prefrontal cortex as popular accounts have tended to suggest. Its chemical action includes modulating levels of dopamine in the frontal lobes. Sustained attention also depends on noradrenaline and acetylcholine, especially in distracting environments—this is the chemistry underlying the concentration it takes to focus. And while you're focusing attention on the task at hand, acetylcholine in the right prefrontal cortex helps to improve the quality of the work done by the attentional filter. Acetylcholine density in the brain changes rapidly—at the subsecond level—and its release is tied to the detection of something you're searching for. Acetylcholine also plays a role in sleep: It reaches a peak during REM sleep, and helps to prevent outside inputs from disturbing your dreaming.

In the last few years, we've learned that acetylcholine and noradrenaline appear to be integrated into the brain's circuitry via heteroreceptors—chemical receptors inside a neuron that can accept more than one type of trigger (as distinguished from the more typical autoreceptors that function like a lock and key, letting only one specific neurotransmitter into the synapse). Through this mechanism, acetylcholine and noradrenaline can influence the release of each other.

The attentional filter comprises a network in the frontal lobes and sensory cortices (auditory and visual cortex). When we're searching for something, the filter can retune neurons to match the characteristics of the thing we're searching for, such as the red and white stripes of Waldo, or the size and shape of your car keys. This allows search to be very rapid and to filter out things that are irrelevant. But due to neural noise, it doesn't always work perfectly—we sometimes look right at the thing we're searching for without realizing what it is. The attentional filter (or *Where's Waldo?* network) is controlled in part by neurons with nicotinic receptors located in a part of the brain called the substantia innominata. Nicotinic receptors are so named because they respond to nicotine, whether smoked or chewed, and they're spread throughout the brain. For all the problems it causes to our overall health, it's well established that nicotine can improve the rate of signal detection when a person has been misdirected—that is, nicotine creates a state of vigilance that allows one to become more detail oriented and less dependent on top-down expectations. The attentional filter also communicates closely with the insula, so that it can activate the switch there in order to pull us out of the mind-wandering mode and into the stay-on-task mode when necessary. In addition, it's strongly coupled to the cingulate, facilitating rapid access to the motor system to make an appropriate behavioral response—like jumping out of the way—when a dangerous object comes at you.

Recall from earlier that the attentional filter incorporates a warning system so that important, life-altering signals can break through your mind-wandering or your focused-task mode. If you're driving along and your thoughts start to wander, this is the system that snaps to when a large truck suddenly crosses over into your lane, and gives you a shot of adrenaline at the same time. The warning system is governed by noradrenaline in the frontal and parietal lobes. Drugs, such as guanfacine (brand names Tenex and Intuniv) and clonidine, that are prescribed for hypertension, ADHD, and anxiety disorders can block noradrenaline release, and in turn block your alerting to warning signals. If you're a sonar operator in a submarine, or a forest ranger on fire watch, you want your alerting system to be functioning at full capacity. But if you are suffering from a disorder that causes you to hear noises that aren't there, you want to attenuate the warning system, and guanfacine can do this.

The attentional switch that Vinod Menon and I located in the insula helps to turn the spotlight of attention from one thing to another, and is governed by noradrenaline and cortisol (the stress hormone). Higher levels of dopamine here and in surrounding tissue appear to enhance the functioning of the mind-wandering network. The locus coeruleus and noradrenaline system also modulate these behavioral states. The noradrenaline system is evolutionarily very old and is found even in crustaceans, where some researchers believe it serves a similar role.

Where Memory Comes From

The way neuroscientists talk about these attentional systems, you might think they are modes that affect the whole brain in an all-or-none fashion: You're either in the central executive mode or see-sawing into the mind-wandering mode. You're either awake or asleep. After all, we *know* when we're awake, don't we? And when we're asleep, we are completely off-line, and realize we've been asleep only after we wake up. This is not the way it works.

In stark contrast to this misperception, neuroscientists have recently discovered that parts of the brain can fall asleep for a few moments or longer without our realizing it. At any given moment, some circuits in the brain may be off-line, slumbering, recouping energy, and as long as we're not calling on them to do something for us, we don't notice. This applies just as well to the four parts of the attentional system—any or all of them can be partially functioning. This is likely responsible for a great proportion of things we misplace or lose: The part of our brain that should be attending to where we put them is either asleep or distracted by something else. It's what happens when we miss something we're searching for or look right at it and don't recognize it; it happens when we're daydreaming and it takes us a beat to shift back to alertness.

Thus many things get lost when we are not attending to the moment of putting them down. The remedy is to practice mindfulness and attentiveness, to train ourselves to a Zen-like focus of living in the moment, of paying attention whenever we put things down or put things away. That little bit of focus goes a long way in training the brain (specifically the hippocampus) to remember where we put things, because we're invoking the central executive to help with encoding the moment. Having systems like key hooks, cell phone trays, and a special hook or drawer for sunglasses externalizes the effort so that we don't have to keep everything in our heads. Externalizing memory is an idea that goes back to the Greeks, and its effectiveness has been confirmed many times over by contemporary neuroscience. The extent to which we do it already is astounding when you think about it. As Harvard psychologist Dan Wegner noted, "Our walls are filled with books, our file cabinets with papers, our notebooks with jottings, our homes with artifacts and souvenirs." The word *souvenir,* not coincidentally, comes from the French word for "to remember." Our computers are filled with data records, our calendars with appointments and birthdays, and students scribble answers to tests on their hands.

One current view among some memory theorists is that a very large number of the things you've consciously experienced in your life is encoded in your brain—many of the things you've seen, heard, smelled, thought, all those conversations, bicycle rides, and meals are potentially in there somewhere, provided you paid attention to them. If it's all in there, why do we forget? As Patrick Jane of *The Mentalist* described it, rather eloquently, "Memory is unreliable because the untrained brain has a crappy filing system. It takes everything that happens to you and throws it all willy-nilly into a big dark closet—when you go in there looking for something, all you can find are the big obvious things, like when your mom died, or stuff that you don't really need. Stuff that you're not looking for, like the words to 'Copacabana.' You can't find what you need, but don't panic, because it's still there."

How is this possible? When we experience any event, a unique network of neurons is activated depending on the nature of the event. Watching a sunset? Visual centers that represent shadows and light, pink, orange, and yellow are activated. That same sunset a half hour earlier or later looks different, and so invokes correspondingly different neurons for representing it. Watching a tennis game? Neurons fire for face recognition for the players, motion detection for the movements of their bodies, the ball, the rackets, while higher cognitive centers keep track of whether they stayed in bounds and what the score is. Each of our thoughts, perceptions, and experiences has a unique neural correlate—if it didn't, we would perceive the events as identical; it is the difference in neuronal activations that allows us to distinguish events from one another.

The act of remembering something is a process of bringing back on line those neurons that were involved in the original experience. The neurons represent the world to us as the thing is happening, and as we recall it, those same neurons *re*-present the thing to us. Once we get those neurons to become active in a fashion similar to how they were during the original event, we experience the memory as a lower-resolution replay of the original event. If only we could get every one of those original neurons active in *exactly* the same way they were the first time, our recollections would be strikingly vivid and realistic. But the remembering is imperfect; the instructions for which neurons need to be gathered and how exactly they need to fire are weak and degraded, leading to a representation that is only a dim and often inaccurate copy of the real experience. Memory is fiction. It may present itself to us as fact, but it is highly susceptible to distortion. Memory is not just a replaying, but a rewriting.

Adding to the difficulty is the fact that many of our experiences share similarities with one another, and so when trying to re-create them in memory, the brain can get fooled by competing items. Thus, our memory tends to be poor most of the time, not because of the limited capacity of our brains to store the information but because of the nature of memory retrieval, which can easily become distracted or confounded by other, similar items. An additional problem is that memories can become altered. When they are retrieved they are in a labile or vulnerable state and they need to be reconsolidated properly. If you're sharing a memory with a friend and she says, "No, the car was green, not blue," *that* information gets grafted onto the memory. Memories in this labile state can also vanish if something interferes with their reconsolidation, like lack of sleep, distraction, trauma, or neurochemical changes in the brain.

Perhaps the biggest problem with human memory is that we don't always know when we're recalling things inaccurately. Many times, we have a strong feeling of certainty that accompanies an incorrect, distorted memory. This faulty confidence is widespread, and difficult to extinguish. The relevance to organizational systems is that the more we can externalize memory through physical records out-there-in-the-world, the less we must rely on our overconfident, underprecise memory.

Is there any rhyme or reason about which experiences we'll be able to remember accurately versus those that we won't? The two most important rules are that the best-remembered experiences are distinctive/unique or have a strong emotional component.

Events or experiences that are out of the ordinary tend to be remembered better because there is nothing competing with them when your brain tries to access them from its storehouse of remembered events. In other words, the reason it can be difficult to remember what you ate for breakfast two Thursdays ago is that there was probably nothing special about that Thursday or that particular breakfast—consequently, all your breakfast memories merge together into a sort of generic impression of a breakfast. Your memory merges similar events not only because it's more efficient to do so, but also because this is fundamental to how we learn things—our brains extract abstract rules that tie experiences together. This is especially true for things that are routine. If your breakfast is always the same—cereal with milk, a glass of orange juice, and a cup of coffee for instance—there is no easy way for your brain to extract the details from one particular breakfast. Ironically, then, for behaviors that are routinized, you can remember the generic content of the behavior (such as the things you ate, since you always eat the same thing), but particulars to that one instance can be very difficult to call up (such as the sound of a garbage truck going by or a bird that passed by your window) *unless* they were especially distinctive or emotional. On the other hand, if you did something unique that broke your routine—perhaps you had leftover pizza for breakfast and spilled tomato sauce on your dress shirt—you are more likely to remember it.

A key principle, then, is that memory retrieval requires our brains to sift through multiple, competing instances to pick out just the ones we are trying to recollect. If there are similar events, it retrieves many or all of them, and usually creates some sort of composite, generic mixture of them without our consciously knowing it. This is why it is difficult to remember where we left our glasses or car keys—we've set them down in so many different places over so many years that all those memories run together and our brains have a difficult time finding the relevant one.

On the other hand, if there are no similar events, the unique one is easily distinguished from others and we are able to recollect it. This is in direct proportion to how distinctive the event was. Having pizza for breakfast may be relatively unusual; going out for breakfast with your boss may be more unusual. Having breakfast served to you in bed on your twenty-first birthday by a new, naked, romantic partner is even more unusual. Other unusual events that are typically easy for people to remember include life cycle events such as the birth of a sibling, a marriage, or the death of a loved one. As an amateur bird-watcher, I remember exactly where I was when I saw a pileated woodpecker for the first time, and I remember details about what I was doing a few minutes before and after seeing him. Similarly, many of us remember the first time we saw identical twins, the first time we rode a horse, or the first time we were in a thunderstorm.

Evolutionarily, it makes sense for us to remember unique or distinctive events because they represent a potential change in the world around us or a change in our understanding of it—we need to register these in order to maximize our chances for success in a changing environment.

The second principle of memory concerns emotions. If something made us incredibly frightened, elated, sad, or angry—four of the primary human emotions—we're more likely to remember it. This is because the brain creates neurochemical tags, or markers, that accompany the experience and cause it to become labeled as important. It's as though the brain took a yellow fluorescent highlighter to the text of our day, and selectively marked up the important parts of the day's experiences. This makes evolutionary sense—the emotionally important events are probably the ones that we *need* to remember in order to survive, things like the growl of a predator, the location of a new freshwater spring, the smell of rancid food, the friend who broke a promise.

These chemical tags, tied to emotional events, are the reason we so readily remember important national events such as the assassination of President Kennedy, the space shuttle *Challenger* explosion, the attacks of 9/11, or the election and inauguration of President Obama. These were emotional events for most of us, and they became instantly tagged with brain chemicals that put them in a special neural status facilitating access and retrieval. And these neurochemical tags work for personal memories as well as national ones. You might not be able to remember when you last did your laundry, but you probably remember the person with whom you had your first kiss and exactly where it took place. And even if you are sketchy on some of the details, it is likely you'll remember the emotion associated with the memory.

Unfortunately, the existence of such emotional tags, while making memory retrieval quicker and easier, does not guarantee that the memory retrieval will be more accurate. Here is an example. If you are like most Americans, you remember right where you were when you first learned that the World Trade Center Twin Towers in New York City had been attacked on September 11, 2001. You probably remember the room you were in, roughly the time of day (morning, afternoon, evening), and perhaps even who you were with or who you spoke to that day. You probably also remember watching the horrifying television images of an airplane crashing into the first tower (the North Tower), and then, about twenty minutes later, the image of a second plane crashing into the second tower (the South Tower). Indeed, according to a recent survey, 80% of Americans share this memory. But it turns out this memory is completely false. The television networks broadcasted real-time video of the South Tower collision on September 11, but video of the North Tower collision wasn't available and didn't appear on broadcast television until the following day, on September 12. Millions of Americans saw the videos out of sequence, seeing the video of the South Tower impact twenty-four hours earlier than the video of the North Tower impact. But the narrative we were told and knew to be true, that the North Tower was hit about twenty minutes *before* the South Tower, causes our memory to stitch together the sequence of events as they happened, not as we experienced them. This caused a false memory so compelling that even President George W. Bush falsely recalled seeing the North Tower get hit on September 11, although the television archives show this to be impossible.

As a demonstration of the fallibility of memory, try this exercise. First, get a pen or pencil and a piece of paper. Below, you'll see a list of words. Read each one out loud at a rate of one word per second. That is, don't read as quickly as you can, but take your time and focus on each one as you read it.

REST
TIRED
AWAKE
DREAM
SNORE
BED
EAT
SLUMBER
SOUND
COMFORT
PILLOW
WAKE
NIGHT

Now, without going back to look, write down as many as you can here, and turn the page when you're done. It's okay, you can write on the page. This is a science book and you are making an empirical record. (If you're reading this as an e-book, use the annotate function. And if this is a library book, well, get a separate sheet of paper.)

Rest Pillow
Tired Bed
Sleep

Did you write down *rest? Night? Aardvark? Sleep?*

If you're like most people, you remembered a few of the words. Eighty-five percent of people write down *rest. Rest* is the first word you saw, and this is consistent with the *primacy* effect of memory: We tend to remember best the first entry on a list. Seventy percent of people remember the word *night.* It was the last word you saw, and is consistent with the *recency* effect: We tend to remember the most recent items we encountered on a list, but not as well as the first item. For lists of items, scientists have documented a serial position curve, a graph showing how likely it is that an item will be remembered as a function of its position in a list.

You almost certainly didn't write down *aardvark,* because it wasn't on the list—researchers typically throw in test questions like that to make sure their subjects are paying attention. About 60% of the people tested write down *sleep.* But if you go back and look now, you'll see that *sleep* wasn't on the list! You've just had a false memory, and if you're like most people, you were confident when you wrote down *sleep* that you had seen it. How did this happen?

It's due to the associational networks described in the Introduction—the idea that if you think of *red,* it might activate other memories (or conceptual nodes) through a process called spreading activation. The same principle is at work here; by presenting a number of words that are *related* to the idea of sleep, the word *sleep* became activated in your brain. In effect, this is a false memory, a memory you have for something that didn't actually happen. The implications of this are far-reaching. Skillful attorneys can use this, and principles like it, to their clients' advantage by implanting ideas and memories in the minds of witnesses, juries, and even judges.

Changing a single word in a sentence can cause witnesses to falsely remember seeing broken glass in a picture. Psychologist Elizabeth Loftus showed videos of a minor car accident to participants in an experiment. Later, she asked half of them, "How fast were the cars going when they hit each other?" and she asked the other half, "How fast were the cars going when they smashed into each other?" There were dramatically different estimates of speed, depending on that one word (*smashed* versus *hit*). She then had the participants back one week later and asked, "Was there any broken glass at the scene?" (There was no broken glass in the video.) People were more than twice as likely to respond yes to the question if they had been asked, a week earlier, about the cars' speed with the word *smashed* in the question.

To make matters worse, the act of recalling a memory thrusts it into a labile state whereby new distortions can be introduced; then, when the memory is put back or re-stored, the incorrect information is grafted to it as though it were there all along. For example, if you recall a happy memory while you're feeling blue, your mood at the time of retrieval can color the memory to the point that when you re-store it in your memory banks, the event gets recoded as slightly sad. Psychiatrist Bruce Perry of the Feinberg School of Medicine sums it up: "We know today that, just like when you open a Microsoft Word file on your computer, when you retrieve a memory from where it is stored in the brain, you automatically open it to 'edit.' You may not be aware that your current mood and environment can influence the emotional tone of your recall, your interpretation of events, and even your beliefs about which events actually took place. But when you 'save' the memory again and place it back into storage, you can inadvertently modify it. . . . [This] can bias how and what you recall the next time you pull up that 'file.'" Over time, incremental changes can even lead to the creation of memories of events that never took place.

With the exception of the fact that memories can be so easily distorted and overwritten—a problematic and potentially troublesome affair—the brain organizes past events in an ingenious fashion, with multiple access points and multiple ways to cue any given memory. And if the more audacious theorists are right, everything you've experienced is "in there" somewhere, waiting to be accessed. Then why don't we become overwhelmed by memory? Why is it that when you think of hash browns, your brain doesn't automatically deliver up *every single time you've ever had hash browns?* It's because the brain organizes similar memories into categorical bundles.

Why Categories Matter

Eleanor Rosch has shown that the act of categorizing is one of cognitive economy. We treat things as being of a kind so that we don't have to waste valuable neural processing cycles on details that are irrelevant for our purposes. When looking out at the beach, we don't typically notice individual grains of sand, we see a collective, and one grain of sand becomes grouped with all the others. It doesn't mean that we're incapable of discerning differences among the individual grains, only that for most practical purposes our brains automatically group like objects together. Similarly, we see a bowl of peas as containing aggregated food, as peas. As I wrote earlier, we regard the peas as interchangeable for practical purposes—they are functionally equivalent because they serve the same purpose.

Part of cognitive economy is that we aren't flooded with all the possible terms we could use to refer to objects in the world—there exists a natural, typical term that we use most often. This is the term that is appropriate in most situations. We say that noise coming from around the corner is a *car*, not a 1970 Pontiac GTO. We refer to that *bird* that made a nest in the mailbox, not that rufous-sided towhee. Rosch called this the basic-level category. The basic level is the first term that babies and children learn, and the first one we typically learn in a new language. There are exceptions of course. If you walk into a furniture store, you might ask the greeter where the chairs are. But if you walk into a store called Just Chairs and ask the same question, it sounds odd; in this context, you'd burrow down to a subordinate level from the basic level and ask where the office chairs are, or where the dining room chairs are.

As we specialize or gain expert knowledge, we tend to drop down to the subordinate level in our everyday conversation. A sales agent at Just Chairs won't call the stockroom and ask if they have any accent chairs, he'll ask for the mahogany Queen Anne replica with the yellow tufted back. A bird-watcher will text other bird-watchers that there's a rufous-sided towhee watching a nest in my mailbox. Our knowledge thus guides our formation of categories and the structure they take in the brain.

Cognitive economy dictates that we categorize things in such a way as not to be overwhelmed by details that, for most purposes, don't matter. Obviously, there are certain things on which you want detailed information right now, but you never want all the details all the time. If you're trying to sort through the black beans to pull out the hard, undercooked ones, you see them for the moment as individuals, not functionally equivalent. The ability to go back and forth between these modes of focus, to change lenses from the collective to the individual, is a feature of the mammalian attentional system, and highlights the hierarchical nature of the central executive. Although researchers tend to treat the central executive as a unitary entity, in fact it can be best understood as a collection of different lenses that allow us to zoom in and zoom out during activities we're engaged in, to focus on what is most relevant at the moment. A painter needs to see the individual brushstroke or point she is painting but be able to cycle back and forth between that laserlike focus and the painting-as-a-whole. Composers work at the level of individual pitches and rhythms, but need to apprehend the larger musical phrase and the entire piece in order to ensure that everything fits together. A cabinetmaker working on a particular section of the door is still mindful of the cabinet-as-a-whole. In all these cases and many more—an entrepreneur launching a company, an aircraft pilot planning a landing—the person performing the work holds an image or ideal in mind, and attempts to get it manifested in the real world so that the appearance of the thing matches the mental image.

The distinction between appearance and a mental image traces its roots back to Aristotle and Plato and was a cornerstone of classic Greek philosophy. Aristotle and Plato both spoke of a distinction between how something appears and how it really and truly is. A cabinetmaker can use a veneer to make plywood *appear* to be solid mahogany. The cognitive psychologist Roger Shepard, who was my teacher and mentor (and who drew the monster illusion in Chapter 1), pushed this further in his theory that adaptive behavior depends on an organism being able to make three appearance-reality distinctions.

First, some objects, though different in presentation, are inherently identical. That is, different views of the same object that strike very different retinal images, ultimately refer to the same object. This is an act of categorization—the brain has to integrate different views of an object into a coherent, unified representation, binding them into a single category.

We do this all the time when we're interacting with other people—their faces appear to us in profile, straight on, and at angles, and the emotions their faces convey project very different retinal images. The Russian psychologist A. R. Luria reported on a famous patient who could *not* synthesize these disparate views and had a terrible time recognizing faces on account of a brain lesion.

Second, objects that are similar in presentation are inherently different. For example, in a scene of horses grazing in a meadow, each horse may look highly similar to others, even identical in terms of its retinal image, but evolutionarily adaptive behavior requires that we understand each one is an individual. This principle doesn't involve categorization; in fact, it requires a kind of unbundling of categorization, a recognition that although these objects may be functionally and practically equivalent, there are situations in which it behooves us to understand that they are distinct entities (e.g., if only one approaches you at a rapid trot, there is probably much less danger than if the entire herd comes toward you).

Third, objects although different in presentation may be of the same natural kind. If you saw one of the following crawling on your leg or in your food,

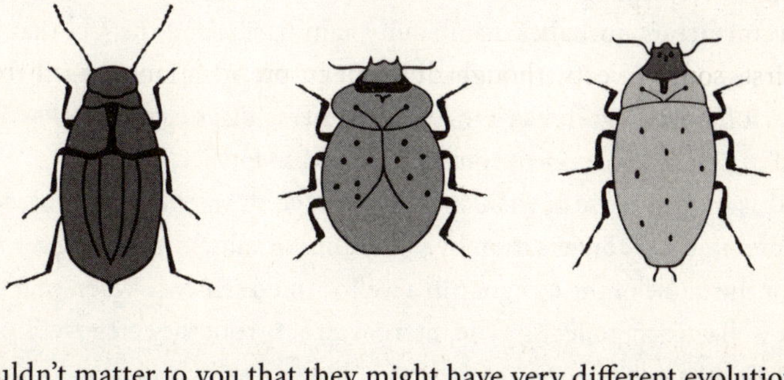

it wouldn't matter to you that they might have very different evolutionary histories, mating habits, or DNA. They may not share a common evolutionary ancestor within a million years. All you care about is that they belong to the category of "things I do not want crawling on me or in my food."

Adaptive behavior, therefore, according to Shepard, depends on cognitive economy, treating objects as equivalent when indeed they are. To categorize an object means to consider it equivalent to other things in that category, and different—along some salient dimension—from things that are not.

The information we receive from our senses, from the world, typically has structure and order, and is not arbitrary. Living things—animals and plants—typically exhibit correlational structure. For example, we can perceive attributes of animals, such as wings, fur, beaks, feathers, fins, gills, and lips. But these do not occur at random. Wings typically are covered in feathers rather than fur. This is an empirical fact provided by the world. In other words, combinations do not occur uniformly or randomly, and some pairs are more probable than others.

Where do categories fit into all of this? Categories often reflect these co-occurrences: The category *bird* implies that wings and feathers will be present on the animal (although there are counterexamples, such as the wingless kiwi of New Zealand and certain now-extinct featherless birds).

We all have an intuitive sense of what constitutes a category member and how well it fits the category, even from a young age. We use linguistic hedges to indicate the unusual members of the category. If you're asked, "Is a penguin a bird?" it would be correct to respond yes, but many of us would respond using a hedge, something like "a penguin is *technically* a bird." If we wanted to elaborate, we might say, "They don't fly, they swim." But we wouldn't say, "A sparrow is technically a bird." It is not just technically a bird, it is a bird par excellence, among the very best examples of birds in North America, due to several factors, including its ubiquity, familiarity, and the fact that it has the largest number of attributes in common with other members of the category: It flies, it sings, it has wings and feathers, it lays eggs, it makes a nest, it eats insects, it comes to the bird feeder, and so forth.

This instant sense of what constitutes a "good" member of a category is reflected in daily conversation by our ability to substitute a category *member* for the name of the category in a well-formed sentence when that member is well chosen, reflecting the internal structure of the category. Take the following sentence:

> Twenty or so birds often perch on the telephone wire outside my window and tweet in the morning.

I can take out the word *birds* and substitute *robins, sparrows, finches,* or *starlings* with no loss of correctness. But if I substitute *penguins, ostriches,* or *turkeys,* it sounds absurd.

Similarly, consider:

> The schoolboy took the piece of fruit out of his lunch box and took several bites before eating his sandwich.

We can substitute *apple, banana,* or *orange* without loss of correctness, but we cannot just as easily substitute *cucumber* or *pumpkin* without the sentence seeming odd. The point is that when we use preexisting categories, or create new ones, there are often clear exemplars of objects that obviously belong to or are central to the category, and other cases that don't fit as well. This ability to recognize diversity and organize it into categories is a biological reality that is absolutely essential to the organized human mind.

How are categories formed in our brains? Generally, there are three ways. First, we categorize them based on either *gross or fine appearance*. Gross appearance puts all pencils together in the same bin. Fine appearance may separate soft-lead from hard-lead pencils, gray ones from colored ones, golf pencils from schoolwork pencils. A feature of all categorization processes used by the human brain, including appearance-based categorization, is that they are expandable and flexible, subject to multiple levels of resolution or graininess. For example, zooming in on pencils, you may desire to have maximal separation like they do at the stationery store, separating them both by manufacturer and by the softness of their lead: 3H, 2H, H, HB, B. Or you may decide to separate them by how much of the eraser is left, whether they have bite marks on them or not (!), or by their length. Zooming out, you may decide to put all pencils, pens, felt markers, and crayons into a single broad category of writing implements. As soon as you decide to identify and name a category, the brain creates a representation of that category and separates objects that fall inside from objects that fall outside the category. If I say, "A mammal is an animal that gives birth to live young and that nurses its young," it is easy to quickly categorize ostrich (no), whale (yes), salmon (no), and orangutan (yes). If I tell you that there exist five species of mammal that lay eggs (including the platypus and echidna), you can quickly accommodate the new information about these exceptions, and this seems perfectly ordinary.

A second way we categorize is based on *functional equivalence* when objects lack similarity of appearance. In a pinch, you can use a crayon to write a note—it becomes functionally equivalent to a pen or pencil. You can use an opened-up paper clip to post something to a corkboard, an untwisted coat hanger to unclog your kitchen sink; you can bunch up your down jacket to use it as a pillow while you're camping. A classic functional equivalence concerns food. If you're driving on the highway and pull into a gas station, hungry, you may be willing to accept a range of products as functionally equivalent for relieving hunger, even though they don't resemble one another: fresh fruit, yogurt, a bag of mixed nuts, a granola bar, muffin, or premade burrito. If you've ever used the back of a stapler or a shoe to pound a nail, you've employed a functional equivalence for a hammer.

A third way we categorize is in conceptual categories that address *particular situations*. Sometimes these are done on the fly, leading to ad hoc categories. For example: What do the following items have in common? Your wallet, childhood photographs, cash, jewelry, and the family dog. They don't have any physical similarities, and they lack functional similarities. What binds them together is that they are "things you might take out of your house in case of a fire." You may never have thought about their going together or being conceptually bound until that moment when you have to make a quick decision about what to take. Alternatively, these situational categories can be planned far in advance. A shelf devoted to emergency preparedness items (water, canned foods, can opener, flashlight, wrench for turning off natural gas, matches, blanket) exemplifies this.

Each of these three categorization methods informs how we organize our homes and work spaces, how we allocate shelf and drawer space, and how we can sort things to make them easy and quick to find. Each time we learn or create a new category, there is neural activity in a circuit that invokes a prefrontal cortex–thalamic loop, alongside the caudate nucleus. It contains low-resolution maps of perceptual space (linking to the hippocampus); it associates a categorization space with a perceptual stimulus. Dopamine release strengthens synapses when you correctly categorize items according to a rule. If you change a classification rule—say you decide to sort your clothes by color rather than by season—the cingulate cortex (part of the central executive) becomes activated. Of course we also cross-classify, placing things in more than one category. In one situation, you might think of yogurt as a dairy product; in another, you might think of it as a breakfast item. The former is based on a taxonomic classification, the latter on a functional category.

But how important are categories? Is making them really that profound? What if mental categories like this are actually manifested in neural tissue? Indeed they are.

More than 50,000 years ago, our human ancestors categorized the world around them, making distinctions and divisions about things that were relevant to their lives: edible versus nonedible, predator versus prey, alive versus dead, animate versus inanimate. As we saw in Chapter 1, their biological categories grouped together objects based on appearance or characteristics. In addition, they would have used conceptual, ad hoc categories for things that lacked physical similarities but shared functional features—for example, "things you don't want in your food," a heterogeneous category that could include worms, insects, a clump of dirt, tree bark, or your little brother's stinky feet.

In the last few years, we've learned that the formation and maintenance of categories have their roots in known biological processes in the brain. Neurons are living cells, and they can connect to one another in trillions of different ways. These connections don't just lead to learning—the connections *are* the learning. The number of possible brain states that each of us can have is so large that it exceeds the number of known particles in the universe. The implications of this are mind-boggling: Theoretically, you should be able to represent uniquely in your brain every known particle in the universe, and have excess capacity left over to organize those particles into finite categories. Your brain is just the tool for the information age.

Neuroimaging technology has uncovered the biological substrates of categorization. Volunteers placed inside a scanning machine are asked to create or think of different kinds of categories. These categories might contain natural objects like plants and animals or human-made artifacts like tools and musical instruments. The scanning technology allows us to pinpoint, usually within one cubic millimeter, where particular neural activity is taking place. This research has shown that the categories we form are real, biological entities, with specific locations in the brain. That is, specific and replicable regions of the brain become active both when we recall previously made categories and when we make them up on the spot. This is true whether the categories are based on physical similarities (e.g., "*edible leaves*") or only conceptual ones ("*things I could use as a hammer*"). Additional evidence for the biological basis of categories comes from case studies of people with brain lesions. Disease, strokes, tumors, or other organic brain trauma sometimes cause a specific region of the brain to become damaged or die. We've now seen patients whose brain damage is so specific that they may lose the ability to use and understand a single category, such as *fruits,* while retaining the ability to use and understand a related category, such as *vegetables.* The fact that a specific category can become lost in this way points to its biological basis in millions of years of evolution, and the importance of categorization in our lives today.

Our ability to use and create categories on the spot is a form of cognitive economy. It helps us by consolidating like things, freeing us from having to make decisions that can cause energy depletion, those hundreds of inconsequential decisions such as "Do I want this pen or that pen?" or "Is this exactly the pair of socks that I bought?" or "Have I mixed nearly identical socks in attempting to match them?"

Functional categories in the brain can have either hard (sharply defined) or fuzzy boundaries. Triangles are an example of a hard boundary category. To be a member of the category, an object must be a two-dimensional closed figure with three sides, the sum of whose interior angles must equal exactly 180 degrees. Another hard boundary is the outcome of a criminal proceeding—with the exception of hung juries and mistrials, the defendant is found either guilty or not guilty; there is no such thing as 70% guilty. (During sentencing, the judge can accommodate different degrees of punishment, or assign degrees of responsibility, but she's generally not parsing degrees of guilty. In civil law, however, there can be degrees of guilt.)

An example of a fuzzy boundary is the category "*friendship.*" There are clear and obvious cases of people who you know are friends, and clear cases of people who you know are not—strangers, for example. But "*friends*" is a category that, for most of us, has fuzzy boundaries. It depends to some degree on context. We invite different people to our homes for a neighborhood barbecue than for a birthday party; we'll go out for drinks with people from work but not invite them to our homes. Like many categories, inclusion depends on context. The category "*friends*" has permeable, fuzzy boundaries, unlike the triangle category for which polygons are either in or out. We consider some people to be friends for some purposes and not for others.

Hard boundaries apply mostly to formal categories typically found in mathematics and law. Fuzzy boundaries can occur in both natural and human-made categories. Cucumbers and zucchinis are technically fruits, but we allow them to permeate the fuzzy boundary "*vegetable*" because of context—we tend to eat them with or in lieu of "proper" vegetables such as spinach, lettuce, and carrots. The contextual and situational aspect of categories is also apparent when we talk about temperature—104 degrees Fahrenheit is too hot for the bedroom when we're trying to sleep, but it's the perfect temperature for a hot tub. That same 104 would seem not quite hot enough if it were coffee.

A classic case of a fuzzy category is "*game*," and the twentieth-century philosopher Ludwig Wittgenstein spent a great deal of time thinking about it, concluding that there was no list of attributes that could unambiguously define the category. Is a game something you do for leisure? That definition would exclude professional football and the Olympic Games. Something you do with other people? That lets out solitaire. An activity done for fun, and bound by certain rules, that is sometimes practiced competitively for fans to watch? That lets out the children's game Ring around the Rosies, which is not competitive, nor does it have any rules, yet really does seem like a game. Wittgenstein concluded that something is a *game* when it has a family resemblance to other games. Think of a hypothetical family, the Larsons, at their annual family reunion. If you know enough Larsons, you might be able to easily tell them from their non-Larson spouses, based on certain family traits. Maybe there's the Larson dimpled chin, the aquiline nose, the large floppy ears and red hair, and the tendency to be over six feet tall. But it's possible, likely even, that no one Larson has *all* these attributes. They are not *defining* features, they are *typical* features. The fuzzy category lets in anyone who resembles the prototypical Larson, and in fact, the prototypical Larson, the Larson with all the noted features, may not actually exist as anything other than a theoretical, Platonic ideal.

The cognitive scientist William Labov demonstrated the fuzzy category/family resemblance concept with this series of drawings:

The object in the upper left is clearly a cup. As we move to the right on the top row, the cup gets wider and wider until at number 4 it has a greater resemblance to a bowl than a cup. What about number 3? It could be in either the *cup* or the *bowl* category, depending on context. Similarly, as the cups get taller, moving downward, they begin to look less and less like cups and more like pitchers or vases. Other variations, such as adding a stem (number 17) make it look more like a goblet or wineglass. Changing the shape (numbers 18 and 19), however, makes it look like a peculiar cup, but a cup all the same. This illustrates the underlying notion that category boundaries are flexible, malleable, and context-dependent. If I serve you wine in number 17 and I make it out of glass instead of porcelain or ceramic, you're more likely to accept it as a goblet. But even if I make number 1 out of glass, the object it still most closely resembles is a cup, regardless of whether I fill it with coffee, orange juice, wine, or soup.

Fuzzy categories are instantiated biologically in the brain, and are as real as hard categories. Being able to create, use, and understand both kinds of categories is something that our brains are hardwired to do—even two-year-olds do it. As we think about organizing our lives and the spaces we inhabit, creating categories and bins for things is an act of cognitive economy. It's also an act of great creativity if we allow it to be, leading to organizational systems that range from the rigid classification of a military warehouse and the perfect sock drawer to whimsical categories that reflect playful ways of looking at the world and all of the objects in it.

Getting Part of Your Mind Outside Your Body

The brain organizes information in its own idiosyncratic way, a way that has served us very well. But in an age of information overload, not to mention decision overload, we need systems outside our heads to help us. Categories can off-load a lot of the difficult work of the brain into the environment. If we have a drawer for baking supplies, we don't need to remember separately where ten different items are—the rolling pin, the cookie cutters, the sifter, and so on—we just remember that we have a category for baking tools, and it is in the third drawer down underneath the coffeemaker. If we're planning two separate birthday parties, one at the office and one at home, the category of "*people I work with*" in our mental recollection, Outlook file, or contacts app on our smartphone helps prompt the memory of whom to include and whom not to.

Calendars, smartphones, and address books are also brain extenders, externalizing onto paper or into computer chips myriad details that we no longer have to keep in our heads. Historically, the ultimate brain extenders were books, keeping track of centuries' worth of collected knowledge that we can access when we need it. Perhaps they still are.

People at the top of their professions, in particular those known for their creativity and effectiveness, use systems of attention and memory external to their brain as much as they can. And a surprising number of them, even in high-tech jobs, use decidedly low-tech solutions for keeping on top of things. Yes, you can embed a microchip in your keys that will let you track them with a cell phone app, and you can create electronic checklists before you travel to ensure you take everything you need. But many busy and effective people say that there is something different, something visceral in using old-fashioned physical objects, rather than virtual ones, to keep track of important things from shopping lists to appointments to ideas for their next big project.

One of the biggest surprises I came upon while working on this book was the number of such people who carry around a pen and notepads or index cards for taking physical notes, and their insistence that it is both more efficient and more satisfying than the electronic alternatives now on offer. In her autobiography, *Lean In*, Sheryl Sandberg reluctantly admits to carrying a notebook and pen around to keep track of her To Do list, and confesses that at Facebook, where she is the COO, this is "like carrying around a stone tablet and chisel." Yet she and many others like her persist in this ancient technology. There must be something to it.

Imagine carrying a stack of 3 x 5 index cards with you wherever you go. When you get an idea for something you're working on, you put it on one card. If you remember something you need to do later, you put that on a card. You're sitting on a bus and suddenly remember some people you need to call and some things you need to pick up at the hardware store—that's several more cards. You've figured out how to solve that problem your sister is having with her husband—that goes on a card. Every time any thought intrudes on what you're doing, you write it down. David Allen, the efficiency expert and author of books, including *Getting Things Done,* calls this kind of note-taking "clearing the mind."

Remember that the mind-wandering mode and the central executive work in opposition and are mutually exclusive states; they're like the little devil and angel standing on opposite shoulders, each trying to tempt you. While you're working on one project, the mind-wandering devil starts thinking of all the other things going on in your life and tries to distract you. Such is the power of this task-negative network that those thoughts will churn around in your brain until you deal with them somehow. Writing them down gets them out of your head, clearing your brain of the clutter that is interfering with being able to focus on what you want to focus on. As Allen notes, "Your mind will remind you of all kinds of things when you can do nothing about them, and merely thinking about your concerns does not at all equate to making any progress on them."

Allen noticed that when he made a big list of everything that was on his mind, he felt more relaxed and better able to focus on his work. This observation is based in neurology. When we have something on our minds that is important—especially a To Do item—we're afraid we'll forget it, so our brain rehearses it, tossing it around and around in circles in something that cognitive psychologists actually refer to as the rehearsal loop, a network of brain regions that ties together the frontal cortex just behind your eyeballs and the hippocampus in the center of your brain. This rehearsal loop evolved in a world that had no pens and paper, no smartphones or other physical extensions of the human brain; it was all we had for tens of thousands of years and during that time, it became quite effective at remembering things. The problem is that it works too well, keeping items in rehearsal until we attend to them. Writing them down gives both implicit and explicit permission to the rehearsal loop to let them go, to relax its neural circuits so that we can focus on something else. "If an obligation remained recorded only mentally," Allen says, "some part of me constantly kept thinking that it should be attended to, creating a situation that was inherently stressful and unproductive."

Writing things down conserves the mental energy expended in worrying that you might forget something and in trying not to forget it. The neuroscience of it is that the mind-wandering network is competing with the central executive, and in such a battle, the mind-wandering default mode network usually wins. Sometimes it's as if your brain has a mind of its own. If you want to look at this from a Zen point of view, the Masters would say that the constant nagging in your mind of undone things pulls you out of the present—tethers you to a mind-set of the future so that you're never fully in the moment and enjoying what's now. David Allen notes that many of his clients spin their wheels at work, worrying about things they need to do at home, and when they're at home, they are worried about work. The problem is that you're never really in either place.

"Your brain needs to engage on some consistent basis with all of your commitments and activities," Allen says. "You must be assured that you are doing what you need to be doing, and that it's OK to be not doing what you're not doing. If it's on your mind, then your mind isn't clear. Anything you consider unfinished in any way must be captured in a trusted system outside your mind. . . ." That trusted system is to write it down.

For the 3 x 5 system to work best, the rule is one idea or task per card—this ensures that you can easily find it and dispose of it when it's been dealt with. One piece of information per card allows for rapid sorting and resorting, and it provides random access, meaning that you can access any idea on its own, take it out of the stack without dislocating another idea, and put it adjacent in the stack to similar ideas. Over time, your idea of what is similar or what binds different ideas together may change, and this system—because it is random and not sequential—allows for that flexibility.

Robert Pirsig inspired a generation to philosophical reflection—and organizing their thoughts—with his hugely popular novel *Zen and the*

Art of Motorcycle Maintenance, published in 1974. In a somewhat less well-known later book (nominated for a Pulitzer Prize), *Lila: An Inquiry into Morals,* he endeavors to establish a way of thinking about metaphysics. Phaedrus, the author's alter ego and the story's protagonist, uses the index card system for organizing his philosophical notions. The size of the index cards, he says, makes them preferable to full-size sheets of paper because they provide greater random access. They fit into a shirt pocket or purse. Because they're all the same size, they're easy to carry and organize. (Leibniz complained about all the slips of paper that he had ideas on getting lost because they were all different sizes and shapes.) And importantly, "when information is organized in small chunks that can be accessed and sequenced at random it becomes much more valuable than when you have to take it in serial form. . . . They [the index cards] ensured that by keeping his head empty and keeping sequential formatting to a minimum, no fresh new unexplored ideas would be forgotten or shut out." Of course our heads can never be truly empty, but the idea is powerful. We should off-load as much information to the external world as possible.

Once you have a stack of index cards, you make it a point to sort them regularly. When there are a small number, you simply put them in the order in which you need to deal with them. With a larger number, you assign the index cards to categories. A modified version of the system that Ed Littlefield had me use for sorting his mail works:

- Things to do today
- Things to do this week
- Things that can wait
- Junk drawer

It isn't the names of the categories that are critical, it is the process of external categorization. Maybe your categories are more like some of these:

- Shopping lists
- Errands
- Things to do at home
- Things to do at work
- Social
- Things to ask Pat to do

- Things related to Mom's health care
- Phone calls to make

David Allen recommends this mnemonic for fine sorting your To Do list into four actionable categories:

Do it

Delegate it

Defer it

Drop it

Allen suggests the two-minute rule: If you can attend to one of the things on your list in less than two minutes, do it now (he recommends setting aside a block of time every day, thirty minutes for example, just to deal with these little tasks, because they can accumulate quickly to the point of overload). If a task can be done by someone else, delegate it. Anything that takes more than two minutes to deal with, you defer. You might be deferring only until later today, but you defer it long enough to get through your list of two-minute tasks. And there are some things that just aren't worth your time anymore—priorities change. While going through the daily scan of your index cards, you can decide to drop them.

At first it may sound like busywork. You can keep these things all in your head, right? Well, yes, you *can*, but the point is that the anatomy of your brain makes it less effective to do so. And the busywork is not so onerous. It's a time for reflection and healthy mind-wandering. To distinguish the cards that go in one category versus another, a header card can be placed as the first card in the new category. If your 3 x 5 cards are white, your header cards can be blue, for example, to make finding them easy. Some people go crazy with the index card system and extend this to use different-colored cards for the different categories. But this makes it more difficult to move a card from one category to another, and the whole point of the 3 x 5 system is to maximize flexibility—any card should be able to be put anywhere in the stack. As your priorities change, you simply reorder the cards to put them in the order and the category you want. Little bits of information each get their own index card. Phaedrus wrote a whole book by putting ideas, quotes, sources, and other research results on index cards, which he called slips. What begins as a daunting task of trying to figure out what goes where in a report becomes simply a matter of ordering the slips.

> Instead of asking "Where does this metaphysics of the universe begin?"—which was a virtually impossible question—all he had to do was just hold up two slips and ask, "Which comes first?" This was easy and he always seemed to get an answer. Then he would take a third slip, compare it with the first one, and ask again, "Which comes first?" If the new slip came after the first one he compared it to the second. Then he had a three-slip organization. He kept repeating this process with slip after slip.

People who use the index card system find it liberating. Voice recorders require you to listen back, and even on a sped-up playback, it takes longer to listen to a note than it does to read it. Not terribly efficient. And the voice files are not easily sorted. With index cards, you can sort and re-sort to your heart's content.

Pirsig continues, describing Phaedrus's organizational experiments. "At various times he'd tried all kinds of different things: colored plastic tabs to indicate subtopics and sub-subtopics; stars to indicate relative importance; slips split with a line to indicate both emotive and rational aspects of their subject; but all of these had increased rather than decreased confusion and he'd found it clearer to include their information elsewhere."

One category that Phaedrus allowed for was *unassimilated*. "This contained new ideas that interrupted what he was doing. They came in on the spur of the moment while he was organizing the other slips or sailing or working on the boat or doing something else that didn't want to be disturbed. Normally your mind says to these ideas, 'Go away, I'm busy,' but that attitude is deadly to Quality." Pirsig recognized that some of the best ideas you'll have will come to you when you're doing something completely unrelated. You don't have time to figure out how to use the idea because you're busy with something else, and taking time to contemplate all the angles and ramifications takes you out of the task you're working on. For Phaedrus, an *unassimilated* pile helped solve the problem. "He just stuck the slips there on hold until he had the time and desire to get to them." In other words, this is the junk drawer, a place for things that don't have another place.

You don't need to carry all the cards with you everywhere of course—the abeyance or future-oriented ones can stay in a stack on your desk. To maximize the efficiency of the system, the experts look through their cards every morning, reordering them as necessary, adding new ones if sifting through the stack gives them new ideas. Priorities change and the random access nature of the cards means you can put them wherever they will be most useful to you.

For many of us, a number of items on our To Do lists require a decision and we feel we don't have enough information to make the decision. Say that one item on your To Do list was "Make a decision about assisted living facilities for Aunt Rose." You've already visited a few and gathered information, but you haven't yet made the decision. On a morning scan of your cards, you find you aren't ready to do it. Take two minutes now to think about what you need in order to make the decision. Daniel Kahneman and Amos Tversky said that the problem with making decisions is that we are often making them under conditions of uncertainty. You're uncertain of the outcome of putting Rose in a home, and that makes the decision difficult. You also fear regret if you make the wrong decision. If more information will remove that uncertainty, then figure out what that information is and how to obtain it, then—to keep the system working for you—put it on an index card. Maybe it's talking to a few more homes, maybe it's talking to other family members. Or maybe you just need time to let the information set in. In that case, you put a deadline on the decision card, say four days from now, and try to make the decision then. The essential point here is that during your daily sweep through the cards, you have to do something with that index card—you do something about it now, you put it in your abeyance pile, or you generate a new task that will help to move this project forward.

The index card system is merely one of what must be an infinite number of brain extension devices, and it isn't for everyone. Paul Simon carries a notebook with him everywhere to jot down lines or phrases that he might use later in a song, and John R. Pierce, the inventor of satellite communication, carried around a lab book that he used as a journal for everything he had to do as well as for research ideas and names of people he met. A number of innovators carried pocket notebooks to record observations, reminders, and all manner of what-not; the list includes George S. Patton (for exploring ideas on leadership and war strategy, as well as to record daily affirmations), Mark Twain, Thomas Jefferson, and George Lucas. These are serial forms of information storage, not random access; everything in them is chronological. It involves a lot of thumbing through pages, but it suits their owners.

As humble and low-tech as it may seem, the 3 x 5 card system is powerful. That is because it builds on the neuroscience of attention, memory, and categorization. The task-negative or mind-wandering mode is responsible for generating much useful information, but so much of it comes at the wrong time. We externalize our memory by putting that information on index cards. We then harness the power of the brain's intrinsic and evolutionarily ancient desire to categorize by creating little bins for those external memories, bins that we can peer into whenever our central executive network wishes to. You might say categorizing and externalizing our memory enables us to balance the yin of our wandering thoughts with the yang of our focused execution.

PART TWO

3

ORGANIZING OUR HOMES

Where Things Can Start to Get Better

Few of us feel that our homes or work spaces are perfectly organized. We lose our car keys, an important piece of mail; we go shopping and forget something we needed to buy; we miss an appointment we thought we'd be sure to remember. In the best case, the house is neat and tidy, but our drawers and closets are cluttered. Some of us still have unpacked boxes from our last move (even if it was five years ago), and our home offices accumulate paperwork faster than we know what to do with it. Our attics, garages, basements, and the junk drawers in our kitchens are in such a state that we hope no one we know ever takes a peek inside of them, and we fear the day we may need to actually find something there.

These are obviously not problems that our ancestors had. When you think about what your ancestors might have lived like a thousand years ago, it's easy to focus on the technological differences—no cars, electricity, central heating, or indoor plumbing. It's tempting to picture homes as we know them now, meals more or less the same except for the lack of prepackaged food. More grinding of wheat and skinning of fowl, perhaps. But the anthropological and historical record tells a very different story.

In terms of food, our ancestors tended to eat what they could get their hands on. All kinds of things that we don't eat today, because they don't taste very good by most accounts, were standard fare only because they were available: rats, squirrels, peacocks—and don't forget locusts! Some foods that we consider haute cuisine today, such as lobster, were so plentiful in the 1800s that they were fed to prisoners and orphans, and ground up into fertilizer; servants requested written assurance that they would not be fed lobster more than twice a week.

Things that we take for granted—something as basic as the kitchen—didn't exist in European homes until a few hundred years ago. Until 1600, the typical European home had a single room, and families would crowd around the fire most of the year to keep warm. The number of possessions the average person has now is far greater than we had for most of our evolutionary history, easily by a factor of 1,000, and so organizing them is a distinctly modern problem. One American household studied had more than 2,260 *visible* objects in just the living room and two bedrooms. That's not counting items in the kitchen and garage, and all those that were tucked inside a drawer, cabinet, or in boxes. Including those, the number could easily be three times as high. Many families amass more objects than their houses can hold. The result is garages given over to old furniture and unused sports equipment, home offices cluttered with boxes of stuff that haven't yet been taken to the garage. Three out of four Americans report their garages are too full to put a car into them. Women's cortisol levels (the stress hormone) spike when confronted with such clutter (men's, not so much). Elevated cortisol levels can lead to chronic cognitive impairment, fatigue, and suppression of the body's immune system.

Adding to the stress is that many of us feel organizing our possessions has gotten away from us. Bedside tables are piled high with stuff. We don't even remember what's in those unpacked boxes. The TV remote needs a new battery, but we don't know where the new batteries are. Last year's bills are piled high on the desk of our home office. Few of us feel that are homes are as well organized as, say, Ace Hardware. How do they do it?

The layout and organization of products on shelves in a well-designed hardware store exemplify the principles outlined in the previous chapters. It practices putting together conceptually similar objects, putting together functionally associated objects, and all the while maintaining cognitively flexible categories.

John Venhuizen is president and CEO of Ace Hardware, a retailer with more than 4,300 stores in the United States. "Anyone who takes retailing and marketing seriously has a desire to know more about the human brain," he says. "Part of what makes the brain get cluttered is capacity—it can only absorb and decipher so much. Those *big box stores* are great retailers and we can learn a lot from them, but our model is to strive for a smaller, navigable store because it is easier on the brain of our customers. This is an endless pursuit." Ace, in other words, employs the use of flexible categories to create cognitive economy.

Ace employs an entire category-management team that strives to arrange the products on the shelves in a way that mirrors the way consumers think and shop. A typical Ace store carries 20,000–30,000 different items, and the chain as a whole inventories 83,000 different items. (Recall from Chapter 1 that there are an estimated one million SKUs in the United States. This means that the Ace Hardware chain stocks nearly 10% of all the available products in the country.)

Ace categorizes its items hierarchically into departments, such as *lawn & garden, plumbing, electrical,* and *paint.* Then, beneath those categories are subdivisions such as *fertilizers, irrigation,* and *tools* (under *lawn & garden),* or *fixtures, wire,* and *bulbs* (under *electrical).* The hierarchy digs down deep. Under the *Hand & Power Tools Department*, Ace lists the following, nested subcategories:

- Power Tools
- Consumer Power Tools | Heavy-Duty Power Tools | Wet/Dry Vacs
- Corded Drills
- Craftsman
- Black & Decker
- Makita
- And so on

What works for inventory control, however, isn't necessarily what works for shelving and display purposes. "We learned long ago," Venhuizen says, "that hammers sell with nails because when the customer is buying nails and they see a hammer on the shelf, it reminds them that they need a new one. We used to rigidly keep the hammers with other hand tools; now we put a few with the nails for just that reason."

Suppose you want to repair a loose board in your fence and you need a nail. You go to the hardware store, and typically there will be an entire aisle for fasteners (the superordinate category). Nails, screws, bolts, and washers (basic-level categories) take up a single aisle, and within that aisle are hierarchical subdivisions with subsections for concrete nails, drywall nails, wood nails, carpet tacks (the subordinate categories).

Suppose now that you want to buy laundry line. This is a type of rope with special properties: It has to be made of a material that won't stain wet clothes; it has to be able to be left outside permanently and so must withstand the elements; it has to have the tensile strength to hold a load of laundry without breaking or stretching too much. Now, you could imagine that the hardware store would have a single aisle for rope, string, twine, cord, and cable, where all of these like things are kept together (as with nails), and they do, but the merchants leverage our brains' associative memory networks by also placing a stock of laundry line near the Tide detergent, ironing boards, irons, and clothespins. That is, some laundry line is kept with "things you need to do your laundry," a functional category that mirrors the way the brain organizes information. This makes it easy not just to find the product you want, but to remember that you need it.

How about clothing retailers organizing their stock? They tend to use a hierarchical system, too, like Ace Hardware. They may also use functional categories, putting rainwear in one section, sleepwear in another. The categorization problem for a clothing retailer is this: There are at least four important dimensions on which their stock differs—the gender of the intended buyer, the kind of clothing (pants, shirts, socks, hats, etc.), color, and size. Clothing stores typically put the pants in one section and the shirts in another, and so on. Then, dropping down a level in the hierarchy, dress shirts are separated from sports shirts and T-shirts. Within the pants department, the stock tends to be arranged by size. If a department employee has been especially punctilious in reordering after careless browsers have gone through the stock, within each size category the pants are arranged by color. Now it gets a bit more complicated because men's pants are sized using two numbers, the waist and the inseam length. In most clothing stores, the waist is the *categorization number:* All the pants of a particular waist size are grouped together. So you walk into the Gap, you ask for the pants department, and you're directed to the back of the store, where you find rows and rows of square boxes containing thousands of pairs of pants. Right away you notice a subdivision. The jeans are probably stocked separately from the khakis, which are stocked separately from any other sporty, dressy, or more upscale pants.

Now, all the jeans with a 34-inch waist will be clearly marked on the shelf. As you look through them, the inseam lengths should be in increasing order. And color? It depends on the store. Sometimes, all the black jeans are in one contiguous set of shelves, all the blue are in another. Sometimes, within a size category, all the blues are stacked on top of all the blacks, or they're intermixed. The nice thing about color is that it is easy to spot—it pops out because of your attentional filter (the *Where's Waldo?* network)—and so, unlike size, you don't have to hunt for a tiny label to see what color you've got. Note that the shelving is hierarchical and also divided. Men's clothes are in one part of the store and women's in another. It makes sense because this is usually a coarse division of the "selection space" in that, most of the time, the clothes we want are in one gender category or the other and we don't find ourselves hopping back and forth between them.

Of course not all stores are so easy to navigate for customers. Department stores often organize by designer—Ralph Lauren is here, Calvin Klein is there, Kenneth Cole is one row beyond—then within designer, they re-sort to implement a hierarchy, grouping clothes first by type (pants versus shirts) and then by color and/or size. The makeup counters in department stores tend to be vendor driven—Lancôme, L'Oréal, Clinique, Estée Lauder, and Dior each have their own counter. This doesn't make it easy for the shopper looking for a particular shade of red lipstick to match a handbag. Few shoppers walk into Macy's thinking, "I've just got to get a *Clinique* red." It's terribly inconvenient racing back and forth between one area of the store and another. But the reason Macy's does it this way is because they rent out the floor space to the different makeup companies. The Lancôme counter at Macy's is a miniature store-within-a-store and the salespeople work for Lancôme. Lancôme provides the fixtures and the inventory, and Macy's doesn't have to worry about keeping the shelves organized or ordering new products; they simply take a small part of the profits from each transaction.

Our homes are not typically as well organized as, say, Ace Hardware, the Gap, or the Lancôme counter. There is the world driven by market forces in which people are paid to keep things organized, and then there is your home.

One solution is to put systems in place at home that will tame the mess—an infrastructure for keeping track of things, sorting them, placing them in locations where they will be found and not lost. The task of organizational systems is to provide maximum information with the least cognitive effort. The problem is that putting systems in place for organizing our homes and work spaces is a daunting task; we fear they'll take too much time and energy to initiate, and that, like a New Year's Day diet resolution, we won't be able to stick with them for long. The good news is that, to a limited extent, all of us already have organizational systems in place that protect us from the creeping chaos that surrounds us. We seldom lose forks and knives because we have a silverware drawer in the kitchen where such things go. We don't lose our toothbrushes because they are used in a particular room and have a particular place to be stored there. But we do lose bottle openers when we carry them from the kitchen to the rec room or the living room and then forget where they last were. The same thing happens to hairbrushes if we are in the habit of taking them out of the bathroom.

A great deal of losing things then arises from structural forces—the various nomadic things of our lives not being confined to a certain location as is the lowly toothbrush. Take reading glasses—we carry them with us from room to room, and they are easily misplaced because they have no designated place. The neurological foundation of this is now well understood. We evolved a specialized brain structure called the hippocampus just for remembering the spatial location of things. This was tremendously important throughout our evolutionary history for keeping track of where food and water could be found, not to mention the location of various dangers. The hippocampus is such an important center for place memory that it's found even in rats and mice. A squirrel burying nuts? It's his hippocampus that helps him retrieve nuts several months later from hundreds of different locations.

In a paper now famous among neuroscientists, the hippocampus was studied in a group of London taxi drivers. All London taxi drivers are required to take a knowledge test of routes throughout the city, and preparation can take three or four years of study. Driving a taxi in London is especially difficult because it is not laid out on a grid system like most American cities; many streets are discontinuous, stopping and starting up again with the same name some distance away, and many streets are one-way or can be accessed only by limited routes. To be an effective taxi driver in London requires superior spatial (place) memory. Across several experiments, neuroscientists found that the hippocampus in London taxi drivers was larger than in other people of comparable age and education—it had increased in volume due to all the location information they needed to keep track of. More recently, we've discovered that there are dedicated cells in the hippocampus (called dentate granule cells) to encode memories for specific places.

Place memory evolved over hundreds of thousands of years to keep track of things that didn't move, such as fruit trees, wells, mountains, lakes. It's not only vast but exquisitely accurate for stationary things that are important to our survival. What it's not so good at is keeping track of things that move from place to place. This is why you remember where your toothbrush is but not your glasses. It's why you lose your car keys but not your car (there are an infinity of places to leave your keys around the house, but relatively fewer places to leave the car). The phenomenon of place memory was known already to the ancient Greeks. The famous mnemonic system they devised, the method of loci, relies on our being able to take concepts we want to remember and attach them to our vivid memories of well-known spaces, such as the rooms in our home.

Recall the Gibsonian affordances from Chapter 1, ways that our environment can serve as mental aids or cognitive enhancers. Simple affordances for the objects of our lives can rapidly ease the mental burden of trying to keep track of where they are, and make keeping them in place—taming their wandering ways—aesthetically and emotionally pleasing. We can think of these as *cognitive prosthetics*. For keys, a bowl or hook near the door you usually use solves the problem (featured in *Dr. Zhivago* and *The Big Bang Theory*). The bowl or hook can be decorative, to match the decor of the room. The system depends on being compulsive about it. Whenever you are home, that is where the keys should be. As soon as you walk in the door, you hang them there. No exceptions. If the phone is ringing, hang the keys up first. If your hands are full, put the packages down and hang up those keys! One of the big rules in not losing things is the *rule of the designated place*.

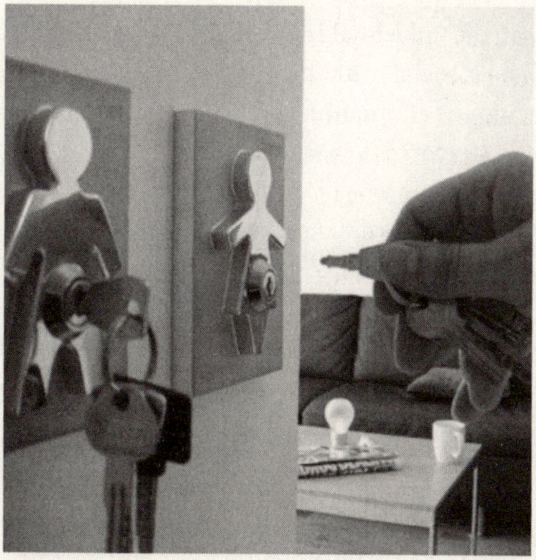

A tray or shelf that is designated for a smartphone encourages you to put your phone there and not somewhere else. The same is true for other electronic objects and the daily mail. Sharper Image, Brookstone, SkyMall, and the Container Store have made a business model out of this neurological reality, featuring products spanning an amazing range of styles and price points (plastic, leather, or sterling silver) that function as *affordances* for keeping your wayward objects in their respective homes. Cognitive psychology theory says spend as much as you can on these: It's very difficult to leave your mail scattered about when you've spent a lot of money for a special tray to keep it in.

But simple affordances don't always require purchasing new stuff. If your books, CDs, or DVDs are organized and you want to remember where to put back the one you just took out, you can pull out the one just to the left of it about an inch and then it becomes an affordance for you to easily see where to put back the one you "borrowed" from your library. Affordances aren't just for people with bad memories, or people who have reached their golden years—many people, even young ones with exceptional memories, report that they have trouble keeping track of everyday items. Magnus Carlsen is the number one rated chess player in the world at only twenty-three years old. He can keep ten games going at once just in his memory—without looking at the board—but, he says, "I forget all kinds of [other] stuff. I regularly lose my credit cards, my mobile phone, keys, and so on."

B. F. Skinner, the influential Harvard psychologist and father of behaviorism, as well as a social critic through his writings, including *Walden Two*, elaborated on the affordance. If you hear on the weather report in the evening that it's supposed to rain tomorrow, he said, put an umbrella near the front door so you won't forget to take it. If you have letters to mail, put them near your car keys or house keys so that when you leave the house, they're right there. The principle underlying all these is off-loading the information from your brain and into the environment; *use the environment itself to remind you of what needs to be done.* Jeffrey Kimball, formerly a vice president of Miramax and now an award-winning independent filmmaker, says, "If I know I might forget something when I leave the house, I put it in or next to my shoes by the front door. I also use the 'four' system—every time I leave the house I check that I have four things: keys, wallet, phone, and glasses."

If you're afraid you'll forget to buy milk on the way home, put an empty milk carton on the seat next to you in the car or in the backpack you carry to work on the subway (a note would do, of course, but the carton is more unusual and so more apt to grab your attention). The other side to leaving physical objects out as reminders is to put them away when you don't need them. The brain is an exquisite change detector and that's why you notice the umbrella by the door or the milk carton on the car seat. But a corollary to that is that the brain habituates to things that don't change—this is why a friend can walk into your kitchen and notice that the refrigerator has developed an odd humming noise, something you no longer notice. If the umbrella is by the door all the time, rain or shine, it no longer functions as a memory trigger, because you don't notice it. To help remember where you parked your car, parking lot signs at the San Francisco airport recommend taking a cell phone photo of your spot. Of course this works for bicycle parking as well. (In the new heart of the tech industry, Google cars and Google Glass will probably be doing this for us soon enough.)

When organized people find themselves running between the kitchen and the home office all the time to get a pair of scissors, they buy an extra pair. It might seem like cluttering rather than organizing, but buying duplicates of things that you use frequently and in different locations helps to prevent you from losing them. Perhaps you use your reading glasses in the bedroom, the home office, and the kitchen. Three pairs solves the problem if you can create a designated place for them, a special spot in each room, and always leave them there. Because the reading glasses are no longer moving from room to room, your place memory will help you recall within each room where they are. Some people buy an extra set for the glove compartment of the car to read maps, and put another pair in their purse or jacket to have when they're at a restaurant and need to read the menu. Of course prescription reading glasses can be expensive, and three pairs all the more so. Alternatively, a tether for the reading glasses, a neck cord, keeps them with you all the time. (Contrary to the frequently observed correlation, there is no scientific evidence that these little spectacle lanyards make your hair go gray or create an affinity for cardigans.) The neurological principle remains. Be sure that when you untether them, they go back to their one spot; the system collapses if you have several spots.

Either one of these overall strategies—providing duplicates or creating a rigidly defined special spot—works well for many everyday items:

lipstick, hair scrunchies, pocketknives, bottle openers, staplers, Scotch tape, scissors, hairbrushes, nail files, pens, pencils, and notepads. The system doesn't work for things you can't duplicate, like your keys, computer, iPad, the day's mail, or your cell phone. For these, the best strategy is to harness the power of the hippocampus rather than trying to fight it: Designate a specific location in your house that will be *home* to these objects. Be strict about adhering to it.

Many people may be thinking, "Oh, I'm just not a detail-oriented person like that—I'm a *creative* person." But a creative mind-set is not antithetical to this kind of organization. Joni Mitchell's home is a paragon of organizational systems. She installed dozens of custom-designed, special-purpose drawers in her kitchen to better organize just exactly the kinds of things that tend to be hard to locate. One drawer is for rolls of Scotch tape, another for masking tape. One drawer is for mailing and packing products; another for string and rope; another for batteries (organized by size in little plastic trays); and a particularly deep drawer holds spare lightbulbs. Tools and implements for baking are separate from those for sautéing. Her pantry is similarly organized. Crackers on one shelf, cereal on another, soup ingredients on a third, canned goods on a fourth. "I don't want to waste energy *looking* for things," she says. "What good is that? I can be more efficient, productive and in a better mood if I don't spend those frustrating extra minutes searching for something." Thus, in fact, many creative people find the time to be creative precisely because of such systems unburdening and uncluttering their minds.

A large proportion of successful rock and hip-hop musicians have home studios, and despite the reputation they may have for being anything-goes, hard-drinking rebels, their studios are meticulously organized. Stephen Stills's home studio has designated drawers for guitar strings, picks, Allen wrenches, jacks, plugs, equipment spare parts (organized by type of equipment), splicing tape, and so on. A rack for cords and cables (it looks something like a necktie rack) holds electrical and musical instrument cords of various types in a particular order so that he can grab what he needs even without looking. Michael Jackson fastidiously catalogued every one of his possessions; among the large staff he employed was someone with the job title *chief archivist.* John Lennon kept boxes and boxes of work tapes of songs in progress, carefully labeled and organized.

There's something almost ineffably comforting about opening a drawer and seeing things all of one kind in it, or surveying an organized closet. Finding things without rummaging saves mental energy for more important creative tasks. It is in fact physiologically comforting to avoid the stress of wondering whether or not we're ever going to find what we're looking for. Not finding something thrusts the mind into a fog of confusion, a toxic vigilance mode that is neither focused nor relaxed. The more carefully constructed your categories, the more organized is your environment and, in turn, your mind.

From the Junk Drawer to the Filing Cabinet and Back

The fact that our brains are inherently good at creating categories is a powerful lever for organizing our lives. We can construct our home and work environments in such a way that they become extensions of our brains. In doing so, we must accept the capacity limitations of our central executive. The standard account for many years was that working memory and attention hit a limit at around five to nine unrelated items. More recently, a number of experiments have shown that the number is realistically probably closer to four.

The key to creating useful categories in our homes is to limit the number of types of things they contain to one or at most *four* types of things (respecting the capacity limitations of working memory). This is usually easy to do. If you've got a kitchen drawer that contains cocktail napkins, shish kebab skewers, matches, candles, and coasters, you can conceptualize it as "*things for a party.*" Conceptualizing it that way ties together all these disparate objects at a higher level. And then, if someone gives you special soaps that you want to put out only when you entertain, you know what drawer to keep them in.

Our brains are hardwired to make such categories, and these categories are cognitively flexible and can be arranged hierarchically. That is, there are different levels of resolution for what constitutes a kind, and they are context-dependent. Your bedroom closet probably contains clothes and then is subdivided into specialized categories such as underwear, shirts, socks, pants, and shoes. Those can be further subdivided if all your jeans are in one place and your fancy pants in another. When tidying the house, you might throw anything clothing-related into the closet and perform a finer subsort later. You might put anything tool-related in the garage, separating nails from hammers, screws from screwdrivers at a later time. The important observation is that we can create our own categories, and they're maximally efficient, neurologically speaking, if we can find a single thread that ties together all the members of a particular category.

David Allen, the efficiency expert, observes that what people usually mean when they say they want to get organized is that they need to get *control* of their physical and psychic environments. A germane finding in cognitive psychology for gaining that control is to make visible the things you need regularly, and hide things that you don't. This principle was originally formulated for the design of objects like television remote controls. Set aside your irritation with the number of buttons that remain on those gadgets for a moment—it is clear that you don't want the button that changes the color balances to be right next to the button that changes channels, where you might press it by mistake. In the best designs, the seldom-used setup controls are hidden behind a flip panel, or at least out of the way of the buttons you use daily.

In organizing your living space, the goals are to off-load some of the memory functions from your brain and into the environment; to keep your environment visually organized, so as not to distract you when you're trying to relax, work, or find things; and to create designated places for things so that they can be easily located.

Suppose you have limited closet space for your clothes, and some articles of clothing you wear only rarely (tuxedos, evening gowns, ski clothes). Move them to a spare closet so they're not using up prime real estate and so you can organize your daily clothes more efficiently. The same applies in the kitchen. Rather than putting all your baking supplies in one drawer, it makes organizational sense to put your Christmas cookie cutters in a special drawer devoted to Christmas-y things so you reduce clutter in your daily baking drawer—something you use only two weeks out of the year shouldn't be in your way fifty weeks out of the year. Keep stamps, envelopes, and stationery together in the same desk drawer because you use them together.

The display of liquor bottles in busy bars and taverns (places that many call home!) follows this principle. The frequently used liquors are within arm's reach of the bartender in what is called the *speed rack* attached to the base of the bar; little movement or mental energy is wasted in searching for these when making popular drinks from the speed rack. Less frequently used bottles are off to the side, or on a back shelf. Then, within this system, bottles of like spirits are placed side by side. The three or four most popular bourbons will be within arm's reach next to one another; the three or four most popular blended Scotches are next to them, and the single malts next to those. The configuration of both what's in the speed rack and what's on display will take account of local preferences. A bar in Lexington, Kentucky, would have many well-known brands of bourbon prominently displayed; a college town bar would have more tequila and vodka on display.

In a well-organized system, there is a balance between category size and category specificity. In other words, if you have only a handful of nails, it would be silly to devote an entire drawer just to them. It's more efficient and practical, then, to combine items into conceptual categories such as "home repair items." When the number of nails you have reaches critical mass, however, so that you're spending too much time every Sunday trying to find the precise nail you want, it makes sense to sort them by size into little bins the way they do at the hardware store. Time is an important consideration, too: Do you expect to be using these things more or less in the next few years?

Following Phaedrus, maintain the kind of flexibility that lets you create "everything else" categories—a junk drawer. Even if you have an exquisitely organized system where every drawer, shelf, and cubbyhole in your kitchen, office, or workshop is labeled, there will often be things that just don't fit into any existing system. Or alternatively, you might have too few things to devote an entire drawer or shelf to. From a purely obsessive-compulsive standpoint, it would be nice to have an entire drawer or shelf devoted to spare lightbulbs, another to adhesives (glue, contact cement, epoxy, double-sided tape), and another to your collection of candles. But if all you have is a single lightbulb and a half- used tube of Krazy Glue, there's no point.

Two neurologically based steps for setting up home information systems are, first, the categories you create need to reflect how you use and interact with your possessions. That is, the categories have to be meaningful to *you*. They should take into account your life stage. (All those hand-tied fisherman's flies that your grandfather left you might stay in the tackle box unsorted until you take up fly-fishing in a few decades, then you'll want to arrange the flies in a finer-grained way.) Second, avoid putting too many dissimilar items into a drawer or folder unless you can come up with an overarching theme. If you can't, MISCELLANEOUS or JUNK or UNCLASSIFIABLE are OK. But if you find yourself having four or five junk drawers, it's time to re-sort and regroup their contents, into MISC HOUSEHOLD versus MISC GARDEN versus MISC KIDS' STUFF for example.

Beyond those practical personalized steps, follow these general three rules of organization.

> Organization Rule 1: A mislabeled item or location is worse than an unlabeled item.

>> In a burst of energy, Jim labels one drawer in his office STAMPS AND ENVELOPES and another BATTERIES. After a couple of months, he swaps the contents of the drawers because he finds it difficult to bend over and distinguish AAA from AA batteries. He doesn't swap the labels because it's too much trouble, and he figures it doesn't matter because *he* knows where they are. This is a slippery slope! If you allow two drawers to go mislabeled, it's only a matter of time before you loosen your grip on creating "a place for everything and everything in its place." It also makes it difficult for anyone else to find anything. Something that is *unlabeled* is actually preferable because it causes a conversation such as "Jim, where do you keep your batteries?" or, if Jim isn't around, a systematic search. With mislabeled drawers, you don't know which ones you can trust and which ones you can't.

> Organization Rule 2: If there is an existing standard, use it.

>> Melanie has a recycling bin and a garbage bin under her kitchen sinks. One of them is blue and the other is gray. Outside, the bins that the city sanitation department gave her are blue (for recycling) and gray (for garbage). She should stick with that color-coded system because it is a standard, and then she doesn't have to try to memorize two different, opposing systems.

> Organization Rule 3: Don't keep what you can't use.

>> If you don't need it or it's broken and unfixable, get rid of it. Avery picks a ballpoint pen out of her pen drawer, and it doesn't write. She

> tries everything she knows to get it to work—moistening the tip, heating it with a lighter, shaking it, and making swirls on a piece of paper. She concludes it doesn't work, and then puts it right back in the drawer and takes another pen. Why did she (and why do we) do this? Few of us have an accurate knowledge of what makes a pen work or not work. Our efforts to get them to write are rewarded randomly—sometimes we get them working, sometimes we don't. We put them back in the drawer, thinking to ourselves "Maybe it'll work next time." But the clutter of a drawer full of mixed pens, some of which write and some of which don't, is a brain drain. Better to throw out the nonworking pen. Or, if you just can't *stand* the thought of that, designate a special box or drawer for recalcitrant pens that you will attempt to reform someday. If you're keeping the spare rubber feet that came with your TV set, and the TV set is no longer working, get rid of those rubber feet.

I am assuming people will still be watching something called TV when this book is published.

The Digital Home

Decades of research have shown that human learning is influenced by context and by the location where the learning takes place. Students who studied for an exam in the room they later took it in did better than students who studied somewhere else. We go back to our childhood home after a long absence, and a flood of forgotten memories is released. This is the reason it's important to have a designated place for each of our belongings—the hippocampus does the remembering for us if we associate an object with a particular spatial location. What happens when the information in the home is substantially, increasingly digital? There are a number of important implications in an age when so many more of us work from home or do office work at home.

One way to exploit the hippocampus's natural style of memory storage is to create different work spaces for the different kinds of work we do. But we use the same computer screen for balancing our checkbook, responding to e-mails from our boss, making online purchases, watching videos of cats playing the piano, storing photos of our loved ones, listening to our favorite music, paying bills, and reading the daily news. It's no wonder we can't remember everything—the brain simply wasn't designed to have so much information in one place. This advice is probably a luxury for a select few, but soon it will be possible as the cost of computers goes down: If you can, it's helpful to have one device dedicated to one domain of things. Instead of using your computer for watching videos and listening to music, have a dedicated media device (iPod, iPad). Have one computer for personal business (checking accounts and taxes), and a second computer for personal and leisure activities (planning trips, online purchases, storing photos). And a third computer for work. Create different desktop patterns on them so that the visual cues help to remind you, and put you in the proper place-memory context, of each computer's domain.

The neurologist and writer Oliver Sacks goes one further: If you're working on two completely separate projects, dedicate one desk or table or section of the house for each. Just stepping into a different space hits the reset button on your brain and allows for more productive and creative thinking.

Short of owning two or three separate computers, technology now allows for portable pocket drives that hold your entire hard disk—you can plug in a "leisure" pocket drive, a "work" pocket drive, or a "personal finance" pocket drive. Or instead, different user modes on some computers change the pattern of the desktop, the files on it, and the overall appearance to facilitate making these kinds of place-based, hippocampus-driven distinctions.

Which brings us to the considerable amount of information that hasn't been digitized yet. You know, on that stuff they call paper. Two schools of thought about how to organize the paper-based business affairs of your home are now battling over this area. In this category are included operating manuals for appliances and various electrical or electronic devices, warranties for purchased products and services, paid bills, canceled checks, insurance policies, other daily business documents, and receipts.

Microsoft engineer Malcolm Slaney (formerly of Yahoo!, IBM, and Apple) advocates scanning everything into PDFs and keeping them on your computer. Home scanners are relatively inexpensive, and there are strikingly good scanning apps available on cell phones. If it's something you want to keep, Malcolm says, scan it and save it under a filename and folder that will help you find it later. Use OCR (optical character recognition) mode so that the PDF is readable as text characters rather than simply a photograph of the file, to allow your computer's own search function to find specific keywords you're looking for. The advantage of digital filing is that it takes up virtually no space, is environmentally friendly, and is electronically searchable. Moreover, if you need to share the document with someone (your accountant, a colleague) it's already in a digital format and so you can simply attach it to an e-mail.

The second school of thought is advocated by someone I'll call Linda, who for many years served as the executive assistant to the president of a Fortune 100 company. She has asked to remain anonymous to protect the privacy of her boss. (What a great executive assistant!) Linda prefers to keep paper copies of everything. The chief advantage of paper is that it is almost permanent. Because of rapidly changing technology, digital files are rarely readable for more than ten years; paper, on the other hand, lasts for hundreds of years. Many computer users have become alerted to a rude surprise after their old computers failed: It's often not possible to buy a computer with the old operating system on it, and the new operating system can't open all your old files! Financial records, tax returns, photos, music—all of it gone. In large cities, it's possible to find services that will convert your files from old to new formats, but this can be costly, incomplete, and imperfect. Electrons are free, but you get what you pay for.

Other advantages of paper are that it can't be as easily edited or altered, or corrupted by a virus, and you can read it when the power's out. And although paper can be destroyed by a fire, so can your computer.

Despite their committed advocacy, even Malcolm and Linda keep many of their files in the nonpreferred format. In some cases, this is because they come to us that way—receipts for online purchases are sent as digital files by e-mail; bills from small companies still arrive by U.S. mail on paper.

There are ways of sorting both kinds of information, digital and paper, that can maximize their usefulness. The most important factor is the ease with which they can be retrieved.

For physical paper, the classic filing cabinet is still the best system known. The state of the art is the hanging file folder system, invented by Frank D. Jonas and patented in 1941 by the Oxford Filing Supply Company, which later became the Oxford Pendaflex Corporation. Oxford and secretarial schools have devised principles for creating file folders, and they revolve around making things easy to store and easy to retrieve. For a small number of files, say fewer than thirty, labeling them and sorting them in alphabetical order by topic is usually sufficient. More than that and you're usually better off alphabetizing your folders within higher-order categories, such as HOME, FINANCIAL, KIDS, and the like. Use the physical environment to separate such categories—different drawers in the filing cabinet, for example, can contain different higher-order categories; or within a drawer, different colored file folders or file folder tabs make it possible to visually distinguish categories very quickly. Some people, particularly those with attention deficit disorder, panic when they can't see all of their files in front of them, out in the open. In these cases, open filing carts and racks exist so that the files don't need to be hidden behind a drawer.

An often-taught practical rule about traditional filing systems (that is, putting paper into hanging file folders) is that you don't want to have a file folder with only one piece of paper in it—it's too inefficient. The goal is to group paperwork into categories such that your files contain five to twenty or so separate documents. Fewer than that and it becomes difficult to quickly scan the numerous file folder labels; more than that and you lose time trying to finger through the contents of one file folder. The same logic applies to creating categories for household and work objects.

Setting up a home filing system is more than just slapping a label on a folder. It's best to have a plan. Take some time to think about what the different kinds of papers are that you're filing. Take that stack of papers on your desk that you've been meaning to do something with for months and start sorting them, creating high-level categories that subsume them. If the sum total of all your file folders is less than, say, twenty, you could just have a folder for each topic and put them in alphabetical order. But more than that, and you're going to waste time searching for folders when you need them. You might have categories such as FINANCES, HOME STUFF, PERSONAL, MEDICAL, and MISCELLANEOUS (the junk drawer of your system for things that don't fit anywhere else: pet vaccination records, driver's license renewal, brochures for that trip you want to take next spring). Paperwork from specific correspondents should get its own folder. In other words, if you have a separate savings account, checking account, and retirement account, you don't want a folder labeled BANK STATEMENTS; you want folders for each account. The same logic applies across all kinds of objects.

Don't spend more time filing and classifying than you'll reap on searching. For documents you need to access somewhat frequently, say health records, make file folders and categories that facilitate finding what you're looking for—separate folders for each household member, or folders for GENERAL MEDICAL, DENTISTRY, EYE CARE, and so on. If you've got a bunch of file folders with one piece of paper in them, consolidate into an overarching theme. Create a dedicated file for important documents you need regularly to access, such as a visa, birth certificate, or health insurance policy.

All of the principles that apply to physical file folders of course also apply to the virtual files and folders on your computer. The clear advantage of the computer, however, is that you can keep your files entirely unorganized and the search function will usually help you find them nearly instantly (if you can remember what you named them). But this imposes a burden on your memory—it requires that you register and recall every filename you've ever used. Hierarchically organized files and folders have the big advantage that you can browse them to rediscover files you had forgotten about. This externalizes the memory from your brain to the computer.

If you really embrace the idea of making electronic copies of your important documents, you can create tremendously flexible relational databases and hyperlinks. For example, suppose you do your personal accounting in Excel and you've scanned all of your receipts and invoices to PDF files. Within Excel, you can link any entry in a cell to a document on your computer. Looking for the warranty and receipt on your Orvis fishing tackle jacket? Search Excel for *Orvis*, click on the cell, and you have the receipt ready to e-mail to the Customer Service Department. It's not just financial documents that can be linked this way. In a Word document in which you're citing research papers, you can create live links to those papers on your hard disk, a company server, or in the cloud.

Doug Merrill, former chief information officer and VP of engineering at Google, says "organization isn't—nor should it be—the same for everybody." However, there are fundamental things like To Do lists and carrying around notepaper or index cards, or "putting everything in a certain place and remembering where that place is."

But wait—even though many of us have home offices and pay our bills at home, all this doesn't sound like home. Home isn't about filing. What do you love about being at home? That feeling of calm, secure control over how you spend your time? What do you do at home? If you're like most Americans, you are multitasking. That buzzword of the aughts doesn't happen just on the job anymore. The smartphones and tablets have come home to roost.

Our cell phones have become Swiss Army knife–like appliances that include a dictionary, calculator, Web browser, e-mail client, Game Boy, appointment calendar, voice recorder, guitar tuner, weather forecaster, GPS, texter, tweeter, Facebook updater, and flashlight. They're more powerful and do more things than the most advanced computer at IBM corporate headquarters thirty years ago. And we use them all the time, part of a twenty-first-century mania for cramming everything we do into every single spare moment of downtime. We text while we're walking across the street, catch up on e-mail while standing in line, and while having lunch with friends, we surreptitiously check to see what our *other* friends are doing. At the kitchen counter, cozy and secure in our domicile, we write our shopping lists on smartphones while we are listening to that wonderfully informative podcast on urban beekeeping.

But there's a fly in the ointment. Although we think we're doing several things at once, multitasking, this has been shown to be a powerful and diabolical illusion. Earl Miller, a neuroscientist at MIT and one of the world experts on divided attention, says that our brains are "not wired to multitask well. . . . When people think they're multi-tasking, they're actually just switching from one task to another very rapidly. And every time they do, there's a cognitive cost in doing so." So we're not actually keeping a lot of balls in the air like an expert juggler; we're more like a bad amateur plate spinner, frantically switching from one task to another, ignoring the one that is not right in front of us but worried it will come crashing down any minute. Even though we think we're getting a lot done, ironically, multitasking makes us demonstrably less efficient.

Multitasking has been found to increase the production of the stress hormone cortisol as well as the fight-or-flight hormone adrenaline, which can overstimulate your brain and cause mental fog or scrambled thinking. Multitasking creates a dopamine-addiction feedback loop, effectively rewarding the brain for losing focus and for constantly searching for external stimulation. To make matters worse, the prefrontal cortex has a novelty bias, meaning that its attention can be easily hijacked by something new—the proverbial shiny objects we use to entice infants, puppies, and kittens. The irony here for those of us who are trying to focus amid competing activities is clear: The very brain region we need to rely on for staying on task is easily distracted. We answer the phone, look up something on the Internet, check our e-mail, send an SMS, and each of these things tweaks the novelty-seeking, reward-seeking centers of the brain, causing a burst of endogenous opioids (no wonder it feels so good!), all to the detriment of our staying on task. It is the ultimate empty-caloried brain candy. Instead of reaping the big rewards that come from sustained, focused effort, we instead reap empty rewards from completing a thousand little sugarcoated tasks.

In the old days, if the phone rang and we were busy, we either didn't answer or we turned the ringer off. When all phones were wired to a wall, there was no expectation of being able to reach us at all times—one might have gone out for a walk or be between places, and so if someone couldn't reach you (or you didn't feel like being reached), that was considered normal. Now more people have cell phones than have toilets. This has created an implicit expectation that you should be able to reach someone when it is convenient for *you,* regardless of whether it is convenient for them. This expectation is so ingrained that people in meetings routinely answer their cell phones to say, "I'm sorry, I can't talk now, I'm in a meeting." Just a decade or two ago, those same people would have let a landline on their desk go unanswered during a meeting, so different were the expectations for reachability.

Just having the *opportunity* to multitask is detrimental to cognitive performance. Glenn Wilson of Gresham College, London, calls it infomania. His research found that being in a situation where you are trying to concentrate on a task, and an e-mail is sitting unread in your inbox, can reduce your effective IQ by 10 points. And although people claim many benefits to marijuana, including enhanced creativity and reduced pain and stress, it is well documented that its chief ingredient, cannabinol, activates dedicated cannabinol receptors in the brain and interferes profoundly with memory and with our ability to concentrate on several things at once. Wilson showed that the cognitive losses from multitasking are even *greater* than the cognitive losses from pot smoking.

Russ Poldrack, a neuroscientist at Stanford, found that learning information while multitasking causes the new information to go to the wrong part of the brain. If students study and watch TV at the same time, for example, the information from their schoolwork goes into the striatum, a region specialized for storing new procedures and skills, not facts and ideas. Without the distraction of TV, the information goes into the hippocampus, where it is organized and categorized in a variety of ways, making it easier to retrieve it. MIT's Earl Miller adds, "People can't do [multitasking] very well, and when they say they can, they're deluding themselves." And it turns out the brain is very good at this deluding business.

Then there are the metabolic costs of switching itself that I wrote about earlier. Asking the brain to shift attention from one activity to another causes the prefrontal cortex and striatum to burn up oxygenated glucose, the same fuel they need to stay on task. And the kind of rapid, continual shifting we do with multitasking causes the brain to burn through fuel so quickly that we feel exhausted and disoriented after even a short time. We've literally depleted the nutrients in our brain. This leads to compromises in both cognitive and physical performance. Among other things, repeated task switching leads to anxiety, which raises levels of the stress hormone cortisol in the brain, which in turn can lead to aggressive and impulsive behaviors. By contrast, staying on task is controlled by the anterior cingulate and the striatum, and once we engage the central executive mode, staying in that state uses less energy than multitasking and actually reduces the brain's need for glucose.

To make matters worse, lots of multitasking requires decision-making: Do I answer this text message or ignore it? How do I respond to this? How do I file this e-mail? Do I continue what I'm working on now or take a break? It turns out that decision-making is also very hard on your neural resources and that little decisions appear to take up as much energy as big ones. One of the first things we lose is impulse control. This rapidly spirals into a depleted state in which, after making lots of insignificant decisions, we can end up making truly bad decisions about something important. Why would anyone want to add to their daily weight of information processing by trying to multitask?

In discussing information overload with Fortune 500 leaders, top scientists, writers, students, and small business owners, e-mail comes up again and again as a problem. It's not a philosophical objection to e-mail itself, it's the mind-numbing amount of e-mails that comes in. When the ten-year-old son of my neuroscience colleague Jeff Mogil was asked what his father does for a living, he responded, "He answers e-mails." Jeff admitted after some thought that it's not so far from the truth. Workers in government, the arts, and industry report that the sheer volume of e-mail they receive is overwhelming, taking a huge bite out of their day. We feel obligated to answer our e-mails, but it seems impossible to do so and get anything else done.

Before e-mail, if you wanted to write to someone, you had to invest some effort in it. You'd sit down with pen and paper, or at a typewriter, and carefully compose a message. There wasn't anything about the medium that lent itself to dashing off quick notes without giving them much thought, partly because of the ritual involved, and the time it took to write a note, find and address an envelope, add postage, and walk the letter to a mailbox. Because the very act of writing a note or letter to someone took this many steps, and was spread out over time, we didn't go to the trouble unless we had something important to say. Because of e-mail's immediacy, most of us give little thought to typing up any little thing that pops in our heads and hitting the send button. And e-mail doesn't cost anything. Sure, there's the money you paid for your computer and your Internet connection, but there is no incremental cost to sending one more e-mail. Compare this with paper letters. Each one incurred the price of the envelope and the postage stamp, and although this doesn't represent a lot of money, these were in limited supply—if you ran out of them, you'd have to make a special trip to the stationery store and the post office to buy more, so you didn't use them frivolously. The sheer ease of sending e-mails has led to a change in manners, a tendency to be less polite about what we ask of others. Many professionals tell a similar story. Said one, "A large proportion of e-mails I receive are from people I barely know asking me to do something for them that is outside what would normally be considered the scope of my work or my relationship with them. E-mail somehow apparently makes it OK to ask for things they would never ask by phone, in person, or in snail mail."

There are also important differences between snail mail and e-mail on the receiving end. In the old days, the only mail we got came once a day, which effectively created a cordoned-off section of your day to collect it from the mailbox and sort it. Most importantly, because it took a few days to arrive, there was no expectation that you would act on it immediately. If you were engaged in another activity, you'd simply let the mail sit in the box outside or on your desk until you were ready to deal with it. It even seemed a bit odd to race out to the mailbox to get your mail the moment the letter carrier left it there. (It had taken days to get this far, why would a few more minutes matter?) Now e-mail arrives continuously, and most e-mails demand some sort of action: Click on this link to see a video of a baby panda, or answer this query from a coworker, or make plans for lunch with a friend, or delete this e-mail as spam. All this activity gives us a sense that we're getting things done—and in some cases we are. But we are sacrificing efficiency and deep concentration when we interrupt our priority activities with e-mail.

Until recently, each of the many different modes of communication we used signaled its relevance, importance, and intent. If a loved one communicated with you via a poem or a song, even before the message was apparent, you had a reason to assume something about the nature of the content and its emotional value. If that same loved one communicated instead via a summons, delivered by an officer of the court, you would have expected a different message before even reading the document. Similarly, phone calls were typically used to transact different business from that of telegrams or business letters. The medium was a clue to the message. All of that has changed with e-mail, and this is one of its overlooked disadvantages—because it is used for everything. In the old days, you might sort all of your postal mail into two piles, roughly corresponding to personal letters and bills. If you were a corporate manager with a busy schedule, you might similarly sort your telephone messages for callbacks. But e-mails are used for *all* of life's messages. We compulsively check our e-mail in part because we don't know whether the next message will be for leisure/amusement, an overdue bill, a "to do," a query . . . something you can do now, later, something life-changing, something irrelevant.

This uncertainty wreaks havoc with our rapid perceptual categorization system, causes stress, and leads to decision overload. Every e-mail requires a decision! Do I respond to it? If so, now or later? How important is it? What will be the social, economic, or job-related consequences if I don't answer, or if I don't answer *right now?*

Now of course e-mail is approaching obsolescence as a communicative medium. Most people under the age of thirty think of e-mail as an outdated mode of communication used only by "old people." In its place they text, and some still post to Facebook. They attach documents, photos, videos, and links to their text messages and Facebook posts the way people over thirty do with e-mail. Many people under twenty now see Facebook as a medium for the older generation. For them, texting has become the primary mode of communication. It offers privacy that you don't get with phone calls, and immediacy you don't get with e-mail. Crisis hotlines have begun accepting calls from at-risk youth via texting and it allows them two big advantages: They can deal with more than one person at a time, and they can pass the conversation on to an expert, if needed, without interrupting the conversation.

But texting sports most of the problems of e-mail and then some. Because it is limited in characters, it discourages thoughtful discussion or any level of detail. And the addictive problems are compounded by texting's hyperimmediacy. E-mails take some time to work their way through the Internet, through switches and routers and servers, and they require that you take the step of explicitly opening them. Text messages magically appear on the screen of your phone and demand immediate attention from you. Add to that the social expectation that an unanswered text feels insulting to the sender, and you've got a recipe for addiction: You receive a text, and that activates your novelty centers. You respond and feel rewarded for having completed a task (even though that task was entirely unknown to you fifteen seconds earlier). Each of those delivers a shot of dopamine as your limbic system cries out "More! More! Give me more!"

In a famous experiment, my McGill colleague Peter Milner and James Olds placed a small electrode in the brains of rats, in a small structure of the limbic system called the nucleus accumbens. This structure regulates dopamine production and is the region that "lights up" when gamblers win a bet, drug addicts take cocaine, or people have orgasms—Olds and Milner called it the pleasure center. A lever in the cage allowed the rats to send a small electrical signal directly to their nucleus accumbens. Do you think they liked it? Boy howdy! They liked it so much that they did nothing else. They forgot all about eating and sleeping. Long after they were hungry, they ignored tasty food if they had a chance to press that little chrome bar; they even ignored the opportunity for sex. The rats just pressed the lever over and over again, until they died of starvation and exhaustion. Does that remind you of anything? A thirty-year-old man died in Guangzhou (China) after playing video games continuously for three days. Another man died in Daegu (Korea) after playing video games almost continuously for fifty hours, stopped only by his going into cardiac arrest.

Each time we dispatch with an e-mail in one way or another, we feel a sense of accomplishment, and our brain gets a dollop of reward hormones telling us we accomplished something. Each time we check a Twitter feed or Facebook update, we encounter something novel and feel more connected socially (in a kind of weird impersonal cyber way) and get another dollop of reward hormones. But remember, it is the dumb, novelty-seeking portion of the brain driving the limbic system that induces this feeling of pleasure, not the planning, scheduling, higher-level thought centers in the prefrontal cortex. Make no mistake: E-mail, Facebook, and Twitter checking constitute a neural addiction.

The secret is to put systems in place to trick ourselves—to trick our *brains*—into staying on task when we need them to. For one, set aside certain times of day when you'll do e-mail. Experts recommend that you do e-mail only two or three times a day, in concerted clumps rather than as they come in. Many people have their e-mail programs set to put through arriving e-mails automatically or to check every five minutes. Think about that: If you're checking e-mail every five minutes, you're checking it 200 times during the waking day. This has to interfere with advancing your primary objectives. You might have to train your friends and coworkers not to expect immediate responses, to use some other means of communication for things like a meeting later today, a lunch date, or a quick question.

For decades, efficient workers would shut their doors and turn off their phones for "productivity hours," a time when they could focus without being disturbed. Turning off our e-mail follows in that tradition and it does soothe the brain, both neurochemically and neuroelectrically. If the type of work you do really and truly doesn't allow for this, you can set up e-mail filters in most e-mail programs and phones, designating certain people whose mail you want to get through to you right away, while other mail just accumulates in your inbox until you have time to deal with it. And for people who really can't be away from e-mail, another effective trick is to set up a special, private e-mail account and give that address only to those few people who need to be able to reach you right away, and check your other accounts only at designated times.

Lawrence Lessig, a law professor at Harvard, and others have promoted the idea of e-mail bankruptcy. At a certain point, you realize that you're never going to catch up. When this happens, you delete or archive everything in your inbox, and then send out a mass e-mail to all your correspondents, explaining that you're hopelessly behind in e-mail and that if whatever they were e-mailing you about is still important, they should e-mail you again. Alternatively, some people set up an automatic reply that gets sent in response to any incoming e-mail message. The reply might say something along the lines of "I will try to get to your e-mail within the next week. If this is something that requires immediate action, please telephone me. If it still requires my reply and you haven't heard from me in a week, please resend your message with '2nd attempt' in the subject line."

As shadow work increases and we are called upon to do more of our own personal business management, the need to have accounts with multiple companies has mushroomed. Keeping track of your login information and passwords is difficult because different websites and service providers impose wildly different restrictions on these parameters. Some providers insist that you use your e-mail address as a login, others insist you don't; some require that your password contains special characters such as $&*#, and others won't allow any at all. Additional restrictions include not being able to repeat a character more than twice (so that *aaa* would not be allowed in your password string anywhere) or not being allowed to use the same password you've used in the past six months. Even if logins and passwords could be standardized, however, it would be a bad idea to use the same login and password for all your accounts because if one account gets compromised, then all of them do.

Several programs exist for keeping track of your passwords. Many of them store the information on servers (in the cloud), which poses a potential security threat—it's only a matter of time before hackers break in and steal millions of passwords. In recent months, hackers stole the passwords of 3 million Adobe customers, 2 million Vodafone customers in Germany, and 160 million Visa credit and debit card customers. Others reside on your computer, which make them less vulnerable to external attack (although still not 100% secure), yet more vulnerable if your computer is stolen. The best of the programs generate passwords that are fiendishly hard to guess, and then store them in an encrypted file so that even if someone gets their hands on your computer, they can't crack your passwords. All you have to remember is the one password to unlock the password file—and that should ideally be an unholy mess of upper- and lowercase letters, numbers, and special symbols, something like Qk8$#@iP{%mA. Writing down passwords on a piece of paper or in a notebook is not recommended because that is the first place thieves will look.

One option is to keep passwords stored on your computer in an encrypted password management program that will recognize the websites you visit and will automatically log you in; others will simply allow you to retrieve your password if you forget it. A low-cost alternative is simply to save all your passwords in an Excel or Word file and password-protect that file (make sure to choose a password that you won't forget, and that isn't the same as other passwords you're using).

Don't even think about using your dog's name or your birthday as a password, or, for that matter, any word that can be found in a dictionary. These are too easy to hack. A system that optimizes both security and ease of use is to generate passwords according to a formula that you memorize, and then write down on a piece of paper or in an encrypted file only those websites that require an alteration of that basic formula. A clever formula for generating passwords is to think of a sentence you'll remember, and then use the first letters of each word of the sentence. You can customize the password for the vendor or website. For example, your sentence might be "My favorite TV show is *Breaking Bad*."

Turning that into an actual password, taking the first letter of each word, would yield

M f T V s i B B

Now replace one of those letters with a special symbol, and add a number in the middle, just to make it particularly safe:

M f T V $ 6 i B B

You now have a secure password, but you don't want to use the same password for every account. You can customize the password by adding on to the beginning or the end the name of the vendor or website you're accessing. If you were using this for your **C**itibank **c**hecking **a**ccount, you might take the three letters *C c a* and start your password with them to yield

C c a M f T V $ 6 i B B

For your <u>U</u>nited <u>A</u>irlines <u>M</u>ileage <u>P</u>lus account, the password would be

U A M P M f T V $ 6 i B B

If you encounter a website that won't allow special characters, you simply remove them. The password for your Aetna health care account might then be

A M f T V i B B

Then, all you have to write down on a piece of paper are the deviations from the standard formula. Because you haven't written down the actual formula, you've added an extra layer of security in case someone discovers your list. Your list might look something like this:

Aetna health insurance	std formula w/o special char or number
Citibank checking	std formula
Citibank Visa card	std formula w/o number
Liberty Mutual home insurance	std formula w/o spec char
Municipal water bill	std formula
Electric utility	first six digits of std formula
Sears credit card	std formula + month

Some websites require that you change your password every month. Just add the month to the end of your password. Suppose it was your Sears credit card. For October and November, your passwords might be:

S M f T V $ 6 i B B Oct
S M f T V $ 6 i B B Nov

If all this seems like a lot of trouble, IBM predicts that by 2016, we'll no longer need passwords because we'll be using biometric markers such as an iris scan (currently being used by border control agencies in the United States, Canada, and other countries), fingerprint, or voice recognition, yet many consumers will resist sharing biometrics out of privacy concerns. So maybe passwords are here to stay, at least for a little while longer. The point is that even with something as intentionally unorganizable as passwords, you can actually, quite easily become mentally organized.

Home Is Where I Want to Be

Losing certain objects causes a great deal more inconvenience or stress than losing others. If you lose your Bic pen, or forget that crumpled-up dollar bill in your pants when you send it to the laundry, it's not a calamity. But locking yourself out of your house in the middle of the night during a snowstorm, not being able to find your car keys in an emergency, or losing your passport or cell phone can be debilitating.

We are especially vulnerable to losing things when we travel. Part of the reason is that we're outside of our regular routine and familiar environment, so the affordances we have in place at home are not there. There is added demand on our hippocampal place memory system as we try to absorb a new physical environment. In addition, losing things in the information age can pose certain paradoxes or catch-22s. If you lose your credit card, what number do you call to report it? It's not that easy because the number was written on the back of the card. And most credit card call centers ask you to key in your card number, something that you can't do if you don't have the card right in front of you (unless you've memorized that sixteen-digit number *plus* the three-digit secret card verification code on the back). If you lose your wallet or purse, it can be difficult to obtain any cash because you no longer have ID. Some people worry about this much more than others. If you're among the millions of people who do lose things, organizing fail-safes or backups might clear your mind of this stress.

Daniel Kahneman recommends taking a proactive approach: Think of the ways you could lose things and try to set up blocks to prevent them. Then, set up fail-safes, which include things like:

- Hiding a spare house key in the garden or at a neighbor's house
- Keeping a spare car key in your top desk drawer
- Using your cell phone camera to take a close-up picture of your passport, driver's license, and health insurance card, and both sides of your credit card(s)

- Carrying with you a USB key with all your medical records on it
- When traveling, keeping one form of ID and at least some cash or one credit card in a pocket, or somewhere separate from your wallet and other cards, so that if you lose one, you don't lose everything
- Carrying an envelope for travel receipts when you're out of town so that they're all in one place, and not mixed in with other receipts.

And what to do when things *do* get lost? Steve Wynn is the CEO of the Fortune 500 company that bears his name, Wynn Resorts. The designer of the award-winning luxury hotels the Bellagio, Wynn, and Encore in Las Vegas, and the Wynn and Palace in Macau, he oversees an operation with more than 20,000 employees. He details a systematic approach.

> Of course, like anyone else, I lose my keys or my wallet or passport. When that happens, I try to go back to one truth. Where am I *sure* that I saw my passport last? I had it upstairs when I was on the phone. Then I creep through the activities since then. I was on the phone upstairs. Is the phone still there? No, I brought the phone downstairs. What did I do when I was downstairs? While I was talking I fiddled with the TV. To do that I needed to have the remote. OK, where is the remote? Is my passport with it? No, it's not there. Oh! I got myself a glass of water from the fridge. There it is, the passport is next to the fridge—I set it down while I was on the phone and not thinking.
>
> Then there is the whole process of trying to remember something. I have the name of that actor on the tip of my tongue. I *know* that I know it, I just can't get it. And so I think about it systematically. I remember that it began with a "D." So let's see, dă, day, deh, dee, dih, die, dah, doe, due, duh, dir, dar, daw . . . I think hard like I'm trying to lift a weight, going through each combination until it comes.

Many people over the age of sixty fear that they're suffering memory deficits, fighting off early-onset Alzheimer's, or simply losing their marbles because they can't remember something as simple as whether they took that multivitamin at breakfast or not. But—neuroscience to the rescue—it is probably just that the act of taking the pill has become so commonplace that it is forgotten almost immediately afterward. Children don't usually forget when they've taken pills because the act of pill taking is still novel to them. They focus intently on the experience, worry about choking or ending up with a bad taste in their mouths, and all these things serve two purposes: First, they reinforce the novelty of the event at the moment of the pill taking, and second, they cause the child to focus intently on that moment. As we saw earlier, attention is a very effective way of entering something into memory.

But think about what we adults do when taking a pill, an act so commonplace that we can do it without thinking (and often do). We put the pill in our mouths, take a drink, swallow, all while thinking about six other things: Did I remember to pay the electric bill? What new work will my boss give me to do today at that ten o'clock meeting? I'm getting tired of this breakfast cereal, I have to remember to buy a different one next time I'm at the store. . . . All of this cross talk in our overactive brains, combined with the lack of attention to the moment of taking the pill, increases the probability that we'll forget it a few short minutes later. The childlike sense of wonder that we had as children, the sense that there is adventure in each activity, is partly what gave us such strong memories when we were young—it's not that we're slipping into dementia.

This suggests two strategies for remembering routine activities. One is to try to reclaim that sense of newness in everything we do. Easier said than done of course. But if we can acquire a Zen-like mental clarity and pay attention to what we're doing, letting go of thoughts of the future and past, we will remember each moment because each moment will be special. My saxophone teacher and friend Larry Honda, head of the Music Department at Fresno City College and leader of the Larry Honda Quartet, gave me this remarkable gift when I was only twenty-one years old. It was the middle of summer, and I was living in Fresno, California. He came over to my house to give me my weekly saxophone lesson. My girlfriend, Vicki, had just harvested another basket of strawberries, which were particularly plentiful that year, from our garden, and as Larry came up the walkway, she offered him some. When other friends had come by and Vicki had offered them strawberries, they ate them while continuing to talk about whatever they were talking about before the appearance of the berries, their minds and bodies trying to eat and talk at the same time. This is hardly unusual in modern Western society.

But Larry had his way of doing things. He stopped and looked at them. He picked one up and stroked the leafy stem with his fingers. He closed his eyes and took in a deep breath, with the strawberry just under his nostrils. He tasted it and ate it slowly with all his focus. He was so far into the unfolding of the moment, it drew me in, too, and I remember it clearly thirty-five years later. Larry approached music the same way, which I think made him a great saxophone player.

The second, more mundane way to remember these little moments is much less romantic, and perhaps less spiritually satisfying, but no less effective (you've heard it before): Off-load the memory functions into the physical world rather than into your crowded mental world. In other words, write it down on a piece of paper, or if you prefer, get a system. By now, most of us have seen little plastic pill holders with the names of the days of the week written on them, or the times of day, or both. You load up your pills in the proper compartment, and then you don't have to remember anything at all except that an empty compartment confirms you took your dose. Such pillboxes aren't foolproof (as the old saying goes, "Nothing is foolproof because fools are ingenious"), but they reduce errors by unloading mundane, repetitive information from the frontal lobes into the external environment.

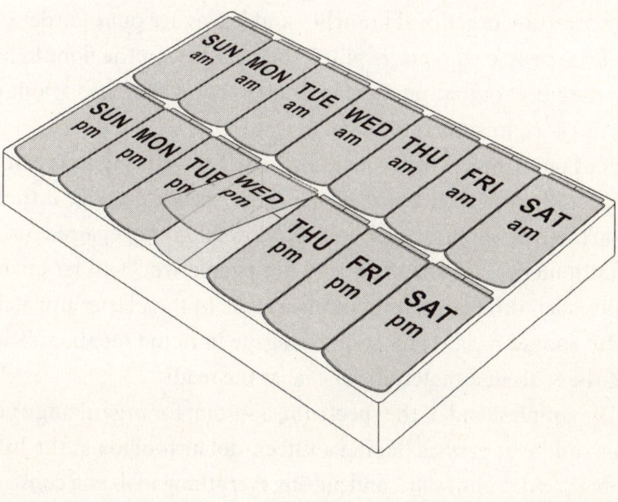

In addition to designating a special place for things you're likely to misplace (like the key hook near the front door), it's helpful to put things where you are most likely to need them. This off-loads the burden of memory entirely, and is similar to Skinner's plan of leaving the umbrella by the door on days when the forecast calls for rain. For instance, the specialized tools that come with appliances and furniture, such as a garbage disposal wrench, IKEA furniture wrench, and adjustment wrench for your exercise bicycle, can be attached to the object using duct tape or nylon gripper ties. If you attach your IKEA wrench to a leg support underneath the table, it will be right where you need it if the table starts to wobble and you need to tighten the screw. This is in keeping with the principle of cognitive efficiency: Why have to remember where something is? Put it precisely where you will need it. Flashlight manufacturers started doing this decades ago when they tucked a spare bulb inside the cap you screw off to change the batteries—you can't lose it because it's right where you need it. What if you can't do that for the objects you'll need? Put them in individual ziplock bags along with a piece of notepaper stating what object they're for and keep all these bags in a shoe box labeled THINGS I WILL NEED.

Humans differ from one another along thousands of dimensions, including variously defined levels of stress and security, but one thing most of us have in common is a drive toward order in our immediate environment. This is a trait found even in many lower species, including some birds and rodents who can tell if an intruder has entered their living space by whether carefully organized branches and leaves are out of order on their return. Even people who prefer piling their clothes on the floor to hanging them in the closet or folding them in drawers know that the various clothes piles have a certain system to them.

Part of our sense of order manifests itself in wanting to repair simple things when we can. Here again, people differ. At one extreme is the fanatic who won't let the slightest nick in a windowsill go unrepaired, or a loose faucet untightened. At the other end are people who will let burned-out lightbulbs stay unreplaced for months, cracks in the plaster unpatched for years. But sooner or later, most of us engage in home repair, and we keep some of the tools and materials for that at the ready.

At the simplest end of the spectrum, a system for organizing and keeping tools can be as easy as buying a fifteen-dollar toolbox at the hardware store or big box discount store, and putting everything tool- and construction-related into it. At the other end, many people build a system of drawers, cabinets, and racks in the garage for keeping track—a single drawer for different kinds of hammers; a drawer for adjustable wrenches; a drawer for fixed wrenches, and so on. In the middle of the spectrum, several catalogues and hardware stores sell a kind of "all-in-one" home repair kit with a starter set of tools in a form-fit box—every tool has a designated place in the box and so it's obvious when one's missing. These all-in-one kits typically include the most commonly used screws and nails, too.

James L. Adams, a creativity consultant and retired mechanical engineering professor at Stanford, is one of the popularizers of the phrase "thinking outside the box." In his spare time, Adams rebuilds and restores antique tractors and trucks. He recommends Harbor Freight Tools and similar merchants as a cost-effective way to buy and organize tools. Harbor Freight Tools, a mail order company with a network of walk-in stores throughout the United States, specializes in hard-to-find tools, telescoping mirrors and parts grabbers, EZ outs (a tool for removing stuck bolts), as well as hand tools, power tools, workbenches, and heavy tools, such as engine lifters and auto ramps (to drive your car up onto while you change the oil). Many tools come in cases that facilitate keeping them organized. One set of products that vastly simplifies and reorganizes the life of an active home-repair person are "storehouses." For example, Harbor Freight sells a nut-and-bolt storehouse that contains a few of virtually every size of nut and bolt that you would ever use; screw and nail storehouses are also available, as well as a "washer storehouse" that contains 141 pieces for $4.99. The 1001 Piece Nut and Bolt Storehouse including all the pieces plus a plastic storage chest (and preprinted drawer labels!) cost $19.95 as of this writing.

To many, the idea of having 1,001 nuts and bolts organized in carefully created little drawers, each with subdivided compartments, sounds like OCD overkill. But it's helpful to analyze this logically. Suppose you finally have the time to repair that crooked cabinet in your kitchen and you see that a screw is missing from the hinge. You don't have the right screw, so you drive or take the bus to the hardware store, eating up at least half an hour of your day and a few dollars of transportation costs, not to mention the cost of the screw. Just two trips like this and the screw storehouse has paid for itself. The washer storehouse saves a few trips to the store when your garden hose starts leaking. The next time you're out doing errands and you're near your local hardware store *anyway*, you can replace the parts you used from the storehouse. And if you find spare nuts, screws, washers, and such around the house, you have a place to keep them, all in order. Creating your own miniature hardware store all at once is a big savings on time and energy, compared to buying things piecemeal as you need them. Many successful people report that they experience mental benefits from organizing or reorganizing their closets or drawers when they are stressed. And we now understand the neurological substrates: This activity allows our brains to explore new connections among the things that clutter our living spaces, while simultaneously allowing the mind-wandering mode to recontextualize and recategorize those objects' relationships to one another and our relationship to them.

That said, it is important to accept that humans differ from one another along many dimensions, and what makes one person feel secure can drive another person insane. To a minimalist antimaterialist, the idea of accumulating a thousand nuts and bolts to *maybe* be used *someday* not only causes stress but contradicts her self-image. At the other extreme, survivalist freaks are stressed out without twenty gallons of water and a forty-day supply of vacuum-packed protein. There are those two kinds of people, plus everybody in between. It is important to harmonize your organizational style and systems with your personality.

With thousands of different objects in the modern home, these are not the kinds of problems our ancestors faced. But our ancestors faced different stressors than we do, including the very real threat of an early demise. We need to be proactive about reducing stress by doing things that reset our working brains—experiencing nature and art, allowing the mind-wandering mode to kick in regularly, and spending time with friends. So how do we organize that?

4

ORGANIZING OUR SOCIAL WORLD

How Humans Connect Now

On July 16, 2013, a mentally unstable New York woman abducted her seven-month-old son from a foster care agency in Manhattan. In such abduction cases, experience has shown that the chances of finding the child diminish drastically with each passing hour. Police feared for the infant boy's safety, and with no leads, they turned to a vast social network created for national emergency alerts—they sent text messages to millions of cell phones throughout the city. Just before four A.M., countless New Yorkers were awakened by the text message:

The alert, which showed the license plate number of the car used to abduct the infant, resulted in someone spotting the car and calling the New York City Police Department, and the infant was safely recovered. The message broke through people's attentional filter.

Three weeks later, the California Highway Patrol issued a regional, and later statewide, Amber Alert after two children were abducted near San

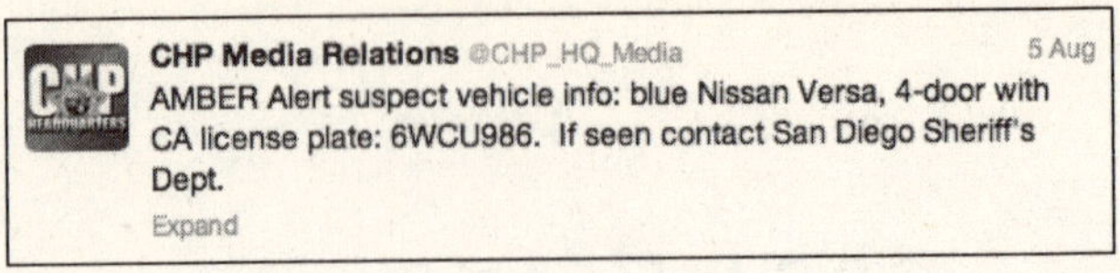
CHP Media Relations @CHP_HQ_Media 5 Aug
AMBER Alert suspect vehicle info: blue Nissan Versa, 4-door with CA license plate: 6WCU986. If seen contact San Diego Sheriff's Dept.
Expand

Diego. The alert was texted to millions of cell phones in California, tweeted by the CHP, and repeated above California freeways on large displays normally used to announce traffic conditions. Again the victim was safely recovered.

It's not just technology that has made this possible. We humans are hard-wired to protect our young, even the young of those not related to us. Whenever we read of terrorist attacks or war atrocities, the most wrenching and visceral reactions are to descriptions of children being harmed. This feeling appears to be culturally universal and innate.

The Amber Alert is an example of crowdsourcing—outsourcing to a crowd—the technique by which thousands or even millions of people help to solve problems that would be difficult or impossible to solve any other way. Crowdsourcing has been used for all kinds of things, including wildlife and bird counts, providing usage examples and quotes to the editors of the *Oxford English Dictionary*, and helping to decipher ambiguous text. The U.S. military and law enforcement have taken an interest in it because it potentially increases the amount of data they get by turning a large number of civilians into team members in information gathering. Crowdsourcing is just one example of organizing our social world—our social networks—to harness the energy, expertise, and physical presence of many individuals for the benefit of all. In a sense, it represents another form of externalizing the human brain, a way of linking the activities, perceptions, and cognitions of a large number of brains to a joint activity for the collective good.

In December 2009, DARPA offered $40,000 to anyone who could locate ten balloons that they had placed in plain sight around the continental United States. DARPA is the Defense Advanced Research Projects Agency, an organization under the U.S. Department of Defense. DARPA created the Internet (more precisely, they designed and built the first computer network, ARPANET, on which the current World Wide Web is modeled). At issue was how the United States might solve large-scale problems of national security and defense, and to test the country's capacity for mobilization during times of urgent crisis. Replace "balloons" with "dirty bombs" or other explosives, and the relevance of the problem is clear.

On a predesignated day, DARPA hid ten large, red weather balloons, eight feet in diameter, in various places around the country. The $40,000 prize would be awarded to the first person or team anywhere in the world who could correctly identify the precise location of all ten balloons. When the contest was first announced, experts pointed out that the problem would be impossible to solve using traditional intelligence-gathering techniques.

There was great speculation in the scientific community about how the problem would be solved—for weeks, it filled up lunchroom chatter at universities and research labs around the world. Most assumed the winning team would use satellite imagery, but that's where the problem gets tricky. How would they divide up the United States into surveillable sections with a high-enough resolution to spot the balloons, but still be able to navigate the enormous number of photographs quickly? Would the satellite images be analyzed by rooms full of humans, or would the winning team perfect a computer-vision algorithm for distinguishing the red balloons from other balloons and from other round, red objects that were not the target? (Effectively solving the *Where's Waldo?* problem, something that computer programs couldn't do until 2011.)

Further speculation revolved around the use of reconnaissance planes, telescopes, sonar, and radar. And what about spectrograms, chemical sensors, lasers? Tom Tombrello, physics professor at Caltech, favored a sneaky approach: "I would have figured out a way to get to the balloons before they were launched, and planted GPS tracking devices on them. Then finding them is trivial."

The contest was entered by 53 teams totaling 4,300 volunteers. The winning team, a group of researchers from MIT, solved the problem in just under nine hours. How did they do it? Not via the kinds of high-tech satellite imaging or reconnaissance that many imagined, but—as you may have guessed—by constructing a massive, ad hoc social network of collaborators and spotters—in short, by crowdsourcing. The MIT team allocated $4,000 to finding each balloon. If you happened to spot the balloon in your neighborhood and provided them with the correct location, you'd get $2,000. If a friend of yours whom you recruited found it, your friend would get the $2,000 and you'd get $1,000 simply for encouraging your friend to join the effort. If a friend of your friend found the balloon, you'd get $500 for this third-level referral, and so on. The likelihood of any one person spotting a balloon is infinitesimally small. But if everyone you know recruits everyone they know, and each of them recruits everyone *they* know, you build a network of eyes on the ground that theoretically can cover the entire country. One of the interesting questions that social networking engineers and Department of Defense workers had wondered about is how many people it would take to cover the entire country in the event of a real national emergency, such as searching for an errant nuclear weapon. In the case of the DARPA balloons, it required only 4,665 people and fewer than nine hours.

A large number of people—the public—can often help to solve big problems outside of traditional institutions such as public agencies. Wikipedia is an example of crowdsourcing: Anyone with information is encouraged to contribute, and through this, it has become the largest reference work in the world. What Wikipedia did for encyclopedias, Kickstarter did for venture capital: More than 4.5 million people have contributed over $750 million to fund roughly 50,000 creative projects by filmmakers, musicians, painters, designers, and other artists. Kiva applied the concept to banking, using crowdsourcing to kick-start economic independence by sponsoring microloans that help start small businesses in developing countries. In its first nine years, Kiva has given out loans totaling $500 million to one million people in seventy different countries, with crowdsourced contributions from nearly one million lenders.

The people who make up the crowd in crowdsourcing are typically amateurs and enthusiastic hobbyists, although this doesn't necessarily have to be the case. Crowdsourcing is perhaps most visible as a form of consumer ratings via Yelp, Zagat, and product ratings on sites such as Amazon.com. In the old, pre-Internet days, a class of workers existed who were expert reviewers and they would share their impressions of products and services in newspaper articles or magazines such as *Consumer Reports*. Now, with TripAdvisor, Yelp, Angie's List, and others of their ilk, ordinary people are empowered to write reviews about their own experiences. This cuts both ways. In the best cases, we are able to learn from the experiences of hundreds of people about whether this motel is clean and quiet, or that restaurant is greasy and has small portions. On the other hand, there were advantages to the old system. The pre-Internet reviewers were professionals—they performed reviews for a living—and so they had a wealth of experience to draw on. If you were reading a restaurant review, you'd be reading it from someone who had eaten in *a lot* of restaurants, not someone who has little to compare it to. Reviewers of automobiles and hi-fi equipment had some expertise in the topic and could put a product through its paces, testing or paying attention to things that few of us would think of, yet might be important—such as the functioning of antilock brakes on wet pavement.

Crowdsourcing has been a democratizing force in reviewing, but it must be taken with a grain of salt. Can you trust the crowd? Yes and no. The kinds of things that everybody likes may not be the kinds of things *you* like. Think of a particular musical artist or book you loved but that wasn't popular. Or a popular book or movie that, in your opinion, was awful. On the other hand, for quantitative judgments, crowds can come close. Take a large glass jar filled with many hundreds of jelly beans and ask people to guess how many are in it. While the majority of answers will probably be very wrong, the group average comes surprisingly close.

Amazon, Netflix, Pandora, and other content providers have used the wisdom of the crowd in a mathematical algorithm called collaborative filtering. This is a technique by which correlations or co-occurrences of behaviors are tracked and then used to make recommendations. If you've seen a little line of text on websites that says something like "customers who bought *this* also enjoyed *that,*" you've experienced collaborative filtering firsthand. The problem with these algorithms is that they don't take into account a host of nuances and circumstances that might interfere with their accuracy. If you just bought a gardening book for Aunt Bertha, you may get a flurry of links to books about gardening—*recommended just for you!*—because the algorithm doesn't know that you hate gardening and only bought the book as a gift. If you've ever downloaded movies for your children, only to find that the website's movie recommendations to you became overwhelmed by G-rated fare when you're looking for a good adult drama, you've seen the downside.

Navigation systems also use a form of crowdsourcing. When the Waze app on your smartphone, or Google Maps, is telling you the best route to the airport based on current traffic patterns, how do they know where the traffic is? They're tracking your cell phone and the cell phones of thousands of other users of the applications to see how quickly those cell phones move through traffic. If you're stuck in a traffic jam, your cell phone reports the same GPS coordinates for several minutes; if traffic is moving swiftly, your cell phone moves as quickly as your car and these apps can recommend routes based on that. As with all crowdsourcing, the quality of the overall system depends crucially on there being a large number of users. In this respect they're similar to telephones, fax machines, and e-mail: If only one or two people have them, they are not much good—their utility increases with the number of users.

Artist and engineer Salvatore Iaconesi used crowdsourcing to understand treatment options for his brain cancer by placing all of his medical records online. He received over 500,000 responses. Teams formed, as physicians discussed medical options with one another. "The solutions came from all over the planet, spanning thousands of years of human history and traditions," says Iaconesi. Wading through the advice, he chose conventional surgery in combination with some alternative therapies, and the cancer is now in remission.

One of the most common applications of crowdsourcing is hidden behind the scenes: reCAPTCHAs. These are the distorted words that are often displayed on websites. Their purpose is to prevent computers, or "bots," from gaining access to secure websites, because such problems are difficult to solve for computers and usually not too difficult for humans. (CAPTCHA is an acronym for **C**ompletely **A**utomated **P**ublic **T**uring test to tell **C**omputers and **H**umans **A**part. reCAPTCHAs are so-named for recycling—because they recycle human processing power.) reCAPTCHAs act as sentries against automated programs that attempt to infiltrate websites to steal e-mail addresses and passwords, or just to exploit weaknesses (for example, computer programs that might buy large numbers of concert tickets and then attempt to sell them at inflated prices). The source of these distorted words? In many cases they are pages from old books and manuscripts that Google is digitizing and that Google's computers have had difficulty in deciphering. Individually, each reCAPTCHA takes only about ten seconds to solve, but with more than 200 million of them being solved every day, this amounts to over 500,000 hours of work being done *in one day*. Why *not* turn all this time into something productive?

The technology for automatically scanning written materials and turning them into searchable text is not perfect. Many words that a human being can discern are misread by computers. Consider the following example from an actual book being scanned by Google:

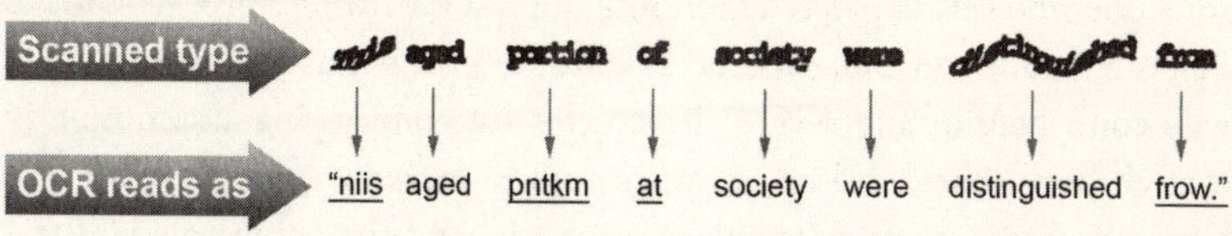

After the text is scanned, two different OCR (for optical character recognition) programs attempt to map these blotches on the page to known words. If the programs disagree, the word is deemed unsolved, and then reCAPTCHA uses it as a challenge for users to solve. How does the system know if you guessed an unknown word correctly? It doesn't! But reCAPTCHAs pair the unknown words with known words; they assume that if you solve the known word, you're a human, and that your guess on the unknown word is reasonable. When several people agree on the unknown word, it's considered solved and the information is incorporated into the scan.

Amazon's Mechanical Turk is typically used for tasks that computers aren't particularly good at but humans would find repetitively dull or boring. A recent cognitive psychology experiment published in *Science* used Amazon's Mechanical Turk to find experimental participants. Volunteers (who were paid three dollars each) had to read a story and then take a test that measured their levels of empathy. Empathy requires the ability to switch between different perspectives on the same situation or interaction. This requires using the brain's daydreaming mode (the task-negative network), and it involves the prefrontal cortex, cingulate, and their connections to the temporoparietal junction. Republicans and Democrats don't use these empathy regions of their brains when thinking of one another. The research finding was that people who read literary fiction (as opposed to popular fiction or nonfiction) were better able to detect another person's emotions, and the theory proposed was that literary fiction engages the reader in a process of decoding the characters' thoughts and motives in a way that popular fiction and nonfiction, being less complex, do not. The experiment required hundreds of participants and would have taken a great deal more time to accomplish using physical participants in the laboratory.

Of course it is also a part of human nature to cheat, and anyone using crowdsourcing has to put into play checks and balances. When reading an online review of a restaurant, you can't know that it was written by someone who actually dined there and not just the owner's brother-in-law. For Wikipedia, those checks and balances are the sheer number of people who contribute to and review the articles. The underlying assumption is that cheaters, liars, and others with mild to extreme sociopathy are the minority in any given assemblage of people, and the white hats will triumph over the black hats. This is unfortunately not always true, but it appears to be true enough of the time for crowdsourcing to be useful and mostly trustworthy. It's also, in many cases, a cost-saving alternative to a phalanx of paid experts.

Pundits have argued that "the crowd is always right," but this is demonstrably not true. Some people in the crowd can be stubborn and dogmatic while simultaneously being misinformed, and having a panel of expert overseers can go a long way toward improving the accuracy and success of crowdsourced projects such as Wikipedia. As *New Yorker* essayist Adam Gopnik explains,

> When there's easy agreement, it's fine, and when there's widespread disagreement on values or facts, as with, say, the origins of capitalism, it's fine too; you get both sides. The trouble comes when one side is right and the other side is wrong and doesn't know it. The Shakespeare authorship [Wikipedia] page and the Shroud of Turin page are scenes of constant conflict and are packed with unreliable information. Creationists crowd cyberspace every bit as effectively as evolutionists, and extend their minds just as fully. Our trouble is not the overall absence of smartness but the intractable power of pure stupidity.

Modern social networks are fraught with dull old dysfunction and wonderfully new opportunities.

Aren't Modern Social Relations Too Complex to Organize?

Some of the largest changes we are facing as a society are cultural, changes to our social world and the way we interact with one another. Imagine you are living in the year 1200. You probably have four or five siblings, and another four or five who died before their second birthday. You live in a one-room house with a dirt floor and a fire in the center for warmth. You share that house with your parents, children, and an extended family of aunts, uncles, nephews, and nieces all crowded in. Your daily routines are intimately connected to those of about twenty family members. You know a couple hundred people, and you've known most of them all your life. Strangers are regarded with suspicion because it is so very unusual to encounter them. The number of people you'd encounter in a lifetime was fewer than the number of people you'd walk past during rush hour in present-day Manhattan.

By 1850, the average family group in Europe had dropped from twenty people to ten living in close proximity, and by 1960 that number was just five. Today, 50% of Americans live alone. Fewer of us are having children, and those who do are having fewer children. For tens of thousands of years, human life revolved around the family. In most parts of the industrialized world, it no longer does. Instead, we create multiple overlapping social worlds—at work, though hobbies, in our neighborhoods. We become friends with the parents of our children's friends, or with the owners of our dog's friends. We build and maintain social networks with our friends from college or high school, but less and less with family. We meet more strangers, and we incorporate them into our lives in very new ways.

Notions of privacy that we take for granted today were very different just two hundred years ago. It was common practice to share rooms and even beds at roadside inns well into the nineteenth century. Diaries tell of guests complaining about late-arriving guests who climbed into bed with them in the middle of the night. As Bill Bryson notes in his intimately detailed book *At Home*, "It was entirely usual for a servant to sleep at the foot of his master's bed, regardless of what his master might be doing within the bed."

Human social relations are based on habits of reciprocity, altruism, commerce, physical attraction, and procreation. And we have learned much about these psychological realities from the behavior of our nearest biological relatives, the monkeys and great apes. There are unpleasant by-products of social closeness—rivalry, jealousy, suspicion, hurt feelings, competition for increased social standing. Apes and monkeys live in much smaller social worlds than we do nowadays, typically with fewer than fifty individuals living in a unit. More than fifty leads to rivalries tearing them apart. In contrast, humans have been living together in towns and cities with tens of thousands of people for several thousand years.

A rancher in Wyoming or a writer in rural Vermont might not encounter anyone for a week, while a greeter at Walmart might make eye contact with 1,700 people a day. The people we see constitute much of our social world, and we implicitly categorize them, divvying them up into an almost endless array of categories: family, friends, coworkers, service providers (bank teller, grocery store clerk, dry cleaner, auto mechanic, gardener), professional advisors (doctors, lawyers, accountants). These categories are further subdivided—your family includes your nuclear family, relatives you look forward to seeing, and relatives you don't. There are coworkers with whom you might go out for a beer after work, and those you wouldn't. And context counts: The people you enjoy socializing with at work are not necessarily people you want to bump into on a weekend at the beach.

Adding to the complexity of social relationships are contextual factors that have to do with your job, where you live, and your personality. A rancher in Wyoming may count in his social world a small number of people that is more or less constant; entertainers, Fortune 500 CEOs, and others in the public eye may encounter hundreds of new people each week, some of whom they will want to interact with again for various personal or professional reasons.

So how do you keep track of this horde of people you want to connect with? Celebrity attorney Robert Shapiro recommends this practical system. "When I meet someone new, I make notes—either on their business card or on a piece of paper—about where and how I met them, their area of expertise, and if we were introduced by someone, who made the introduction. This helps me to contextualize the link I have to them. If we had a meal together, I jot down who else was at the meal. I give this all to my secretary and she types it up, entering it into my contacts list.

"Of course the system gets more elaborate for people I interact with regularly. Eventually as I get to know them, I might add to the contacts list the name of their spouse, their children, their hobbies, things we did together with places and dates, maybe their birthday."

David Gold, regional medical product specialist for Pfizer, uses a related technique. "Suppose I met Dr. Ware in 2008. I write down what we talked about in a note app on my phone and e-mail it to myself. Then if I see him again in 2013, I can say 'Remember we were talking about *naltrexone* or such-and-such.'" This not only provides context to interactions, but continuity. It grounds and organizes the minds of both parties, and so, too, the interaction.

Craig Kallman is the chairman and CEO of Atlantic Records in New York—his career depends on being able to stay in touch with an enormous number of people: agents, managers, producers, employees, business colleagues, radio station managers, retailers, and of course the many musicians on his label, from Aretha Franklin to Flo Rida, from Led Zeppelin to Jason Mraz, Bruno Mars, and Missy Elliott. Kallman has an electronic contacts list of 14,000 people. Part of the file includes when they last spoke and how they are connected to other people in his database. The great advantage that the computer brings to a database of this size is that you can search along several different parameters. A year from now, Kallman might remember only one or two things about a person he just met, but he can search the contacts list and find the right entry. He might remember only that he had lunch with him in Santa Monica about a year ago, or that he met a person through Quincy Jones. He can sort by the last date of contact to see whom he hasn't caught up with in a while.

As we saw in Chapter 2, categories are often most useful when they have flexible, fuzzy boundaries. And social categories benefit from this greatly. The concept of "friend" depends on how far you are from home, how busy your social life is, and a number of other circumstances. If you run into an old high school friend while touring Prague, you might enjoy having dinner with him. But back home, where you know lots of people with whom you prefer spending time, you might never get together with him.

We organize our friendships around a variety of motivations and needs. These can be for historical reasons (we stay in touch with old friends from school and we like the sense of continuity to earlier parts of our lives), mutual admiration, shared goals, physical attractiveness, complementary characteristics, social climbing. . . . Ideally, friends are people with whom we can be our true selves, with whom we can fearlessly let our guard down. (Arguably, a close friend is someone with whom we can allow ourselves to enter the daydreaming attentional mode, with whom we can switch in and out of different modes of attention without feeling awkward.)

Friendships obviously also revolve around shared likes and dislikes—it's easier to be friends with people when you like doing the same things. But even this is relative. If you're a quilting enthusiast and there's only one other in town, the shared interest may bring you together. But at a quilting convention, you may discover someone whose precise taste in quilts matches yours more specifically, hence more common ground and a potentially tighter bond. This is why that friend from back home is a welcome companion in Prague. (Finally! Someone else who speaks English and can talk about the Superbowl!) It's also why that same friend is less interesting when you get back home, where there are people whose interests are more aligned with yours.

Because our ancestors lived in social groups that changed slowly, because they encountered the same people throughout their lives, they could keep almost every social detail they needed to know in their heads. These days, many of us increasingly find that we can't keep track of all the people we know and new people we meet. Cognitive neuroscience says we should externalize information in order to clear the mind. This is why Robert Shapiro and Craig Kallman keep contact files with contextual information such as where they met someone new, what they talked about, or who introduced them. In addition, little tags or notes in the file can help to organize entries—work friends, school friends, childhood friends, best friends, acquaintances, friends of friends—and there's no reason you can't put multiple tags in an entry. In an electronic database, you don't need to sort the entries, you can simply search for any that contain the keyword you're interested in.

I recognize that this can seem like a lot of busywork—you're spending your time *organizing* data about your social world instead of actually spending time with people. Keeping track of birthdays or someone's favorite wine isn't mutually exclusive with a social life that enjoys spontaneity, and it doesn't imply having to tightly schedule every encounter. It's about organizing the information you have to allow those spontaneous interactions to be more emotionally meaningful.

You don't have to have as many people in your contact list as the CEO of Atlantic Records does to feel the squeeze of job, family, and time pressures that prevent you from having the social life you want. Linda, the executive assistant introduced in the last chapter, suggests one practical solution for staying in touch with a vast array of friends and social contacts—use a *tickler.* A tickler is a reminder, something that tickles your memory. It works best as a note in your paper or electronic calendar. You set a frequency—say every two months—that you want to check in with friends. When the reminder goes off, if you haven't been in touch with them since the last time, you send them a note, text, phone call, or Facebook post just to check in. After a few of these, you'll find you settle into a rhythm and begin to look forward to staying in touch this way; they may even start to call you reciprocally.

Externalizing memory doesn't have to be in physical artifacts like calendars, tickler files, cell phones, key hooks, and index cards—it can include other people. The professor is the prime example of someone who may act as a repository for arcane bits of information you hardly ever need. Or your spouse may remember the name of that restaurant you liked so much in Portland. The part of external memory that includes other people is technically known as *transactive memory*, and includes the knowledge of who in your social network possesses the knowledge you seek—knowing, for example, that if you lost Jeffrey's cell phone number, you can get it from his wife, Pam, or children, Ryder and Aaron. Or that if you can't remember when Canadian Thanksgiving will be this year (and you're not near the Internet), you can ask your Canadian friend Lenny.

Couples in an intimate relationship have a way of sharing responsibility for things that need to be remembered, and this is mostly implicit, without their actually assigning the task to each other. For example, in most couples, each member of the couple has an area of expertise that the other lacks, and these areas are known to both partners. When a new piece of information comes in that concerns the couple, the person with expertise accepts responsibility for the information, and the other person lets the partner do so (relieving themselves of having to). When information comes in that is neither partner's area of expertise, there is usually a brief negotiation about who will take it on. These transactive memory strategies combine to ensure that information the couple needs will always be captured by at least one of the partners. This is one of the reasons why, after a very long relationship, if one partner dies, the other partner can be left stuck not knowing how vast swaths of day-to-day life are navigated. It can be said that much of our data storage is within the small crowd of our personal relationships.

A large part of organizing our social world successfully, like anything else, is identifying what we want from it. Part of our primate heritage is that most of us want to feel that we fit in somewhere and are part of a group. Which group we're part of may matter less to some of us than others, as long as we're part of a group and not left entirely on our own. Although there are individual differences, being alone for too long causes neurochemical changes that can result in hallucinations, depression, suicidal thoughts, violent behaviors, and even psychosis. Social isolation is also a risk factor for cardiac arrest and death, even more so than smoking.

And although many of us *think* we prefer being alone, we don't always know what we want. In one experiment, commuters were asked about their ideal commute: Would they prefer to talk to the person next to them or sit quietly by themselves? Overwhelmingly, people said they'd rather sit by themselves—the thought of having to make conversation with their seatmate was abhorrent (I admit I would have said the same thing). Commuters were then assigned either to sit alone and "enjoy their solitude" or to talk to the person sitting next to them. Those who talked to their seatmate reported having a significantly more pleasant commute. And the findings weren't due to differences in personality—the results held up whether the individuals were outgoing or shy, open or reserved.

In the early days of our species, group membership was essential for protection from predators and enemy tribes, for the sharing of limited food resources, the raising of children, and care when injured. Having a social network fulfills a deep biological need and activates regions of the brain in the anterior prefrontal cortex that help us to position ourselves in relation to others, and to monitor our social standing. It also activates emotional centers in the brain's limbic system, including the amygdala, and helps us to regulate emotions. There is comfort in belonging.

Enter social networking sites. From 2006 to 2008, MySpace was the most visited social networking site in the world, and was the most visited website of any kind in the United States, surpassing even Google. Today, it is the Internet equivalent of a ghost town with digital tumbleweeds blowing through its empty streets. Facebook rapidly grew to be the dominant social networking site and currently has more than 1.2 billion regular monthly users, more than one out of every seven people on the planet. How did it do this? It appealed to our sense of novelty, and our drive to connect to other people. It has allowed us to keep in touch with a large number of people with only a small investment of time. (And for those people who really just want to be left alone, it allows them to stay connected with others without having to actually see them in person!)

After a whole lifetime of trying to keep track of people, and little slips of paper with their phone numbers and addresses on them, now you can look people up by name and see what they're doing, and let them know what you're doing, without any trouble. Remember that, historically, we grew up in small communities and everyone we knew as children we knew the rest of our lives. Modern life doesn't work this way. We have great mobility. We go off to college or to work. We move away when we start a family. Our brains carry around a vestigial primordial longing to know where all these people in our lives ended up, to reconnect, to get a sense of resolution. Social networking sites allow us to do all this without demanding too much time. On the other hand, as many have observed, we lost touch with these people for a reason! There was a natural culling; we didn't keep up with people whom we didn't like or whose relevance to our lives diminished over time. Now they can find us and have an expectation that we can be found. But for millions of people, the pluses outweigh the minuses. We get news feeds, the equivalent of the town crier or hair salon gossip, delivered to our tablets and phones in a continuous stream. We can tailor those streams to give us contact with what or whom we most care about, our own personal social ticker tape. It's not a replacement for personal contact but a supplement, an easy way to stay connected to people who are far-flung and, well, just busy.

There is perhaps an illusion in all of this. Social networking provides breadth but rarely depth, and in-person contact is what we crave, even if online contact seems to take away some of that craving. In the end, the online interaction works best as a supplement, not a replacement for in-person contact. The cost of all of our electronic connectedness appears to be that it limits our biological capacity to connect with other people. Another see-saw in which one replaces the other in our attention.

Apart from the minimum drive to be part of a group or social network, many of us seek something more—having friends to do things with, to spend leisure or work time with; a circle of people who understand difficulties we may be encountering and offer assistance when needed; a relationship providing practical help, praise, encouragement, confidences, and loyalty.

Beyond companionship, couples seek intimacy, which can be defined as allowing another person to share and have access to our private behaviors, personal thoughts, joys, hurts, and fears of being hurt. Intimacy also includes creating shared meaning—those inside jokes, that sideways glance that only your sweetie understands—a kind of telepathy. It includes the freedom to be who we are in a relationship (without the need to project a false sense of ourselves) and to allow the other person to do the same. Intimacy allows us to talk openly about things that are important to us, and to take a clear stand on emotionally charged issues without fear of being ridiculed or rejected. All this describes a distinctly Western view—other cultures don't view intimacy as a necessity or even define it in the same way.

Not surprisingly, men and women have different images of what intimacy entails: Women are more focused than men on commitment and continuity of communication, men on sexual and physical closeness. Intimacy, love, and passion don't always go together of course—they belong to completely different, multidimensional constructs. We hope friendship and intimacy involve mutual trust, but they don't always. Just like our chimpanzee cousins, we appear to have an innate tendency to deceive when it is in our own self-interest (the cause of untold amounts of frustration and heartache, not to mention sitcom plots).

Modern intimacy is much more varied, plural, and complex than it was for our ancestors. Throughout history and across cultures, intimacy was rarely regarded with the importance or emphasis we place on it now. For thousands of years—the first 99% of our history—we didn't do much of anything except procreate and survive. Marriage and pair-bonding (the term that biologists use) was primarily sought for reproduction and for social alliances. Many marriages in historical times took place to create bonds between neighboring tribes as a way to defuse rivalries and tensions over limited resources.

A consequence of changing definitions of intimacy is that today, many of us ask more than ever of our romantic partners. We expect them to be there for emotional support, companionship, intimacy, and financial support, and we expect at various times they will function as confidante, nurse, sounding board, secretary, treasurer, parent, protector, guide, cheerleader, masseuse or masseur, and through it all we expect them to be consistently alluring, sexually appealing, and to stay in lockstep with our own sexual appetites and preferences. We expect our partners to help us achieve our full potential in life. And increasingly they do.

Our increased desire for our partners to do all these things is rooted in a biological need to connect deeply with at least one other person. When it is missing, making such a connection becomes a high priority. When that need is fulfilled by a satisfying intimate relationship, the benefits are both psychological and physiological. People in a relationship experience better health, recover from illnesses more quickly, and live longer. Indeed, the presence of a satisfying intimate relationship is one of the strongest predictors of happiness and emotional well-being that has ever been measured. How do we enter into and maintain intimate relationships? One important factor is the way that personality traits are organized.

Of the thousands of ways that human beings differ from one another, perhaps the most important trait for getting along with others is agreeableness. In the scientific literature, to be agreeable is to be cooperative, friendly, considerate, and helpful—attributes that are more or less stable across the lifetime, and show up early in childhood. Agreeable people are able to control undesirable emotions such as anger and frustration. This control happens in the frontal lobes, which govern impulse control and help us to regulate negative emotions, the same region that governs our executive attention mode. When the frontal lobes are damaged—from injury, stroke, Alzheimer's, or a tumor, for example—agreeableness is often among the first things to go, along with impulse control and emotional stability. Some of this emotional regulation can be learned—children who receive positive reinforcement for impulse control and anger management become agreeable adults. As you might imagine, being an agreeable person is a tremendous advantage for maintaining positive social relationships.

During adolescence, when behavior is somewhat unpredictable and strongly influenced by interpersonal relations, we react and are guided by what our friends are doing to a much larger degree. Indeed, a sign of maturity is the ability to think independently and come to one's own conclusions. It turns out that having a best friend during adolescence is an important part of becoming a well-adjusted adult. Those without one are more likely to be bullied and marginalized and to carry these experiences into becoming disagreeable adults. And although being agreeable is important for social outcomes later in life, just having a *friend* who is agreeable also protects against social problems later in life, even if you yourself are not. Both girls and boys benefit from having an agreeable friend, although girls benefit more than boys.

Intimate relationships, including marriage, are subject to what behavioral economists call strong sorting patterns along many different attributes. For example, on average, marriage partners tend to be similar in age, education level, and attractiveness. How do we find each other in an ocean of strangers?

Matchmaking or "romantic partner assistance" is not new. The Bible describes commercial matchmakers from over two thousand years ago, and the first publications to resemble modern newspapers in the early 1700s carried personal advertisements of people (mostly men) looking for a spouse. At various times in history, when people were cut off from potential partners—early settlers of the American West, Civil War soldiers, for example—they took to advertising for partners or responding to ads placed by potential partners, providing a list of attributes or qualities. As the Internet came of age in the 1990s, online dating was introduced as an alternative to personals ads and, in some cases, to matchmakers, via sites that advertised the use of scientific algorithms to increase compatibility scores.

The biggest change in dating between 2004 and 2014 was that one-third of all marriages in America began with online relationships, compared to a fraction of that in the decade before. Half of these marriages began on dating sites, the rest via social media, chat rooms, instant messages, and the like. In 1995, it was still so rare for a marriage to have begun online that newspapers would report it, breathlessly, as something weirdly futuristic and kind of freakish.

This behavioral change isn't so much because the Internet itself or the dating options have changed; it's because the population of Internet users has changed. Online dating used to be stigmatized as a creepier extension of the somewhat seedy world of 1960s and 1970s personal ads—the last resort for the desperate or undatable. The initial stigma associated with online dating became irrelevant as a new generation of users emerged for whom online contact was already well known, respectable, and established. And, like fax machines and e-mail, the system works only when a large number of people use it. This started to occur around 1999–2000. By 2014, twenty years after the introduction of online dating, younger users have a higher probability of embracing it because they have been active users of the Internet since they were little children, for education, shopping, entertainment, games, socializing, looking for a job, getting news and gossip, watching videos, and listening to music.

As already noted, the Internet has helped some of us to become more social and to establish and maintain a larger number of relationships. For others, particularly heavy Internet users who are introverted to begin with, the Internet has led them to become less socially involved, lonelier, and more likely to become depressed. Studies have shown a dramatic decline in empathy among college students, who apparently are far less likely to say that it is valuable to put oneself in the place of others or to try and understand their feelings. It is not just because they're reading less literary fiction, it's because they're spending more time alone under the illusion that they're being social.

Online dating is organized differently from conventional dating in four key ways—access, communication, matching, and asynchrony. Online dating gives us access to a much larger and broader set of potential mates than we would have encountered in our pre-Internet lives. The field of eligibles used to be limited to people we knew, worked with, worshipped with, went to school with, or lived near. Many dating sites boast millions of users, dramatically increasing the size of the pool. In fact, the roughly two billion people who are connected to the Internet are potentially accessible. Naturally, access to millions of profiles doesn't necessarily mean access to electronic or face-to-face encounters; it simply allows users to see who else is available, even though the availables may not be reciprocally interested in you.

The communication medium of online dating allows us to get to know the person, review a broad range of facts, and exchange information before the stress of meeting face-to-face, and perhaps to avoid an awkward face-to-face meeting if things aren't going well. Matching typically occurs via mathematical algorithms to help us select potential partners, screening out those who have undesirable traits or lack of shared interests.

Asynchrony allows both parties to gather their thoughts in their own time before responding, and thus to present their best selves without all of the pressure and anxiety that occurs in synchronous real-time interactions. Have you ever left a conversation only to realize hours later the thing you wish you had said? Online dating solves that.

Taken together, these four key features that distinguish Internet dating are not always desirable. For one thing, there is a disconnect between what people find attractive in a profile and what they find in meeting a person face-to-face. And, as Northwestern University psychologist Eli Finkel points out, this streamlined access to a pool of thousands of potential partners "can elicit an evaluative, assessment-oriented mind-set that leads online daters to objectify potential partners and might even undermine their willingness to commit to one of them."

It can also cause people to make lazy, ill-advised decisions due to cognitive and decision overload. We know from behavioral economics—and decisions involving cars, appliances, houses, and yes, even potential mates—that consumers can't keep track of more than two or three variables of interest when evaluating a large number of alternatives. This is directly related to the capacity limitations of working memory, discussed in Chapter 2. It's also related to limitations of our attentional network. When considering dating alternatives, we necessarily need to get our minds to shuttle back and forth between the central executive mode—keeping track of all those little details—and the daydreaming mode, the mode in which we try to picture ourselves with each of the attractive alternatives: what our life would be like, how good they'll feel on our arm, whether they'll get along with our friends, and what our children will look like with his or her nose. As you now know, all that rapid switching between central executive calculating and dreamy mind-wandering depletes neural resources, leading us to make poor decisions. And when cognitive resources are low, we have difficulty focusing on relevant information and ignoring the irrelevant. Maybe online dating is a form of social organization that has gone off the rails, rendering decision-making more difficult rather than less.

Staying in any committed, monogamous relationship, whether it began online or off, requires fidelity, or "forgoing the forbidden fruit." This is known to be a function of the availability of attractive alternatives. The twist with the advent of online dating, however, is that there can be many thousands of times more in the virtual world than in the off-line world, creating a situation where temptation can exceed willpower for both men and women. Stories of people (usually men) who "forgot" to take their dating profile down after meeting and beginning a serious relationship with someone are legion.

With one-third of people who get married meeting online, the science of online courtship has recently come into its own. Researchers have shown what we all suspected: Online daters engage in deception; 81% lie about their height, weight, or age. Men tend to lie about height, women about weight. Both lie about their age. In one study, age discrepancies of ten years were observed, weight was underreported by thirty-five pounds, and height was overreported by two inches. It's not as though these things would be undiscovered upon meeting in person, which makes the misrepresentations more odd. And apparently, in the online world, political leaning is more sensitive and less likely to be disclosed than age, height, or weight. Online daters are significantly more likely to admit they're fat than that they're Republicans.

In the vast majority of these cases, the liars are aware of the lies they're telling. What motivates them? Because of the large amount of choice that online daters have, the profile results from an underlying tension between wanting to be truthful and wanting to put one's best face forward. Profiles often misrepresent the way you were sometime in the recent past (e.g., employed) or the way you'd like to be (e.g., ten pounds thinner and six years younger).

Social world organization gone awry or not, the current online dating world shows at least one somewhat promising trend: So far, there is a 22% lower risk of marriages that began online ending in divorce. But while that may sound impressive, the actual effect is tiny: Meeting online reduces the overall risk of divorce from 7.7% to 6%. If all the couples who met off-line met online instead, only 1 divorce for every 100 marriages would be prevented. Also, couples who met on the Web tend to be more educated and are more likely to be employed than couples who met in person, and educational attainment and employment tend to predict marital longevity. So the observed effect may not be due to Internet dating per se, but to the fact that Internet daters tend to be more educated and employed, as a group, than conventional daters.

As you might expect, couples who initially met via e-mail tend to be older than couples who met their spouse through social networks and virtual worlds. (Young people just don't use e-mail very much anymore.) And like DARPA, Wikipedia, and Kickstarter, online dating sites that use crowdsourcing have cropped up. ChainDate, ReportYourEx, and the Lulu app are just three examples of a kind of Zagat-like rating system for dating partners.

Once we are in a relationship, romantic or platonic, how well do we know the people we care about, and how good are we at knowing their thoughts? Surprisingly bad. We are barely better than 50/50 in assessing how our friends and coworkers feel about us, or whether they even like us. Speed daters are lousy at assessing who wants to date them and who does not (so much for intuition). On the one hand, couples who thought they knew each other well correctly guessed their partner's reactions four out of ten times—on the other hand, they *thought* they were getting *eight* out of ten correct. In another experiment, volunteers watched videos of people either lying or telling the truth about whether they were HIV positive. People believed that they were accurate in detecting liars 70% of the time, but in fact, they did no better than 50%. We are very bad at telling if someone is lying, even when our lives depend on it.

This has potentially grave consequences for foreign policy. The British believed Adolf Hitler's assurance in 1938 that peace would be preserved if he was given the land just over the Czech border. Thus the British discouraged the Czechs from mobilizing their army. But Hitler was lying, having already prepared his army to invade. The opposite misreading of intentions occurred when the United States believed Saddam Hussein was lying about not having any weapons of mass destruction—in fact, he was telling the truth.

Outside of military or strategic contexts, where lying is used as a tactic, why do people lie in everyday interactions? One reason is fear of reprisal when we've done something we shouldn't. It is not the better part of human nature, but it is human nature to lie to avoid punishment. And it starts early—six-year-olds will say, "I didn't do it," while they're in the middle of doing it! Workers on the Deepwater Horizon oil rig in the gulf waters off of Louisiana knew of safety problems but were afraid to report them for fear of being fired.

But it is also human nature to forgive, especially when we're given an explanation. In one study, people who tried to cut in line were forgiven by others even if their explanation was ridiculous. In a line for a copy machine, "I'm sorry, may I cut in? I need to make copies" was every bit as effective as "I'm sorry, may I cut in? I'm on deadline."

When doctors at the University of Michigan hospitals started disclosing their mistakes to patients openly, malpractice lawsuits were cut in half. The biggest impediment to resolution had been requiring patients to *imagine* what their doctors were thinking, and having to sue to find out, rather than just allowing doctors to explain how a mistake happened. When we're confronted with the human element, the doctor's constraints and what she is struggling with, we're more likely to understand and forgive. Nicholas Epley, a professor at the University of Chicago Booth School of Business (and author of *Mindwise*), writes, "If being transparent strengthens the social ties that make life worth living, and enables others to forgive our shortcomings, why not do it more often?"

People lie for other reasons of course, not just fear of reprisals. Some of these include avoiding hurting other people's feelings, and sometimes little white lies become the social glue that prevents tempers from flaring and minimizes antagonism. In this context, we are surprisingly good at telling when people are lying, and we go along with it, cooperatively, every day. It has to do with the gentle way we ask for things when we want to avoid confrontations with people—indirect speech acts.

Why People Are Indirect with Us

A large part of human social interaction requires that we subdue our innate primate hostilities in order to get along. Although primates in general are among the most social species, there are few examples of primate living groups that support more than eighteen males within the group—the interpersonal tensions and dominance hierarchies just become too much for them and they split apart. And yet humans have been living in cities containing tens of thousands of males for several millennia. How do we do it? One way of helping to keep large numbers of humans living in close proximity is through the use of nonconfrontational speech, or indirect speech acts. Indirect speech acts don't say what we actually want, but they imply it. The philosopher Paul Grice called these *implicatures.*

Suppose John and Marsha are both sitting in an office, and Marsha's next to the window. John feels hot. He could say, "Open the window," which is direct and may make Marsha feel a little weird. If they're workplace equals, who is John to tell Marsha what to do or to boss her around, she might think. If instead John says, "Gosh, it's getting warm in here," he is inviting her into a cooperative venture, a simple but not trivial unwrapping of what he said. He is implying his desire in a nondirective and nonconfrontational manner. Normally, Marsha plays along by inferring that he'd like her to open the window, and that he's not simply making a meteorological observation. At this point, Marsha has several response choices:

a. She smiles back at John and opens the window, signaling that she's playing this little social game and that she's cooperating with the charade's intent.
b. She says, "Oh really? I'm actually kind of chilly." This signals that she is still playing the game but that they have a difference of opinion about the basic facts. Marsha's being cooperative, though expressing a different viewpoint. Cooperative behavior on John's part at this point requires him to either drop the subject or to up the ante, which risks raising levels of confrontation and aggression.
c. Marsha can say, "Oh yes—it is." Depending on *how* she says it, John might take her response as flirtatious and playful, or sarcastic and rude. In the former case, she's inviting John to be more explicit, effectively signaling that they can drop this subterfuge; their relationship is solid enough that she is giving John permission to be direct. In the latter case, if Marsha uses a sarcastic tone of voice, she's indicating that she agrees with the premise—it's hot in there—but she doesn't want to open the window herself.
d. Marsha can say, "Why don't you take off your sweater." This is noncooperative and a bit confrontational—Marsha is opting out of the game.
e. Marsha can say, "I was hot, too, until I took off my sweater. I guess the heating system finally kicked in." This is less confrontational. Marsha is agreeing with the premise but not the implication of what should be done about it. It is partly cooperative in that she is helping John to solve the problem, though not in the way he intended.
f. Marsha can say, "Screw you." This signals that she doesn't want to play the implicature game, and moreover, she is conveying aggression. John's options are limited at this point—either he can ignore her (effectively backing down) or he can up the ante by getting up, stomping past her desk, and forcefully opening the damn window. (Now it's war.)

The simplest cases of speech acts are those in which the speaker utters a sentence and means exactly and literally what he says. Yet *indirect* speech acts are a powerful social glue that enables us to get along. In them, the speaker means exactly what she says but also something more. The something more is supposed to be apparent to the hearer, and yet it remains unspoken. Hence, the act of uttering an indirect speech act can be seen as inherently an act of play, an invitation to cooperate in a game of verbal hide-and-seek of "Do you understand what I'm saying?" The philosopher John Searle says the mechanism by which indirect speech acts work is that they invoke in both the speaker and the hearer a shared representation of the world; they rely on shared background information that is both linguistic and social. By appealing to their shared knowledge, the speaker and listener are creating a pact and affirming their shared worldview.

Searle asks us to consider another type of case with two speakers, A and B.

A: Let's go to the movies tonight.

B: I have to study for an exam tonight.

Speaker A is not making an implicature—it can be taken at face value as a direct request, as marked by the use of *let's*. But Speaker B's reply is clearly indirect. It is meant to communicate both a literal message ("I'm studying for an exam tonight") and an unspoken implicature ("Therefore I can't go to the movies"). Most people agree that B is employing a gentler way of resolving a potential conflict between the two people by avoiding confrontation. If instead, B said

B1: No.

speaker A feels rejected, and without any cause or explanation. Our fear of rejection is understandably very strong; in fact, social rejection causes activation in the same part of the brain as physical pain does, and—perhaps surprisingly and accordingly—Tylenol can reduce people's experience of social pain.

Speaker B makes the point in a cooperative framework, and by providing an explanation, she implies that she really would like to go, but simply cannot. This is equivalent to the person cutting in line to make copies and providing a meaningless explanation that is better received than no explanation at all. But not all implicatures are created equal. If instead, B had said

B2: I have to wash my hair tonight.

or

B3: I'm in the middle of a game of solitaire that I really must finish.

then B is expecting that A will understand these as rejections, and offers no explanatory niceties—a kind of conversational slap in the face, albeit one that extends the implicature game. B2 and B3 constitute slightly gentler ways of refusing than B1 because they do not involve blatant and outright contradiction.

Searle extends the analysis of indirect speech acts to include utterances whose meaning may be thoroughly indecipherable but whose intent, if we're lucky, is one hundred percent clear. He asks us to consider the following. Suppose you are an American soldier captured by the Italians during World War II while out of uniform. Now, in order to get them to release you, you devise a plan to convince them that you are a German officer. You could say to them in Italian, "I am a German officer," but they might not believe it. Suppose further that you don't speak enough Italian in the first place to say that.

The ideal utterance in this case would be for you to say, in perfect German, "I am a German officer. Release me, and be quick about it." Suppose, though, that you don't know enough German to say that, and all you know is one line that you learned from a German poem in high school: "Kennst du das Land, wo die Zitronen blühen?" which means "Knowest thou the land where the lemon trees bloom?" If your Italian captors don't speak any German, your saying "Kennst du das Land, wo die Zitronen blühen?" has the *effect* of communicating that you are German. In other words, the literal meaning of your speech act becomes irrelevant, and only the implied meaning is at work. The Italians hear what they recognize only as German, and you hope they will make the logical leap that you must indeed be German and therefore worthy of release.

Another aspect of communication is that information can become updated through social contracts. You might mention to your friend Bert that Ernie said such-and-such, but Bert adds the new information that we now know Ernie's a liar and can't be trusted. We learned that Pluto is no longer a planet when a duly authorized panel, empowered by society to make such decisions and judgments, said so. Certain utterances have, by social contract, the authority to change the state of the world. A doctor who pronounces you dead changes your legal status instantly, which has the effect of utterly changing your life, whether you're in fact dead or not. A judge can pronounce you innocent or guilty and, again, the truth doesn't matter as much as the force of the pronouncement, in terms of what your future looks like. The set of utterances that can so change the state of the world is limited, but they are powerful. We empower these legal or quasi-legal authorities in order to facilitate our understanding of the social world.

Except for these formal and legalistic pronouncements, Grice and Searle take as a premise that virtually all conversations are a cooperative undertaking and that they require both literal and implied meanings to be processed. Grice systematized and categorized the various rules by which ordinary, cooperative speech is conducted, helping to illuminate the mechanisms by which indirect speech acts work. The four Gricean maxims are:

1. Quantity. Make your contribution to the conversation as informative as required. Do not make your contribution more informative than is required.
2. Quality. Do not say what you believe to be false. Do not say that for which you lack adequate evidence.
3. Manner. Avoid obscurity of expression (don't use words that your intended hearer doesn't know). Avoid ambiguity. Be brief (avoid unnecessary prolixity). Be orderly.
4. Relation. Make your contribution relevant.

The following three examples demonstrate violations of maxim 1, quantity, where the second speaker is not making a contribution that is informative enough:

A: Where are you going this afternoon?

B: Out.

A: How was your day?

B: Fine.

A: What did you learn in school today?

B: Nothing.

Even if we don't know about Gricean maxims, we intuitively recognize these replies as being noncooperative. The first speaker in each case is *implying* that he would like a certain level of detail in response to his query, and the second speaker is opting out of any cooperative agreement of the sort.

As another example, suppose Professor Kaplan is writing a recommendation for a pupil who is applying to graduate school.

"Dear Sir, Mr. X's command of English is fine and his attendance in my class has been regular. Very truly yours, Professor Kaplan."

By violating the maxim of quantity—not providing enough information—Professor Kaplan is implying that Mr. X is not a very good student, without actually saying it.

Here's an example of the other extreme, in which the second speaker provides too much information:

A: Dad, where's the hammer?

B: On the floor, two inches from the garage door, lying in a puddle of water where you left it three hours ago after I told you to put it back in the toolbox.

The second speaker in this case, by providing too much information, is implying more than the facts of the utterance, and is signaling annoyance.

A is standing by an obviously immobilized car when B walks by.

A: I'm out of gas.

B: There's a garage just about a quarter mile down the street.

B is violating the maxim of quality if, in fact, there is no garage down the street, or if the speaker knows that the garage is open but has no gasoline. Suppose B wants to steal the tires from A's car. A assumes that B is being truthful, and so walks off, giving B enough time to jack up the car and unmount a tire or two.

A: Where's Bill?

B: There's a yellow VW outside Sue's house. . . .

B flouts the maxim of relevance, suggesting that A is to make an inference. A now has two choices:

1. Accept B's statement as flouting the maxim of relevance, and as an invitation to cooperate. A says (to himself): Bill drives a yellow VW. Bill knows Sue. Bill must be at Sue's house (and B doesn't want to come right out and say so for some reason; perhaps this is a delicate matter or B promised not to tell).
2. Withdraw from B's proposed dialogue and repeat the original question, "Yes, but where's Bill?"

Of course B has other possible responses to the question "Where's Bill?":

B1: At Sue's house. (no implicature)

B2: Well, I saw a VW parked at Sue's house, and Bill drives a VW. (a mild implicature, filling in most of the blanks for A)

B3: What an impertinent question! (direct, somewhat confrontational)

B4: I'm not supposed to tell you. (less direct, still somewhat confrontational)

B5: I have no idea. (violating quality)

B6: [Turns away] (opting out of conversation)

Indirect speech acts such as these reflect the way we actually use language in everyday speech. There is nothing unfamiliar about these exchanges. The great contribution of Grice and Searle was that they organized the exchanges, putting them into a system whereby we can analyze and understand how they function. This all occurs at a subconscious level for most of us. Individuals with autism spectrum disorders often have difficulty with indirect speech acts because of biological differences in their brains that make it difficult for them to understand irony, pretense, sarcasm, or any nonliteral speech. Are there neurochemical correlates to getting along and keeping social bonds intact?

There's a hormone in the brain released by the back half of the pituitary gland, oxytocin, that has been called by the popular press the love hormone, because it used to be thought that oxytocin is what causes people to fall in love with each other. When a person has an orgasm, oxytocin is released, and one of the effects of oxytocin is to make us feel bonded to others. Evolutionary psychologists have speculated that this was nature's way of causing couples to want to stay together after sex to raise any children that might result from that sex. In other words, it is clearly an evolutionary advantage for a child to have two caring, nurturing parents. If the parents feel bonded to each other through oxytocin release, they are more likely to share in the raising of their children, thus propagating their tribe.

In addition to difficulty understanding any speech that isn't literal, individuals with autism spectrum disorders don't feel attachment to people the way others do, and they have difficulty empathizing with others. Oxytocin in individuals with autism shows up at lower than normal levels, and the administration of oxytocin causes them to become more social, and improves emotion recognition. (It also reduces their repetitive behaviors.)

Oxytocin has additionally been implicated in feelings of trust. In a typical experiment, people watch politicians making speeches. The observers are under the influence of oxytocin for half the speeches they watch, and a placebo for the other half (of course they don't know which is which). When asked to rate whom they trust the most, or whom they would be most likely to vote for, people select the candidates they viewed while oxytocin was in their system.

There's a well-established finding that people who receive social support during illness (simple caring and nurturing) recover more fully and more quickly. This simple social contact when we're sick also releases oxytocin, in turn helping to improve health outcomes by reducing stress levels and the hormone cortisol, which can cripple the immune system.

Paradoxically, levels of oxytocin also increase during gaps in social support or poor social functioning (thus absence does make the heart grow fonder—or at least more attached). Oxytocin may therefore act as a distress signal prompting the individual to seek out social contact. To reconcile this paradox—is oxytocin the love drug or the without-love drug?—a more recent theory gaining traction is that oxytocin regulates the salience of social information and is capable of eliciting positive and negative social emotions, depending on the situation and individual. Its real role is to organize social behavior. Promising preliminary evidence suggests that oxytocin pharmacotherapy can help to promote trust and reduce social anxiety, including in people with social phobia and borderline personality disorder. Nondrug therapies, such as music, may exert similar therapeutic effects via oxytocinergic regulation; music has been shown to increase oxytocin levels, especially when people listen to or play music together.

A related chemical in the brain, a protein called arginine vasopressin, has also been found to regulate affiliation, sociability, and courtship. If you think your social behaviors are largely under your conscious control, you're underestimating the role of neurochemicals in shaping your thoughts, feelings, and actions. To wit: There are two species of prairie voles; one is monogamous, the other is not. Inject vasopressin in the philandering voles and they become monogamous; block vasopressin in the monogamous ones and they become as randy as Gene Simmons in a John Holmes movie.

Injecting vasopressin also causes innate, aggressive behaviors to become more selective, protecting the mate from emotional (and physical) outbursts.

Recreational drugs such as cannabis and LSD have been found to promote feelings of connection between people who take those drugs and others, and in many cases, a feeling of being more connected to the world-as-a-whole. The active ingredient in marijuana activates specialized neural receptors called cannabinoid receptors, and it has been shown experimentally in rats that they increase social activity (when the rats could get up off the couch). LSD's action in the brain includes stimulating dopamine and certain serotonin receptors while attenuating sensory input from the visual cortex (which may be partly responsible for visual hallucinations). Yet the reason LSD causes feelings of social connection is not yet known.

In order to feel socially connected to others, we like to think we know them, and that to some extent we can predict their behavior. Take a moment to think about someone you know well—a close friend, family member, spouse, and so on, and rate that person according to the three options below.

The person I am thinking of tends to be:

a.	subjective	analytic	depends on the situation
b.	energetic	relaxed	depends on the situation
c.	dignified	casual	depends on the situation
d.	quiet	talkative	depends on the situation
e.	cautious	bold	depends on the situation
f.	lenient	firm	depends on the situation
g.	intense	calm	depends on the situation
h.	realistic	idealistic	depends on the situation

Now go back and rate yourself on the same items.

Most people rate their friend in terms of traits (the first two columns) but rate themselves in terms of situations (the third column). Why? Because by definition, we see only the public actions of others. For our own behaviors, we have access not just to the public actions but to our private actions, private feelings, and private thoughts as well. Our own lives seem to us to be more filled with rich diversity of thoughts and behaviors because we are experiencing a wider range of behaviors in ourselves while effectively having only one-sided evidence about others. Harvard psychologist Daniel Gilbert calls this the "invisibility" problem—the inner thoughts of others are invisible to us.

In Chapter 1, cognitive illusions were compared to visual illusions. They are a window into the inner workings of the mind and brain, and reveal to us some of the substructure that supports cognition and perception. Like visual illusions, cognitive illusions are automatic—that is, even when we know they exist, it is difficult or impossible to turn off the mental machinery that gives rise to them. Cognitive illusions lead us to misperceive reality and to make poor decisions about choices we are presented with, medical options, and interpreting the behaviors of other people, particularly those who comprise our social world. Misinterpreting the motivations of others leads to misunderstandings, suspicion, and interpersonal conflict and, in the worst cases, war. Fortunately, many cognitive illusions can be overcome with training.

One of the most well established findings in social psychology concerns how we interpret the actions of others, and it's related to the demonstration above. There are two broad classes of explanation for why people do what they do—*dispositional* or *situational.* Dispositional explanations embrace the idea that all of us have certain traits (dispositions) that are more or less stable across our lifetimes. As you just saw, we have a tendency to describe the people we know in trait terms: They're extroverts or introverts, agreeable or disagreeable, the life of the party or a stick-in-the-mud.

Situational explanations, on the other hand, acknowledge that momentary circumstances sometimes contribute to our responses and can override any innate predispositions. These oppositional approaches are sometimes characterized as "the person versus the situation." Dispositional explanations say, "I was born (or made) that way." Situational ones (to quote comedian Flip Wilson) say, "The devil made me do it."

In one famous study, students at the Princeton Theological Seminary were asked to come into an office to provide their opinions on "religious education and vocations." After they had filled out a series of questionnaires, the experimenter explained that questionnaires tend to be oversimplified, and so for the final part of the study, the students would be asked to record a three- to five-minute talk based on a short piece of text. The students were then given one of two things to read, either a paragraph exploring whether "ministering" can be effective within the professional clergy these days, or the parable of the Good Samaritan from the New Testament (who stopped to help an injured man after a priest and a Levite had passed him by on the road).

Now, in social psychology experiments, things are not usually as they seem—the experimenters go to great lengths to hide what they're really up to, in order to reduce the possibility that participants will be able to tailor their behavior to the experiment. In this case, the experimenter told the participants that space was tight in the building they were in, and consequently he had made arrangements for the talk to be recorded in an office building next door (this was part of the deception). The experimenter then drew a map for the participants, showing them how to get there.

Thirteen participants in each reading group were told that they should hurry because an assistant in the adjacent building had expected them a few minutes earlier. Thirteen others were told, "It'll be a few minutes before they're ready for you, but you might as well head on over." This constitutes a situational factor—some students are in a hurry, some are not. Some people are more helpful than others, a dispositional trait that we assume is more or less stable across a person's lifetime. But this particular group—seminary students—are no doubt more helpful than the average person because they are studying to become members of the clergy, a helping profession. We assume that differences in the traits of helpfulness and compassion are minimized in this particular population, and moreover, any remaining individual differences would be evenly distributed across the two conditions of the study because the experimenters randomly assigned students to one condition or the other. The design of the experiment cleverly pits dispositional against situational factors.

Between the two Princeton campus buildings, the experimenters had placed a confederate—a research assistant—who sat slumped in a doorway and who appeared to be in need of medical attention. When each theological student passed by, the confederate coughed and groaned.

If you believe that a person's traits are the best predictor of behavior, you would predict that all or most of the seminary students would stop and help this injured person. And, as an added, elegant twist to the experiment, half have just read the story of the Good Samaritan who stopped to help someone in a situation *very much like this.*

What did the experimenters find? The students who were in a hurry were six times more likely to keep on walking and pass by the visibly injured person without helping than the students who had plenty of time. The amount of time the students had was the situational factor that predicted how they would behave, and the paragraph they read had no significant effect.

This finding comes as a surprise to most people. There have been dozens of demonstrations of people making incorrect predictions, overweighting the influence of traits and undervaluing the power of the situation when attempting to explain people's behavior. This cognitive illusion is so powerful it has a name: the fundamental attribution error. An additional part of the fundamental attribution error is that we fail to appreciate that the roles people are forced to play in certain situations constrain their behavior.

In a clever demonstration of this, Lee Ross and his colleagues staged a mock game show at Stanford. Ross plucked a handful of students from his classroom and randomly assigned half of them to be Questioners and half to be Contestants in a trivia game. The Questioners were asked to come up with general knowledge questions that were difficult but not impossible to answer—they could draw from any area in which they had an interest or expertise—for example, movies, books, sports, music, literature, their coursework, or something they read in the news. Ross reminded them that they each had some knowledge that was likely not held by everyone in the classroom. Perhaps they collected coins, and a fair question might have to do with what years the United States minted pennies out of steel instead of copper. Or perhaps they were taking an elective course on Virginia Woolf in the English Department and a fair question might be what decade "A Room of One's Own" was published in. An unfair question would be something like "What was the name of my second-grade teacher?"

The Questioners then stood in front of the class and asked the Contestants the questions as the rest of the class looked on. They mined general knowledge, trivia, and factoids such as we see on television game shows like *Jeopardy!*, questions such as "What do the initials in W. H. Auden's name stand for?"; "What is the current form of government in Sri Lanka?"; "What is the longest glacier in the world?"; "Who was the first runner to break the four-minute mile"; and "What team won the 1969 World Series?"

The Contestants did not do particularly well in answering the questions. A crucial point here is that the manipulation about who was a Questioner and who was a Contestant was made obvious to all concerned, because it was by random assignment. After the game was over, Ross asked the observers in the class to answer the following questions: "On a scale of one to ten, how smart would you say the Questioner was compared to the average Stanford student?" and "On a scale of one to ten, how smart would you say the Contestant was compared to the average Stanford student?"

We humans are hardwired to attend to individual differences. This probably served us well throughout evolutionary history as we made decisions about whom to mate with, whom to go hunting with, and whom to trust as allies. Traits such as *nurturing, affectionate, emotionally stable, reliable, trustworthy,* and *intelligent* would have been important criteria. If we were sitting in Lee Ross's Stanford class, observing this mock game show, our overwhelming impression would likely be surprise at all the arcane knowledge displayed by the Questioners—how could they know so much?

And about so many different things? It wasn't just the *Contestants* who didn't know the answers to the questions; most of the *observers* didn't either!

An important feature of the experiment is that it was designed to confer a self-presentation advantage upon the Questioners relative to the Contestants or observers. When Ross tallied the data, he found that the observer students in the classroom rated the Questioners to be genuinely smarter than the average Stanford student. Moreover, they rated the Contestants to be below average. The raters were attributing the performance they observed to stable dispositions. What they were failing to do—the cognitive illusion—was to realize that the role played by the Questioners virtually guaranteed that they would appear knowledgeable, and similarly, the role played by the Contestants virtually guaranteed that they would seem ignorant. The role of Questioner conferred a great advantage, an opportunity to make a self-serving, image-building display. No right-minded Questioner would ask a question that he didn't already know the answer to, and because he was encouraged to generate difficult and obscure questions, it was unlikely the Contestant would know many of the answers.

Not only was the game rigged, but so were the mental reactions of the participants—indeed, the mental responses of all of us. We succumb to the cognitive illusion of the fundamental attribution error regularly. Knowing that it exists can help us to overcome it. Suppose you're walking down the halls of your office and pass a new coworker, Kevin. You say hello and he doesn't respond. You could attribute his behavior to a stable personality trait and conclude that he is shy or that he is rude. Or you could attribute his behavior to a situational factor—perhaps he was lost in thought or was late for a meeting or is angry at you. The science doesn't say that Kevin rarely responds to situational factors, just that observers tend to discount them. Daniel Gilbert has gone on to show that this fundamental attribution error is produced by information overload. Specifically, the more cognitive load one is experiencing, the more likely one is to make errors in judgment about the causes of an individual's behavior.

Another way to contextualize the results of the Stanford experiment is that the participants drew a conclusion that was overly influenced by the outcome of the game, and made an outcome-bias-based inference. If you hear that Jolie passed a difficult college course and Martina failed it, you might conclude that Jolie is smarter, worked harder, or is a better student. Most people would. The outcome appears to be a cogent indicator of something related to academic ability. But what if you found out that Jolie and Martina had different instructors for the class? Both Jolie and Martina got an equal number of questions correct on their exams, but Jolie's instructor was lenient and passed everyone in the class, while Martina's instructor was strict and failed nearly everyone. Even knowing this, outcome bias is so powerful that people continue to conclude that Jolie is smarter. Why is it so powerful if it is sometimes wrong?

Here's the twist. It's because most of the time, the outcome has predictive value and operates as a simple inferential cue when we're making judgments. Reliance on such primal unconscious cues is efficient, typically yielding accurate judgments with much less effort and cognitive load. In an era of information overload, sometimes outcome-based biases save time, but we need to be aware of them because sometimes they just make us wrong.

On the Edge of Your Social World

Another cognitive illusion that concerns social judgments is that we tend to have a very difficult time ignoring information that has been shown later to be false. Suppose you're trying to decide between job A and job B; you've been offered positions in both companies at the same rate of pay. You start making inquiries, and a friend tells you that the people at company A are very difficult to get along with and that, moreover, there have been a number of sexual harassment suits filed against the company's management. It's very natural to start reviewing in your mind all the people you met at company A, trying to imagine who is difficult and who might have been implicated in the harassment claims. A few days later, you and your friend are talking, and your friend apologizes, saying that she confused company A with a different company with a similar name—the evidence on which your first conclusion was made has been summarily removed. Dozens of experiments have shown that the original knowledge—now known to be false—exerts a lingering influence on your judgments; it is impossible to hit the reset button. Lawyers know this well, and often plant the seeds of a false idea in the minds of jurors and judges. After opposing counsel objects, the judge's admonition, "The jury will disregard that last exchange," comes too late to affect impression formation and judgment.

A vivid example of this comes from another experiment by psychologist Stuart Valins. This experiment shows its age—the 1960s—and is not even remotely politically correct by today's standards. But the data it provided are valid and have been robustly replicated in dozens of conceptually similar studies.

Undergraduate men were brought into the laboratory to take part, they were told, in an experiment on what the average college man considers to be attractive in a woman. They were placed in a chair and wired up with electrodes on their arms and a microphone on their chests. The experimenter explained that the electrodes and microphone would measure physiological arousal in response to a set of *Playboy* magazine centerfolds that they would be shown one at a time. Each participant saw the same pictures as every other participant, but in a different order. A loudspeaker played back the sounds of the participants' heartbeat. One by one, the participants looked at the pictures displayed by the experimenter, and the audible heartbeat clearly increased or decreased in response to how attractive the men found each woman's picture.

Unbeknownst to the participants, the electrodes on their arms and the microphone on their chests were not connected to the loudspeaker—it was all a ruse. The heartbeat they thought they heard was actually a tape recording of a synthesizer pulse, and the fluctuations in rate had been predetermined by the experimenter. When the experiment was over, the experimenter showed them that the heartbeat sounds were, in fact, synthesized pulses, and not at all tied to the participant's own heartbeat. The experimenter showed the participants the tape recorder playback system, and that the chest microphone and arm electrodes were not actually hooked up to anything.

Consider this from the participant's point of view. For a brief moment, he was given the impression that real physiological responses of his body showed that he found a particular woman particularly attractive. Now the evidence for that impression has been completely annulled. Logically, if he were engaging in rational decision-making, he'd hit the reset button on his impressions and conclude that there was no reason to trust the sound coming out of the speakers. The payoff of the experiment came next, when the experimenter allowed the participant to select pictures to take home as compensation for helping out with the experiment. Which pictures did the men pick? Overwhelmingly, they chose the pictures for which the loudspeaker played the highest heart rate. The belief they held, and for which all evidence was now removed, persevered, clouding their judgment. Valins believes that the mechanism by which this occurs is self-persuasion. People invest a significant amount of cognitive effort generating a belief that is consistent with the physiological state they are experiencing. Having done so, the results of this process are relatively persistent and resistant to change, but they do represent an insidious error of judgment. Nicholas Epley says that we are unaware of the construction of our beliefs and the mental processes that lead to them, in most cases. Consequently, even when evidence is explicitly removed, the beliefs persist.

Belief perseverance shows up in everyday life with gossip. Gossip is nothing new of course. It is among the earliest human foibles documented in writing, in the Old Testament and other ancient sources from the dawn of literacy. Humans gossip for many reasons: It can help us feel superior to others when we are otherwise feeling insecure about ourselves. It can help us to forge bonds with others to test their allegiance—if Tiffany is willing to join in the gossip with me against Britney, I can perhaps count on Tiffany as an ally. The problem with gossip is that it can be false. This is especially the case when the gossip is passed through the ears and mouths of several people, each of whom embellishes it. Due to belief perseverance, faulty social information, based on an outright lie or a distortion of the facts, can be very difficult to eradicate. And careers and social relationships can become difficult to repair afterward.

In addition to our brains holding an innate predisposition toward making trait attributions and enjoying gossip, humans tend to be innately suspicious of outsiders, where an outsider is anyone different from us. "Different from us" can be described by many dimensions and qualities: religion, skin color, hometown, the school from which we graduated, our income level, the political party we belong to, the kinds of music we listen to, the athletic team we root for. In high schools all around America, students tend to break off into cliques based on some salient (to them) dimension of difference. The primary dividing dimension is typically between students who affiliate with and buy into the whole idea that school will help them, and those who, for reasons of background, family experience, or socioeconomic status, believe that school is a waste of time. Beyond this primary division, high schoolers typically break into dozens of subcliques based on further partitioning of what constitutes "people like us."

This partitioning of social group membership arises at a time when our brains and bodies are undergoing dramatic neural and hormonal changes. Socially, we are coming to understand that we can have our own tastes and desires. We don't have to like what our parents like or say we should like—we explore and subsequently develop and refine our *own* tastes in music, clothing, films, books, and activities. This is a factor in why elementary schools tend to have relatively few social groups or extracurricular clubs and why high schools have so many.

But along with the many other cognitive illusions that lead to faulty social judgments is a phenomenon known as the in-group/out-group bias. We tend—erroneously of course—to think of people who are members of *our* group, whatever that group may be, as individuals, while we think of members of out-groups as a less well differentiated collective. That is, when asked to judge how disparate are the interests, personalities, and proclivities of the people in our group (the in-group) versus another group (the out-group), we tend to overestimate the similarities of out-group members.

So, for example, if Democrats are asked to describe how similar Democrats are to one another, they might say something like "Oh, Democrats come from all walks of life—we're a very diverse group." If then asked to describe Republicans, they might say, "Oh, those Republicans—all they care about is lower taxes. They're all alike." We also tend to prefer members of our own group. In general, a group will be perceived differently, and more accurately, by its own members than by outsiders.

In-group and out-group effects have a neurobiological basis. Within an area of the brain called the medial prefrontal cortex, there is a group of neurons that fire when we think about ourselves and people who are like us. This neural network is related to the daydreaming mode described in Chapter 2—the daydreaming mode is active when we think about ourselves in relation to others, and when we engage in perspective taking.

One plausible explanation for in-group/out-group effects is that they are merely a product of exposure—we know lots of different people in our group and we know them better than we know the people in the other group. This has to be true by definition; we associate with members of the in-group and not the out-group. Therefore, on a regular basis, we're confronted with the complexity and diversity of our friends, whom we know well, and while we wrongly believe that the people we don't know are less complex and diverse. We're better able to engage the medial prefrontal cortex with in-group members because their behaviors are simply easier for our brains to visualize in all their nuance.

But this hypothesis is contradicted by the striking fact that what constitutes an in-group or out-group can be defined on the flimsiest of premises, such as which of two randomly defined groups won a coin toss. One criterion for having a sense of group belongingness is interdependence of fate. After establishing common fate by the coin toss—one group would win a small prize and the other would not—students in an experiment were then asked to judge how similar or different members of each group were. There was a robust in-group/out-group effect even in this ad hoc grouping. Members of the in-group reported that people in their group—people they had just met—had more desirable qualities, and that they'd rather spend time with them. Other studies showed that similar flimsy manipulations lead in-group members to rate themselves as more different from one another than out-group members. It appears that the partitioning of people into mutually exclusive categories activates the perception that "we" are better than "they" even when there is no rational basis for it. That's just the way "we" are.

When we think about organizing our social world, the implication of in-group/out-group bias is clear. We have a stubborn tendency to misjudge outsiders and hence diminish our abilities to forge new, cooperative, and potentially valuable social relations.

Racism is a form of negative social judgment that arises from a combination of belief perseverance, out-group bias, categorization error, and faulty inductive reasoning. We hear about a particular undesirable trait or act on the part of an individual, and jump to the false conclusion that this is something completely predictable for someone of that ethnic or national background. The form of the argument is:

1.0. The media report that Mr. A did this.
1.1. I don't like this thing he did.
1.2. Mr. A is from the country of Awfulania.
1.3. Therefore, everyone from Awfulania must do this thing that I don't like.

There is nothing wrong of course with statements 1.0 or 1.1. Statement 1.2 seems to violate (flout) the Gricean maxim of relevance, but this is not, in and of itself, a logical violation. Noticing where someone is from is neither moral nor immoral in and of itself. It exists as a fact, outside morality. How one uses the information is where the morality enters the picture. One might notice a person's religion or country of origin as a step toward rapprochement, toward better understanding of cultural differences. Or one may use it for racist generalizations. From a logical standpoint, the real problem occurs at 1.3, a generalization from a single specific instance. For a number of historical and cognitive reasons, humans evolved an unfortunate tendency to do this, and in some instances it is adaptive. I eat a piece of fruit I've never eaten before, I get sick, I then assume (inductive reasoning) that *all* pieces of this particular fruit are potentially inedible. We make generalizations about entire classes of people or things because the brain is a giant inferencing machine, and it uses whatever data it has in its attempt to ensure our survival.

In the late 1970s, social psychologist Mick Rothbart taught a class on race relations that had approximately equal numbers of black and white students. A white student would often begin a question with the preface, "Don't black people feel . . ." and Mick would think to himself, "That's a good question." But if a black student started a question with "Don't white people feel . . ." Mick found himself thinking, "What do they mean, 'white people'? There are all kinds of white people, some conservative, some liberal, some Jewish, some gentile, some sensitive to the problems of minorities, and some not. 'White people' is too broad and meaningless a category to use, and there is no way I can respond to . . . the question . . . in its existing form."

Of course the same thoughts were likely going through the minds of the black students in the class when the question began with "Don't black people feel . . ." In cases of in-group/out-group bias, each group thinks of the other as homogeneous and monolithic, and each group views itself as variegated and complex. You're probably thinking that a cure for this is increased exposure—if members of groups get to know one another better, the stereotypes will fall away. This is true to a large degree, but in-group/out-group bias, being so deeply rooted in our evolutionary biology, is hard to shake completely. In one experiment, men and women judging one another as a group still fell prey to this cognitive bias. "It is impressive," Mick Rothbart wrote, "to have demonstrated this phenomenon with two groups who have almost continual contact, and a wealth of information about one another." Once we have a stereotype, we tend not to reevaluate the stereotype; we instead discard any new, disconfirming evidence as "exceptions." This is a form of belief perseveration.

The serious problems of famine, war, and climate change that we face will require solutions involving all of the stakeholders in the future of the world. No one country can solve these issues, and no collection of countries can if they view each other as out-groups rather than in-groups. You might say the fate of the world depends (among other things) on abolishing out-group bias. In one particular case, it did.

October 1962 was perhaps the time in world history when we were closest to complete destruction of the planet, as President Kennedy and Chairman Khrushchev were engaged in a nuclear standoff known in the United States as the Cuban Missile Crisis. (Or, as the Soviets called it, the Caribbean Crisis of 1962.)

A key aspect of the conflict's resolution was a back-channel, private communication between JFK and Khrushchev. This was the height of the cold war. Officials on each side believed that the other was trying to take over the world and couldn't be trusted. Kennedy saw himself and all Americans as the *in-group* and Khrushchev and the Soviets as the *out-group*. All of the biases we've seen accrued: Americans saw themselves as trustworthy, and any aggressive behaviors by the United States (even as judged by international standards) were justified; any aggressive behaviors by the Soviets showed their true nature as vicious, heartless, and irrational agents bent on destruction.

The turning point came when Khrushchev broke through all of the bravado and rhetoric and asked Kennedy to consider things from *his* perspective, to use a little empathy. He implored Kennedy several times to "try to put yourself in our place." He then pointed out their similarities, that both of them were leaders of their respective countries: "If you are really concerned about the peace and welfare of your people, and this is your responsibility as President, then I, as the Chairman of the Council of Ministers, am concerned for my people. Moreover, the preservation of world peace should be our joint concern, since if, under contemporary conditions, war should break out, it would be a war not only between the reciprocal claims, but a world wide cruel and destructive war."

In effect, Khrushchev pointed to a group in which he and Kennedy were both members—leaders of major world powers. In so doing, he turned Kennedy into an *in-group* member from an *out-group* member. This was the turning point in the crisis, opening up the possibility for a compromise solution that resolved the crisis on October 26, 1962.

Military action is often misguided. During World War II, the Nazis bombed London, hoping to induce a surrender; it had the opposite effect, increasing the British resolve to resist. In 1941, the Japanese tried to prevent the United States from entering the war by attacking Pearl Harbor, which backfired when it impelled the United States to enter the war. In the 1980s, the U.S. government provided funds for military action against Nicaragua to obtain political reform. During late 2013 and early 2014, three years after the start of the Egyptian revolt for democracy, the acting government was locked in a vicious cycle of terrorism and repression with the Muslim Brotherhood that hardened the determination of both sides.

Why are these interventions so often unsuccessful? Because of in-group and out-group bias, we tend to think that coercion will be more effective with our enemies than with ourselves, and conciliation will be more effective with ourselves than our enemies. Former secretary of state George Shultz, reflecting on forty years of United States foreign policy from 1970 to the present, said, "When I think about all the money we spent on bombs and munitions, and our failures in Viet Nam, Iraq, Afghanistan and other places around the world . . . Instead of advancing our agenda using force, we should have instead built schools and hospitals in these countries, improving the lives of their children. By now, those children would have grown into positions of influence, and they would be grateful to us instead of hating us."

When We Want to Escape a Social World

In an organized and civilized society, we depend on one another in a variety of interdependent ways. We assume that people won't throw their garbage willy-nilly on the sidewalk in front of our house, that neighbors will let us know if they see suspicious activity when we're out of town, and that if we need urgent medical help, someone will stop to dial 9-1-1. The act of living in cities and towns together is fundamentally an act of cooperation. The government, at various levels (federal, state, county, municipal), passes laws to define civil behavior, but at best they can address only the most extreme cases at the margins of civility. We rely on each other not just to observe the law but to be basically helpful and cooperative beyond the law. Few jurisdictions have a law that says if you see Cedric's four-year-old fall off her bicycle in the street, you must help her or notify Cedric, but it would be widely seen as monstrous if you didn't. (Argentina is one country that legally requires assisting those in need.)

Nevertheless, social interactions are complex and a number of experiments have demonstrated that we tend either to act in our own self-interest or just plain don't want to get involved. Take the case, for example, of witnessing a mugging, holdup, or other dangerous situation. There are clear societal norms about helping the victim in a situation like this. But there are also perfectly justifiable fears about what might happen to the person who intervenes. Pitted against societal norms and cooperative inclinations are several psychological forces that pull us toward inaction. As the social psychologists John Darley and Bibb Latané say, "'I didn't want to get involved' is a familiar comment, and behind it lies fears of physical harm, public embarrassment, involvement with police procedures, lost work days and jobs, and other unknown dangers."

In addition, there are many circumstances in which we are not the only ones witnessing an event where intervention seems called for, such as in public places. As a highly social species living in close proximity with thousands of others, we want to fit in. This desire in turn causes us to look about to others for cues about what is acceptable in a given situation. We see someone across the street who appears to be getting mugged. We look around and see dozens of other people viewing the same situation and none of them are doing anything about it. "Maybe," we think to ourselves, "this isn't as it seems. None of these other people are reacting, and maybe they know something I don't. Maybe it isn't really a mugging; it's just two people who know each other having an impromptu wrestling match. I should respect their privacy." Unknown to us, the dozens of other people are also looking around and having a similar internal dialogue, and reaching the same conclusion that it is against the societal norm to get involved in this particular conflict. These are not just textbook problems. In 2011, sixty-one-year-old Walter Vance, a man with a heart condition, died after collapsing in a Target store in West Virginia while hundreds of shoppers walked by and even over him. In 2013, shoppers at a QuickStop convenience store in Kalamazoo, Michigan, stepped over a man who had been shot and lay dying in the doorway. The cashier failed to check if the victim was alive, continuing to serve customers instead.

This tendency to not get involved is driven by three powerful, interrelated psychological principles. One is the strong desire to conform to others' behavior in the hope that it will allow us to gain acceptance within our social group, to be seen as cooperative and agreeable. The second is social comparison—we tend to examine our behavior in terms of others.

The third force pushing us toward inaction is diffusion of responsibility. This is based on very natural and ingrained feelings about equity and wanting to punish freeloaders: "Why should *I* stick my neck out if all these other people aren't—*they* could do something about it just as well as I could." Darley and Latané conducted a classic experiment designed to replicate a real-life medical emergency. Participants were nearly three times as likely to seek rapid help for a victim having a seizure when they thought they were the only witnesses than when they thought four other people were also there. Diffusion of responsibility extends to diffusion of blame for inaction, and the very real possibility that somebody else, unknown to us, has already initiated a helping action, for example, calling the police. As Darley and Latané say,

> When only one bystander is present in an emergency, if help is to come, it must come from him. Although he may choose to ignore it (out of concern for his personal safety, or desires "not to get involved"), any pressure to intervene focuses uniquely on him. When there are several observers present, however, the pressures to intervene do not focus on any one of the observers; instead the responsibility for intervention is shared among all the onlookers and is not unique to any one. As a result, no one helps.

Of course this is not a particularly admirable form of moral reasoning, but it does capture an essential part of human nature and, admittedly, is not our proudest moment as a species. We are not just a social species but often a selfish one. As one participant in the Darley and Latané experiment said, with respect to the person having a seizure, "It's just my kind of luck, something has to happen to me!" That is, she failed to empathize with the victim, considering only the inconvenience to her in having to be impeded by a crisis. Thankfully, we are not all this way, and not in every situation. Humans and other animals are often unselfish. Geese will come to the aid of one another at great personal risk; vervet monkeys broadcast alarm calls when predators are near, greatly increasing their own visibility to those predators, and meerkats stand guard for predators while the rest of their pack are eating. What is the neurochemical mechanism that supports this altruistic sentinel behavior? Oxytocin—the same social-affiliative hormone that increases trust and social cooperation among humans.

The distinction between our selfish and altruistic responses can be seen as a categorization error. When we are engaging in conformity, social comparison, or diffusion of responsibility, we are categorizing ourselves with the larger group as opposed to the victim. We see ourselves as standing with *them*, and they become our in-group. We fail to identify with the victim, who becomes a mistrusted, or at the very least misunderstood, member of an out-group. This is why Darley and Latané found that so many of their participants raced to help when they thought they were the sole witnesses—with no social group to categorize themselves in, they were free to identify with the victim. Knowing these principles can help us to overcome them, to empathize with the victim, and to squash the tendency to say, "I don't want to get involved."

Your social world is your social world. Who can say how to organize it? We are all increasingly interconnected, and our happiness and well-being is increasingly interdependent. One measure of the success of a society is how engaged its citizens are in contributing to the common good. If you see an Amber Alert on the highway and then see a matching license plate, call the police. Try to be agreeable. For all the digitization of our social life, we are still all in this together.

5

ORGANIZING OUR TIME

What Is the Mystery?

Ruth was a thirty-seven-year-old married mother of six. She was planning dinner for her brother, her husband, and her children to be served at six P.M. At 6:10, when her husband walked into the kitchen, he saw that she had two pots going on the stove, but the meat was still frozen and the salad was only partly made. Ruth had just picked up a tray of dessert and was getting ready to serve it. She had no awareness that she was doing things in the wrong order, or in fact that a proper order existed.

Ernie began his career as an accountant and was promoted to comptroller of a home building firm at age thirty-two. His friends and family considered him to be especially responsible and reliable. At age thirty-five he abruptly put all his savings into a partnership with a sketchy businessman and soon after had to declare bankruptcy. Ernie drifted through job after job and was fired from each for being late, disorganized, and a general deterioration of his ability to plan anything or to properly prioritize his tasks. He required more than two hours to get ready for work in the morning, and often spent entire days doing nothing more than shaving and washing his hair. Ernie suddenly had lost the ability to properly evaluate future needs: He adamantly refused to get rid of useless possessions such as five broken television sets, six broken fans, assorted dead houseplants, and three bags crammed full of empty frozen orange juice cans.

Peter had been a successful architect with a graduate degree from Yale, a special talent for math and science, and an IQ 25 points above average.

Given a simple assignment of reorganizing a small office space, he found himself utterly perplexed. He spent nearly two hours preparing to begin the project, and once he started, he inexplicably kept starting over. He made several preliminary sketches of idea fragments but was unable to connect those ideas or to refine the sketches. He was well aware of his disordered thinking. "I know what I want to draw, but I just don't do it. It's crazy . . . it's as if I'm getting a train of thought and then I start to draw it, and then I lose the train of thought. And, then, I have another train of thought that's in a different direction and the two don't [meet] . . . and this is a very simple problem."

What Ruth, Ernie, and Peter have in common is that shortly before these episodes, all three suffered damage to their prefrontal cortex. This is the part of the brain I wrote about before, which, along with the anterior cingulate, basal ganglia, and insula, helps us to organize time and engage in planning, to maintain attention and stick with a task once we've started it. The networked brain is not a mass of undifferentiated tissue—damage to discrete regions of it often results in very specific impairments. Damage to the prefrontal cortex wreaks havoc with the ability to plan a sequence of events and thereby sustain calm, productive effort resulting in the accomplishment of

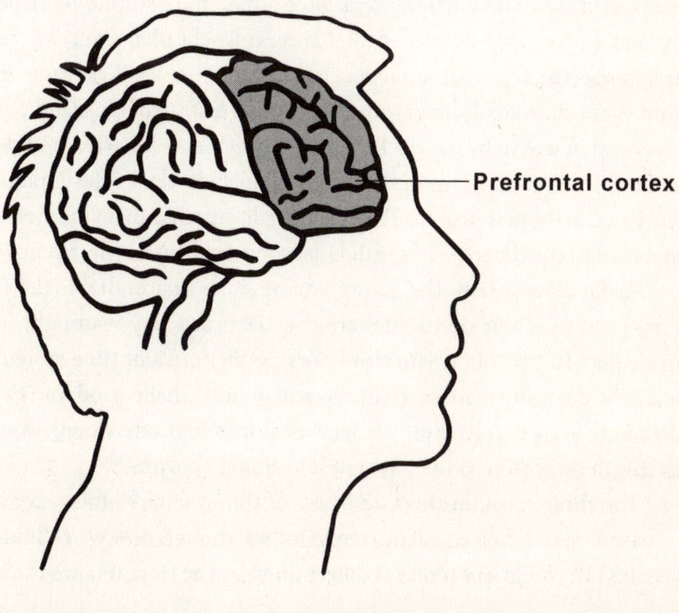

the goals we've set ourselves in the time we have. But even the healthiest of us sometimes behave as though we've got frontal lobe damage, missing appointments, making silly mistakes now and then, and not making the most of our brain's evolved capacity to organize time.

The Biological Reality of Time

Both mystics and physicists tell us that time is an illusion, simply a creation of our minds. In this respect, time is like color—there is no color in the physical world, just light of different wavelengths reflecting off of objects; as Newton said, the light waves themselves are colorless. Our entire sense of color results from the visual cortex in our brains processing these wavelengths and interpreting them as color. Of course that doesn't make it subjectively any less real—we look at a strawberry and it *is* red, it doesn't just *seem* red. Time can be thought of similarly as an interpretation that our brains impose on our experience of the world. We feel hungry after a certain amount of time has passed, sleepy after we've been awake for a certain amount of time. The regular rotation of the earth on its axis and around the sun leads us to organize time as a series of cyclical events, such as day and night and the four seasons, that in turn allow us to mentally register the passage of time. And having registered time, more so than ever before in human history, we divide up that time into chunks, units to which we assign specific activities and expectations for what we'll get done in them. And these chunks of time are as real to us as a strawberry is red.

Most of us live by the clock. We make appointments, wake and sleep, eat, and organize our time around the twenty-four-hour clock. The duration of the day is tied to the period of rotation of the earth, but what about the idea to divide that up into equal parts—where did that come from? And why twenty-four?

As far as we know, the Sumerians were the first to divide the day into time periods. Their divisions were one-sixth of a day's sunlight (roughly equivalent to two of our current hours). Other ancient time systems reckoned the day from sunrise to sunset, and divided that period into two equal divisions. As a result, these ancient mornings and afternoons would vary in length by season as the days got longer and shorter.

The three most familiar divisions of time we make today continue to be based on the motions of heavenly bodies, though now we call this astrophysics. The length of a year is determined by the time it takes the earth to circle the sun; the length of a month is (more or less) the time it takes the moon to circle the earth; the length of a day is the time it takes the earth to rotate on its axis (and observed by us as the span between two successive sunrises or sunsets). But further divisions are not based on any physical laws and tend to be based on historical factors that are largely arbitrary. There is nothing inherent in any biological or astrophysical cycle that would lead to the division of a day into twenty-four equal segments.

The current practice of dividing the clock into twenty-four comes from the ancient Egyptians, who divided the day into ten parts and then added an hour for each of the ambiguous periods of twilight, yielding twelve parts. Egyptian sundials in archeological sites testify to this. After nightfall, time was kept by a number of means, including tracking the motion of the stars, the burning of candles, or the amount of water that flowed through a small hole from one vessel to another. The Babylonians also used fixed duration with twenty-four hours in a day, as did Hipparchus, the ancient Greek mathematician and astronomer.

The division of the hour into sixty minutes, and the minutes into sixty seconds is also arbitrary, deriving from the Greek mathematician Eratosthenes, who divided the circle into sixty parts for an early cartographic system representing latitudes.

For most of human history, we did not have clocks or indeed any way of accurately reckoning time. Meetings and ritual get-togethers would be arranged by referencing obvious natural events, such as "Please drop by our camp when the moon is full" or "I'll meet you at sunset." Greater precision than that wasn't possible, but it wasn't needed, either. The kind of precision we've become accustomed to began after railroads were built. You might think the rationale is that railroad operators wanted to make departure times accurate and standardized as a convenience for customers, but it really grew out of safety concerns. After a series of railroad collisions in the early 1840s, investigators sought ways to improve communication and reduce the risk of accidents. Prior to that, timekeeping was considered a local matter for each city or town. Because there did not exist rapid forms of communication or transportation, there was no practical disadvantage to one location being desynchronized from another—and no way to really tell! Sir Sandford Fleming, a Scottish engineer who had helped design many of the railroads in Canada, came upon the idea of worldwide standard time zones, which were adopted by all Canadian and U.S. railroads in late 1883. The United States Congress didn't make it into law until the Standard Time Act was passed thirty-five years later.

Still, what we call hours, minutes, and days are arbitrary: There is nothing physically or biologically critical about the day being divided into twenty-four parts, or the hour and minute being divided into sixty parts. They were easy to adopt because these divisions don't contradict any inherent biological process.

Are there any biological constants to time? Our life span appears to be limited to about one hundred years (plus or minus twenty) due to aging. One theory used to be that life span limits are programmed into the genes to limit population size, but this has been dismissed because, in the harsh conditions of the wild, most species don't live long enough to age, so there would be no threat of overpopulation. A few species don't age at all and so are technically immortal. These include some species of jellyfish, flatworms (planaria), and hydra; the only causes of death in them are from injury or disease. This is in stark contrast to humans—of the roughly 150,000 people who die in the world each day, two-thirds die from age-related causes, and this number can reach 90% in peaceful industrialized nations, where war or disease is less likely to shorten life.

Natural selection has very limited or no opportunities to exert any direct influence on the aging process. Natural selection will tend to favor genes that have good effects on the organism early in life, prior to reproductive age, even if they have bad effects at older ages. Once an individual has reproduced and passed on his or her genes to the next generation, natural selection no longer has a means by which to operate on that person's genome. This has two consequences. If an early human inherited a gene mutation that rendered him less likely to reproduce—a gene that made him vulnerable to early disease or simply made him an unattractive mate—that gene would be less likely to show up in the next generation. On the other hand, suppose there are two gene mutations that each conferred a survival advantage and made this early human especially attractive, but one of them has the side effect of causing cancer at age seventy-five, decades after the most likely age at which an individual reproduces. Natural selection has no way to discourage the cancer-causing gene because the gene doesn't show itself until long after it has been passed on to the next generation. Thus, genetic variations that challenge survival at an old age—variations such as a susceptibility to cancer, or weakening of the bones—will tend to accumulate as one gets older and farther away in time from the peak age of reproduction. (This is because such a small percentage of organisms reproduce after a certain age that any investment in genetic mechanisms for survival beyond this age benefits a very small percentage of the population.) There is also the Hayflick limit, which states that cells can divide only a maximum number of times due to errors that accumulate during successive cell divisions. The fact that we not only die but are aware that our time is limited has different effects on us across the life span—something I write about at the end of this chapter.

At the level of hours and minutes, the most relevant constants are: human heart rates, which normally vary from 60 to 100 beats per minute; the need to spend roughly one-third of our time sleeping in order to function properly; and without cues from the sun, our bodies will drift toward a twenty-five-hour day. Biologists and physiologists still don't know why this is so. Moving down to the level of time that occurs at 1/1000 of a second are biological constants with respect to the temporal resolution of our senses. If a sound has a gap in it shorter than 10 milliseconds, we will tend not to hear it, because of resolution limits of the auditory system. For a similar reason, a series of clicks ceases to sound like clicks and becomes a musical note when the clicks are presented at a rate of about once every 25 milliseconds. If you're flipping through static (still) pictures, they must be presented slower than about once every 40 milliseconds in order for you to see them as separate images. Any faster than that and they exceed the temporal resolution of our visual system and we perceive motion where there is none (this is the basis of flipbooks and motion pictures).

Photographs are interesting because they can capture and preserve the world at resolutions that exceed those of our visual system. When this happens, they allow us to see a view of the world that our eyes and brains would never see on their own. Shutter speeds of 125 and 250 provide samples of the world in 8 millisecond and 4 millisecond slices, and this is part of our fascination with them, particularly as they capture human movement and human expressions. These sensory limits are constrained by a combination of neural biology and the physical mechanics of our sensory organs. Individual neurons have a range of firing rates, on the order of once per millisecond to once every 250 milliseconds or so.

We have a more highly developed prefrontal cortex than any other species. It's the seat of many behaviors that we consider distinctly human:

logic, analysis, problem solving, exercising good judgment, planning for the future, and decision-making. It is for these reasons that it is often called the central executive, or CEO of the brain. Extensive two-way connections between the prefrontal cortex and virtually every other region of the brain place it in a unique position to schedule, monitor, manage, and manipulate nearly every activity we undertake. Like real CEOs, these cerebral CEOs are highly paid in metabolic currency. Understanding how they work (and exactly how they get paid) can help us to use their time more effectively.

It's natural to think that because the prefrontal cortex is orchestrating all this activity and thought, it must have massive neural tracts for back-and-forth communication with other brain regions so that it can excite them and bring them on line. In fact, most of the prefrontal cortex's connections to other brain regions are not excitatory; they're the opposite: inhibitory. That's because one of the great achievements of the human prefrontal cortex is that it provides us with impulse control and, consequently, the ability to delay gratification, something that most animals lack. Try dangling a string in front of a cat or throwing a ball in front of a retriever and see if they can sit still. Because the prefrontal cortex doesn't fully develop in humans until after age twenty, impulse control isn't fully developed in adolescents (as many parents of teenagers have observed). It's also why children and adolescents are not especially good at planning or delaying gratification.

When the prefrontal cortex becomes damaged (such as from disease, injury, or a tumor), it leads to a specific medical condition called dysexecutive syndrome.

The condition is recognized by the kinds of planning and time coordination deficits that Ruth the homemaker, Ernie the accountant, and Peter the architect suffered from. It is also often accompanied by an utter lack of inhibition across a range of behaviors, particularly in social settings. Patients may blurt out inappropriate remarks, or go on binges of gambling, drinking, or sex with inappropriate partners. And they tend to act on what is right in front of them. If they see someone moving, they have difficulty inhibiting the urge to imitate them; if they see an object, they pick it up and use it.

What does all this have to do with organizing time? If your inhibitions are reduced, and you're impaired at seeing the future consequences of your actions, you tend to do things now that you might regret later, or that make it difficult to properly complete projects you're working on. Binge-watch an entire season of *Mad Men* instead of working on the Pensky file? Eat a donut (or two) instead of sticking to your diet? That's your prefrontal cortex not doing its job. In addition, damage to the prefrontal cortex causes an inability to effectively go forward or backward in time in one's mind—remember Peter the architect's description of starting over and over and not being able to move forward. Dysexecutive syndrome patients often get stuck in the present, doing something over and over again, perseverating, revealing a failure in temporal control. They can be terrible at organizing their calendars and *To Do* lists due to a double whammy of neural deficits. First, they're unable to place events in the correct temporal order. A patient with severe damage might attempt to bake the cake before having added all the ingredients. And many frontal lobe patients are not aware of their deficit; a loss of insight is associated with these frontal lobe lesions, such that patients generally underestimate their impairment. Having an impairment is bad enough, but if you don't know you have it, you're liable to go headlong into situations without taking proper precautions, and end up in trouble.

As if that weren't enough, advanced prefrontal cortex damage interferes with the ability to make connections and associations between disparate thoughts and concepts, resulting in a loss of creativity. The prefrontal cortex is especially important for generating creative acts in art and music. *This* is the region of the brain that is most active when creative artists are functioning at their peak.

If you're interested in seeing what it's like to have prefrontal cortex damage, there's a simple, reversible way: Get drunk. Alcohol interferes with the ability of prefrontal cortex neurons to communicate with one another, by disrupting dopamine receptors and blocking a particular kind of neuron called an NMDA receptor, mimicking the damage we see in frontal lobe patients. Heavy drinkers also experience the frontal lobe system double whammy: They may lose certain capabilities, such as impulse control or motor coordination or the ability to drive safely, but they aren't aware that they've lost them—or simply don't care—so they forge ahead anyway.

An overgrowth of dopaminergic neurons in the frontal lobes leads to autism (characterized by social awkwardness and repetitive behaviors), which mimics frontal lobe damage to some degree. The opposite, a reduction of dopaminergic neurons in the frontal lobes, occurs in Parkinson's disease and attention deficit disorder (ADD). The result then is scattered thinking and a lack of planning, which can sometimes be improved by the administration of L-dopa or of methylphenidate (also known by its brand name Ritalin), drugs that increase dopamine in the frontal lobes. From autism and Parkinson's, we've learned that too much or too little dopamine causes dysfunction. Most of us live in a Goldilocks zone where everything is just right. That's when we plan our activities, follow through on our plans, and inhibit impulses that would take us off track.

It may be obvious, but the brain coordinates a large share of the body's housekeeping and timekeeping functions—regulating heart rate and blood pressure, signaling when it's time to sleep and wake up, letting us know when we're hungry or full, and maintaining body temperature even as the outside temperature changes. This coordination takes place in the so-called reptilian brain, in structures we share with all vertebrates. In addition to this, there are the higher cognitive functions of the brain handled by the cerebral cortex: reasoning, problem solving, language, music, precision athletic movement, mathematical ability, art, and the mental operations that support them, including memory, attention, perception, motor planning, and categorization. The entire brain weighs three pounds (1.4 kg) and so is only a small percentage of an adult's total body weight, typically 2%. But it consumes 20% of all the energy the body uses. Why? The perhaps oversimplified answer is that time is energy.

Neural communication is very rapid—it has to be—reaching speeds of over 300 miles per hour, and with neurons communicating with one another hundreds of times per second. The voltage output of a single resting neuron is 70 millivolts, about the same as the line output of an iPod. If you could hook up a neuron to a pair of earbuds, you could actually hear its rhythmic output as a series of clicks. My colleague Petr Janata did this many years ago with neurons in the owl's brain. He attached small thin wires to neurons in the owl's brain and connected the other end of the wires to an amplifier and a loudspeaker. Playing music to the owl, Petr could hear in the neural firing pattern the same pattern of beats and pitches that were in the original music.

Neurochemicals that control communication between neurons are manufactured in the brain itself. These include some relatively well-known ones such as serotonin, dopamine, oxytocin, and epinephrine, as well as acetylcholine, GABA, glutamate, and endocannabinoids. Chemicals are released in very specific locations and they act on specific synapses to change the flow of information in the brain. Manufacturing these chemicals, and dispersing them to regulate and modulate brain activity, requires energy—neurons are living cells with a metabolism, and they get that energy from glucose. No other tissue in the body relies solely on glucose for energy except the testes. (This is why men occasionally experience a battle for resources between their brains and their glands.)

A number of studies have shown that eating or drinking glucose improves performance on mentally demanding tasks. For example, experimental participants are given a difficult problem to solve, and half of them are given a sugary treat and half of them are not. The ones who get the sugary treat perform better and more quickly because they are supplying the body with glucose that goes right to the brain to help feed the neural circuits that are doing the problem solving. This doesn't mean you should rush out and buy armloads of candy—for one thing, the brain can draw on vast reserves of glucose already held in the body when it needs them. For another, chronic ingestion of sugars—these experiments looked only at short-term ingestion—can damage other systems and lead to diabetes and sugar crash, the sudden exhaustion that many people feel later when the sugar high wears off.

But regardless of where it comes from, the brain burns glucose, as a car burns gasoline, to fuel mental operations. Just how much energy does the brain use? In an hour of relaxing or daydreaming, it uses eleven calories or fifteen watts—about the same as one of those new energy-efficient lightbulbs. Using the central executive for reading for an hour takes about forty-two calories. Sitting in class, by comparison, takes sixty-five calories—not from fidgeting in your seat (that's not factored in) but from the additional mental energy of absorbing new information. Most brain energy is used in synaptic transmission, that is, in connecting neurons to one another and, in turn, connecting thoughts and ideas to one another. What all this points to is that good time management should mean organizing our time in a way that maximizes brain efficiency. The big question many of us ask today is: Does that come from doing one thing at a time or from multitasking? If we only do one thing at a time, can we ever hope to catch up?

Mastering the See-Saw of Events

The brain "only takes in the world little bits and chunks at a time," says MIT neuroscientist Earl Miller. You may think you have a seamless thread of data coming in about the things going on around you, but the reality is your brain "picks and chooses and anticipates what it thinks is going to be important, what you should pay attention to."

In Chapters 1 and 3, I talked about the metabolic costs of multitasking, such as reading e-mail and talking on the phone at the same time, or social networking while reading a book. It takes more energy to shift your attention from task to task. It takes less energy to focus. That means that people who organize their time in a way that allows them to focus are not only going to get more done, but they'll be less tired and less neurochemically depleted after doing it. Daydreaming also takes less energy than multitasking. And the natural intuitive see-saw between focusing and daydreaming helps to recalibrate and restore the brain. Multitasking does not.

Perhaps most important, multitasking by definition disrupts the kind of sustained thought usually necessary for problem solving and for creativity. Gloria Mark, professor of informatics at UC Irvine, explains that multitasking is bad for innovation. "Ten and a half minutes on one project," she says, "is not enough time to think in-depth about anything." Creative solutions often arise from allowing a sequence of altercations between dedicated focus and daydreaming.

Further complicating things is that the brain's arousal system has a novelty bias, meaning that its attention can be hijacked easily by something new—the proverbial shiny objects we use to entice infants, puppies, and cats. And this novelty bias is more powerful than some of our deepest survival drives: Humans will work just as hard to obtain a novel experience as we will to get a meal or a mate. The difficulty here for those of us who are trying to focus amid competing activities is clear: The very brain region we need to rely on for staying on task is easily distracted by shiny new objects. In multitasking, we unknowingly enter an addiction loop as the brain's novelty centers become rewarded for processing shiny new stimuli, to the detriment of our prefrontal cortex, which wants to stay on task and gain the rewards of sustained effort and attention. We need to train ourselves to go for the long reward, and forgo the short one. Don't forget that the awareness of an unread e-mail sitting in your inbox can effectively reduce your IQ by 10 points, and that multitasking causes information you want to learn to be directed to the wrong part of the brain.

There are individual differences in cognitive style, and the trade-off present in multitasking often comes down to focus versus creativity. When we say that someone is focused, we usually mean they're attending to what is right in front of them and avoiding distraction, either internal or external. On the other hand, creativity often implies being able to make connections between disparate things. We consider a discovery to be creative if it explores new ideas through analogy, metaphor, or tying together things that we didn't realize were connected. This requires a delicate balance between focus and a more expansive view. Some individuals who take dopamine-enhancing drugs such as methylphenidate report that it helps them to stay motivated to work, to stay focused, and to avoid distractions, and that it facilitates staying engaged with repetitious tasks. The downside, they report, is that it can destroy their ability to make connections and associations, and to engage in expansive, creative thinking—underscoring the see-saw relationship between focus and creativity.

There is an interesting gene known as COMT that appears to modulate the ease with which people can switch tasks, by regulating the amount of dopamine in the prefrontal cortex. COMT carries instructions to the brain for how to make an enzyme (in this case, catechol-O-methyltransferase, hence the abbreviation COMT) that helps the prefrontal cortex to maintain optimal levels of dopamine and noradrenaline, the neurochemicals critical to paying attention. Individuals with a particular version of the COMT gene (called Val158Met) have *low* dopamine levels in the prefrontal cortex and, at the same time, show greater cognitive flexibility, easier task switching, and more creativity than average. Individuals with a different version of the COMT gene (called Val/Val homozygotes) have *high* dopamine levels, less cognitive flexibility, and difficulty task switching. This converges with anecdotal observations that many people who appear to have attention deficit disorder—characterized by low dopamine levels—are more creative and that those who can stay very focused on a task might be excellent workers when following instructions but are not especially creative. Keep in mind that these are broad generalizations based on aggregates of statistical data, and there are many individual variations and individual differences.

Ruth, Ernie, and Peter were stymied by everyday events such as cooking a meal, clearing the house of broken, unwanted items, or redecorating a small office. Accomplishing any task requires that we define a beginning and an ending. In the case of more complex operations, we need to break the whole thing into manageable chunks, each with its own beginning and ending. Building a house, for example, might seem impossibly complicated. But builders don't look at it that way—they divide the project into stages and chunks: grading and preparing the site, laying the foundation, framing the super structure and supports, plumbing, electrical, installing drywall, floors, doors, cabinets, painting. And then each of those stages is further divided into manageable chunks. Prefrontal cortex damage, among other things, can lead to deficits both in event segmentation—that's why Peter had trouble rearranging the office—and in stitching the segmented events back into the proper order—why Ruth was cooking the food out of order.

One of the most complicated things that humans do is to put the components of a multipart sequence in their proper temporal order. To accomplish temporal ordering, the human brain has to set up different scenarios, a series of what-ifs, and juggle them in different configurations to figure out how they affect one another. We estimate completion times and work backward. Temporal order is represented in the hippocampus alongside memory and spatial maps. If you're planting flowers, you dig a hole first, *then* take the flowers out of their temporary pots, *then* put the flowers in the ground, *then* fill the hole with dirt, *then* water them. This seems obvious for something we do all the time, but anyone who has ever tried to put together IKEA furniture knows that if you do things in the wrong order, you might have to take it apart and start all over from the beginning. The brain is adept at this kind of ordering, requiring communication between the hippocampus and the prefrontal cortex, which is working away busily assembling a mental image of the finished outcome alongside mental images of partly finished outcomes and—subconsciously most of the time—picturing what would happen if you did things out of sequence. (You really don't want to whip the cream *after* you've spooned it onto the pie—what a mess!)

More cognitively taxing is being able to take a set of separate operations, each with their own completion time, and organize their start times so that they are all completed at the same time. Two common human activities where this is done make an odd couple: cooking and war.

You know from experience that you can't serve the pie just as it comes out of the oven because it will be too hot, or that it takes some time for your oven to preheat. Your goal of being able to serve the pie at the right time means you need to take into account these various timing parameters, and so you probably work out a quick, seat-of-the-pants calculation about how long the combined pie cooking and cooling period is, how long it will take everyone to eat their soup and their pasta, and what an appropriate period might be to wait between the time everyone finishes the main course and when they'll want dessert (if you serve it too quickly, they may feel rushed;

if you wait too long, they may grow impatient). From here, we work backward from the time we want to serve the pie to when we need to preheat the oven to ensure the timing is right.

Wartime maneuvers also require essentially the same precise organization and temporal planning. In World War II, the Allies took the German army by surprise, using a series of deceptions and the fact that there was no harbor at the invasion site; the Germans assumed it would be impossible to maintain an offensive without shipborne materials. Unprecedented amounts of supplies and personnel were spirited to Normandy in secret so that artificial, portable harbors could be swiftly constructed at Saint-Laurent-sur-Mer and Arromanches. The harbors, code-named Mulberry, were assembled like an enormous jigsaw puzzle and, when fully operational, could move 7,000 tons of vehicles, supplies, and personnel per day. The operation required 545,000 cubic yards of concrete, 66,000 tons of reinforcing steel, 9,000 standards of timber (approximately 1.5 million cubic feet), 440,000 square yards of plywood, and 97 miles of steel wire rope, taking 20,000 men to build it, all of which had to arrive in the proper order and at the proper time. Building it and transporting it to Normandy without detection or suspicion is considered one of the greatest engineering and military feats in human history and a masterpiece of human planning and timing—thanks to connections between the frontal lobes and the hippocampus.

The secret to planning the invasion of Normandy was that, like all projects that initially seem overwhelmingly difficult, it was broken up deftly into small tasks—thousands of them. This principle applies at all scales: If you have something big you want to get done, break it up into chunks—meaningful, implementable, doable chunks. It makes time management much easier; you only need to manage time to get a single chunk done. And there's neurochemical satisfaction at the completion of each stage.

Then there is the balance between doing and monitoring your progress that is necessary in any multistep project. Each step requires that we stop the actual work every now and then to view it objectively, to ensure we're carrying it out properly and that we're happy with the results so far. We step back in our mind's eye to inspect what we did, figure out whether we need to redo something, whether we can move forward. It's the same whether we're sanding a fine wood cabinet, kneading dough, brushing our hair, painting a picture, or building a PowerPoint presentation. This is a familiar cycle: We work, we inspect the work, we make adjustments, we push forward. The prefrontal cortex coordinates the comparison of what's out-there-in-the-world with what's in your head. Think of an artist who evaluates whether the paint she just applied had a desirable effect on the painting. Or consider something as simple as mopping the floor—we're not just blindly swishing the mop back and forth; we're ensuring that the floor comes clean. And if it doesn't, we go back and scrub certain spots a little more. In many tasks, both creative and mundane, we must constantly go back and forth between work and evaluation, comparing the ideal image in our head with the work in front of us.

This constant back-and-forth is one of the most metabolism-consuming things that our brain can do. We step out of time, out of the moment, and survey the big picture. We like what we see or we don't, and then we go back to the task, either moving forward again, or backtracking to fix a conceptual or physical mistake. As you now know well, such attention switching and perspective switching is depleting, and like multitasking, it uses up more of the brain's nutrients than staying engaged in a single task.

In situations like this, we are functioning as both the boss and the employee. Just because you're good at one doesn't mean you'll be any good at the other. Every general contractor knows painters, carpenters, or tile setters capable of great work, but only when someone is standing by to give perspective. Many subcontractors actually doing the work have neither the desire nor the ability to think about budgets or make decisions about the optimum trade-off between time and money. Indeed, left to their own devices, some are such perfectionists that nothing ever gets finished. I once worked with a recording engineer who blew through a budget trying to make one three-minute song perfect before I was able to stop him and remind him that we still had eleven other songs to do. In the world of music, it's no accident that only a few artists produce themselves effectively (Stevie Wonder, Paul McCartney, Prince, Jimmy Page, Joni Mitchell, and Steely Dan). Many, many PhD students fall into this category, never finishing their degrees because they can't move forward—they're too perfectionistic. The real job in supervising PhD students isn't teaching them facts; it's keeping them on track.

Planning and doing require separate parts of the brain. To be both a boss and a worker, one needs to form and maintain multiple, hierarchically organized attentional sets and then bounce back and forth between them. It's the central executive in your brain that notices that the floor is dirty. It forms an *executive* attentional set for "mop the floor" and then constructs a *worker* attentional set for doing the actual mopping. The executive set cares only that the job is done and is done well. It might find the mop, a bucket the mop fits into, the floor cleaning product. Then, the worker set gets down to wetting the mop, starting the job, monitoring the mop head so you know when it's time to put it back in the bucket, rinsing the head now and then when it gets too dirty. A good worker will be able to call upon a level of attention subordinate to all that and momentarily become a kind of detail-oriented worker who sees a spot that won't come out with the mop, gets down on his hands and knees, and scrapes or scrubs or uses whatever method necessary to get that spot out. This detail-oriented worker has a different mind-set and different goals from those of the regular worker or boss. If your spouse walks in, after the detail guy has been working for fifteen minutes on a smudge off in the corner, and says, "What—are you crazy!? You've got the entire floor left to do and the guests will be here in fifteen minutes!" the detail guy is pulled up into the perspective of the boss and sees the big picture again.

All this level shifting, from boss down to worker down to detail worker and back again, is a shifting of the attentional set and it comes with the metabolic costs of multitasking. It's exactly the reason a good hand car wash facility has these jobs spread out among three classes of workers. There are the car washers who do just the broad strokes of soaping down and rinsing the whole car. When they're done, the detail guys come in and look closely to see if there are any leftover dirty spots, to clean the wheels and bumpers, and present the car to you. There's also a boss who's looking over the whole operation to make sure that no worker spends too much or too little time at any one point or on any one car. By dividing up the roles in this way, each worker forms one, rather than three, attentional sets and can throw himself into that role without worrying about anything at a different level.

We can all learn from this because we all have to be workers in one form or another at least some of the time. The research says that if you have chores to do, put similar chores together. If you've collected a bunch of bills to pay, just pay the bills—don't use that time to make big decisions about whether to move to a smaller house or buy a new car. If you've set aside time to clean the house, don't also use that time to repair your front steps or reorganize your closet. Stay focused and maintain a single attentional set through to completion of a job. Organizing our mental resources efficiently means providing slots in our schedules where we can maintain an attentional set for an extended period. This allows us to get more done and finish up with more energy.

Related to the manager/worker distinction is that the prefrontal cortex contains circuits responsible for telling us whether *we're* controlling something or someone else is. When we set up a system, this part of the brain marks it as self-generated. When we step into someone else's system, the brain marks it that way. This may help explain why it's easier to stick with an exercise program or diet that someone else sets up: We typically trust them as "experts" more than we trust ourselves. "My trainer told me to do three sets of ten reps at forty pounds—he's a trainer, he must know what he's talking about. I can't design my own workout—what do I know?" It takes Herculean amounts of discipline to overcome the brain's bias against self-generated motivational systems. Why? Because as with the fundamental attribution error we saw in Chapter 4, we don't have access to others' minds, only our own. We are painfully aware of all the fretting and indecision, all the nuances of our internal decision-making process that led us to reach a particular conclusion. (I really need to get serious about exercise.) We don't have access to that (largely internal) process in others, so we tend to take their certainty as more compelling, in many cases, than our own. (Here's your program. Do it every day.)

To perform all but the simplest tasks requires flexible thinking and adaptiveness. Along with the many other distinctly human traits discussed, the prefrontal cortex allows us the flexibility to change behavior based on context. We alter the pressure required to slice a carrot versus slicing cheese; we explain our work differently to our grandma than to our boss; we use a pot holder to take something out of the oven but not out of the refrigerator. The prefrontal cortex is necessary for such adaptive strategies for living daily life, whether we're foraging for food on the savanna or living in skyscrapers in the city.

The balance between flexible thinking and staying on task is assessed by neuropsychologists using a test called the Wisconsin Card Sorting Test. People are asked to sort a deck of specially marked cards according to a rule. In the example below, the instruction might be to sort the new, unnumbered card according to the shade of gray, in which case it should be put on pile 1. After getting used to sorting a bunch of cards according to this rule, you're then given a new rule, for example, to sort by shape (in which case the new card should be put on pile 4) or to sort by number (in which case the new card should be put on pile 2).

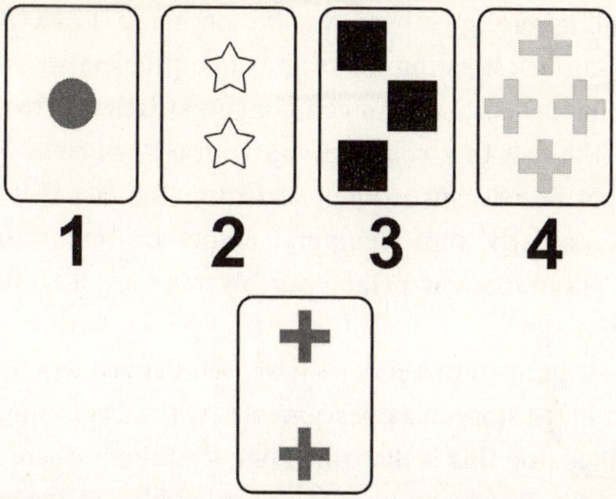

People with frontal lobe deficits have difficulty changing the rule once they've started; they tend to perseverate, applying an old rule after a new one is given. Or they show an inability to stick to a rule, and err by suddenly applying a new rule without being prompted. It was recently discovered that holding a rule in mind and following it is accomplished by networks of neurons that synchronize their firing patterns, creating a distinctive brain wave. For example, if you're following the shading rule in the card sorting task, your brain waves will oscillate at a particular frequency until you switch to follow shape, and then they'll oscillate at a different frequency. You can think of this by analogy to radio broadcasts: It's as though a given rule operates in the brain on a particular frequency so that all the instructions and communication of that rule can remain distinct from other instructions and communications about other rules, each of which is transmitted and coordinated on its own designated frequency band.

Reaching our goals efficiently requires the ability to selectively focus on those features of a task that are most relevant to its completion, while successfully ignoring other features or stimuli in the environment that are competing for attention. But how do you know what factors are relevant and what factors aren't? This is where expertise comes in—in fact, it could be said that what distinguishes experts from novices is that they know what to pay attention to and what to ignore. If you don't know anything at all about cars and you're trying to diagnose a problem, every screech, sputter, and knock in the engine is potential information and you try to attend to them all. If you're an expert mechanic, you home in on the one noise that is relevant and ignore the others. A good mechanic is a detective (as is a good physician), investigating the origins of a problem so as to learn the story of what happened. Some car components are relevant to the story and some aren't. The fact that you filled up with a low-octane gasoline this morning might be relevant to the backfiring. The fact that your brakes squeak isn't. Similarly, some temporal events are important and some aren't. If you put in that low-octane gas this morning, it's different than if you did it a year ago.

We take for granted that movies have well-defined temporal frames—scenes—parts of the story that are segmented with a beginning and an end. One way of signaling this is that when one scene ends, there is a break in continuity—a cut. Its name comes from analog film; in the editing room, the film would be physically cut at the end of one event, and spliced to the beginning of another (nowadays, this is done digitally and there is no physical cutting, but the digital editing tools use a little scissors icon to represent the action, and we still call this a cut, just as we "cut and paste" with our word processors). Without cuts signifying the end of a scene, it would be difficult for the brain to process and digest the material as it became a single onslaught of information, 120 minutes long. Of course modern filmmaking, particularly in action movies, uses far more cuts than was previously the norm, as a way to engage our ever hungrier appetite for visual stimulation.

Movies use the cut in three different ways, which we've learned to interpret by experience. A cut can signify a discontinuity in time (the new scene begins three hours later), in place (the new scene begins on the other side of town), or in perspective (as when you see two people talking and the camera shifts from looking at one face to looking at the other).

These conventions seem obvious to us. But we've learned them through a lifetime of exposure to comics, TV, and films. They are actually cultural inventions that have no meaning for someone outside our culture. Jim Ferguson, an anthropologist at Stanford, describes his own empirical observation of this when he was doing fieldwork in sub-Saharan Africa:

> When I was living among the Sotho, I went into the city one day with one of the villagers. The city is something he had no experience with. This was an intelligent and literate man—he had read the Bible, for example. But when he saw a television for the first time in a shop, he couldn't make heads or tails of what was going on. The

> narrative conventions that we use to tell a story in film and TV were completely unknown to him. For example, one scene would end and another would begin at a different time and place. This gap was completely baffling to him. Or during a single scene, the camera would focus on one person, then another, in order to take another perspective. He struggled, but simply couldn't follow the story. *We* take these for granted because we grew up with them.

Film cuts are extensions of culturally specific storytelling conventions that we also see in our plays, novels, and short stories. Stories don't include every single detail about every minute in a character's life—they jump to salient events, and we have been trained to understand what's going on.

Our brains encode information in scenes or chunks, mirroring the work of writers, directors, and editors. To do that, the information packets, like movie scenes, must have a beginning and an ending. Implicit in our management of time is that our brains automatically organize and segment the things we see and do into chunks of activity. Richard is not building a house today or even building the bathroom, he is preparing the kitchen floor for the tile. Even Superman chunks—he may wake up every morning and tell Lois Lane, "I'm off to save the world today, honey," but what he tells himself is the laundry list of chunked tasks that need to be done to accomplish that goal, each with a well-defined beginning and ending. (1. Capture Lex Luthor. 2. Dispose of Kryptonite safely. 3. Hurl ticking bomb into outer space. 4. Pick up clean cape from dry cleaner.)

Chunking fuels two important functions in our lives. First, it renders large-scale projects doable by giving us well-differentiated tasks. Second, it renders the experiences of our lives memorable by segmenting them with well-defined beginnings and endings—this in turn allows memories to be stored and retrieved in manageable units. Although our actual waking time is continuous, we can easily talk about the events of our lives as being differentiated in time. The act of having breakfast has a more or less well differentiated beginning and ending, as does your morning shower. They don't bleed into one another in your memory because the brain does the editing, segmenting, and labeling for you. And we can subdivide these scenes at will. We make sense of the events in our lives by segmenting them, giving them temporal boundaries. We don't treat our daily lives as undifferentiated moments, we group moments into salient events such as "brushing my teeth," "eating breakfast," "reading the newspaper," and "driving to the train station." That is, our brains implicitly impose a beginning and an ending to events. Similarly, we don't perceive or remember a football game as a continuous sequence of action, we remember the game in terms of its quarters, downs, and specific important plays. And it's not just because the rules of the game create these divisions. When talking about a particular play, we can further subdivide: We remember the running back peeling off into the open; the quarterback dodging the defensive linemen; the arm of the quarterback stretched back and ready to throw; the fake throw; and then the quarterback suddenly running, stride-by-stride, for a surprise touchdown.

There is a dedicated portion of the brain that partitions long events into chunks, and it is in—you guessed it—the prefrontal cortex. An interesting feature of this event segmentation is that hierarchies are created without our even thinking about them, and without our instructing our brains to make them. That is, our brains automatically create multiple, hierarchical representations of reality. And we can review these in our mind's eye from either direction—from the top down, that is, from large time scales to small, or from the bottom up, from small time scales to large.

Consider a question such as asking a friend, "What did you do yesterday?" Your friend might give a simple, high-level overview such as "Oh, yesterday was like any other day. I went to work, came home, had dinner, and then watched TV." Descriptions like these are typical of how people talk about events, making sense of a complex dynamic world in part by segmenting it into a modest number of meaningful units. Notice how this response implicitly skips over a lot of detail that is probably generic and unremarkable, concerning how your friend woke up and got out of the house. And the description jumps right to his or her workday. This is followed by two more salient events: eating dinner and watching TV.

The proof that hierarchical processing exists is in the fact that normal, healthy people can subdivide their answer into increasingly smaller parts if you ask them to. Prompt them with "Tell me more about the dinner?" and you might get a response like "Well, I made a salad, heated up some leftovers from the party we had the night before, and then finished that nice Bordeaux that Heather and Lenny brought over, even though Lenny doesn't drink."

And you can drill down still more: "How exactly did you prepare the salad? Don't leave anything out."

"I took some lettuce out of the crisper in the refrigerator, washed it, sliced some tomatoes, shredded some carrots, and then added a can of hearts of palm. Then I put on some Kraft Italian dressing."

"Tell me in even more detail how you prepared the lettuce. As though you were telling someone who has never done this before."

"I took out a wooden salad bowl from the cupboard and wiped it clean with a dish towel. I opened the refrigerator and took out a head of red leaf lettuce from the vegetable crisper. I peeled off layers of lettuce leaves, looked carefully to make sure that there weren't any bugs or worms, tore the leaves into bite-size pieces, then soaked them in a bowl of water for a bit. Then I drained the water, rinsed the leaves under running water, and put them in a salad spinner to dry them. Then I put all the now-dry lettuce into the salad bowl and added the other ingredients I mentioned."

Each of these descriptions holds a place in the hierarchy, and each can be considered an event with a different level of temporal resolution. There is a natural level at which we tend to describe these events, mimicking the natural level of description I wrote about in Chapter 2—the *basic level* of categories in describing things like birds and trees. If you use a level of description that is too high or too low in the hierarchy—which is to say, a level of description that is unexpected or atypical—it is usually to make some kind of point. It seems aberrant to use the wrong level of description, and it violates the Gricean maxim of quantity.

Artists often flout these norms to make an artistic gesture, to cause the audience to see things differently. We can imagine a film sequence in which someone is preparing a salad, and every little motion of tearing lettuce leaves is shown as a close-up. This might seem to violate a storytelling convention of recounting information that moves the story forward, but in surprising us with this seemingly unimportant lettuce tearing, the filmmaker or storyteller creates a dramatic gesture. By focusing on the mundane, it may convey something about the mental state of the character, or build tension toward an impending crisis in the story. Or maybe we see a centipede in the lettuce that the character doesn't notice.

The temporal chunking that our brains create isn't always explicit. In films, when the scene cuts from one moment to another, our brains automatically fill in the missing information, often as a result of a completely separate set of cultural conventions. In television shows from the relatively modest 1960s (Rob and Laura Petrie slept in separate twin beds!), a man and a woman might be seen sitting on the edge of the bed kissing before the scene fades to black and cuts to the next morning, when they wake up together. We're meant to infer a number of intimate activities that occurred between the fade-out and the new scene, activities that could not be shown on network TV in the 1960s.

A particularly interesting example of inference occurs in many single-panel comics. Often the humor requires you to imagine what happened in the instant immediately before or immediately after the panel you're being shown. It's as though the cartoonist devised a series of four or five panels to tell the story and has chosen to show you only one—and typically not even the funniest one but the one right before or right after what would be the funniest panel. It's this act of audience participation and imagination that makes the single-panel comic so engaging and so rewarding—to get the joke, you actually have to figure out what some of those missing panels must be.

Take this example from *Bizarro*:

The humor is not so much in what the judge is saying but in our imagining what must have gone on in the courtroom moments before to elicit such a warning! Because we are coparticipants in figuring out the joke, cartoons like these are more memorable and pleasurable than ones in which every detail is handed to us. This follows a well-established principle of cognitive psychology called levels of processing: Items that are processed at a deeper level, with more active involvement by us, tend to become more strongly encoded in memory. This is why passive learning through textbooks and lectures is not nearly as effective a way to learn new material as is figuring it out for yourself, a method called *peer instruction* that is being introduced into classrooms with great success.

Sleep Time

You go to bed later or get up earlier. A daily time-management tactic we all use and barely notice revolves around that large block of lost time that can make all of us feel unproductive: sleep. It's only recently that we've begun to understand the enormous amount of cognitive processing that occurs while we're asleep. In particular, we now know that sleep plays a vital role in the consolidation of events of the previous few days, and therefore in the formation and protection of memories.

Newly acquired memories are initially unstable and require a process of neural strengthening or consolidation to become resistant to interference, and to become accessible to us for retrieval. For a memory to be accessible means that we can retrieve it using a variety of different cues. Take, for example, that lunch of shrimp scampi I had at the beach a few weeks ago with my high-school buddy Jim Ferguson. If my memory system is functioning normally, by today, any of the following queries should be able to evoke one or more memories associated with the experience:

- Have I ever eaten shrimp scampi?
- When's the last time I had seafood?
- When's the last time I saw my friend Jim Ferguson?
- Does Jim Ferguson have good table manners?
- Are you still in touch with any friends from high school?
- Do you ever go out to lunch?
- Is it windy at the beach this time of year?
- What were you doing last Wednesday at one P.M.?

In other words, there are a variety of ways that a single event such as a lunch with an old friend can be contextualized. For all of these attributes to be associated with the event, the brain has to toss and turn and analyze the experience after it happens, extracting and sorting information in complex ways. And this new memory needs to be integrated into existing conceptual frameworks, integrated into old memories previously stored in the brain (shrimp is seafood, Jim Ferguson is a friend from high school, good table manners do *not* include wiping shrimp off your mouth with the tablecloth).

In the last few years, we've gained a more nuanced understanding that these different processes are accomplished during distinct phases of sleep. These processes both preserve memories in their original form, and extract features and meaning from the experiences. This allows new experiences to become integrated into a more generalized and hierarchical representation of the outside world that we hold inside our heads. Memory consolidation requires that our brains fine-tune the neural circuits that first encountered the new experience. According to one theory that is gaining acceptance, this has to be done when we're asleep, or otherwise the activity in those circuits would be confused with an actually occurring experience. All of this tuning, extraction, and consolidation doesn't happen during one night but unfolds over several sequential nights. Disrupted sleep even two or three days after an experience can disrupt your memory of it months or years later.

Sleep experts Matthew Walker (from UC Berkeley) and Robert Stickgold (from Harvard Medical School) note the three distinct kinds of information processing that occur during sleep. The first is *unitization*, the combining of discrete elements or chunks of an experience into a unified concept. For example, musicians and actors who are learning a new piece or scene might practice one phrase at a time; unitization during sleep binds these together into a seamless whole.

The second kind of information processing we accomplish during sleep is *assimilation*. Here, the brain integrates new information into the existing network structure of other things you already knew. In learning new words, for example, your brain works unconsciously to construct sample sentences with them, turning them over and experimenting with how they fit into your preexisting knowledge. Any brain cells that used a lot of energy during the day show an increase of ATP (a neural signaling coenzyme) during sleep, and this has been associated with assimilation.

The third process is *abstraction*, and this is where hidden rules are discovered and then entered into memory. If you learned English as a child, you learned certain rules about word formation such as "add *s* to the end of a word to make it plural" or "add *ed* to the end of a word to make it past tense." If you're like most learners, no one taught you this—your brain abstracted the rule by being exposed to it in multiple instances. This is why children make the perfectly logical mistake of saying "he goed" instead of "he went," or "he swimmed" instead of "he swam." The abstraction is correct; it just doesn't apply to these particular irregular verbs. Across a range of inferences involving not just language but mathematics, logic problems, and spatial reasoning, sleep has been shown to enhance the formation and understanding of abstract relations, so much so that people often wake having solved a problem that was unsolvable the night before. This may be part of the reason why young children just learning language sleep so much.

Thus, many different kinds of learning have been shown to be improved after a night's sleep, but not after an equivalent period of being awake. Musicians who learn a new melody show significant improvement in performing it after one night's sleep. Students who were stymied by a calculus problem the day it was presented are able to solve it more easily after a night's sleep than an equivalent amount of waking time. New information and concepts appear to be quietly practiced while we're asleep, sometimes showing up in dreams. A night of sleep more than doubles the likelihood that you'll solve a problem requiring insight.

Many people remember the first day they played with a Rubik's Cube. That night they report that their dreams were disturbed by images of those brightly colored squares and of them rotating and clicking in their sleep. The next day, they are much better at the game—while asleep, their brains had extracted principles of where things were, relying on both their conscious perceptions of the previous day and myriad unconscious perceptions. Researchers found the same thing when studying Tetris players' dreams. Although the players reported dreaming about Tetris, especially early on in their learning, they didn't dream about specific games or moves they had made; rather, they dreamed about abstract elements of the game. The researchers hypothesized that this created a template by which their brains could organize and store just the sort of generalized information that would be necessary to succeed at the game.

This kind of information consolidation happens all the time in our brains, but it happens more intensely for tasks we are more engaged with.

Those calculus students didn't simply glance at the problem during the day, they tried actively to solve it, focused attention on it, and then reapproached it after a night's sleep. If you are only dimly engaged in your French language tapes, it is unlikely your sleep will help you to learn grammar and vocabulary. But if you struggle with the language for an hour or more during the day, investing your focus, energy, and emotions in it, then it will be ripe for replay and elaboration during your sleep. This is why language immersion works so well—you're emotionally invested and interpersonally engaged with the language as you attempt to survive in the new linguistic environment. This kind of learning, in a way, is hard to manufacture in the classroom or language laboratory.

Perhaps the most important principle of memory is that we tend to remember best those things we care about the most. At a biological level, neurochemical tags are created and attached to experiences that are emotionally important; and those appear to be the ones that our dreams grab hold of.

All sleep isn't created equal when it comes to improving memory and learning. The two main categories of sleep are REM (rapid eye movement) and NREM (non-REM), with NREM sleep being further divided into four stages, each with a distinct pattern of brain waves. REM sleep is when our most vivid and detailed dreams occur. Its most obvious feature is temporary selective muscle suppression (so that if you're running in your dream, you don't get out of bed and start running around the house). REM sleep is also characterized by low-voltage brain wave patterns (EEG), and the rapid, flickering eyelid movements for which it is named. It used to be thought that all our dreaming occurs during REM sleep, but there is newer evidence that we can dream during NREM sleep as well, although those dreams tend to be less elaborate. Most mammals have physiologically similar states, and we assume they're dreaming, but we can't know for sure. Additional dreamlike states can occur just as we're falling asleep and just as we're waking up; these can feature vivid auditory and visual imagery that seem like hallucinations.

REM sleep is believed to be the stage during which the brain performs the deepest processing of events—the unitization, assimilation, and abstraction mentioned above. The brain chemicals that mediate it include decreases in noradrenaline and increased levels of acetylcholine and cortisol. A preponderance of theta wave activity facilitates associative linking between disparate brain regions during REM. This has two interesting effects. The first is that it allows our brains to draw out connections, deep underlying connections, between the events in our lives that we might not otherwise perceive, through activating thoughts that are far-flung in our consciousness and unconsciousness. It's what lets us perceive, for example, that clouds look a bit like marshmallows, or that "Der Kommissar" by Falco uses the same musical hook as "Super Freak" by Rick James. The second effect is that it appears to cause dreams in which these connections morph into one another: You dream you're eating a marshmallow and it suddenly floats up to the sky and becomes a rain cloud; you're watching Rick James on TV and he's driving a Ford Falcon (the brain can be a terrible punster—Falco becomes Falcon); you're walking down a street and suddenly the street is in a completely different town, and the sidewalk turns to water. These distortions are a product of the brain exploring possible relations among disparate ideas and things. And it's a good thing they happen only while you're asleep or your view of reality would be unreliable.

There's another kind of distortion that occurs when we sleep—time distortion. What may seem like a long, elaborate dream spanning thirty minutes or more may actually occur within the span of a single minute. This may be due to the fact that the body's own internal clock is in a reduced state of activation (you might say it is asleep, too) and so becomes unreliable.

The transition between REM and NREM sleep is believed to be mediated by GABAergic neurons near the brainstem, those same neurons that act as inhibitors in the prefrontal cortex. Current thinking is that these and other neurons in the brain act as switches, bringing us from one state to the other. Damage to one part of this brain region causes a dramatic reduction in REM sleep, while damage to another causes an increase.

A normal human sleep cycle lasts about 90–100 minutes. Around 20 of those minutes on average are spent dreaming in REM sleep, and 70–80 are NREM sleep, although the length varies throughout the night. REM periods may be only 5–10 minutes at the beginning of the night and expand to 30 minutes or more later in the early morning hours. Most of the memory consolidation occurs in the first two hours of slow-wave, NREM sleep, and during the last 90 minutes of REM sleep in the morning. This is why drinking and drugs (including sleep medications) can interfere with memory, because that crucial first sleep cycle is compromised by intoxication. And this is why sleep deprivation leads to memory loss—because the crucial 90 minutes of sleep at the end is either interrupted or never occurs. And you can't make up for lost sleep time. Sleep deprivation after a day of learning prevents sleep-related improvement, even three days later following two nights of good sleep. This is because recovery sleep or rebound sleep is characterized by abnormal brain waves as the dream cycle attempts to resynchronize with the body's circadian rhythm.

Sleep may also be a fundamental property of neuronal metabolism. In addition to the information consolidation functions, a new finding in 2013 showed that sleep is necessary for cellular housekeeping. Like the garbage trucks that roam city streets at five A.M., specific metabolic processes in the glymphatic system clear neural pathways of potentially toxic waste products that accumulate during waking thought. As discussed in Chapter 2, we also know that it is not an all-or-none phenomenon: Parts of the brain sleep while others do not, leading to not just the sense but the reality that sometimes we are half-asleep or sleeping only lightly. If you've ever had a brain freeze—momentarily unable to remember something obvious—or if you've ever found yourself doing something silly like putting orange juice on your cereal, it may well be that part of your brain is taking a nap. Or it could just be that you're thinking about too many things at once, having overloaded your attentional system.

Several factors contribute to feelings of sleepiness. First, the twenty-four-hour cycle of light and darkness influences the production of neurochemicals specifically geared to induce wakeful alertness or sleepiness. Sunlight impinging on photoreceptors in the retina triggers a chain reaction of processes resulting in stimulation of the suprachiasmatic nucleus and the pineal gland, a small gland near the base of the brain, about the size of a grain of rice. About one hour after dark, the pineal gland produces melatonin, a neurohormone partly responsible for giving us the urge to sleep (and causing the brain to go into a sleep state).

The sleep-wake cycle can be likened to a thermostat in your home. When the temperature falls to a certain point, the thermostat closes an electrical circuit, causing your furnace to turn on. Then, when your preset, desired temperature is reached, the thermostat interrupts the circuit and the furnace turns off again. Sleep is similarly governed by neural switches. These follow a homeostatic process and are influenced by a number of factors, including your circadian rhythm, food intake, blood sugar level, condition of your immune system, stress, sunlight and darkness. When your homeostat increases above a certain point, it triggers the release of neurohormones that induce sleep. When your homeostat decreases below a certain point, a separate set of neurohormones are released to induce wakefulness.

At one time or another, you've probably thought that if only you could sleep less, you'd get so much more done. Or that you could just borrow time by sleeping one hour less tonight and one hour more tomorrow night. As enticing as these seem, they're not borne out by research. Sleep is among *the* most critical factors for peak performance, memory, productivity, immune function, and mood regulation. Even a mild sleep reduction or a departure from a set sleep routine (for example, going to bed late one night, sleeping in the next morning) can produce detrimental effects on cognitive performance for many days afterward. When professional basketball players got ten hours of sleep a night, their performance improved dramatically: Free-throw and three-point shooting each improved by 9%.

Most of us follow a sleep-waking pattern of sleeping for 6–8 hours followed by staying awake for approximately 16–18. This is a relatively recent invention. For most of human history, our ancestors engaged in two rounds of sleep, called segmented sleep or bimodal sleep, in addition to an afternoon nap. The first round of sleep would occur for four or five hours after dinner, followed by an awake period of one or more hours in the middle of the night, followed by a second period of four or five hours of sleep. That middle-of-the-night waking might have evolved to help ward off nocturnal predators. Bimodal sleep appears to be a biological norm that was subverted by the invention of artificial light, and there is scientific evidence that the bimodal sleep-plus-nap regime is healthier and promotes greater life satisfaction, efficiency, and performance.

To many of us raised with the 6–8 hour, no-nap sleep ideal, this sounds like a bunch of hippie-dippy, flaky foolishness at the fringe of quackery. But it was discovered (or rediscovered, you might say) by Thomas Wehr, a respected scientist at the U.S. National Institute of Mental Health. In a landmark study, he enlisted research participants to live for a month in a room that was dark for fourteen hours a day, mimicking conditions before the invention of the lightbulb. Left to their own devices, they ended up sleeping eight hours a night but in two separate blocks. They tended to fall asleep one or two hours after the room went dark, slept for about four hours, stayed awake for an hour or two, and then slept for another four hours.

Millions of people report difficulty sleeping straight through the night. Because uninterrupted sleep appears to be our cultural norm, they experience great distress and ask their doctors for medication to help them stay asleep. Many sleep medications are addictive, have side effects, and leave people feeling drowsy the next morning. They also interfere with memory consolidation. It may be that a simple change in our expectations about sleep and a change to our schedules can go a long way.

There are large individual differences in sleep cycles. Some people fall asleep in a few minutes, others take an hour or more at night. Both are considered within the normal range of human behavior—what is important is what is normal for you, and to notice if there is a sudden change in your pattern that could indicate disease or disorder. Regardless of whether you sleep straight through the night or adopt the ancient bimodal sleep pattern, how much sleep should you get? Rough guidelines from research suggest the following, but these are just averages—some individuals really do require more or less than what is indicated, and this appears to be hereditary. Contrary to popular myth, the elderly do not need less sleep; they are just less able to sleep for eight hours at a stretch.

AVERAGE SLEEP NEEDS

Age	**Needed sleep**
Newborns (0–2 months)	12–18 hours
Infants (3–11 months)	14–15 hours
Toddlers (1–3 years)	12–14 hours
Preschoolers (3–5 years)	11–13 hours
Children (5–10 years)	10–11 hours
Preteens and Teenagers (10–17)	8 1/2–9 1/4 hours
Adults	6–10 hours

One out of every three working Americans gets less than six hours' sleep per night, well below the recommended range noted above. The U.S. Centers for Disease Control and Prevention (CDC) declared sleep deprivation a public health epidemic in 2013.

The prevailing view until the 1990s was that people could adapt to chronic sleep loss without adverse cognitive effects, but newer research clearly says otherwise. Sleepiness was responsible for 250,000 traffic accidents in 2009, and is one of the leading causes of friendly fire—soldiers mistakenly shooting people on their own side. Sleep deprivation was ruled to be a contributing factor in some of the most well-known global disasters: the nuclear power plant disasters at Chernobyl (Ukraine), Three Mile Island (Pennsylvania), Davis-Besse (Ohio), and Rancho Seco (California); the oil spill from the *Exxon Valdez;* the grounding of the cruise ship *Star Princess;* and the fatal decision to launch the *Challenger* space shuttle. Remember that Air France plane that crashed into the Atlantic Ocean in June 2009, killing all 288 people on board? The captain had been running on only one hour of sleep, and the copilots were also sleep deprived.

In addition to loss of life, there is the economic impact. Sleep deprivation is estimated to cost U.S. businesses more than $150 billion a year in absences, accidents, and lost productivity—for comparison, that's roughly the same as the annual revenue of Apple Corporation. If sleep-related economic losses were a business, it would be the sixth-largest business in the country. It's also associated with increased risk for heart disease, obesity, stroke, and cancer. Too much sleep is also detrimental, but perhaps the most important factor in achieving peak alertness is consistency, so that the body's circadian rhythms can lock into a consistent cycle. Going to bed just one hour late one night, or sleeping in for an hour or two just one morning, can affect your productivity, immune function, and mood significantly for several days after the irregularity.

Part of the problem is cultural—our society does not value sleep. Sleep expert David K. Randall put it this way:

> While we'll spend thousands on lavish vacations to unwind, grind away hours exercising and pay exorbitant amounts for organic food, sleep remains ingrained in our cultural ethos as something that can be put off, dosed or ignored. We can't look at sleep as an

investment in our health because—after all—it's just sleep. It is hard to feel like you're taking an active step to improve your life with your head on a pillow.

Many of us substitute drugs for good sleep—an extra cup of coffee to take the place of that lost hour or two of sleep, and a sleeping pill if all that daytime caffeine makes it hard to fall asleep at night. It is true that caffeine enhances cognitive function, but it works best when you've been maintaining a consistent sleep pattern over many days and weeks; as a substitute for lost sleep, it may keep you awake, but it will not keep you alert or performing at peak ability. Sleeping pills have been shown to be counterproductive to both sleep and productivity. In one study, cognitive behavior therapy—a set of practices to change thought and behavior patterns—was found to be significantly more effective than the prescription drug Ambien in combating insomnia. In another study, sleeping pills allowed people on average to sleep only eleven minutes longer. More relevant, the quality of sleep with sleeping pills is poor, disrupting the normal brain waves of sleep, and there is usually a sleeping pill hangover of dulled alertness the next morning. Because medication-induced sleep quality is poor, memory consolidation is affected, so we experience short-term memory loss—we don't remember that we didn't get a good night's sleep, and we don't remember how groggy we were upon waking up.

One of the most powerful cues our body uses to regulate the sleep-wake cycle is light. Bright light in the morning signals the hypothalamus to release chemicals that help us wake up, such as orexin, cortisol, and adrenaline. For this reason, if you're having trouble sleeping, it's important to avoid bright lights right before bedtime, such as those from the TV or computer screen.

Here are some guidelines for a good night's sleep: Go to bed at the same time every night. Wake up at the same time every morning. Set an alarm clock if necessary. If you have to stay up late one night, still get up at your fixed time the next morning—in the short run, the consistency of your cycle is more important than the amount of sleep. Sleep in a cool, dark room. Cover your windows if necessary to keep out light.

What about those delicious afternoon stretches on the couch? There's a reason they feel so good: They're an important part of resetting worn-out neural circuits. People differ widely in their ability to take naps and in whether they find naps helpful. For those who do, they can play a large role in creativity, memory, and efficiency. Naps longer than about forty minutes can be counterproductive, though, causing sleep inertia. For many people, five or ten minutes is enough.

But you can't take naps just any old time—not all naps are created equal. Those little micronaps you take in between hitting the snooze button on your morning alarm? Those are counterproductive, giving you abnormal sleep that fails to settle into a normal brain wave pattern. Napping too close to bedtime can make it difficult or impossible to fall asleep at night.

In the United States, Great Britain, and Canada, napping tends to be frowned upon. We're aware that members of Latino cultures have their naps—siestas—and we consider this a cultural oddity, not for us. We try to fight it off by having another cup of coffee when the drowsiness overtakes us. The British have institutionalized this fighting-off with four o'clock teatime. But the benefits of napping are well established. Even five- or ten-minute "power naps" yield significant cognitive enhancement, improvement in memory, and increased productivity. And the more intellectual the work, the greater the payoff. Naps also allow for the recalibration of our emotional equilibrium—after being exposed to angry and frightening stimuli, a nap can turn around negative emotions and increase happiness. How does a nap do all that? By activating the limbic system, the brain's emotional center, and reducing levels of monoamines, naturally occurring neurotransmitters that are used in pill form to treat depression, anxiety, and schizophrenia. Napping has also been shown to reduce the incidence of cardiovascular disease, diabetes, stroke, and heart attacks. A number of companies now encourage their employees to take short naps—fifteen minutes is the corporate norm—and many companies have dedicated nap rooms with cots.

The emerging consensus is that sleep is not an all-or-nothing state. When we are tired, parts of our brain may be awake while other parts sleep, creating a kind of paradoxical mental state in which we think we're awake, but core neural circuits are off-line, dozing. One of the first neural clusters to go off-line in cases like these is memory, so even though you think you're awake, your memory system isn't. This causes failures of retrieval (what was that word again?) and failures of storage (I know you just introduced yourself, but I forgot what you said your name is).

Normally, our body establishes a circadian rhythm synchronized to the sunrise and sunset of our local time zone, largely based on cues from sunlight and, to a lesser degree, mealtimes. This rhythm is part of a biological clock in the hypothalamus that also helps to regulate core body temperature, appetite, alertness, and growth hormones. Jet lag occurs when that circadian cycle becomes desynchronized from the time zone you're in. This is partly due to the sunrise and sunset occurring at different times than your body clock expects, thus giving unexpected signals to the pineal gland. Jet lag is also due to our disrupting our circadian rhythm by waking, exercising, eating, and sleeping according to the new local time rather than to the home time our body clock is adjusted for. In general, the body clock is not easily shifted by external factors, and this resistance is what causes many of the difficulties associated with jet lag. These difficulties include clumsiness, fuzzy thinking, gastrointestinal problems, poor decision-making, and the most obvious one, being alert or sleepy at inappropriate times.

It's been only in the past 150 years that we've been able to jump across time zones, and we haven't evolved a way to adapt yet. Eastward travel is more difficult than westward because our body clock prefers a twenty-five-hour day. Therefore, we can more easily stay awake an extra hour than fall asleep an hour early. Westward travel finds us having to delay our bedtime, which is not so difficult to do. Eastward travel finds us arriving in a city where it's bedtime and we're not yet tired. Traveling east is difficult even for people who do it all the time. One study of nineteen Major League Baseball teams found a significant effect: Teams that had just traveled eastward gave up more than one run on average in every game. Olympians have shown significant deficits after traveling across time zones in either direction, including reductions in muscle strength and coordination.

As we age, resynchronizing the clock becomes more difficult, partly due to reductions in neuroplasticity. Individuals over the age of sixty have much greater difficulty with jet lag, especially on eastbound flights.

Aligning your body clock to the new environment requires a phase shift. It takes one day per time zone to shift. Advance or retard your body clock as many days before your trip as the number of time zones you'll be crossing. Before traveling east, get into sunlight early in the day. Before traveling west, avoid sunlight early by keeping the curtains drawn, and instead expose yourself to bright light in the evening, to simulate what would be late afternoon sun in your destination.

Once you're on the plane, if you're westbound, keep the overhead reading lamp on, even if it is your home bedtime. When you arrive in the western city, exercise lightly by taking a walk in the sun. That sunlight will delay the production of melatonin in your body. If you're on an eastbound plane, wear eye shades to cover your eyes two hours or so before sunset in your destination city, to acclimate yourself to the new "dark" time.

Some research suggests that taking melatonin, 3–5 milligrams, two to three hours before bedtime can be effective, but this is controversial, for other studies have found no benefit. No studies have examined the long-term effects of melatonin, and young people and pregnant women have been advised to avoid it entirely. Although it is sometimes marketed as a sleep aid, melatonin will not help you sleep if you have insomnia because, by bedtime, your body has already produced as much melatonin as it can use.

When We Procrastinate

Many highly successful people claim to have ADD, and some genuinely meet the clinical definition. One of them was Jake Eberts, a film producer whose works include *Chariots of Fire, Gandhi, Dances with Wolves, Driving Miss Daisy, A River Runs through It, The Killing Fields,* and *Chicken Run,* and whose films received sixty-six Oscar nominations and seventeen Oscar wins (he passed away in 2012). By his own admission, he had a short attention span and very little patience, and he was easily bored. But his powerful intellect found him graduating from McGill University at the age of twenty and leading the engineering team for the European company Air Liquide before earning his MBA from Harvard Business School at age twenty-five. Early on, Jake identified his chief weakness: a tendency to procrastinate. He is of course not alone in this, and it is not a problem unique to people with attention deficit disorder. To combat it, Jake adopted a strict policy of "do it now." If Jake had a number of calls to make or things to attend to piling up, he'd dive right in, even if it cut into leisure or socializing time. And he'd do the most unpleasant task—firing someone, haggling with an investor, paying bills—the first thing in the morning to get it out of the way. Following Mark Twain, Jake called it eating the frog: Do the most unpleasant task first thing in the morning when gumption is highest, because willpower depletes as the day moves on. (The other thing that kept Jake on track was that, like most executives, he had executive assistants. He didn't have to remember due dates or small items himself; he could just put a given task in "the Irene bucket" and his assistant, Irene, would take care of it.)

Procrastination is something that affects all of us to varying degrees. We rarely feel we're caught up on everything. There are chores to do around the house, thank-you notes to write, synchronizing and backing up of our computers and smartphones to do. Some of us are affected by procrastination only mildly, others severely. Across the whole spectrum, all procrastination can be seen as a failure of self-regulation, planning, impulse control, or a combination of all three. By definition, it involves delaying an activity, task, or decision that would help us to reach our goals. In its mildest form, we simply start things at a later time than we might have, and experience unneeded stress as a deadline looms closer and we have less and less time to finish. But it can lead to more problematic outcomes. Many people, for instance, delay seeing their doctors, during which time their condition can become so bad that treatment is no longer an option, or they put off writing wills, filling out medical directives, installing smoke detectors, taking out life insurance, or starting a retirement savings plan until it's too late.

The tendency to procrastinate has been found to be correlated with certain traits, lifestyles, and other factors. Although the effects are statistically significant, none of them is very large. Those who are younger and single (including divorced or separated) are slightly more likely to procrastinate. So are those with a Y chromosome—this could be why women are far more likely to graduate from college than men; they are less likely to procrastinate. As mentioned earlier, being outside in natural settings—parks, forests, the beach, the mountains, and the desert—replenishes self-regulatory mechanisms in the brain, and accordingly, living or spending time in nature, as opposed to urban environments, has been shown to reduce the tendency to procrastinate.

A related factor is what Cambridge University psychologist Jason Rentfrow calls selective migration—people are apt to move to places that they view as consistent with their personalities. Large urban centers are associated with a tendency to be better at critical thinking and creativity, but also with procrastination. This could be because there are so many things to do in a large urban center, or because the increased bombardment of sensory information reduces the ability to enter the daydreaming mode, the mode that replenishes the executive attention system. Is there a brain region implicated in procrastination? As a failure of self-regulation, planning, and impulse control, if you guessed the prefrontal cortex, you'd be right: Procrastination resembles some of the temporal planning deficits we saw following prefrontal damage, at the beginning of this chapter. The medical literature reports many cases of patients who suddenly developed procrastination after damage to this region of the brain.

Procrastination comes in two types. Some of us procrastinate in order to pursue restful activities—spending time in bed, watching TV—while others of us procrastinate certain difficult or unpleasant tasks in favor of those that are more fun or that yield an immediate reward. In this respect, the two types differ in activity level: The rest-seeking procrastinators would generally rather not be exerting themselves at all, while the fun-task procrastinators enjoy being busy and active all the time but just have a hard time starting things that are not so fun.

An additional factor has to do with delayed gratification, and individual differences in how people tolerate that. Many people work on projects that have a long event horizon—for example, academics, businesspeople, engineers, writers, housing contractors, and artists. That is, the thing they're working on can take weeks or months (or even years) to complete, and after completion, there can be a very long period of time before they get any reward, praise, or gratification. Many people in these professions enjoy hobbies such as gardening, playing a musical instrument, and cooking because those activities yield an immediate, tangible result—you can *see* the patch of your flower bed where you removed the weeds, you can *hear* the Chopin piece you've just played, and you can *taste* the rhubarb pie you just baked. In general, activities with a long time to completion—and hence a long time to reward—are the ones more likely to be started late, and those with an immediate reward are less likely to be procrastinated.

Piers Steel is an organizational psychologist, one of the world's foremost authorities on procrastination and a professor at the Haskayne School of Business at the University of Calgary. Steel says that two underlying factors lead us to procrastinate:

> Humans have a low tolerance for frustration. Moment by moment, when choosing what tasks to undertake or activities to pursue, we tend to choose not the most rewarding action but the easiest. This means that unpleasant or difficult things get put off.

We tend to evaluate our self-worth in terms of our achievements. Whether we lack self-confidence in general—or confidence that this particular project will turn out well—we procrastinate because that allows us to delay putting our reputations on the line until later. (This is what psychologists call an ego-protective maneuver.)

The low tolerance for frustration has neural underpinnings. Our limbic system and the parts of the brain that are seeking immediate rewards come into conflict with our prefrontal cortex, which all too well understands the consequences of falling behind. Both regions run on dopamine, but the dopamine has different actions in each. Dopamine in the prefrontal cortex causes us to focus and stay on task; dopamine in the limbic system, along with the brain's own endogenous opioids, causes us to feel pleasure. We put things off whenever the desire for immediate pleasure wins out over our ability to delay gratification, depending on which dopamine system is in control.

Steel identifies what he calls two faulty beliefs: first, that life should be easy, and second, that our self-worth is dependent on our success. He goes further, to build an equation that quantifies the likelihood that we'll procrastinate. If our self-confidence *and* the value of completing the task are both high, we're less likely to procrastinate. These two factors become the denominator of the procrastination equation. (They're in the denominator because they have an inverse relationship with procrastination—when they go up, procrastination goes down, and vice versa.) They are pitted against two other factors: how soon in time the reward will come, and how distractible we are. (Distractibility is seen as a combination of our need for immediate gratification, our level of impulsivity, and our ability to exercise self-control.) If the length of time it will take to complete the task is high, *or* our distractibility is high, this leads to an increase in procrastination.

$$\text{Procrastination} = \frac{\text{time to complete task} \times \text{distractibility}}{\text{self-confidence} \times \text{task value}}$$

To refine Steel's equation, I've added delay, the amount of time one has to wait to receive positive feedback for completion of the task. The greater the delay, the greater the likelihood of procrastination:

$$\text{Procrastination} = \frac{\text{time to complete task} \times \text{distractibility} \times \text{delay}}{\text{self-confidence} \times \text{task value}}$$

Certain behaviors may look like procrastination but arise due to different factors. Some individuals suffer from initiation deficits, an inability to get started. This problem is distinct from planning difficulties, in which individuals fail to begin tasks sufficiently early to complete them because they have unrealistic or naïve ideas about how long it will take to complete subgoals. Others may fail to accomplish tasks on time because they don't have the required objects or materials when they finally sit down to work. Both of these latter difficulties arise from a lack of planning, not from procrastination per se. On the other hand, some individuals may be attempting a challenging task with which they have no previous experience; they may simply not know where or how to begin. In these cases, having supervisors or teachers who can help them break up the problem into component parts is very helpful and often essential. Adopting a systematic, componential approach to assignments is effective in reducing this form of procrastination.

Finally, some individuals suffer from a chronic inability to finish projects they've started. This is not procrastination, because they don't put off *starting* projects; rather, they put off ending them. This can arise because the individual doesn't possess the skills necessary to properly complete the job with acceptable quality—many a home hobbyist or weekend carpenter can testify to this. It can also arise from an insidious perfectionism in which the individual has a deep, almost obsessive belief that their work products are never good enough (a kind of failure in satisficing). Graduate students tend to suffer from this kind of perfectionism, no doubt because they are comparing themselves with their advisors, and comparing their thesis drafts with their advisors' finished work. It is an unfair comparison of course. Their advisors have had more experience, and the advisor's setbacks, rejected manuscripts, and rough drafts are hidden from the graduate student's view—all the graduate student ever sees is the finished product and the gap between it and her own work. This is a classic example of the power of the *situation* being underappreciated in favor of an attribution about stable traits, and it shows up as well in the workplace. The supervisor's role virtually guarantees that she will appear smarter and more competent than the supervisee. The supervisor can choose to show the worker her own work when it is finished and polished. The worker has no opportunity for such self-serving displays and is often required to show work at draft and interim stages, effectively guaranteeing that the worker's product won't measure up, thus leaving many underlings with the feeling they aren't good enough. But these situational constraints are not as predictive of ability as students and other supervisees make them out to be. Understanding this cognitive illusion can encourage individuals to be less self-critical and, hopefully, to emancipate themselves from the stranglehold of perfectionism.

Also important is to disconnect one's sense of self-worth from the outcome of a task. Self-confidence entails accepting that you might fail early on and that it's OK, it's all part of the process. The writer and polymath George Plimpton noted that successful people have paradoxically had many more failures than people whom most of us would consider to be, well, *failures.* If this sounds like double-talk or mumbo jumbo, the resolution of the paradox is that successful people (or people who eventually become successful) deal with failures and setbacks very differently from everyone else. The unsuccessful person interprets the failure or setback as a career breaker and concludes, "I'm no good at this." The successful person sees each setback as an opportunity to gain whatever additional knowledge is necessary to accomplish her goals. The internal dialogue of a successful (or eventually successful) person is more along the lines of "I thought I knew everything I needed to know to achieve my goals, but this has taught me that I don't. Once I learn this, I can get back on track." The kinds of people who become successful typically know that they can expect a rocky road ahead and it doesn't dissuade them when those bumps knock them off kilter—it's all part of the process. As Piers Steel would say, they don't subscribe to the faulty belief that life should be easy.

The frontal lobes play a role in one's resilience to setbacks. Two subregions involved in self-assessment and judging one's own performance are the dorsolateral prefrontal cortex and the orbital cortex. When they are overactive, we tend to judge ourselves harshly. In fact, jazz musicians need to turn *off* these regions while improvising, in order to freely create new ideas without the nagging self-assessment that their ideas are not good enough. When these regions are damaged, they can produce a kind of hyperresilience. Prior to damage, one patient was unable to get through a standard battery of test problems without weeping, even after correctly completing them. After the damage to the prefrontal cortex, she was utterly unable to complete the same problems, but her attitude differed markedly: She would continue to try the problems over and over again, beyond the patience of the examiner, making mistake after mistake without the least indication of embarrassment or frustration.

Reading the biographies of great leaders—corporate CEOs, generals, presidents—the sheer number and magnitude of failures many have experienced is staggering. Few thought that Richard Nixon would recover from his embarrassing defeat in the 1962 California gubernatorial election. ("You won't have Nixon to kick around anymore.") Thomas Edison had more than one thousand inventions that were unsuccessful, compared to only a small number that were successful. But the successful ones were wildly influential: the lightbulb, phonograph, and motion picture camera. Billionaire Donald Trump has had as many high-profile failures as successes: dead-end business ventures like Trump Vodka, *Trump* magazine, Trump Airlines, and Trump Mortgage, four bankruptcies, and a failed presidential bid. He is a controversial figure, but he has demonstrated resilience and has never let business failures reduce his self-confidence. Too much self-confidence of course is not a good thing, and there can be an inner tug-of-war between self-confidence and arrogance that can, in some cases, lead to full-scale psychological disorders.

Self-confidence appears to have a genetic basis, and is a trait that is relatively stable across the life span, although like any trait, different situations can trigger different responses in the individual, and environmental factors can either build up or chip away at it. One effective strategy is *acting as if.* In other words, even those who lack an inner sense of self-confidence can act as if they are self-confident by not giving up, working hard at tasks that seem difficult, and trying to reverse temporary setbacks. This can form a positive feedback loop wherein the additional effort actually results in success and helps to gradually build up the person's sense of agency and competence.

Creative Time

Here's a puzzle: What word can be joined to all of these to create three new compound words?

crab *sauce* *pine*

Most people try to focus on the words intently and come up with a solution. Most of them fail. But if they start to think of something else and let their mind wander, the solution comes in a flash of insight. (The answer is in the *Notes* section.) How does this happen?

Part of the answer has to do with how comfortable we are in allowing ourselves to enter the daydreaming mode under pressure of time. Most people say that when they're in that mode, time seems to stop, or it feels that they have stepped outside of time. Creativity involves the skillful integration of this time-stopping daydreaming mode and the time-monitoring central executive mode. When we think about our lives as a whole, one theme that comes up over and over is whether we feel we made any contributions with our lives, and it is usually the creative contributions, in the broadest sense, that we're most proud of. In the television series *House*, Wilson is dying of cancer, with only five months to live. Knowing he's going to die, he implores Dr. House, "I need you to tell me that my life was worthwhile." We learn that his sense of his life's worth comes from having effected new and creative solutions for dozens of patients who wouldn't otherwise be alive.

Achieving insight across a wide variety of problems—not just word problems but interpersonal conflicts, medical treatments, chess games, and music composition, for example—typically follows a pattern. We focus all our attention on the aspects of the problem as it is presented, or as we understand it, combing through different possible solutions and scenarios with our left prefrontal cortex and anterior cingulate. But this is merely a preparatory phase, lining up what we know about a problem. If the problem is sufficiently complex or tricky, what we already know won't be enough. In a second phase, we need to relax, let go of the problem, and let networks in the right hemisphere take over. Neurons in the right hemisphere are more broadly tuned, with longer branches and more dendritic spines—they are able to collect information from a larger area of cortical space than left hemisphere neurons, and although they are less precise, they are better connected. When the brain is searching for an insight, these are the cells most likely to produce it. The second or so preceding insight is accompanied by a burst of gamma waves, which bind together disparate neural networks, effectively binding thoughts that were seemingly unrelated into a coherent new whole. For all this to work, the relaxation phase is crucial.

That's why so many insights happen during warm showers. Teachers and coaches always say to relax. This is why.

If you're engaged in any kind of creative pursuit, one of the goals in organizing your time is probably to maximize your creativity. We've all had the experience of getting wonderfully, blissfully lost in an activity, losing all track of time, of ourselves, our problems. We forget to eat, forget that there is a world of cell phones, deadlines, and other obligations. Abraham Maslow called these peak experiences in the 1950s, and more recently the psychologist Mihaly Csikszentmihalyi (pronounced MEE-high, CHEECH-sent-mee-high) has famously called this the flow state. It feels like a completely different state of being, a state of heightened awareness coupled with feelings of well-being and contentment. It's a neurochemically and neuroanatomically distinct state as well. Across individuals, flow states appear to activate the same regions of the brain, including the left prefrontal cortex (specifically, areas 44, 45, and 47) and the basal ganglia. During flow, two key regions of the brain *deactivate:* the portion of the prefrontal cortex responsible for self-criticism, and the amygdala, the brain's fear center. This is why creative artists often report feeling fearless and as though they are taking creative risks they hadn't taken before—it's because the two parts of their brain that would otherwise prevent them from doing so have significantly reduced activity.

People experience flow in many kinds of work, from looking at the tiniest cells to exploring the largest scales of the universe. Cell biologist Joseph Gall described flow looking through a microscope; astronomers describe it looking through telescopes. Similar flow states are described by musicians, painters, computer programmers, tile setters, writers, scientists, public speakers, surgeons, and Olympic athletes. People experience it playing chess, writing poetry, rock climbing, and disco dancing. And almost without exception, the flow state is when one does his or her best work, in fact, work that is above and beyond what one normally thinks of as his or her best.

During the flow state, attention is focused on a limited perceptual field, and that field receives your full concentration and complete investment. Action and awareness merge. You cease thinking about yourself as separate from the activity or the world, and you don't think of your actions and your perceptions as being distinct—what you *think* becomes what you *do*. There are psychological aspects as well. During flow, you experience freedom from worry about failure; you are aware of what needs to be done, but you don't feel that *you* are doing it—the ego is not involved and falls away completely. Rosanne Cash described writing some of her best songs in this state. "It didn't feel like *I* was writing it. It was more like, the song was already there and I just had to hold up my catcher's mitt and grab it out of the air." Parthenon Huxley, a lead vocalist for The Orchestra (the current incarnation of the British band ELO) recalled a concert they played in Mexico City. "I opened my mouth to sing and all kinds of fluidity was there—I couldn't believe the notes that were coming out of my mouth, couldn't believe it was me."

Flow can occur during either the planning or the execution phase of an activity, but it is most often associated with the execution of a complex task, such as playing a trombone solo, writing an essay, or shooting baskets. Because flow is such a focused state, you might think that it involves staying inside either the planning phase or the execution phase, but in fact it usually allows for the seamless integration of them—what are normally separate tasks, boss and worker tasks, become permeable, interrelated tasks that are part of the same gesture. One thing that characterizes flow is a lack of distractibility—the same old distractions are there, but we're not tempted to attend to them. A second characteristic of flow is that we monitor our performance without the kinds of self-defeating negative judgments that often accompany creative work. Outside of flow, a nagging voice inside our heads often says, "That's not good enough." In flow, a reassuring voice says, "I can fix that."

Flow states don't occur for just any old task or activity. They can occur only when one is deeply focused on the task, when the task requires intense concentration and commitment, contains clear goals, provides immediate feedback, and is perfectly matched to one's skill level. This last point requires that your own skills and abilities are matched in a particular way to the level of difficulty before you. If the task you are engaged in is too simple, holding no challenge, you'll get bored. That boredom will break your attention to the task, and your mind will wander into the default mode. If the task is too difficult and holds too many challenges, you'll become frustrated and experience anxiety. The frustration and anxiety will also break your attention. It's when the challenge is just right for you—given your own particular set of skills—that you have a chance of reaching flow. There's no guarantee that you will, but if this condition isn't met, if the challenge isn't just right for you, it surely won't happen.

In the graph below, challenge is shown on the y-axis, and you can see that high challenge leads to anxiety and low challenge to boredom. Right in the middle is the area where flow is possible. The funnel shape of the flow region is related to the level of your own acquired skills, running along the x-axis. What this shows is that the greater your skills, the greater the opportunity to achieve flow. If you have low skill, the challenge window opening is small; if you have high skill, there is a much wider range of possibility for you to achieve flow. This is because the flow state is characterized by a total lack of conscious awareness, a merging of your self with the project itself, a seamless melding of thought, action, movement, and result. The higher your skill level, the more easily you can practice those skills automatically, subconsciously, and then the more easily you can disengage your conscious mind, your ego, and other enemies of flow. Flow states occur more regularly for those who are experts or who have invested a great deal of time to train in a given domain.

Engagement is what flow is defined by—high, high levels of engagement. Information access and processing seem effortless—facts that we need are at our fingertips, even long-lost ones we didn't know we knew; skills we didn't know we had begin to emerge. With no need to exercise self-control to stay focused, we free neural resources to the task at hand. And this is where something paradoxical occurs in the brain. During flow states, we

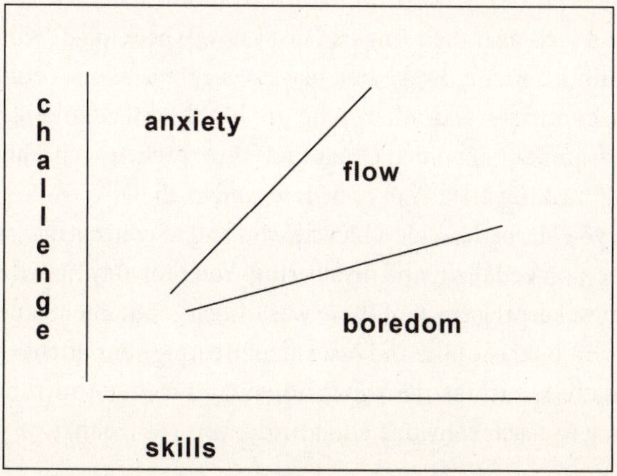

no longer need to exert ourselves to stay on task—it happens automatically as we enter this specialized attentional state. It takes less energy to be in flow—in a peak of creative engagement—than to be distracted. This is why flow states are periods of great productivity and efficiency.

Flow is a chemically different state as well, involving a particular neurochemical soup that has not yet been identified. It appears there needs to be a balance of dopamine and noradrenaline, particularly as they are modulated in a brain region known as the striatum (seat of the attentional switch), serotonin (for freedom to access stream-of-consciousness associations), and adrenaline (to stay focused and energized). GABA neurons (sensitive to gamma-Aminobutyric acid) that normally function to inhibit actions and help us to exercise self-control need to reduce their activity so that we aren't overly critical of ourselves in these states and so that we become less inhibited in the production of ideas. Finally, some of the processes involved in homeostasis, particularly sexual drive, hunger, and thirst, need to be reduced so that we're not distracted by bodily functions. In very high flow states, we lose complete awareness of our environment. Csikszentmihalyi notes one case in which the roof fell in during an operation and the surgeon didn't notice it until after the operation was over.

Flow occurs when you are not explicitly thinking about what you're doing; rather, your brain is in a special mode of activity in which procedures and operations are performed automatically without your having to exert conscious control. This is why practice and expertise are prerequisites for flow. Musicians who have learned their scales can play them without explicitly concentrating on them, based on motor memory. Indeed, they report that it feels as if their fingers "just know where to go" without their having to think about it. Basketball players, airplane pilots, computer programmers, gymnasts, and others who are highly skilled and highly practiced report similar phenomena, that they have reached such a high level of ability that thinking seems not to be involved at all.

When you learned to ride a bicycle, you had to concentrate on keeping your balance, on pedaling, and on steering. You probably tipped over a few times because keeping track of these was difficult. But after some practice, you could climb on the bike and just ride, directing your attention to more pleasant matters, such as the view and your immediate surroundings. If you then try to teach someone *else* to ride, you realize that very much of what you know is not available to conscious introspection or description. Circuits in the brain have become somewhat autonomous in carrying it out and they don't require direction from the central executive system in your prefrontal cortex. We just press START in our brain, and the bike-riding sequence takes over. People report similar automaticity with tying their shoes, driving a car, and even solving differential equations.

We all have brain programs like these. But trying to think about what you're doing can quickly interfere, ending the automaticity and high performance level you've enjoyed. The easiest way to get someone to fall off a bicycle is to ask him to concentrate on how he's staying up, or to describe what he's doing. The great tennis player John McEnroe used this to his advantage on the courts. When an opponent was performing especially well, for example by using a particularly good backhand, McEnroe would compliment him on it. McEnroe knew this would cause the opponent to think about his backhand, and this thinking disrupted the automatic application of it.

Flow is not always good; it can be disruptive when it becomes an addiction, and it is socially disruptive if flow-ers withdraw from others and stay in their own cocoon. Jeannette Walls, in *The Glass Castle,* describes her mother being so absorbed in painting that she would ignore her hungry children's cries for food. Three-year-old Jeannette accidentally set herself on fire while standing on a chair in front of the stove, attempting to cook hot dogs in a boiling pot while her artist mother was absorbed in painting. Even after Jeannette returned from six weeks in the hospital, her mother couldn't be bothered to step outside the flow she was in while painting, to cook for the child.

Creative people often arrange their lives to maximize the possibility that flow periods will occur, and to be able to stay in flow once they arrive there. The singer and songwriter Neil Young described it best. Wherever he is, no matter what he is doing, if a song idea comes to him, he "checks out" and stops doing whatever he is doing and creates the time and space then and there to work on the song. He pulls over to the side of the road, abruptly leaves dinner parties, and does whatever it takes to stay connected to the muse, to stay on task. If he ends up getting a reputation for being flaky, and not always being on time, it's the price to pay for being creative.

It seems, then, that in some respects, creativity and conscientiousness are incompatible. If you want to indulge your creative side, it means you can't also be punctilious about keeping appointments. Of course, one could counter that Neil is being exceptionally conscientious about his art and giving *it* all he's got. It's not a lack of conscientiousness; it's just that his conscientiousness serves a different priority.

Stevie Wonder practices the same kind of self-imposed separation from the world to nourish his creativity. He described it in terms of emotion—when he feels a groundswell of emotion inside him upon learning of tragic news or spending time with someone he loves, for example—he goes with it, stays in the emotional experience, and doesn't allow himself to become distracted, even if it means missing an appointment. If he can write a song about the emotion at that moment, he does; otherwise, he tries later to fully immerse himself in that same emotional state so that it will infuse the song. (He also has a poor reputation for being on time.)

Sting organizes and partitions his time to maximize creative engagement. On tours, his time is well structured by others to give him maximum freedom. He doesn't need to think about anything at all except music. Where he has to be, what he has to do, when he eats, all these parts of the day are completely scheduled for him. Importantly, he has a few hours of personal time every day that is sacrosanct. Everyone knows not to interrupt him then, and he knows that there is nothing pressing or more important to do than to use the time for creative and creativity-restoring acts. He'll use the time for yoga, songwriting, reading, and practicing. By combining his exceptional self-discipline and focus with a world in which distractions have been dramatically reduced, he can more easily become absorbed in creative pursuits. Sting also did something interesting to help him handle the disorienting (and creativity-crushing) effects of travel. Working closely with an interior designer, he found curtains, pillows, rugs, and other decorative objects that resemble in style, color, and texture those he enjoys at home. Every day on the road, his tour staff create a virtual room out of interlocking aluminum poles and curtains, a private space inside the concert venue that is exactly the same from city to city so there is a great deal of comfort and continuity in the midst of all the change. This promotes a calm and distraction-free state of mind. There's a fundamental principle of neuroscience behind this: As we noted earlier, the brain is a giant change detector. Most of us are easily distracted by newness, the prefrontal cortex's novelty bias. We can help ourselves by molding our environments and our schedules to facilitate and promote creative inspiration. Because his senses aren't being bombarded daily by new sights, colors, and spatial arrangements—at least during his four-hour personal time—Sting can let his brain and his mind relax and more easily achieve a flow state.

There's an old saying that if you really need to get something done, give it to a busy person. It sounds paradoxical, but busy people tend to have systems for getting things done efficiently, and the purpose of this section is to uncover what those systems are. Even inveterate procrastinators benefit from having more to do—they'll dive into a task that is more appealing than the one they're trying to avoid, and make great progress on a large number of projects. Procrastinators seldom do absolutely nothing. Robert Benchley, the *Vanity Fair* and *New Yorker* writer, wrote that he managed to build a bookshelf and pore through a pile of scientific articles when an article was due.

A large part of efficient time management revolves around avoiding distractions. An ironic aspect of life is how easily we can be harmed by the things we desire. Fish are seduced by a fisherman's lure, a mouse by cheese. But at least these objects of desire look like sustenance. This is seldom the case for us. The temptations that can disrupt our lives are often pure indulgences. None of us needs to gamble, or drink alcohol, read e-mail, or compulsively check social networking feeds to survive. Realizing when a diversion has gotten out of control is one of the great challenges of life.

Anything that tempts us to break the extended concentration required to perform well on challenging tasks is a potential barrier to success. The change and novelty centers in your brain also feed you chemical rewards when you complete tasks, no matter how trivial. The social networking addiction loop, whether it's Facebook, Twitter, Vine, Instagram, Snapchat, Tumblr, Pinterest, e-mail, texting, or whatever new thing will be adopted in the coming years, sends chemicals through the brain's pleasure center that are genuinely, physiologically addicting. The greatest life satisfaction comes from completing projects that required sustained focus and energy. It seems unlikely that anyone will look back at their lives with pride and say with satisfaction that they managed to send an extra thousand text messages or check social network updates a few hundred extra times while they were working.

To successfully ignore distractions, we have to trick ourselves, or create systems that will encourage us to stick with the work at hand. The two kinds of distractions we need to deal with are external—those caused by things in the world that beckon us—and internal—those caused by our mind wandering back to the default daydreaming mode.

For external distractions, the strategies already mentioned apply. Set aside a particular time of day to work, with the phone turned off and your e-mail and browser shut down. Set aside a particular place to work that allows you to focus. Make it a policy to not respond to missives that come in during your productivity time. Adopt the mental set that this thing you're doing now is the most important thing you could be doing. Remember the story of presidential candidate Jimmy Carter in Chapter 1—his aides managed time and space for him. They evaluated, in real time, whether the greatest value would be gained by continuing to talk to the person in front of him or someone else who was waiting, whether he should be here or there. This allowed Carter to let go of his time-bound cares completely, to live in the moment and attend one hundred percent to the person in front of him. Similarly, executive assistants often schedule the time of their bosses so that the boss knows that whatever is in front of her is *the* most important thing she could be doing right now. She doesn't need to worry about projects or tasks that are going unattended, because the assistant is keeping track of them for her. This is similar to the situation described above with construction workers: Great productivity and increased quality result if the person doing the work and the person scheduling or supervising the work are not the same person.

For those of us without executive assistants, we have to rely on our own wits, and on the prefrontal cortex's central executive.

To combat internal distractions, the most effective thing you can do is the mind-clearing exercise I wrote about in Chapter 3. Difficult tasks benefit from a sustained period of concentration of fifty minutes or more, due to the amount of time it takes your brain to settle into and maintain a focused state. The best time-management technique is to ensure you have captured every single thing that has your attention, or should have your attention, by writing it down. The goal is to get projects and situations off your mind but not to lose any potentially useful ideas—externalizing your frontal lobes. Then you can step back and look at your list from an observer standpoint and not let yourself be driven by what's the latest and loudest in your head.

Taking breaks is also important. Experts recommend getting up to walk around at least once every ninety minutes, and scheduling daily physical activity. By now, even the most vegetative, TV-bingeing couch potatoes among us have heard that daily exercise is important. We try to tell ourselves that we're doing just fine, our pants still fit (sort of), and all this physical fitness stuff is overrated. But actuarial and epidemiological studies show unquestionably that physical activity is strongly related to the prevention of several chronic diseases and premature death, and enhances the immune system's ability to detect and fend off certain types of cancer. And although twenty years ago, the recommendations were for the sort of vigorous activity that few people over the age of forty-five are motivated to undertake, current findings suggest that even moderate activity such as brisk walking for thirty minutes, five days a week, will yield significant effects. Older adults (fifty-five to eighty) who walked for forty minutes three days a week showed significant increases in the size of their hippocampus, enhancing memory. Exercise has also been shown to prevent age-related cognitive decline by increasing blood flow to the brain, causing increases in the size of the prefrontal cortex and improvements in executive control, memory, and critical thinking.

There is one mistake that many of us make when we have a looming deadline for a big project, a project that is very important and will take many many hours or days or weeks to complete. The tendency is to put everything else on hold and devote all our time to that big project—it seems as though every minute counts. But doing this means that lots of little tasks will go undone, only to pile up and create problems for you later. You know you should be attending to them, a little voice in your head or entry on your To Do list nags at you; it takes a great deal of conscious effort to *not* do them. This carries a tangible psychological strain as your brain keeps trying to tamp them down in your consciousness, and you end up using more mental energy to *not* do them than you would have used to do them.

The solution is to follow the *five-minute rule*. If there is something you can get done in five minutes or less, do it now. If you have twenty things that would only take five minute each, but you can spare only thirty minutes now, prioritize them and do the others later or tomorrow, or delegate them. The point is that things you can deal with now are better off being dealt with, rather than letting them accumulate. A good tip is to set aside some time each day to deal with such things—whether it's picking up clothes off the floor, making an unpleasant phone call, or giving a quick response to an e-mail. If this seems to contradict the discussion above, about not allowing yourself to get distracted by unimportant tasks, note the critical distinction: I'm proposing here that you set aside a designated block of time to deal with all these little things; don't intersperse them within a block of time you've set aside to focus on a single, large project.

One thing that many successful people do for time management is to calculate how much their time is subjectively worth to them. This is not necessarily what it is worth in the marketplace, or what their hourly pay works out to, although it might be informed by these—this is how much they feel their time is worth to them. When deciding, for example, whether to steam clean your carpets or hire someone to do it, you might take into account what else you could be doing with your time. If a free weekend day is rare, and you are really looking forward to spending it bicycling with friends, or going to a party, you may well decide that it's worth it to pay someone else to do it. Or if you're a consultant or attorney earning upward of $300 an hour, spending $100 to join one of those priority services that bypasses the long line at airport security seems well worth it.

If you calculate what your time is worth to you, it simplifies a great deal of decision-making because you don't have to reassess each individual situation. You just follow your rule: "If I can spend $XX and save an hour of my time, it is worth it." Of course this assumes that the activity is something you don't find pleasurable. If you like steam-cleaning carpets and standing in airport lines, then the calculation doesn't work. But for tasks or chores about which you are indifferent, having a time-value rule of thumb is very helpful.

Related to knowing how much your time is worth is the following rule: Do not spend more time on a decision than it's worth. Imagine you're clothes shopping and find a shirt you particularly like, and it is just at the limit of what you decided you'd spend. The salesperson comes over and shows you another shirt that you like just as much. Here, you're willing to invest a certain amount of time trying to choose between the two because you have a limited amount of money. If the salesperson offers to throw in the second shirt for only five dollars more, you'll probably jump at the chance to buy both because, at that point—with a small amount of money at stake—agonizing over the decision isn't worth the time.

David Lavin, a former chess champion and now president of the international speakers agency bearing his name, articulates it this way: "A colleague once complained 'you made a decision without having all the facts!' Well, getting all the facts would take me an hour and the amount of income at stake means that this decision is only worth ten minutes of my time."

Time management also requires structuring your future with reminders. That is, one of the secrets to managing time in the present is to anticipate future needs so that you're not left scrambling and playing catch-up all the time. Linda (whom we met in Chapter 3), the executive assistant for the president of a $20 billion Fortune 100 company, describes how she managed the executive offices, and in particular her boss's schedule, his assignments, and his To Do list. She is among the most efficient and most organized people I've ever met.

"I use a lot of abeyance or *tickler files,*" Linda says, things that remind her about some future obligation well in advance. The tickler file is either a physical file on her desk or, increasingly, an alert on her calendar. "I use the calendar as the primary way to organize my boss's schedule. I use it for my own schedule, too. When I come in in the morning, the calendar tells me what needs to be done today, as well as what future things we need to be thinking about today.

"If a new project comes across his desk, I find out how long he thinks he'll need to complete it, and when it is due. Say he thinks he needs two weeks to do it. I'll set a tickler, a reminder in the calendar three weeks before it's due—that's a week before the two weeks he needs to do it—so that he can start thinking about it and know that it's coming up. Then another tickler on the day he's supposed to start working on it, and ticklers every day to make sure he's doing it.

"Of course many of his projects require input from other people, or have components that other people need to provide. I sit down with him and he tells me who else will contribute to the project, and when he needs to have their input by, in order for him to make his deadline. I make reminders on the calendar to contact all of them."

For all this to work, it's important to put *everything* in the calendar, not just some things. The reason is simple: If you see a blank spot on the calendar, you and anyone else looking at it would reasonably assume that the time is available. You can't just *partially* use a calendar, keeping some of your appointments in your head—that's a recipe for double booking and missed appointments. The best strategy is to enter events, notes, and reminders in the calendar as soon as they come up or, alternatively, gather all of your calendar entries on index cards or slips of paper and set aside one or two times each day to update your calendar en masse.

Linda says that she prints out every calendar entry on paper as well, in case the computer goes down for some reason, or crashes. She maintains multiple calendars: one that her boss sees and one that is just for her to see—hers includes reminders to herself that she doesn't need to bother him with—and she also keeps separate calendars for her personal business (unrelated to work) and for key people with whom her boss interacts.

Linda also uses the calendar to organize things that need to be done prior to an appointment. "If it's a medical appointment and there are things required in advance of the appointment—tests, for example—I find out how long it takes for the test results to come in, and then put in a reminder to get the tests done well in advance of the actual medical appointment. Or if it's a meeting and certain documents need to be reviewed in advance of the meeting, I figure out how long they'll take to read and schedule time in the calendar for that." These days, most computer calendars can synchronize with the calendar on an Android, iPhone, BlackBerry, or other smartphone, so that every reminder or some selected subset of them also shows up on the phone.

Special dates become part of the calendar, along with tickler files in advance of those dates. "Birthdays go on the calendar," Linda says, "with a tickler a week or two in advance to remind us to buy a present or send a card. Actually, any social event or business meeting that will require a gift gets two calendar entries—one for the event itself and one in advance so that there's time to select a gift."

Of course, there are things you want to spend time on, but just not now. Remembering to complete time-sensitive tasks and doing them at the most convenient times is becoming easier, because externalizing them is becoming easier. Some programs allow you to compose an e-mail or text message but send it at a later date—this works effectively as a tickler file: You compose an e-mail or text on the day you're thinking about it, to remind you on a particular day in the future that you need to do something or start working on a project. Work flow apps such as Asana allow you to do the same thing, with the option of tagging coworkers and friends if you're engaged in a joint project that requires input from others. Asana then automatically sends e-mails to remind people when and what needs to be done.

As a time-saver, cognitive psychologist Stephen Kosslyn recommends that if you are not the kind of person who overspends—that is, if you know you can live within your means—stop balancing your checkbook. Banks seldom make errors anymore, he notes, and the average size of the error is likely to be minuscule compared to the hours you'll spend squaring every purchase. He advises to go over the statement quickly to identify any unauthorized charges, then file it and be done with it. If you set up automatic overdraft protection, you don't need to worry about checks bouncing. Second, set up automatic bill payments for every recurring bill: your Visa card, cell phone, electric bill, mortgage. The hours a month you used to spend paying bills is free time gained.

Life Time

As people grow older, they frequently say that time seems to pass more quickly than when they were younger. There are several hypotheses about this. One is that our perception of time is nonlinear and is based on the amount of time we've already lived. A year in the life of a four-year-old represents a larger proportion of the time she's already been alive than it does for a forty-year-old. Experiments suggest that the formula for calculating subjective time is a power function, and the equation states that the passing of a year should seem twice as long for a ten-year-old than for a forty-year-old. You may recall trying to be still for an entire minute as a child, and now a minute goes by very quickly.

Another factor is that after the age of thirty, our reaction time, cognitive processing speed, and metabolic rate slow down—the actual speed of neural transmission slows. This leaves the impression that the world is racing by, relative to our slowed-down thought processes.

The way we choose to fill our time naturally changes across the life span as well. When we're young, we are driven by novelty and motivated to learn and experience new things. Our teens and twenties can be seen as a time when we want to learn as much about ourselves and the world as possible, so that we can come to know, out of an infinity of possibilities, what we like and how we'd like to spend our time. Am I someone who likes parachuting? Martial arts? Modern jazz? As we get older and approach our fifties and sixties, most of us place a higher priority on actually *doing* the things we already know we like rather than trying to discover new things we like. (Individuals vary tremendously of course; some older people are more interested in new experiences than others.)

These different views of how we want to spend time are partly fueled by how much time we feel we have left. When time is perceived as open-ended, the goals that become most highly prioritized are those that are preparatory, focused on gathering information, on experiencing novelty, and on expanding one's breadth of knowledge. When time is perceived as constrained, the highest-priority goals will be those that can be realized in the short-term and that provide emotional meaning, such as spending time with family and friends. And although it's well documented that older people tend to have smaller social networks and reduced interests, and are less drawn to novelty than younger people, the older people are just as happy as the younger ones—they've found what they like and they spend their time doing it. Research shows clearly that this is *not* due to aging per se but to a sense of time running out. Tell a twenty-year-old that he has only five years left to live and he tends to become more like a seventy-five-year-old—not particularly interested in new experiences, instead favoring spending time with family and friends and taking time for familiar pleasures. It turns out that young people with terminal diseases tend to view the world more like old people. There's a certain logic to this based on risk assessment: If you have a limited number of meals left, for example, why would you order a completely new dish you've never tried before, running the risk that you'll hate it, when you can order something you know you like? Indeed, prisoners on death row tend to ask for familiar foods for their last meals: pizza, fried chicken, and burgers, not crêpes suzette or cassoulet de canard. (At least American prisoners. There are no data on what French prisoners requested. France abolished the death penalty in 1981.)

A related difference in time perception is driven by differences in attention and emotional memory. Older adults show a special preference for emotionally positive memories over emotionally negative memories, while younger adults show the opposite. This makes sense because it has long been known that younger people find negative information more compelling and memorable than the positive. Cognitive scientists have suggested that we tend to learn more from negative information than from positive—one obvious case is that positive information often simply confirms what we already know, whereas negative information reveals to us areas of ignorance. In this sense, the drive for negative information in youth parallels the thirst for knowledge that wanes as we age. This age-related positivity bias is reflected in brain scans: Older adults activate the amygdala only for positive information, whereas younger adults activate it for both positive and negative information.

One way to stave off the effects of aging is to stay mentally active, to perform tasks you've never done before. This sends blood to parts of your brain that wouldn't otherwise get it—the trick is to get the blood flowing in every nook and cranny. People with Alzheimer's disease show deposits in the brain of amyloids, proteins that erroneously interact, forming small, fibrous microfilaments in the brain. People who were more cognitively active in their lives have less amyloid in their brains, suggesting that mental activity protects against Alzheimer's. And it's not just being active and learning new things in your seventies and eighties that counts—it's a lifetime pattern of learning and exercising the brain. "We tend to focus on what people do at seventy-five in terms of dementia," says William Jagust, a neuroscientist at UC Berkeley. But there is more evidence that what you do in your life, at forty or fifty, is probably more important."

"Retaining lots of social interaction is really important," adds Arthur Toga, a neuroscientist at the University of Southern Califomia. "It involves so much of the brain. You have to interpret facial expressions and understand new concepts." In addition, there is pressure to react in real time, and to assimilate new information. As with cognitive activity, having a history of social interaction across the life span is protective against Alzheimer's.

For people of any age, the world is becoming increasingly linear—a word I'm using in its figurative rather than mathematical sense. Nonlinear thinkers, including many artists, are feeling more marginalized as a result. As a society, it seems we take less time for art. In doing so, we may be missing out on something that is deeply valuable and important from a neurobiological standpoint. Artists recontextualize reality and offer visions that were previously invisible. Creativity engages the brain's daydreaming mode directly and stimulates the free flow and association of ideas, forging links between concepts and neural nodes that might not otherwise be made. In this way, engagement in art as either a creator or consumer helps us by hitting the reset button in our brains. Time stops. We contemplate. We reimagine our relationship to the world.

Being creative means allowing the nonlinear to intrude on the linear, and to exercise some control over the output. The major achievements in science and art over the last several thousand years required induction, rather than deduction—required extrapolating from the known to the unknown and, to a large extent, blindly guessing what should come next and being right some of the time. In short, they required great creativity combined with a measure of luck. There is a mystery to how these steps forward are made, but we can stack the decks in our favor. We can organize our time, and our minds, to leave time for creativity, for mind-wandering, for each of us to make our own unique contribution in our time here.

In contrast to creative thinking is rational decision-making. Unfortunately, the human brain didn't evolve to be very good at this, and evolutionary biologists and psychologists can only speculate why this might be so. We have a limited attentional capacity to deal with large amounts of information, and as a consequence, evolution has put into place time- and attention-saving strategies that work much of the time but not all of the time. The better we do in life, and the more we become like the HSPs (those highly successful persons) we dream of being, the more perplexing some decisions become. We could all use better decision-making strategies. The next chapter examines how we can better organize scientific and medical information, to teach ourselves to be our own best advocates in times of illness, and to make more evidence-based choices when they matter most.

6

ORGANIZING INFORMATION FOR THE HARDEST DECISIONS

When Life Is on the Line

"Nothing comes to my desk that is perfectly solvable," President Obama observed. "Otherwise, someone else would have solved it."

Any decision for which the solution is obvious—a no-brainer—is going to be made by someone lower down the line than the president. No one wants to waste his, which is after all our, valuable time. The *only* decisions that come to him are the ones that have stumped everyone down the line before him.

Most of the decisions that a president of the United States has to make have serious implications—potential loss of life, escalation of tensions between countries, changes in the economy that could lead to loss of jobs. And they typically arrive with impoverished or imperfect information. His advisors don't need him to brainstorm about new possibilities—although occasionally he may do that. The advisors pass a problem upward not because they're not smart enough to solve it, but because it invariably involves a choice between two losses, two negative outcomes, and the president has to decide which is more palatable. At that point, President Obama says, "you wind up dealing with probabilities. Any given decision you make, you'll wind up with a thirty to forty percent chance that it isn't going to work."

I wrote about Steve Wynn, the CEO of Wynn Resorts, in Chapter 3. About decision-making, he says, "In any sufficiently large organization, with an effective management system in place, there is going to be a pyramid shape with decision makers at every level. The only time I am brought in is when the only known solutions have a downside, like someone losing their job, or the company losing large sums of money. And usually the decision is already framed for me as two negatives. I'm the one who has to choose which of those two negatives we can live with."

Medical decision-making often feels a lot like that—choosing between two negatives. We face a gamble: either the possibility of declining health if we do nothing, or great potential discomfort, pain, and expense if we choose a medical procedure. Trying to evaluate the outcomes rationally can be taxing.

Most of us are ill-equipped to calculate such probabilities on our own. We're not just ill-equipped to calculate probabilities, we are not trained to evaluate them rationally. We're faced with decisions every day that impact our livelihood, our happiness, and our health, and most of these decisions—even if we don't realize it at first—come down to probabilities. If a physician starts explaining medical choices probabilistically, it is likely the patient will not grasp the information in a useful way. The news is delivered to us during a period of what can be extreme emotional vulnerability and cognitive overload. (How do you feel when you get a diagnosis?) While the physician is explaining a 35% chance of this and a 5% chance of that, our minds are distracted, racing with thoughts of hospital bills and insurance, and how we'll ask for time off work. The doctor's voice fades into the background as we imagine pain, discomfort, whether our will is up to date, and who's going to look after the dog while we're in the hospital.

This chapter provides some simple tools for organizing information about health care, and they apply to all the hardest decisions we face. But the complexity of medical information inevitably provokes strong emotions while we grapple with unknowns and even the meaning of our lives. Medical decision-making presents a profound challenge to the organized mind, no matter how many assistants you have, or how competent you are at everything else you do.

Thinking Straight About Probabilities

Decision-making is difficult because, by its nature, it involves uncertainty. If there was no uncertainty, decisions would be easy! The uncertainty exists because we don't know the future, we don't know if the decision we make will lead to the best possible outcome. Cognitive science has taught us that relying on our gut or intuition often leads to bad decisions, particularly in cases where statistical information is available. Our guts and our brains didn't evolve to deal with probabilistic thinking.

Consider a forty-year-old woman who wants to have children. She reads that, compared to someone younger, she is five times more likely to have a child with a particular birth defect. At first glance, this seems like an unacceptable risk. She is being asked to pit her strong emotional desire for children against an intellectual knowledge of statistics. Can knowledge of statistics bridge this gap and lead her to the right conclusion, the one that will give her the happiest life?

Part of maintaining an organized mind and organized life requires that we make the *best decisions possible.* Bad decisions sap strength and energy, not to mention the time we might have to invest in revisiting the decision when things go wrong. Busy people who make a lot of high-stakes decisions tend to divide their decision-making into categories, performing triage, similar to what I wrote about for list making and list sorting in Chapter 3:

1. Decisions you can make right now because the answer is obvious
2. Decisions you can delegate to someone else who has more time or expertise than you do
3. Decisions for which you have all the relevant information but for which you need some time to process or digest that information. This is frequently what judges do in difficult cases. It's not that they don't have the information—it's that they want to mull over the various angles and consider the larger picture. It's good to attach a deadline to these.
4. Decisions for which you need more information. At this point, either you instruct a helper to obtain that information or you make a note to yourself that *you* need to obtain it. It's good to attach a deadline in either case, even if it's an arbitrary one, so that you can cross this off your list.

Medical decision-making sometimes falls into category 1 (*do it now*), such as when your dentist tells you that you have a new cavity and she wants to fill it. Fillings are commonplace and there is not much serious debate about alternatives. You probably have had fillings before, or know people who have, and you're familiar with the procedures. There are risks, but these are widely considered to be outweighed by the serious complications that could result from leaving the cavity unfilled. The word *widely* here is important; your dentist doesn't have to spend time explaining alternatives or the consequences of not treating. Most physicians who deal with serious diseases don't have it this easy because of the uncertainty about the best treatment.

Some medical decision-making falls into category 2 (*delegate it*), especially when the literature seems either contradictory or overwhelming. We throw up our hands and ask, "Doc, what would *you* do?" essentially delegating the decision to her.

Category 3 (*mull it over*) can seem like the right option when the problem is first presented to you, or after categories 2 and 4 (*get more information*) have been implemented. After all, for decisions that affect our time on this planet, it is intuitively prudent not to race to a decision.

Much of medical decision-making falls into category 4—you simply need more information. Doctors can provide some of it, but you'll most likely need to acquire additional information and then analyze it to come to a clear decision that's right for you. Our gut feelings may not have evolved to deal instinctively with probabilistic thinking, but we can train our brain in an afternoon to become a logical and efficient decision-making machine. If you want to make better medical decisions—particularly during a time of crisis when emotional exhaustion can cloud the decision-making process—you need to know something about probabilities.

We use the term *probability* in everyday conversation to refer to two completely different concepts, and it's important to separate these. In one case, we are talking about a mathematical calculation that tells us the likelihood of a particular outcome from among many possible ones—an objective calculation. In the other case, we're referring to something subjective—a matter of opinion.

Probabilities of the first kind describe events that are calculable or countable, and—importantly—they are theoretically repeatable. We might be describing events such as tossing a coin and getting three heads in a row, or drawing the king of clubs from a deck of cards, or winning the state lottery. *Calculable* means we can assign precise values in a formula and generate an answer. *Countable* means we can determine the probabilities empirically by performing an experiment or conducting a survey and counting the results. To say that they're repeatable simply means we can do the experiment over and over again and expect similar descriptions of the probabilities of the events in question.

For many problems, calculating is easy. We consider all possible outcomes and the outcome we're interested in and set up an equation. The probability of drawing the king of clubs (or any other single card) from a full deck is 1 out of 52 because it is possible to draw any of the 52 cards in a deck and we're interested in just 1 of them. The probability of picking *any* king from a full deck is 4 out of 52 because there are 52 cards in the deck and we're interested in 4 of them. If there are 10 million tickets sold in a fresh round of a sweepstakes and you buy 1 ticket, the probability of your winning is 1 out of 10 million. It's important to recognize, both in lotteries and medicine, you can do things that change a probability by a large amount but with no real-world, practical significance. You can increase the odds of winning that state lottery by a factor of 100 by buying 100 lottery tickets. But the chance of winning remains so incredibly low, 1 in 100,000, that it hardly seems like a reasonable investment. You might read that the probability of getting a disease is reduced by 50% if you accept a particular treatment. But if you only had a 1 in 10,000 chance of getting it anyway, it may not be worth the expense, or the potential side effects, to lower the risk.

Some probabilities of the objective type are difficult to calculate, but they are countable, at least in principle. For example, if a friend asked you the probability of drawing a straight flush—any sequence of five cards of the same suit—you might not know how to work this out without consulting a probability textbook. But in theory, you could count your way to an answer. You would deal cards out of decks all day long for many days and simply write down how often you get a straight flush; the answer would be very close to the theoretical probability of .0015% (15 chances in 1,000,000). And the longer you make the experiment—the more trials you have—the closer your counted observations are likely to come to the true, calculated probability. This is called the law of large numbers: Observed probabilities tend to get closer and closer to theoretical ones when you have larger and larger samples. The big idea is that the probability of getting a straight flush is both countable and repeatable: If you get friends to perform the experiment, they should come up with similar results, provided they perform the experiment long enough for there to be a large number of trials.

Other kinds of outcomes are not even theoretically calculable, but are still countable. The probability of a baby being born a boy, of a marriage ending in divorce, and of a house on Elm Street catching fire all fall into this category. For questions like these, we resort to observations—we count because there's no formula that tells us how to calculate the probability. We check the records of births in area hospitals, we look at fire reports over a ten-year period in the neighborhood. An automobile manufacturer can obtain failure data from hundreds of thousands of fuel injectors to find out the probability of failure after a given amount of use.

Whereas objective probabilities involve a calculation from theory or counting from observation, the second kind of probability—the subjective—is neither calculable nor countable. In this case, we are using the word *probability* to express our subjective confidence in a future event. For example, if I say there is a 90% chance that I'm going to Susan's party next Friday, this wasn't based on any calculation I performed or indeed that anyone *could* perform—there is nothing to measure or calculate. Instead, it is an expression of how confident I am that this outcome will occur. Assigning numbers like this gives the impression that the estimate is precise, but it isn't.

So even though one of these two kinds of probability is objective and the other is subjective, almost nobody notices the difference—we use the word *probability* in everyday speech, blindly going along with it, and treating the two different kinds of probability as the *same thing*.

When we hear things like "There is a sixty percent chance that the conflict between these two countries will escalate to war" or "There is a ten percent probability that a rogue nation will detonate an atomic device in the next ten years," these are not calculated probabilities of the first kind; they are *subjective* expressions of the second kind, about how confident the speaker is that the event will occur. Events of this second kind are not replicable like the events of the first kind. And they're not calculable or countable like playing cards or fires on Elm Street. We don't have a bunch of identical rogue nations with identical atomic devices to observe to establish a count. In these cases, a pundit or educated observer is making a guess when they talk about "probability," but it is not a probability in the mathematical sense. Competent observers may well disagree about this kind of probability, which speaks to their subjectivity.

Drawing the king of clubs two times in a row is unlikely. Just how unlikely? We can calculate the probability of two events occurring by multiplying the probability of one event by the probability of the other. The probability of drawing the king of clubs from a full deck is $1/52$ for both the first and second drawing (if you put the first king back after drawing it, to make the deck full again). So $1/52 \times 1/52 = 1/2704$. Similarly, the probability of getting three heads in a row in tossing a coin is calculated by taking the probability of each event, ½, and multiplying them together three times: $1/2 \times 1/2 \times 1/2 = 1/8$. You could also set up a little experiment where you toss a coin three times in a row many times. In the long run, you'll get three heads in a row about one-eighth of the time.

For this multiplication rule to work, the events have to be independent. In other words, we assume that the card I draw the first time doesn't have anything to do with the card I draw the second time. If the deck is shuffled properly, this should be true. Of course there are cases when the events are not independent. If I see that you put the king of clubs on the bottom of the deck after my first pick, and I choose the bottom of the deck the second time, the events aren't independent. If a meteorologist forecasts rain today and rain tomorrow, and you want to know the probability that it will rain two days in a row, those events are not independent, because weather fronts take some time to pass through an area. If the events are not independent, the math gets a bit more complicated—although not terribly so.

Independence needs to be considered carefully. Getting struck by lightning is very unusual—according to the U.S. National Weather Service, the chance is 1 in 10,000. So, is the chance of getting struck by lightning *twice* $1/10{,}000 \times 1/10{,}000$ (1 chance in 100 million)? That holds only if the events are independent, and they probably are not. If you live in an area with a lot of lightning storms and you tend to stay outdoors during them, you are more likely to be struck by lightning than someone who lives in a different locale and takes more precautions. One man was hit by lightning twice within two minutes, and a Virginia park ranger was hit seven times during his lifetime.

It would be foolish to say, "I've already been hit by lightning once, so I can walk around in thunderstorms with impunity." Yet this is the sort of pseudo logic that is trotted out by people unschooled in probability. I overheard a conversation at a travel agency some years ago as a young couple were trying to decide which airline to fly. It went something like this (according to my no doubt imperfect memory):

Alice: "I'm not comfortable taking Blank Airways—they had that crash last year."

Bob: "But the odds of a plane crash are one in a million. Blank Airways just had their crash. It's not going to happen to them again."

Without knowing more about the circumstances of the Blank Airways crash, Alice's statement indeed constitutes a perfectly reasonable fear. Airplane crashes are usually not random events; they potentially indicate some underlying problem with an airline's operations—poorly trained pilots, careless mechanics, an aging fleet. The likelihood of Blank Airways having two crashes in a row cannot be considered independent events. Bob is using "gut reasoning" and not logical reasoning, like saying that since you just got hit by lightning, it can't happen again. Following this pseudologic to an extreme, you can imagine Bob arguing, "The chances of a bomb being on this plane are one in a million. Therefore I'll bring a bomb on the plane with me because the chance of *two* bombs being on the plane are astronomically high."

Even if plane crashes were independent, to think that it won't happen now "because it just happened" is to fall for a form of the gambler's fallacy, thinking that a safe flight is now "due." The gods of chance are not counting flights to make sure that one million go by before the next crash, and neither are they going to ensure that the next crashes are evenly distributed among the remaining air carriers. So the likelihood of any airline having two crashes in a row cannot be considered independent.

An objectively obtained probability is not a guarantee. Although in the long run, we expect a coin to come up heads half the time, probability is not a self-correcting process. The coin has no memory, knowledge, willpower, or volition. There is not some overlord of the theory of probability making sure that everything works out just the way you expect. If you get "heads" ten times in a row, the probability of the coin coming up "tails" on the next toss is still 50%. Tails is not more likely and it is not "due." The notion that chance processes correct themselves is part of the gambler's fallacy, and it has made many casino owners, including Steve Wynn, very wealthy. Millions of people have continued to put money into slot machines under the illusion that their payout is due. It's true that probabilities tend to even out, but only in the long run. And that long run can take more time and money than anyone has.

The confusing part of this is that our intuition tells us that getting eleven heads in a row is very unlikely. That is right—but only partially right.

The flaw in the reasoning results from confusing the rarity of ten heads in a row with the rarity of eleven heads in a row—in fact, they are not all that different. Every sequence of ten heads in a row has to be followed by either another head or another tail, each of which is equally likely.

Humans have a poor sense of what constitutes a random sequence. When asked to generate a random sequence, we tend to write down far more alternations (heads—tails—heads—tails) and far fewer runs (heads—heads—heads) than appear in actual random sequences. In one experiment, people were asked to write down what they thought a random sequence would look like for 100 tosses of a coin. Almost no one put down runs of seven heads or tails in a row, even though there is a greater than 50% chance that they will occur in 100 tosses. Our intuition pushes us toward evening out the heads/tails ratio even in short sequences, although it can take very long sequences—millions of tosses—for the stable 50/50 ratio to show up.

Fight that intuition! If you toss a coin three times in a row, it is true that there is only a 1/8 chance that you'll get three heads in a row. But this is confounded by the fact that you're looking at a short sequence. On average, only 14 flips are required to get three heads in a row, and in 100 flips, there's a greater than 99.9% chance there will be three heads in a row at least once.

The reason we get taken in by this illogical thinking—the thinking that probabilities change in sequences—is that in some cases they do actually change. Really! If you're playing cards and you've been waiting for an ace to show up, the probability of an ace increases the longer you wait. By the time 48 cards have been dealt, the probability of an ace on the next card is one (all that is left are aces). If you're a hunter-gatherer searching for that stand of fruit trees you saw last summer, each section of land you search without finding it increases your chance of finding it in the next one. Unless you stop to think carefully, it is easy to confuse these different probability models.

Many things we are interested in have happened before, and so we can usually count or observe how often they tend to occur. The base rate of something is the background rate of its occurrence. Most of us have an intuitive sense for this. If you bring your car to the mechanic because the engine is running rough, before even looking at it, your mechanic might say something like "It's probably the timing—that's what it is in ninety percent of the cars we see. It could also be a bad fuel injector, but the injectors hardly ever fail." Your mechanic is using informed estimations of the base rate that something occurs in the world.

If you're invited to a party at Susan's house with a bunch of people you've never met, what are the chances that you'll end up talking to a doctor versus a member of the president's cabinet? There are many more doctors than there are cabinet members. The base rate for doctors is higher, and so if you know nothing at all about the party, your best guess is you'll run into more doctors than cabinet members. Similarly, if you suddenly get a headache and you're a worrier, you may fear that you have a brain tumor. Unexplained headaches are very common; brain tumors are not. The cliché in medical diagnostics is "When you hear hoofbeats, think horses, not zebras." In other words, don't ignore the base rate of what is most likely, given the symptoms.

Cognitive psychology experiments have amply demonstrated that we typically ignore base rates in making judgments and decisions. Instead, we favor information we think is diagnostic, to use a medical term. At Susan's party, if the person you're talking to has an American flag lapel pin, is very knowledgeable about politics, and is being trailed by a U.S. Secret Service agent, you might conclude that she is a cabinet member because she has the attributes of one. But you'd be ignoring base rates. There are 850,000 doctors in the United States and only fifteen cabinet members. Out of 850,000 doctors, there are bound to be some who wear American flag label pins, are knowledgeable about politics, and are even trailed by the Secret Service for one reason or another. For example, sixteen members of the 111th Congress were doctors—far more than there are cabinet members. Then there all the doctors who work for the military, the FBI, and the CIA, and doctors whose spouses, parents, or children are high-profile public servants—some of whom may qualify for Secret Service protection. Some of those 850,000 doctors may be up for security clearances or are being investigated in some matter, which would account for the Secret Service agent. This error in reasoning is so pervasive that it has a name—the representativeness heuristic. It means that people or situations that appear to be representative of one thing effectively overpower the brain's ability to reason, and cause us to ignore the statistical or base rate information.

In a typical experiment from the scientific literature, you're given a scenario to read. You're told that in a particular university, 10% of the students are engineers and 90% are not. You go to a party and you see someone wearing a plastic pocket protector (unstated in the description is that many people consider this a stereotype for engineers). Then you're asked to rate how likely you think it is that this person is an engineer. Many people rate it as a certainty. The pocket protector seems so diagnostic, such conclusive evidence, that it is hard to imagine that the person could be anything else. But engineers are sufficiently rare in this university that we need to account for that fact. The probability of this person being an engineer may not be as low as the base rate, 10%, but it is not as high as 100%, either—other people might wear pocket protectors, too.

Here's where it gets interesting. Researchers then set up the same scenario—a party at a university where 10% of the students are engineers and 90% are not—and then explain: "You run into someone who might be wearing a plastic pocket protector or not, but you can't tell because he has a jacket on." When asked to rate the probability that he is an engineer, people typically say "fifty-fifty." When asked to explain why, they say, "Well, he could be wearing a pocket protector or not—we don't know." Here again is a failure to take base rates into account. If you know nothing at all about the person, then there is a 10% chance he is an engineer, not a 50% chance. Just because there are only two choices doesn't mean they are equally likely.

To take an example that might be intuitively clearer, imagine you walk into your local grocery store and bump into someone without seeing them. It could either be Queen Elizabeth or not. How likely is it that it is Queen Elizabeth? Most people don't think it is 50-50. How likely is it that the queen would be in *any* grocery store, let alone the one I shop at? Very unlikely. So this shows we're capable of using base rate information when events are extremely unlikely. It's when they're only mildly unlikely that our brains freeze up. Organizing our decisions requires that we combine the base rate information with other relevant diagnostic information. This type of reasoning was discovered in the eighteenth century by the mathematician and Presbyterian minister Thomas Bayes, and bears his name: Bayes's rule.

Bayes's rule allows us to refine estimates. For example, we read that roughly half of marriages end in divorce. But we can refine that estimate if we have additional information, such as the age, religion, or location of the people involved, because the 50% figure holds only for the aggregate of all people. Some subpopulations of people have higher divorce rates than others.

Remember the party at the university with 10% engineers and 90% non-engineers? Some additional information could help you to estimate the probability that someone with a pocket protector is an engineer. Maybe you know that the host of the party had a bad breakup with an engineer, so she no longer invites them to her parties. Perhaps you learn that 50% of premed and medical students at this school wear pocket protectors. Information like this allows us to update our original base rate estimates with the new information. Quantifying this updated probability is an application of Bayesian inferencing.

We're no longer asking the simple, one-part question "What is the probability that the person with a pocket protector is an engineer?" Instead, we're asking the compound question "What is the probability that the person with a pocket protector is an engineer, *given* the information that fifty percent of the premeds and medical students at the school wear pocket protectors?" The rarity of engineers is being pitted against the added circumstantial information about the ubiquity of pocket protectors.

We can similarly update medical questions such as "What is the likelihood that this sore throat indicates the flu, *given* that three days ago I visited someone who had the flu?" or "What is the likelihood that this sore throat indicates hay fever, *given* that I was just outdoors gardening at the height of pollen season?" We do this kind of updating informally in our heads, but there are tools that can help us to quantify the effect of the new information. The problem with doing it informally is that our brains are not configured to generate accurate answers to these questions intuitively. Our brains evolved to solve a range of problems, but Bayesian problems are not among them yet.

Oh, No! I Just Tested Positive!

How serious is news like this? Complex questions like this are easily solvable with a trick I learned in graduate school—fourfold tables (also known as contingency tables). They are not easily solved using intuition or hunches. Say you wake up with blurred vision one morning. Suppose further that there exists a rare disease called optical blurritis. In the entire United States, only 38,000 people have it, which gives it an incidence, or base rate, of 1 in 10,000 (38,000 out of 380 million). You just read about it and now you fear you have it. Why else, you are thinking, would I have blurry vision?

You take a blood test for blurritis and it comes back positive. You and your doctor are trying to decide what to do next. The problem is that the cure for blurritis, a medication called chlorohydroxelene, has a 5% chance of serious side effects, including a terrible, irreversible itching just in the part of your back that you can't reach. (There's a medication you can take for itching, but it has an 80% chance of raising your blood pressure through the roof.) Five percent doesn't seem like a big chance, and maybe you're willing to take it to get rid of this blurry vision. (That 5% is an objective probability of the first kind—not a subjective estimate but a figure obtained from tracking tens of thousands of recipients of the drug.) Naturally, you want to understand precisely what the chances are that you actually have the disease before taking the medication and running the risk of being driven crazy with itching.

The fourfold table helps to lay out all this information in a way that's easy to visualize, and doesn't require anything more complicated than eighth-grade division. If numbers and fractions make you want to run screaming from the room, don't worry—the Appendix contains the details, and this chapter gives just a birds'-eye view (a perhaps blurry one, since after all, you're suffering from the symptoms of blurritis right now).

Let's look at the information we have.

- The base rate for blurritis is 1 in 10,000, or .0001.
- Chlorohydroxelene use ends in an unwanted side effect 5% of the time, or .05.

You might assume that if the test came back positive, it means you have the disease, but tests don't work that way—most are imperfect. And now that you know something about Bayesian thinking, you might want to ask the more refined question "What is the probability that I *actually* have the disease, *given* that the test came out positive?" Remember, the base rate tells us that the probability of having the disease for anyone selected at random is .0001. But you're not just anyone selected at random. Your vision was blurry, and your doctor had you take the test.

We need more information to proceed. We need to know what percentage of the time the test is wrong, and that it can be wrong in two ways. It can indicate you have the disease when you don't—a *false positive*—or it can indicate that you don't have the disease when you do—a *false negative*. Let's assume that both of these figures are 2%. In real life, they can be different from each other, but let's assume 2% for each.

We start by drawing four squares and labeling them like this:

TEST RESULTS

		Pos.	Neg.	
Disease	Yes			
	No			
	Totals			

The column headings represent the fact that the test result can be either positive or negative. We set aside for the moment whether those results are accurate or not—that's what we'll use the table to conclude. The row headings show that the disease can be either present or absent in a given patient. Each square represents a conjunction of the row and column headings. Reading across, we see that, of the people who have the disease (the "Disease yes" row), some of them will have positive results (the ones in the upper left box) and some will have negative test results (the upper right box). The same is true of the "Disease no" row; some people will have positive test results and some will have negative. You're hoping that even though you tested positive (the left column), you don't have the disease (the lower left square).

After filling in the information we were given (I walk through it more slowly in the Appendix), we can answer the question "What is the probability that I have the disease, *given* that I had a positive test result?"

TEST RESULTS

		Pos.	Neg.	
Disease	Yes	1	0	1
	No	200	9,799	9,999
	Totals	201	9,799	10,000

Consider the column that shows people who have a positive test result:

TEST RESULTS

		Pos.	Neg.	
Disease	Yes	1	0	1
	No	200	9,799	9,999
	Totals	201	9,799	10,000

You can see that out of 10,000 people, 201 of them (the total in the margin below the left column) had a positive test result like yours. But of those 201 people, only 1 has the disease—there is only 1 chance in 201 that you actually have the disease. We can take 1/201 × 100 to turn it into a percent, and we obtain about 0.49%—not a high likelihood however you put it. . . . Your chances were 1 in 10,000 before you went in for the test. Now they are 1 in 201. There is still a roughly 99.51% chance you do not have the disease. If this reminds you of the lottery ticket example above, it should. Your odds have changed dramatically, but this hasn't affected the real-world outcome in any appreciable way. The take-home lesson is that the results of the test don't tell you everything you need to know—you need to also apply the base rate and error rate information to give you an accurate picture. This is what the fourfold table allows you to do. It doesn't matter whether the disease produces moderate symptoms, such as blurry vision, or very severe symptoms, such as paralysis; the table still allows you to organize the information in an easily digestible format. Ideally, you would also work closely with your physician to take into account any comorbid conditions, co-occurring symptoms, family history, and so on to make your estimate more precise.

Let's look at that other piece of information, the miracle drug that can cure blurritis, chlorohydroxelene, which has a 1 in 5 chance of side effects (20% side effects is not atypical for real medications). If you take the medicine, you need to compare the 1 in 5 chance of a relentlessly itchy back with the 1 in 201 chance that it will offer you a cure. Put another way, if 201 people take the drug, only 1 of them will experience a cure (because 200 who are prescribed the drug don't actually have the disease—yikes!). Now, of those same 201 people who take the drug, 1 in 5, or 40, will experience the side effect. So 40 people end up with that back itch they can't reach, for every 1 person who is cured. Therefore, if you take the drug, you are 40 times more likely to experience the side effect than the cure. Unfortunately, these numbers are typical of modern health care in the United States. Is it any wonder that costs are skyrocketing and out of control?

One of my favorite examples of the usefulness of fourfold tables comes from my teacher Amos Tversky. It's called the two-poison problem. When Amos administered a version of it to MDs at major hospitals and medical schools, as well as to statisticians and business school graduates, nearly every one of them got the answer so wrong that the hypothetical patients would have died! His point was that probabilistic reasoning doesn't come naturally to us; we have to fight our knee-jerk reaction and learn to work out the numbers methodically.

Imagine, Amos says, that you go out to eat at a restaurant and wake up feeling terrible. You look in the mirror and see that your face has turned blue. Your internist tells you that there are two food-poisoning diseases, one that turns your face blue and one that turns your face green (we assume for this problem that there are no other possibilities that will turn your face blue or green). Fortunately, you can take a pill that will cure you. It has no effect if you are healthy, but if you have one of these two diseases and you take the wrong pill, you die. Imagine that, in each case, the color your face turns is consistent with the disease 75% of the time, and that the green disease is five times more common than the blue disease. What color pill do you take?

Most people's hunch (and the hunch shared by medical professionals whom Amos asked) is that they should take the blue pill because (a) their face is blue, and (b) the color their face turns is consistent most of the time, 75%. But this ignores the base rates of the disease.

We fill in a fourfold table. We aren't told the size of the population we're dealing with, so to facilitate the construction of the table, let's assume a population of 120 (that's the number that goes in the lower right area outside the table). From the problem, we have enough information to fill in the rest of the table.

If the green disease is five times more common than the blue disease, that means that out of 120 people who have one or the other, 100 must have the green disease and 20 must have the blue disease.

YOUR FACE

		Blue	Green	
Disease	Blue			20
	Green			100
	Totals			120

Because the color of your face is consistent with the disease 75% of the time, 75% of the people with blue disease have a blue face; 75% of 20 = 15. The rest of the table is filled in similarly.

YOUR FACE

		Blue	Green	
Disease	Blue	15	5	20
	Green	25	75	100
	Totals	40	80	120

Now, before you take the blue pill—which could either cure or kill you—the Bayesian question you need to ask is "What is the probability that I have the blue disease, *given* that I have a blue face?" The answer is that out of the 40 people who have a blue face, 15 of them have the disease: 15/40 = 38%. The probability that you have the *green* disease, given that you have a blue face, is 25/40, or 62%. You're much better off taking the green pill *regardless of what color your face is.* This is because the green face disease is far more common than the blue face disease. Again, we are pitting base rates against symptoms, and we learned that base rates should not be ignored. It is difficult to do this in our heads—the fourfold table gives a way of organizing the information visually that is easy to follow. Calculations like this are why doctors will often start patients on a course of antibiotics before they receive test results to know exactly what is wrong—certain antibiotics work against enough common diseases to warrant them.

In the example of blurritis that I began with, 201 people will test positive for a disease that only 1 person has. In many actual health-care scenarios, all 201 people will be given medication. This illustrates another important concept in medical practice: the *number needed to treat.* This is the number of people who have to take a treatment, such as a medication or surgery, before one person can be cured. A number needed to treat of 201 is not unusual in medicine today. There are some routinely performed surgeries where the number needed to treat is 48, and for some drugs, the number can exceed 300.

Blue faces and tests for imaginary diseases aside, what about the decisions that confront one's mortality directly? Your doctor says these meds will give you a 40% chance of *living* an extra five years. How do you evaluate *that*?

There is a way to think about this decision with the same clear rationality that we applied to the two-poison problem, using the concept of "expected value." The expected value of an event is its probability multiplied by the value of the outcome. Business executives routinely evaluate financial decisions with this method. Suppose someone walks up to you at a party and offers to play a game with you. She'll flip a fair coin, and you get $1 every time it comes up heads. How much would you pay to play this game? (Assume for the moment that you don't particularly enjoy the game, though you don't particularly mind it—what you're interested in is making money.) The expected value of the game is 50 cents, that is, the probability of the coin coming up heads (.5) times the payoff ($1). Note that the expected value is often not an amount that you can actually win in any one game: Here you either win $0 or you win $1. But over many hundreds of repetitions of the game, you should have earned close to 50 cents per game. If you pay less than 50 cents per game to play, in the long run you'll come out ahead.

Expected values can also be applied to losses. Suppose you're trying to figure out whether to pay for parking downtown or take the chance of getting a ticket by parking in a loading zone. Imagine that the parking lot charges $20 and that the parking ticket is $50, but you know from experience that there's only a 25% chance you'll get a ticket. Then the expected value of going to the parking lot is -$20: You have a 100% chance of having to pay the attendant $20 (I used a minus sign to indicate that it's a loss).

The decision looks like this:

a. Pay for parking: A 100% chance of losing $20
b. Don't pay for parking: A 25% chance of losing $50

The expected value of the parking ticket is 25% × -$50, which is -$12. 50. Now of course you hate parking tickets and you want to avoid them. You might be feeling unlucky today and want to avoid taking chances. So *today* you might pay the $20 for parking in order to avoid the possibility of being stuck with a $50 ticket. But the rational way to evaluate the decision is to consider the long term. We're faced with hundreds of decisions just like this in the course of our daily lives. What really matters is how we're going to make out *on average*. The expected value for this particular decision is that you will come out ahead in the long run by paying parking tickets: a loss of $12.50 on average versus a loss of $20. Over a year of parking once a week on this particular street, you'll spend $650 on parking tickets versus $1,040 on parking lots—a big difference. Of course, on any particular day, you can apply Bayesian updating. If you see a meter reader inching along the street toward your parking spot in the loading zone, that's a good day to go to the parking lot.

Expected value also can be applied to nonmonetary outcomes. If two medical procedures are identical in their effectiveness and long-term benefits, you might choose between them based on how much time they'll take out of your daily routine.

Procedure 1: A 50% chance of requiring 6 weeks of recovery and a 50% chance of requiring only 2 weeks

Procedure 2: A 10% chance of requiring 12 weeks and a 90% chance of requiring only 0.5 weeks

Again I use a minus sign to indicate the *loss* of time. The expected value (in time) of procedure 1 is therefore

$(.5 \times -6 \text{ weeks}) + (.5 \times -2 \text{ weeks}) = -3 + -1 = \mathbf{-4\ weeks.}$

The expected value of procedure 2 is

$(.1 \times -12) + (.9 \times -.5) = -1.2 + -.45 = \mathbf{-1.65\ weeks.}$

Ignoring all other factors, you're better off with procedure 2, which will have you out of commission for only about a week and a half (on average), versus procedure 1, which will have you out for 4 weeks (on average).

Of course you may not be able to ignore all other factors; minimizing the amount of recovery time may not be your only concern. If you've just booked nonrefundable tickets on an African safari that leaves in 11 weeks, you can't take the chance of a 12-week recovery. Procedure 1 is better because the worst-case scenario is you're stuck in bed for 6 weeks. So expected value is good for evaluating averages, but it is often necessary to consider best- and worst-case scenarios. The ultimate extenuating circumstance is when one of the procedures carries with it a risk of fatality or serious disability. Expected value can help organize this information as well.

Risks Either Way

At some point in your life, it is likely you'll be called upon to make critical decisions about your health care or that of someone you care about. Adding to the difficulty is that the situation is likely to cause physical and psychological stress, reducing the sharpness of your decision-making abilities. If you ask your doctor for the accuracy of the test, he may not know. If you try to research the odds associated with different treatments, you may find that your doctor is ill-equipped to walk through the statistics. Doctors are clearly essential in diagnosing an illness, in laying out the different treatment options, treating the patient, and following up to make sure the treatment is effective. Nevertheless, as one MD put it, "Doctors generate better knowledge of efficacy than of risk, and this skews decision-making." Moreover, research studies focus on whether or not an intervention provides a cure, and the issue of side effects is less interesting to those who have designed the studies. Doctors educate themselves about the success of procedures but not so much the drawbacks—this is left to you to do, another form of shadow work.

Take cardiac bypass surgery—there are 500,000 performed in the United States every year. What is the evidence that it is helpful? Randomized clinical trials show no survival benefit in most patients who had undergone the surgery. But surgeons were unconvinced because the logic of the procedure to them was justification enough. "You have a plugged vessel, you bypass the plug, you fix the problem, end of story." If doctors think a treatment *should* work, they come to believe that it *does* work, even when the clinical evidence isn't there.

Angioplasty went from zero to 100,000 procedures a year with no clinical trials—like bypass surgery, its popularity was based simply on the logic of the procedure, but clinical trials show no survival benefit. Some doctors tell their patients that angioplasty will extend their life expectancy by ten years, but for those with stable coronary disease, it has not been shown to extend life expectancy by even one day.

Were all these patients stupid? Not at all. But they were vulnerable. When a doctor says, "You have a disease that could kill you, but I have a treatment that works," it is natural to jump at the chance. We ask questions, but not too many—we want our lives back, and we're willing to follow the doctor's orders. There is a tendency to shut down our own decision-making processes when we feel overwhelmed, something that has been documented experimentally. People given a choice along with the opinion of an expert stop using the parts of the brain that control independent decision-making and hand over their decision to the expert.

On the other hand, life expectancy isn't the whole story, even though this is the way many cardiologists sell the bypass and angioplasty to their patients. Many patients report dramatically improved quality of life after these procedures, the ability to do things they love. They may not live longer, but they live better. This is a crucial factor in any medical choice, one that should not be swept under the rug. Ask your doctor not just about efficacy and mortality, but quality of life and side effects that may impact it. Indeed, many patients value quality of life more than longevity and are willing to trade one for the other.

A potent example of the pitfalls in medical decision-making comes from the current state of prostate cancer treatments. An estimated 2.5 million men in the United States have prostate cancer, and 3% of men will die from it. That doesn't rank it in the Top Ten causes of death, but it is the second leading cause of cancer death for men, after lung cancer. Nearly every urologist who delivers the news will recommend radical surgery to remove the prostate. And on first blush, it sounds reasonable—we see cancer, we cut it out.

Several things make thinking about prostate cancer complicated. For one, it is a particularly slow-progressing cancer—most men die *with* it rather than *of* it. Nevertheless, the C-word is so intimidating and frightening that many men just want to "cut it out and be done with it." They are willing to put up with the side effects to know that the cancer is gone. But wait, there is a fairly high incidence of *recurrence* following surgery. And what about the side effects? The incident rate—how often side effects occur among patients after surgery—are in parentheses:

- inability to maintain an erection sufficient for intercourse (80%)
- shortening of the penis by one inch (50%)
- urinary incontinence (35%)
- fecal incontinence (25%)
- hernia (17%)
- severing of urethra (6%)

The side effects are awful. Most people would say they're better than death, which is what they think is the alternative to surgery. But the numbers tell a different story. First, because prostate cancer is slow moving and doesn't even cause symptoms in most of the people who have it, it can safely be left untreated in some men. How many men? Forty-seven out of 48. Put another way, for every 48 prostate surgeries performed, only one life is extended—the other 47 patients would have lived just as long anyway, and not had to suffer the side effects. Thus, the number needed to treat to get one cure is 48. Now, as to the side effects, there's over a 97% chance a patient will experience at least one of those listed above. If we ignore the sexual side effects—the first two—and look only at the others, there is still more than a 50% chance that the patient will experience at least one of them, and a pretty big chance he'll experience two. So, of the 47 people who were not helped by the surgery, roughly 24 are going to have at least one side effect. To recap: For every 48 prostate surgeries performed, 24 people who would have been fine without surgery experience a major side effect, while 1 person is cured. You are 24 times more likely to be harmed by the side effect than helped by the cure. Of men who undergo the surgery, 20% regret their decision. Clearly, it is important to factor quality of life into the decision.

So why, then, does nearly every urologist recommend the surgery? For one, the surgery is one of the most complicated and difficult surgeries known. You might think this is a good reason for them *not* to recommend it, but the fact is that they have an enormous amount invested in learning to do it. The training required is extensive, and those who have mastered it are valued for this rare skill. In addition, patients and their families carry expectations that a physician will *do* something. Patients tend to be dissatisfied with a practitioner who says, "We'll keep an eye on it." People who go to an internist with a cold are measurably unhappy if they walk out of the office empty-handed, without a prescription. Multiple studies show that these patients feel their doctor didn't take them seriously, wasn't thorough, or both.

Another reason surgery is pushed is that the surgeon's goal is to eradicate the cancer and to do so with the lowest possible incidence of recurrence. Patients are complicit in this: "It's very hard to tell a surgeon 'I'd like to leave a cancer in place,'" explains Dr. Jonathan Simons, president of the Prostate Cancer Foundation. Medical schools teach that surgeries are the gold standard for most cancers, with survival rates higher than other methods, and much higher than ignoring the problem. They use a summary statistic of how many people die of the cancer they were treated for, five and ten years after surgery. But this summary ignores important data such as susceptibility to other maladies, quality of life after surgery, and recovery time.

Dr. Barney Kenet, a Manhattan dermatologist, finds all this fascinating. "Surgeons are taught that 'a chance to cut is a chance to cure,'" he says. "It's part of the DNA of their culture. In the examples you've been giving me about cancer, with the odds and statistics all carefully analyzed, the science of treatment is in collision with the art of practicing medicine—and it is an art."

Medical schools and surgeons may not worry so much about quality of life, but you should. Much of medical decision-making revolves around your own willingness to take risks, and your threshold for putting up with inconveniences, pain, or side effects. How much of your time are you willing to spend driving to and from medical appointments, sitting in doctors' offices, fretting about results? There are no easy answers, but statistics can go a long way toward clarifying the issues here. To return to prostate surgeries, the advised recovery period is six weeks. That doesn't seem like an unreasonable amount of time, considering that the surgery can save your life.

But the question to ask is not "Am I willing to invest six weeks to save my life?" but rather "Is my life actually being saved? Am I one of the forty-seven people who don't need the surgery or am I the one who does?" Although the answer to that is unknowable, it makes sense to rely on the probabilities to guide your decision; it is statistically unlikely that you will be helped by the surgery unless you have specific information that your cancer is aggressive. Here's an additional piece of information that may bring the decision into sharp focus: The surgery extends one's life, on average, by only six weeks. This number is derived from the average of the forty-seven people whose lives were not extended at all (some were even shortened by complications from the surgery) and the one person whose life was saved by the surgery and has gained five and a half years. The six-week life extension in this case exactly equals the six-week recovery period! The decision, then, can be framed in this way: Do you want to spend those six weeks *now*, while you're younger and healthier, lying in bed recovering from a surgery you probably didn't need? Or would you rather take the six weeks off the end of your life when you're old and less active?

Many surgical procedures and medication regimens pose just this trade-off: The amount of time in recovery can equal or exceed the amount of life you're saving. The evidence about the life-extending benefits of exercise is similar. Don't get me wrong—exercise has many benefits, including mood enhancement, strengthening of the immune system, and improving muscle tone (and hence overall appearance). Some studies show that it even improves clarity of thought through oxygenation of the blood. But let's examine one claim that has received a lot of attention in the news, that if you perform aerobic exercise an hour a day and reach your target heart rate, you will extend your life. Sounds good, but by how much? Some studies show you extend your life by one hour for every hour you exercise. If you love exercise, this is a great deal—you're doing something you love and it's extending your life by the same amount. This would be like saying that for every hour you have sex, or every hour you eat ice cream, you'll live an extra hour. Easy choice—the hour you spend on the activity is essentially "free" and doesn't count against the number of hours you've been allotted in this life. But if you *hate* exercise and find it unpleasant, the hour you're spending amounts to an hour lost. There are enormous benefits to daily exercise, but extending your life is not one of them. That's no reason not to exercise—but it's important to have reasonable expectations for the outcome.

Two objections to this line of thinking are often posed. The first is that talking about averages in a life-or-death decision like this doesn't make sense because no actual prostate surgery patient has their life extended by the average quoted above of six weeks. One person has his life extended by five and a half years, and forty-seven have their lives extended by nothing at all. This "average" life extension of six weeks is simply a statistical fiction, like the parking example.

It is true, no one person gains by this amount; the average is often a number that doesn't match a single person. But that doesn't invalidate the reasoning behind it. Which leads to the second objection: "You can't evaluate this decision the way you evaluate coin tosses and card games, based on probabilities. Probabilities and expected values are only meaningful when you are looking at many, many trials and many outcomes." But the rational way to view such decisions is to consider these offers not as "one-offs," completely separated from time and life experience, but as part of a string of decisions that you will need to make throughout your life. Although each individual decision may be unique, we are confronted with a lifetime of propositions, each one carrying a probability and an expected value. You are not making a decision about that surgical procedure in isolation from other decisions in your life. You are making it in the context of thousands of decisions you make, such as whether to take vitamins, to exercise, to floss after every meal, to get a flu shot, to get a biopsy. Strictly rational decision-making dictates that we pay attention to the expected value of each decision.

Each decision carries uncertainty and risks, often trading-off time and convenience now for some unknown outcome later. Of course if you were one hundred percent convinced that you'd enjoy perfect oral health if you flossed after every meal, you would do so. Do you expect to get that much value from flossing so often? Most of us aren't convinced, and flossing three times a day (plus more for snacks) seems, well, like more trouble than it's worth.

Obtaining accurate statistics may sound easy but often isn't. Take biopsies, which are commonplace and routinely performed, and carry risks that are poorly understood even by many of the surgeons who perform them. In a biopsy, a small needle is inserted into tissue, and a sample of that tissue is withdrawn for later analysis by a pathologist who looks to see if the cells are cancerous or not. The procedure itself is not an exact science—it's not like on *CSI* where a technician puts a sample in a computer and gets an answer out the other end.

The biopsy analysis involves human judgment and what amounts to a "Does it look funny?" test. The pathologist or histologist examines the sample under a microscope and notes any regions of the sample that, in her judgment, are not normal. She then counts the number of regions and considers them as a proportion of the entire sample. The pathology report may say something like "5% of the sample had abnormal cells" or "carcinoma noted in 50% of the sample." Two pathologists often disagree about the analysis and even assign different grades of cancer for the same sample. That's why it's important to get a second opinion on your biopsy—you don't want to start planning for surgery, chemotherapy, or radiation treatment until you're really sure you need it. Nor do you want to grow too complacent about a negative biopsy report.

To stick with the prostate cancer example, I spoke with six surgeons at major university teaching hospitals and asked them about the risks of side effects from prostate biopsy. Five of them said the risk of side effects from the biopsy was around 5%, the same as what you can read for yourself in the medical journals. The sixth said there was no risk—that's right, none at all. The most common side effect mentioned in the literature is sepsis; the second most common is a torn rectum; and the third is incontinence. Sepsis is dangerous and can be fatal. The biopsy needle has to pass through the rectum, and the risk of sepsis comes from contamination of the prostate and abdominal cavity with fecal material. The risk is typically reduced by having the patient take antibiotics prior to the procedure, but even with this precaution, there still remains a 5% risk of an unwanted side effect.

None of the physicians I spoke to chose to mention a recovery period for the biopsy, or what they euphemistically refer to as side effects of "inconvenience." These are not health-threatening, simply unpleasant. It was only when I brought up a 2008 study in the journal *Urology* that they admitted that one month after biopsy, 41% of men experienced erectile dysfunction, and six months later, 15% did. Other side effects of "inconvenience" include diarrhea, hemorrhoids, gastrointestinal distress, and blood in the semen that can last for several months. Two of the physicians sheepishly admitted that they deliberately withhold this information. As one put it, "We don't mention these complications to patients because they might be discouraged from getting the biopsy, which is a very important procedure for them to have." This is the kind of paternalism that many of us dislike from doctors, and it also violates the core principle of informed consent.

Now, that 5% risk of serious side effects may not sound so bad, but consider this: Many men who have been diagnosed with early-stage or low-grade prostate cancer are choosing to live with the cancer and to monitor it, a plan known as watchful waiting or active surveillance. In active surveillance, the urologist may call for biopsies at regular intervals, perhaps every twelve to twenty-four months. For a slow-moving disease that may not show any symptoms for over a decade, this means that some patients will undergo five or more biopsies. What is the risk of sepsis or another serious side effect during one or more biopsies if you have five biopsies, each one carrying a risk of 5%?

This calculation doesn't follow the multiplication rule I outlined above; we'd use *that* if we wanted to know the probability of a side effect on all five biopsies—like getting heads on a coin five times in a row. And it doesn't require a fourfold table because we're not asking a Bayesian question such as "What is the probability I have cancer, *given* that the biopsy was positive?" (Pathologists sometimes make mistakes—this is equivalent to the diagnosticity of the blood tests we saw earlier.) To ask about the risk of a side effect in at least one out of five biopsies—or to ask about the probability of getting at least one head on five tosses of a coin—we need to use something called the binomial theorem. The binomial can tell you the probability of the bad event happening at least one time, all five times, or any number you like. If you think about it, the most useful statistic in a case like this is not the probability of your having an adverse side effect *exactly one time* out of your five biopsies (and besides, we already know how to calculate this, using the multiplication rule). Rather, you want to know the probability of having an adverse side effect *at least one time*, that is, on one or more of the biopsies. These probabilities are different.

The easiest thing to do here is to use one of the many available online calculators, such as this one: http://www.stat.tamu.edu/~west/applets/binomialdemo.html.

To use it, you enter the following information into the onscreen boxes:

> *n* refers to the number of times you are undergoing a procedure (in the language of statistics, these are "trials").
>
> *p* refers to the probability of a side effect (in the language of statistics, these are "events").
>
> *X* refers to how many times the event occurs.

Using the example above, we are interested in knowing the probability of having at least one bad outcome (the event) if you undergo the biopsy five times. Therefore,

> $n = 5$ (5 biopsies)
>
> $p = 5\%$, or .05
>
> $X = 1$ (1 bad outcome)

Plugging these numbers into the binomial calculator, we find that if you have five biopsies, the probability of having a side effect at least once is 23%.

Of the five surgeons who acknowledged that there was a 5% risk of side effects from the prostate biopsy, only one understood that the risk increased with each biopsy. Three of them said that the 5% risk applied to a lifetime of having biopsies—you could have as many as you want, and the risk never increased.

I explained that each biopsy represented an independent event, and that two biopsies presented a greater risk than one. None of them were buying it. The first of my conversations went like this:

"I read that the risk of serious complications from the biopsy is five percent."

"That's right."

"So if a patient has biopsies five times, that increases their risk to nearly twenty-five percent."

"You can't just add the probabilities together."

"I agree, you can't. You need to use the binomial theorem, and you come up with twenty-three percent—very close to twenty-five percent."

"I've never heard of the binomial theorem and I'm sure it doesn't apply here. I don't expect you to understand this. It requires statistical training."

"Well, I've had some statistical training. I think I can understand."

"What is it you do for a living again?"

"I'm a research scientist—a neuroscientist. I lecture in our graduate statistics courses and I've published some statistical methods papers."

"But you're not an MD like I am. The problem with you is that you don't understand medicine. You see, medical statistics are different from other statistics."

"What?"

"I've had twenty years of experience in medicine. How much have you had? I'm dealing in the real world. You can have all the *theories* you want, but you don't know anything. I see patients every day. I know what I'm seeing."

Another surgeon, a world expert in the da Vinci "robot" guided surgery, told me, "These statistics don't sound right. I've probably done five hundred biopsies and I don't think I've seen more than a couple of dozen cases of sepsis in my whole career."

"Well, twenty-four out of five hundred is about five percent."

"Oh. Well, I'm sure it wasn't that many, then. I would have noticed if it was five percent."

Either a glutton for punishment, or an optimist, I visited the department head for oncology at another leading hospital. If a person had prostate cancer, I pointed out, they're better off not having surgery because of the number needed to treat: Only 2% of patients are going to benefit from the surgery.

"Suppose it was you with the diagnosis," he said. "You wouldn't want to forgo the surgery! What if you're in that two percent?"

"Well . . . I probably wouldn't be."

"But you don't know that."

"You're right, I don't *know* it, but by definition, it is unlikely—there's only a two percent chance that I'd be in the two percent."

"But you wouldn't *know* that you're not. What if you were? Then you'd want the surgery. What's the matter with you?"

I discussed all this with the head of urological oncology at yet another university teaching hospital, a researcher-clinician who publishes studies on prostate cancer in scientific journals and whose papers had an expert's command of statistics. He seemed disappointed, if unsurprised, at the stories about his colleagues. He explained that part of the problem with prostate cancer is that the commonly used test for it, the PSA, is poorly understood and the data are inconsistent as to its effectiveness in predicting outcomes. Biopsies are also problematic because they rely on sampling from the prostate, and some regions are easier to sample from than others. Finally, he explained, medical imaging is a promising avenue—magnetic resonance imaging and ultrasound for example—but there have been too few long-term studies to conclude anything about their effectiveness at predicting outcomes. In some cases, even high-resolution MRIs miss two-thirds of the cancers that show up in biopsies. Nevertheless, biopsies for diagnosis, and surgery or radiation for treatment, are still considered the gold standards for managing prostate cancer. Doctors are trained to treat patients and to use effective techniques, but they are not typically trained in scientific or probabilistic thinking—you have to apply these kinds of reasoning yourself, ideally in a partnership with your physician.

What Doctors Offer

But wait a minute—if MDs are so bad at reasoning, how is it that medicine relieves so much suffering and extends so many lives? I have focused on some high-profile cases—prostate cancer, cardiac procedures—where medicine is in a state of flux. And I've focused on the kinds of problems that are famously difficult, that exploit cognitive weaknesses. But there are many successes: immunization, treatment of infection, organ transplants, preventive care, and neurosurgery (like Salvatore Iaconesi's, in Chapter 4), to name just a few.

The fact is that if you have something wrong with you, you don't go running to a statistics book, you go to a doctor. Practicing medicine is both an art and a science. Some doctors apply Bayesian inferencing without really knowing they're doing it. They use their training and powers of observation to engage in pattern matching—knowing when a patient matches a particular pattern of symptoms and risk factors to inform a diagnosis and prognosis.

As Scott Grafton, a top neurologist at UC Santa Barbara, says, "Experience and implicit knowledge really matter. I recently did clinical rounds with two emergency room doctors who had fifty years of clinical experience between them. There was zero verbal gymnastics or formal logic of the kind that Kahneman and Tversky tout. They just *recognize* a problem. They have gained skill through extreme reinforcement learning, they become exceptional pattern recognition systems. This application of pattern recognition is easy to understand in a radiologist looking at X-rays. But it is also true of any great clinician. They can generate extremely accurate Bayesian probabilities based on years of experience, combined with good use of tests, a physical exam, and a patient history." A good doctor will have been exposed to thousands of cases that form a rich statistical history (Bayesians call this a prior distribution) on which they can construct a belief around a new patient. A great doctor will apply all of this effortlessly and come to a conclusion that will result in the best treatment for the patient.

"The problem with Bayes and heuristics arguments," Grafton continues, "is they fail to recognize that much of what physicians learn to do is to extract information from the patient directly, and to individualize decision-making from this. It is extremely effective. A good doctor can walk into a hospital room and *smell* impending death." When many doctors walk into an ICU room, for example, they look at the vital signs and the chart. When Grafton walks into an ICU room, he looks at the patient, leveraging his essential human capacity to understand another person's mental and physical state.

Good doctors talk to their patients to understand the history and symptoms. They elegantly use pattern matching. The science informs their judgments, but they don't rely on any one test. In the two-poison and optical blurritis stories, I've glossed over an important fact about how real medical decisions are made. Your doctor wouldn't have ordered the test unless he thought, based on his examination of you and your history, that you might have the disease. For my made-up blurritis, although the base rate in the general population is 1 in 38,000, that's not the base rate of the disease for people who have blurry vision, end up in a doctor's office and end up taking the test. If that base rate is, say, 1 in 9,500, you can redo the table and find out that the chance of your having blurritis drops from 1 in 201 to about 1 in 20. This is what Bayesian updating is all about—finding statistics that are relevant to your particular circumstance and using them. You improve your estimates of the probability by constraining the problem to a set of people who more closely resemble you along pertinent dimensions. The question isn't "What is the probability that I'll have a stroke?" for example, but "What is the probability that someone my age, gender, blood pressure, and cholesterol level will have a stroke." This involves combining the science of medicine with the art of medicine.

And although there are things that medicine is not particularly good at, it is hard to argue with the overwhelming successes of medicine over the past hundred years. The U.S. Centers for Disease Control and Prevention (CDC) in Atlanta reports nearly complete eradication—a 99% decrease in morbidity—between 1900 and 1998 for nine diseases that formerly killed hundreds of thousands of Americans: smallpox, diphtheria, tetanus, measles, mumps, rubella, *Haemophilus influenzae*, pertussis, and polio. Diphtheria fell from 175,000 cases to one, measles from 500,000 to about 90. For most of human history, from around 10,000 BCE to 1820, our life expectancy was capped at about twenty-five years. World life expectancy since then has increased to more than sixty years, and since 1979, U.S. life expectancy has risen from seventy-one to seventy-nine.

What about cases where doctors are more directly involved with patients? After all, life span may be attributable to other factors, such as improved hygiene. In the battlefield, even while weapons have become more damaging, a soldier's odds of being successfully treated for a wound have increased dramatically: Through the Civil War and both world wars, the odds of dying from a wound were around 1 in 2.5; during the Iraq War, they had fallen to 1 in 8.2. Infant, neonatal, and postneonatal mortality rates have all been reduced. In 1915, for every 1,000 births, 100 infants would die before their first birthday; in 2011, that number had dropped to 15. And although prostate cancer, breast cancer, and pancreatic cancer have been particularly challenging to manage, survival rates for childhood leukemia have risen from near 0% in 1950 to 80% today.

Clearly, medicine is doing a lot right, and so is the science behind it. But there remains a gray, shadowy area of pseudomedicine that is problematic because it clouds the judgment of people who need real medical treatment and because the area is, well, disorganized.

Alternative Medicine: A Violation of Informed Consent

One of the core principles of modern medicine is informed consent—that you have been fully briefed on all the pros and cons of any treatment you submit to, that you have been given all of the information available in order to make an informed decision.

Unfortunately, informed consent is not truly practiced in modern health care. We are bombarded with information, most of it incomplete, biased, or equivocal, and at a time when we are least emotionally prepared to deal with it. This is especially true with alternative medicine and alternative therapies.

An increasing number of individuals seek alternatives to the professional medical-hospital system for treating illness. Because the industry is unregulated, figures are hard to come by, but *The Economist* estimates that it is a $60 billion business worldwide. Forty percent of Americans report using alternative medicines and therapies; these include herbal and homeopathic preparations, spiritual or psychic healing practices, and various nonmedical manipulations of body and mind with a healing intent. Given its prominence in our lives, there is some basic information anyone consenting to this kind of health care should have.

Alternative medicine is simply medicine for which there is no evidence of effectiveness. Once a treatment has been scientifically shown to be effective, it is no longer called *alternative*—it is simply called *medicine.* Before a treatment becomes part of conventional medicine, it undergoes a series of rigorous, controlled experiments to obtain evidence that it is both safe and effective. To be considered alternative medicine, nothing of the kind is required. If someone holds a belief that a particular intervention works, it becomes "alternative." Informed consent means that we should be given information about a treatment's efficacy and any potential hazards, and this is what is missing from alternative medicine.

To be fair, saying that there is no evidence does not mean that the treatment is ineffective; it simply means its effectiveness has not yet been demonstrated—we are agnostic. But the very name "alternative medicine" is misleading. It is alternative but it is not medicine (which begs the question What is it an alternative to?).

How is science different from pseudoscience? Pseudoscience often uses the terminology of science and observation but does not use the full rigor of controlled experiments and falsifiable hypotheses. A good example is homeopathic medicine, a nineteenth-century practice that entails giving extremely small doses (or actually no dose at all) of harmful substances that are claimed to provide a cure. It is based on two beliefs. First is that when a person shows symptoms such as insomnia, stomach distress, fever, cough, or tremors, administering a substance which, in normal doses, causes those symptoms, can cure it. There is no scientific basis for that claim. If you have poison ivy, and I give you more poison ivy, all I've done is given you more poison ivy. It is not a cure—it is the problem! The second belief is that diluting a substance repeatedly can leave remnants of the original substance that are active and have curative properties, and that the more dilute the substance is, the more effective or powerful it is. According to homeopaths, the "vibrations" of the original substance leave their imprint on water molecules.

And the dilution has to be accomplished according to a very specific procedure. A homeopathic technician takes one part of the chemical substance and dilutes it in ten parts of water, then shakes it up and down ten times, back and forth ten times, and from side to side ten times. Then he takes one part of that solution and dilutes it in ten parts of water, and performs the shaking routine again. He does this at least twenty times altogether, resulting in a solution in which there is one part of the original substance for 100,000,000,000,000,000,000 parts of water. For retail homeopathic products, dilutions are routinely 1 followed by 30 zeros, and often 1 followed by—get this—1,500 zeros. This is equivalent to taking one grain of rice, crushing it into a powder, and dissolving it in a sphere of water the size of our solar system. Oh, I forgot: and then repeating *that* process twenty-six times. Homeopathy was invented before the Italian scientist Amedeo Avogadro discovered a mathematical constant that now bears his name, expressing the number of atoms or molecules that are retained in dilutions (6.02×10^{23}). The point is that in standard, retail homeopathic dilutions, there is *nothing* remaining of the original substance. But that's supposed to be good because, remember, the more dilute the homeopathic medicine is, the stronger it is. All this has led professional skeptic James Randi to the observation that the way to overdose on homeopathic medicine is to not take any at all. (Randi has offered $1 million for more than a decade to anyone who can provide evidence that homeopathy works.)

Homeopathy is pseudoscience because (a) it doesn't stand up to controlled experiments, (b) it uses the language of science such as dilution and molecule, and (c) it makes no sense within a scientific understanding of cause and effect.

Setting homeopathy aside, when it comes to serious illness, such as cancer, infection, Parkinson's disease, pneumonia, or even milder illnesses like common colds and flu, there is no evidence that alternative medicine is effective. Edzard Ernst, a British research scientist, reviewed hundreds of studies and found that 95% of the treatments were indistinguishable from no treatment at all—equivalent to placebo. (The other 5%, which do work, may represent experimental error, according to traditional thresholds for success in scientific research.) Vitamins and supplements fare no better. After extensive clinical trials spanning decades and many different research labs and protocols, it's been found that multivitamins are not effective for anything at all. In fact, vitamins can harm. In the doses contained in vitamin pills, Vitamin E and folic acid are associated with *increased* risk for cancer. Excess Vitamin D is associated with an increased risk for cardiac inflammation, and excess Vitamin B6 is associated with nerve damage. In dietary amounts—what you get from a normal diet as opposed to taking supplements—these vitamins are not a problem, but the amounts typically found in supplements and over-the-counter vitamin pills can be harmful. And in spite of the fact that millions of Americans take Vitamin C or echinacea when they feel a cold coming on, there is little evidence that these help. Why do we *think* they do?

Our forebrains have evolved to notice co-occurrences of events, but not a lack of occurrences. This relates to the fourfold tables we looked at earlier: Our brains are biased to focus on what's in the upper left square—psychologists call this *illusory correlation.*

The reason the correlations are illusory is that the upper left square doesn't tell us all we need to know to draw the best conclusion. Imagine you feel a cold coming on so you start taking lots of echinacea. You notice that the cold never develops. This happens to you at five different times and so you conclude that the echinacea has helped. Your fourfold table looks like this:

		FEEL HEALTHY NEXT DAY	
		Yes	No
Take Echinacea	Yes	5	
	No		
	Totals		

Pretty impressive! Here are some problems. A certain number of colds are going to go away if you do nothing. And there might be times when you felt a cold coming on, did nothing, and promptly forgot about it. If you were part of a scientific study, there would be more meticulous data collection than most of us do by ourselves. Here is what the rest of the table might look like if you filled it in as part of a study:

		FEEL HEALTHY NEXT DAY	
		Yes	No
Take Echinacea	Yes	5	10
	No	180	5
	Totals		

Note that in order to have a complete picture, you need to know on how many days you did not take echinacea and you did *not* get a cold—that's most of the time! Needing to know this seems counterintuitive—but that's the whole point here, that our forebrains have a hard time making sense of this kind of information. Just looking at the table, you can see that a cold is twice as likely to develop if you take echinacea as not (the right column of the table). To put this into Bayesian form, the probability of getting a cold, *given* that you took echinacea, still equals .67.

By the way, the placebo effect—that we feel better and often *get* better just from taking something, even if it has no medicinal ingredients—is very real and very strong. Larger pills have a bigger placebo effect than small pills. Sham injections have a larger effect than pills. A great deal of the effect of products with no known medicinal value may simply be this placebo effect. This is why double-blind, randomized clinical control trials are necessary: Everyone in the study gets a pill and nobody knows who got what. Many of the people taking the "empty" pill are going to improve relative to people who got nothing, but if the medicine really works, it should work even better than placebo. This is how new treatments are approved.

It's not just echinacea and Vitamin C that wreak havoc with our causal reasoning. We fall prey to illusory correlations all the time. Have you ever had the experience that you were thinking of someone, someone you hadn't thought of in a long time, and then suddenly the phone rings and—wow! There they are! Before jumping to the conclusion that psychic powers are involved, you'd need to know three other pieces of information: How often do you think of people who *don't* call you, how often do you *not* think of people who *do* call you, and finally, how often do you *not* think of someone and then they *don't* call! If you work all this out in a fourfold table, it is likely you'll find that the occasionally vivid coincidences are swamped by events of the other three kinds, making the point that these correlations are illusory.

Our brains evidently have evolved to focus on the upper left cell, the hits, and remember nothing else. One of my former teachers, Paul Slovic, dubbed this *denominator neglect*. Slovic says we imagine the numerator—the tragic story you saw on the news about a car crash—and don't think about the denominator—the overwhelming number of automobile trips that end safely. Denominator neglect shows up in very odd ways. In one study, people were told that a disease kills 1,286 people out of every 10,000. They judged this as more dangerous than did people who were told of a disease that kills 24.14% of the population. Note that 1,286/10,000 is just under 13%. So, in reality, it's only about half as dangerous. But in the first case, we focus on the numerator, the 1,286 individuals who will be stricken with the disease. We may try to picture that many people in hospital beds. In the second case, we hear 24.14% and the brain tends to treat it as an abstract statistic with no human beings attached.

Denominator neglect leads to a tendency to catastrophize, to imagine the worst possible scenario without placing it in proper statistical perspective. As Daniel Kahneman writes, "Every parent who has stayed up waiting for a teenage daughter who is late from a party will recognize the feeling. You may know that there is really (almost) nothing to worry about, but you cannot help images of disaster from coming to mind."

The vividness with which we can recall catastrophes, coupled with denominator neglect, can lead to truly terrible decisions. In the two months following the terrorist attacks of September 11, 2001, so many people in the United States were afraid to fly that they took to their cars for trips they otherwise would have taken by plane. There were no more airplane crashes in October or November, but 2,170 more people died in automobile crashes during that period than usually do. These people focused on the numerator (four horrible airplane crashes, 246 people aboard them) but not the denominator (ten million safe commercial flights per year in the United States). As one researcher put it, "Terrorists can strike twice—first, by directly killing people, and second, through dangerous behaviors induced by fear in people's minds."

Related to this is that we tend to overweight rare events. Kahneman describes this scenario: Imagine that intelligence officers determine that suicide bombers have entered two different cities and are ready to strike. One city has one suicide bomber, the other city has two. Logically, the citizens of the first city should feel twice as safe. But they probably don't. The image is so vivid that the fear is roughly the same. Now, if there were one hundred suicide bombers, that would be a different story, but the point is that we are not sensitive to the math because our brains weren't built that way. Fortunately, we can train them.

Which brings us back to alternative medicine and the fact that many of its claims rest on illusory correlations, based on denominator neglect. The appeal of alternative medicine is at least in part because a growing number of people are suspicious of "Western medicine," and they seek alternatives. Overwhelmed by the imperfections in the way modern health care is managed, they feel a need to rebel against those who have supplied us with imperfectly effective and expensive drugs. They are suspicious of the large profits that pharmaceutical companies (and some hospitals) make, and are wary of treatments that are recommended within a strong culture of maximizing profits—the concern being that some treatments may be prescribed not because they are best for the patient but because they are best for those who stand to gain financially. Unfortunately, recent news stories have shown that this is sometimes true.

Alternative medicine enthusiasts also complain about the paternalistic or arrogant manner of some doctors ("I know what's right for you and you don't need to understand it"), exemplified by the urological oncologist I spoke to who became hostile when asked to discuss his statistical reasoning about biopsy. At one of the leading hospitals in the United States, breast cancer patients who undergo radiation treatment aren't told about the high probability of experiencing painful radiation burns, evidently because the oncologists have decided for the patient that the benefits of the treatment outweigh the pain and discomfort of it. But this violates the principle of informed consent. All patients should be given all the information available so they can decide what they are willing to accept and what they are not.

Another thing to worry about is a lack of calibration among some doctors. In one study, physicians making a prognosis were accurate only 20% of the time. In another study, researchers collected autopsy results of patients who died in the hospital. They then compared these to the diagnosis made by the patients' physicians while they were still alive. The elegant part of this experiment is that the physicians also reported their confidence in the diagnosis they had given. Looking only at those cases in which the doctors were "completely certain" of the diagnosis, they were wrong for about 40% of their patients. Being wrong about so many diagnoses is understandable and perhaps forgivable, given that medical cases can be very complicated, and what we've already seen about the imperfection of tests. But being so overconfident is less understandable, because it means the doctors are not paying attention to outcomes.

The appeal of alternative medicine, then, is that it plays into the genuine feelings of distrust that many people feel for the medical establishment. It offers the perhaps romanticized hope of natural products providing natural, noninvasive cures. The use of alternative medicine often feeds a nativist belief that if something is plant-based or natural, it must be good. (But of course this is false: Think hemlock, castor bean seeds, jasmine berries, and poisonous mushrooms.) An additional problem is that herbal and plant-based medicines are not regulated in the United States or in many other countries. The U.S. Food and Drug Administration (FDA) estimates that basic quality control standards are not adhered to by 70% of the companies. And while quality control is a serious problem, with contaminants and fillers being found present in a large number of samples, the supplements themselves can and do cause harm even when they are not compromised by poor manufacturing. A seventeen-year-old Texas youth, Christopher Herrera, showed up at the emergency room of a Houston hospital in 2012 with his chest, face, and eyes bright yellow, "almost highlighter yellow," according to Dr. Shreena Patel, the doctor who treated him. He had suffered liver damage after using a green tea extract he'd bought at a nutrition store as a fat-burning supplement, and the damage was so severe that he required a liver transplant. Dietary supplements now account for 20% of drug-related liver injuries, tripling the rate from ten years ago.

Yet most of us know someone who claims to have been cured by some form of alternative medicine, whether for a cold, backache, or even cancer. A dear friend of mine was diagnosed with prostate cancer and was told he had six months to live. "Get your affairs in order and do something you've always wanted to do," they said. "A vacation in Hawaii, perhaps." He told them, "What I've always wanted to do is live a long life," and he walked out.

My friend heard about a doctor specializing in alternative medicine. The doctor did extensive "alternative" blood tests and as a result prescribed a very specific diet and exercise. The list of permitted and forbidden foods was so restrictive, it would take my friend three or four hours a day just to prepare his meals. He followed the diet and exercise program with the same kind of commitment and focus he had applied to every aspect of his life, the kind of discipline that had led him to become the president of a well-known international company when he was only thirty-eight years old.

The six-month death sentence was given twelve years ago. My friend is thriving, doing better than ever before. He went back to his dream-team oncologists two years after they had said he'd be dead and they ran a battery of tests. His PSA was down to nearly zero and his other biomarkers were all normal and stable. They refused to believe he had cured himself with diet and exercise. "There must have been something wrong with our tests when you came in last time" was all they could muster.

I know a half dozen people who have similar stories. They are compelling. I'm grateful that my friends have lived. The important point is that these are not scientific studies, they are just stories. They are uplifting, quizzical, mysterious, challenging stories but just stories. The plural of *anecdote* is not *data*. There were no experimental controls, the patients were not randomly assigned to one condition or another, there was no scientist keeping careful records of the progression of either the disease or the cure. We don't have the opportunity to know what would have happened if my friend *hadn't* changed his diet and started exercising—he might have lived just as long and not had to spend eighty hours a month chopping vegetables in his kitchen. Or he might be dead. Not long ago, I asked him if he had gone back for a biopsy or medical imaging to be sure the cancer was really gone. "Why would I do that?" he asked. "I'm healthier than I've ever been, I feel great, and it's not like I would do anything differently based on what they find."

My friend beating cancer with diet and exercise is neither consistent nor inconsistent with science; it stands outside of scientific scrutiny because the data were not collected in a scientific way.

Like the doctors who were eager to believe in coronary bypass and angioplasties because they had a plausible mechanism, we're willing to believe that diet and exercise can beat cancer without any scientific support. It's just plausible enough and it makes intuitive sense to us. None of us has a complete understanding of the relation between diet, exercise, disease, and health. We hear the story and we think, "Yeah, there just might be something to that." To see that we're basing this on the plausibility of the mechanism rather than the data, consider that if, instead of diet and exercise, my friend slept upside down in a tent the shape of a pyramid, we'd say that was just crazy.

One of the nice things about science is that it is open to stories like my friend's so as not to miss out on important new cures. Most scientific findings begin with a simple observation, often serendipitous, that is followed up with careful study; think Newton's apple or Archimedes displacing the water in his bathtub.

Lying in wait within "alternative medicine" may well be a cure for cancer or other ailments. Research is under way in hundreds of laboratories throughout the world testing herbal preparations, alternative medicines and therapies. But until they are shown to be effective, they carry the danger that they may cause patients to delay seeking treatments that have been shown to work, and consequently delay a cure sometimes beyond the point of no return. This is what happened to Steve Jobs—he rejected surgery to follow an alternative regime of acupuncture, dietary supplements, and juices that he later realized didn't work and that delayed the conventional treatment that experts say would probably have prolonged his life.

Thousands of people die in the United States every year from diseases that were preventable or curable with "Western medicine." The scientific method has brought civilization further in the last two hundred years than all other methods over the previous ten thousand years. Medical researchers understand that patients' lives are at stake in their experiments—often, even before a clinical trial is completed, scientists will see a clear benefit and call off the trial early in order to make the medicine available sooner rather than make patients wait, some of whom are so sick that waiting is not an option.

Indeed, because some of the alternative therapies, such as diet and exercise, *do* make so much sense, and because there are so very many stories like my friend's, the U.S. National Institutes of Health (NIH) has set up a division for complementary and alternative medicine to explore such treatments, using all the tools of modern science. So far, the NIH reports many cases of no effects or tiny effects, translating to only small numbers of people who benefit from alternative therapies and an enormous number who don't. In one typical study, for example, nearly 100,000 individuals were randomly assigned to Vitamin D versus none or placebo, in order to test the hypothesis that Vitamin D is preventive against cancer and cardiovascular disease. The results found that 150 people need to be treated with Vitamin D for five years for one life to be saved, but among those 149 who were not helped, there were a host of unwanted side effects, including kidney stones, fatigue, pancreatitis, and bone pain. We don't know about the long-term effects of Vitamin D therapy, and newer evidence now links an excess of Vitamin D to mortality. There remains much work to do.

How You Think, What You Do

When it comes to choosing which treatment option is best for you, you may find yourself largely on your own. You'll have to gather information and apply the fourfold table. For alternatives that carry similar risks, the decision can be difficult. Part of the reason for this is that people differ greatly in the amount of risk they are willing to take, and the amount of discomfort (both psychological and physical) they're willing to endure. This side of the patient decision-making process is covered very well in Jerome Groopman and Pamela Hartzband's book *Your Medical Mind.*

What are your biases regarding medicine? We all have them. Groopman and Hartzband describe four types of patients: minimalist, maximalist, naturalist, and technologist. A medical minimalist tries to interact with medicine and doctors as little as possible. A maximalist thinks every problem, every ache and pain, has a medical solution. A naturalist believes the body can cure itself, perhaps with the aid of plant-based and spiritual remedies. A technologist believes there are always new drugs or procedures that are better than anything that came before them, and that they will be the most effective route to follow.

These represent extreme types; most of us have some of each of these in us. You might be a minimalist regarding your dental care, but a maximalist for botox and other "youth preservation" procedures. You could be a naturalist when it comes to colds and flus, but a technologist if you need surgery for a ruptured appendix. And these orientations interact. There are certainly maximalist naturalists who have shelves of herbal remedies, and there are minimalist technologists who do as little as possible but, if they need surgery, will request the latest high-tech robot-guided laser surgery with the 1.21 gigawatt flux capacitor guidance system. Understanding your own biases can lead to more efficient decision-making, and a far more productive doctor-patient dialogue. It can be especially helpful to tell your doctor outright which of these styles you lean toward.

But the value of simply understanding the probabilities, how the numbers look on a fourfold table, is always useful and will prove to be so again and again no matter what your personality.

You will hear that if you take some remedy, or follow some new regimens, you will reduce your risk of getting disease *X* by 50%. That sounds like a no-brainer. But keep those base rates in mind. Consider the forty-year-old woman who was contemplating children, and was told that, given her age (a Bayesian way of framing the problem), a particular birth defect is 5 times more likely. Suppose there was only a 1 in 50,000 chance for a younger woman to have a child with this birth defect, and the chance for the forty-year-old has risen to 1 in 10,000. It is still a very unlikely occurrence. The base rate of the defect is sufficiently low that even a fivefold increase in risk, although impressive in percentage terms, doesn't have any practical implications. If this reminds you of the statistical shenanigans in Chapter 4 concerning lower divorce rates for people who met online, you're absolutely right. A 25% reduction in a divorce rate, from 7.7% to 6%, doesn't have any real-world significance. An increase or reduction in risk like this can pass tests of statistical significance (mainly of concern to researchers) but still not make a meaningful difference.

Alternatively, if you are facing an 80% chance of a catastrophic outcome and you can reduce that by 25%, to a 60% chance, this seems worth doing—the 25% reduction is more meaningful at the top end of the scale. Just about all of us have this personality. We know because of ideas worked out in psychology and behavioral economics, known as prospect theory and expected utility. For most of us nonrational human decision-makers, losses loom larger than gains. In other words, the pain of losing $100 is greater than the pleasure of winning $100. To put it another way, most of us would do more to avoid losing a year of life than we would to gain a year.

One of Kahneman and Tversky's many great insights was that both gains and losses are nonlinear, meaning that the same amount of gain (or loss) does not cause equal happiness (or sadness)—they're relative to your current state. If you are broke, gaining one dollar is very important. If you are a millionaire, it is not. There are other nonlinearities: Suppose you've just been diagnosed with a particular disease, and your doctor recommends a treatment that will increase your chance of recovery by ten percentage points. The 10% increase *feels* different, depending on your initial chance of recovery. Consider the following scenarios:

a. Increase your chance of recovery from 0% to 10%.
b. Increase your chance of recovery from 10% to 20%.
c. Increase your chance of recovery from 45% to 55%.
d. Increase your chance of recovery from 90% to 100%.

If you're like most people, scenarios A and D seem more compelling than B and C. Scenario A changes a certainty of death to a possibility of life. It's a small possibility, but we are programmed to cling to life and to look at the bright side when faced with alternatives such as this. Scenario D changes a possibility of death to a certainty of life. We jump at the chance of A or D; we want more information about B and C to decide if they're worth it.

Our intuitive system is not well configured to understand statistics or to make rational decisions in every case—this is the principal point behind Daniel Kahneman's *Thinking, Fast and Slow.* As an example, most of us are so sensitive to how a problem is presented—the way it is framed—that simple, even ridiculous manipulations can dramatically influence choices and preferences. For example, consider the following hypothetical data about outcomes of cancer surgery versus radiation. Which would you choose?

1a. Of 100 people having surgery, 90 live through the procedure, and 34 are alive at the end of five years.
1b. Of 100 people having radiation therapy, all live through the treatment, and 22 are alive at the end of five years.

If you chose surgery, you're like most people—the five-year outcome seems more appealing, even when pitted against the fact that the immediate outcome is better with the radiation.

Now the data are reframed in terms of mortality instead of survival—which would you prefer?

2a. Of 100 people having surgery, 10 die during the procedure, and 66 die by the end of five years.
2b. Of 100 people having radiation therapy, none dies during treatment, and 78 die by the end of five years.

These two formulations of the problem, or frames, are clearly identical mathematically—10 people out of 100 dying is the same as 90 people out of 100 living—but they are *not* identical psychologically. People are more likely to choose surgery in the first case and radiation in the second. In the first pair of scenarios, our attention is apparently drawn to the difference in five-year outcomes, where 34% are alive from surgery but only 22% from radiation. The framing of the second pair of scenarios apparently draws our attention to the difference in risk of the procedure itself: Radiation reduces the risk of immediate death from 10% to 0%. The framing effect was observed not just in patients but in experienced physicians and statistically sophisticated businesspeople.

Another aspect of framing is that most of us are better with pictures than with raw numbers, one of the motivations for changing the university calculus curriculum to use graphic-based presentations of difficult material. One way that has been tried by doctors to help patients better understand risks is to display visually the various outcomes for a hypothetical group of 100 patients. Here, in this example, are the risks and benefits of treatment with antibiotics for a middle-ear infection (otitis media). The number needed to treat is 20 (out of 100 people who are given antibiotics, 5 people will benefit). In addition, 9 people will not be cured and will need further follow-up. Of the group, 86 are neither helped nor harmed—at least not physically (perhaps financially). This is a lot of antibiotics being taken for such a small benefit. But graphics like these help patients to understand the risk and make better decisions because they can *see* the proportion of people in each category.

Another aspect of everyone's decision-making psychology is regret. Amos Tversky taught that risk aversion is driven by regret, a powerful psychological force. We tend to make decisions to avoid the regret that may come from having made the wrong decision, even if the choices were starkly contrasted in terms of expected value. Although treatment *X* may have

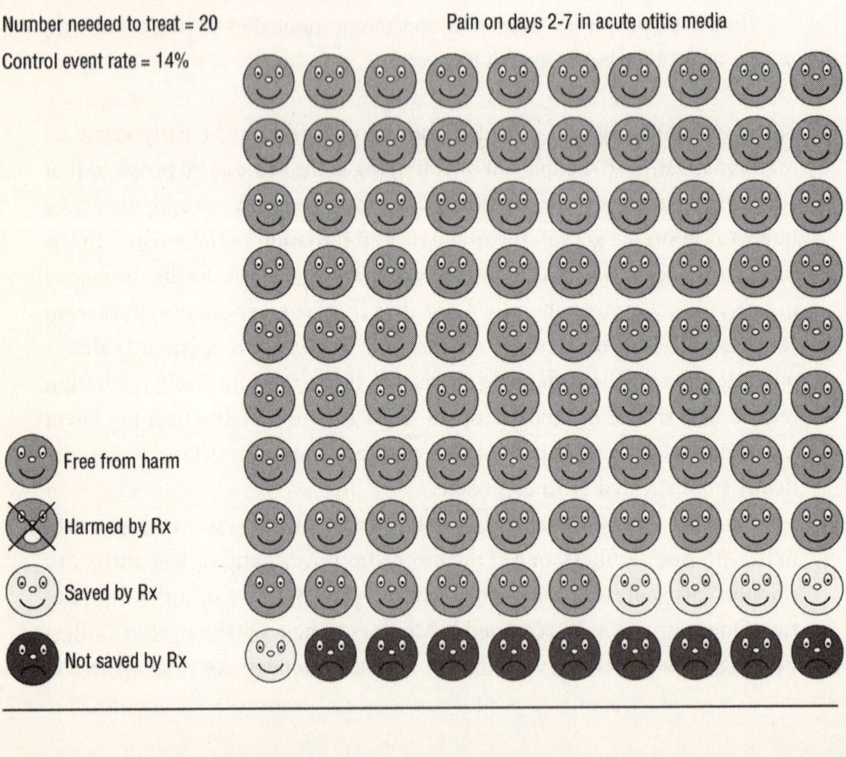

only a 10% chance of helping, and a high risk of side effects, you may choose it rather than live with the regret of learning later that *you* were among the 10% who would benefit from it. The emotional cost of regret can be enormous. As one breast cancer survivor put it, "They told me that they didn't know whether radiation therapy following the surgery would help or not. But I just kept thinking: What if the breast cancer returns and I didn't get it? I'd feel like such an idiot."

The two front tires on my car are five years old and there is still plenty of tread in the center, but I noticed some wear on the edges (this can occur from underinflation or lots of mountain driving). I asked a tire specialist about it and he pointed out that after five years, the rubber in tires becomes brittle and can crack, leading the tread and belts to separate from the rest of the tire. Coupled with the low edge tread, the tires have very little protection against hazards and could blow.

Now, I've driven for many years, and many hundreds of thousands of miles, and I've had only two or three tires blow out in my life. These were not dangerous situations, but they were inconvenient. You pull over, jack up the car, put on a spare, and if all goes well, you're only half an hour late to an appointment and you've only gotten your clothes a little dirty. On the other hand, if this had happened during a rainstorm, or on a mountain road or highway with no shoulder, it would have been much more unpleasant and possibly unsafe. Neither my mechanic nor the U.S. Department of Transportation can give me an accurate probability that my particular tires will blow before the center tread wears down to the point that they need to be replaced anyway. Even without that information, my hunch—and the hunch of my mechanic—is that the expected value or benefit of replacing the two tires is much lower than the cost of replacing them.

My friend Allan delights in saving money. I mean, he *loves* saving money, and always tells us how he bought his dishes at the Dollar Store and clothes at the Salvation Army store. It's not that he can't afford more—he has plenty of money—it's just that he feels like he's a champion in defying the consumer culture of the modern world. Allan would take great pleasure in boasting that he saved $200 by keeping his old tires, and he's willing to take his chances on an unknown probability of a future inconvenience. My disposition is that I'm more willing to trade money for convenience and safety. Others like the added assurance and are willing to pay for it. This is essentially what insurance is—if fire insurance were such a good deal for home owners, insurance companies would not be the rich multinational corporations they are; make no mistake, it is a good deal for *them*. But we like the peace of mind insurance offers. I bought the new tires. (Allan has read this passage and wants me to tell you that he thinks I made a decision driven by irrational fears and that I worry too much over nothing.)

Regret plays a huge role in decisions like this. If I ruin a nice picnic or a nice set of clothes or end up in a crash because I didn't spend that $200, I'm going to feel like an idiot. If Allan can get two more years of wear out of a pair of old tires, he will gleefully wave $200 cash in my face and tell me I was foolish for being such a worrywart.

Of course medical decision-making is also driven by fear of regret. Some of us are willing to trade inconvenience and discomfort now to avoid even a small, 5% chance of something going wrong and the regret of "If only I had done that thing the doctor recommended! What's wrong with me?—my *life* was at stake!" Allan, on the other hand, wants to maximize his pleasure in the moment and values the freedom to do what he pleases, unencumbered by health regimens or medical procedures that are not absolutely necessary *today*.

The best strategy for organizing medical information in cases like these is to arm yourself with the most accurate statistics attainable, as well as understanding your own biases and your stomach for risks and regret. If you find yourself lost and confused, friends and family are often helpful in reminding you of the core values you have lived your life by.

Medicine, Math, and Making Meaningful Choices

The other chapters in this book have been particularly concerned with attention and memory, but the great boon to making decisions about things that matter is mathematics, the so-called queen of the sciences. It might seem like dull, lifeless arithmetic at times, but to get organized in our thinking about life, we are ultimately going to have to let go of our abiding distaste for what sometimes seems like the inhumanity of probability analysis and mathematical calculations.

At that point in life, when facing a difficult choice with the most serious consequences, when we are scared, perplexed, and frustrated, when life is actually on the line, put your faith in the numbers. Try to gather as much information as you can and work through it with experts. If you need surgery, get it done by someone who has done a lot of them. As the CEO of your own health care, you need to understand how to take the information the doctors give you and analyze it in these fourfold tables, applying Bayesian reasoning, because that will take a lot of the guesswork out of medical decision-making, turning it into numbers that we can easily evaluate, since most of us don't have the refined intuitions of a Dr. Gregory House.

Take some time to make the decision, and consider it from a mathematical perspective. Talk it over with your doctor, and if your doctor isn't comfortable discussing statistics, find one who is. It's important to overcome your reluctance to ask questions or to argue with the doctor. Bring a loved one with you to back you up. Be sure the appointment is long enough—ask the doctor, "How long will you have for me?"

When we're sick or injured, our life seems to become controlled by experts, but it doesn't have to be that way. We can take charge of our own diseases, learn as much as we can about them and seek advice from more than one doctor. Doctors are people, too, of course, and they come with many different personalities, styles, and strengths. It's worth finding one whose style matches your own, who understands your needs and can help you meet them. Your relationship with a doctor shouldn't be one of parent and child, but one of partners who can work together in the business of achieving a common goal.

7

ORGANIZING THE BUSINESS WORLD

How We Create Value

At midday on September 30, 2006, the de la Concorde overpass at Laval outside of Montreal collapsed onto Quebec Autoroute 19, a major north-south artery. Five people were killed and six others were seriously injured when their cars were thrown over the edge. During the bridge's construction, the contractors had installed the steel reinforcing bars in the concrete incorrectly and, to save money, unilaterally decided to use a lower-quality concrete, which didn't meet design specifications. The ensuing government inquiry determined that this caused the bridge to collapse. Several other cases of low-quality concrete used in bridges, overpasses, and highways were identified in Quebec during a government inquiry into corruption in the construction industry. The history of shoddy construction practices is long—the wooden amphitheater in Fidenae near ancient Rome was built on a poor foundation, in addition to being improperly constructed, causing its collapse in 27 CE with 20,000 casualties. Similar disasters have occurred around the world, including the Teton Dam in Idaho in 1976, the collapse of Sichuan schools in the Chinese earthquake of 2008, and the failure of the Myllysilta Bridge in Turku, Finland, in 2010.

When they work properly, large civic projects like these involve many specialists and levels of checks and balances. The design, decision-making, and implementation are structured throughout an organization in a way that increases the chances for success and value. Ideally, what everyone is working for is a situation in which both human and material resources are allocated to achieve maximum value. (When all the components of a complex system achieve maximum value, and when it is impossible to make any one component of the system better without making at least one other component worse, the system can be said to have reached the Pareto optimum.) The asphalt worker paving a city street shouldn't normally make the decision about what quality of paving materials to use or how thick the layer should be—these decisions are made by higher-ups who must optimize, taking into account budgets, traffic flow, weather conditions, projected years of use, standard customs and practices, and potential lawsuits if potholes develop. These different aspects of information gathering and decision-making are typically distributed throughout an organization and may be assigned to different managers who then report to their higher-ups, who in turn balance the various factors to achieve the city's long-term goals, to satisfice this particular decision. As Adam Smith wrote in *The Wealth of Nations* in 1776, one of the greatest advances in work productivity was the division of labor. Dividing up tasks in any large human enterprise has proved extremely influential and useful.

Up until the mid 1800s, businesses were primarily small and family-run, serving only a local market. The spread of telegraph and railroads beginning in the mid 1800s made it possible for more companies to reach national and international markets, building on progress in maritime trade that had been developing for centuries. The need for documentation and functional specialization or cross-training grew dramatically along with this burgeoning long-distance commerce. The aggregate of letters, contracts, accounting, inventory, and status reports presented a new organizational challenge: How do you find that piece of information you need this afternoon inside this new mountain of paper? The Industrial Revolution ushered in the Age of Paperwork.

A series of railroad collisions in the early 1840s provided an urgent push toward improved documentation and functional specialization. Investigators concluded that the accidents resulted from communications among engineers and operators of various lines being handled too loosely. No one was certain who had authority over operations, and acknowledging receipt of important messages was not common practice. The railroad company investigators recommended standardizing and documenting operating procedures and rules. The aim was to transcend dependence upon the skills, memory, or capacity of any single individual. This involved writing a precise definition of duties and responsibilities for each job, coupled with standardized ways of performing these duties.

Functional specialization within the workforce became increasingly profitable and necessary so that things wouldn't grind to a halt if that lone worker who knew how to do this one particular thing was out sick. This led to functionally compartmentalized companies, and an even greater need for paperwork so workers could communicate with their bosses (who might be a continent away), and so that one division of a company could communicate with other divisions. The methods of record keeping and the management style that worked for a small family-owned company simply didn't scale to these new, larger firms.

Because of these developments, managers suddenly had greater control over the workers, specifically, over who was doing the work. Processes and procedures that had been kept in workers' heads were now recorded in handbooks and shared within the company, giving each worker an opportunity to learn from prior workers and to add improvements. Such a move follows the fundamental principle of the organized mind: externalizing memory. This involves taking the knowledge from the heads of a few individuals and putting it (such as in the form of written job descriptions) out-there-in-the-world where others can see and use it.

Once management obtained detailed task and job descriptions, it was possible to fire a lazy or careless employee and replace him or her with someone else without a great loss of productivity—management simply communicated the details of the job and where things had been left off. This was essential in building and repairing the railroads, where great distances existed between the company headquarters and the workers in the field. Yet soon the drive to systematize jobs extended to managers, so managers became as replaceable as workers, a development promoted by the English efficiency engineer Alexander Hamilton Church.

The trend toward systematizing jobs and increasing organization efficiency led the Scottish engineer Daniel McCallum to create the first organizational charts in 1854 as a way to easily visualize reporting relationships among employees. A typical org chart shows who reports to whom; the downward arrows indicate a supervisor-to-supervisee relationship.

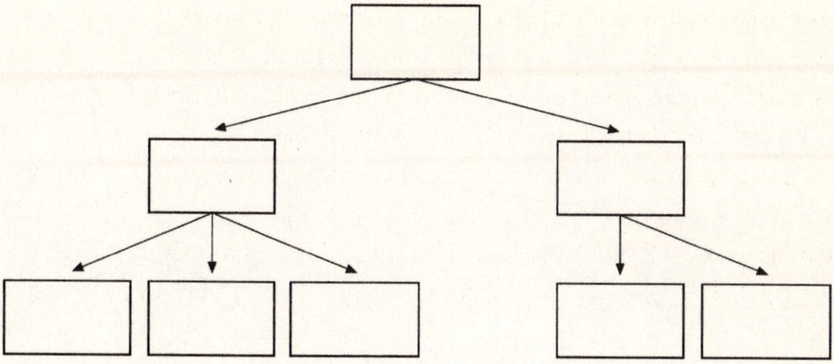

Org charts represent reporting hierarchies very well, but they don't show how coworkers interact with one another; and although they show business relationships, they do not show personal relationships. Network diagrams were first introduced by the Romanian sociologist Jacob Moreno in the 1930s. They are more useful in understanding which employees work with and know one another, and they're often used by management consultants to diagnose problems in structural organization, productivity, or efficiency.

Below is the network diagram from a one-month survey of an Internet start-up company (the company was eventually sold to Sony). The diagram shows who interacted with whom during the month surveyed; the interactions shown are dichotomous, without attention to the number or quality of interactions. The diagram reveals that the founder (the node at the top) interacted with only one other person, his COO; the founder was on a fund-raising trip this particular month. The COO interacted with three people. One of them was in charge of product development, and he interacted with an employee who oversaw a network of seven consultants. The consultants interacted with one another a great deal.

Creating a network map allowed management to see that there was one person whom nobody ever talked to, and two people who interacted extensively with each other but no one else. Various forms of network diagrams are possible, including using "heat maps" in which colors indicate the degree of interaction (hotter colors mean more interaction along a node, colder colors mean less). Network maps can be used in conjunction with hierarchical organization charts to identify which members of an organization

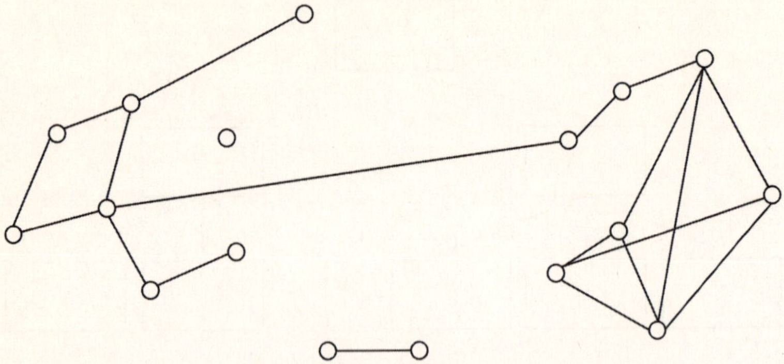

already know one another, which in turn can facilitate creating project teams or reorganizing certain functions and reporting structures. Standard organizational behavior practice is to split up teams that aren't functioning efficiently and to try to replicate teams that are. But because team efficiency isn't simply a matter of who has what skills, and is more a matter of interpersonal familiarity and who works well together, the network diagram is especially useful; it can track not just which team members work together but which, if any, socialize together outside of work (and this could be represented differentially with color or dotted lines, or any number of standard graphing techniques).

Organizations can have either flat (horizontal) or deep (vertical) hierarchies, which can have a great impact on employee and manager efficiency and effectiveness. Compare these two different org charts, for a flat company (left) with only three levels and a vertical company (right) with five levels:

The command structure in corporate and military organizations can take either form, and each system has advantages and disadvantages (conventional military structure is vertical, but terrorist and other cell-based groups typically use flat structure with decentralized control and communications).

A flat structure encourages people to work together and allows for overlap in effort, often empowering employees to do what needs to be done and apply their talents outside of formal command or task structure. A drawback of flat structure is that there may be only one person who has effective decision-making authority, and that person will have too many decisions to make. Due to the lack of a hierarchy, extra effort is needed to establish who has responsibility for which tasks. Indeed, some form of

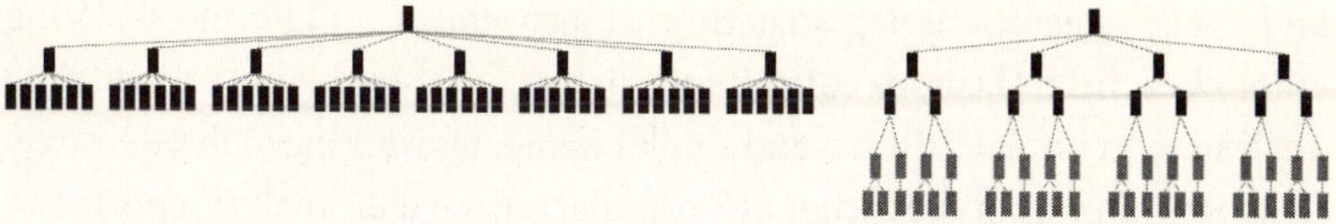

vertical structure is essential to achieve coordination among the employees and their projects, to avoid duplication of effort, and to ensure coherence across different components of a project. The additional advantage of vertical structure is that employees can more easily be held accountable for their decisions and their work product.

Tall vertical systems usually encourage specialization and the efficiencies that come from it. But tall structures can also result in employees being isolated from one another and working in silos, unaware of what others are doing that might be closely related to their own work. When a vertical system becomes too tall (too many levels), it can take too much time for instructions to filter down to the ground from higher up, or vice versa. Railroad companies led the way to more complex organization in the business world, and in the last fifty years the level of complexity has grown so that in many cases it is impossible to keep track of what everyone is doing. Fifty companies in the world have more than a quarter million employees, and seven companies in the world have more than one million.

Companies can be thought of as transactive memory systems. Part of the art of fitting into a company as a new employee, indeed part of becoming an effective employee (especially in upper management), is learning who holds what knowledge. If you want the 2014 sales figures for the southeastern region, you call Rachel, but she has the figures only for framistans; if you want to include your company's business in selling gronespiels, you need to call Scotty; if you want to know if United Frabezoids ever got paid, you call Robin in accounts payable. The company as a whole is a large repository of information, with individual humans effectively playing the role of neural networks running specialized programs. No one person has all the knowledge, and indeed, no one person in a large company even knows whom to ask for every bit of knowledge it takes to keep the company running.

A typical story: Booz Allen Hamilton (a consulting firm) was given a big contract by the Fortune 100 company where Linda worked as the executive assistant to the CEO. Their assignment was to study the organization and make suggestions for structural improvement. While interviewing employees there, the Booz consultants discovered three highly trained data analysts with similar skill sets and similar mandates working in three entirely separate columns of the company's org chart. Each data analyst reported to an assistant manager, who reported to a district manager, who reported to a division manager, who reported to a vice president. Each data analyst was ultimately responsible to an entirely different vice president, making it virtually impossible for them, their bosses, or even their bosses' bosses to know about the existence of the others. (They even worked in different buildings.) Booz consultants were able to bring the analysts together for weekly meetings where they pooled their knowledge, shared certain tricks they had learned, and helped one another solve common technical problems they were facing. This led to great efficiencies and cost savings for the company.

Vertical structures are necessary when a high degree of control and direct supervision over employees are required. Nuclear power plants, for example, tend to have very tall vertical structures because supervision is extremely important—even a small error can result in a disaster. The vertical structure allows managers to constantly check and cross-check the work of lower-level managers to ensure that rules and procedures are followed accurately and consistently.

RBC Royal Bank of Canada is a $30 billion company, serving 18 million customers. Its corporate culture places a high value on mentorship, on managers developing subordinates, improving their chances of being promoted, and ensuring gender equity. Its vertical structure allows for close supervision of employees by their managers. Liz Claiborne, Inc., was the first Fortune 500 company to be founded by a woman. When Liz Claiborne was designing the structure of her company, she chose flat—four levels for four thousand employees—in order to keep the company nimble and able to respond quickly to changing fashion trends. There is no evidence that structure in and of itself affects the profitability of a company; different structures work best for different companies.

The size of an organization tends to predict how many levels it will have, but the relationship is logarithmic. That is, while an organization with 1,000 employees on average has four hierarchical levels, increasing the number of employees by a factor of 10 does not increase the number of levels by 10; rather, it increases the number of levels by a factor of 2. And after an organization reaches 10,000 employees, an asymptote is reached: Organizations with 12,000, 100,000, or 200,000 employees rarely have more than nine or ten levels in their hierarchy. The principle of minimum chain of command states that an organization should choose the fewest number of hierarchical levels possible.

These same descriptions of structure—flat and vertical—can be applied to a corporate website, or the file system on your own computer. Imagine that the flat and vertical structure drawings on page 273 are site maps for two different versions of a company's website. Both sites might present visitors with the same data, but the visitors' experience will be very different. With a well-designed flat organization, the visitor can obtain summary information in one click, and more detailed information in two clicks. With the vertical organization, that same visitor might also locate desired summary information in one or two clicks, but the detailed information will require four clicks. Of course sites aren't always designed well or in a way that allows a visitor to find what she's looking for—Web designers are not typical users, and the labels, menus, and hierarchies they use might not be obvious to anyone else. Hence the user may end up doing a great deal of searching, fishing, and backtracking. The flat organization makes it easier to backtrack; the vertical makes it easier to locate a hard-to-find file if the visitor can be sure she's in the correct subnode. Still, there are limits to flat organizations' ease of use: If the number of middle-level categories becomes too great, it takes too long to review them all, and because they themselves are not hierarchically organized, there can be redundancies and overlap. Visitors can easily become overwhelmed by too many choices—deep hierarchy offers fewer choices at once. The same analysis applies to the folders within folders on your hard drive.

But the organization of people is radically different from the organization of a website. Even in a deep vertical structure, people can and need to have agency from time to time. The lowliest transit worker sometimes needs to jump on the track to rescue a woman who fell; an investment bank secretary needs to be a whistle-blower; a mailroom worker needs to notice the disgruntled coworker who showed up with a rifle. All those actions fulfill a part of the company's objectives—safety and ethical dealings.

In any hierarchically organized firm or agency, the task of carrying out the company's objectives typically falls to the people at the lowest levels of the hierarchy. Cell phones aren't built by the engineer who designed them or the executive who is in charge of marketing and selling them but by technicians on an assembly line. A fire isn't put out by the fire chief but by the coordinated efforts of a team of firefighters on the street. While managers and administrators do not typically *do* the main work of a company, they play an essential role in accomplishing the company's objectives. Even though it is the machine gunner and not the major who fights battles, the major is likely to have a greater influence on the outcome of a battle than any single machine gunner.

Decision-Making Throughout the Hierarchy

Anyone who has ever owned something of high value that needs repairs—a home or a car, for example—has had to contend with compromises and has seen how a management perspective is necessary to the decision-making process. Do you buy the thirty-year roof or the twenty-year roof? The top-of-the-line washing machine or the bargain brand? Suppose your mechanic tells you that you need a new water pump for your car and that, in descending order of price, he can install an original equipment manufacturer (OEM) part from the dealer, a functionally identical part from an overseas company, or a warrantied used part from a junkyard. He can't make the decision for you because he doesn't know your disposable income or your plans for the car. (Are you getting ready to sell it? Restoring it for entry in a car show? Planning to drive it through the Rockies next July, where the cooling system will be pushed to its limits?) In short, the mechanic doesn't have a high-level perspective on your long-range plans for your car or your money. Any decision other than the OEM part installed by an authorized dealer is a compromise, but one that many people are willing to make in the interest of satisficing.

Standard models of decision-making assume that a decision maker—especially in economic and business contexts—is not influenced by emotional considerations. But neuroeconomics research has shown this is not true: Economic decisions produce activity in emotional regions of the brain, including the insula and amygdala. The old cartoon image of the angel on one shoulder and the devil on the other, giving competing advice to a flummoxed head in the middle, is apt here. Benefits are evaluated deep inside the brain, in a part of the striatum closest to your spine (which includes the brain's reward center, the nucleus accumbens), while costs are simultaneously evaluated in the amygdala, another deep structure, commonly thought of as the brain's fear center (the region responsible for the fight-or-flight response during threats to survival and other dangers). Taking in this competing information about costs and benefits, the prefrontal cortex acts as the decider. This isn't the same thing as the experience we have of consciously trying to decide between two alternatives; decision-making is often very rapid, outside our conscious control, and involves heuristics and cognitive impulses that have evolved to serve us in a wide range of situations. The rationality we think we bring to decision-making is partly illusory.

Major decisions are usually not made by any one individual, nor by any easily defined group of individuals. They emerge through a process of vastly distributed discussion, consultation, and sharing of information. This is both a positive and a negative feature of large organizations. When they work well, great things can be accomplished that would be impossible for a small number of people to do: designing and building the Hoover Dam, the plasma TV, or Habitat for Humanity. But, as suggested at the beginning of this chapter, when communications or the exercise of competent and ethically based authority do not work well, or the optimal checks and balances aren't in place, you end up with bridge collapses, Enron, or Chernobyl.

In general, in a multilevel vertical organization, the chain of authority and direction travels downward with increasing specificity. The CEO may articulate a plan to one of his VPs; that VP adds some specificity about how best he thinks the plan can be accomplished and hands it to a division manager with experience and expertise in these sorts of operations. This continues on, down the line, until it reaches the individuals who actually do the work.

We see this in the organization of military authority. The general or commander defines a goal. The colonel assigns tasks to each battalion in his command; the major to each company in his battalion; the captain to each platoon in his company. Each officer narrows the scope and increases the specificity of the instructions he passes on. Still, the modern army gives a fair degree of situational control and discretion to the soldiers on the ground. Perhaps surprisingly, the U.S. Army has been among the organizations most adaptable to change, and has thought deeply about how to the apply findings of psychological science to organizational behavior. Its current policy strives to empower people throughout the chain of command, "allowing subordinate and adjacent units to use their common understanding of the operational environment and commander's intent, in conjunction with their own initiative, to synchronize actions with those of other units without direct control from the higher headquarters."

The value of limited local autonomy and the exercise of discretion by subordinates is not a recent development in organizational strategy, for companies or for the military. Nearly one hundred years ago, the 1923 U.S. Army Field Service Regulations manual expected that subordinates would have a degree of autonomy in matters of judgment, stating that "an order should not trespass upon the province of a subordinate."

Smooth operation within the military or a company requires trust between subordinates and superiors and an expectation that subordinates will do the right thing. The current edition of the U.S. Army Training Manual puts it this way:

> Our fundamental doctrine for command requires trust throughout the chain of command. Superiors trust subordinates and empower them to accomplish missions within their intent. Subordinates trust superiors to give them the freedom to execute the commander's intent and support their decisions. The trust between all levels depends upon candor. . . .
>
> Army doctrine stresses mission command, the conduct of military operations that allows subordinate leaders maximum initiative. It acknowledges that operations in the land domain are complex and often chaotic, and micromanagement does not work. Mission command emphasizes competent leaders applying their expertise to the situation as it exists on the ground and advancing the mission based on their commander's intent. Mission command fosters a culture of trust, mutual understanding, and a willingness to learn from mistakes. . . . Commanders . . . provide subordinates as much leeway for initiative as possible while keeping operations synchronized.

Superiors often resist delegating authority or decisions. They rationalize this by saying that they are more highly skilled, trained, or experienced than the subordinate. But there are good reasons for delegating decision-making. First, the superior is more highly paid, and so the cost of the decision must be weighed against the benefit of having such a high-paid individual make it. (Remember the maxim from Chapter 5: How much is your time worth?) Along the same lines, the superior has to conserve his time so that he can use it for making more important decisions. Secondly, subordinates are often in a better position to make decisions because the facts of the case may be directly available to them and not to the superior. General Stanley McChrystal articulated this with respect to his leadership during the United States–Iraq conflict:

> In my command, I would push down the ability and authority to act. It doesn't mean the leader abrogates responsibility but that the team members are partners, not underlings. They'd wake me up in the middle of the night and ask "Can we drop this bomb?" and I'd ask "Should we?" Then they'd say, "That's why we're calling you!" But I don't know anything more than they're telling me, and I'm probably not smart enough to add any value to the knowledge they already have from the field.

Steve Wynn's management philosophy endorses the same idea:

> Like most managers, I'm at the top of a large pyramidal structure, and the people who are below me make most of the decisions. And most of the time, the decisions that they make are of the "A or B" type: Should we do A or should we do B? And for most of those, the decision is obvious—one outcome is clearly better than the other. In a few cases, the people below me have to think hard about which one to do, and this can be challenging. They might have to consult with someone else, look deeper into the problem, get more information.
>
> Once in a while a decision comes along where both outcomes look bad. They have a choice between A and B and neither one is going to be good, and they can't figure out which one to choose.

> That's when they end up on my calendar. So when I look at my calendar, if the Director of Food Services is on there, I know it's something bad. Either he's going to quit, or he's got to make a decision between two very bad outcomes. My job when that happens is not to make the decision for them as you might think. By definition, the people who are coming to me are the real experts on the problem. They know lots more about it, and they are closer to it. All I can do is try to get them to look at the problem in a different light. To use an aviation metaphor, I try to get them to see things from 5,000 feet up. I tell them to back up and find out *one truth that they know is indisputable.* However many steps they might have to back up, I talk it over with them until they find the deep truth underlying all of it. The truth might be something like "the most important thing at our hotel is the guest experience," or "no matter what, we cannot serve food that is not 100% fresh." Once they identify that core truth, we creep forward slowly through the problem and often a solution will emerge. But I don't make the decision for them. They're the ones who have to bring the decision to the people under them, and they're the ones who have to live with it, so they need to come to the decision themselves and be comfortable with it.

It is just as important to recognize the value of making difficult decisions when necessary. As former New York mayor Michael Bloomberg notes:

> A leader is someone willing to make decisions. Politicians can get elected if voters think they will do things, even if they don't support all those things. W [President George W. Bush] was elected not because everyone agreed with him but because they knew he was sincere and would do what he thought needed to be done.

Ethics necessarily come into play in corporate and military decision-making. What is good for one's own self-interests, or the company's interests, is not always consonant with what is good for the community, the populace, or the world. Humans are social creatures, and most of us unconsciously modify our behavior to minimize conflict with those around us. Social comparison theory models this phenomenon well. If we see other cars parking in a no-parking zone, we are more likely to park there ourselves. If we see other dog owners ignoring the law to clean up after their dogs, we are more likely to ignore it, too. Part of this comes from a sense of equity and fairness that has been shown to be innately wired into our brains, a product of evolution. (Even three-year-olds react to inequality.) In effect, we think, "Why should *I* be the chump who picks up dog poo when everyone else just leaves theirs all over the Boston Commons?" Of course the argument is specious because good behaviors are just as contagious as bad, and if we model correct behavior, others are likely to follow.

Organizations that discuss ethics openly, and that model ethical behavior throughout the organization, create a culture of adhering to ethical norms because it is "what everyone does around here." Organizations that allow employees to ignore ethics form a breeding ground for bad behavior that tempts even the most ethically minded and strong-willed person, a classic case of the power of the situation overpowering individual, dispositional traits. The ethical person may eventually find him- or herself thinking, "I'm fighting a losing battle; there's no point in going the extra mile because no one notices and no one cares." Doing the right thing when no one is looking is a mark of personal integrity, but many people find it very difficult to do.

The army is one of the most influential organizations to have addressed this, and they do so with surprising eloquence:

> All warfare challenges the morals and ethics of Soldiers. An enemy may not respect international conventions and may commit atrocities with the aim of provoking retaliation in kind. . . . All leaders shoulder the responsibility that their subordinates return from a campaign not only as good Soldiers, but also as good citizens. . . . Membership in the Army profession carries with it significant responsibility—the effective and ethical application of combat power.

Ethical decision-making invokes different brain regions than economic decision-making and again, because of the metabolic costs, switching between these modes of thought can be difficult for many people. It's difficult therefore to simultaneously weigh various outcomes that have both economic and ethical implications. Making ethical or moral decisions involves distinct structures within the frontal lobes: the orbitofrontal cortex (located just behind the eyes) and the dorsolateral prefrontal cortex just above it. These two regions are also required for understanding ourselves in relation to others (social perception), and the compliance with social norms. When damaged, they can lead to socially inappropriate behavior such as swearing, walking around naked, and saying insulting things to people right to their faces. Making and evaluating ethical decisions also involves distinct subregions of the amygdala, the hippocampus (the brain's memory index), and the back portion of the superior temporal sulcus, a deep groove in the brain that runs from front to back behind the ears. As with economic decisions involving costs and benefits, the prefrontal cortex acts as the decider between the moral actions being contemplated.

Neuroimaging studies have shown that ethical behavior is processed in the same way regardless of whether it involves helping someone in need or thwarting an unethical action. In one experiment, participants watched videos of people being compassionate toward an injured individual, or aggressive toward a violent assailant. As long as the people in the video were behaving in an ethically appropriate and socially sanctioned way, the same brain regions were active in the participants who watched the videos. Moreover, such brain activations are universal across people—different people contemplating the same ethical acts show a high degree of synchronization of their brain activity; that is, their neurons fire in similar, synchronous patterns. The neuronal populations affected by this include those in the insula (mentioned above in the discussion of economic decision-making), our friend the prefrontal cortex, and the precuneus, a region at the top and back of the head associated with self-reflection and perspective taking, and which exists not just in humans but in monkeys.

Does this mean that even monkeys have a moral sense? A recent study by one of the leading scientists of animal behavior, Frans de Waal, asked just this question. He found that monkeys have a highly developed sense of what is and is not equitable. In one study, brown capuchin monkeys who participated in an experiment with another monkey could choose to reward only themselves (a selfish option) or both of them (an equitable, prosocial option). The monkeys consistently chose to reward their partner. And this was more than a knee-jerk response. De Waal found convincing evidence that the capuchins were performing a kind of moral calculation.

When the experimenter "accidentally" overpaid the partner monkey with a better treat, the deciding monkey withheld the reward to the partner, evening out the payoffs. In another study, monkeys performed tasks in exchange for food rewards given by the experimenters. If the experimenter gave a larger reward to one monkey than another for the same task, the monkey with the smaller reward would suddenly stop performing the task and sulk. Think about this: These monkeys were willing to *forgo* a reward entirely (a tempting piece of food) simply because they felt the organization of the reward structure was unfair.

Those In Charge

Conceptions of leadership vary from culture to culture and across time, including figures as diverse as Julius Caesar and Thomas Jefferson, Jack Welch of GE and Herb Kelleher of Southwest Airlines. Leaders can be reviled or revered, and they gain followers through threat of punishment (economic, psychological, or physical), or a combination of personal magnetism, motivation, and inspiration. In modern companies, government, or the military, a good leader might be best defined as anyone who inspires and influences people to accomplish goals and to pursue actions for the greater good of the organization. In a free society, an effective leader motivates people to focus their thinking and efforts in ways that allow them to do their best and to produce work that pushes them to the highest levels of their abilities. In some cases, people so inspired discover previously unseen talents and achieve great satisfaction from their work and their interactions with coworkers.

A broader definition of leadership promoted by Harvard psychologist Howard Gardner includes individuals who significantly affect the thoughts, feelings, or behaviors of a significant number of individuals indirectly, through the works they create—these can be works of art, recipes, technological artifacts and products . . . almost anything. In this conception, influential leaders would include Amantine Dupin (George Sand), Picasso, Louis Armstrong, Marie Curie, and Martha Graham. These leaders typically work outside of any corporate structure, although like anyone, they have to work with big business at some contractual level. Nevertheless, they don't fit the standard business-school profile of a leader who has significant economic impact.

Both kinds of leaders, those inside and outside the corporate world, possess certain psychological traits. They tend to be adaptable and responsive, high in empathy, and able to see problems from all sides. These qualities require two distinct forms of cognition: social intelligence and flexible, deep analytic intelligence. An effective leader can quickly understand opposing views, how people came to hold them, and how to resolve conflicts in ways that are perceived to be mutually satisfying and beneficial. Leaders are often adept at bringing people together—suppliers, potential adversaries, competitors, characters in a story—who appear to have conflicting goals. A great business leader uses her empathy to allow people or organizations to save face in negotiations so that each side in a completed negotiation can feel they got what they wanted (and a gifted negotiator can make each side feel they got a little bit more than the other party). In Gardner's model, it is no coincidence that many great leaders are also great storytellers—they motivate others around them with a compelling narrative, one that they themselves embody. Leaders show greater integration of electrical activity in the brain across disparate regions, meaning that they use more of their brain in a better-orchestrated fashion than the rest of us. Using these measures of neural integration, we can identify leaders in athletics and music, and in the next few years, the techniques promise to be refined enough to use as screening for leadership positions.

Great leaders can turn competitors into allies. Norbert Reithofer, CEO of BMW, and Akio Toyoda, CEO of Toyota—clearly competitors—launched a collaboration in 2011 to create an environmentally friendly luxury vehicle and a midsize sports car. The on-again, off-again partnership and strategic alliance between Steve Jobs at Apple and Bill Gates at Microsoft strengthened both companies and allowed them to better serve their customers.

As is obvious from the rash of corporate scandals in the United States over the last twenty years, negative leadership can be toxic, resulting in the collapse of companies or the loss of reputation and resources. It is often the result of self-centered attitudes, a lack of empathy for others within the organization, and a lack of concern for the organization's long-term health. The U.S. Army recognizes this in military and civic organizations as well: "Toxic leaders consistently use dysfunctional behaviors to deceive, intimidate, coerce, or unfairly punish others to get what they want for themselves." Prolonged use of these tactics undermines and erodes subordinates' will, initiative, and morale.

Leaders are found in all levels of the company—one doesn't have to be the CEO to exert influence and affect corporate culture (or to be a storyteller with the power to motivate others). Again, some of the best thinking on the subject comes from the U.S. Army. The latest version of their *Mission Command* manual outlines five principles that are shared by commanders and top executives in the most successful multinational businesses:

- Build cohesive teams through mutual trust.
- Create shared understanding.
- Provide a clear and concise set of expectations and goals.
- Allow workers at all levels to exercise disciplined initiative.
- Accept prudent risks.

Trust is gained or lost through everyday actions, not through grand or occasional gestures. It takes time to build—coming from successful shared experiences and training—a history of two-way communication, the successful completion of projects, and achievement of goals.

Creating shared understanding refers to company management communicating with subordinates at all levels the corporate vision, goals, and the purpose and significance of any specific initiatives or projects that must be undertaken by employees. This helps to empower employees to use their discretion because they share in a situational understanding of the overriding purpose of their actions. Managers who hide this purpose from underlings, out of a misguided sense of preserving power, end up with unhappy employees who perform their jobs with tunnel vision and who lack the information to exercise initiative.

At McGill University, the dean of science undertook an initiative several years ago called *STARS (Science Talks About Research for Staff)*. These were lunchtime talks by professors in the science department who described their research to the general staff: secretaries, bookkeepers, technicians, and the custodial staff. These jobs tend to be very far removed from the actual science. The initiative was successful by any measure—the staff gained an understanding of the larger context of what they were doing. A bookkeeper realized she wasn't just balancing the books for any old research lab but for one that was on the cusp of curing a major disorder. A secretary discovered that she was supporting work that uncovered the cause of the 2011 tsunami and that could help save lives with better tsunami predictions. The effect of *Soup and Science* was that everyone felt a renewed sense of purpose for their jobs. One custodian commented later that he was proud to be part of a team doing such important work. His work improved and he began to take personal initiative that improved the research environment in very real and tangible ways.

The third of the army's five command principles concerns providing a clear and concise expression of expectations and goals, the purpose of particular tasks, and the intended end state. This furnishes focus to staff and helps subordinates and their superiors to achieve desired results without extensive further instructions. The senior manager's intent provides the basis for unity of effort throughout the larger workforce.

Successful managers understand that they cannot provide guidance or direction for all conceivable contingencies. Having communicated a clear and concise expression of their intent, they then convey the boundaries within which subordinates may exercise disciplined initiative while maintaining unity of effort. *Disciplined initiative* is defined as taking action in the absence of specific instructions when existing instructions no longer fit the situation, or unforeseen opportunities arise.

Prudent risk is the deliberate exposure to a negative outcome when the employee judges that the potential positive outcome is worth the cost. It involves making careful, calculated assessments of the upsides and downsides of different actions. As productivity expert Marvin Weisbord notes, "There are no technical alternatives to personal responsibility and cooperation in the workplace. What's needed are more people who will stick their necks out."

Some employees are more productive than others. While some of this variation is attributable to differences in personality, work ethic, and other individual differences (which have a genetic and neurocognitive basis), the nature of the job itself can play a significant role. There are things that managers can do to improve productivity, based on recent findings in neuroscience and social psychology. Some of these are obvious and well known, such as setting clear goals and providing high-quality, immediate feedback. Expectations need to be reasonable or employees feel overwhelmed, and if they fall behind, they feel they can never catch up. Employee productivity is directly related to job satisfaction, and job satisfaction in turn is related to whether employees experience that they are doing a good job in terms of both quality and quantity of output.

There's a part of the brain called Area 47 in the lateral prefrontal cortex that my colleague Vinod Menon and I have been closely studying for the last fifteen years. Although no larger than your pinky finger, it's a fascinating area just behind your temples that has kept us busy. Area 47 contains prediction circuits that it uses in conjunction with memory to form projections about future states of events. If we can predict some (but not all) aspects of how a job will go, we find it rewarding. If we can predict *all* aspects of the job, down to the tiniest minutiae, it tends to be boring because there is nothing new and no opportunity to apply the discretion and judgment that management consultants and the U.S. Army have justly identified as components to finding one's work meaningful and satisfying. If some but not too many aspects of the job are surprising in interesting ways, this can lead to a sense of discovery and self-growth.

Finding the right balance to keep Area 47 happy is tricky, but the most job satisfaction comes from a combination of these two: We function best when we are under some constraints and are allowed to exercise individual creativity within those constraints. In fact, this is posited to be *the* driving force in many forms of creativity, including literary and musical. Musicians work under the very tight constraints of a tonal system—Western music uses only twelve different notes—and yet within that system, there is great flexibility. The composers widely regarded as among the most creative in musical history fit this description of balancing creativity within constraints. Mozart didn't invent the symphony (Torelli and Scarlatti are credited with that) and The Beatles didn't invent rock 'n' roll (Chuck Berry and Little Richard get the credit, but its roots go back clearly to Ike Turner and Jackie Brenston in 1951, Louis Jordan and Lionel Hampton in the 1940s). It's what Mozart and The Beatles did within the tight constraints of those forms, the enormous creativity and ingenuity they brought to their work, that pushed at the boundaries of those forms, leading to them being redefined.

But there is a critical point about differences between individuals that exerts arguably more influence on worker productivity than any other. The factor is locus of control, a fancy name for how people view their autonomy and agency in the world. People with an internal locus of control believe that they are responsible for (or at least can influence) their own fates and life outcomes. They may or may not feel they are leaders, but they feel that they are essentially in charge of their lives. Those with an external locus of control see themselves as relatively powerless pawns in some game played by others; they believe that other people, environmental forces, the weather, malevolent gods, the alignment of celestial bodies—basically any and all external events—exert more influence on their lives than they themselves do. (This latter view is artistically conveyed in existential novels by Kafka and Camus, not to mention Greek and Roman mythology.) Of course these are extremes, and most people fall somewhere along a continuum between them. But locus of control turns out to be a significant moderating variable in a trifecta of life expectancy, life satisfaction, and work productivity. This is what the modern U.S. Army has done in allowing subordinates to use their own initiative: They've shifted a great deal of the locus of control in situations to the people actually doing the work.

Individuals with an internal locus of control will attribute success to their own efforts ("I tried really hard") and likewise with failure ("I didn't try hard enough"). Individuals with an external locus of control will praise or blame the external world ("It was pure luck" or "The competition was rigged"). In school settings, students with a high internal locus of control believe that hard work and focus will result in positive outcomes, and indeed, as a group they perform better academically. Locus of control also affects purchasing decisions. For example, women who believe they can control their weight respond most favorably to slender advertising models, and women who believe they can't respond better to larger-size models.

Locus of control also shows up in gambling behaviors: Because people with a high external locus of control believe that things happen *to* them capriciously (rather than being the agents of their own fortunes), they are more likely to believe that events are governed by hidden and unseen outside forces such as luck. Accordingly, they are likely to take more chances, try riskier bets, and bet on a card or roulette number that hasn't come up in a long time, under the mistaken notion that this outcome is now due; this is the so-called gambler's fallacy. They are also more likely to believe that if they need money, gambling can provide it.

Locus of control appears to be a stable internal trait that is not significantly affected by experiences. That is, you might expect that people who experience a great deal of hardship would give up any notions of their own agency in the face of overwhelming evidence to the contrary and become externals. And you might expect that those who experience a great deal of success would become internals, self-confident believers that they were the agents of that success all along. But the research doesn't bear this out. For example, researchers studied small independent business owners whose shops were destroyed by Hurricane Agnes in 1972, at the time, the costliest hurricane to hit the United States. Over one hundred business owners were assessed for whether they tended toward internal or external locus of control. Then, three and a half years after the hurricane, they were reassessed. Many realized big improvements in their businesses during the recovery years, but many did not, seeing once thriving businesses deteriorate dramatically; many were thrown into ruin.

The interesting finding is that on the whole, none of these individuals shifted their views about internal versus external locus of control as a function of how their fortunes changed. Those who were internals to begin with remained internals regardless of whether their business performance improved or not during the intervening time. Same with the externals. Interestingly, however, those internals whose performance improved showed a shift toward *greater* internality, meaning they attributed the improvement to their hard work. Those who were externals and who experienced setbacks and losses showed a shift toward greater externality, meaning they attributed their failures to a deepening of the situational factors and bad luck that they felt they had experienced throughout their lives. In other words, a change of fortune following the hurricane that confirmed their beliefs only caused them to increase the strength of those beliefs; a change in fortune that went counter to their beliefs (an internal losing everything, an external whose business recovered) did nothing to change their beliefs.

The locus-of-control construct is measurable with standard psychological tests and turns out to be predictive of job performance. It also influences the managerial style that will be effective. Employees who have an external locus of control believe their own actions will not lead to the attainment of rewards or the avoidance of punishment, and therefore, they don't respond to rewards and punishments the way others do. Higher managers tend to have a high internal locus of control.

Internals tend to be higher achievers, and externals tend to experience more stress and are prone to depression. Internals, as you might expect, exert greater effort to influence their environment (because, unlike externals, they believe their efforts will amount to something). Internals tend to learn better, seek new information more actively, and use that information more effectively, and they are better at problem solving. Such findings may lead managers to think they should screen for and hire only people with an internal locus of control, but it depends on the particular job. Internals tend to exhibit less conformity than externals, and less attitude change after being exposed to a persuasive message. Because internals are more likely to initiate changes in their environment, they can be more troublesome to supervise. Moreover, they're sensitive to reinforcement, so if effort in a particular job doesn't lead to rewards, they may lose motivation more than an external, who has no expectation that his or her effort really matters anyway.

Industrial organization scientist Paul Spector of the University of South Florida says that internals may attempt to control work flow, task accomplishment, operating procedures, work assignments, relationships with supervisors and subordinates, working conditions, goal setting, work scheduling, and organizational policy. Spector summarizes: "Externals make more compliant followers or subordinates than do internals, who are likely to be independent and resist control by superiors and other individuals. . . . Externals, because of their greater compliance, would probably be easier to supervise as they would be more likely to follow directions." So the kind of employee who will perform best depends on the kind of work that needs to be done. If the job requires adaptability and complex learning, independence and initiative, or high motivation, internals would be expected to perform better. When the job requires compliance and strict adherence to protocols, the external would perform better.

The combination of high autonomy and an internal locus of control is associated with the highest levels of productivity. Internals typically "make things happen," and this, combined with the opportunity to do so (through high autonomy), delivers results. Obviously, some jobs that involve repetitive, highly constrained tasks such as some assembly-line work, toll taking, stockroom, cashier, and manual labor are better suited to people who don't desire autonomy. Many people prefer jobs that are predictable and where they don't have to take personal responsibility for how they organize their time or their tasks. These workers will perform better if they can simply follow instructions and are not asked to make any decisions. Even within these kinds of jobs, however, the history of business is full of cases in which a worker exercised autonomy in a job where it was not typically found and came up with a better way of doing things, and a manager had the foresight to accept the worker's suggestions. (The sandpaper salesman Richard G. Drew, who invented masking tape and turned 3M into one of the largest companies, is one famous case.)

On the other hand, workers who are self-motivated, proactive, and creative may find jobs with a lack of autonomy to be stifling, frustrating, and boring, and this may dramatically reduce their motivation to perform at a high level. This means that managers should be alert to the differences in motivational styles, and take care to provide individuals who have an internal locus of control with autonomous jobs, and individuals who have an external locus of control with more constrained jobs.

Related to autonomy is the fact that most workers are motivated by intrinsic rewards, not paychecks. Managers tend to think they are uniquely motivated by intrinsic matters such as pride, self-respect, and doing something worthwhile, believing that their employees don't care about much other than getting paid. But this is not borne out by the research. By attributing shallow motives to employees, bosses overlook the actual depth of their minds and then fail to offer their workers those things that truly motivate them. Take the GM auto plant in Fremont, California. In the late 1970s it was the worst-performing GM plant in the world—defects were rampant, absenteeism reached 20%, and workers sabotaged the cars. Bosses believed that the factory workers were mindless idiots, and the workers behaved that way. Employees had no control over their jobs and were told only what they needed to know to do their narrow jobs; they were told nothing about how their work fit into the larger picture of the plant or the company. In 1982, GM closed the Fremont plant. Within a few months, Toyota began a partnership with GM and reopened the plant, hiring back 90% of the original employees. The Toyota management method was built around the idea that, if only given the chance, workers wanted to take pride in their work, wanted to see how their work fit into the larger picture and have the power to make improvements and reduce defects. Within one year, with *the same workers*, the plant became number one in the GM system and absenteeism dropped to below 2%. The only thing that changed was management's attitude toward employees, treating them with respect, treating them more like managers treated one another—as intrinsically motivated, conscientious members of a team with shared goals.

Who was the most productive person of all time? This is a difficult question to answer, largely because productivity itself is not well defined, and conceptions of it change through the ages and over different parts of the world. But one could argue that William Shakespeare was immensely productive. Before dying at the age of fifty-two, he composed thirty-eight plays, 154 sonnets, and two long narrative poems. Most of his works were produced in a twenty-four-year period of intense productivity. And these weren't just any works—they are some of the most highly respected works of literature ever produced in the history of the world.

One could also make a case for Thomas Edison, who held nearly eleven hundred patents, including many that changed history: electric light and power utilities, sound recordings, and motion pictures. He also introduced pay-per-view in 1894. One thing these two have in common—and share with other greats like Mozart and Leonardo da Vinci—is that they were their own bosses. That means to a large degree the locus of control for their activities was internal. Sure, Mozart had commissions, but within a system of constraints, he was free to do what he wanted in the way he wanted to do it. Being one's own boss requires a lot of discipline, but for those who can manage it, greater productivity appears to be the reward.

Other factors contribute to productivity, such as being an early riser: Studies have shown that early birds tend to be happier, more conscientious and productive, than night owls. Sticking to a schedule helps, as does making time for exercise. Mark Cuban, the owner of Landmark Theatres and the Dallas Mavericks, echoes what many CEOs and their employees say about meetings: They're usually a waste of time. An exception is if you're negotiating a deal or soliciting advice from a large number of people. But even then, meetings should be short, drawn up with a strict agenda, and given a time limit. Warren Buffett's datebook is nearly completely empty and has been for twenty-five years—he rarely schedules anything of any kind, finding that an open schedule is a key to his productivity.

The Paperwork

Organizing people is a good start to increasing value in any business. But how can the people—and that's each of us—begin to organize the constant flood of documents that seem to take over every aspect of our work and our private lives? Managing the flow of paper and electronic documents is increasingly important to being effective in business. By now, weren't we supposed to have the paperless office? That seems to have gone the way of jet packs and Rosie the Robot. Paper consumption has increased 50% since 1980, and today the United States uses 70 million tons of paper in a year. That's 467 pounds, or 12,000 sheets, of paper for every man, woman, and child. It would take six trees forty feet tall to replenish it. How did we get here and what can we do about it?

After the mid 1800s, as companies grew in size, and their employees spread out geographically, businesses found it useful to keep copies of outgoing correspondence either by hand-copying each document or through the use of a protocopier called the letter press. Incoming correspondence tended to be placed in pigeonhole desks and cabinets, sometimes sorted but often not. Cogent information, such as the sender, date, and subject, might be written on the outside of the letter or fold to help in locating it later. With a small amount of incoming correspondence, the system was manageable—one might have to search through several letters before finding the right one, but this didn't take too much time and could have been similar to the children's card game Concentration.

Concentration is a game based on a 1960s television game show hosted by Hugh Downs. In the home version, players set up a matrix of cards facedown—perhaps six across and five down for a total of thirty cards. (You start with two decks of cards and select matched pairs, so that every card in your matrix has an identical mate.) The first player turns over two cards. If they match, the player keeps them. If they don't, the player turns them back over, facedown, and it is the next player's turn. Players who can remember where previously turned-over cards were located are at an advantage. The ability to do this resides in the hippocampus—remember, it's the place-memory system that increases in size in London taxicab drivers.

All of us use this hippocampal spatial memory every day, whether trying to find a document or a pair of scissors. We often have a clear idea of where the item is, relative to others. The cognitive psychologist Roger Shepard's entire filing system was simply stacks and stacks of paper all through his office. He knew which pile a given document was in, and roughly how far down into the pile it was, so he could minimize his search time using this spatial memory. Similarly, the early system of finding unsorted letters filed in cubbyholes relied on the office worker's spatial memory of where that letter was. Spatial memory can be very, very good. Squirrels can locate hundreds of nuts they buried—and they're not just using smell. Experiments show that they preferentially look for nuts that *they* buried in the places they buried them, not for nuts buried by other squirrels. Nevertheless, with any large amount of paperwork or correspondence, finding the right piece in the nineteenth century could easily become time-consuming and frustrating.

The cubbyhole filing system was among the first modern attempts to externalize human memory and extend our brains' own processing capacity. Important information was written down and could then be consulted later for verification. The limitation was that human memory had to be used to remember where the document was filed.

The next development in the cubbyhole filing system was . . . more cubbyholes! The Wooton Desk (patent 1874) featured over one hundred storage places, and advertising promised the businessman he would become "master of the situation." If one had the prescience to label the cubbyholes in an organized fashion—by client last name, by due date for order, or through some other logical scheme—the system could work very well.

But still the big problem was that each individual document needed to be folded to fit in the cubbyholes, meaning that it had to be unfolded to be identified and used. The first big improvement on this was the flat file, introduced in the late 1800s. Flat files could be kept in drawers, in bound book volumes, or in cabinets, and they increased search efficiency as well as capacity. Flat files were either bound or unbound. When bound, documents tended to be stored chronologically, which meant that one needed to know roughly when a document arrived in order to locate it. More flexible were flat files that were filed loosely in boxes and drawers; this allowed them to be arranged, rearranged, and removed as needed, just like the 3 x 5 index cards favored by Phaedrus (and many HSPs) in Chapter 2.

The state of the art for flat file storage by the late nineteenth century was a system of letter-size file boxes, similar to the kind still available today at most stationery stores. Correspondence could be sewn in, glued in, or otherwise inserted into alphabetical or chronological order. By 1868, flat file cabinets had been introduced—these were cabinets containing several dozen drawers of the dimensions of a flat letter, something like oversize library card catalogues. These drawers could be organized in any of the ways already mentioned, typically chronologically, alphabetically, or topically, and the contents of the drawers could be further organized. Often, the drawer contents were left unsorted, requiring the user to have to look through the contents to find the right document. JoAnne Yates, professor of management at MIT and a world expert in business communication, articulates the problems:

> To locate correspondence in an opened box file or a horizontal cabinet file, all the correspondence on top of the item sought had to be lifted up. Since the alphabetically or numerically designated drawers in horizontal cabinet files filled up at different rates, correspondence was transferred out of active files into back-up storage at different rates as well. And the drawers could not be allowed to get too full, since then papers would catch and tear as the drawers were opened. Letter boxes had to be taken down from a shelf and opened up, a time-consuming operation when large amounts of filing were done.

As Yates notes, keeping track of whether a given document or pile of documents was deemed *active* or *archival* was not always made explicit. Moreover, if the user wanted to expand, this might require transferring the contents of one box to another in an iterative process that might require dozens of boxes being moved down in the cabinet, to make room for the new box.

To help prevent document loss, and to keep documents in the order they were filed, a ring system was introduced around 1881, similar to the three-ring binders we now use. The advantages of ringed flat files were substantial, providing random access (like Phaedrus's 3 x 5 index card system) and minimizing the risk of document loss. With all their advantages, binders did not become the dominant form of storage. For the next fifty years, horizontal files and file books (both bound and glued) were the standard in office organization. Vertical files that resemble the ones we use today were first introduced in 1898. A confluence of circumstances made them useful. Copying technology improved, increasing the number of documents to be filed; the "systematic management movement" required increasing documentation and correspondence; the Dewey Decimal System, introduced in 1876 and used in libraries for organizing books, relied on index cards that were kept in drawers, so the furniture for holding vertical files was already familiar. The invention of the modern typewriter increased the speed at which documents could be prepared, and hence the number of them needing to be filed. The Library Bureau, founded by Melvil Dewey, created a system for filing and organizing documents that consisted of vertical files, guides, labels, folders, and cabinetry and won a gold medal at the 1893 World's Fair in Chicago.

Vertical files function best when alphabetized. One factor that prevented their earlier invention was that, up through the eighteenth century, the alphabet was not universally known. The historian James Gleick notes, "A literate, book-buying Englishman at the turn of the seventeenth century could live a lifetime without ever encountering a set of data ordered alphabetically." So alphabetizing files was not the first organizational scheme that came to mind, simply because the average reader could not be expected to know that *H* came after *C* in the alphabet. We take it for granted now because all schoolchildren are taught to memorize the alphabet. Moreover, spelling was not regarded as something that could be right or wrong until the eighteenth and nineteenth centuries, so alphabetizing was not practical. The first dictionaries were faced with the puzzling problem of how to arrange the words.

When vertical files became the standard around 1900—followed by their offspring, the hanging file folders invented by Frank D. Jonas in 1941—they offered a number of organizational advantages that probably seem obvious to us now, but they were an innovation hundreds of years in the making:

1. Papers could be left open and not folded, so their contents could be easily inspected.
2. Handling and ease of access: Papers filed on edge were easier to handle; papers before them in the sequence didn't have to be removed first.
3. Papers that were related to one another could be kept in the same folder, and then subcategorized within the folder (e.g., by date, or alphabetically by topic or author).
4. Whole folders could be removed from the cabinet for ease of use.
5. Unlike the bound systems previously in use, documents could be taken out of the system individually, and could be re-sorted or refiled at will (the Phaedrus principle).
6. When folders became full, their contents could be easily redistributed.
7. The system was easily expandable.
8. Transparency: If properly labeled and implemented, the system could be used by anyone encountering it for the first time.

Vertical files don't solve every problem, of course. There is still the decision to make about how to organize the files and folders, not to mention how to organize drawers within a filing cabinet, and if you have multiple filing cabinets, how to organize *them*. Running a strictly alphabetical system across a dozen different cabinets is efficient if every folder is sorted by name (as in a doctor's office), but suppose you're filing different kinds of things? You may have files for customers and for suppliers, and it would be more effective to separate them into different cabinets.

HSPs typically organize their files by adopting a hierarchical or nested system, in which topic, person, company, or chronology is embedded in another organization scheme. For example, some companies organize their files first geographically by region of the world or country, and then by topic, person, company, or chronology.

How would a nested system look today in a medium-size business? Suppose you run an automotive parts company and you ship to the forty-eight states of the continental United States. For various reasons, you treat the Northeast, Southeast, West Coast, and "Middle" of the country differently. This could be because of differential shipping costs, or different product lines specific to those territories. You might start out with a four-drawer filing cabinet, with each of the drawers labeled for one of the four territories. Within a drawer, you'd have folders for your customers arranged alphabetically by customer surname or company name. As you expand your business, you may eventually need an entire filing cabinet for each territory, with drawer 1 for your alphabetical entries A–F, drawer 2 for G–K, and so on. The nesting hierarchy doesn't need to stop there. How will you arrange the documents within a customer's file folder? Perhaps reverse chronologically, with the newest items first.

If you have many pending orders that take some time to fill, you may keep a folder of pending orders at the front of each territory's drawer, filing those pending orders chronologically so that you can quickly see how long the customer who has been waiting the longest has been without their order. There are of course infinite variations to filing systems. Rather than file drawers for territory, with customer folders inside, you could make your top-level file drawers strictly alphabetical and then subdivide within each drawer by region. For example, you'd open up the A file drawer (for customers whose surnames or company names begin with *A*) and you would have drawer dividers inside, for the territorial regions of Northeast, Southeast, West Coast, and Middle. There is no single rule for determining what the most efficient system will be for a given business. A successful system is one that requires the minimum amount of searching time, and that is most transparent to new employees. It will be a system that can be easily described. Again, an efficient system is one in which you've exploited affordances by off-loading as many memory functions as possible from your brain into a well-labeled and logically organized collection of external objects.

This can take many forms, limited only by your imagination and ingenuity. If you find you're often confusing one file folder for another, make the folders different colors to easily distinguish them. A business that depends heavily on telephone or Skype calls, and has clients, colleagues, or suppliers in different time zones, organizes all the materials related to these calls in time-zone order so that it's easy to see whom to call at which times of day. Lawyers file case material in numbered binders or folders that correspond to statute numbers. This makes reviewing precedents very easy. Sometimes simple and whimsical ordering is more memorable—a clothing retailer keeps files related to shoes in the bottom drawer, pants one drawer up, shirts and jackets above that, and hats in the top drawer.

Linda describes the particularly robust system that she and her colleagues used at an $8 billion company with 250,000 employees. Documents of different kinds were separated into designated cabinets in the executive offices. One or more cabinets were dedicated to personnel files, others for shareholder information (including annual reports), budgets and expenses for the various units, and correspondence. The correspondence filing was an essential part of the system.

> The system for correspondence was that I would keep hard copies of everything in triplicate. One copy of a letter would go in a chronological file, one in a topic file, and one alphabetically by the name of the correspondent. We kept these in three-ring binders, and there would be alphabetical tabs inside, or for a particularly large or often-used section, a custom tab with the name of that section. The outside of the binder was clearly labeled with the contents.

In addition to the hard copies, Linda kept a list of all correspondence, with keywords, in a database program (she used FileMaker, but Excel would work as well). When she needed to locate a particular document, she'd look it up in her computer database by searching for a keyword. That would tell her which three binders the document was in (e.g., chron file for February 1987, topic binder for the Larch project, volume 3, or alpha binder by letter writer's last name). If the computers were down, or she couldn't find it in the database, it was nearly always found by browsing through the binders.

The system is remarkably effective, and the time spent maintaining it is more than compensated for by the efficiencies of retrieval. It cleverly exploits the principle of associative memory (the fire truck example from the Introduction, Robert Shapiro's and Craig Kallman's annotated contacts lists in Chapter 4), that memory can be accessed through a variety of converging nodes. We don't always remember everything about an event, but if we can remember one thing (such as the approximate date, or where a given document fell roughly in sequence with respect to other documents, or which person was involved in it), we can find what we're looking for by using the associative networks in our brains.

Linda's decision to move correspondence to three-ring binders reflects a fundamental principle of file folder management: Don't put into a file folder more than will fit, and generally not more than fifty pages. If your file folders contain more than that, experts advise splitting up the contents into subfolders. If you truly need to keep more pages than that in one place, consider moving to a three-ring binder system. The advantage of the binder system is that pages are retained in order—they don't fall or spill out—and via the Phaedrus principle, they provide random access and can be reordered if necessary.

In addition to these systems, HSPs create systems to automatically divide up paperwork and projects temporally, based on how urgent they are. A small category of "now" items, things that they need to deal with right away, is close by. A second category of "near-term" items is a little farther away, perhaps on the other side of the office or down the hall. A third category of reference or archival papers can be even farther away, maybe on another floor or off-site. Linda adds that anything that needs to be accessed regularly should be put in a special RECURRENCE folder so that it is easy to get to. This might include a delivery log, a spreadsheet updated weekly with sales figures, or staff phone numbers.

An essential component of setting up any organizational system in a business environment is to allow for things that fall through the cracks, things that don't fit neatly into any of your categories—the miscellaneous file or junk drawer, just as you might have at home in the kitchen. If you can't come up with a logical place for something, it does not represent a failure of cognition or imagination; it reflects the complex, intercorrelated structure of the many objects and artifacts in our lives, the fuzzy boundaries, and the overlapping uses of things. As Linda says, "The miscellaneous folder is progress, not a step backward." That list of frequent flyer numbers you constantly refer to? Put it in the RECURRENCE folder or a MISCELLANEOUS folder in the front of the drawer. Say you take a tour of a vacant office building across town. You're not really looking to move, but you want to save the information sheet you received just in case. If your filing system doesn't have a section for *relocating, office lease,* or *physical plant,* it would be wasteful to create one, and if you create a single file folder for this, with a single piece of paper in it, where will you file the folder?

Ed Littlefield (my old boss from Utah International) was a big proponent of creating a STUFF I DON'T KNOW WHERE TO FILE file. He'd check it once a month or so to refresh his memory of what's in it, and occasionally he'd have accumulated a critical mass of materials with a theme to create a new, separate file for them. One successful scientist (and member of the Royal Society) keeps a series of junk drawer–like files called THINGS I WANT TO READ, PROJECTS I'D LIKE TO START, and MISCELLANEOUS IMPORTANT PAPERS. At home, that little bottle of auto body paint the shop gives you after a collision repair? If you keep a drawer or shelf for automotive supplies, that's the obvious place to put it, but if you have *zero* automotive supplies except this little bottle, it doesn't make sense to create a categorical spot just for one item. Better to put it in a junk drawer with other hard-to-categorize things.

Of course CEOs, Supreme Court judges, and other HSPs don't have to do all this themselves. They simply ask their executive assistants for the Morrow file or, more often, their EAs bring them a file with instructions about what needs to be done on it and by when. But their EAs need to follow logical systems, and there is often room for improvement in these. Key is that the system be transparent so that if an assistant falls ill, someone else, even without specific training, can find what the CEO needs.

Linda says that in training new EAs, the biggest point is to "remember that you're organizing people, not files and documents. You need to get to know your boss's routines—they might tend to put things in piles and you might have to go through their things, or you might have to keep copies for them if they tend to lose things. If you're working for more than one person—or if your boss interacts with others on a regular basis—it's a good idea to have a separate folder on your desk for each one of them so that if they drop by unexpectedly, you've got the essential information right in front of you."

Linda's advice for time management from Chapter 5 is worth revisiting here. "For deadlines, you might need to keep a tickler file. For example, as soon as you learn about any kind of deadline, you need to talk to the boss about it and see how long they think they'll need. Then you put a tickler on the calendar on the day they're supposed to start working on it." Other EAs even put a tickler a few days before that so their boss can start thinking in advance about the project he'll be working on.

"The things that typically require organization in an office are correspondence, business documents, presentations, things you need for meetings (including information in advance that needs to be reviewed), to do lists, the calendar, contacts, and books and journals," Linda adds. The first four are usually best organized in files, folders, boxes, or binders. To Do lists, calendars, and contacts are important enough that she recommends the redundancy of keeping them on paper and on the computer. This only works if the number of contacts is small enough to fit on paper—Craig Kallman, the CEO of Atlantic Records, who has 14,000 contacts, has to rely on his computer for the entire list, but he keeps frequently used ones stored in his cell phone. If he kept more than the frequently used ones, it would be too cumbersome and time-consuming to search them.

E-mail filing and sorting is increasingly time-consuming as many HSPs report receiving hundreds of e-mails a day *after* the spam filter has gotten rid of nuisance mail. Craig Kallman gets about six hundred e-mails every day. If he spent only one minute on each of them, it would take him ten hours a day to get through them. He uses weekends as catch-up time and, when possible, forwards e-mails to others to attend to. But, as with many HSPs, he got into his line of work because he actually loves the work. Delegating a project lessens his involvement with it and the joy he derives from it, not to mention that his expertise and experience are not easily matched by others—the work product benefits from his involvement, but the e-mail stream alone, apart from telephone calls, snail mail, and meetings, is a big time commitment.

How does the White House organize communications? To begin with, the president and vice president do not have piles of documents on their desks, and they do not use e-mail, both for national security reasons. All communications go through the executive secretary, who decides what has priority and what needs to be worked on now. The president and vice president do receive briefing books about particular topics. For example, if the president wants to know everything about a pipeline project in Minnesota, staffers pull together information that has been obtained from phone calls, meetings, e-mails, faxes, letters, and so on and put it into the binder.

Each individual staffer has the autonomy to decide how he will sort or file the papers and communications that they need to do their work—there is no "White House Standard" or anything like that. As long as they can put their hands on a needed communication, they can organize it as they please. This distributed system of organization is a powerful reminder that a top-down approach (like that used in the Fremont GM plant) is not always the most effective.

Mike Kelleher, the director of the Office of Correspondence in the White House during the first Obama administration, says that every week the office received 65,000 paper letters, 500,000 e-mails, 5,000 faxes, and 15,000 phone calls. Spending even just one minute on each of these would require 9,750 person hours, or the equivalent of 244 employees working full-time. Numbers like this require the kind of quick sort and prioritizing system that Ed Littlefield used for his mail when he served on the boards of Wells Fargo, Chrysler, and Utah International. Kelleher's office employs 49 full-time staff, 25 interns, and a small army of volunteers. Paper letters get sorted into one of more than a hundred bins or cubbyholes, as in the back of a post office, depending on recipient (first lady, first dog, children, VP, cabinet offices, such as HUD, DOT, DOD). With these kinds of numbers, delegation is essential. The White House can't declare e-mail bankruptcy, as Lawrence Lessig suggested in Chapter 3. As you might imagine, although hundreds of thousands of letters and e-mails are addressed to the president, many of the questions are about policies that come under the jurisdiction or mandate of specific departments within the administration. Questions about health care, economic policy, or veterans' benefits are referred to their respective departments. Much of the correspondence includes requests for the president to write letters of congratulations for various life events, such as making Eagle Scout, turning one hundred, being married fifty years, and so on, which the White House does try to honor. These end up in the Office of Presidential Correspondence. And again, there are no centralized guidelines for sorting and filing e-mails; staffers use whatever method they see fit—as long as they can produce an e-mail when requested.

Increasingly, people who use e-mail have separate accounts. HSPs might have two business accounts, one for the people they deal with regularly and another that their EAs monitor and sort, in addition to one or two personal accounts. Having separate accounts helps to organize and compartmentalize things, and to restrict interruptions: You may want to turn off all your e-mail accounts during a productivity hour except for the one your assistant and your boss use to reach you right away. An efficient way to deal with multiple accounts is to use a single computer program to collect them all. Most e-mail programs, including Outlook, Apple Mail, Gmail, and Yahoo!, allow you to download into their interface any mail from any provider. The advantage is that if all your different accounts show up in one interface, it's easier to locate what you're looking for if you don't have to log into several accounts to find a specific e-mail or document. Also, categories have fuzzy boundaries. That dinner invitation from a coworker might have shown up in your business account, but you need to coordinate with her husband, who sent his schedule to your personal account.

To reiterate a point from Chapter 3, some people, particularly those with attention deficit disorder, panic when they can't see all of their files out in the open in front of them. The idea of filing e-mails on a computer is stressful, and so for them, adopting Linda's system of printing them out is often necessary. Open filing carts and racks exist so that physical files don't need to be hidden behind a drawer. Other people simply cannot set up or maintain filing systems. The idea of putting things in little compartments is incompatible with their cognitive style, or disengages their creative mode. This relates to the two attentional systems introduced in Chapter 2. Creative people are at their most innovative while engaging the daydreaming mode. Putting things into little compartments requires not only engaging but staying in the central executive mode. Recall that these modes operate in a see-saw relationship—if you're in one mode, you are not in the other. Consequently, many creative people resist the kinds of geeky, compartmentalized systems outlined here. Compartment-resistant people are found across all walks of life, in a variety of professions, from the law to medicine, and from science to art. In these cases, they either hire assistants to do all their filing for them, or they declare filing bankruptcy and just let piles accumulate.

Jeff Mogil is a very creative and productive behavioral geneticist. His desk is preternaturally clear and the only things ever on top of it are things he's working on at the moment, arranged in neat piles. His filing system is impeccable. At the other extreme is Roger Shepard, whose office always looked like the aftermath of a natural disaster. Piles of papers had covered his desk for so long that even he didn't remember what color the surface was. The piles extended to every available space in the office, including a coffee table, the floor, and windowsills. He had barely enough room to walk a path from the door to his desk. But he knew where everything was, thanks to an exquisite temporal and spatial memory. "These piles over here are from five years ago," he said, "and these are from this month." When I was a student, walking down the hall from Roger Shepard's office to Amos Tversky's was a sobering study in contrasts. Amos had the kind of clean and tidy office that visitors found incredibly intimidating; there was never *anything* on his desk. Years later, a colleague confided, "Yes, the desk was clean. But you wouldn't want to look into his drawers and cabinets!" Neat and organized are not necessarily the same thing.

Lew Goldberg, a personality psychologist who is known as the father of the Big Five personality dimensions, devised a system for filing correspondence and for reprints of articles by other scientists. The reprint collection had seventy-two topic categories, and each article was represented on—you guessed it—a 3 x 5 index card. The cards lived in wooden library card catalogues and were cross-referenced by author, title, and topic. He'd look up an item in his catalogue, which would direct him to one of several hundred three-ring binders that took up a wall in his office from floor to ceiling. While his system has worked for him for fifty years, he acknowledges that it isn't for everyone. His University of Oregon colleague Steve Keele, a pioneer in the study of timing mechanisms in the brain, was a Roger Shepard–like piler and stacker. "Steve was reputed to have had the world's messiest office, and yet he could always find everything. Piles and piles and piles all over. You could walk in and say, 'Steve, I know this isn't your area, but I've developed an interest in how humans fixate on a moving visual target.' And he would say, 'Oh, I happen to have a student who wrote a paper about this in 1975, and I haven't graded it yet, but it's right . . . here.'"

But there are piles and then there are *piles.* Oftentimes, pile and stack makers are procrastinating on a decision about whether to keep something or throw it out, whether it is relevant or not. It's important to go through piles on a regular basis to whittle them down, trim them, or re-sort them—not everything in them remains relevant forever.

Recall the system that Microsoft senior research fellow Malcolm Slaney advocated in Chapter 3, to keep everything on your computer. Jason Rentfrow, a scientist at Cambridge University, agrees, adding that "although Gmail doesn't organize your files, it does allow very easy access and searchability to them. In some ways that—and 'spotlight' or 'find' on your computer—is like applying a Google Internet search strategy to your own computer. Maybe it's not even worth bothering having folders anymore—you could have just one folder with everything in it and then use search functions to find anything you want. You can limit to date, content, name, etc."

From Multitasking to Planning for Failure

In Chapter 5, I wrote about some of the evidence against multitasking as a strategy for getting more work done. But is it realistic to give it up—isn't it what we have to do in the business world? Stanford professor Clifford Nass assumed, as most people do, that multitaskers were superhumans, capable of doing many things at once with high success: juggling phone calls, e-mails, live conversations, texting. He further assumed that they had an unusually high ability to switch attention from one task to another and that their memories could differentiate the multiple tasks in an orderly way.

> We all bet high multitaskers were going to be stars at something. We were absolutely shocked. We lost all our bets. It turns out multitaskers are terrible at every aspect of multitasking. They're terrible at ignoring irrelevant information; they're terrible at keeping information in their head nicely and neatly organized; and they're terrible at switching from one task to another.

We all want to believe that we can do many things at once and that our attention is infinite, but this is a persistent myth. What we really do is shift our attention rapidly from task to task. Two bad things happen as a result: We don't devote enough attention to any one thing, and we decrease the quality of attention applied to any task. When we do one thing—uni-task—there are beneficial changes in the brain's daydreaming network and increased connectivity. Among other things, this is believed to be protective against Alzheimer's disease. Older adults who engaged in five one-hour training sessions on attentional control began to show brain activity patterns that more closely resembled those of younger adults.

You'd think people would realize they're bad at multitasking and would quit. But a cognitive illusion sets in, fueled in part by a dopamine-adrenaline feedback loop, in which multitaskers *think* they are doing great. Part of the problem is that workplaces are misguidedly encouraging workers to multitask. Nass notes a number of societal forces that encourage multitasking. Many managers impose rules such as "You must answer e-mail within fifteen minutes" or "You must keep a chat window open," but this means you're stopping what you're doing, fragmenting concentration, Balkanizing the vast resources of your prefrontal cortex, which has been honed over tens of thousands of years of evolution to *stay on task*. This stay-on-task mode is what gave us the pyramids, mathematics, great cities, literature, art, music, penicillin, and rockets to the moon (and hopefully—soon—*jet packs*). Those kinds of discoveries cannot be made in fragmented two-minute increments.

It is a testament to our cognitive flexibility and neural plasticity that we are able to go against all this evolution, but at least until the next evolutionary leap in our prefrontal cortex, multitasking leads to not more work but less, not better work but sloppier work. Adding to this, every day we are confronted with new Facebook and Instagram updates, new YouTube videos, Twitter streams, and whatever new technology will replace them in the next year or two. As of this writing, there were thirteen hundred apps for mobile devices being released *every day*. "Cultural forces, and the expectation that people will respond instantly, and chat and talk and do all these things all at once, means all the pressure is going that way," Nash says.

The companies that are winning the productivity battle are those that allow their employees productivity hours, naps, a chance for exercise, and a calm, tranquil, *orderly* environment in which to do their work. If you're in a stressful environment where you're asked to produce and produce, you're unlikely to have any deep insights. There's a reason Google puts Ping-Pong tables in their headquarters. Safeway, a $4 billion grocery chain in the United States and Canada, has doubled sales in the last fifteen years under the leadership of Steven Burd, who, among other things, encouraged employees to exercise at work, through salary incentives, and installed a full gym at corporate headquarters. Studies have found that productivity goes up when the number of hours per week of work goes down, strongly suggesting that adequate leisure and refueling time pays off for employers and for workers. Overwork—and its companion, sleep deprivation—have been shown to lead to mistakes and errors that take longer to fix than the overtime hours worked. A sixty-hour work week, although 50% longer than a forty-hour work week, reduces productivity by 25%, so it takes two hours of overtime to accomplish one hour of work. A ten-minute nap can be equivalent to an extra hour and a half of sleep at night. And vacations?

Ernst & Young found that for each additional ten hours of vacation their employees took, their year-end performance ratings from their supervisors improved by 8%.

It is now well known that some of the most productive companies—Google, Twitter, Lucasfilm, *Huffington Post*—provide perks such as in-house gyms, gourmet dining rooms, nap rooms, and flexible hours. Google paid for 100,000 free employee massages, and its campus boasts wellness centers and a seven-acre sports complex with basketball, bowling, bocce ball, and roller hockey. The statistical software giant SAS and Toyota distributor JM Family Enterprises feature in-house health care; Atlantic Health System offers on-site acupressure massage; Microsoft's campus has a spa; SalesForce.com provides free yoga classes; Intuit lets employees spend 10% of their time on any project they're passionate about; Deloitte encourages employees to donate time to nonprofits for up to six months by offering full benefits and 40% of pay. Giving employees environments like these seems to pay, and it makes sense from a neurobiological standpoint. Sustained concentration and effort is most effective not when fragmented into little pieces by multitasking, but when apportioned into big focused chunks separated by leisure, exercise, or other mentally restorative activities.

Multitasking results from information overload, trying to attend to too many things at once. When the many things we're attending to require a decision, how much information do we need to make optimal decisions? Optimal complexity theory states that there is an inverted U function for how much information or complexity is optimal.

Too little is no good, but so is too much. In one study, experimenters simulated a military exercise. Players in the simulated game were college students in teams who were either invading or defending a small island country. Players were allowed to control the amounts of information with which to make their decisions—they received a document that read:

> The information you are receiving is prepared for you in the same way it would be prepared for real commanders by a staff of intelligence officers. These persons have been instructed to inform you only of important occurrences. You may feel that these men do not give you sufficient information or do not give you adequate detail. On the other hand, you may feel that the information you

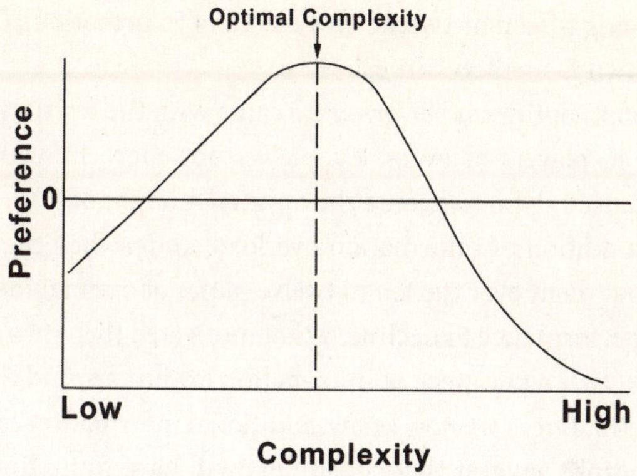

are receiving is too detailed and you are presented with some unimportant information. You may instruct these intelligence officers to increase or decrease the amount of information they present to you. We would like you to decide this matter for yourself. Please do not consult the other commanders on this issue at any time. We will adjust the information flow according to the majority opinion in your group. Please check your preference in comparison to the immediately preceding game period:

I would prefer to:
receive much more information
receive a little more information
receive about the same amount of information
receive a little less information
receive much less information

In actuality, the players did not have control over the information, but their response was used to study optimal levels of information. They received either two, five, eight, ten, twelve, fifteen, or twenty-five pieces of information within the thirty-minute period of the game.

According to the theory of optimal information, players would perform better with about ten to twelve pieces of information during the course of the game, and the experiment confirmed this. The amount of additional information players requested decreased for those who were already receiving fifteen or twenty-five pieces of information. This leads to the upside-down U-shaped curve.

But although optimum *performance* came with the ten to twelve pieces of information, players at every level *asked* for more information, even though this caused them to exceed the optimal amount of information and enter into a condition of information overload, and—when that additional information put them over the ten to twelve pieces of optimal information—caused their performance to decline. What motivated them to ask may have been the belief that a key piece of information lay just around the corner in the next bulletin. But as we now know, additional information carries a cost.

These findings suggest that consumers will have finite limits for how much information they can absorb and process within a given period of time. Let's call it the *load effect.* In fact, this has been shown empirically—consumers make poorer choices with more information. This mechanism is similar to the load effect we saw in Chapter 4 that leads to incorrect social judgments. A separate study examined the effects of additional information on the decision to purchase a home. It found the maximum number of parameters that can be processed is around ten. The interesting thing is that the parameters can be either attributes of choice or alternatives. In other words, if you are trying to decide between two houses, you don't want to be keeping track of more than ten pieces of information about them combined. Or, if you can trim your list to two pieces of information you're interested in—perhaps square footage and quality of the school district—you can compare ten houses. In the home-buying studies, consumers were given up to twenty-five attributes to keep track of on up to twenty-five different homes. Their decision-making ability began to suffer when *either* parameter was greater than ten. Above ten, however, it didn't matter if there were fifteen, twenty, or twenty-five parameters—once the consumer hits information overload, still more information doesn't significantly affect the already saturated system. This limit of ten is the *maximum.* The optimal number is closer to five and is consistent with processing limits of the brain's central executive. This may remind you of the problem with online dating sites mentioned in Chapter 4—that more information is not always better and, in that context, has been found to lead to poorer selectivity and poorer choices as online daters become overwhelmed by irrelevant information and suffer both cognitive overload and decision fatigue.

Another important factor, shown by Duke economist and author Dan Ariely, is that consumers perform better when they have a particular type of internal locus of control, that is, when they can actually control the type of information they receive. In a series of experiments, he demonstrated that if the consumer can choose which parameters to receive information about, as well as how much, they make better decisions. This is primarily because the consumer can choose information that is relevant to them or that they are best able to understand. For example, in shopping for cameras, Consumer *X* may care mainly about size and price, while Consumer *Y* may care mainly about resolution (number of pixels) and type of lens. Information that would be distracting or impossible to interpret for one type of consumer causes information overload and interferes with optimal decision processing. Separate research by Kahneman and Tversky shows that people are unable to ignore information that is not relevant to them, so there is a real neural cost of being presented with information you don't care about and can't use.

Then the question becomes not one of how many things you can do at once, but how orderly you can make the information environment. There is considerable research into the difference in utility between simple and complex information. Claude Shannon, an electrical engineer who worked at Bell Laboratories, developed information theory in the 1940s. Shannon information theory is among the most important mathematical ideas of the twentieth century; it has profoundly affected computing and telecommunications, and is the basis for the compression of sound, image, and movie files (e.g., MP3, JPEG, and MP4 respectively).

A fundamental problem in telecommunications, signaling, and security is how to transmit a message as briefly as possible, to pack the maximum amount of data into the minimum amount of time or space; this packing is called data compression. Back when telephone service was carried along a single pair of copper wires (what telecommunications nerds call POTS, for "plain old telephone service"), there was a limited amount of call volume that could be carried across the main telephone wires (trunks), and the cost of running new lines was prohibitively expensive. This led to perceptual experiments and the finding that the telephone company didn't need to transmit the entire frequency range of the human voice for speech to remain intelligible. The so-called telephone band transmitted only

300–3300 hertz, a subset of the full range of human hearing, which spans 20–20,000 hertz, and gave telephone transmissions their characteristic "tinny" sound. It wasn't hi-fi, but it was intelligible enough for most purposes—it satisficed. But if you've ever tried to explain on POTS that you're talking about the letter *f* and not the letter *s*, you've experienced the bandwidth limitation, because the acoustical difference of those two letters is entirely within the range that Bell cut out. But in doing so, the telephone company could squeeze several conversations into the space of one, maximizing the efficiency of their network and minimizing hardware costs. Cell phones continue to be band limited for the same reason, to maximize the ability of cell towers to carry multiple conversations. This bandwidth limitation is most apparent if you try to listen to music over the telephone—the low frequencies of the bass and the high frequencies of cymbals are almost completely absent.

Information theory came up in Chapter 1 in discussing the number of simultaneous conversations that a person can follow, and the information processing limits of human attention being estimated at around 120 bits per second. It is a way to *quantify* the amount of information contained in any transmission, instruction, or sensory stimulus. It can apply to music, speech, paintings, and military orders. The application of information theory generates a number that allows us to compare the amount of information contained in one transmission with that contained in another.

Suppose that you want to convey instructions to someone on how to construct a chessboard. You could say

> Make a square and color it white. Now make another square adjacent to that and color it black. Make a square adjacent to that and color it white. Make a square adjacent to that and color it black. Make a square adjacent to that . . .

You could continue this type of instruction until you get to eight squares (completing one row) and then you'd have to instruct your friend to go back to the first square and put a black square just above it, and then proceed square by square to fill the second row, and so on. This is a cumbersome way to convey the instructions, and not very streamlined. Compare that to

> Make an 8 x 8 matrix of squares, alternately coloring them black and white.

The first instruction refers to each of the 64 squares individually. In binary arithmetic, 64 pieces of information requires 6 bits of information (the number of bits is the exponent of the equation $2^n = 64$. In this example, $n = 6$ because $2^6 = 64$). But implementing a rule such as "alternately color the squares" requires only 1 bit: A given square is either black or white and so there are two choices. Because $2^1 = 2$, we need only 1 bit (1 is the exponent, which determines the amount of information). The two additional facts that the grid is eight squares wide and eight squares long makes for a total of three pieces of information, which take 2 bits. If you want to specify what pieces are on which squares, you're back up to 6 bits because each bit needs to be specified individually. So an empty chess board can be fully specified in 2 bits, a chessboard with its 32 pieces on it takes 6 bits. There is more information on a loaded chess board than on an empty one, and now we have a way to quantify how much more. Even though Shannon and his colleagues at Bell Labs were working in an analog, precomputer world, they were thinking ahead to when computers would be used for telecommunications. Because computers are based on binary arithmetic, Shannon opted to use the measurement units of digital computers, the bit. But it doesn't have to be that way—we could talk about all this in regular numbers and leave bits out of it if we wanted to: The instructions to make an empty chess board require a minimum of 3 pieces of information, and the instructions to re-create a loaded chess board require a minimum of 64 pieces of information.

The same logic applies to re-creating photographs and pictures on your computer. When you are looking at a JPEG or other image file on your screen, you're looking at a *re-creation* of that file—the image was created right there, on the spot, as soon as you double-clicked on the filename. If you were to look into the actual file, the computer file that your operating system uses to construct the picture, you'd see a string of zeros and ones. No picture, just zeros and ones, the vocabulary of binary arithmetic. In a black-and-white picture, every little dot on the screen—the pixels—can be either black or white, and the zeros and ones are telling your computer whether to make a pixel black or white. Color pictures take more instructions because they are represented by five different possibilities: black, white, red, yellow, and cyan. That's why color picture files are larger than black-and-white picture files—they contain more information.

Information theory doesn't tell us how much information we *could* use to describe things, it tells us the *minimum* amount of information we need—remember, Shannon was trying to figure out how to cram as much telephone conversation onto a single pair of copper wires as he could, to maximize Ma Bell's capacity and to minimize the investment in new infrastructure (telephone poles, wires, network switches).

Computer scientists spend a lot of time trying to condense information in this way so that their programs can run more efficiently. Another way of looking at Shannon information theory is to consider two strings of letters 64 characters long:

1. abababababababababababababababababababababababababababababababab
2. qicnlnwmpzoimbpimiqznvposmsoetycqvnzrxnobseicndhrigaldjguuwknhid

Number 1 can be represented with a 2-bit instruction:

64 items, ab, alternate

Number 2, being a random sequence, requires 64 individual instructions (6 bits) because the instruction itself must be exactly the same as the string:

qicnlnwmpzoimbpimiqznvposmsoetycqvnzrxnobseicndhrigald jguuwknhid

How do we determine whether or not a sequence of numbers or letters is random? The Russian mathematician Andrey Kolmogorov introduced an influential idea about this. He said that a string is random if there is no way to describe it or represent it in an abbreviated form. By his definition, number 1 above is not random because we can come up with a scheme (computer scientists call this an algorithm) to represent it in brief. Number 2 is random because there is no scheme we can come up with apart from simply listing every element, one at a time, as it is in the actual sequence.

Kolmogorov complexity theory encapsulates it this way: Something is random when you cannot explain how to derive a sequence using any fewer than the number of elements in the sequence itself. This definition of complexity meshes with our everyday, lay use of the term. We say that a car is more complex than a bicycle, and surely it takes a far larger set of instructions to build a car than a bicycle.

Information theory can be applied to organizational systems like the file and folder hierarchy on your computer, or to org charts in a company. And, according to Kolmogorov complexity theory, if the org chart can be described by a small number of simple rules, the company is said to be highly structured. Compare these two descriptions. For company one, starting at the top with the CEO, everyone supervises three people, and this extends all the way down through four levels, after which everyone supervises fifty to one hundred people. This model might apply to a telephone, water, electric, or gas company that has four layers of management and then a large number of workers out in the field repairing or installing lines, or reading meters. This could also be a technology company with customer service and technical assistance agents at the bottom level. This org chart could be completely and accurately specified in 2 bits.

A company with a less systematic and regular structure requires as

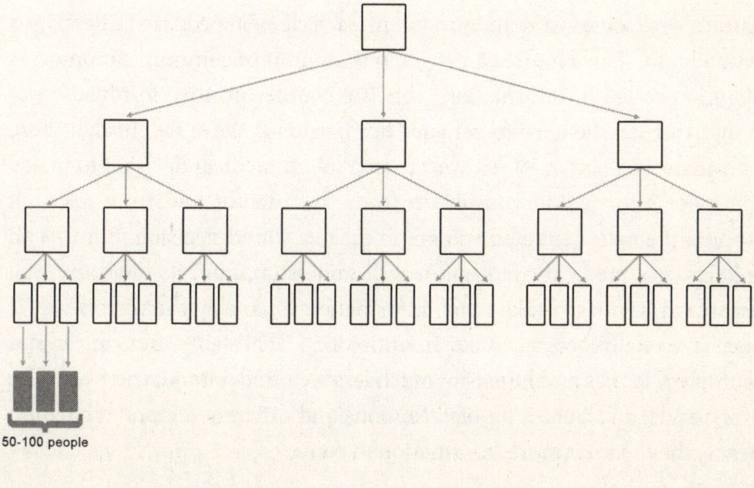

many bits as there are elements because there is no discernible pattern, similar to the random letters in example number 2 above:

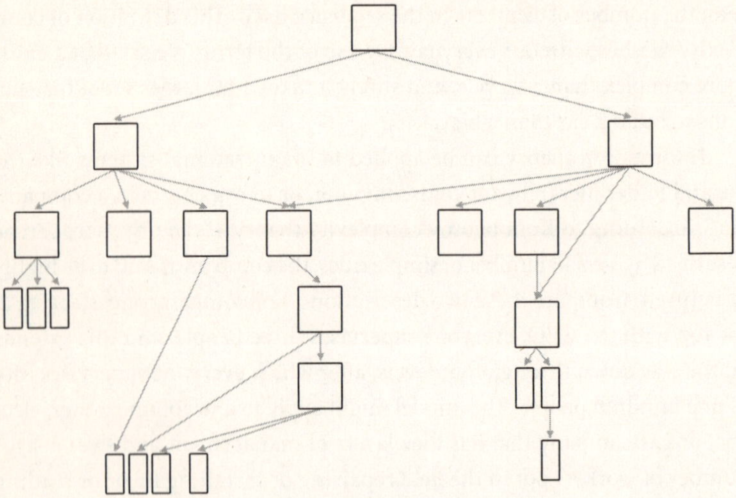

The more structured a system is, the less information required to describe it. Conversely, more information is required to describe a disorganized or unstructured system. At the extreme, the most disorganized system possible is a random arrangement of everything—because there is no pattern whatsoever in a random system, each element needs to be described individually. This requires an enormous amount of communication or, as Shannon called it, information. This is a counterintuitive formulation of things that can be hard to get your head around. We're taught that more information is better. When you've got a tough medical decision to make, the more information you obtain from your doctor and from research studies, the better situated you are to make a sound decision. But this all coheres. If a medical condition is well understood and its literature well organized, it doesn't take much information to convey the treatment. "If you have pneumococcus, take an antibiotic." That's easy. But cancer and multiple sclerosis and lupus are much less well understood; there are a lot of ifs, ands, and buts, a lot of exceptions and different factors to balance; hence, they require more information to convey.

The power of information theory is that it can be applied to anything—website structure, legal and ethical domains, even directions you give to someone trying to find your house. Recall the discussion of flat versus vertical organization as applied to websites or computer file hierarchies. Shannon information theory can be applied to quantify the level of structure or information they contain (here, we're talking about the information in the hierarchical structure itself, as distinct from the information *content* contained on the website).

Or take legal systems. They contain a great number of redundancies, exceptions, and specifics because they are attempting to cover all possible cases. Nearly all civilized societies have laws against rape, murder, robbery, extortion, maiming, assault, battery, and slander, for example. The codes take up a great deal of space as they are encoded in books and on computers. From an information theoretic standpoint, these could all be minimized with a short algorithm: Don't do anything to someone who would not want it done to them (this is essentially the Golden Rule).

Similarly, compare two ways of a friend giving you directions to his house:

1. Take Highway 40 East to Highway 158 East, then turn left on Main Street, right on Basil Avenue, left on South Lake Road, continue straight on North Lake Road, a slight right on Main Street (not the same Main Street you were on before) to a quick left on Big Falls Road, a right on 8th Trail until you get to number 66 on your right, just before the park.
2. Take Highway 40 East and follow the signs to Big Falls Regional Park—my house is just before the entrance.

Algorithm 2 has less Kolmogorov complexity. Notice that it accomplishes this in part by following a dictum of Chapter 2: Off-load as much information as possible to the external world—here, the road signs that already exist.

Given an org chart, then, one can compute the amount of information contained in it and use that as a measure of the organization's complexity, or by using the reciprocal of the measure, one can calculate the *degree of structure* (or organization) within a business, military unit, or any other work or social unit. Here, structure is high when complexity is low—this is equivalent to saying that the Shannon information content is low. Again, this may seem counterintuitive, but a business has a greater degree of structural organization if its org chart can be described in a simple rule containing few words, and there are no exceptions to the rule.

Whether the *degree of structure* of a company predicts efficiency, profitability, or job satisfaction remains an empirical question, one that has not been investigated. On the one hand, individuals clearly differ in their ability to supervise others, and so, naturally, some bosses will have more employees simply because they are adept at handling more. Individuals also differ widely in their skills, and a nimble and efficient organization should allow employees to use their strengths for the good of the company. This can lead to ad hoc reporting structures and special arrangements. Even the best-planned hierarchies become circumvented for the larger good of the company.

One such case occurred in Linda's company. A data analyst had a set of skills unavailable elsewhere in the company, and his supervisor arranged for him to take on a special project, for which he reported to a manager two levels above him and in a different vertical column on the company org chart. This ad hoc arrangement would require 2 extra bits to represent in the company structure, but the arrangement was profitable for the corporation, ultimately allowing them to introduce a new product that greatly increased revenues. Incentives figure into such arrangements. Those increased revenues were accrued to the account of the divisional manager where the work was completed, not to the account of the divisional manager who lent out the skilled data analyst. As in many large corporations, the organizational structure and incentive schemes put too much emphasis on profits accorded to a district or division, and not enough emphasis on the shared goals of the entire company. As I wrote earlier, Booz Allen Hamilton spent several months interviewing employees at Linda's company to better understand their skills, the kinds of problems they were working on, and their job descriptions. After they reported their recommendations, the incentive structure and corporate vision statement were reworked to include cross-division teamwork. It seems obvious to us, but in a company with 250,000 employees, big ideas can get lost.

Ad hoc reporting arrangements can facilitate collaboration, but there are downsides. Too many exceptions to the straightforward org chart become difficult to follow; employees with too many bosses can be difficult to manage, and their hours can be difficult to track. In general, a business that is highly structured is more resilient under stress. If a manager leaves her job, smooth, continuous operation of the company is achieved if the replacement can step into a well-defined job with clear reporting structure and fewer ad hoc arrangements. Clearly defined roles promote continuity and efficiency, and give upper management more flexibility in reassigning managers and workers. It is also easier to keep track of and remember who is who in a highly systematic, well-structured organization because, by definition, it can be communicated in very few words, such as "Every division manager has four districts."

In setting up any kind of structured system—the way file folders are arranged within drawers, or files on a computer, or employees within a company, a successful system is one that requires the minimum amount of searching time and is transparent to anyone who walks in the room. It will be easily described. This reduces the Shannon information content and reduces Kolmogorov complexity. Work flow charts can be similarly analyzed using the same approach:

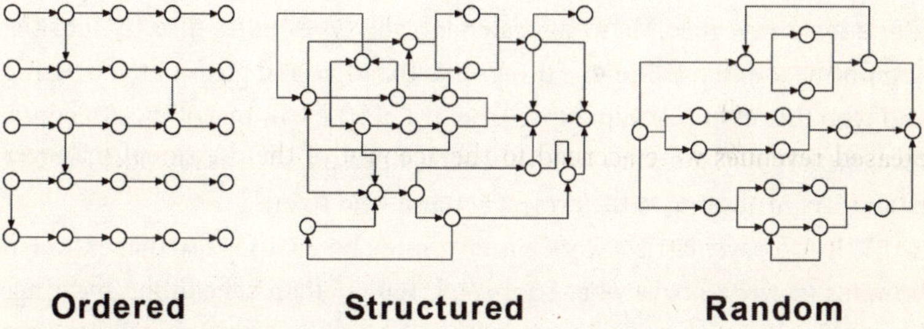

We can make our business worlds more orderly by paying close attention to information flows and escaping the illusions of multitasking. But is that enough? Chapter 3 introduced the idea of planning for failure, a strategy session in which you try to figure out anything that could possibly go wrong and how it would go wrong, and then put systems in place to either prevent it or recover from it. At home, the kinds of things that go wrong typically cause inconvenience for us and our families. At work, things that go wrong can affect thousands of people and cost serious money. The planning-for-failure procedure is to think about everything that could go wrong. Then, come up with a way to minimize the likelihood of those things happening, and a backup or fail-safe plan in the event that they do happen. Leaving your keys by the front door minimizes the likelihood of your forgetting to take them with you. Hiding a key in the garden allows you to gracefully recover (without breaking a window or calling a locksmith) if you do forget the key. What does planning for failure mean in the business world?

One simple thing that can go wrong at the office, just as at home, is to miss a deadline or important appointment. Electronic calendar reminders scheduled to appear on your computer *and* on your cell phone are effective, and a phone call or in-person interruption from a colleague or EA is an effective backup for the most important appointments.

To ensure you'll be able to locate important documents, former Google VP and CIO Douglas Merrill recommends making search a forethought rather than an afterthought. That is, file things, either electronic or physical, in a way that will allow you to quickly retrieve them. Ask yourself, "Where will I look for this when I need it?" or "How can I tag or label this item so that I'll be able to find it?" Related is preparing for the possibility that you'll show up at a meeting with no idea what it's about or why you're there. "I make sure all my calendar entries contain some context," Merrill says. "When my assistant adds a new meeting to my calendar, she types notes directly into the appointment entry, telling me things like the topic and goals of the meeting and who the other participants will be. If I don't know one of the attendees, my assistant may add a few notes about that person, such as job title, what he or she is contributing to the project at hand, and so on."

Why do psychiatrists work a fifty-minute hour? They use that extra ten minutes to write down what happened. Rather than scheduling meetings back-to-back, experts advise giving yourself ten minutes to write down what happened, to make notes about what needs to be done, and other comments that will orient you to this project when you next start to work on it. And to give yourself ten minutes *before* a meeting to review what is going to happen there. Because attention switching is metabolically costly, it's good neural hygiene for your brain to give it time to switch into the mind-set of your next meeting gradually and in a relaxed way before the meeting starts. When interrupted during a project, experts recommend making notes about where you left off so you can get back into the project more quickly later.

This is good advice, but there is an underlying point. Thinking ahead about what could go wrong, looking at the future and foreseeing threats—this is what an organized business mind can do, should do, must do.

Some threats are bigger than others. The smooth functioning of businesses is threatened by computer failure to a degree that many people have never taken seriously. Hard drives crash, and Internet servers go down (either your own or ones that you rely on from third parties). Many customers at restaurants, in taxicabs, or at clothing stores have experienced an unanticipated "failure to connect" of the electronic credit card machine. Taxi drivers in big cities, who can't afford to lose a payment due to a faulty connection, often carry around an old-style plastic credit card press, a machine that makes an impression of the credit card numbers on a specially designed form from the credit card company. This illustrates planning for failure par excellence, the result of effective planning for failure. The optimists who think nothing will go wrong experience the lost sales and financial setbacks, and the realists who are prepared for things to go wrong retain revenue in spite of technological hiccups.

More serious is the loss of important records and data or, just as bad, an inability to open files that have become corrupted or outdated. There are two hazards here to worry about—disk failure and file format obsolescence. A rigorous planning-for-failure approach to your data requires thinking about the ways you can lose access to that data, and how you can set systems in place to prevent or at least minimize that loss.

As of this writing, 90% of the world's data is stored on magnetic disks. These are vulnerable to magnetic field variations just like recording tape—prolonged exposure to magnets (such as found in loudspeakers) or radiation can corrupt the data, and temperature changes as small as 15 degrees Centigrade can double failure rates. Copying and backing up files can also introduce transcription errors—for many types of files, one wrong bit in the header can render the file completely unreadable. Beyond that, hard disks, thumb drives, CDs, and other storage media eventually all fail. (An old disk drive that has been sitting on a shelf, even one in a dust-proof, magnetically shielded case, can stop working after a few years if its bearings freeze.) And just having multiple copies of your files on the same hard drive doesn't protect you if the hard drive fails. Probabilities that a hard drive will fail within five years reach 50% or more. A study by Microsoft engineers found that 25% of all servers suffer a disk failure within two years. These are reasons to back up your data—many IT experts have an aphorism, "It's not *if* your hard drive will fail—it's *when*." For any business, having unimpeded access to all its files, both current and historical, is important. For a publicly traded company or government agency, it's essential for legal and regulatory reasons. USB flash drives and solid state drives are more expensive than magnetic drives, but are more robustly sensitive to changes in the environment.

The recommended solution is to back up your files to at least *two* different hard disks, and check those hard disks regularly—once every three months is a good rule of thumb—to be sure they're still functioning. Many companies use rolling backups and maintain an archive of files one day old, one week old, one month old, two months old, and so on, and they keep these in duplicate, triplicate, or more. If one fails, you've got a backup of the backup. It's unlikely that all would fail at the same time. The only way *that* is likely to happen is if there's a fire, flood, nuclear explosion, or other event that wipes out everything in a particular location. For this reason, governmental organizations and large companies spread the risk by keeping their hard disk backups in different locations. For a small business without vast resources, this is still within reach. If you've got a customer or close colleague (or even relative) in another city, you can hook up a remotely accessible backup disk at their home or place of business and schedule automatic backups and restores from your home base.

Backing up to the cloud, that is, to remote servers accessible via the Internet, is another way to maintain copies of files. It's also efficient for primary access when you use several different devices and want to keep them synchronized. Suppose you have a laptop, home computer, office computer, smartphone, and tablet. How do you keep track of where certain files are, or which computer has the most recent version of the Pensky file? Tech writer Paul Boutin sums up the dispersion that is indicative of a modern digital life: "Some photos are on your smartphone. Others sit on your home computer. Your digital work documents, favorite Web clippings and notes from meetings? Scattered like confetti after New Year's Eve." The solution is to synchronize all your devices, but few of us actually take the time to do that. After a long day at work, it's hard to motivate yourself to plug your phone into your computer, let alone to set up the synchronization program to function correctly, in automatic mode, in the first place. Cloud storage mitigates this problem to a large degree—you simply set all your devices to automatically upload and synchronize their files to a digital storage locker maintained by a third-party company, and when you're looking for that photo of your dog wearing sunglasses, or the shopping list you made on the subway on your way to work, you have to search only one place and it comes to you instantly (provided you have an Internet connection).

Perry R. Cook, professor of computer science at Princeton University, points out that there are pluses and minuses to backing up your files to the cloud. The advantage is that someone *else* is taking responsibility for maintaining the hardware, backing up those big servers (they're not just keeping *one* copy of your tax documents and family photos but multiple copies), and keeping everything running smoothly. On the other hand, Perry notes, "one of the issues of cloud storage is accessibility. MegaUpload, in addition to allowing people to store backup files, became a huge piracy site. When it was shut down by the U.S. Department of Justice in 2012, no one could get their files. All their clients, including professional photographers and moviemakers, lost everything. It's like making a deal with your neighbor to store your lawn mower, and he gets raided by the Feds for growing pot and everything is seized. You lose your lawn mower. With MegaUpload, courts wouldn't open it up even long enough to let legitimate users get their stuff. With the cloud, the companies could go under or be subject to regulatory or judicial restrictions and you're out of luck. The moral: keep your own data."

Back to planning for failure: You've backed up your files, but what if you upgrade your system and they won't open?! Cook advises having a plan for migrating files.

File migration refers to the process of making readable files that are no longer readable due to system, software, and hardware updates—basically, many computer file formats become obsolete. This follows from the rapid developments in the tech sector. Both hardware and software manufacturers have an incentive to create faster and more powerful products. These cause incompatibilities with old systems. It is likely that you, or someone you know, has experienced this. Your old computer stops working and when you go to get it repaired, the technician tells you that he can't fix it because the parts are no longer available—motherboards, logic boards, whatever. He suggests you buy a new computer. You do, and when you get it home, you realize that it comes with a wholly new and unfamiliar operating system. The new operating system won't open files from your old computer, and you can't simply reinstall your old operating system because the computer's hardware won't run it. Now you have a hard disk full of files that you can't open—your tax returns, family photos, correspondence, projects from work—all of them unreadable.

To be proactive about file migration, you keep track of all the different file types you have on your computer. When a new operating system comes out, or a new version of a software application you use, don't just blindly hit the upgrade-now button on your computer screen. It's necessary to test your old files to see if they'll open before you commit to the new system. You don't need to test all of them, just a sample of each kind by trying to open them. (Do this on a different machine or external hard drive than the one you're currently using.) There are three typical possibilities about what could happen.

1. The files will open without any issue and your new software uses the same file format as the old software.
2. The files open slowly because they require a conversion to the new software. The new software has a different format now (as when Microsoft moved from .doc to .docx format). If this happens, you need to begin migrating, that is, translating your files to the new format.
3. The files don't open at all. You need to wait until a translation program becomes available (this happens some of the time) or figure out a way to save your old files in a different format that will render them readable on the new computer (as when you save a Word document as .rtf, a more highly readable file type, although some page formatting can be lost).

Who needs to worry about migration? It's potentially a legal issue for corporations, publicly traded companies, research labs, and journalists to be able to put their hands on archival materials. For the rest of us who use our computers as digital archives of our lives, migration is just ordinary everyday planning-for-failure thinking.

Perry Cook counsels businesses and conscientious individuals to keep legacy (old) machines around, or to be sure that you have access to them, as well as any printers they worked with in their day (old printers don't typically work with modern computers). If there is no way to translate an old file to a currently readable format, you can always print it out. "It's a very retro, caveman approach to modern technology," Perry says. "But it works. So if you want to keep that e-mail from Aunt Bertha, print it out." Perry advises against throwing away an old computer when you upgrade but instead, making a bootable disk image and checking on your old machine every three to six months. There are still companies who kept vital information on 9 millimeter tape back in the era of big mainframes, or on 5-1/2-inch floppy disks in the first era of PCs, who never migrated. There are services for file migration in many major cities, but they're expensive. These media are so old now that few machines exist that can read them, and the process requires several steps of translating the file up through several different formats. Librarians and IT departments in large corporations recommend having one or more full-time people just for file migration (independent of anyone who handles backups, which are a different matter).

Finally, Perry says, "It helps if your file formats are open source. Why? Microsoft and Adobe files are very fragile—if one bit is off, the computer can't open the file at all. If it's plain text (.txt files), almost any program can open and inspect it, and if there's an error, it's just one character. If it's Open Source, somewhere there is a computer geek who can figure out how to open the file for you."

Another aspect of planning for failure, especially for business travelers, is that we often find ourselves stuck on a plane, in an airport, or in a hotel room for longer than we thought we'd be. There's not much we can do to prevent these un-anticipatable events, but as part of a planning-for-failure approach, we can control how we cope with it. HSPs might assemble a pouch with everything they need to make a mobile office:

- extra chargers for phone and computer
- USB key
- pen
- pencil, eraser, pencil sharpener
- mini stapler
- notepad
- Post-its
- extra computer connector cables that you often use

The key to this working is to keep it stocked up. Don't raid it if you're home—it is sacrosanct! Along the same lines, seasoned business travelers assemble a little emergency food pack: nuts, dried fruit, PowerBar. And they assemble a toilet kit with duplicates so that they're not having to pack stuff from the bathroom in the rush and haze right before a trip—that's how things get forgotten.

Planning for failure is a necessary way of thinking in the age of information overload. It is what CEOs, COOs, and their attorneys do, as well as military officers and strategists, and leaders of public institutions. Performing artists do it, too. Musicians carry extra guitar strings, reeds, electronic connectors—anything that might break in the middle of a performance and bring the show to a screeching halt. All these people spend a great deal of time trying to think about all the ways that something might go wrong, how they might prevent it, and how they would recover if it does. Humans are the only species that possess this capacity. As described in Chapter 5, no other animal plans for the future or strategizes about how to act in situations that haven't yet occurred. This kind of planning is not important just for being personally organized but is essential to successful business. It comes down to locus of control: An effective organization is one that takes steps to manage its own future rather than allowing external forces—human, environmental, or otherwise—to dictate its course.

PART THREE

8

WHAT TO TEACH OUR CHILDREN

The Future of the Organized Mind

Five years ago, two teenagers from the Midwest decided they wanted to build an airplane from scratch. Not just a glider, but a twin-engine jet that would carry fifty passengers and fly above five thousand feet. The fact that neither of them knew anything about principles of flight, or engines, or had ever built *anything* didn't daunt them—they reasoned that if other people could build jets, they could, too. They sought out books on the subject, but they decided early on that they didn't want to be constrained by what other people had done before—that their own intuitions should carry just as much weight as a textbook. After all, they reasoned, early airplane designers such as the Wright brothers didn't have textbooks to rely on, did they, and *their* airplanes turned out just fine.

They set up a work area in an open field in town. A few weeks into the project, the kids invited members of their high school and the larger community to participate. People could come by any time of the day or night and add to the airplane, or, if they were so inclined, they could take away something that didn't seem right to them, and either replace it or leave it to the next person to do so. A posted sign instructed passersby that the construction project was open to anyone, regardless of background or ability, that it was a true community project with equal access to all. Why should airplane construction be the domain of an elite few? Anyone with a desire to contribute was encouraged to do so.

At one point, an aeronautical engineer visiting relatives in the town passed by the project and was concerned (*horrified* might be a better word).

He added an emergency shutoff valve to the fuel system, and installed an oil cooler he found at a nearby junkyard. Before leaving town, he left extensive instructions about wing design and jet engine control, along with warnings and cautions that he said must be heeded before attempting to fly the plane. A few days later, an eleven-year-old county champion of paper airplane making, with a do-it-yourself attitude, brought a wrench to the building site and removed the oil cooler the engineer installed, and then threw away all of the engineer's instructions and warnings. Of course, this was all well within the ethos of the project, so no one stopped him.

The airplane was completed after two years, and a test flight was arranged for ten lucky members of the community. They drew straws to see who the pilot would be, reasoning that this was another job that was overrated and should be given to anyone who was interested.

Would you like to be a passenger in this plane? Of course not! But why not exactly?

For one thing, you might find the blatant disregard for expertise to be off-putting. Most of us believe that building (not to mention flying) an airplane requires special training, that it cannot be left to just anyone. In an organized society, we set up specialized schools to provide aeronautical training. These schools need to be accredited and certified by independent agencies in order to guarantee that the training provided is sound. We endorse *in general* a system in which licenses and certifications of various kinds need to be issued to surgeons, lawyers, electricians, construction companies, and the like. They assure us that high standards of quality and safety have been met. In short, we accept that there are experts in the world who know more than we do, that this expertise is valuable and indeed necessary to undertake important projects.

This story is entirely fictional, but it is a very close analogue to what Wikipedia does. I say this with some trepidation because Wikipedia has done at least two very admirable things: It has made information massively, unprecedentedly, ridiculously accessible, and it has made it free. I wholeheartedly agree that information should be accessible, and moreover, I believe that this is the foundation of a successful society—informed citizens are better able to make decisions about our mutual governance, and better able to become happy and productive members of their community.

But there was a trade-off: an antipathy toward expertise. This is according to no less an authority than Lawrence Sanger, the cofounder (with Jimmy Wales) of Wikipedia! The problem, he notes, is that anyone—*anyone*—can edit a Wikipedia article, regardless of their knowledge or training. There is no central authority of credentialed experts who review the articles to ensure that they are factual or that they are being edited by someone with knowledge on the topic. As a reader of Wikipedia, you have no way to know whether you're reading something accurate or not. And this isn't an unwitting side effect; it was part of Wikipedia's very design. Jimmy Wales has stated that experts should be accorded no more respect than novices, that there should be "no elite, and no hierarchy" of them to get in the way of newcomers who want to participate in Wikipedia.

If you were looking at the rudder of that community jet plane, you'd have no way to know whether it was designed by an expert or a novice, especially if you yourself were a novice. And when a true expert did come by, the visiting aeronautical engineer, his work and contributions were given no more weight ultimately than those of an eleven-year-old. Moreover, if you were coming upon the airplane for the first time and knew nothing of its history, you might very reasonably assume that it was designed by a professional because that is our expectation when we see such a considerable capital project in this country. We expect bridges not to collapse, car gas tanks not to explode, and dams to hold.

Conventional encyclopedias employ editors who are recognized leaders in their respective fields. The editors in turn identify and hire world-renowned experts in various domains to write the topic entries. Those entries are then reviewed for accuracy and bias by still other world experts in the field, who have to buy into the treatment of the subject. The authors sign their work with their academic credentials so that any reader can see who was responsible for the article and what their qualifications are. The system is not foolproof. At least three sources of inaccuracy emerge in articles: intrinsic bias, maintaining the status quo, and a preselection effect in those who agree to write the articles. An expert on Chinese art may devalue Korean art (intrinsic bias); new ideas and scholarship that challenge well-established ones may take some time to become accepted by the entrenched experts who have risen to a sufficient prominence in their field to be considered encyclopedia authors (a drive to maintain the status quo); scientists with active research programs and who are the most knowledgeable about emerging trends may not take the time to write encyclopedia articles, which are not considered "important" scholarship by their academic peers (preselection effect).

But although the system is not foolproof, its failures occur within a value system that both acknowledges and respects expertise, a system that both implicitly and explicitly establishes a meritocracy in which those who demonstrably know more about a topic are placed in a position to share their knowledge. I can't put too fine a point on this. Under the Wikipedia model, a neurosurgeon has as much say about an entry on brain aneurisms as a high school dropout. No rational person would choose the high school dropout as their brain surgeon, but if Wikipedia is to be the de facto and default source of information about technical topics such as aneurisms (and nontechnical ones as well), we should all be able to have confidence in its articles' origins.

Sure, eventually, someone knowledgeable may come along to correct the high school dropout's inexpert advice, but when? And how can you know that it's been done? It might be just before or just after you consult the article. Also, without overseers or curators, the entries have little consistency. Details that have grabbed the attention of a single individual can loom large in an entry, while important things can get much less treatment if no one has the knowledge or interest to fill out those sections. What is lacking is an editorial hand to make a decision on questions such as "Is this fact worth knowing about this entry and is it more important than other facts?" In the extreme, an encyclopedia entry could tell you every possible fact about a person or place, leaving nothing out—but such an entry would be too unwieldy to be useful. The usefulness of most professional summaries is that someone with perspective has used their best judgment about what, in the scheme of things, should be included. The person most involved in editing the entry on Charles Dickens may have no connection to the person writing the entry on Anton Chekhov, and so we end up with idiosyncratic articles that don't give equivalent weight to their lives, their works, their influences, and their historical place.

For scientific, medical, and technical topics, even in peer-reviewed journals, the information sources aren't always clearly on display. Technical articles can be difficult to understand without specific training, and there are controversies in many fields that require experience to understand and resolve. An expert knows how to weigh different sources of information and to resolve such apparent contradictions.

Some of the most relentless contributors to Wikipedia revisions appear to be people who have simply read a contrary account in a textbook or were taught something different in high school than what current experts believe. ("If it's in a textbook, it must be right!") What many novices don't know is that it can take five years or more for new information to filter down to textbooks, or that their high school teachers were not always right. As Lawrence Sanger puts it, Wikipedia articles can end up being "degraded in quality by the majority of people, whose knowledge of the subject is based on paragraphs in books and mere mentions in college classes." Articles that may have started out accurate can be hacked into inaccuracy by hordes of nonexperts, many of whom are inclined to believe fervently that their own intuitions, memories, or feelings ought to hold just as much weight as a scientific paper or the opinions of true experts. The root problem, Lawrence Sanger says, is a "lack of respect for expertise." As one Wikipedia commentator noted, "Why would an expert bother contributing his valuable time to a project that can be ruined by any random idiot on the net?"

Wikipedia does have two clear advantages over conventional encyclopedias. One is that it is nimble. When there is breaking news—an outbreak of violence in a troubled country, an earthquake, the death of a celebrity—Wikipedia is quick to respond and can report on those events within minutes or hours, unlike print encyclopedias, which take so long to compile. A second advantage is that topics that might not rate inclusion in a print encyclopedia can exist in an online format where space and printed pages are not limiting factors. There are thousands of words written about the computer game Dungeons & Dragons and the TV show *Buffy the Vampire Slayer*, far more than is written about President Millard Fillmore or Dante's *Inferno*. For popular TV shows, Wikipedia features plot summaries for each episode, and includes rather extensive information about guest stars and cast. Entries like these are examples of its strength and where the crowdsourcing ethos can shine. Anyone who is moved by the performance of a particular bit actor on *CSI* can look for her name in the credits at the end of the show and add her to the Wikipedia entry for that episode, all this without having to be an expert of any kind. Other fans of the show who are engaged with it can be trusted to correct faulty information, relying on the broadcast credits for the program.

This fan-based kind of editing is related to fan fiction, the recent phenomenon of fans writing works featuring their favorite characters from popular TV shows and films, or adding to existing stories to fill in plot holes or story lines that they feel were insufficient in the original work. This all began with a *Star Trek* fanzine (of course). This fan-based kind of literature may demonstrate a human need for community storytelling. We are, after all, a social species. We become joined by common stories, whether they are origin stories of humanity or of the country in which we live. Wikipedia clearly answers a need for making storytelling a participatory and communal act, and it inspires millions of people to contribute their enthusiasm and interest (and, yes, often expertise) in the service of what may be one of the most ambitious projects of scholarship ever.

One way to significantly improve Wikipedia would be to hire a panel of editors to supervise the entries and editing process. These experts could ensure uniformity and quality, and moderate disputes. Novices could still contribute—which is part of the fun and excitement of Wikipedia—but an expert panel would have the last word. Such a move would be possible only if Wikipedia had a larger source of income available, either through subscriptions or usage fees, or a benefactor. A loose affiliation of millionaires and billionaires, philanthropists, government agencies, book publishers, and universities could perhaps finance the endeavor, but it is difficult to challenge the grassroots ethos that has grown up around Wikipedia, that its content is democratically determined, and that all information should be free, all the time.

The lack of sympathy for a paid model is similar to a situation that arose in the psychedelic 1960s. When the music impresario Bill Graham started organizing some of the first outdoor rock concerts in Golden Gate Park in San Francisco, many of the hippies complained vigorously about his charging admission to the concerts. "Music should be free," they cried. Some added that music's ability to soothe the mortal soul, or its status as the "voice of the universe" virtually mandated that it should be free. Graham patiently pointed out the problem. "OK," he said, "let's assume for the moment that the musicians are willing to play for free, that they don't have to worry about how to pay their rent, or pay for their musical instruments. Do you see that stage? We built it here in the park. It took a team of carpenters and the wood and other materials had to be trucked in. Are they all going to work for free, too? And what about the truck drivers and the gas that their trucks use? Then there are the electricians, sound engineers, lighting, the portable toilets . . . are all of those people going to work for free, too?"

Of course, as detailed here, this free ethos for Wikipedia leads to all kinds of problems. So for now, the situation is at an impasse, with one notable exception—the emergence of organized and curated editing sessions by public institutions. The Smithsonian American Art Museum in Washington, DC, holds daylong "editathons" to improve the quality of entries by inviting Wikipedia editors, authors, and other volunteers to use the institution's extensive archives and resources alongside Smithsonian employees. Unfortunately, like the rodents in the Olds and Milner experiment, which repeatedly pressed a bar for a reward, a recalcitrant user can undo all of that curated editing with a single mouse click.

Do the advantages of being able to get a lot of information free outweigh the disadvantages? It depends on how important it is to you that information be accurate. By some definitions of the word, something can be considered "information" only if it *is* accurate. An important part of information literacy, and keeping information organized, is to know what is true and what isn't, and to know something about the weight of evidence supporting claims. Although it is important to be respectful of other points of view—after all, this is the way we can learn new things—it is also important to acknowledge that not all points of view are necessarily equally valid: Some really do come from true scholarship and expertise. Someone can believe wholeheartedly that Russia is in the middle of South America, but that doesn't make it true.

The world has changed for school-age children (not to mention university students and everyone else). Just fifteen years ago, if you wanted to learn a new fact, it took some time. Say, for example, you wanted to know the range of your favorite bird, the scarlet tanager, or the value of Planck's constant. In the old, pre-Internet days, either you had to find someone who knew or you had to find it yourself in a book. To do the latter, you first had to figure out what book might contain the information. You'd march down to a bricks-and-mortar library and spend a fair amount of time at the card catalogue to get, if not to the right book, at least to the right section of the library. There, you'd no doubt browse several books until you found the answer. The entire process could take literally hours. Now these two searches take seconds.

The acquisition of information, a process that used to take hours or even days, has become virtually instantaneous. This utterly changes the role of the classroom teacher from K–12 through graduate school. It no longer makes sense for teachers to consider their primary function to be the transmission of information. As the *New Yorker* essayist Adam Gopnik put it, nowadays, by the time a professor explains the difference between *elegy* and *eulogy*, everyone in the class has already Googled it.

Of course not everything is so easy to find. The immediate access to information that Wikipedia, Google, Bing, and other Internet tools provide has created a new problem that few of us are trained to solve, and *this* has to be our collective mission in training the next generation of citizens. This has to be what we teach our children: how to evaluate the hordes of information that are out there, to discern what is true and what is not, to identify biases and half-truths, and to know how to be critical, independent thinkers. In short, the primary mission of teachers must shift from the dissemination of raw information to training a cluster of mental skills that revolve around critical thinking. And one of the first and most important lessons that should accompany this shift is an understanding that there exist in the world experts in many domains who know more than we do. They should not be trusted blindly, but their knowledge and opinions, if they pass certain tests of face validity and bias, should be held in higher regard than those who lack special training. The need for education and the development of expertise has never been greater. One of the things that experts spend a great deal of their time doing is figuring out which sources of information are credible and which are not, and figuring out what they know versus what they don't know. And these two skills are perhaps the most important things we can teach our children in this post-Wikipedia, post-Google world. What else? To be conscientious and agreeable. To be tolerant of others. To help those less fortunate than they. To take naps.

As soon as a child is old enough to understand sorting and organizing, it will enhance his cognitive skills and his capacity for learning if we teach him to organize his own world. This can be stuffed animals, clothes, pots and pans in the kitchen. Make it into a game to sort and re-sort, by color, by height, by shininess, by name—all as an exercise in seeing the attributes one by one. Recall that being organized and conscientious are predictive of a number of positive outcomes, even decades later, such as longevity, overall health, and job performance. Being organized is a far more important trait than ever before.

Procrastination is a pervasive problem and is more widespread among children than adults. Every parent knows the difficulties encountered in trying to get a child to do homework when a favorite TV show is on, to clean her room when friends are outside playing, or even just to go to bed at the designated bedtime. These difficulties arise for two reasons—children are more likely to want immediate gratification, and they are less likely to be able to foresee the future consequences of present inaction; both of these are tied to their underdeveloped prefrontal cortices, which don't fully mature until after the age of twenty (!). This also makes them more vulnerable to addiction.

To some extent, most children can be taught to *do it now* and to shun procrastination. Some parents even make a game out of it. Recall the motto of Jake Eberts, the film producer who taught his children: "Eat the frog. Do that unpleasant thing first thing in the morning and you feel free for the rest of the day."

There are a number of critical thinking skills that are important, and teaching them is relatively straightforward. Indeed, most of them are already taught in law schools and graduate schools, and in previous generations they were taught in college preparatory–oriented grades 6–12 schools. The most important of these skills are not beyond the reach of the average twelve-year-old. If you like watching courtroom dramas (*Perry Mason, L.A. Law, The Practice*), many of the skills will be familiar, for they closely resemble the kinds of evaluations that are made during court cases. There, a judge, jury, and the attorneys for both sides must decide what to admit into the court, and this is based on considerations such as the source of the information, its credibility, whether or not a witness possesses the necessary expertise to make certain judgments, and the plausibility of an argument.

My colleague Stephen Kosslyn, a cognitive neuroscientist who was formerly chair of Harvard's Psychology Department and is now dean of the faculty at the Minerva Schools at KGI, calls these collectively *foundational concepts and habits of mind*. They are mental habits and reflexes that should be taught to all children and reinforced throughout their high school and college years.

Information Literacy

There is no central authority that controls how websites or blogs are named, and it is easy to create a fictitious identity or claim phony credentials. The president of Whole Foods posed as a regular guy customer to praise the store's pricing and policies. There are many stories like this. Just because a website is named U.S. Government Health Service doesn't mean it is run by the government; a site named Independent Laboratories doesn't mean that it is independent—it could well be operated by an automobile manufacturer who wants to make its cars look good in not-so-independent tests.

Newspapers and magazines such as *The New York Times, The Washington Post, The Wall Street Journal,* and *Time* strive to be neutral in their coverage of news. Their reporters are trained to obtain information with independent verifications—a cornerstone of this kind of journalism. If one government official tells them something, they get corroboration from another source. If a scientist makes a claim, reporters contact other scientists who don't have any personal or professional relationship with the first scientist, in order to get independent opinions. Few would take at face value a claim about the health benefits of almonds published by the Almond Growers Association of the United States but nowhere else.

It is true that reputable sources are somewhat conservative about wanting to be certain of facts before running with them. Many sources have emerged on the Web that do not hold to the same traditional standards of truth, and in some cases, they can break news stories and do so accurately before the more traditional and conservative media. *TMZ* ran the story of Michael Jackson's death before anyone else because they were willing to publish the story based on less evidence than *CNN* or *The New York Times.* In that particular case, they turned out to be right, but it doesn't always work out that way.

During fast-breaking news events, like the Arab Spring, journalists aren't always on site. Reports from regular citizens hit the Web through Twitter, Facebook, and blogs. These *can* be reliable sources of information, especially when considered as a collection of observations. Nonprofessional journalists—citizens who are swept up in a crisis—provide timely, firsthand accounts of events. But they don't always distinguish in their reports what they've perceived firsthand from what they've simply heard through rumor or innuendo. Our hunger for instant updates on breaking news stories leads to inaccuracies that become settled only later. Early reports contain false or unverified information that doesn't get sorted out until some hours or days after the event. In the pre-Internet days, journalists had time to gather the necessary information and verify it before going to press. Because newspapers published only once a day, and network TV news had its primary broadcast only once a day, there was not the rush we see now to run with a story before all the facts are in.

During the August 2013 chemical attacks in Syria, the information flow available via social media was contaminated with misinformation, some of it deliberately planted. With no trained investigative journalists to organize the conflicting and contradictory accounts, it was difficult for anyone to make sense of what was happening. As former *New York Times* editor Bill Keller noted, "It took an experienced reporter familiar with Syria's civil war, my colleague C. J. Chivers, to dig into the technical information in the U.N. report and spot the evidence—compass bearings for two chemical rockets—that established the attack was launched from a Damascus redoubt of Assad's military." Chivers himself: "Social media isn't journalism, it's information. *Journalism* is what you do with it."

Two sources of bias can affect articles. One is the bias of the writer or editors. As humans, they have their own political and social opinions, and for serious journalism, these are supposed to be left at the door. This isn't always easy. One difficulty with preparing a neutral news story is that there can be many subtleties and nuances, many parts of the story that don't fit neatly into a brief summary. The choice about what parts of an article to leave out—elements that complicate the story—is just as important as deciding what to include, and the conscious or subconscious biases of the writers and editors can come into play in this selection.

Some news sources, such as *National Review* or *Fox* (on the right) and *MSNBC* or *The Nation* (on the left) appeal to us because they have a particular political leaning. Whether or not this is the result of a conscious filtering of information isn't obvious. Some of their reporters may feel they are the *only* neutral and unbiased journalists in the business. Others may feel it is their responsibility to seek out views on their side of the political spectrum to counter what they perceive as a pernicious political bias in the so-called mainstream media.

My former professor Lee Ross of Stanford University conducted a study that revealed an interesting fact about such politically and ideologically based biases in news reporting, dubbed the *hostile media effect*. Ross and his colleagues, Mark Lepper and Robert Vallone, found that partisans on any side of an issue tend to find reporting to be biased in favor of their opponents. In their experiment, they showed a series of news reports about the 1982 Beirut massacre to Stanford students who had pre-identified themselves as either pro-Israeli or pro-Palestinian. The pro-Israeli students complained that the reporting was strongly biased toward the Palestinian point of view. They said that the news reports held Israel to stricter standards than other countries, and that the reporters were clearly biased against Israel. Finally, the students counted only a few pro-Israeli references in the reports, but many anti-Israeli references. The pro-Palestinian students, on the other hand, reported exactly the opposite bias from watching the same news reports—they judged the reports to be strongly biased toward Israel, and counted far fewer pro-Palestinian references and far more anti-Palestinian references. They, too, felt that the reporters were biased, but against the Palestinians, not the Israelis. Both groups were worried that the reports were so biased that previously neutral viewers would turn against their side after viewing them. In fact, a neutral group of students watching the same clips held opinions that fell between the opinions of the partisan students, testifying to the neutrality of the clips.

These experiments were conducted with reports that were close to being objectively neutral (as indexed by the neutral students' responses). It is easy to imagine, then, that a partisan watching a news report that is skewed toward his or her beliefs will find *that* to be neutral. This is arguably a factor in the new prominence of so-called ideologically driven news commentary such as those by Ann Coulter and Rachel Maddow, a form of journalism that has probably always existed as long as there was news to convey. Herodotus, in ancient Greece, is not only recognized as among the first historians, but the first who allowed partisan bias to enter into his reports, and he was taken to task by Aristotle, Cicero, Josephus, and Plutarch for it. Biases come in many forms, including what is deemed newsworthy, the sources cited, and the use of selective rather than comprehensive information.

We are not always seeking neutrality when finding information on the Web, but it is important to understand who is providing the information, what organizations they are sponsored by or affiliated with (if any), and whether the website content is sanctioned by or provided by officials, experts, partisans, amateurs, or people posing as someone they're not.

Because the Internet is like the Wild West—largely lawless and self-governed—it is the responsibility of each Internet user to be on guard against being taken in by the digital equivalent of crooks, con artists, and snake-oil salesmen. If this is beginning to sound like still another instance of shadow work, it is. The work of authenticating information used to be done, to varying degrees, by librarians, editors, and publishers. In many universities, a librarian holds an advanced degree and a rank equivalent to that of a professor. A good librarian is a scholar's scholar, familiar with the difference between a rigorously reviewed journal and a vanity press, and is up to date on controversies in many different fields that arise due to lapses in scholarship, credibility, and where to look for impartial perspectives.

Librarians and other information specialists have developed user's guides to evaluating websites. These include questions we should ask, such as "Is the page current?" or "What is the domain?" (A guide prepared by NASA is particularly helpful.) Critical thinking requires that we not take at face value the content we find on the Web. The usual cues we evolved to use when interacting with people—their body language, facial expressions, and overall demeanor—are absent. People re-post articles and alter them for their own gain; advertising endorsements are disguised as reviews; and impostors are difficult to detect. Is the page merely an opinion? Is there any reason you should believe its content more than that of any other page? Is the page a rant, an extreme view, possibly distorted or exaggerated?

In evaluating scientific and medical information, the report should include footnotes or other citations to peer-reviewed academic literature. Facts should be documented through citations to respected sources. Ten years ago, it was relatively easy to know whether a journal was reputable, but the lines have become blurred with the proliferation of open-access journals that will print anything for a fee in a parallel world of pseudo-academia. As Steven Goodman, a dean and professor at Stanford School of Medicine, notes, "Most people don't know the journal universe. They will not know from a journal's title if it is for real or not." How do you know if you're dealing with a reputable journal or not? Journals that appear on indexes such as PubMed (maintained by the U.S. National Library of Medicine) are selected for their quality; articles on Google Scholar are not. Jeffrey Beall, a research librarian at the University of Colorado Denver, has developed a blacklist of what he calls predatory open-access journals. His list has grown from twenty publishers four years ago to more than three hundred today.

Suppose your doctor recommends that you take a new drug and you're trying to find more information about it. You enter the name of the drug into your favorite search engine, and one of the first sites that comes up is

RxList.com. You haven't seen this site before and you want to validate it. From the "*About RxList*" page, you learn, "Founded by pharmacists in 1995, RxList is the premier Internet Drug Index resource." A link sends you to a list of contributing writers and editors, with further links to brief bios, showing their academic degrees or professional affiliations so that you can decide for yourself if their expertise is suitable. You can also enter RxList .com into Alexa.com, a free data mining and analysis service, where you learn that the site is mostly used by people with only "some college" and, compared to other Internet sites, it is less used by people with college or graduate degrees. This tells you that it is a resource for the typical layperson, which might be just what you're looking for—a way to avoid the technical jargon in medical descriptions of pharmaceutical products—but for more sophisticated users, it serves as a warning that the information may not be vetted. How reliable is the information? According to Alexa, the top five sites that link to RxList.com are:

yahoo.com

wikipedia.org

blogger.com

reddit.com

bbc.co.uk

Only one of these informs us about the site's validity, the link from the BBC news service. If you follow the link, however, it turns out to be on a message board portion of the site, and is nothing more than a comment by a reader. A Google search of .gov sites that link to RxList.com is more helpful, revealing 3,290 results. Of course the number itself is meaningless—they could be subpoenas or court proceedings of actions against the company, but a random sampling shows they are not. Among the first reported links is from the National Institutes of Health on a page of recommended resources for clinical medicine, as well as links from the State of New York, the State of Alabama, the U.S. Food and Drug Administration, the National Cancer Institute (of the NIH), and other organizations that lend legitimacy and a seal of approval to RxList.com.

Because the Web is unregulated, the burden is on each user to apply critical thinking when using it. You can remember the three aspects of Web literacy by an English word used to express good wishes on meeting or parting: *ave*. Authenticate, validate, and evaluate.

Much of the information we encounter about health, the economy, our favorite sports, and new product reviews involves statistics, even if it isn't dressed up that way. One source of misleading data comes from a bias in the way the data were obtained. This most often occurs in statistical summaries that we encounter, but it can also occur in regular news stories. The bias refers to cases when an unrepresentative sample is collected (of people, germs, foods, incomes, or whatever quantity is being measured and reported on). Suppose a reporter wanted to measure the average height of people in the city of Minneapolis, for an investigative story on whether alleged contaminants in the water supply have led to a decrease in height of the population. The reporter decides to stand on a street corner and measure passersby. If the reporter stands in front of a basketball court, the sample is likely to be taller than the average person; if the reporter stands in front of the Minneapolis Society for Short People, the sample is likely to be shorter than the average.

Don't laugh—this type of sampling error is pervasive (though admittedly not always as obvious) even in respected scientific journals! The types of people who volunteer for experimental drug trials are undoubtedly different from those who don't; they may be from lower on the socioeconomic spectrum and need the money, and socioeconomic status is known to correlate with a range of overall health measures due to differences in childhood nutrition and access to regular health care. When only a certain subset of all possible experimental participants walk through the laboratory door, the sampling bias is called a *preselection* effect. As another example, if the researchers advertise for participants for a new drug experiment, and a precondition is that they cannot drink any alcohol for eight weeks during the trials, the researchers end up bypassing the average person and preselecting people who have a certain lifestyle and all that goes with it (they may be super stressed from not having the relief of an occasional drink; they may be alcoholics in a treatment program; they may be unusually healthy people who are exercise fanatics).

Harvard University routinely publishes data on the salaries earned by recent graduates. The type of mental training that we should be teaching, starting in childhood, would cause anyone to ask the question: Is there a possible source of bias in Harvard's data? Could those salary figures somehow be inaccurate, due to a latent bias in the data-gathering methods? For example, if Harvard relied on surveys mailed to recent graduates, it might miss any recent graduates who are homeless, indigent, or in prison. Of those who did receive the survey, not all may be willing to return it. It seems plausible that those recent Harvard graduates who are unemployed or working at menial jobs or simply not making much money might be too embarrassed to return the survey. This would lead to an overestimate of the true average salary of recent graduates. And of course there is another source of error—shocker—people lie (even Harvard students). In a survey like this, recent grads may overstate their income to impress whoever might be reading the survey, or out of guilt that they're not making more.

Imagine that a stockbroker sends an unsolicited letter to your home.

> Dear neighbor,
>
> I've just moved into the area and I'm an expert at predicting the stock market. I've already made a fortune, and I would like you to be able to benefit from the system that I've developed over many years of hard work.
>
> I'm not asking for any of your money! I'm just asking that you give me a chance to prove myself without any commitment from you at all. Over the next several months, I will make predictions about the market through the mail, and all you have to do is wait to see whether they are true or not. At any time, you can ask me to stop sending letters. But if my predictions are right, you can contact me at the number below and I'll be happy to take you on as a client and help you to make riches beyond your wildest dreams.
>
> To get started, I predict that IBM stock will go up in the next month. I'll send you another letter in four weeks with my next prediction.

A month later, you get another letter.

> Dear neighbor,
>
> Thanks for opening this letter. As you'll recall, I predicted last month that IBM stock would go up—and it did! My next prediction is that Dow Chemical will go up. Talk to you next month.

A month after that, you get another letter, with the broker pointing out that he was correct again, and making a new prediction. This goes on for six months in a row—every time, he called the market exactly as he said he would. At this point, the average person would be thinking that they should give him some money. Some might even be thinking of mortgaging their houses and giving him *all* their money. Six times in a row! This guy is a genius! You know from Chapter 6 that the odds of him getting it right by chance is only $1/2^6$ or 1 in 64.

But you're not the average person. You've been trained in habits of mind and to ask the question, Is there missing information? Is there a logical, alternative explanation for this broker's success that doesn't rely on his having unheard-of abilities in predicting the market? What information might be missing, or obscured from your view?

Consider that in this particular case, you're seeing only those letters he chose to send you—you're not seeing the letters he sent to anyone else. Statisticians call this selective windowing. The case I'm describing actually occurred, and the broker was imprisoned for fraud. At the beginning of the whole scheme, he sent out *two* sets of letters: One thousand people received a letter predicting that IBM stock would go up, and one thousand received a letter predicting that it would go down. At the end of the month, he simply waits to see what happens. If IBM went down, he forgets about the thousand people who received a wrong prediction, and he sends follow-up letters only to those thousand who received the correct prediction. He tells half of them that Dow Chemical will go up and he tells the other half that Dow Chemical will go down. After six iterations of this, he's got a core group of thirty-one people who have received six correct predictions in a row, and who are ready to follow him anywhere.

Selective windowing occurs in less nefarious and deliberate ways as well. A video camera trained on a basketball player making ten free throws in a row may selectively window the successes, and the one hundred misses surrounding it aren't shown. A video of a cat playing a recognizable melody on the piano may show only ten seconds of random music out of several hours of nonsense.

We often hear reports about an intervention—a pill someone takes to improve their health, a government program that defuses tensions in a foreign country, an economic stimulus package that puts many people back to work. What's usually missing in these reports is a control condition, that is, what would have happened *without* the intervention? This is especially important if we want to draw conclusions about causality, that the one event caused the other. We can't know this without a proper control. "I took Vitamin C and my cold was gone in four days!" But how long would it have taken for your cold to go away if you *didn't* take Vitamin C? If the peculiar flight and maneuvering pattern a witness attributed to a UFO could be replicated in a conventional aircraft, it takes some of the juice out of the argument that the aircraft could only have been a UFO.

For decades, the professional magician and skeptic James Randi has followed self-proclaimed psychics around the world and has replicated *exactly* their feats of mind reading. His aim? To counter the argument that the psychics *must* be using extrasensory perception and mysterious psychic powers because there is no other explanation for their extraordinary feats. By accomplishing the same thing with magic, Randi is offering a more logical, parsimonious explanation for the phenomena. He is not proving that psychic powers don't exist, only that psychics can't do anything that he can't do using ordinary magic. His is a control condition, one in which psychic powers are not used. This leaves the following logical possibilities:

1. Both psychic powers and magic exist, and they are able to produce the same feats.
2. Psychic powers don't exist—psychics use magic and then lie about it.
3. Magic doesn't exist—magicians use psychic powers and then lie about it.

Two of these options require you to toss out everything that is known about science, cause and effect, and the way the world works. One of these asks you only to believe that some people in the world are willing to lie about what they do or how they do it in order to make a living. To make matters more interesting, Randi has offered a $1 million prize to anyone who can do something with psychic powers that he cannot replicate with magic. The only restriction is that the psychics have to perform their demonstrations under controlled conditions—using cards or other objects that are neutral (not ones that they provide or have a chance to doctor)—and with video cameras taping them. More than four hundred people have tried to claim the prize, but their psychic powers mysteriously fail them under these conditions, and the money sits in an escrow account. As Stanford psychologist Lee Ross says, "If psychic powers exist, they are impish, and do not want to be discovered in the presence of a scientist."

When two quantities vary together in some kind of clear relationship, we say they are correlated. Taking multivitamins was correlated, in some older studies, with longer life span. But this doesn't mean that multivitamins *cause* you to live longer. They could be entirely unrelated, or there could be a third factor *x* that causes both. It's called *x* because it is, at least initially, unidentified. There could be a cluster of behaviors called health conscientiousness. People who are health conscientious see their doctors regularly, eat well, and exercise. This third factor *x* might cause those people to take vitamins and to live longer; the vitamins themselves may be an artifact in the story that does not cause longer life. (As it happens, the evidence that multivitamins are associated with longer life appears to be faulty, as mentioned in Chapter 6.)

The results of Harvard's salary survey are no doubt intended to lead the average person to infer that a Harvard education is responsible for the high salaries of recent graduates. This may be the case, but it's also possible that the kinds of people who go to Harvard in the first place come from wealthy and supportive families and therefore might have been likely to obtain higher-paying jobs regardless of where they went to college. Childhood socioeconomic status has been shown to be a major quantity correlated with adult salaries. Correlation is not causation. Proving causation requires carefully controlled scientific experiments.

Then there are truly spurious correlations—odd pairings of facts that have no relationship to each other and no third factor *x* linking them. For example, we could plot the relationship between the global average temperature over the past four hundred years and the number of pirates in the world and conclude that the drop in the number of pirates is caused by global warming.

The Gricean maxim of relevance implies that no one would construct such a graph (below) unless they felt these two were related, but this is where critical thinking comes in. The graph shows that they are correlated, but not that one causes the other. You could spin an ad hoc theory—pirates can't stand heat, and so, as the oceans became warmer, they sought other employment. Examples such as this demonstrate the folly of failing to separate correlation from causation.

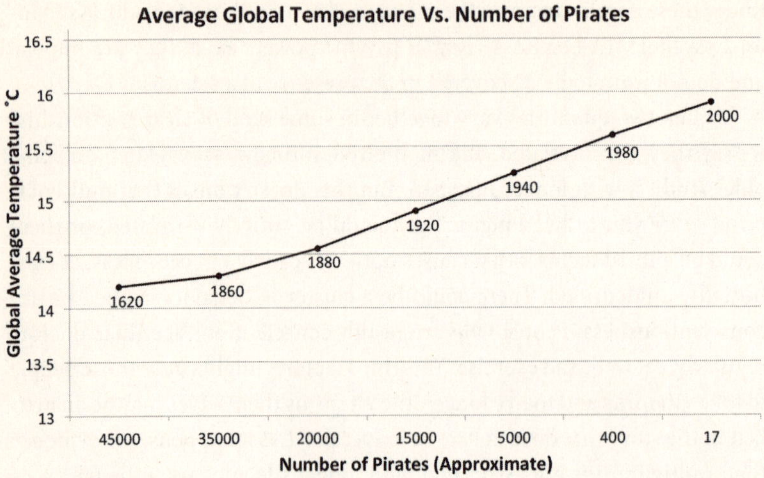

It is easy to confuse cause and effect when encountering correlations. There is often that third factor *x* that ties together correlative observations. In the case of the decline in pirates being related to the increase in global warming, factor *x* might plausibly be claimed to be industrialization. With industrialization came air travel and air cargo; larger, better fortified ships; and improved security and policing practices. Pirates declined because the way we transport valuable goods across long distances changed, and law enforcement improved. The industrialization that led to these developments also led to increases in carbon-based emissions and greenhouse gases, which in turn led to global climate change.

The reason we end up with correlational data so much of the time is that conducting controlled experiments can be impractical or unethical. A controlled experiment is the gold standard in science, and it requires random assignment of "treatment units" to experimental conditions. To study the effects of smoking cigarettes on lung cancer, the "treatment units" are people, and the experimental conditions are smoking or not smoking. The only scientifically rigorous way to study the issue would be to randomly assign some people to the *smoking* condition, and then force them to smoke a certain number of cigarettes per day, while another group of people is randomly assigned to the *no smoking* condition. Then the researcher simply has to wait to see how many people in each group contract lung cancer.

This type of experiment is performed routinely with experimental medicines, and people are naturally quite willing to volunteer to be in the drug condition if they think it will help cure their illness. But if the experiment carries with it the threat of harm, such as smoking, it is unethical to perform it. The logic behind random assignment is this: There might be some people who are more likely to show an effect in your experiment than others, and random assignment helps to distribute them evenly across the different experimental groups. We know that people who work in coal mines or who live in areas with serious air pollution are more likely to contract lung cancer; it wouldn't be a fair test of smoking if all of them ended up in the *smoking* group or in the *no smoking* group—the researcher randomly assigns subjects to even out the potential effects of any preexisting condition, personality type, or other factor that could bias the results.

It can be all too tempting to infer causation from correlational data, especially when controlled experiments can't be done. When we can imagine a plausible, underlying mechanism, the temptation is even greater. The data linking smoking and lung cancer in humans are correlational. The data were obtained by looking retrospectively at people who die from lung cancer and tracking back to see whether or not they were smokers and how much they smoked. The correlation is not perfect: Not every smoker dies of lung cancer and not everyone who dies of lung cancer was a smoker. Some smokers live long lives and die of other things—there are many people who continue to smoke into their eighties and nineties. Some lung cancers appear in nonsmokers, and could be based on genetic or epigenetic factors, exposure to radiation, or other factors. But the correlation between smoking and lung cancer is strong—90% of lung cancers occur among smokers—and scientists have identified a plausible underlying mechanism: toxic chemicals within the smoke-damaged lung tissue. No one has proven that smoking causes lung cancer with a controlled experiment, but we infer causation. It's important to know the difference.

Consider an alternative account, championed by the scientist (and smoker) Hans Eysenck. He has proposed that there is a certain personality type that is prone to smoking. This seems reasonable. Now suppose that there is a gene associated with this personality type and *also* associated with a propensity to get lung cancer. The gene becomes a third factor *x*—it increases the likelihood that people will take up smoking and it also increases the likelihood that they'll get lung cancer. Note that if this is true, those people would have gotten lung cancer *whether or not they smoked*—but because the gene causes them to smoke, we'll never know for sure if they would have contracted lung cancer without smoking. Few scientists take this view seriously, but it is possible that Eysenck is right.

An example of a third-factor-*x* explanation that turned out to be true is the story of high-tension power lines and childhood leukemia rates in suburban Denver. In the 1980s, the Centers for Disease Control and Prevention became alarmed that the incidence of childhood leukemia was several times greater in certain Denver suburbs than in other parts of the country. An investigation was launched. Researchers discovered that the neighborhoods that had the highest leukemia rates were those with high-tension power lines. And the closer a house was to power lines with a transformer, the greater the risk of leukemia. It was suggested that the strong electromagnetic fields of the power lines disrupted the cellular membrane in children, making the cells more vulnerable to mutation and hence cancer. Here was a correlation and a plausible underlying mechanism. The mechanism was that the power lines were causing the leukemia. A several-years-long epidemiological investigation, however, concluded there was a third factor *x* that accounted for most of the increase in leukemia rates: socioeconomic status. Because the lines are unsightly, and because much of suburban Denver has power lines buried underground, the houses near visible power lines were less expensive. People who lived near these power lines were thus more likely to be lower on the socioeconomic scale; they had poorer diets, poorer access to health care, and, on average, unhealthy lifestyles. The correlation between living near power lines and developing leukemia was real, but the initial explanation of the cause was not accurate—socioeconomic status was driving both.

Fish oil, rich in omega-3 fatty acids, has been found to be protective against cardiovascular disease, and the American Heart Association has been recommending the consumption of fish twice a week and the supplementation of fish oil capsules, for over ten years. Long-chain omega-3 fatty acids, found in oily fish such as herring, sardines, salmon, and mackerel, are considered essential for human health. They decrease inflammation and have been associated with improved mood, cognitive ability, and energy, and they strengthen heart function. Although some recent studies have cast doubt on the efficacy of fish oil, there is still a body of evidence pointing to its benefits, so many doctors continue to recommend it to their patients.

In the summer of 2013, a study came out that found a strong link between omega-3s and increased risk of prostate cancer in men. Men who were already diagnosed with prostate cancer were found to have higher levels of chemicals found in fatty fish than did cancer-free men. Those blood levels were associated with a 43% increase in the risk of developing prostate cancer. Of course, in a correlational study, there could be some third factor *x* that is leading to both, and this has not been identified (nor much mentioned in the articles reporting on this finding). Doctors are split as to whether to continue recommending fish oil for their male patients.

The situation is confusing, to say the least. One of the most vocal critics of the study, Dr. Mark Hyman, has a potential conflict of interest: He runs a laboratory that makes its money testing people's blood for omega-3 fatty acids, and operates a website that sells omega-3 capsules. But that doesn't mean he's wrong. He notes that the data are correlational, not the result of a controlled study. He voices concern about the way the blood samples were analyzed. There are many unknowns here, and the various risks and benefits are not well quantified, making the kinds of fourfold table analysis of Chapter 6 unreliable, although not undoable. Thus, a fairly solid body of evidence does suggest that fish oil protects against heart disease, and this is now pitted against a single new study suggesting that fish oil may promote prostate cancer.

To find out how physicians were handling the news, I talked to cardiologists, urological oncologists, and internists. The cardiologists and oncologists were generally split along party lines, with the cardiologists recommending fish oil supplements for the protective effects, and the oncologists recommending against them for the increased cancer risk. An extreme reading of the state of the decision would be: "Die of heart disease or prostate cancer? You get to choose!" Dr. Katsuto Shinohara, a urological oncologist at UC San Francisco, broke the tie among the various physicians, noting that "it is prudent not to put too much stock in a single study." That single study will surely be followed up on and replicated in the coming years. The evidence for the protective effects of fish oil across dozens of studies, he feels, outweighs the risks of fish oil shown in a single study.

Still, men with previously diagnosed prostate cancer may wish to be especially careful. For them (and perhaps men over fifty who have not received such a diagnosis), the situation presents no clear solution. If one waits until the new fish oil studies come in, there are risks in the meantime of taking omega-3s and of not taking them. Incidentally, the American Heart Association also recommends eating tofu and soybeans for their beneficial cardiological effects, and some studies show that soy is preventive against prostate cancer. Other studies have shown that soy doesn't reduce prostate cancer recurrence, and that it can be associated with loss of mental acuity in older men.

The fish oil question is perhaps one for the decision-making equivalent of the junk drawer, a decision that cannot easily be categorized with what we know at present. Sometimes, critical thinking leads to a conclusion that there is no certain answer. And yet we then must make a certain choice.

Whenever we encounter information in the form of numbers, it is important to do a quick mental check to see if the numbers reported are even *plausible*. To do this, you need to be familiar with certain bits of world knowledge. Every one of us has a mental file drawer full of trivia, such as the population of the United States, the normal operating speed of a car, how long it takes to lose weight, or the amount of time a normal human pregnancy lasts. And any fact of this sort that you haven't committed to memory is just a few hundred milliseconds from finding through a Web search. Performing a quick check of the plausibility of numerical information is one of the easiest and most important parts of critical thinking.

If someone says that 400 million people voted in the last U.S. federal election, that a new economy car has a top speed of four hundred miles per hour, or that so-and-so lost fifty pounds in two days with a juice fast, your general knowledge of the world and your inherent numeracy should raise a red flag about these numerical values.

One of the most important skills, then, that we can teach our children is to think about numbers logically and critically, and enable this sort of querying and verification. The goal of these skills is not to see if the number you've encountered is *exactly* correct, but only to see if it is *approximately* correct—that is, close enough to be *plausible*.

There's a quick trick for evaluating numerical information that is rarely written about in the critical thinking literature: Set *boundary conditions*. A boundary condition describes what the *lowest* and *highest* answers could possibly be. Suppose I ask you how tall Shaquille O'Neal is, and you don't know the answer. Is he taller than four feet? Well, certainly he must be, you might reason; he is a famous member of the NBA, and basketball players tend to be tall. Is he taller than five feet? Again, this is almost certainly true. Is he shorter than ten feet? You may catch yourself searching your memory; you've probably never heard of *anyone* who is ten feet tall, so yes, you would say he is shorter than ten feet. A quick and not-terribly-precise pair of boundary conditions, then, are that Shaq is somewhere between five feet and ten feet tall. If you know a bit about the NBA and the heights of players, and you know something about human physiological limitations, you might be able to refine your boundary conditions to say that he is probably between five feet six inches and seven feet eight inches. The art in setting boundary conditions is to get them as close as possible to each other while maintaining confidence in your answer. According to the NBA, Shaq is seven feet one inch.

Setting boundary conditions is an essential part of scientific and everyday critical thinking, and is crucial to decision-making. We do this all the time without even knowing it. If you go to the grocery store and buy a bag of groceries, and the checkout clerk tells you that the bill is five cents, you instantly know that something is wrong without having to sum up the cost of every item in your bag. Similarly, if she tells you the price is $500, you also know that something is wrong. Effective approximating is being able to set boundary conditions that aren't so ludicrously far apart. Based on your shopping habits, you might know that 90% of the time a typical bag of groceries at your regular market costs between $35 and $45; you'd be surprised if the total was $15 or if it was $75. So we would say that the *boundary conditions* for your bag of groceries are $35–$45. Scientists would describe this as your *90% confidence interval*—that is, you are 90% sure that the register total should fall within this interval. The closer together your boundary conditions are, the more helpful your approximation is of course.

Part of setting boundary conditions is using your knowledge of the world or acquiring a few landmarks to help in your estimation. If you had to estimate a friend's height, you could use the fact that the average door frame in North America is about eighty inches; how tall is the person compared to the door? Alternatively, if you were speaking to her, would you look her in the eye or have to look up or down? If you need to estimate the width of a car or bus, or the size of a room, imagine yourself lying down in it—would you be able to lie down without curling up? How many of you would fit in the space?

Scientists talk about *order of magnitude* estimates. An order of magnitude is a power of ten. In other words, as a first rough estimate, we try to decide how many zeros there are in the answer. Suppose I ask you how many tablespoons of water are in a cup of coffee. Here are some "power of ten" possibilities:

a. 2
b. 20
c. 200
d. 2,000
e. 20,000

For the sake of completeness, we might also include fractional powers of ten:

f. 1/20
g. 1/200
h. 1/2000

Now you can quickly rule out the fractions: 1/20 of a tablespoon is a very small amount, and 1/200 is even smaller than that. You could probably easily rule out 2 tablespoons as the answer. What about 20 tablespoons? You might not be so sure, and you might find yourself trying to mentally convert 20 tablespoons to some other, more useful measure like cups or ounces. Let's shelve that for a minute to work on the basis of intuition first, and calculation and conversion second. To recap: You're sure there are more than 2 tablespoons; you're not sure if there are more or less than 20 tablespoons. What about 200 tablespoons? This seems like a lot, but again, you may not be sure. But it must be clear that 2,000 tablespoons is too many. Of the eight estimates listed, you've quickly converged on two of them as plausible: 20 and 200 tablespoons. This is actually quite remarkable. It is a question you may never have considered before, and with a little bit of reasoning and intuition, you were able to narrow the answer down to these two possibilities.

Now let's calculate. If you bake, you may know that there are 2 tablespoons in 1/8 cup, and therefore 2 × 8 = 16 tablespoons in a cup. The true answer is not any of those listed above, but the correct answer, 16, is closer to 20 than to any of the others. The idea of these powers of ten, of the order of magnitude estimates, is that we don't let ourselves get hung up on unnecessary precision when we're approximating. It is useful enough for the purposes of this thought experiment to know that *the answer is closer to 20 than it is to 2 or to 200*. That is what an order of magnitude estimate is.

If you didn't know how many tablespoons are in a cup, you might picture a tablespoon and a cup and try to imagine how many times you'd have to fill your tablespoon and empty it into the cup before the cup would be full. Not everyone has the former fact at their command, and not everyone is able to visualize these quantities, and so that process may end for a lot of people right here. You might simply say that the answer could be 20 or 200 and you're not sure. You've narrowed your answer to two orders of magnitude, which is not bad at all.

We set boundary conditions unconsciously many times a day. When you step on the scale, you expect it to read within a few pounds of what it read yesterday. When you step outside, you expect the temperature to be within a certain number of degrees of what it was the last time you were out. When your teenager tells you that it took forty minutes to get home from school, you know whether this is within the normal range of times or not. The point is that you don't have to count every single item in your grocery bag to know whether or not the total is *reasonable*; you don't need to carry a stopwatch to know if your commute time is radically longer or shorter than usual. We round, we estimate, we fudge the numbers, and this is a crucial operation for knowing quickly whether what we observe is reasonable.

Approximately OK

One of the most important tools in critical thinking about numbers is to grant yourself permission to generate wrong answers to mathematical problems you encounter. Deliberately wrong answers! Engineers and scientists do it all the time, so there's no reason we shouldn't all be let in on their little secret: the art of approximating, or the "back of the napkin" calculation. Such deliberately wrong answers can get you close enough to the right answer to make a decision in just a fraction of the time. As the British writer Saki wrote, "a little bit of inaccuracy saves a great deal of explanation."

For over a decade, when Google conducted job interviews, they'd ask their applicants questions that have no answers. Google is a company whose very existence depends on innovation—on inventing things that are new and didn't exist before, and on refining existing ideas and technologies to allow consumers to do things they couldn't do before. Contrast this with how most companies conduct job interviews: In the skills portion of the interview, the company wants to know if you can actually do the things that they need doing.

In a restaurant, the necessary skill might be chopping vegetables or making a soup stock. In an accounting firm, it might be an awareness of tax codes and an ability to properly fill out tax forms. But Google doesn't even know what skills they need new employees to have. What they need to know is whether an employee can think his way through a problem. Students who graduate from top universities in technical or quantitative fields such as computer science, electrical engineering, economics, or business know how to apply what they've learned, and know how to look for information they need. But relatively few can effectively think and reason for themselves.

Consider the following question that has been asked at actual Google job interviews: How much does the Empire State Building weigh?

Now, there is no correct answer to this question in any practical sense because no one knows the answer. There are too many variables, too many unknowns, and the problem is unwieldy. Google isn't interested in *the answer*, though; they're interested in the *process*, in how a prospective employee would go about solving it. They want to see a reasoned, rational way of approaching the problem to give them insight into how an applicant's mind works, how organized a thinker she is.

There are four common responses to the problem. People throw up their hands and say "That's impossible," or they try to look up the answer somewhere. Although an answer to this is out there on the Web by now (it has become a somewhat famous problem within the computer science community), Google wants to hire employees who can answer questions that haven't been answered before—*that* requires a certain kind of mind prone to methodical thinking. Fortunately, this kind of thinking can be taught, and it is not beyond the reach of the average person. George Polya, in his influential book *How to Solve It*, showed how the average person can solve complicated mathematical problems without specific training in math. The same is true for this class of crazy, unknowable problems.

The third response? Asking for more information. By "weight of the Empire State Building," do you mean with or without furniture? With or without fixtures? Do I count the people in it? But questions like this are a distraction. They don't bring you any closer to solving the problem; they only postpone being able to start it, and soon you are right back where you began, wondering how in the world you would figure out something such as this.

The fourth response is the correct one, using approximating, or what some people call guesstimating. These types of problems are also called estimation problems or Fermi problems, after the physicist Enrico Fermi, who was famous for being able to make estimates with little or no actual data, for questions that seemed impossible to answer. Examples of Fermi problems include "How many basketballs will fit into a city bus?" "How many Reese's Peanut Butter Cups would it take to encircle the globe at the equator?" and "How many piano tuners are there in Chicago?" Approximating involves making a series of educated guesses systematically by partitioning the problem into manageable chunks, identifying assumptions, and then using your general knowledge of the world to fill in the blanks.

How would you solve the problem of "How many piano tuners are there in Chicago?" Google wants to know how people make sense of the problem—how they divide up the knowns and unknowns systematically. Remember, you can't simply call the Piano Tuners Union of Chicago and ask; you have to work this from facts (or reasonable guesses) that you can pull out of your head. Breaking down the problem into manageable units is the fun part. Where to begin? As with many Fermi problems, it's often helpful to estimate some intermediate quantity, not the one you're being asked to estimate, but something that will help you get where you want to go. In this case, it might be easier to start with the number of *pianos* that you think are in Chicago and then figure out how many tuners it would take to keep them in tune.

In any Fermi problem, we first lay out what it is we need to know, then list some assumptions. To solve this problem, you might start by trying to estimate the following numbers:

1. How often pianos are tuned (How many times per year is a given piano tuned?)
2. How long it takes to tune a piano
3. How many hours a year the average piano tuner works
4. The number of pianos in Chicago

Knowing these will help you arrive at an answer. If you know how often pianos are tuned and how long it takes to tune a piano, you know how many hours a year are spent tuning one piano. Then you multiply that by the number of pianos in Chicago to find out how many hours are spent every year tuning Chicago's pianos. Divide this by the number of hours each tuner works, and you have the number of tuners.

Assumption 1: The average piano owner tunes his piano once a year.

Where did this number come from? I made it up! But that's what you do when you're approximating. It's certainly within an order of magnitude: The average piano owner isn't tuning only one time every ten years, nor ten times a year. Some piano owners tune their pianos four times a year, some of them zero, but one time a year seems like a reasonable guesstimate.

Assumption 2: It takes 2 hours to tune a piano. A guess. Maybe it's only 1 hour, but 2 is within an order of magnitude, so it's good enough.

Assumption 3: How many hours a year does the average piano tuner work? Let's assume 40 hours a week, and that the tuner takes 2 weeks' vacation every year: 40 hours a week × 50 weeks is a 2,000-hour work year. Piano tuners travel to their jobs—people don't bring their pianos in—so the piano tuner may spend 10%–20% of his or her time getting from house to house. Keep this in mind and take it off the estimate at the end.

Assumption 4: To estimate the number of pianos in Chicago, you might guess that 1 out of 100 people have a piano—again, a wild guess, but probably within an order of magnitude. In addition, there are schools and other institutions with pianos, many of them with multiple pianos. A music school could have 30 pianos, and then there are old-age homes, bars, and so on. This estimate is trickier to base on facts, but assume that when these are factored in, they roughly equal the number of private pianos, for a total of 2 pianos for every 100 people.

Now to estimate the number of people in Chicago. If you don't know the answer to this, you might know that it is the third-largest city in the United States after New York (8 million) and Los Angeles (4 million). You might guess 2.5 million, meaning that 25,000 people have pianos. We decided to double this number to account for institutional pianos, so the result is 50,000 pianos.

So, here are the various estimates:

1. There are 2.5 million people in Chicago.
2. 1 out of 100 people have a piano.
3. There is 1 institutional piano for every 100 people.
4. Therefore, there are 2 pianos for every 100 people.
5. There are 50,000 pianos in Chicago.
6. Pianos are tuned once a year.
7. It takes 2 hours to tune a piano.
8. Piano tuners work 2,000 hours a year.
9. In one year, a piano tuner can tune 1,000 pianos (2,000 hours per year ÷ 2 hours per piano).
10. It would take 50 tuners to tune 50,000 pianos (50,000 pianos ÷ 1,000 pianos tuned by each piano tuner).
11. Add 15% to that number to account for travel time, meaning that there are approximately 58 piano tuners in Chicago.

What is the real answer? The Yellow Pages for Chicago lists 83. This includes some duplicates (businesses with more than one phone number are listed twice), and the category includes piano and organ technicians who are not tuners. Deduct 25 for these anomalies, and an estimate of 58 appears to be very close. Even without the deduction, the point is that it is within an order of magnitude (because the answer was neither 6 nor 600).

Back to the Google interview and the Empire State Building question. If you were sitting in that interview chair, your interviewer would ask you to think out loud and walk her through your reasoning. There is an infinity of ways one might solve the problem, but to give you a flavor of how a bright, creative, and systematic thinker might do it, here is one possible "answer." And remember, the final number is not the point—the thought process, the set of assumptions and deliberations, is the answer.

Let's see. One way to start would be to estimate its size, and then estimate the weight based on that.

I'll begin with some assumptions. I'm going to calculate the weight of the building empty—with no human occupants, no furnishings, appliances, or fixtures. I'm going to assume that the building has a square base and straight sides with no taper at the top, just to simplify the calculations.

For size I need to know height, length, and width. I don't know how tall the Empire State Building is, but I know that it is definitely more than 20 stories tall and probably less than 200 stories. I don't know how tall one story is, but I know from other office buildings I've been in that the ceiling is at least 8 feet inside each floor and that there are typically false ceilings to hide electrical wires, conduits, heating ducts, and so on. I'll guess that these are probably 2 feet. So I'll approximate 10–15 feet per story. I'm going to refine my height estimate to say that the building is probably more than 50 stories high. I've been in lots of buildings that are 30–35 stories high. My boundary conditions are that it is between 50 and 100 stories; 50 stories work out to being 500–750 feet tall (10–15 feet per story), and 100 stories work out to be 1,000–1,500 feet tall. So my height estimate is between 500 and 1,500 feet. To make the calculations easier, I'll take the average, 1,000 feet.

Now for its footprint. I don't know how large its base is, but it isn't larger than a city block, and I remember learning once that there are typically 10 city blocks to a mile. A mile is 5,280 feet, so a city block is 1/10 of that, or 528 feet. I'm going to guess that the Empire State Building is about half of a city block, or about 265 feet on each side. If the building is square, it is 265 × 265 feet in its length × width. I can't do that in my head, but I know how to calculate 250 × 250 (that is, 25 × 25 = 625, and I add two zeros to get 62,500). I'll round this total to 60,000, an easier number to work with moving forward.

Now we've got the size. There are several ways to go from here. All rely on the fact that most of the building is empty—that is, it is hollow. The weight of the building is mostly in the walls and floors and ceilings. I imagine that the building is made of steel (for the walls) and some combination of steel and concrete for the floors. I'm not really sure. I know that it is probably not made of wood.

The volume of the building is its footprint times its height. My footprint estimate above was 60,000 square feet. My height estimate was 1,000 feet. So 60,000 × 1,000 = 60,000,000 cubic feet. I'm not accounting for the fact that it tapers as it goes up.

I could estimate the thickness of the walls and floors and estimate how much a cubic foot of the materials weighs and come up then with an estimate of the weight per story. Alternatively, I could set boundary conditions for the volume of the building. That is, I can say that it weighs more than an equivalent volume of solid air and less than an equivalent volume of solid steel (because it is mostly empty). The former seems like a lot of work. The latter isn't satisfying because it generates numbers that are likely to be very far apart. Here's a hybrid option: I'll assume that on any given floor, 95% of the volume is air, and 5% is steel. I'm just pulling this estimate out of the air, really, but it seems reasonable. If the width of a floor is about 265 feet, 5% of 265 ≈ 13 feet. That means that the walls on each side, and any interior supporting walls, total 13 feet. As an order of magnitude estimate, that checks out—the total walls can't be a mere 1.3 feet (one order of magnitude smaller) and they're not 130 feet (one order of magnitude larger).

I happen to remember from school that a cubic foot of air weighs 0.08 pounds. I'll round that up to 0.1. Obviously, the building is not all air, but a lot of it is—virtually the entire interior space—and so this sets the minimum boundary for the weight. The volume times the weight of air gives an estimate of 60,000,000 cubic feet × 0.1 pounds = 6,000,000 pounds.

I don't know what a cubic foot of steel weighs. But I can estimate that, based on some comparisons. It seems to me that 1 cubic foot of steel must certainly weigh more than a cubic foot of wood. I don't know what a cubic foot of wood weighs either, but when I stack firewood, I know that an armful weighs about as much as a 50-pound bag of dog food. So I'm going to guess that a cubic foot of wood is about 50 pounds and that steel is about 10 times heavier than that. If the entire Empire State Building were steel, it would weigh 60,000,000 cubic feet × 500 pounds = 30,000,000,000 pounds.

This gives me two boundary conditions: 6 million pounds if the building were all air, and 30 billion pounds if it were solid steel. But as I said, I'm going to assume a mix of 5% steel and 95% air.

$$
\begin{array}{r}
5\% \times 30 \text{ billion} = 1{,}500{,}000{,}000 \\
+\ 95\% \times 6 \text{ million} = 5{,}700{,}000 \\
\hline
1{,}505{,}700{,}000 \text{ pounds}
\end{array}
$$

or roughly 1.5 billion pounds. Converting to tons, 1 ton = 2,000 pounds, so 1.5 billion pounds/2,000 = 750,000 tons.

This hypothetical interviewee stated her assumptions at each stage, established boundary conditions, and then concluded with a *point estimate* at the end, of 750,000 tons. Nicely done!

Another job interviewee might approach the problem much more parsimoniously. Using the same assumptions about the size of the building, and assumptions about its being empty, a concise protocol might come down to this:

> Skyscrapers are constructed from steel. Imagine that the Empire State Building is filled up with cars. Cars also have a lot of air in them, they're also made of steel, so they could be a good proxy. I know that a car weighs about 2 tons and it is about 15 feet long, 5 feet wide, and 5 feet high. The floors, as estimated above, are about 265 × 265 feet each. If I stacked the cars side by side on the floor, I could get 265/15 = 18 cars in one row, which I'll round to 20 (one of the beauties of guesstimating). How many rows will fit? Cars are about 5 feet wide, and the building is 265 feet wide, so 265/5 = 53, which I'll round to 50. That's 20 cars x 50 rows = 1,000 cars on each floor. Each floor is 10 feet high and the cars are 5 feet high, so I can fit 2 cars up to the ceiling. 2 × 1,000 = 2,000 cars per floor. And 2,000 cars per floor × 100 floors = 200,000 cars. Add in their weight, 200,000 cars × 4,000 pounds = 800,000,000 pounds, or in tons, 400,000 tons.

These two methods produced estimates that are relatively close—one is a bit less than twice the other—so they help us to perform an important sanity check. The first gave us 750,000 tons, the second gave us about a half million tons. Because this has become a somewhat famous problem (and a frequent Google search), the Empire State Building's website has taken to giving their estimate of the weight, and it comes in at 365,000 tons. So we find that both guesstimates brought us within an order of magnitude of the official estimate, which is just what was required.

Neither of these methods comes up with *the* weight of the building. Remember, the point is not to come up with a number, but to come up with a line of reasoning, an *algorithm* for figuring it out. Much of what we teach graduate students in computer science is just this—how to create algorithms for solving problems that have never been solved before. How much capacity do we need to allow for on this trunk of telephone lines going into the city? What will the ridership be of a new subway that is being built? If there is a flood, how much water will spill into the community and how long will it take for the ground to reabsorb it? These are problems that have no known answer, but skilled approximating can deliver an answer that is of great practical use.

The president of a well-known Fortune 500 company proposed the following solution. While not conforming strictly to the rules of the problem, it is nevertheless very clever:

> I would find the company or companies that financed the construction of the Empire State Building and ask to see the supplies manifests . . . the list of every material that was delivered to the construction site. Assuming 10%–15% waste, you could then estimate the weight of the building by the materials that went into it. Actually, even more accurate would be this: Remember that every truck that drives along a freeway has to be weighed because the trucking companies pay a usage tax to the roads department based on their weight. You could check the weight of the trucks and have all the information you need right there. The weight of the building is the weight of all the materials trucked in to construct it.

Is there ever a case where you'd need to know the weight of the Empire State Building? If you wanted to build a subway line that ran underneath it, you would want to know the weight so you could properly support the ceiling of your subway station. If you wanted to add a heavy new antenna to the top of the building, you would need to know the total weight of the building to calculate whether or not the foundation can support the additional weight. But practical considerations are not the point. In a world of rapidly increasing knowledge, unimaginable amounts of data, and rapid technological advance, the architects of the new technologies are going to need to know how to solve unsolvable problems, how to break them up into smaller parts. The Empire State Building problem is a window into how the mind of a creative and technically oriented person works, and probably does a better job of predicting success in these kinds of jobs than grades in school or scores on an IQ test.

These so-called back-of-the-envelope problems are just one window into assessing creativity. Another test that gets at both creativity and flexible thinking without relying on quantitative skills is the "name as many uses" test. For example, how many uses can you come up with for a broomstick? A lemon? These are skills that can be nurtured beginning at a young age. Most jobs require some degree of creativity and flexible thinking. As an admissions test for flight school for commercial airline pilots, the name-as-many-uses test was used because pilots need to be able to react quickly in an emergency, to be able to think of alternative approaches when systems fail. How would you put out a fire in the cabin if the fire extinguisher doesn't work? How do you control the elevators if the hydraulic system fails? Exercising this part of your brain involves harnessing the power of free association—the brain's daydreaming mode—in the service of problem solving, and you want pilots who can do this in a pinch.

Novelist Diane Ackerman describes playing one session of this game with her husband, Paul, in her book *One Hundred Names for Love:*

> What can you do with a pencil—other than write?
>
> I'd begun. "Play the drums. Conduct an orchestra. Cast spells. Ball yarn. Use as a compass hand. Play pick-up sticks. Rest one eyebrow on it. Fasten a shawl. Secure hair atop the head. Use as the mast for a Lilliputian's sailboat. Play darts. Make a sundial. Spin vertically on flint to spark a fire. Combine with a thong to create a slingshot. Ignite and use as a taper. Test the depth of oil. Clean a pipe. Stir paint. Work a Ouija board. Gouge an aqueduct in the sand. Roll out dough for a pie crust. Herd balls of loose mercury. Use as the fulcrum for a spinning top. Squeegee a window. Provide a perch for your parrot. . . . Pass the pencil-baton to you. . . ."

> "Use as a spar in a model airplane," Paul had continued. "Measure distances. Puncture a balloon. Use as a flagpole. Roll a necktie around. Tamp the gunpowder into a pint-size musket. Test bonbons for contents. . . . Crumble, and use the lead as a poison."

This type of thinking can be taught and practiced, and can be nurtured in children as young as five years old. It is an increasingly important skill in a technology-driven world with untold unknowns. There are no right answers, just opportunities to exercise ingenuity, to find new connections, and to allow whimsy and experimentation to become a normal and habitual part of our thinking, which will lead to better problem solving.

It is important to teach our children to become lifelong learners, curious and inquisitive. Equally important is to instill in children a sense of play, that thinking isn't just serious, it can be fun. This entails giving them the freedom to make mistakes, to explore new thoughts and ideas outside of the ordinary—divergent thinking will be increasingly necessary to solve some of the biggest problems facing the world today. Benjamin Zander, conductor of the Boston Philharmonic, teaches young musicians that self-criticism is the enemy of creativity: "When you make a mistake say to yourself '*how interesting!*' A mistake is an opportunity to learn!"

Where You Get Your Information

As with many concepts, "*information*" has a special and specific meaning to mathematicians and scientists: It is anything that reduces uncertainty. Put another way, information exists wherever a pattern exists, whenever a sequence is not random. The more information, the more structured or patterned the sequence appears to be. Information is contained in such diverse sources as newspapers, conversations with friends, tree rings, DNA, maps, the light from distant stars, and the footprints of wild animals in the forest. Possessing information is not enough. As the American Library Association presciently concluded in their 1989 report *Presidential Committee on Information Literacy*, students must be taught to play an *active* role in knowing, identifying, finding, evaluating, organizing, and using information. Recall the words of *New York Times* editor Bill Keller—it's not having the information that's important, it's what you *do* with it.

To *know* something entails two things: for there to be no doubt, and for it to be true. "Religious fanatics 'know' no less than we scientists," Daniel Kahneman says. "The question might be 'How do we know?' What I believe in science is because people have told me things, people I know and whom I trust. But if I liked and trusted other things, I would believe and 'know' other things. 'Knowing' is the absence of alternatives of other beliefs." This is why education and exposure to many different ideas are so important. In the presence of alternatives of other beliefs, we can make an informed and evidence-based choice about what is true.

We should teach our children (and one another) to be more understanding of others and of other points of view. The biggest problems the world faces today, of famine, poverty, and aggression, will require careful cooperation among people who don't know one another well and, historically, have not trusted one another. Recall the many health benefits of being an agreeable person. This does not mean being agreeable in the face of views that are harmful or patently wrong, but it means keeping an open mind and trying to see things from another's perspective (as Kennedy did in his conflict with Khrushchev).

The Internet, that great equalizer, may actually be making this more difficult to do than ever. Most everyone knows by now that Google, Bing, Yahoo!, and other search engines track your search history. They use this information for auto-complete, so that you don't have to type the entire search term in the find window the next time. They use this information in two additional ways—one, to target advertising (that's why if you searched for new shoes online, a shoe ad shows up the next time you log into Facebook), and the other, to improve the search results for each individual user. That is, after you search for a particular thing, the search engines keep track of which of the results you ended up clicking on so that they can place those higher up in the results list, saving you time the next time you do a similar search. Imagine now that the search engines have not just a few days' or weeks' worth of your searches, but twenty years of searches. Your search results have been iteratively refined to become ever more personal. The net result is that you are more likely to be given results that support your world view and less likely to encounter results that challenge your views. While you may seek to maintain an open mind and consider alternate opinions, the search engines will be narrowing down what you actually see. An unintended consequence, perhaps, but one worth worrying about in a world where global cooperation and understanding are increasingly important.

There are three ways we can learn information—we can absorb it implicitly, we can be told it explicitly, or we can discover it ourselves. Implicit learning, such as when we learn a new language through immersion, is usually the most efficient. In classroom settings and at work, most information is conveyed in one of the two latter ways—being told explicitly or discovering ourselves.

The last two decades of research on the science of learning have shown conclusively that we remember things better, and longer, if we discover them ourselves rather than being told them explicitly. This is the basis for the flipped classroom described by physics professor Eric Mazur in his book *Peer Instruction*. Mazur doesn't lecture in his classes at Harvard. Instead, he asks students difficult questions, based on their homework reading, that require them to pull together sources of information to solve a problem. Mazur doesn't give them the answer; instead, he asks the students to break off into small groups and discuss the problem among themselves. Eventually, nearly everyone in the class gets the answer right, and the concepts stick with them because they had to reason their own way to the answer.

Something similar happens in art. When we read well-written literary fiction, for example, our prefrontal cortex begins to fill in aspects of the characters' personalities, to make predictions about their actions, in short, we become active participants in figuring out the story. Reading gives our brains time to do that because we can proceed at our own pace. We've all had the experience of reading a novel and finding that we slow down in places to contemplate what was just written, to let our minds wander, and think about the story. This is the action of the daydreaming mode (in opposition to the central executive mode) and it is healthy to engage it—remember, it is the brain's "default" mode.

In contrast, sometimes entertainment comes at us so rapidly that our brains don't have time to engage in thoughtful reflection or prediction. This can be true of certain television programs and video games. Such rapidly presented events capture attention in a bottom-up fashion, involving the sensory rather than the prefrontal cortices. But it would be wrong to focus on the medium and conclude "books good, movies bad." Many nonliterary, or pulp fiction, and nonfiction books, even though they allow us to proceed at our own pace, present information in a direct way that lacks the nuance and complexity of literary fiction, and this was the finding of the study briefly described in Chapter 4: Reading literary fiction, but not pulp fiction or nonfiction, increased the reader's empathy and emotional understanding of other people.

A striking parallel distinction was found in a study of children's television shows. Angeline Lillard and Jennifer Peterson of the University of Virginia had four-year-olds watch just nine minutes of *SpongeBob SquarePants* cartoons, a fast-paced television program, versus watching the slower-paced public television cartoon *Caillou,* or drawing pictures on their own for nine minutes. They found that the fast-paced cartoon had an immediate negative impact on children's executive function, a collection of prefrontal cortical processes including goal-directed behavior, attentional focus, working memory, problem solving, impulse control, self-regulation, and delay of gratification. The researchers point not just to the fast pace itself, but to the "onslaught of fantastical events" which are, by definition, novel and unfamiliar. Encoding such events is likely to be particularly taxing on cognitive resources, and the fast pace of programs like *SpongeBob* don't give children the time to assimilate the new information. This can reinforce a cognitive style of not thinking things through or following new ideas to their logical conclusion.

As in many psychological studies, there are important caveats. First, the researchers didn't test attentional capacity in the three groups of children prior to testing (although they did use the well-accepted method of random assignment, meaning that any a priori attentional differences should be equally distributed across the experimental groups). Second, *SpongeBob* is designed for six- to eleven-year-olds, and so its effect on four-year-olds may be limited just to that age group; the study didn't look at other age groups. Finally, the participants were an uncommonly homogeneous group of largely white, upper-middle-class kids drawn from a university community, and the findings may not be generalizable. (On the other hand, these kinds of issues arise in nearly all experiments in the psychological literature and they are no different for the Lillard and Peterson study than the limitations on most of what we know about human behavior.)

The tentative and intriguing take-home message is that reading high-quality fiction and literary nonfiction, and perhaps listening to music, looking at art, and watching dance, may lead to two desirable outcomes: increased interpersonal empathy and better executive attentional control.

What matters today, in the Internet era, is not whether you know a particular fact but whether you know where to look it up, and then, how to verify that the answer is reasonable. On the Web, anything goes. Conspiracy theorists say that McDonald's restaurants are part of a multinational, diabolical plan to decimate social security, put power in the hands of a liberal elite, and hide the fact that aliens are among us. But in the real world, facts are facts: Columbus sailed the ocean blue in 1492, not 1776. Red light has a longer wavelength than blue. Aspirin may cause stomach upset, but not autism. Facts matter, and tracing the source of them has simultaneously become increasingly easier and more difficult. In the old, pre-Internet days, you went to a library (just as Hermione does at Hogwarts) and looked things up. There might have been only a handful of written sources, perhaps an encyclopedia article written by an eminent scholar, or a few peer-reviewed articles, to verify a fact. Having found your verification, you could rest easy. You had to go out of your way to find opinions that were at the fringe of society or were just dead wrong. Now there are thousands of opinions, and the correct ones are no more likely to be encountered than the incorrect ones. As the old saying goes, a man with one watch always knows what time it is; a man with two watches is never sure. We are now less sure of what we know and don't know. More so than at any other time in history, it is crucial that each of us takes responsibility for verifying the information we encounter, testing it and evaluating it. This is the skill we must teach the next generation of citizens of the world, the capability to think clearly, completely, critically, and creatively.

9

EVERYTHING ELSE

The Power of the Junk Drawer

To many people, being organized means "a place for everything and everything in its place." This is an important principle for organizing files, tools, objects in the home and office, and so on. But it's equally important for our organizational systems and infrastructure to allow for fuzzy categories, for things that fall through the cracks—the miscellaneous folder in your filing system, the junk drawer in your kitchen. As Doug Merrill says, organization gives us the freedom to be a bit disorganized. A typical American kitchen junk drawer holds pens, matches, slips of paper, maybe a hammer, chopsticks, a tape measure, picture hooks. There are certain design constraints at work that legitimize a catchall drawer: You're not going to redesign the kitchen just to have a small drawer or cubby for chopsticks and another for matches. The junk drawer is a place where things collect until you have time to organize them, or because there is no better place for them. Sometimes what looks like a mess may not have to be physically reorganized at all, if you can slow down and observe the organization in the thicket of details.

As I've emphasized throughout this book, the most fundamental principle of organization, the one that is most critical to keeping us from forgetting or losing things, is this: Shift the burden of organizing from our brains to the external world. If we can take some or all of the process out of our brains and put it into the physical world, we are less likely to make mistakes. But the organized mind enables you to do much more than merely avoid mistakes. It enables you to do things and go places you might not otherwise imagine. Externalizing information doesn't always involve writing it down or encoding it in some external medium. Often it has already been done for you. You just have to know how to read the signs.

Take the numbering of the U.S. Interstate Highway System. On the surface, it may look like a mess, but in fact it's a hightly organized system. It was initiated by President Dwight D. Eisenhower and construction began in 1956. Today, it comprises nearly 50,000 miles of roadway. The numbering of interstate highways follows a set of simple rules. If you know the rules, it is easier to figure out where you are (and harder to get lost) because the rules off-load information from your memory and put it into a system that is out-there-in-the-world. In other words, you don't need to memorize a set of seemingly arbitrary facts such as *Highway 5 runs north-south* or *Highway 20 runs east-west in the southern part of the country.* Instead, you learn a set of rules that applies to all the numbers, and then the highway numbers themselves tell you how they run:

1. One- and two-digit highway numbers less than 100 identify major routes (e.g., 1, 5, 70, 93) that cross state lines.
2. Even numbers are east-west routes, odd numbers are north-south.
3. Even numbers increase as they move from south to north; odd numbers increase as they move from west to east.
4. Route numbers that are multiples of 5 are major arteries that extend over long distances. For example, I-5 is the westernmost major artery carrying north-south traffic between Canada and Mexico; I-95 is the easternmost major artery carrying north-south traffic between Canada and Florida. I-10 is the southernmost major artery carrying west-east traffic from California to Florida, and I-90 is the northernmost, carrying west-east traffic from Washington State to New York State.
5. Three-digit numbers identify loops, or auxiliary, supplementary routes in or around a city. If the first digit is even, it is a route through or around a city that breaks off of and eventually rejoins the main route. If the first digit is odd, it is a spur into or out of a city and does not rejoin the main route (if you're afraid of getting lost, the auxiliary highways with an even-numbered first digit are thus always a safer bet). Generally, the second and third digits refer to the principal interstate served by the three-digit route. For example, if you are in Northern California and you find yourself on something called I-580, you can deduce the following:

It is a supplement to route I-80.
It is running east-west (even number).
It is a spur into the city (first digit odd) and will not rejoin route I-80.

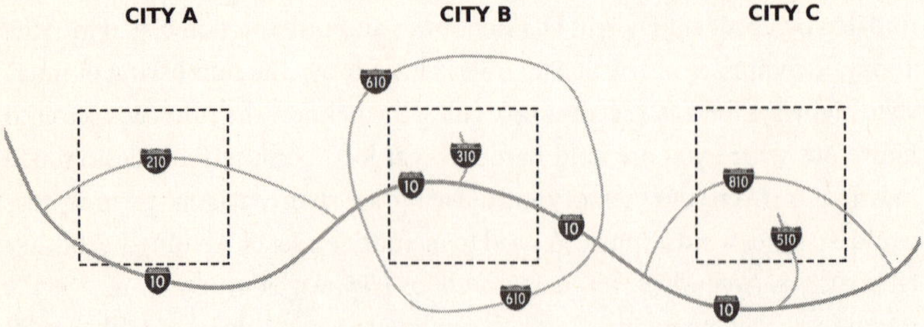

In New York State, I-87 is a principal north-south highway. It's not a multiple of 5, so it is not considered a major route like the nearby parallel highway I-95. Up near Albany, I-87 joins I-787, which splits off to bring drivers right into the city. The system of rules is slightly difficult to memorize, but it is logical and structured, and far easier to memorize than the direction and nature of all the different highways in the country.

The periodic table of the elements makes apparent the relationships and certain regularities latent in the world that might otherwise be missed. From left to right, elements are presented in increasing order of their atomic number (the number of protons in the nucleus). Elements with the same core or nuclear charge, as determined by the number of electrons in the outermost shell, appear in the same column and have similar properties; moving from top to bottom, the number of electron shells increases. Moving from left to right along a row, each element adds one proton and one electron, and becomes less metallic. Elements with similar physical properties tend to be grouped together, with metals in the lower left and nonmetals in the upper right; elements with intermediate properties (such as semiconductors) fall between them.

One of the unanticipated and exciting consequences of constructing the periodic table was that, as scientists placed elements within this structure, they discovered gaps in the chart where they assumed elements should go—elements with one more proton than the one to the left of it and one less than the one to the right of it—but no known elements fit that description. This led scientists to search for the missing elements, and in every case, they found them, either in nature or through laboratory synthesis.

Group → / ↓Period	1	2	3	4	5	6	7	8	9	10	11	12	13	14	15	16	17	18
1	1 H																	2 He
2	3 Li	4 Be											5 B	6 C	7 N	8 O	9 F	10 Ne
3	11 Na	12 Mg											13 Al	14 Si	15 P	16 S	17 Cl	18 Ar
4	19 K	20 Ca	21 Sc	22 Ti	23 V	24 Cr	25 Mn	26 Fe	27 Co	28 Ni	29 Cu	30 Zn	31 Ga	32 Ge	33 As	34 Se	35 Br	36 Kr
5	37 Rb	38 Sr	39 Y	40 Zr	41 Nb	42 Mo	43 Tc	44 Ru	45 Rh	46 Pd	47 Ag	48 Cd	49 In	50 Sn	51 Sb	52 Te	53 I	54 Xe
6	55 Cs	56 Ba		72 Hf	73 Ta	74 W	75 Re	76 Os	77 Ir	78 Pt	79 Au	80 Hg	81 Tl	82 Pb	83 Bi	84 Po	85 At	86 Rn
7	87 Fr	88 Ra		104 Rf	105 Db	106 Sg	107 Bh	108 Hs	109 Mt	110 Ds	111 Rg	112 Cn	113 Uut	114 Fl	115 Uup	116 Lv	117 Uus	118 Uuo
Lanthanides			57 La	58 Ce	59 Pr	60 Nd	61 Pm	62 Sm	63 Eu	64 Gd	65 Tb	66 Dy	67 Ho	68 Er	69 Tm	70 Yb	71 Lu	
Actinides			89 Ac	90 Th	91 Pa	92 U	93 Np	94 Pu	95 Am	96 Cm	97 Bk	98 Cf	99 Es	100 Fm	101 Md	102 No	103 Lr	

The elegance of the periodic table is difficult to duplicate but worth trying, even in rather mundane settings. A machine shop that organizes taps and dies, or nuts and bolts, along two dimensions of length and width can easily find gaps in the collection where items are missing. The systematic organization also makes it easy to notice misfiled items.

The fundamental principle of externalizing information applies universally. Airline pilots formerly had two controls that looked strikingly similar but performed different functions for the flaps and the landing gear. After a series of accidents, human-factors engineers came up with the idea of externalizing the information about the actions of those controls: The flap control was made to look like a miniature flap, and the landing gear control was made into a round wheel, resembling the landing gear. Rather than the pilots having to rely on their memories of which control was where, the control itself reminded them of what it was for, and pilots made fewer errors as a result.

But what happens when you can't externalize the information—for example, when meeting new people? Surely there's a way to remember their names better. It happens to all of us: You meet someone, you get into a truly interesting conversation, make lots of eye contact, exchange some personal confidences, only to realize you've forgotten their name. Now it's too embarrassing to ask, so you wander off sheepishly, not sure what to do next.

Why is it so difficult? Because of the way memory works: We encode new information only if we pay attention to it, and we aren't always paying attention at the moment we're introduced. In that instant of meeting a new person, many of us become preoccupied with the impression we're making on them—we think about how we're dressed or whether our breath stinks, or we try to read their body language to see how they're sizing us up. This makes encoding any new information, such as a name, impossible. And for the self-assured, task-oriented person meeting someone new, thoughts may turn to "Who is this person, what important information might I glean from this conversation?" and a whole internal dialogue is off to the races, not paying attention to that brief 500 milliseconds when the name is said once.

To remember a new name, you need to allow yourself time for encoding; five seconds or so is usually about right. Rehearse the name silently to yourself over and over. While you're doing that, look at the person's face, and concentrate on associating the name to the face. Remember, you've (probably) heard the name before, so you're not having to learn a new *name*, you just need to associate a familiar name with a new face. If you're lucky, the person's face will remind you of someone else you know with that name. If not the whole face, maybe a feature will. Maybe this new Gary you're meeting has eyes like another friend Gary, or this new Alyssa has the same high cheekbones of your high school friend Alyssa. If you can't make an associative connection like these, try to superimpose someone you know with that name on the current person's face, creating a chimera. This will help it become memorable.

What if the person says his name and then goes silent? Five seconds is a lot of dead air hanging out there. If that happens, ask your new acquaintance a question about where he's from or what he does—but you're not really interested in paying attention to that; you're giving yourself that buffer to encode his name (don't worry, the ancillary information usually gets encoded, too).

If you meet someone who has a name you've never heard, it's only slightly more complicated. The encoding time is the key here. Ask her to spell the name and then spell it back to her, and say the name again back to her. During this whole exchange, you're repeating the name to yourself, and gaining valuable rehearsal time. Simultaneously, try to create in your mind a vivid picture of something that reminds you of the name and imagine the person in that picture. For example, if you meet a man named Adiel (pronounced "a deal"), you might think of that old television game show *Let's Make a Deal*. If you picture Adiel as a contestant on the game show during your five seconds of encoding (saying "*Adiel, Adiel, Adiel, Adiel, Adiel*" to yourself while picturing the stage), it will be easier to remember him later. If you meet someone named Ye-Sho, you might picture an old English street corner act, with your new acquaintance holding a sign that reads YE OLDE SHOW. These gimmicky techniques work. The more absurd or distinctive the mental image you create, the more memorable will be the name. To further instantiate the name, once you've learned it, use it! If you're at a party, you can introduce your new acquaintance to others, giving you more opportunities to practice the name. Or start a sentence with it: "Courtney—let me ask you this . . ."

Externalizing information organizes the mind and allows it to be more creative. The history of science and culture is filled with stories of how many of the greatest scientific and artistic discoveries occurred while the creator was not thinking about what he was working on, not consciously anyway—the daydreaming mode solved the problem for him, and the answer appeared suddenly as a stroke of insight. John Lennon recalled in an interview how he wrote "Nowhere Man." After working five hours trying to come up with something, he gave up. "Then, 'Nowhere Man' came, words and music, the whole damn thing as I lay down." James Watson uncovered the structure of DNA, and Elias Howe the automatic sewing machine, in their dreams. Salvador Dali, Paul McCartney, and Billy Joel created some of their most loved works from dreams. Mozart's, Einstein's, and Wordsworth's own descriptions of their creative process emphasize the role of the daydreaming mode in supporting their insights. The three books of *Thus Spake Zarathustra* by Friedrich Nietzsche were composed in three separate ten-day bursts of inspiration. As Pulitzer Prize–winning novelist Marilynne Robinson observes:

> Every writer wonders where fictional ideas come from. The best of them often appear very abruptly after a period of imaginative drought. And, mysteriously, they really are good ideas, much superior to the contrivances of conscious invention.

Many creative artists and scientists report that they don't know where their best ideas came from and that they feel like mere copyists, transcribing the idea. When Haydn heard the first public performance of his oratorio *The Creation,* he reportedly burst into tears and cried, "*I* have not written this." In the see-saw of attention, Western culture overvalues the central executive mode, and undervalues the daydreaming mode. The central executive approach to problem solving is often diagnostic, analytic, and impatient, whereas the daydreaming approach is playful, intuitive, and relaxed.

Browsing and Serendipity

Microsoft senior research fellow Malcolm Slaney and Cambridge University professor Jason Rentfrow advocated (in Chapter 7) dispensing with physical copies of documents and mail, and all the filing, sorting, and locating that they entail. Computer-based digital archives are more efficient in terms of storage space, and generally quicker in terms of retrieval.

But many of us still find something soothing and satisfying about handling physical objects. Memory is multidimensional, and our memories for objects are based on multiple attributes. Think back to your experience with file folders, the physical kind. You might have had an old beat-up one that didn't look like the others and that—quite apart from what was inside it or written on it—evoked your memories of what was in it. Physical objects tend to look different from one another in a way that computer files don't. All bits are created equal. The same 0s and 1s on your computer that render junk mail also render the sublime beauty of Mahler's fifth symphony, Monet's Water Lilies, or a video of a Boston terrier wearing reindeer antlers. There is nothing in the medium itself that carries a clue to the message. So much so that if you looked at the digital representation of any of these—or this paragraph, for example—you would not even know that those zeros and ones were representing images rather than text or music. Information has thus become separated from meaning.

We don't have a system in the computer world that mimics the satisfying real-world experience that worked so well for us. More than ten years ago, software applications allowed people to personalize their file and folder icons, but the idea never really caught on, probably because the lack of a physical folder object, with all its nuanced variations, made all the computer icons still look too heterogeneous or just plain silly. This is one of the objections many older people have to MP3 files—they all look alike. There is nothing to distinguish them other than their names. LPs and CDs had the additional cue of color and size to help remind us what was inside. Apple introduced Album Art to help, but many people feel it's not the same as holding a physical object. The procedural and cognitive trade-off at stake concerns searchability (with digital files) versus the viscerally and aesthetically satisfying act of employing the kinds of visual and tactile cues our species evolved to use. Technology writer Nicholas Carr writes, "The medium does matter. As a technology, a book focuses our attention, isolates us from the myriad distractions that fill our everyday lives. A networked computer does precisely the opposite." Faster is not always desirable, and going straight to what you want is not always better.

There is a peculiar irony in all of this: Small libraries are far more useful than large ones. The Library of Congress may have one copy of every book ever published, but it is very unlikely that you will serendipitously find a book you did not know about and that will delight you. There is just too much there. A small library, carefully curated and tended by a librarian, will have made some deliberate choices about what books to include. When you reach for a copy of one book, you'll see books adjacent on the shelf that may spark your interest, or you may find your eye caught by a title in a completely separate, unrelated section of the library and start browsing there. No one browses the Library of Congress—it is too massive, too complete. As Augustus De Morgan said of the libraries at the British Museum, if a work is wanted, "it can be asked for; but to be wanted, it must be known." And what chance has any single work to be known to be there? Minuscule. Historian James Gleick notes, "too much information, and so much of it lost."

Many people today report that they discovered some of their favorite music and books by browsing the (limited) collections of friends. If instead you were to spin the roulette wheel of the great jukebox in the sky to randomly choose a song or book from the millions that exist in the cloud, it's unlikely you'd find something appealing.

Gleick, in his thorough history *The Information*, observes, "There is a whiff of nostalgia in this sort of warning, along with an undeniable truth: that in the pursuit of knowledge, slower can be better. Exploring the crowded stacks of musty libraries has its own rewards. Reading—even browsing—an old book can yield sustenance denied by a database search." It is perhaps fitting that I stumbled upon this paragraph by accident in the library at Auburn College, where I was looking for something else entirely, and the spine of Gleick's book caught my eye. Many scientific careers were fueled by ideas that came to researchers by stumbling upon articles that captured their attention while searching for something else that turned out to be far more boring and less useful. Many students today do not know the pleasure of serendipity that comes from browsing through stacks of old academic journals, turning past "irrelevant" articles on the way to the one they're looking for, finding their brain attracted to a particularly interesting graph or title. Instead, they insert the name of the journal article they want and the computer delivers it to them with surgical precision, effortlessly. Efficient, yes. Inspiring, and capable of unlocking creative potential, not so much.

Some computer engineers have noted this and taken steps to address it. StumbleUpon is one of several websites that allow people to discover content (new websites, photos, videos, music) through recommendations of other users with similar patterns of interests and tastes, a form of collaborative filtering. Wikipedia has a random-article button, and the MoodLogic music recommendation service used to have a surprise-me button. But these are too broad in their scope and don't respect the organizational systems that sentient, cognitive humans have imposed on materials. When we stumble upon an article in a journal, it is nearby the article we were looking for because an editor deemed the two articles to be similar along some dimension, of broad relevance to the same kinds of people. In the library, either the Dewey Decimal cataloguing system or the Library of Congress system place books in the same section that have, at least in the minds of their creators, overlapping themes. Librarians in small libraries across North America are now experimenting with "modified Dewey" shelving so as to better serve browsers walking through their particular library space rather than flipping through a card catalogue or online search engine. The electronic serendipity buttons so far are too unconstrained to be helpful. Wikipedia could and should know your history of browsing topics so that the random-article button takes you to something that might be at least *broadly* construed as within your interests. Instead, it treats all topics equally—all bits are equal—and you're just as likely to get an article on the tributary to a small river in Southern Madagascar as you are to get one on the prefrontal cortex.

Another thing that has been lost with digitization and free information is an appreciation for the objects in a collection. A person's music library was once, not so long ago, a collection to admire, possibly envy, and a way to learn something about its owner. Because record albums had to be purchased one by one, because they were relatively expensive and took up space, music lovers compiled such libraries deliberately, with thought and planning. We educated ourselves about musical artists so that we could become more careful consumers. The costs of making a mistake encouraged us to think carefully before adding a clunker to the collection. High school and college students would look at a new friend's record collection and wander through it, allowing themselves a glimpse of their new friend's musical tastes and the musical paths that he or she presumably crossed to acquire this particular collection of music. Now we download songs we've never heard of, and might not enjoy, if iTunes happens to stumble upon them in shuffle mode, but the cost of making a mistake has been rendered negligible. Gleick conceptualizes the issue this way: There used to be a line between what one possessed and what one did not. This distinction no longer exists. When the sum total of every song ever recorded is available—every version, every outtake, every subtle variation—the problem of acquisition becomes irrelevant, but the problem of selection becomes impossible. How will I decide what to listen to? And of course this is a global information problem not confined to music. How do I decide what film to watch, what book to read, what news to keep up with? The twenty-first century's information problem is one of selection.

There are really only two strategies for selection in the face of this—*searching* and *filtering*. Together these can be more parsimoniously thought of as one strategy, filtering, and the only variable is who does the filtering, you or someone else. When *you* search for something, you start out with an idea of what you want, and you go out and try to find it. In the Internet age, "go out" may not be more than typing a few keystrokes on your laptop while you sit propped up in bed with your slippers on, but you are effectively going out into the digital world to find what you're looking for. (Computer scientists call this pull because you are pulling information from the Internet, as opposed to push, where the Internet automatically sends information to you.) You or your search engine filter and prioritize the results, and if all goes well, you have what you're looking for instantly. We tend not to keep a copy of it, virtual or physical, because we know it will be there later for us when we need it. No curating, no collecting, and no serendipity.

This is a downside to digital organization, and it makes opportunities to daydream perhaps more important than ever. "The greatest scientists are artists as well," said Albert Einstein. Einstein's own creativity arrived as sudden insight following daydreaming, intuition, and inspiration. "When I examine myself and my methods of thought," he said, "I come close to the conclusion that the gift of imagination has meant more to me than any talent for absorbing absolute knowledge. . . . All great achievements of science must start from intuitive knowledge. I believe in intuition and inspiration. . . . At times I feel certain I am right while not knowing the reason." The importance of creativity to Einstein was encapsulated in his motto, "Imagination is more important than knowledge."

Many of the world's problems—cancer, genocide, repression, poverty, violence, gross inequities in the distribution of resources and wealth, climate change—will require great creativity to solve. Recognizing the value of nonlinear thinking and the daydreaming mode, the National Cancer Institute (NCI) sponsored a brainstorming session with artists, scientists, and other creative people in Cold Spring Harbor during a few days in 2012. The NCI acknowledged that after decades of research costing billions of dollars, a cure for cancer was still very far off. They handpicked people who had no knowledge or expertise in cancer research and paired them with some of the leading cancer researchers in the world. The brainstorming session asked the nonexperts to simply generate ideas, no matter how wild. Several of the ideas generated were deemed brilliant by the experts, and collaborations are currently under way to implement them.

As with Einstein, the key to the NCI initiative is that nonlinear, creative thinking be tethered to rational, linear thinking in order to implement it in the most robust and rigorous way possible—the dreams of men and women paired with the vast resources of computers. Paul Otellini, the recently retired CEO of Intel, puts it this way:

> When I arrived at Intel, the possibility that computers would shape all these aspects of our lives was science fiction. . . . Can

technology solve our problems? Think what the world would be like if Moore's law, the equation that characterizes the tremendous growth of the computing industry, were applied to any other industry. Take the auto industry. Cars would get half a million miles per gallon, go 300,000 mph, and it would be cheaper to throw away a Rolls Royce than to park it.

We already see technology doing things that seemed like science fiction not so long ago. UPS trucks have sensors that detect malfunctions before they occur. To have your own personal genome sequenced used to cost $100K, now it's less than $1,000. By the end of this decade, the equivalent of the human brain, 100 billion neurons, will fit on a single computer chip. Can technology solve our problems? The fascinating, brilliant, curious and diverse individuals who create the technology seem to think so.

Where art, technology, or science alone cannot solve problems, the combination of the three is perhaps the most powerful of all. The ability of technology, when properly guided, to solve intractable global problems has never been higher. The message I take from Otellini is that we are aiming for rewards that we cannot yet even fully imagine.

In doing research for a book idea I had some years ago, *What Your Junk Drawer Says about You*, I looked at dozens of people's junk drawers. They were publicists, authors, composers, attorneys, motivational speakers, homemakers, teachers, engineers, scientists, and artists. I asked each of them to take photographs of their open drawers, then take everything out and arrange it on a table, putting similar things next to each other. I asked them to take another photograph before organizing, re-sorting, refiling the objects, and finally placing them back in what ended up being a much neater and better-organized drawer.

I did the same thing with my own junk drawer. While I meticulously separated the rubble into categories, it occurred to me that our junk drawers provide a perfect metaphor for how we live our lives. How had I accumulated notepads of old friends' shopping lists and broken door handles from my great aunt's rental apartment? Why did I feel the need to hoard five pairs of scissors, three hammers, and two extra dog collars? Was it a strategic decision I made to stockpile various tape brands in the kitchen? Did I use Thomas Goetz's decision tree in deciding to place the NyQuil next to the crescent wrench, or was it an unconscious memory association between the NyQuil (bedtime) and the wrench (crescent moon in the nighttime sky)?

I think not. One's junk drawer, like one's life, undergoes a natural sort of entropy. Every so often, we should perhaps take time out and ask ourselves the following questions:

- Do I really need to hold on to this thing or this relationship anymore? Does it fill me with energy and happiness? Does it serve me?
- Are my communications filled with clutter? Am I direct? Do I ask for what I want and need, or do I hope my partner/friend/coworker will psychically figure it out?
- Must I accumulate several of the same things even though they're identical? Are my friends, habits, and ideas all too similar, or am I open to new people's ideas and experiences?

I found something in my intellectual junk drawer the other day while trying to keep it as ordered as I can. It is from a post on Reddit—a font of information and opinion in the age of information overload—and it is about mathematics, the queen of the sciences and emperor of abstract organization.

> Sometimes, in your mathematics career, you find that your slow progress, and careful accumulation of tools and ideas, has suddenly allowed you to do a bunch of new things that you couldn't possibly do before. Even though you were learning things that were useless by themselves, when they've all become second nature, a whole new world of possibility appears. You have "leveled up," if you will. Something clicks, but now there are new challenges, and now, things you were barely able to think about before suddenly become critically important.
>
> It's usually obvious when you're talking to somebody a level above you, because they see lots of things instantly when those things take considerable work for you to figure out. These are good people to learn from, because they remember what it's like to struggle in the place where you're struggling, but the things they do still make sense from your perspective (you just couldn't do them yourself).

Talking to somebody two or more levels above you is a different story. They're barely speaking the same language, and it's almost impossible to imagine that you could ever know what they know. You can still learn from them, if you don't get discouraged, but the things they want to teach you seem really philosophical, and you don't think they'll help you—but for some reason, they do.

Somebody three levels above is actually speaking a different language. They probably seem less impressive to you than the person two levels above, because most of what they're thinking about is completely invisible to you. From where you are, it is not possible to imagine what they think about, or why. You might think you can, but this is only because they know how to tell entertaining stories. Any one of these stories probably contains enough wisdom to get you halfway to your next level if you put in enough time thinking about it.

Getting organized can bring us all to the next level in our lives.

It's the human condition to fall prey to old habits. We must consciously look at areas of our lives that need cleaning up, and then methodically and proactively do so. And then keep doing it.

Every so often, the universe has a way of doing this for us. We unexpectedly lose a friend, a beloved pet, a business deal, or an entire global economy collapses. The best way to improve upon the brains that nature gave us is to learn to adjust agreeably to new circumstances. My own experience is that when I've lost something I thought was irreplaceable, it's usually replaced with something much better. The key to change is having faith that when we get rid of the old, something or someone even more magnificent will take its place.

APPENDIX

Constructing Your Own Fourfold Tables

As we think about sound medical reasoning, we are often faced with diseases that are so rare that even a positive test doesn't mean you have the disease. Many pharmaceutical products have such a low chance of their working that the risk of side effects is many times greater than the promise of a benefit.

The fourfold table allows us to easily calculate Bayesian probability models, such as the answer to the question "What is the probability that I have a disease, *given* that I already tested positive for it?" or "What is the probability that this medicine will help me, *given* that I have this symptom?"

Here I'll use the example from Chapter 6 of the fictitious disease blurritis. Recall the information given:

- You took a blood test that came back positive for the hypothetical disease blurritis.
- The base rate for blurritis is 1 in 10,000, or .0001.
- The use of the hypothetical drug chlorohydroxelene ends in an unwanted side effect 5% of the time, or .05.
- The blood test for blurritus is wrong 2% of the time, or .02.

The question is, Should you take the medicine or not?

We start by drawing the table and labeling the rows and columns.

TEST RESULTS

		Pos.	Neg.	
Disease	Yes			
	No			
	Totals			

The boxes inside allow us to apportion the data into four mutually exclusive categories:

- people who have the disease who test positive (upper left interior box). We call these CORRECT IDENTIFICATIONS.
- people who have the disease who test negative (upper right interior box). We call these MISSES or FALSE NEGATIVES.
- people who don't have the disease who test positive (lower left interior box). We call these FALSE POSITIVES.
- people who don't have the disease who test negative (lower right interior box). We call these CORRECT REJECTIONS.

TEST RESULTS

		Pos.	Neg.	
Disease	Yes	Correct Identifications	False Negatives	
	No	False Positives	Correct Rejections	
	Totals			

Now we start filling in what we know. The base rate of the disease is 1 in 10,000. In the lower right corner, outside the big box, I'll fill in the "grand total" of 10,000. I call this the population box because it is the number that tells us how many there are in the total population we're looking at (we could fill in 320 million for the population of the United States here, and then work with the total number of cases reported per year—32,000—but I prefer filling in the smaller numbers of the "incident rate" because they're easier to work with).

TEST RESULTS

		Pos.	Neg.	
Disease	Yes			
	No			
	Totals			10,000

What we seek to calculate, with the help of this table, are the numbers in the other boxes, both the boxes inside the outlines and the boxes outside. Of those 10,000 people, we know 1 of them has blurritis. We don't know yet how that person is apportioned by test results, so we fill in the number 1 all the way to the right, corresponding to "Disease: Yes."

TEST RESULTS

		Pos.	Neg.	
Disease	Yes			1
	No			
	Totals			10,000

The way the table is designed, numbers from top to bottom and from left to right are supposed to add up to their "marginal totals" along the outskirts of the figure. This is logical: If the number of people with the disease = 1, and the total number of people under consideration is 10,000, we know the number of people who do *not* have the disease within this population must be: 10,000–1 = 9,999. So we can fill that in the table next.

TEST RESULTS

		Pos.	Neg.	
Disease	Yes			1
	No			9,999
	Totals			10,000

We know from what the doctor told us (above) that 2% of the time, the test is inaccurate. We apply that 2% figure to the totals along the right margin. Of the 9,999 who do not have the disease, 2% of them will be given the wrong diagnosis. That is, although they *don't* have the disease, the test will say they *do* (a false positive, the lower left interior box). We calculate 2% × 9,999 = 199.98, and round that to 200.

TEST RESULTS

		Pos.	Neg.	
Disease	Yes			1
	No	200		9,999
	Totals			10,000

Now, because the numbers need to add up in rows and columns, we can calculate the number of people who don't have the disease and whose test results are negative—the correct rejections. This is 9,999–200 = 9,799.

TEST RESULTS

		Pos.	Neg.	
Disease	Yes			1
	No	200	9,799	9,999
	Totals			10,000

Now we fill in the other misdiagnoses, the 2% false negatives. False negative means you have the disease and the test says you don't—they're in the upper right interior box. Only 1 person has the disease (as we see in the far right margin). We calculate 2% × 1 = .02, or 0 if you round.

TEST RESULTS

		Pos.	Neg.	
Disease	Yes		0	1
	No	200	9,799	9,999
Totals				10,000

And of course that lets us fill in the empty square with 1 (we get that by starting with the margin total, 1, and subtracting the 0 in the top right box, to fill in the empty box on the top left—remember, the numbers need to add up in every row and every column).

TEST RESULTS

		Pos.	Neg.	
Disease	Yes	1	0	1
	No	200	9,799	9,999
Totals				10,000

Now for the sake of completeness, we add the numbers from top to bottom to fill in the margins on the bottom outside the table—the total number of people who got positive test results is simply the sum of those in that column: 1 + 200 = 201. And the total number of people who got negative results is 0 + 9,799 = 9,799.

TEST RESULTS

		Pos.	Neg.	
Disease	Yes	1	0	1
	No	200	9,799	9,999
	Totals	201	9,799	10,000

From here, we can solve the problems as shown in Chapter 6.

1. What is the probability that you have the disease, *given* that you tested positive?

We traditionally replace the word *given* with the symbol | and the word *probability* with the letter *p* to construct a kind of equation that looks like this:

1.1. p(You have the disease | you tested positive)

This format is convenient because it reminds us that the first part of the sentence—everything before the | symbol, becomes the numerator (top part) of a fraction, and everything after the | symbol becomes the denominator.

To answer question 1, we look *only* at the column of people with positive test results, the left column. There is 1 person who actually has the disease out of 201 who tested positive. The answer to question 1 is 1/201, or .49%.

2. What is the probability that you will test positive, *given* that you have the disease?

2.1. p(You test positive | you have the disease)

Here we look only at the top row, and construct the fraction 1/1 to conclude that there is 100% chance that you'll test positive if you really and truly have the disease.

Remember that my hypothetical treatment, chlorohydroxelene, has a 5% chance of side effects. If we treat everyone who tested positive for blurritis—all 201 of them—5%, or 10, will experience the side effect. Remember, only 1 person actually has the disease, so the treatment is 10 times more likely to provide side effects than a cure.

In these two cases I described in Chapter 6, blurritis and the blue face disease, even if you tested positive for them, it is unlikely you have the disease. Of course, if you really have the disease, choosing the right drug is important. What can you do?

You can take the test twice. We apply the multiplicative law of probability here, assuming that the results of the tests are independent. That is, whatever errors might cause you of all people to get an incorrect result are random—it's not as though someone at the testing lab has it in for you—and so if you got an incorrect result once, you're not any more likely to get an incorrect result again than anyone else would be. Recall that I said the test had a 2% chance of being wrong. The probability of its being wrong twice in a row is 2% × 2%, or .0004. If you prefer to work with fractions, the probability was 1/50, and 1/50 × 1/50 = 1/2500. But even this statistic doesn't take into account the base rate, the rarity of the disease. And doing that is the whole point of this section.

The helpful thing to do, of course, is to construct a fourfold table to answer the question "What is the probability that I have the disease, *given* that I tested positive for it twice in a row?"

When we started looking at blurritis, we had just a bunch of numbers and we placed them into a fourfold table; this allowed us to easily calculate our updated probabilities. One of the features of Bayesian inferencing is that you can place those updated probabilities into a new table to update again. With each new update of information, you can build a new table and home in on more and more accurate estimates.

The table looked like this when it was all filled in:

TEST RESULTS

Disease		Pos.	Neg.	
	Yes	1	0	1
	No	200	9,799	9,999
	Totals	201	9,799	10,000

and we read off the following from the table:

Number of people who tested positive: 201

Number of people who tested positive and have the disease: 1

Number of people who tested positive and don't have the disease: 200

Notice that now we're looking only at half the table, the half for people with positive test results. This is because the question we want to answer assumes you tested positive: "What is the probability that I actually have the disease if I test positive for it twice in a row?"

So now we construct a new table using this information. For the table headings, the *second* test result can be positive or negative, you can have or not have the disease, and we're no longer looking at the total population of 10,000; we're looking only at that subset of the 10,000 who tested positive the first time: 201 people. So we put 201 in the population box on the lower right margin.

2ND TEST RESULTS

Disease		Pos.	Neg.	
	Yes			
	No			
	Totals			201

We can also fill in some of the additional information from up above. We know the number of people in this population who do and don't have the disease and so we fill those in on the right margin.

2ND TEST RESULTS

		Pos.	Neg.	
Disease	Yes			1
	No			200
	Totals			201

Now we go back to the original information we were given, that the test makes errors 2% of the time. One person actually has the disease; 2% of the time, it will be incorrectly diagnosed, and 98%, it will be correctly diagnosed: 2% of 1 = .02. I'll round that down to 0—this is the number of people who show false negatives (they have the disease, but it was incorrectly diagnosed the second time). And 98% of 1 is close to 1.

2ND TEST RESULTS

		Pos.	Neg.	
Disease	Yes	1	0	1
	No			200
	Totals			201

Next we apply the same 2% error rate to the people who don't have the disease. 2% of the 200 who don't have the disease will test positive (even though they're healthy): 2% of 200 = 4. That leaves 196 for the correctly diagnosed interior box in the lower right.

2ND TEST RESULTS

		Pos.	Neg.	
Disease	Yes	1	0	1
	No	4	196	200
	Totals			201

We can add up the columns vertically to obtain the marginal totals, which we'll need to compute our new updated probabilities.

2ND TEST RESULTS

		Pos.	Neg.	
Disease	Yes	1	0	1
	No	4	196	200
	Totals	5	196	201

As before, we calculate on the left column, because we're interested only in those people who tested positive a second time.

2ND TEST RESULTS

		Pos.	Neg.	
Disease	Yes	1	0	1
	No	4	196	200
	Totals	5	196	201

Of the 5 people who tested positive a second time, 1 actually has the disease: 1/5 = .20. In other words, the disease is sufficiently rare that even if you test positive *twice in a row*, there is still only a 20% chance you have it, and therefore an 80% chance you don't.

What about those side effects? If we start everyone who tested positive twice in a row on my fictitious chlorohydroxelene with the 5% side effects, 5% of those 5 people, or .25, will experience side effects. So although it's unlikely you have the disease, it's also unlikely all your hair will fall out. For every 5 people who take the treatment, 1 will be cured (because that person actually has the disease) and .25 will have the side effects. In this case, with two tests, you're now about 4 times more likely to experience the cure than the side effects, a nice reversal of what we saw before. (If it makes you uncomfortable to talk about .25 of a person, just multiply all the numbers above by 4.)

We can take Bayesian statistics a step further. Suppose a newly published study shows that if you are a woman, you're ten times more likely to get the disease than if you're a man. You can construct a new table to take this information into account, and to refine the estimate that you actually have the disease.

The calculations of probabilities in real life have applications far beyond medical matters. I asked Steve Wynn, who owns five casinos (at his Wynn and Encore hotels in Las Vegas, and the Wynn, Encore, and Palace in Macau), "Doesn't it hurt, just a little, to see customers walking away with large pots of your money?"

"I'm always happy to see people win. It creates a lot of excitement in the casino."

"Come on, really? It's your money. Sometimes people walk away with *millions*."

"First of all, you know we make a lot more than we pay out. Second, we usually get the money back. In all these years, I've never seen a big winner actually walk away. They come back to the casino and play with what they won, and we usually get it all back. The reason they're there in the first place is that, like most people with a self-indulgence such as golf or fine wine, they like the game more than the money. Winning provides them with capital for the game, without them having to write a check. People lose at 100 cents on the dollar, they win at 99 cents on the dollar. That 1% is our margin."

The expected value of a casino bet always favors the house. Now, there is a psychology of gambling that leads winners who *could* walk away with a fortune to stay and lose it all. Setting this aside, even if all the winners did walk away, the long-run odds are still in favor of the house. Which leads us to extended warranties on things like laser printers, computers, vacuum cleaners, and DVD players. The big discount retailers really push these warranties, and they play upon your quite reasonable reluctance to pay big repair bills on an item you just bought. They promise "worry-free" repairs at a premium price. But make no mistake—this is not a service offered out of the retailer's generosity, but as a moneymaking enterprise. For many retailers, the real profits are not in selling you the initial item but in selling you the warranty to protect it.

Such warranties are almost always a bad deal for you and a good deal for "the house." If there is a 10% chance that you'll use it, and it will save you $300 in repair costs, then its expected value is $30. If they're charging you $90 for it, that $60 above the expected value is a sure profit for the retailer. They try to suck you in with pleas like "If this breaks, the minimum repair charge will be two hundred dollars. The warranty only costs ninety dollars, so you're coming out way ahead." But don't be taken in. *You* only come out ahead if you're one of those 10% who needs it. The rest of the time, *they* come out ahead. Medical decision-making is no different. You can apply expected value calculations to the costs and benefits of various treatment options. There exist strictly mathematical methods for calculating these values of course—there is nothing magic about using these contingency tables. Many people prefer them, though, because they act as a heuristic for organizing the information, and they allow for an easy visual display of the numbers, which in turn helps you to catch any errors you might have made along the way. In fact, much of the advice in this book about staying organized comes down to putting systems in place that will help us catch errors when we make them, or recover from the errors we inevitably all make.

NOTES

NOTE ON THE ENDNOTES

Scientists make their living by evaluating evidence, and come to provisional conclusions based on the weight of that evidence. I say "provisional" because we acknowledge the possibility that new data may come to light that challenge current assumptions and understanding. In evaluating published data, scientists have to consider such things as the quality of the experiment (and the experimenters), the quality of the review process under which the work was assessed, and the explanatory power of the work. Part of the evaluation includes considering alternative explanations and contradictory findings, and forming a (preliminary) conclusion about what all the existing data say. For many claims, it is possible to locate published findings in the research literature that contradict or support a given idea; no single study is ever the whole story. "Cherry-picking" data to make a point is considered one of the cardinal sins of science.

Here, where I cite scientific papers to support a particular scientific point made in this book, I am presenting them as examples of the work that supports the point, not as an exhaustive list. Wherever possible, and to the best of my ability, I have studied a broad range of papers on a topic in order to understand the weight of the evidence for a claim, but have included only representative papers here. Listing every paper I read would make the endnotes section ten times longer, and far less useful to the general reader.

INTRODUCTION

xiv **every conscious experience is stored somewhere in your brain** Goldinger, S. D. (1998). Echoes of echoes? An episodic theory of lexical access. *Psychologial Review, 105*(2), 251.

and, Hintzman, D. L. (1988). Judgments of frequency and recognition memory in a multiple-trace memory model. *Psychological Review, 95*(4), 528.

and, Magnussen, S., Greenlee, M. W., Aslaksen, P. M., & Kildebo, O. Ø. (2003). High-fidelity perceptual long-term memory revisted—and confirmed. (2003). *Psychological Science, 14*(1), 74–76.

and, Nadel, L., Samsonovich, A., Ryan, L., & Moscovitch, M. (2000). Multiple trace theory of human memory: computational, neuroimaging, and neuropsychological results. *Hippocampus, 10*(4), 352–368.

xxv **openness to new experience, conscientiousness** Goldberg, L. R. (1993). The structure of phenotypic personality traits. *American Psychologist, 48*(1), 26–34, p. 26.

xxv **predictor of many important human outcomes** Schmidt, F. L., & Hunter, J. E. (1998). The validity and utility of selection methods in personnel psychology: Practical and theoretical implications of 85 years of research findings. *Psychological Bulletin, 124*(2), 262–274, p. 262.

xxv **including mortality, longevity** Kern, M. L., & Friedman, H. S. (2008). Do conscientious individuals live longer? A quantitative review. *Health Psychology, 27*(5), 505–512, p. 512.

and, Terracciano, A., Löckenhoff, C. E., Zonderman, A. B., Ferrucci, L., & Costa, P. T. (2008). Personality predictors of longevity: Activity, emotional stability, and conscientiousness. *Psychosomatic Medicine, 70*(6), 621–627.

xxv **educational attainment** Hampson, S. E., Goldberg, L. R., Vogt, T. M., & Dubanoski, J. P. (2007). Mechanisms by which childhood personality traits influence adult health status: Educational attainment and healthy behaviors. *Health Psychology, 26*(1), 121–125, p. 121.

xxv **criteria related to career success** Barrick, M. R., & Mount, M. K. (1991). The big five personality dimensions and job performance: A meta-analysis. *Personnel Psychology, 44*(1), 1–26.

and, Roberts, B. W., Chernyshenko, O. S., Stark, S., & Goldberg, L. R. (2005). The structure of conscientiousness: An empirical investigation based on seven major personality questionnaires. *Personnel Psychology, 58*(1), 103–139.

xxv **better recovery outcomes following surgery** Kamran, F. (2013). Does conscientiousness increase quality of life among renal transplant recipients? *International Journal of Research Studies in Psychology, 3*(2), 3–13.

xxv **Conscientiousness in early childhood** Friedman, H. S., Tucker, J. S., Schwartz, J. E., Martin, L. R., Tomlinson-Keasey, C., Wingard, D. L., & Criqui, M. H. (1995). Childhood conscientiousness and longevity: Health behaviors and cause of death. *Journal of Personality and Social Psychology, 68*(4), 696–703, p. 696.

and, Friedman, H. S., Tucker, J. S., Tomlinson-Keasey, C., Schwartz, J. E., Wingard, D. L., & Criqui, M. H. (1993). Does childhood personality predict longevity? *Journal of Personality and Social Psychology, 65*(1), 176–185.

xxv **more Westernized and complex** Goldberg, L. R., personal communication. May 13, 2013.

and, Gurven, M., von Rueden, C., Massenkoff, M., Kaplan, H., & Lero Vie, M. (2013). How universal is the Big Five? Testing the five-factor model of personality variation among forager–farmers in the Bolivian Amazon. *Journal of Personality and Social Psychology, 104*(2), 354–370.

CHAPTER 1

4 **Satisficing:** Simon, H. (1957). Part IV in *Models of man*. New York: Wiley, pp. 196–279.

5 **Warren Buffett's home:** Nye, J. (2013, January 21). Billionaire Warren Buffet still lives in modest Omaha home he bought for $31,500 in 1958. *Daily Mail.*

5 **In 1976, the average supermarket stocked** Waldman, S. (1992, January 27). The tyranny of choice: Why the consumer revolution is ruining your life. *The New Republic*, pp. 22–25.

5 **we need to ignore 39,850 items** Trout, J. (2005, December 5). Differentiate or die. *Forbes.*

5 **one million products** Knolmayer, G. F., Mertens, P., Zeier, A., & Dickersbach, J. T. (2009). Supply chain management case studies. *Supply Chain Management Based on SAP Systems: Architecture and Planning Processes*. Berlin: Springer, pp. 161–188.

5 **showed poorer impulse control** Vohs, K. D., Baumeister, R. F., Schmeichel, B. J., Twenge, J. M., Nelson, N. M., & Tice, D. M. (2008). Making choices impairs subsequent self-control: A limited-resource account of decision-making, self-regulation, and active initiative. *Journal of Personality and Social Psychology, 94*(5), 883–898.

6 **". . . more processing power than the Apollo mission control."** Overbye, D. (2012, June 5). Mystery of big data's parallel universe brings fear, and a thrill. *The New York Times*, p. D3.

6 **the equivalent of 175 newspapers** Alleyne, R. (2011, February 11). Welcome to the information age—174 newspapers a day. *The Telegraph*.

and, Lebwohl, B. (2011, February 10). Martin Hilbert: All human information, stored on CD, would reach beyond the moon. *EarthSky*. Retrieved from http://earthsky.org

6 **34 gigabytes or 100,000 words every day** Bohn, R. E., & Short, J. E. (2010). *How much information? 2009 report on American consumers* (Global Information Industry Center Report). Retrieved from http://hmi.ucsd.edu/

6 **85,000 hours of original programming** Lyman, P., Varian, H. R., Swearingen, K., Charles, P., Good, N., Jordan, L. L., & Pal, J. (2003). *How much information? 2003* (University of California at Berkeley School of Information Management Report). Retrieved from http://www2.sims.berkeley.edu

and, Hilbert, M. (2012). How to measure "how much information"? Theoretical, methodological, and statistical challenges for the social sciences. *International Journal of Communication, 6*, 1042–1055.

6 **6,000 hours of video every hour** Hardy, Q. (2014, January 8). Today's webcams see all (tortoise, we're watching your back). *The New York Times*, p. A1.

6 **It consumes more bytes than all** Nunberg, G. (2011, March 20). James Gleick's history of information. *The New York Times Sunday Book Review*, p. BR1.

7 **120 bits per second** This estimate derives independently from Csikszentmihalyi (2007) and the Bell Labs engineer Robert Lucky, who made an independent estimate that regardless of the modality, the cortex cannot take in more than 50 bits/second—within an order of magnitude of Csikszentmihalyi's. Csikszentmihalyi explains his estimate: "As George Miller and others have suggested, we can process 5–7 bits of information in one apperception; each apperception takes at least 1/15th of a second; hence 7 × 15 = 105 bits/second. Nusbaum has calculated that understanding verbal material takes on the average 60 bits/second."

Csikszentmihalyi, M., & Nakamura, J. (2010). Effortless attention in everyday life: A systematic phenomenology. In B. Bruya (Ed.), *Effortless attention: A new perspective in the cognitive science of attention and action* (pp. 179–189). Cambridge, MA: MIT Press.

and, Csikszentmihalyi, M. (2007, May). Music and optimal experience. In G. Turow (Chair), *Music, rhythm and the brain.* Symposium conducted at the meeting of The Stanford Institute for Creativity and the Arts, Center for Arts, Science and Technology, Stanford, CA.

and, Csikszentmihalyi, M., personal communication, November 8, 2013.

and, Lucky, R. (1989). *Silicon dreams: Information, man, and machine.* New York, NY: St. Martin's Press.

and, Rajman, M., & Pallota, V. (2007). *Speech and language engineering (Computer and Communication Sciences).* Lausanne, Switzerland: EPFL Press.

7 **so much misunderstanding** Csikszentmihalyi, M. (2007, May). Music and optimal experience. In G. Turow (Chair), *Music, rhythm and the brain.* Symposium conducted at the meeting of The Stanford Institute for Creativity and the Arts, Center for Arts, Science and Technology, Stanford, CA.

It's also no wonder that we seek music so purposefully. Music is a rare case of our being able to attend to more than two people at a time because of the structure of harmony and the way in which people can play music *together* without impacting its understandability.

8 **terrestrial vertebrate biomass** Dennett, D. C. (2009). The cultural evolution of words and other thinking tools. In *Cold Spring Harbor Symposia on Quantitative Biology 74,* 435–441.

and, MacCready P. (1999). An ambivalent Luddite at a technological feast. Retrieved from http://www.designfax.net/archives/0899/899trl_2.asp

12 **inattentional blindness:** Mack, A., & Rock, I. (1998). *Inattentional blindness.* Cambridge, MA: The MIT Press.

12 **Gorilla study:** Chabris, C. F., & Simons, D. J. (2011). *The invisible gorilla: And other ways our intuitions deceive us.* New York: Penguin Random House.

12 **Kant and Wordsworth complained** Blair, A. M. (2010). *Too much to know: Managing scholarly information before the modern age.* New Haven, CT: Yale University Press.

13 **categorization reduces mental effort** Direct quote from Rosch, E. (1978). Principles of categorization. In E. Rosch & B. B. Lloyd (Eds.), *Cognition and categorization* (pp. 27–48). Hillsdale, NJ: Lawrence Erlbaum Associates.

13 **For the first 99% of our history** Direct quote from Bryson, B. (2010). *At home: A short history of private life.* New York, NY: Doubleday, p. 34.

13 **an unprecedented volume of business** Almost direct quote from Wright, A. (2008). *Glut: Mastering information through the ages.* Ithaca, NY: Cornell University Press, p. 49.

13 **The first forms of writing emerged** Childe, V. G. (1951). *Man makes himself.* New York, NY: New American Library.

13 **originate from sales receipts** Direct quote from Wright, A. (2008). *Glut: Mastering information through the ages.* Ithaca, NY: Cornell University Press, p. 49.

13 **add up to what we think of as civilization** Direct quote from Bryson, B. (2010). *At home: A short history of private life.* New York, NY: Doubleday, p. 34.

14 **"weaken men's characters . . ."** Wright, A. (2008). *Glut: Mastering information through the ages.* Ithaca, NY: Cornell University Press, p. 6.

14 **Thamus, king of Egypt, argued** Postman, N. (1993). *Technopoly: The surrender of culture to technology.* New York, NY: Vintage, p. 74. Perhaps Thamus was foreshadowing the world of George Orwell's *1984* in which texts were retroactively edited or purged to conform with an ever-changing official version of facts by the government.

14 **Callimachus said books are "a great evil."** Blair, A. M. (2010). *Too much to know: Managing scholarly information before the modern age.* New Haven, CT: Yale University Press, p. 17.

14 **Seneca recommended** Blair (2010), p. 15.

14 **"foolish, ignorant, malignant, libelous . . ."** Blair (2010).

14 **"return to barbarism."** Blair (2010).

14 **"even if all knowledge could be found in books . . ."** Blair, A. M. (2010). *Too much to know: Managing scholarly information before the modern age.* New Haven, CT: Yale University Press. On the topic of too many books, see also, Queenan, J. (2013). *One for the books.* New York, NY: Viking.

15 **these warnings were raised . . . television** Greenstein, J. (1954). Effect of television upon elementary school grades. *The Journal of Educational Research, 48*(3), 161–176.

and, Maccoby, E. E. (1951). Television: Its impact on school children. *Public Opinion Quarterly, 15*(3), 421–444.

and, Scheuer, J. (1992). The sound bite society. *New England Review, 14*(4), 264–267.

and, Witty, P. (1950). Children's, parents' and teachers' reactions to television. *Elementary English, 27*(6), 349–355, p. 396.

15 **these warnings were raised . . . computers** Cromie, W. J. (1999, January 21). Computer addiction is coming on-line. *Harvard Gazette.*

and, Shaffer, H. J., Hall, M. N., & Vander Bilt, J. (2000). "Computer addiction": A critical consideration. *American Journal of Orthopsychiatry, 70*(2), 162–168.

15 **these warnings were raised . . . iPods** Cockrill, A., Sullivan, M., & Norbury, H. L. (2011). Music consumption: Lifestyle choice or addiction. *Journal of Retailing and Consumer Services, 18*(2), 160–166.

and, McFedries, P. (2005). Technically speaking: The iPod people. *IEEE Spectrum, 42*(2), 76.

and, Norbury, H. L. (2008). *A study of Apple's iPod: iPod addiction: Does it exist?* (Master's thesis). Swansea University, Wales.

15 **these warnings were raised . . . iPads** Aldridge, G. (2013, April 21). Girl aged four is Britain's youngest-known iPad addict. *Daily Mirror.*

and, Smith, J. L. (2013, December 28). Switch off—it's time for your digital detox. *The Telegraph.*

15 **these warnings were raised . . . e-mail** Lincoln, A. (2011). FYI: TMI: Toward a holistic social theory of information overload. *First Monday 16*(3).

and, Taylor, C. (2002, June 3). 12 steps for e-mail addicts. *Time.*

15 **these warnings were raised . . . Twitter** Hemp, P. (2009). Death by information overload. *Harvard Business Review, 87*(9), *82–89.*

and, Khang, H., Kim, J. K., & Kim, Y. (2013). Self-traits and motivations as antecedents of digital media flow and addiction: The Internet, mobile phones, and video games. *Computers in Human Behavior, 29*(6), 2416–2424.

and, Saaid, S. A., Al-Rashid, N. A. A., & Abdullah, Z. (2014). The impact of addiction to Twitter among university students. In J. J. Park, I. Stojmenovic, M. Choi, & F. Xhafa (Eds.), *Lecture notes in electrical engineering Vol. 276: Future information technology* (pp. 231–236). Springer.

15 **these warnings were raised . . . Facebook** Pinker, S. (2010, June 11). Mind over mass media. *The New York Times,* p. A31.

and, Saenz, A. (2011, December 13). How social media is ruining your mind. Retrieved from http://singularityhub.com

15 **By 1623, this number** Citing Brian Ogilvie, in Blair, A. M. (2010). *Too much to know: Managing scholarly information before the modern age.* New Haven, CT: Yale University Press, p. 12.

15 **9,000 species of grasses** United States Department of Agriculture. (n.d.). Retrieved from www.usda.gov

15 **2,700 types of palm trees** Fairchild Tropical Botanical Garden, Coral Gables, FL (2011).

15 **And the numbers keep growing** Jowit, J. (2010, September 19). Scientists prune list of world's plants. *The Guardian.*

and, Headrick, D. R. (2000). *When information came of age: Technologies of knowledge in the age of reason and revolution, 1700–1850.* New York, NY: Oxford University Press, p. 20.

15 **increased by at least 3,000** Nervous system squid. (2012, February 8). Internet search: Google Scholar. Retrieved from http://scholar.google.com

Note: Between the time of writing and the time of publication, the number had increased to 58,600 research articles.

15 **Five exabytes (5×10^{18}) of *new* data** Lyman, P., Varian, H. R., Swearingen, K., Charles, P., Good, N., Jordan, L. L., & Pal, J. (2003). *How much information? 2003* (University of California at Berkeley School of Information Management Report). Retrieved from http://www2.sims.berkeley.edu

15 **50,000 times the number of words** Wright, A. (2008). *Glut: Mastering information through the ages.* Ithaca, NY: Cornell University Press, p. 6.

16–17 **This *vigilance* system** In the scientific literature, this is often called the *saliency network* or the *orienting system.*

17 **focus only on that which is relevant** In the scientific literature, this is often called using top-down processing, and in particular, the *alerting* system.

19 ***shadow work*** Illich, I. (1981). *Shadow work*. London, UK: Marion Boyars.

and, Lambert, C. (2011, October 30). Our unpaid, extra shadow work. *The New York Times*, p. SR12.

19 **replaces her cell phone** Manjoo, F. (2014, March 13). A wild idea: Making our smartphones last longer. *The New York Times*, p. B1.

19 **new locations for old menu items** This didn't happen to our ancestors. Your grandparents learned to write with pen and paper, and maybe to type. The medium of pen-and-paper didn't change for centuries. Grandpa didn't have to learn how to use a new pen every few years, or write on a new surface.

19 **better choose our elected officials** Turner, C. (1987). *Organizing information: Principles and practice*. London, UK: Clive Bingley, p. 2.

24 **Human infants between four and nine months** Baillargeon, R., Spelke, E. S., & Wasserman, S. (1985). Object permanence in five-month-old infants. *Cognition, 20*(3), 191–208.

and, Munakata, Y., McClelland, J. L., Johnson, M. H., & Siegler, R. S. (1997). Rethinking infant knowledge: Toward an adaptive process account of successes and failures in object permanence tasks. *Psychological Review, 104*(4), 686–713.

25 **communicate about those systems** Levinson, S. C. (2012). Kinship and human thought. *Science, 336*(6084), 988–989.

25 **6,000 languages known** Levinson, S. C. (2012). Kinship and human thought. *Science, 336*(6084), 988–989.

25 **This is not true in many languages** Trautmann, T. R. (2008). *Lewis Henry Morgan and the invention of kinship*. Lincoln, NE: University of Nebraska Press.

27 **Japanese quails** Wilson, G. D. (1987). *Variant sexuality: Research and theory*. Baltimore, MD: The Johns Hopkins University Press.

28 **patterns in naming plants** Atran, S. (1990). *Cognitive foundations of natural history: Towards an anthropology of science*. New York, NY: Cambridge University Press.

31 **"are interested in all kinds of things . . ."** Atran, S. (1990). *Cognitive foundations of natural history: Towards an anthropology of science*. New York, NY: Cambridge University Press, p. 216.

32 **Out of 30,000 edible plants** Bryson, B. (2010). *At home: A short history of private life*. New York, NY: Doubleday, p. 37.

CHAPTER 2

38 **without registering their content** Schooler, J. W., Reichle, E. D., & Halpern, D. V. (2004). Zoning out while reading: Evidence for dissociations between experience and metaconsciousness. In D. T. Levin (Ed.), *Thinking and seeing: Visual metacognition in adults and children* (pp. 203–226). Cambridge, MA: MIT Press.

38 **daydreaming or mind-wandering network** In particular, the insula. Menon, V., & Uddin, L. Q. (2010). Saliency, switching, attention and control: A network model of insula function. *Brain Structure and Function, 214*(5–6), 655–667.

and, Andrews-Hanna, J. R., Reidler, J. S., Sepulcre, J., Poulin, R., & Buckner, R. L. (2010). Functional-anatomic fractionation of the brain's default network. *Neuron, 65*(4), 550–562.

and, D'Argembeau, A., Collette, F., Van der Linden, M., Laureys, S., Del Fiore, G., Degueldre, C., . . . Salmon, E. (2005). Self-referential reflective activity and its relationship with rest: A PET study. *NeuroImage, 25*(2), 616–624.

and, Gusnard, D. A., & Raichle, M. E. (2001). Searching for a baseline: Functional imaging and the resting human brain. *Nature Reviews Neuroscience, 2*(10), 685–694.

and, Jack, A. I., Dawson, A. J., Begany, K. L., Leckie, R. L., Barry, K. P., Ciccia, A. H., & Snyder, A. Z. (2013). fMRI reveals reciprocal inhibition between social and physical cognitive domains. *NeuroImage, 66,* 385–401.

and, Kelley, W. M., Macrae, C. N., Wyland, C. L., Caglar, S., Inati, S., & Heatherton, T. F. (2002). Finding the self? An event-related fMRI study. *Journal of Cognitive Neuroscience, 14*(5), 785–794.

and, Raichle, M. E., MacLeod, A. M., Snyder, A. Z., Powers, W. J., Gusnard, D. A., & Shulman, G. L. (2001). A default mode of brain function. *Proceedings of the National Academy of Sciences, 98*(2), 676–682.

and, Wicker, B., Ruby, P., Royet, J. P., & Fonlupt, P. (2003). A relation between rest and the self in the brain? *Brain Research Reviews, 43*(2), 224–230.

Note: Tasks requiring mechanical reasoning or objects-in-the-world activate the stay-on-task or central executive network.

38 **That's the daydreaming mode** Raichle, M. E., MacLeod, A. M., Snyder, A. Z., Powers, W. J., Gusnard, D. A., & Shulman, G. L. (2001). A default mode of brain function. *Proceedings of the National Academy of Sciences, 98*(2), 676–682.

38 **the *default mode*** Raichle, M. E., MacLeod, A. M., Snyder, A. Z., Powers, W. J., Gusnard, D. A., & Shulman, G. L. (2001). A default mode of brain function. *Proceedings of the National Academy of Sciences, 98*(2), 676–682.

39 **the mind-wandering mode** In the scientific literature, what I'm calling the mind-wandering mode is referred to as the *default mode* or *task-negative network*, and the central executive is referred to as the *task-positive network.*

39 **These two brain states form a kind of yin-yang** Binder, J. R., Frost, J. A., Hammeke, T. A., Bellgowan, P. S., Rao, S. M., & Cox, R. W. (1999). Conceptual processing during the conscious resting state: A functional MRI study. *Journal of Cognitive Neuroscience, 11*(1), 80–93.

and, Corbetta, M., Patel, G., & Shulman, G. (2008). The reorienting system of the human brain: From environment to theory of mind. *Neuron, 58*(3), 306–324.

and, Fox, M. D., Snyder, A. Z., Vincent, J. L., Corbetta, M., Van Essen, D. C., & Raichle, M. E. (2005). The human brain is intrinsically organized into dynamic, anticorrelated functional networks. *Proceedings of the National Academy of Sciences, 102*(27), 9673–9678.

and, Mazoyer, B., Zago, L., Mellet, E., Bricogne, S., Etard, O., Houde, O., . . . Tzourio-Mazoyer, N. (2001). Cortical networks for working memory and executive functions sustain the conscious resting state in man. *Brain Research Bulletin, 54*(3), 287–298.

and, Shulman, G. L., Fiez, J. A., Corbetta, M., Buckner, R. L., Miezin, F. M., Raichle, M. E., & Petersen, S. E. (1997). Common blood flow changes across visual tasks: II. Decreases in cerebral cortex. *Journal of Cognitive Neuroscience, 9*(5), 648–663.

39 **more the mind-wandering network** Menon, V., & Uddin, L. Q. (2010). Saliency, switching, attention and control: A network model of insula function. *Brain Structure and Function, 214*(5–6), 655–667.

39 **our attentional filter:** I'm here bringing together, for the sake of clarity and parsimony, what the neuroscientific literature considers three different systems: the filter itself, the saliency detector (also called the orienting system or reorienting system), and the alerting or vigilance mode. The distinctions are important to neuroscientists, but they're unimportant for nonspecialists.

39 **mind-wandering mode is a network** Greicius, M. D., Krasnow, B., Reiss, A. L., & Menon, V. (2003). Functional connectivity in the resting brain: A network analysis of the default mode hypothesis. *Proceedings of the National Academy of Sciences, 100*(1), 253–258.

42 **the switch is controlled in a part** Sridharan, D., Levitin, D. J., & Menon, V. (2008). A critical role for the right fronto-insular cortex in switching between central-executive and default-mode networks. *Proceedings of the National Academy of Sciences, 105*(34), 12569–12574.

The insula is also involved in attention, as it helps to regulate physical and emotional urges. Urges often signal a loss of homeostasis and it can be important for us to be aware of this—being thirsty or hungry are obvious examples, or craving protein or a cooler environment. But sustained attention requires that we suppress these urges. Some of us are better than others at this—in some of us, the concentration wins and we end up physically uncomfortable; in others, the urges win and we end up taking multiple trips to the refrigerator when we really should be working. The insula helps to balance these competing demands, and part of its job is to send signals up to consciousness when important urges arise. People with brain damage to the insula who are trying to give up smoking have an easier time of it—the urges aren't being passed up to consciousness.

Naqvi, N. H., Rudrauf, D., Damasio, H., & Bechara, A. (2007). Damage to the insula disrupts addiction to cigarette smoking. *Science, 315*(5811), 531–534.

42 **Switching between two external objects involves the temporal-parietal junction** Corbetta, M., Patel, G., & Shulman, G. L. (2008). The reorienting system of the human brain: From environment to theory of mind. *Neuron, 58*(3), 306–324.

and, Shulman, G. L., & Corbetta, M. (2014). Two attentional networks: Identification and function within a larger cognitive architecture. In M. Posner (Ed.), *The cognitive neuroscience of attention* (2nd ed.) (pp. 113–128). New York, NY: Guilford Press.

For an alternate view, see Geng, J. J., & Vossel, S. (2013). Re-evaluating the role of TPJ in attentional control: Contextual updating? *Neuroscience & Biobehavioral Reviews, 37*(10), 2608–2620.

42 **like a see-saw** Meyer, M. L., Spunt, R. P., Berkman, E. T., Taylor, S. E., & Lieberman, M. D. (2012). Evidence for social working memory from a parametric functional MRI study. *Proceedings of the National Academy of Sciences, 109*(6), 1883–1888.

45 **Daniel Dennett showed** Dennett, D. C. (1991). *Consciousness explained.* New York, NY: Little, Brown and Company.

45 **four or five things at a time** The classic 1956 finding from George Miller that was taught for decades, that attention is limited to 7 ± 2 items, is giving way in contemporary neuroscience to a more restricted view of only four items.

Cowan, N. (2009). Capacity limits and consciousness. In T. Baynes, A. Cleeremans, & P. Wilken (Eds.), *Oxford companion to consciousness* (pp. 127–130). New York, NY: Oxford University Press.

and, Cowan, N. (2010). The magical mystery four: How is working memory capacity limited, and why? *Current Directions in Psychological Science, 19*(1), 51–57.

45 **four components in the human attentional system** Cognitive neuroscientists recognize a fifth component, the *alerting* mode or vigilance. This is conceptually distinct from the attentional filter, but for the purposes of this discussion, I'm treating it as a special case of the on-task mode, where the task is search or vigilance.

This is the state you're in when you're sustaining vigilance—the resting state is replaced by a new state that involves preparation for detecting and responding to an expected signal. We do this when we're waiting for the phone to ring, the traffic light to turn green, or the other shoe to drop. It is characterized by a sense of heightened awareness, sensory sensitivity, and arousal.

45 **The mind-wandering network recruits neurons** Menon, V., & Uddin, L. Q. (2010). Saliency, switching, attention and control: A network model of insula function. *Brain Structure and Function, 214*(5–6), 655–667.

45 **dense mass of fibers connected** Corbetta, M., Patel, G., & Shulman, G. L. (2008). The reorienting system of the human brain: From environment to theory of mind. *Neuron, 58*(3), 306–324.

46 **the inhibitory neurotransmitter GABA** Kapogiannis, D., Reiter, D. A., Willette, A. A., & Mattson, M. P. (2013). Posteromedial cortex glutamate and GABA predict intrinsic functional connectivity of the default mode network. *NeuroImage, 64,* 112–119.

46 **(of a gene called COMT)** Baldinger, P., Hahn, A., Mitterhauser, M., Kranz, G. S., Friedl, M., Wadsak, W., . . . Lanzenberger, R. (2013). Impact of COMT genotype on serotonin-1A receptor binding investigated with PET. *Brain Structure and Function,* 1–12.

46 **The serotonin transporter gene SLC6A4** Bachner-Melman, R., Dina, C., Zohar, A. H., Constantini, N., Lerer, E., Hoch, S., . . . Ebstein, R. P. (2005). AVPR1a and SLC6A4 gene polymorphisms are associated with creative dance performance. *PLoS Genetics, 1*(3), e42.

and, Ebstein, R. P., Israel, S., Chew, S. H., Zhong, S., & Knafo, A. (2010). Genetics of human social behavior. *Neuron, 65*(6), 831–844.

46 **plus the basal ganglia** Posner, M. I., & Fan, J. (2008). Attention as an organ system. In J. R. Pomerantz (Ed.), *Topics in integrative neuroscience: From cells to cognition* (pp. 31–61). New York, NY: Cambridge University Press.

46 **Sustained attention also depends** Sarter, M., Givens, B., & Bruno, J. P. (2001). The cognitive neuroscience of sustained attention: Where top-down meets bottom-up. *Brain Research Reviews, 35*(2), 146–160.

46 **acetylcholine in the right prefrontal cortex** Howe, W. M., Berry, A. S., Francois, J., Gilmour, G., Carp, J. M., Tricklebank, M., . . . Sarter, M. (2013). Prefrontal cholinergic mechanisms instigating shifts from monitoring for cues to cue-guided performance: Converging electrochemical and fMRI evidence from rats and humans. *The Journal of Neuroscience, 33*(20), 8742–8752.

and, Sarter, M., Givens, B., & Bruno, J. P. (2001). The cognitive neuroscience of sustained attention: Where top-down meets bottom-up. *Brain Research Reviews, 35*(2), 146–160.

and, Sarter, M., & Parikh, V. (2005). Choline transporters, cholinergic transmission and cognition. *Nature Reviews Neuroscience, 6*(1), 48–56.

46 **Acetylcholine density in the brain changes rapidly** Howe, W. M., Berry, A. S., Francois, J., Gilmour, G., Carp, J. M., Tricklebank, M., . . . Sarter, M. (2013). Prefrontal cholinergic mechanisms instigating shifts from monitoring for cues to cue-guided performance: Converging electrochemical and fMRI evidence from rats and humans. *The Journal of Neuroscience, 33*(20), 8742–8752.

46 **Acetylcholine also plays a role in sleep** Sarter, M., & Bruno, J. P. (1999). Cortical cholinergic inputs mediating arousal, attentional processing and dreaming: Differential afferent regulation of the basal forebrain by telencephalic and brainstem afferents. *Neuroscience, 95*(4), 933–952.

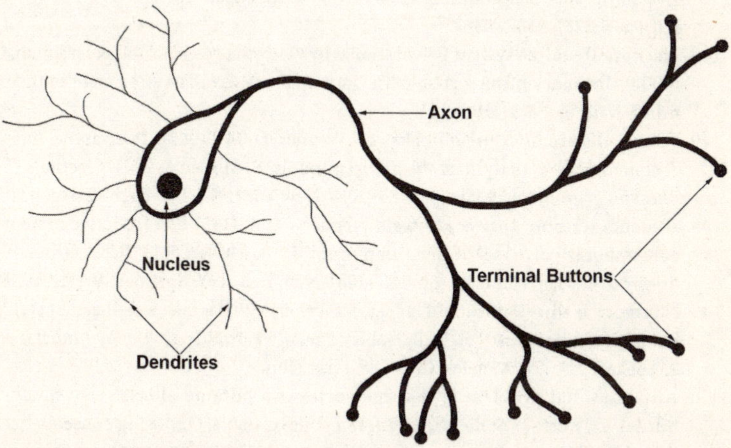

46 **acetylcholine and noradrenaline appear** Sarter, M., personal communication. December 23, 2013.

47 **nicotine can improve the rate of signal detection** Witte, E. A., Davidson, M. C., & Marrocco, R. T. (1997). Effects of altering brain cholinergic activity on covert orienting of attention: Comparison of monkey and human performance. *Psychopharmacology, 132*(4), 324–334.

47 **strongly coupled to the cingulate** Menon, V., & Uddin, L. Q. (2010). Saliency, switching, attention and control: A network model of insula function. *Brain Structure and Function, 214*(5–6), 655–667.

47 **the attentional filter incorporates a warning system** Called the *alerting* system in most of the neuroscientific literature, e.g., Posner, M. I. (2012). *Attention in a social world.* New York, NY: Oxford University Press.

47 **Drugs, such as guanfacine** Marrocco, R. T., & Davidson, M. C. (1998). Neurochemistry of attention. In R. Parasuraman (Ed.), *The attentive brain* (pp. 35–50). Cambridge, MA: MIT Press.

but for a different view see also, Clerkin, S. M., Schulz, K. P., Halperin, J. M., Newcorn, J. H., Ivanov, I., Tang, C. Y., & Fan, J. (2009). Guanfacine potentiates the activation of prefrontal cortex evoked by warning signals. *Biological Psychiatry, 66*(4), 307–312.

48 **governed by noradrenaline and cortisol** Hermans, E. J., van Marle, H. J., Ossewaarde, L., Henckens, M. J., Qin, S., van Kesteren, M. T., . . . Fernández, G. (2011). Stress-related noradrenergic activity prompts large-scale neural network reconfiguration. *Science, 334*(6059), 1151–1153.

and, Frodl-Bauch, T., Bottlender, R., & Hegerl, U. (1999). Neurochemical substrates and neuroanatomical generators of the event-related P300. *Neuropsychobiology, 40*(2), 86–94.

48 **Higher levels of dopamine here** Dang, L. C., O'Neil, J. P., & Jagust, W. J. (2012). Dopamine supports coupling of attention-related networks. *The Journal of Neuroscience, 32*(28), 9582–9587.

48 **The noradrenaline system is evolutionarily** Corbetta, M., Patel, G., & Shulman, G. L. (2008). The reorienting system of the human brain: From environment to theory of mind. *Neuron, 58*(3), 306–324.

49 **"Our walls are filled with books . . ."** Wegner, D. M. (1987). Transactive memory: A contemporary analysis of the group mind. In B. Mullen & G. R. Goethals (Eds.), *Theories of group behavior* (pp. 185–208). New York, NY: Springer-Verlag, p. 187.

49 **students scribble answers to tests** Wegner, D. M. (1987). Transactive memory: A contemporary analysis of the group mind. In B. Mullen & G. R. Goethals (Eds.), *Theories of group behavior* (pp. 185–208). New York, NY: Springer-Verlag, p. 187.

49 **"Memory is unreliable . . ."** Harper, J. (Writer). (2011). Like a redheaded stepchild [television series episode]. In B. Heller (Executive producer), *The Mentalist* (Season 3, Episode 21). Los Angeles, CA: CBS Television.

50 **An additional problem is that memories can become altered** Diekelmann, S., Büchel, C., Born, J., & Rasch, B. (2011). Labile or stable: Opposing consequences for memory when reactivated during waking and sleep. *Nature Neuroscience, 14*(3), 381–386.

and, Nader, K., Schafe, G. E., & LeDoux, J. E. (2000). Reply—Reconsolidation: The labile nature of consolidation theory. *Nature Reviews Neuroscience, 1*(3), 216–219.

53 **even President George W. Bush falsely recalled** Greenberg, D. L. (2004). President Bush's false [flashbulb] memory of 9/11/01. *Applied Cognitive Psychology, 18*(3), 363–370.

and, Talarico, J. M., & Rubin, D. C. (2003). Confidence, not consistency, characterizes flashbulb memories. *Psychological Science, 14*(5), 455–461.

55 **not as well as the first item** In some cases, the first and last items on a list are remembered equally well, and in some cases the last items are remembered better than the first. These differences are primarily due to two variables: how long the list is and whether or not you're *rehearsing* the items as you encounter them. With a long list and no rehearsal, the primacy effect decreases. With an intermediate length list and rehearsal, the primacy effect can be larger than the recency effect

because those early items you encountered receive more rehearsal and encoding than later items.

56 **the word *smashed* in the question** Loftus, E. F., & Palmer, J. C. (1974). Reconstruction of automobile destruction: An example of the interaction between language and memory. *Journal of Verbal Learning and Verbal Behavior, 13*(5), 585–589.

56 **a labile state** Nader, K., & Hardt, O. (2009). A single standard for memory: The case for reconsolidation. *Nature Reviews Neuroscience, 10*(3), 224–234.

56 **". . . the next time you pull up that 'file'"** Perry, B. D., & Szalavitz, M. (2006). *The boy who was raised as a dog and other stories from a child psychiatrist's notebook: What traumatized children can teach us about loss, love, and healing.* New York, NY: Basic Books, p. 156.

57 **typical term that we use most often** Rosch, E. (1978). Principles of categorization. In E. Rosch & B. B. Lloyd (Eds.), *Cognition and categorization* (pp. 27–48). Hillsdale, NJ: Lawrence Erlbaum Associates.

58 **traces its roots back to Aristotle** Irwin, T. H. (1988). *Aristotle's first principles.* New York, NY: Oxford University Press.

and, MacNamara, J. (1999). *Through the rearview mirror: Historical reflections on psychology.* Cambridge, MA: MIT Press, p. 33.

and, Vogt, K. (2010). Ancient skepticism. In E. N. Zalta (Ed.), *The Stanford encyclopedia of philosophy* (Winter 2011 ed.). Retrieved from http://plato.stanford.edu/entries/skepticism-ancient/

62 **caudate nucleus** Maddox, T. (2013, January). Talk presented at the Seventh Annual Meeting of the Auditory Cognitive Neuroscience Society, Tucson, AZ.

63 **taxonomic classification** Ross, B. H., & Murphy, G. L. (1999). Food for thought: Cross-classification and category organization in a complex real-world domain. *Cognitive Psychology, 38*(4), 495–553.

63 **the connections *are* the learning** Seung, S. (2012). *Connectome: How the brain's wiring makes us who we are.* New York, NY: Houghton Mifflin Harcourt.

63 **specific locations in the brain** Although the precise region of activity for mental categories varies from person to person, *within* a person it tends to be stable and confined to a particular location in the brain.

65 **What is a game:** Wittgenstein, L. (2010). *Philosophical investigations.* New York, NY: John Wiley & Sons.

67 **people who carry around a pen and notepads** Not surprisingly, most didn't want their names used in this book, but the list includes several Nobel Prize winners, leading scientists, artists and writers, Fortune 500 CEOs, and national politicians.

68 **"like carrying around a stone tablet and chisel."** Sandberg, S. (2013, March 17). By the book: Sheryl Sandberg. *The New York Times Sunday Book Review,* p. BR8.

68 **"Your mind will remind you . . ."** Allen, D. (2008). *Making it all work: Winning at the game of work and business of life.* New York, NY: Penguin, p. 35.

69 **"If an obligation remained recorded . . ."** Allen, D. (2002). *Getting things done: The art of stress-free productivity.* New York, NY: Penguin, p. 15.

69 **"You must be assured . . ."** Allen, D. (2002). *Getting things done: The art of stress-free productivity.* New York, NY: Penguin.

70 **"when information is organized in small chunks . . ."** Pirsig, R. (1991). *Lila: An inquiry into morals.* New York, NY: Bantam.

72 **"Instead of asking . . ."** Pirsig, R. (1991). *Lila: An inquiry into morals.* New York, NY: Bantam.

72 **With index cards, you can sort and re-sort** Say you have to call ten people today. You put each person's name and phone number on a card, along with a reminder or some salient notes about what you need to discuss. During the second call, you learn of a time-sensitive matter that involves the person who was tenth on your list. You simply take that card and put it on top. Your grocery list? You put it in the stack according to when you expect to get to it, but if you find yourself driving by the grocery store unexpectedly, with time on your hands, you pluck the card out of the stack and put it on top.

73 **Paul Simon carries a notebook** Simon, P., personal communication. September 19, 2013, New York, NY.

73 **John R. Pierce** Pierce, J. R., personal communication. January 3, 1999, Palo Alto, CA.

74 **Mark Twain, Thomas Jefferson, and George Lucas** McKay, B., & McKay, K. (2010, September 13). The pocket notebooks of 20 famous men [Web log message]. Retrieved from http://www.artofmanliness.com/2010/09/13/the-pocket-notebooks-of-20-famous-men/

CHAPTER 3

77 **All kinds of things that we don't eat today** Bryson, B. (2010). *At home: A short history of private life.* New York, NY: Doubleday, pp. 52–53.

and, Steyn, P. (2011). Changing times, changing palates: The dietary impacts of Basuto adaptation to new rulers, crops, and markets, 1830s–1966. In C. Folke Ax, N. Brimnes, N. T. Jensen, & K. Oslund (Eds.), *Cultivating the colonies: Colonial states and their environmental legacies* (pp. 214–236). Columbus, OH: Ohio University Press.

See also, Hopkins, J. (2004). *Extreme cuisine: The weird & wonderful foods that people eat.* North Clarendon, VT: Tuttle Publishing.

78 **servants requested written assurance** Bryson, B. (2010). *At home: A short history of private life.* New York, NY: Doubleday, p. 80.

78 **Until 1600** Bryson, B. (2010). *At home: A short history of private life.* New York, NY: Doubleday, pp. 56–61.

78 **2,260 *visible* objects** Arnold, J. E., Graesch, A. P., Ragazzini, E., & Ochs, E. (2012). *Life at home in the twenty-first century: 32 families open their doors.* Los Angeles, CA: Cotsen Institute of Archaeology Press at UCLA.

and, Segerstrom, S. C., & Miller, G. E. (2004). Psychological stress and the human immune system: a meta-analytic study of 30 years of inquiry. *Psychological Bulletin, 130*(4), 601–630.

78 **garages given over to old furniture** This is nearly a direct quote from Kolbert, E. (2012, July 2). Spoiled rotten. *The New Yorker.*

78 **Three out of four Americans report** Teitell, B. (2012, July 10). Boxed in, wanting out. *The Boston Globe.*

78 **Women's cortisol levels (the stress hormone) spike** Green, P. (2012, June 28). The way we live: Drowning in stuff. *The New York Times*, p. D2.

78 **Elevated cortisol levels can lead to** Kirschbaum, C., Wolf, O. T., May, M., Wippich, W., & Hellhammer, D. H. (1996). Stress- and treatment-induced elevations of

cortisol levels associated with impaired declarative memory in healthy adults. *Life Sciences, 58*(17), 1475–1483.

and, Lupien, S. J., Nair, N. P. V., Brière, S., Maheu, F., Tu, M. T., Lemay, M., . . . Meaney, M. J. (1999). Increased cortisol levels and impaired cognition in human aging: Implication for depression and dementia in later life. *Reviews in the Neurosciences, 10*(2), 117–140.

and, Melamed, S., Ugarten, U., Shirom, A., Kahana, L., Lerman, Y., & Froom, P. (1999). Chronic burnout, somatic arousal and elevated salivary cortisol levels. *Journal of Psychosomatic Research, 46*(6), 591–598.

78 **suppression of the body's immune system** Maule, A. G., Schreck, C. B., & Kaattari, S. L. (1987). Changes in the immune system of coho salmon (Oncorhynchus kisutch) during the parr-to-smolt transformation and after implantation of cortisol. *Canadian Journal of Fisheries and Aquatic Sciences, 44*(1), 161–166.

81 **one gender category or the other** Further differentiation in the pants department might be made for bell-bottoms, boot-cut, button fly, zip fly, prewashed, acid-washed, and so on. This—as with file folder logic—depends on the total number of items. If the store has a large stock, it makes sense to divide it up the way I've described. But if you go to a small boutique, they may have only six pants of all types in each size.

81 **Lancôme provides the fixtures** Interview with MAC counter agent at Macy's San Francisco (Union Square) store, December 30, 2013, 11:15 A.M. (her name is being withheld because she is not authorized to speak on behalf of the company). This was confirmed in an interview with the associate manager.

81 **maximum information** Rosch, E. (1978). Principles of categorization. In E. Rosch & B. B. Lloyd (Eds.), *Cognition and categorization* (pp. 27–48). Hillsdale, NJ: Lawrence Erlbaum Associates.

82 **It's his hippocampus** Lavenex, P., Steele, M. A., & Jacobs, L. F. (2000). Sex differences, but no seasonal variations in the hippocampus of food-caching squirrels: A stereological study. *The Journal of Comparative Neurology, 425*(1), 152–166.

82 **London taxi drivers are required** Harrison, L. (2012, August 6). Taxi drivers and the importance of 'The Knowledge'. *The Telegraph.*

and, *No GPS! Aspiring London taxi drivers memorize a tangle of streets* [Video file]. (2013, April 11). *NBC News.* Retrieved from www.nbcnews.com

82 **the hippocampus in London taxi drivers** Maguire, E. A., Frackowiak, R. S. J., & Frith, C. D. (1997). Recalling routes around London: Activation of the right hippocampus in taxi drivers. *The Journal of Neuroscience, 17*(18), 7103–7110.

and, Maguire, E. A., Gadian, D. G., Johnsrude, I. S., Good, C. D., Ashburner, J., Frackowiak, R. S. J., & Frith, C. D. (2000). Navigation-related structural change in the hippocampi of taxi drivers. *Proceedings of the National Academy of Sciences, 97*(8), 4398–4403.

and, Maguire, E. A., Woollett, K., & Spiers, H. J. (2006). London taxi drivers and bus drivers: A structural MRI and neuropsychological analysis. *Hippocampus, 16*(12), 1091–1101.

82 **dedicated cells in the hippocampus** Deng, W., Mayford, M., & Gage, F. H. (2013). Selection of distinct populations of dentate granule cells in response to inputs as a mechanism for pattern separation in mice. *eLife, 2*, e00312.

83 **The famous mnemonic system** Foer, J. (2011). *Moonwalking with Einstein: The art and science of remembering everything.* New York, NY: Penguin.

83 ***cognitive prosthetics*** Kosslyn, S. M., & Miller, G. W. (2013, October 18). A new map of how we think: Top brain/bottom brain. *The Wall Street Journal.*

83 ***Dr. Zhivago*** Joni Mitchell recalls, "I remember when I first saw that movie. Of course I liked the cinematography, the story, and the outfits. But when Julie Christie walked into her front door and put the keys on a hook, I thought 'there's something I can *use.*' She put her keys right where she wouldn't lose them." Mitchell, J., personal communication. October 4, 2013.

83 **[Untitled photograph of key holders]:** Retrieved January 23, 2014, from http://www.keanmiles.com/key-holder.html. Item can also be found at http://www.moderngent.com/j-me/his_hers_keyholders.php

84 **"I forget all kinds of [other] stuff . . ."** Dominus, S. (2014, January 26). My moves speak for themselves. *The New York Times Sunday Magazine*, p. MM10.

84 **put an umbrella near the front door** Kosslyn, S., personal communication. August, 2013.

85 **If the umbrella is by the door all the time** Along these same lines, efficiency experts recommend leaving things where we're apt to need them.

86 **"I don't want to waste energy . . ."** Conversation with the author, September 7, 2012, British Columbia.

86 **Stephen Stills's home studio** Conversation with the author, January 3, 2013.

86 **Michael Jackson fastidiously catalogued** Logan, L. (Writer). (2013). Michael Jackson's lucrative legacy [television series episode]. In J. Fagar (Executive producer), *60 Minutes.* New York, NY: CBS News.

86 **John Lennon kept boxes and boxes of work tapes** Ono, Yoko (January 18, 1988). Lost Lennon Tapes Premiere Show. (Interview). Westwood One Radio Network.

87 **probably closer to four** Cowan, N. (2010). The magical mystery four: How is working memory capacity limited, and why? *Current Directions in Psychological Science, 19*(1), 51–57.

and, Cowan, N. (2009). Capacity limits and consciousness. In T. Bayne, A. Cleeremans & P. Wilken (Eds.), *Oxford companion to consciousness* (pp. 127–130). New York, NY: Oxford University Press.

88 **they need to get *control*** Direct quote from Allen, D. (2008). *Making it all work: Winning at the game of work and the business of life.* New York, NY: Penguin, p. 18.

88 **make visible the things you need regularly** Norman, D. (2013). *The design of everyday things: Revised and expanded edition.* New York, NY: Basic Books.

88 **In organizing your living space** Four guiding cognitive principles for organizing shelves and drawers are these: Make frequently used objects visible, or at least handy, and as a corollary, put infrequently used objects out of the way so that they don't distract; put similar things together; put together things that are used together, even if they are not similar; organize hierarchically when possible.

88 **The display of liquor bottles** Nearly direct quote from Mutkoski, S. (professor, Cornell School of Hotel Administration), personal communication. May 2, 2013.

89 **A bar in Lexington, Kentucky** Nearly direct quote from Mutkoski, S. (professor, Cornell School of Hotel Administration), personal communication. May 2, 2013.

91 **Students who studied for an exam** Farnsworth, P. R. (1934). Examinations in familiar and unfamiliar surroundings. *The Journal of Social Psychology, 5*(1), 128–129.

and, Smith, S. M. (1979). Remembering in and out of context. *Journal of Experimental Psychology: Human Learning and Memory, 5*(5), 460–471, p. 460.

and, Smith, S. M., & Vela, E. (2001). Environmental context-dependent memory: A review and meta-analysis. *Psychonomic Bulletin & Review, 8*(2), 203–220.

92 **brain simply wasn't designed** I'm using the term *designed* loosely; the brain wasn't designed, it evolved as a collection of special-purpose processing modules.

93 **1941 Oxford Filing Supply Company** by the Jonas, F. D. (1942). U.S. Patent No. 2305710 A. East Williston, NY. U.S. Patent and Trademark Office. Related patents by Jonas and Oxford include US2935204, 2312717, 2308077, 2800907, 3667854, 2318077, and many others.

94 **You might have categories** Creel, R. (2013). How to set up an effective filing system. *Smead Corporation.* Retrieved from http://www.smead.com/hot-topics/filing-system-1396.asp

and, United States Environmental Protection Agency. (2012). Records management tools. Retrieved from http://www.epa.gov

95 **For documents you need to access somewhat frequently** On the other hand, infrequently used documents don't merit this level of attention. You might want to keep sales receipts for household appliances in case you need them for a warranty claim. If your experience with appliances is that they don't break often, a single folder for all the receipts is efficient, as opposed to individual folders labeled for each appliance. On that one day in three years when you need to find the receipt for your washing machine, you can spend two or three minutes sifting through the collected folder of appliance receipts.

95 **"putting everything in a certain place . . ."** Merrill, D. C., & Martin, J. A. (2010). *Getting organized in the Google era: How to get stuff out of your head, find it when you need it, and get it done right.* New York, NY: Crown Business, p. 73.

96 **"not wired to multi-task well . . ."** As quoted in Kastenbaum, S. (2012, May 26). Texting while walking a dangerous experiment in multitasking [audio podcast]. *CNN Radio.*

96 **we're more like a bad amateur plate spinner** Naish, J. (2009, August 11). Is multi-tasking bad for your brain? Experts reveal the hidden perils of juggling too many jobs. *Daily Mail.*

97 **more people have cell phones than have toilets** Six billion of the world's 7 billion people have cell phones, while only 4.5 billion have toilets, according to a United Nations report. Worstall, T. (2013, March 23). More people have mobile phones than toilets. *Forbes.*

97 **reduce your effective IQ by 10 points** Naish, J. (2009, August 11). Is multi-tasking bad for your brain? Experts reveal the hidden perils of juggling too many jobs. *Daily Mail.*

and, Wilson, G. (2010). Infomania experiment for Hewlett-Packard. Retrieved from www.drglennwilson.com

97–98 **the information goes into the hippocampus** Foerde, K., Knowlton, B. J., & Poldrack, R. A. (2006). Modulation of competing memory systems by distraction. *Proceedings of the National Academy of Sciences, 103*(31), 11778–11783.

and, Cohen, N. J., & Eichenbaum, H. (1993). *Memory, amnesia, and the hippocampal system.* Cambridge, MA: MIT Press.

98 **"People can't do [multitasking] very well . . ."** As quoted in Naish, J. (2009, August 11). Is multi-tasking bad for your brain? Experts reveal the hidden perils of juggling too many jobs. *Daily Mail.*

98 **good at this deluding business** See, e.g., Gazzaniga, M. (2008). *Human: The science behind what makes us unique.* New York, NY: HarperCollins.

98 **the metabolic costs of switching itself** Task switching causes large changes in the blood oxygen level-dependent (BOLD) signal in the prefrontal cortex and the anterior cingulate gyrus, as well as other brain areas, and these changes in oxygenation level almost always entail glucose being metabolized.

98 **We've literally depleted the nutrients in our brain** The fatigue that we observe in task-switching might also have a lot to do with the tasks we're switching between—we typically switch between two tasks that are boring (almost by definition, we tend to stay on a task when we find it absorbing). M. Posner, personal communication, April 16, 2014.

98 **repeated task switching leads to anxiety** Nash, J. (2009, August 11). Is multi-tasking bad for your brain? Experts reveal the hidden perils of juggling too many jobs. *Daily Mail.*

98 **can lead to aggressive and impulsive behaviors** Naish, J. (2009, August 11). Is multi-tasking bad for your brain? Experts reveal the hidden perils of juggling too many jobs. *Daily Mail.*

98 **staying on task is controlled by the anterior cingulate and the striatum** Tang, Y-Y., Rothbart, M. K., & Posner, M. I. (2012). Neural correlates of establishing, maintaining, and switching brain states. *Trends in Cognitive Sciences, 16*(6), 330–337.

98 **reduces the brain's need for glucose** Haier, R. J., Siegel, B. V., MacLachlan, A., Soderling, E., Lottenberg, S., & Buchsbaum, M.S. (1992). Regional glucose metabolic changes after learning a complex visuospatial/motor task: A positron emission tomographic study. *Brain Research, 570*(1–2), 134–143.

101 **Crisis hotlines** Kaufman, L. (2014, February 5). In texting era, crisis hotlines put help at youths' fingertips. *The New York Times*, p. A1.

101 **The rats just pressed the lever** Olds, J. (1956). Pleasure centers in the brain. *Scientific American, 195*(4), 105–116.

and, Olds, J., & Milner, P. (1954). Positive reinforcement produced by electrical stimulation of septal area and other regions of rat brain. *Journal of Comparative Physiological Psychology, 47*(6), 419–427.

101 **stopped only by his going into cardiac arrest** Associated Press (2007, September 18). Chinese man drops dead after 3-Day gaming binge.

and, Demick, B. (2005, August 29). Gamers rack up losses. *The Los Angeles Times.*

103 **3 million Adobe customers** Dove, J. (2013, October 3). Adobe reports massive security breach. *PCWorld.*

103 **2 million Vodafone customers** Thomas, D. (2013, September 12). Hackers steal bank details of 2m Vodafone customers in Germany. *Financial Times.*

103 **160 million Visa** Yadron, D., & Barrett, D. (2013, October 3). Jury indicts 13 cyber-attack suspects. *The Wall Street Journal*, p. A2.

104 **A clever formula for generating passwords** Manjoo, F. (2009, July 24). Fix your terrible, insecure passwords in five minutes. *Slate.*

105 **biometric markers** Nahamoo, D. (2011, December 19). IBM 5 in 5: Biometric data will be key to personal security [Web log message]. *IBM Research.* Retrieved from http://ibmresearchnews.blogspot.com/2011/12/ibm-5-in-5-biometric-data-will-be-key.html

106 **Daniel Kahneman recommends taking a proactive approach** Kahneman, D., personal communication. July 11, 2013.

See also, Klein, G. (2003). *The power of intuition: How to use your gut feelings to make better decisions at work.* New York, NY: Crown, pp. 98–101.

and, Kahneman, D. (2011). *Thinking, fast and slow.* New York, NY: Farrar, Straus and Giroux.

107 **USB key with all your medical records** Scan copies of your medical records, history of lab tests, any X-rays that you have, etc., and put them in a PDF file on the USB key. The first page of the PDF document should have vital information, including your name, address, birth date, blood type if you know it, and any drug allergies (this is very important!).

This way, if you are ever in an accident or need emergency medical attention—or if you are far away from home and need routine medical attention—your attending physician doesn't need to wait to get records from your family doctor. USB keys are inexpensive, and PDF files are readable virtually anywhere you go. All manner of misdiagnoses, missteps, and mistakes can be avoided if this information is readily available. To make sure that it's not missed, include a piece of paper in your wallet or purse, next to your health insurance card, that says *All my medical records are on a USB key that I carry with me at all times.*

107 **going through each combination** Wynn, S., personal communication. May 5, 2012, Las Vegas, NV.

110 **trait found even in many lower species** Levitin, D. J. (2008). *The world in six songs: How the musical brain created human nature.* New York, NY: Dutton.

CHAPTER 4

113 **July 16, 2013** Hu, W., & Goodman, J. D. (2013, July 18). Wake-up call for New Yorkers as police seek abducted boy. *The New York Times,* p. A1.

and, Shallwani, P. (2013, July 17). Missing-child hunt sets off wake-up call. *The Wall Street Journal,* p. A19.

113 **The alert, which showed the license plate** "Amber Alert" refers to the Child Abduction Alert System in the United States, named in memory of Amber Hagerman, a nine-year-old abducted and murdered in Texas in 1996.

114 **DARPA offered $40,000** Markoff, J. (2009, December 1). Looking for balloons and insights to online behavior. *The New York Times,* p. D2.

114 **the first computer network, ARPANET** Leiner, B. M., Cerf, V. G., Clark, D. D., Kahn, R. E., Kleinrock, L., Lynch, D. C., . . . Wolff, S. (2009). A brief history of the Internet. *ACM SIGCOMM Computer Communication Review, 39*(5), 22–31.

and, Computer History Museum. (2004). Internet history. Retrieved from http://www.computerhistory.org/internet_history

115 **experts pointed out** Markoff, J. (2010, April 13). New force behind agency of wonder. *The New York Times,* p. D1.

115 **solving the *Where's Waldo?* problem** Buchenroth, T., Garber, F., Gowker, B., & Hartzell, S. (2012, July). Automatic object recognition applied to Where's Waldo? *Aerospace and Electronics Conference (NAECON), 2012 IEEE National,* 117–120.

and, Garg, R., Seitz, S. M., Ramanan, D., & Snavely, N. (2011, June). Where's Waldo: Matching people in images of crowds. *Proceedings of the 24th IEEE Conference on Computer Vision and Pattern Recognition,* 1793–1800.

116 **Wikipedia is an example of crowdsourcing** Ayers, P., Matthews, C., & Yates, B. (2008). *How Wikipedia works: And how you can be a part of it.* San Francisco, CA: No Starch Press, p. 514.

116 **More than 4.5 million people** Kickstarter, Inc. (2014). Seven things to know about Kickstarter. Retrieved from http://www.kickstarter.com

117 **the group average comes** Surowiecki, J. (2005). *The wisdom of crowds.* New York, NY: Penguin.

and, Treynor, J. L. (1987). Market efficiency and the bean jar experiment. *Financial Analysts Journal, 43*(3), 50–53.

118 **the cancer is now in remission** Iaconesi, S. (2012). TED (Producer). (2013). *Why I open-sourced cures to my cancer: Salvatore Iaconesi at TEDGlobal 2013* [Video file]. Available from http://blog.ted.com

and, TEDMED. (2013, July 17). *Salvatore Iaconesi at TEDMED 2013* [Video file]. Retrieved from http://www.youtube.com

and, TEDx Talks. (2012, November 4). *My open source cure: Salvatore Iaconesi at TEDx transmedia* [Video file]. Retrieved from http://www.youtube.com

118 **distorted words that are often displayed on websites** Google. (2014). Digitalizing books one word at a time. Retrieved from http://www.google.com/recaptcha/learnmore

and, von Ahn, L., Maurer, B., McMillen, C., Abraham, D., & Blum, M. (2008). reCAPTCHA: Human-based character recognition via web security measures. *Science, 321*(5895), 1465–1468.

118 **reCAPTCHAs are so-named for recycling—because they recycle human processing power** von Ahn, Luis (co-inventor of reCAPTCHA), personal communication. April 15, 2014, e-mail.

118 **reCAPTCHAs act as sentries** Google. (2014). Digitalizing books one word at a time. Retrieved from http://www.google.com/recaptcha/learnmore

and, von Ahn, L., Maurer, B., McMillen, C., Abraham, D., & Blum, M. (2008). reCAPTCHA: Human-based character recognition via web security measures. *Science, 321*(5895), 1465–1468.

118 **actual book being scanned by Google** This reCaptcha figure has been redrawn to match one in actual use by Google Books, and to highlight some of the difficulties entailed in machine vision.

119 **connections to the temporoparietal junction** Decety, J., & Lamm, C. (2007). The role of the right temporoparietal junction in social interaction: How low-level computational processes contribute to meta-cognition. *The Neuroscientist, 13*(6), 580–593.

120 **"When there's easy agreement . . ."** Gopnik, A. (2014, February 14). The information: How the internet gets inside us. *The New Yorker,* 123–128.

120 **Too Complex to Organize?** Isolated sentences here and there in this section of Chapter 4 first appeared in my review of *Mindwise* in *The Wall Street Journal.* Levitin, D. J. (2014, February 22–23). Deceivers and believers: We are surprisingly terrible at divining what's going on in someone else's mind [Review of the book *Mindwise* by N. Epley]. *The Wall Street Journal,* pp. C5, C6.

121 **twenty family members** Perry, B. D., & Szalavitz, M. (2006). *The boy who was raised as a dog and other stories from a child psychiatrist's notebook: What traumatized children can teach us about loss, love and healing.* New York, NY: Basic Books.

121 **You know a couple hundred people** Perry, B. D., & Szalavitz, M. (2006). *The boy who was raised as a dog and other stories from a child psychiatrist's notebook: What traumatized children can teach us about loss, love and healing.* New York, NY: Basic Books.

121 **By 1850, the average family group** This is nearly a direct quote from Perry, B. D., & Szalavitz, M. (2006). *The boy who was raised as a dog and other stories from a child psychiatrist's notebook: What traumatized children can teach us about loss, love and healing.* New York, NY: Basic Books.

121 **50% of Americans live alone. Fewer of us are having children** Klinenberg, E. (2012, February 12). America: Single, and loving it. *The New York Times,* p. ST10.

121 **It was common practice** Bryson, B. (2010). *At home: A short history of private life.* New York, NY: Doubleday, p. 323.

121 **"It was entirely usual . . ."** Bryson, B. (2010). *At home: A short history of private life.* New York, NY: Doubleday.

122 **1,700 people a day** Statistic Brain. (2013, December 11). Walmart company statistics. Retrieved from http://www.statisticbrain.com

122 **"When I meet someone new, I make notes . . ."** Shapiro, R., personal communication. May 6, 2012, Las Vegas, NV.

122 **"Suppose I met Dr. Ware . . ."** Gold, D., personal communication. November 26, 2013, Montreal, QC.

123 **Craig Kallman is the chairman** Kallman, C., personal communication. September 20, 2013, New York, NY.

125 **arcane bits of information** Wegner, D. M. (1987). Transactive memory: A contemporary analysis of the group mind. In B. Mullen & G. R. Goethals (Eds.), *Theories of group behavior* (pp. 185–208). New York, NY: Springer New York, p. 189.

125 **technically known as *transactive memory*** Wegner, D. M., Giuliano, T., & Hertel, P. (1985). Cognitive interdependence in close relationships. In W. J. Ickes (Ed.), *Compatible and incompatible relationships* (pp. 253–276). New York, NY: Springer-Verlag.

125 **transactive memory strategies** Wegner, D. M. (1987). Transactive memory: A contemporary analysis of the group mind. In B. Mullen & G. R. Goethals (Eds.), *Theories of group behavior* (pp. 185–208). New York, NY: Springer New York, p. 194.

125 **primate heritage** Baumeister, R. F., & Leary, M. R. (1995). The need to belong: Desire for interpersonal attachments as a fundamental human motivation. *Psychological Bulletin, 117*(3), 497–529, p. 497.

126 **being alone for too long causes neurochemical changes** Grassian, S. (1983). Psychopathological effects of solitary confinement. *American Journal of Psychiatry, 140*(11), 1450–1454.

and, Posey, T. B., & Losch, M. E. (1983). Auditory hallucinations of hearing voices in 375 normal subjects. *Imagination, Cognition and Personality, 3*(2), 99–113.

and, Smith, P. S. (2006). The effects of solitary confinement on prison inmates: A brief history and review of the literature. *Crime and Justice, 34*(1), 441–528.

126 **Social isolation is also a risk factor** Epley, N., Akalis, S., Waytz, A., & Cacioppo, J. T. (2008). Creating social connection through inferential reproduction: Loneliness and perceived agency in gadgets, gods, and greyhounds. *Psychological Science, 19*(2), 114–120.

126 **And although many of us *think*** Klinenberg, E. (2012, February 12). America: Single, and loving it. *The New York Times*, p. ST10.

126 **were outgoing or shy, open or reserved** Epley, N. (2014). *Mindwise: How we understand what others think, believe, feel, and want.* New York, NY: Alfred A. Knopf, pp. 58–59.

126 **comfort in belonging** The amygdala used to be called the fight-or-flight fear center of the brain. We now know it isn't just for fear, but rather, for keeping track of salient emotional events of all kinds—the brain's emotional learning and memory consolidation center. Dębiec, J., Doyère, V., Nader, K., & LeDoux, J. E. (2006). Directly reactivated, but not indirectly reactivated, memories undergo reconsolidation in the amygdala. *Proceedings of the National Academy of Sciences, 103*(9), 3428–3433.

and, McGaugh, J. L. (2004). The amygdala modulates the consolidation of memories of emotionally arousing experiences. *Annual Review of Neuroscience, 27*(1), 1–28.

and, Phelps, E. A. (2006). Emotion and cognition: Insights from studies of the human amygdala. *Annual Review of Psychology, 57*(1), 27–53.

126 **surpassing even Google** Cashmore, P. (2006, July 11). MySpace, America's number one. Retrieved from http://www.mashable.com

and, Olsen, S. (2006, July 13) Google's antisocial downside. Retrieved from http://news.cnet.com

126 **1.2 billion regular monthly users** Kiss, J. (2014, February 4). Facebook's 10th birthday: from college dorm to 1.23 billion users. *The Guardian.*

127 **replacement for in-person contact** Marche, S. (2012, May). Is Facebook making us lonely? *The Atlantic.*

and, Turkle, S. (2011). *Alone together: Why we expect more from technology and less from each other.* New York, NY: Basic Books.

127 **cost of all of our electronic connectedness** Fredrickson, B. (2013, March 23). Your phone vs. your heart. *The New York Times*, p. SR14.

127 **having friends to do things with** Buhrmester, D., & Furman, W. (1987). The development of companionship and intimacy. *Child Development, 58*(4), 1101–1113.

127 **assistance when needed; a relationship** George, T. P., & Hartmann, D. P. (1996). Friendship networks of unpopular, average, and popular children. *Child Development, 67*(5), 2301–2316.

and, Hartup, W. W., & Stevens, N. (1997). Friendships and adaptation in the life course. *Psychological Bulletin, 121*(3), 355–370.

127 **encouragement, confidences, and loyalty** Berndt, T. J. (2002). Friendship quality and social development. *Current Directions in Psychological Science, 11*(1), 7–10.

127 **personal thoughts, joys, hurts, and fears of being hurt** Buhrmester, D., & Furman, W. (1987). The development of companionship and intimacy. *Child Development, 58*(4), 1101–1113.

and, L'Abate, L. (2013). [Review of the book *The science of intimate relationships* by Garth Fletcher, Jeffry A. Simpson, Lorne Campbell, and Nikola C. Overall]. *The American Journal of Family Therapy, 41*(5), 456.

See also, Brehm, S. S. (1992). *Intimate relationships: The McGraw-Hill series in social psychology* (2nd ed.). New York, NY: McGraw-Hill.

127 **creating shared meaning** Weingarten, K. (1991). The discourses of intimacy: Adding a social constructionist and feminist view. *Family Process, 30*(3), 285–305.

and, Wynne, L. C. (1984). The epigenesis of relational systems: A model for understanding family development. *Family Process, 23*(3), 297–318.

128 **take a clear stand on emotionally charged issues** This is a close paraphrase of Lerner, H. G. (1989). *The dance of intimacy: A woman's guide to courageous acts of change in key relationships.* New York, NY: Harper Paperbacks, p. 3.

I first encountered it in, Weingarten, K. (1991). The discourses of intimacy: Adding a social constructionist and feminist view. *Family Process, 30*(3), 285–305.

128 **other cultures don't view intimacy as a necessity** Hatfield, E., & Rapson, R. I. (1993). *Love, sex & intimacy: Their psychology, biology & history.* New York, NY: HarperCollins.

and, Hook, M. K., Gerstein, L. H., Detterich, L., & Gridley, B. (2003). How close are we? Measuring intimacy and examining gender differences. *Journal of Counseling & Development, 81*(4), 462–472.

128 **Women are more focused . . . on commitment and continuity** Luepnitz, D.A. (1988). *The family interpreted: Feminist theory in clinical practice.* New York, NY: Basic Books.

128 **men on sexual and physical closeness** Ridley, J. (1993). Gender and couples: Do women and men seek different kinds of intimacy? *Sexual and Marital Therapy* 8(3), 243–253.

128 **Intimacy, love, and passion . . . belong to completely different, multidimensional constructs** Acker, M., & Davis, M. H. (1992). Intimacy, passion and commitment in adult romantic relationships: A test of the triangular theory of love. *Journal of Social and Personal Relationships, 9*(1), 21–50.

and, Graham, J. M. (2011). Measuring love in romantic relationships: A meta-analysis. *Journal of Social and Personal Relationships, 28*(6), 748–771.

and, Sternberg, R. J. (1986). A triangular theory of love. *Psychological Review, 93*(2), 119.

128 **Just like our chimpanzee cousins** Hare, B., Call, J., & Tomasello, M. (2006). Chimpanzees deceive a human competitor by hiding. *Cognition, 101*(3), 495–514.

and, McNally, L., & Jackson, A. L. (2013). Cooperation creates selection for tactical deception. *Proceedings of the Royal Society B: Biological Sciences, 280*(1762).

128 **Modern intimacy is much more varied** Amirmoayed, A. (2012). [Review of the book *Intimacy and power: The dynamics of personal relationships in modern society* by D. Layder]. *Sociology, 46*(3), 566–568.

128 **intimacy was rarely regarded with the importance** Wynne, L. C., & Wynne, A. R. (1986). The quest for intimacy. *Journal of Marital and Family Therapy, 12*(4), 383–394.

128 **99% of our history** Bryson, B. (2010). *At home: A short history of private life.* New York, NY: Doubleday, p. 323.

128–29 **People in a relationship experience better health** Cohen, S., Frank, E., Doyle, W. J., Skoner, D. P., Rabin, B. S., & Gwaltney Jr., J. M., (1998). Types of stressors that increase susceptibility to the common cold in healthy adults. *Health Psychology, 17*(3), 214–223.

and, Hampson, S. E., Goldberg, L. R., Vogt, T. M., & Dubanoski, J. P. (2006). Forty years on: Teachers' assessments of children's personality traits predict self-reported health behaviors and outcomes at midlife. *Health Psychology, 25*(1), 57–64.

129 **recover from illnesses more quickly** Kiecolt-Glaser, J. K., Loving, T. J., Stowell, J. R., Malarkey, W. B., Lemeshow, S., Dickinson, S. L., & Glaser, R. (2005). Hostile marital interactions, proinflammatory cytokine production, and wound healing. *Archives of General Psychiatry, 62*(12), 1377–1384.

129 **live longer** Gallo, L. C., Troxel, W. M., Matthews, K. A., & Kuller, L. H. (2003). Marital status and quality in middle-aged women: Associations with levels and trajectories of cardiovascular risk factors. *Health Psychology, 22*(5), 453–463.
and, Holt-Lunstad, J., Smith, T. B., & Layton, J. B. (2010). Social relationships and mortality risk: A meta-analytic review. *PLoS Medicine, 7*(7), e1000316.

129 **the presence of a satisfying intimate relationship** Diener, E., & Seligman, M. E. P. (2002). Very happy people. *Psychological Science, 13*(1), 81–84. In this paragraph, I'm closely paraphrasing the excellent article by Finkel, et al. Finkel, E. J., Eastwick, P. W., Karney, B. R., Reis, H. T., & Sprecher, S. (2012). Online dating: A critical analysis from the perspective of psychological science. *Psychological Science in the Public Interest, 13*(1), 3–66.

129 **to be agreeable is to be cooperative** Knack, J. M., Jacquot, C., Jensen-Campbell, L. A., & Malcolm, K. T. (2013). Importance of having agreeable friends in adolescence (especially when you are not). *Journal of Applied Social Psychology, 43*(12), 2401–2413.

129 **show up early in childhood** Hampson, S. E., & Goldberg, L. R. (2006). A first large cohort study of personality trait stability over the 40 years between elementary school and midlife. *Journal of Personality and Social Psychology, 91*(4), 763–779.
and, Rothbart, M. K., & Ahadi, S. A. (1994). Temperament and the development of personality. *Journal of Abnormal Psychology, 103*(1), 55–66.
and, Shiner, R. L., Masten, A. S., & Roberts, J. M. (2003). Childhood personality foreshadows adult personality and life outcomes two decades later. *Journal of Personality, 71*(6), 1145–1170.

129 **undesirable emotions such as anger and frustration** Ahadi, S. A., & Rothbart, M. K. (1994). Temperament, development and the Big Five. In C. F. Halverson Jr., G. A. Kohnstamm, & R. P. Martin (Eds.), *The developing structure of temperament and personality from infancy to adulthood* (pp. 189–207). Hillsdale, NJ: Lawrence Erlbaum Associates.

129 **being an agreeable person is a tremendous advantage** Knack, J. M., Jacquot, C., Jensen-Campbell, L. A., & Malcolm, K. T. (2013). Importance of having agreeable friends in adolescence (especially when you are not). *Journal of Applied Social Psychology, 43*(12), 2401–2413.

129 **guided by what our friends are doing** Knack, J. M., Jacquot, C., Jensen-Campbell, L. A., & Malcolm, K. T. (2013). Importance of having agreeable friends in adolescence (especially when you are not). *Journal of Applied Social Psychology, 43*(12), 2401–2413.

129 **a sign of maturity** Kohlberg, L. (1971). Stages of moral development. In C. Beck & E. Sullivan (Eds.), *Moral education* (pp. 23–92). Toronto, ON: University of Toronto Press.

129 **having a *friend* who is agreeable** Boulton, M. J., Trueman, M., Chau, C., Whitehead, C., & Amatya, K. (1999). Concurrent and longitudinal links between friendship and peer victimization: Implications for befriending interventions. *Journal of Adolescence, 22*(4), 461–466.

129 **girls benefit more than boys** Schmidt, M. E., & Bagwell, C. L. (2007). The protective role of friendships in overtly and relationally victimized boys and girls. *Merrill-Palmer Quarterly, 53*(3), 439–460.

129 **strong sorting patterns** Hitsch, G. J., Hortaçsu, A., & Ariely, D. (2010). What makes you click?—Mate preferences in online dating. *Quantitative Marketing and Economics, 8*(4), 393–427.

130 **newspapers in the early 1700s** Cocks, H. G. (2009). *Classified: The secret history of the personal column*. London, UK: Random House.

and, Orr, A. (2004). *Meeting, mating, and cheating: Sex, love, and the new world of online dating*. Upper Saddle River, NJ: Reuters Prentice Hall.

130 **providing a list of attributes or qualities** Orr, A. (2004). *Meeting, mating, and cheating: Sex, love, and the new world of online dating*. Upper Saddle River, NJ: Reuters Prentice Hall.

130 **one-third of all marriages in America** Cacioppo, J. T., Cacioppo, S., Gonzaga, G. C., Ogburn, E. L., & VanderWeele, T. J. (2013). Marital satisfaction and break-ups differ across on-line and off-line meeting venues. *Proceedings of the National Academy of Sciences, 110*(25), 10135–10140.

130 **a fraction of that in the decade before** Fewer than one percent of Americans met romantic partners through personal ads in the 1980s and early 1990s according to national surveys. Laumann, E. O., Gagnon, J. H., Michael, R. T., & Michaels, S. (1994). *The social organization of sexuality: Sexual practices in the United States*. Chicago, IL: University of Chicago Press.

and, Simenauer, J., & Carroll, D. (1982). *Singles: The new Americans*. New York, NY: Simon & Schuster.

130 **Half of these marriages** Cacioppo, J. T., Cacioppo, S., Gonzaga, G. C., Ogburn, E. L., & VanderWeele, T. J. (2013). Marital satisfaction and break-ups differ across on-line and off-line meeting venues. *Proceedings of the National Academy of Sciences, 110*(25), 10135–10140.

130 **In 1995, it was still so rare** Randall, D., Hamilton, C., & Kerr, E. (2013, June 9). We just clicked: More and more couples are meeting online and marrying. *The Independent*.

130 **around 1999–2000** Finkel, E. J., Eastwick, P. W., Karney, B. R., Reis, H. T., & Sprecher, S. (2012). Online dating: A critical analysis from the perspective of psychological science. *Psychological Science in the Public Interest, 13*(1), 3–66.

130 **twenty years after the introduction of online dating** People born before 1960 didn't typically encounter the Internet until they were well into adulthood, and many treated it skeptically at first, based on stories of cybercrime, identity theft, and other problems that still exist. When problems are attached to a new and unfamiliar medium, people are less likely to use it. For people born after 1990, the Internet was so well established that they regarded its hazards as they would hazards of any other

established medium. We know that checking accounts and credit cards are subject to identity theft but they've been around a long time and we accept the risks. If a new alternative emerged—as PayPal did in 1998—the low cost of shifting to it is offset by the perception that it is at least as risky as the status quo. But if PayPal was woven into the fabric of your very first Internet interactions, and presented as simply an alternative to other preexisting financial instruments, the barriers for adopting it are lower.

130 **heavy Internet users who are introverted** Kraut, R., Patterson, M., Lundmark, V., Kiesler, S., Mukophadhyay, T., & Scherlis, W. (1998). Internet paradox: A social technology that reduces social involvement and psychological well-being? *American Psychologist, 53*(9), 1017–1031.

and, Stevens, S. B., & Morris, T. L. (2007). College dating and social anxiety: Using the Internet as a means of connecting to others. *Cyberpsychology & Behavior, 10*(5), 680–688.

131 **decline in empathy among college students** This is a direct quote from Gopnik, A. (2014, February 14). The information: How the internet gets inside us. *The New Yorker,* 123–128.

He goes on to cite Turkle, S. (2011). *Alone together: Why we expect more from technology and less from each other.* New York, NY: Basic Books.

131 **far less likely to say that it is valuable** This is a direct quote from Turkle, S. (2011). *Alone together: Why we expect more from technology and less from each other.* New York, NY: Basic Books.

131 **access, communication, matching, and asynchrony** Finkel, E. J., Eastwick, P. W., Karney, B. R., Reis, H. T., & Sprecher, S. (2012). Online dating: A critical analysis from the perspective of psychological science. *Psychological Science in the Public Interest, 13*(1), 3–66.

131 **The field of eligibles** Kerckhoff, A. C. (1964). Patterns of homogamy and the field of eligibles. *Social Forces, 42*(3), 289–297.

131 **access to millions of profiles** Finkel, E. J., Eastwick, P. W., Karney, B. R., Reis, H. T., & Sprecher, S. (2012). Online dating: A critical analysis from the perspective of psychological science. *Psychological Science in the Public Interest, 13*(1), 3–66.

131 **there is a disconnect** Finkel, E. J., Eastwick, P. W., Karney, B. R., Reis, H. T., & Sprecher, S. (2012). Online dating: A critical analysis from the perspective of psychological science. *Psychological Science in the Public Interest, 13*(1), 3–66.

131 **"can elicit an evaluative, assessment-oriented mind-set . . ."** Finkel, E. J., Eastwick, P. W., Karney, B. R., Reis, H. T., & Sprecher, S. (2012). Online dating: A critical analysis from the perspective of psychological science. *Psychological Science in the Public Interest, 13*(1), 3–66.

132 **cognitive and decision overload** Finkel, E. J., Eastwick, P. W., Karney, B. R., Reis, H. T., & Sprecher, S. (2012). Online dating: A critical analysis from the perspective of psychological science. *Psychological Science in the Public Interest, 13*(1), 3–66.

and, Wilson, T. D., & Schooler, J. W. (1991). Thinking too much: Introspection can reduce the quality of preferences and decisions. *Journal of Personality and Social Psychology, 60*(2), 181–192.

and, Wu, P-L., & Chiou, W-B. (2009). More options lead to more searching and worse choices in finding partners for romantic relationships online: An experimental study. *CyberPsychology, 12*(3), 315–318.

132 **when cognitive resources are low** Martin, L. L., Seta, J. J., & Crelia, R. A. (1990). Assimilation and contrast as a function of people's willingness and ability to expend effort in forming an impression. *Journal of Personality and Social Psychology, 59*(1), 27–37.

There's also a mathematical principle at work: The temptation to search in the hope of finding a better match causes the online dater to read profiles that are increasingly far afield from the good matches, thereby reducing the average quality of matches in the selection set. Decision overload sets in, and daters make poorer choices as they become less selective.

132 **availability of attractive alternatives** Lydon, J. E. (2010). How to forego forbidden fruit: The regulation of attractive alternatives as a commitment mechanism. *Social and Personality Psychology Compass, 4*(8), 635–644.

132 **81% lie** Toma, C. L., Hancock, J. T., & Ellison, N. B. (2008). Separating fact from fiction: An examination of deceptive self-presentation in online dating profiles. *Personality and Social Psychology Bulletin, 34*(8), 1023–1036.

132 **age discrepancies of ten years were observed** Toma, C. L., Hancock, J. T., & Ellison, N. B. (2008). Separating fact from fiction: An examination of deceptive self-presentation in online dating profiles. *Personality and Social Psychology Bulletin, 34*(8), 1023–1036.

133 **they're Republicans** Toma, C. L., Hancock, J. T., & Ellison, N. B. (2008). Separating fact from fiction: An examination of deceptive self-presentation in online dating profiles. *Personality and Social Psychology Bulletin, 34*(8), 1023–1036.

133 **underlying tension** Rosenbloom, S. (2011, November 12). Love, lies and what they learned. *The New York Times*, p. ST1.

133 **22% lower risk** Cacioppo, J. T., Cacioppo, S., Gonzaga, G. C., Ogburn, E. L., & VanderWeele, T. J. (2013). Marital satisfaction and break-ups differ across on-line and off-line meeting venues. *Proceedings of the National Academy of Sciences, 110*(25), 10135–10140.

133 **how well do we know** Epley, N. (2014). *Mindwise: How we understand what others think, believe, feel, and want.* New York, NY: Alfred A. Knopf.

and, Eyal, T., & Epley, N. (2010). How to seem telepathic: Enabling mind reading by matching construal. *Psychological Science, 21*(5), 700–705.

and, Kenny, D. A. (1994). *Interpersonal perception: A social relations analysis.* New York, NY: The Guilford Press, p. 159.

134 ***thought* they were getting *eight* out of ten** Epley, N. (2014). *Mindwise: How we understand what others think, believe, feel, and want.* New York, NY: Alfred A. Knopf, pp. 10–12.

134 **they were accurate in detecting liars 70% of the time** This is a direct quote from Epley, N. (2014). *Mindwise: How we understand what others think, believe, feel, and want.* New York, NY: Alfred A. Knopf, p. 12.

See also, Swann, W. B., Silvera, D. H., & Proske, C. U. (1995). On "knowing your partner": Dangerous illusions in the age of AIDS? *Personal Relationships, 2*(3), 173–186.

134 **We are very bad at telling if someone is lying** Bond Jr., C. F., & DePaulo, B. M. (2006). Accuracy of deception judgments. *Personality and Social Psychology Review, 10*(3), 314–234.

134 **The opposite misreading of intentions** This paragraph quotes nearly directly from Epley, N. (2014). *Mindwise: How we understand what others think, believe, feel, and want.* New York, NY: Alfred A. Knopf.

134 **Deepwater Horizon oil rig** Urbina, I. (2010, July 22). Workers on doomed rig voiced safety concerns. *The New York Times,* p. A1.

134 **malpractice lawsuits were cut in half** Kachalia, A., Kaufman, S. R., Boothman, R., Anderson, S., Welch, K., Saint, S., & Rogers, M. A. M. (2010). Liability claims and costs before and after implementation of a medical error disclosure program. *Annals of Internal Medicine, 153*(4), 213–221.

134 **The biggest impediment to resolution** This is a direct quote from Epley, N. (2014). *Mindwise: How we understand what others think, believe, feel, and want.* New York, NY: Alfred A. Knopf, p. 185.

See also, Chen, P. W. (2010, August 19). When doctors admit their mistakes. *The New York Times.*

and, Kachalia, A., Kaufman, S. R., Boothman, R., Anderson, S., Welch, K., Saint, S., & Rogers, M. A. M. (2010). Liability claims and costs before and after implementation of a medical error disclosure program. *Annals of Internal Medicine, 153*(4), 213–221.

134 **When we're confronted with the human element** This is a paraphrase from Epley of a quote from Richard Boothman, Chief Risk Officer for the University of Michigan hospital that participated in the disclosure study. Epley, N. (2014). *Mindwise: How we understand what others think, believe, feel, and want.* New York, NY: Alfred A. Knopf, p. 185.

135 **little white lies** Camden, C., Motley, M. T., & Wilson, A. (1984). White lies in interpersonal communication: A taxonomy and preliminary investigation of social motivations. *Western Journal of Speech Communication, 48*(4), 309–325.

and, Erat, S., & Gneezy, U. (2012). White lies. *Management Science, 58*(4), 723–733.

and, Scott, G. G. (2006). *The truth about lying: Why and how we all do it and what to do about it.* Lincoln, NE: iUniverse.

and, Talwar, V., Murphy, S. M., & Lee, K. (2007). White lie-telling in children for politeness purposes. *International Journal of Behavioral Development, 31*(1), 1–11.

135 **Paul Grice called these *implicatures*** Grice, H. P. (1975). Logic and conversation. In P. Cole and J. Morgan (Eds.), *Syntax and semantics* (Vol. 3). New York, NY: Academic Press.

also available in, Levitin, D. J. (2010). *Foundations of cognitive psychology: Core readings* (2nd ed.). Boston, MA: Allyn & Bacon.

136 **in which the speaker utters** Searle, J. R. (1991). Indirect speech acts. In S. Davis (Ed.), *Pragmatics: A reader* (pp. 265-277). New York, NY: Oxford University Press.

137 **social rejection causes activation** Eisenberger, N. I., & Lieberman, M. D. (2004). Why rejection hurts: A common neural alarm system for physical and social pain. *Trends in Cognitive Sciences, 8*(7), 294–300.

and, Eisenberger, N. I., Lieberman, M. D., & Williams, K. D. (2003). Does rejection hurt? An fMRI study of social exclusion. *Science, 302*(5643), 290–292.

and, MacDonald, G., & Leary, M. R. (2005). Why does social exclusion hurt? The relationship between social and physical pain. *Psychological Bulletin, 131*(2), 202–223, p. 202.

137 **people's experience of social pain** DeWall, C. N., MacDonald, G., Webster, G. D., Masten, C. L., Baumeister, R. F., Powell, C., . . . Eisenberger, N. I. (2010). Acetaminophen reduces social pain: Behavioral and neural evidence. *Psychological Science, 21*(7), 931–937.

138 **if we're lucky, is one hundred percent clear** Searle, J. R. (1965). What is a speech act? In R. J Stainton (Ed.), *Perspectives in the philosophy of language: A concise anthology, 2000* (pp. 253–268). Peterborough, ON: Broadview Press. I'm paraphrasing and simplifying the story liberally; Searle's own account is much better and funnier.

138 **information can become updated through social contracts** Turner, C. (1987). Organizing information: Principles and practice. London, UK: Clive Bingley.

138 **we now know that Ernie's a liar** Sesame Street (1970, April 23). Ernie eats cake. [Television series episode]. In Sesame Street (Season 1, Episode 119). New York, NY: Children's Television Workshop.

138 **can't be trusted** Turner, C. (1987). *Organizing information: Principles and practice.* London, UK: Clive Bingley.

138 **Pluto is no longer a planet** National Aeronautics and Space Administration. (n.d.). Pluto: Overview. Retrieved from https://solarsystem.nasa.gov/planets/profile.cfm?Object=Pluto

139 **conversations are a cooperative undertaking** Shannon, B. (1987). Cooperativeness and implicature—A reversed perspective. *New Ideas in Psychology, 5*(2), 289–293.

142 **pretense, sarcasm, or any nonliteral speech** Anderson, J. S., Lange, N., Froehlich, A., DuBray, M. B., Druzgal, T. J., Froimowitz, M. P., . . . Lainhart, J. E. (2010). Decreased left posterior insular activity during auditory language in autism. *American Journal of Neuroradiology, 31*(1), 131–139.

and, Harris, G. J., Chabris, C. F., Clark, J., Urban, T., Aharon, I., Steele, S., . . . Tager-Flusberg, H. (2006). Brain activation during semantic processing in autism spectrum disorders via functional magnetic resonance imaging. *Brain and Cognition, 61*(1), 54–68.

and, Wang, A. T., Lee, S. S., Sigman, M., & Dapretto, M. (2006). Neural basis of irony comprehension in children with autism: The role of prosody and context. *Brain, 129*(4), 932–943.

142 **an orgasm, oxytocin is released** Blaicher, W., Gruber, D., Bieglmayer, C., Blaicher, A. M., Knogler, W., & Huber, J. C. (1999). The role of oxytocin in relation to female sexual arousal. *Gynecologic and Obstetric Investigation, 47*(2), 125–126.

and, Carmichael, M. S., Humbert, R., Dixen, J., Palmisano, G., Greenleaf, W., & Davidson, J. M. (1987). Plasma oxytocin increases in the human sexual response. *Journal of Clinical Endocrinology & Metabolism, 64*(1), 27–31.

See also, Diamond, L. M. (2004). Emerging perspectives on distinctions between romantic love and sexual desire. *Current Directions in Psychological Science, 13*(3), 116–119.

and, Young, L. J., & Wang, Z. (2004). The neurobiology of pair bonding. *Nature Neuroscience, 7*(10), 1048–1054.

142 **viewed while oxytocin was in their system** Most of this section is based on information in Chanda, M. L., & Levitin, D. J. (2013). The neurochemistry of music. *Trends in Cognitive Sciences, 17*(4), 179–193.

142 **recover more fully and more quickly** Blazer, D. G. (1982). Social support and mortality in an elderly community population. *American Journal of Epidemiology, 115*(5), 684–694.

and, Broadhead, W. E., Kaplan, B. H., James, S. A., Wagner, E. H., Schoenbach, V. J., Grimson, R., . . . Gehlbach, S. H. (1983). The epidemiologic evidence for a relationship between social support and health. *American Journal of Epidemiology, 117*(5), 521–537.

and, Wills, T. A., & Ainette, M. G. (2012). Social networks and social support. In A. Baum, T. A. A. Revenson, & J. Singer (Eds.), *Handbook of Health Psychology* (pp. 465–492). New York, NY: Psychology Press, p. 465.

143 **[Oxytocin's] real role is to organize social behavior** Oxytocin is not prosocial per se, but rather, regulates stress and anxiety, affective motivational states, and/or perceptual selectivity related to social information.

Bartz, J. A., & Hollander, E. (2006). The neuroscience of affiliation: Forging links between basic and clinical research on neuropeptides and social behavior. *Hormones and Behavior, 50*(4), 518–528.

and, Bartz, J. A., Zaki, J., Bolger, N., & Ochsner, K. N. (2011). Social effects of oxytocin in humans: context and person matter. *Trends in Cognitive Sciences, 15*(7), 301–309.

and, Chanda, M. L., & Levitin, D. J. (2013). The neurochemistry of music. *Trends in Cognitive Sciences, 17*(4), 179–193.

143 **music has been shown to increase oxytocin levels** Grape, C., Sandgren, M., Hansson, L. O., Ericson, M., & Theorell, T. (2003). Does singing promote well-being?: An empirical study of professional and amateur singers during a singing lesson. *Integrative Physiological and Behavioral Science, 38*(1), 65–74.

and, Nilsson, U. (2009). Soothing music can increase oxytocin levels during bed rest after open-heart surgery: A randomised control trial. *Journal of Clinical Nursing, 18*(15), 2153–2161.

143 **mate from emotional (and physical) outbursts** Insel, T. R. (2010). The challenge of translation in social neuroscience: A review of oxytocin, vasopressin, and affiliative behavior. *Neuron, 65*(6), 768–779.

and, Young, L. J., Nilsen, R., Waymire, K. G., MacGregor, G. R., & Insel, T. R. (1999). Increased affiliative response to vasopressin in mice expressing the V1a receptor from a monogamous vole. *Nature, 400*(6746), 766–768.

143 **(when the rats could get up off the couch)** Trezza, V., Baarendse, P. J., & Vanderschuren, L. J. (2010). The pleasures of play: Pharmacological insights into social reward mechanisms. *Trends in Pharmacological Sciences, 31*(10), 463–469.

and, Trezza, V., & Vanderschuren, L. J. (2008). Bidirectional cannabinoid modulation of social behavior in adolescent rats. *Psychopharmacology, 197*(2), 217–227.

144 **themselves in terms of situations** I thank Jason Rentfrow for this demonstration and formulation. Rentfrow, J., personal communication. November 4, 2013.

See also, Rothbart, M., Dawes, R., & Park, B. (1984). Stereotyping and sampling biases in intergroup perception. In J. R. Eiser (Ed.), *Attitudinal judgment* (pp. 109–134). New York, NY: Springer-Verlag, p. 125.

and, Watson, D. (1982). The actor and the observer: How are their perceptions of causality divergent? *Psychological Bulletin, 92*(3), 682–700.

144 **Gilbert calls this the "invisibility" problem** Gilbert, D. T. & Malone, P. S. (1995). The correspondence bias. *Psychological Bulletin, 117*(1), 21–38.

145 **students at the Princeton Theological** Darley, J. M., & Batson, C. D. (1973). "From Jersulem to Jericho": A study of situational and dispositional variables in helping behavior. *Journal of Personality and Social Psychology, 27*(1), 100–108.

146 **"It'll be a few minutes before they're ready . . ."** I'm simplifying here—the actual study had three conditions and forty participants. The three conditions were *high hurry, intermediate hurry,* and *low hurry.* But the starkest contrast and the most interesting two conditions for the hypothesis are the *high* and *low* hurry conditions, and so that is what I'm reporting here.

146 **Lee Ross and his colleagues** Ross, L. D., Amabile, T. M., & Steinmetz, J. L. (1977). Social roles, social control, and biases in social-perception processes. *Journal of Personality and Social Psychology, 35*(7), 485–494, p. 485.

147 **"What team won the 1969 World Series?"** The actual questions from the Ross experiment are not reported in the literature, but these examples illustrate the kind, scope, and breadth of what the Questioners asked. The questions about Auden and glaciers do come from their original report. Ross, L., personal communication. January, 1991.

148 **unlikely the Contestant would know** Ross, L. D., Amabile, T. M., & Steinmetz, J. L. (1977). Social roles, social control, and biases in social-perception processes. *Journal of Personality and Social Psychology, 35*(7), 485–494, p. 485.

148 **the cognitive illusion of the fundamental** The fundamental attribution error has received lots of critiques, including that social, and not just inferential processes are at work, see, e.g. Gawronski, B. (2004). Theory-based bias correction in dispositional inference: The fundamental attribution error is dead, long live the correspondence bias. *European Review of Social Psychology, 15*(1), 183–217.

and also, it may be unique to Western culture, reflecting an individualist bias:

Clarke, S. (2006). Appealing to the fundamental attribution error: Was it all a big mistake? In D. Coady (Ed.), *Conspiracy theories: The philosophical debate* (pp. 130–140). Burlington, VT: Ashgate Publishing.

and, Hooghiemstra, R. (2008). East-West differences in attributions for company performance: A content analysis of Japanese and U.S. corporate annual reports. *Journal of Cross-Cultural Psychology, 39*(5), 618–629.

and, Langdridge, D., & Butt, T. (2004). The fundamental attribution error: A phenomenological critique. *British Journal of Social Psychology, 43*(3), 357–369.

and, Truchot, D., Maure, G., & Patte, S. (2003). Do attributions change over time when the actor's behavior is hedonically relevant to the perceiver? *The Journal of Social Psychology, 143*(2), 202–208.

148 **outcome-bias-based inference** Mackie, D. M., Allison, S. T., Worth, L. T., & Asuncion, A. G. (1992). The generalization of outcome-biased counter-stereotypic inferences. *Journal of Experimental Social Psychology, 28*(1), 43–64.

148 **Jolie passed a difficult college course** This example comes from Mackie, D. M., Allison, S. T., Worth, L. T., & Asuncion, A. G. (1992). The generalization of outcome-biased counter-stereotypic inferences. *Journal of Experimental Social Psychology, 28*(1), 43–64.

149 **people continue to conclude** Allison, S. T., & Messick, D. M. (1985). The group attribution error. *Journal of Experimental Social Psychology, 21*(6), 563–579.

and, Mackie, D. M., Allison, S. T., Worth, L. T., & Asuncion, A. G. (1992). The generalization of outcome-biased counter-stereotypic inferences. *Journal of Experimental Social Psychology, 28*(1), 43–64.

and, Schaller, M. (1992). In-group favoritism and statistical reasoning in social inference: Implications for formation and maintenance of group stereotypes. *Journal of Personality and Social Psychology, 63*(1), 61–74.

149 **Reliance on such primal unconscious cues** Kahneman, D. (2011). *Thinking, fast and slow.* New York, NY: Farrar, Straus and Giroux.

and, Mackie, D. M., Allison, S. T., Worth, L. T., & Asuncion, A. G. (1992). The generalization of outcome-biased counter-stereotypic inferences. *Journal of Experimental Social Psychology, 28*(1), 43–64.

149 **"The jury will disregard that last exchange,"** Rachlinski, J. J., Wistrich, A. J., & Guthrie, C. (2005). Can judges ignore inadmissible information? The difficulty of deliberately disregarding. *University of Pennsylvania Law Review 153*(4), 1251–1345.

149–50 **the data it provided are valid** Anderson, C. A., & Kellam, K. L. (1992). Belief perseverance, biased assimilation, and covariation detection: The effects of hypothetical social theories and new data. *Personality and Social Psychology Bulletin, 18*(5), 555–565.

and, Bonabeau, E. (2009). Decisions 2.0: The power of collective intelligence. *MIT Sloan Management Review, 50*(2), 45–52.

and, Carretta, T. R., & Moreland, R. L. (1982). Nixon and Watergate: A field demonstration of belief perseverance. *Personality and Social Psychology Bulletin, 8*(3), 446–453.

and, Guenther, C. L., & Alicke, M. D. (2008). Self-enhancement and belief perseverance. *Journal of Experimental Social Psychology, 44*(3), 706–712.

Even the emotional qualities of a decision linger when the evidence has been invalidated. Sherman, D. K., & Kim, H. S. (2002). Affective perseverance: The resistance of affect to cognitive invalidation. *Personality and Social Psychology Bulletin, 28*(2), 224–237.

150 **Undergraduate men were brought** Nisbett, R. E., & Valins, S. (1972). Perceiving the causes of one's own behavior. In D. E. Kanouse, H. H. Kelley, R. E. Nisbett, S. Valins, & B. Weiner (Eds.), *Attribution: Perceiving the causes of behavior* (pp. 63–78). Morristown, NJ: General Learning Press.

and, Valins, S. (2007). Persistent effects of information about internal reactions: Ineffectiveness of debriefing. In H. London & R. E. Nisbett (Eds.), *Thought and feeling: The cognitive alteration of feeling states.* Chicago, IL: Aldine Transaction.

See the following for an interesting counter-perspective on the ubiquity of the fundamental attribution error, and the circumstances that will evoke it: Malle, B. F. (2006). The actor-observer asymmetry in attribution: A (surprising) meta-analysis. *Psychogical Bulletin, 132*(6), 895–919.

150 **fluctuations in rate had been predetermined** At a predetermined point in the experiment, the heart rate increased greatly, indicating the highest possible levels of arousal and, by implication, attractiveness. It's not the case that one of the women was universally regarded as more attractive than the others—this factor was randomized so that the heart rate peaked on different pictures for men in the experiment.

151 **the results of this process are relatively persistent** This is nearly a direct quote from Valins, S. (2005). Persistent effects of information about internal reactions: Ineffectiveness of debriefing. *Integrative Physiological & Behavioral Science, 40*(3), 161–165.

151 **Nicholas Epley says** Epley, N. (2014). *Mindwise: How we understand what others think, believe, feel, and want.* New York, NY: Alfred A. Knopf.

151 **primary dividing dimension** Eckert, P. (1989). *Jocks and burnouts: Social categories and identity in the high school.* New York, NY: Teachers College Press.

152 **by its own members than by outsiders** Rothbart, M., Dawes, R., & Park, B. (1984). Stereotyping and sampling biases in intergroup perception. In J. R. Eiser (Ed.), *Attitudinal judgment* (pp. 109–134). New York, NY: Springer-Verlag.

152 **medial prefrontal cortex** D'Argembeau, A., Ruby, P., Collette, F., Degueldre, C., Balteau, E., Luxen, A., . . . Salmon, E. (2007). Distinct regions of the medial prefrontal cortex are associated with self-referential processing and perspective taking. *Journal of Cognitive Neuroscience, 19*(6), 935–944.

and, Mitchell, J. P., Banaji, M. R., & MacRae, C. N. (2005). The link between social cognition and self-referential thought in the medial prefrontal cortex. *Journal of Cognitive Neuroscience, 17*(8), 1306–1315.

and, Northoff, G., & Bermpohl, F. (2004). Cortical midline structures and the self. *Trends in Cognitive Sciences, 8*(3), 102–107.

152 **daydreaming mode is active** D'Argembeau, A., Ruby, P., Collette, F., Degueldre, C., Balteau, E., Luxen, A., . . . Salmon, E. (2007). Distinct regions of the medial prefrontal cortex are associated with self-referential processing and perspective taking. *Journal of Cognitive Neuroscience, 19*(6), 935–944.

and, Gusnard, D. A., Akbudak, E., Shulman, G. L., & Raichle, M. E. (2001). Medial prefrontal cortex and self-referential mental activity: Relation to a default mode of brain function. *Proceedings of the National Academy of Sciences, 98*(7), 4259–4264.

and, Mitchell, J. P., Banaji, M. R., & MacRae, C. N. (2005). The link between social cognition and self-referential thought in the medial prefrontal cortex. *Journal of Cognitive Neuroscience, 17*(8), 1306–1315.

152 **flimsiest of premises** Rabbie, J. M., & Horwitz, M. (1969). Arousal of ingroup-outgroup bias by a chance win or loss. *Journal of Personality and Social Psychology, 13*(3), 269–277, p. 269.

153 **interdependence of fate** Lewin, K. (1948). *Resolving social conflicts: Selected papers on group dynamics.* Oxford, UK: Harper.

153 **similar flimsy manipulations lead** If all this seems far-fetched, the underlying mechanism at work may simply be related to self-esteem. As University of Oregon psychologist Mick Rothbart says, we wish to enhance our own esteem by exalting the groups that are similar to us, and disparaging those that are different. Consider the finding by Robert Cialdini that when people were led by the experimenters to experience a loss of self-esteem, this significantly influenced the way they felt about their favorite sports team: They were more likely to refer to a winning home team as "we" and a losing home team as "they."

Cialdini, R. B., Borden, R. J., Thorne, A., Walker, M. R., Freeman, S., & Sloan, L. R. (1976). Basking in reflected glory: Three (football) field studies. *Journal of Personality and Social Psychology, 34*(3), 366–375.

and, Rothbart, M., Dawes, R., & Park, B. (1984). In J. R. Eiser (Ed.), *Attitudinal judgment* (pp. 109–134). New York, NY: Springer-Verlag.

153 **the partitioning of people** Rothbart, M., & Hallmark, W. (1988). In-group-out-group differences in the perceived efficacy of coercion and conciliation in resolving social conflict. *Journal of Personality and Social Psychology, 55*(2), 248–257.

154 **generalizations about entire classes of people** There are additional explanations for racism beyond the cognitive one I present here. See, for example, Brown, R. (2010). *Prejudice: Its social psychology,* (2nd ed.). Oxford, UK: John Wiley & Sons.

and, Major, B., & O'Brien, L. T. (2005). The social psychology of stigma. *Annual Review of Psychology, 56,* 393–421.

and, Smedley, A., & Smedley, B. D. (2005). Race as biology is fiction, racism as a social problem is real: Anthropological and historical perspectives on the social construction of race. *American Psychologist, 60*(1), 16–26, p. 16.

154 **Mick Rothbart taught a class** Rothbart, M., Dawes, R., & Park, B. (1984). Stereotyping and sampling biases in intergroup perception. In J. R. Eiser (Ed.), *Attitudinal judgment* (pp. 109–134). New York, NY: Springer-Verlag, p. 112.

154 **In cases of in-group/out-group bias** This is nearly a direct quote from Rothbart, M., Dawes, R., & Park, B. (1984). Stereotyping and sampling biases in intergroup perception. In J. R. Eiser (Ed.), *Attitudinal judgment* (pp. 109–134). New York, NY: Springer-Verlag, p. 112.

154 **members of groups get to know one another** This is called intergroup contact theory. Pettigrew, T. F., & Tropp, L. R. (2006). A meta-analytic test of intergroup contact theory. *Journal of Personality and Social Psychology, 90*(5), 751–783.

154 **"to have demonstrated this phenomenon . . ."** Rothbart, M., Dawes, R., & Park, B. (1984). Stereotyping and sampling biases in intergroup perception. In J. R. Eiser (Ed.), *Attitudinal judgment* (pp. 109–134). New York, NY: Springer-Verlag, p. 113.

154 **we tend not to reevaluate the stereotype** Rothbart, M., & Lewis, S. (1988). Inferring category attributes from exemplar attributes: Geometric shapes and social categories. *Journal of Personality and Social Psychology, 55*(5), 861–872.

155 **Caribbean Crisis of 1962** Garthoff, R. L. (1988). Cuban missile crisis: The Soviet story. *Foreign Policy, 72,* 61–80.

155 **"try to put yourself in our place."** Khrushchev, N. (1962, October 24). Letter to President Kennedy. Kennedy Library, President's Office Files, Cuba. No classification marking. This "official translation" prepared in the Department of State and an "informal translation" from the Embassy in Moscow (transmitted in telegram 1070, October 25; Department of State, Presidential Correspondence: Lot 66 D 304) are printed in Department of State Bulletin, November 19, 1973, pp. 637–639.

Office of the Historian, U.S. Department of State. (n.d.). Kennedy-Krushchev exchanges: Document 63. In *Foreign Relations of the United States, 1961–1963* (6). Retrieved from http://history.state.gov/historicaldocuments/frus1961-63v06/d63

155 **"If you are really concerned about the peace . . ."** Khrushchev, N. (1962). Telegram from the Embassy in the Soviet Union to the U.S. Department of State, October 26, 1962, 7 P.M. Kennedy Library, National Security Files, Countries Series, USSR, Khrushchev Correspondence. Secret; Eyes Only; Niact; Verbatim Text. Passed to

the White House at 9:15 P.M. October 26. Other copies of this message are in Department of State, Presidential Correspondence: Lot 66 D 204, and ibid.: Lot 77 D 163. A copy of the Russian-language text is in the former. This "informal translation" and an "official translation" prepared by the Department of State are printed in Department of State Bulletin, November 19, 1973, pp. 640–645.

and, Office of the Historian, U.S. Department of State. (n.d.). Kennedy-Krushchev exchanges: Document 65. In *Foreign Relations of the United States, 1961–1963* (6). Retrieved from http://history.state.gov/historicaldocuments/frus1961-63v06/d65

155 **he turned Kennedy into an *in-group* member** For an experimental replication of this, see Experiment 2 in Rothbart, M., & Hallmark, W. (1988). In-group-out-group differences in the perceived efficacy of coercion and conciliation in resolving social conflict. *Journal of Personality and Social Psychology, 55*(2), 248–257.

156 **During late 2013 and early 2014** Nearly a direct quote from Kirkpatrick, D. D. (2014, January 25). Prolonged fight feared in Egypt after bombings. *The New York Times*, p. A1.

156 **we tend to think that coercion** This sentence, and much of the preceding paragraph are from Rothbart, M., & Hallmark, W. (1988). In-group-out-group differences in the perceived efficacy of coercion and conciliation in resolving social conflict. *Journal of Personality and Social Psychology, 55*(2), 248–257.

156 **"When I think about all the money . . ."** Shultz, G., personal communication. July, 2012, Sonoma County, CA.

156 **(Argentina is one country that . . .)** Articles 106–108 of the Argentine Penal Code, which include the provision in Article 106 "a person who endangers the life or health of another, either by putting a person in jeopardy or *abandoning to their fate a person unable to cope alone who must be cared for* [Author's emphasis] . . . will be imprisoned for between 2 and 6 years." Hassel, G. (n.d.). *Penal especial* [Special penalty]. Retrieved from http://www.monografias.com/trabajos52/penal-especial/penal-especial2.shtml

157 **justifiable fears about what might happen** Darley, J. M., & Latané, B. (1968). Bystander intervention in emergencies: Diffusion of responsibility. *Journal of Personality and Social Psychology, 8*(4), 377–383.

and, Milgram, S., & Hollander, P. (1964). The murder they heard. *The Nation, 198*(15), 602–604.

157 **social psychologists John Darley and Bibb Latané say** Darley, J. M., & Latané, B. (1968). Bystander intervention in emergencies: Diffusion of responsibility. *Journal of Personality and Social Psychology, 8*(4), 377–383, p. 377.

157 **Walter Vance . . . died after collapsing in a Target** *Report: Shoppers unfazed as man dies at Target* [Video file]. (2011, November 26). *NBC News*.

157 **shoppers . . . stepped over a man** Pocklington, R. (2013, Dec. 29). Shocking surveillance footage shows customers stepping over shooting victim as he lay dying in store doorway. *Daily Mirror*.

and, Hall, Jr. R. (2013, Dec. 23). Kalamazoo man convicted of murder in 2012 shooting of Jheryl Wright, 24. *Kalamazoo Gazette*/MLive.com.

157 **strong desire to conform** Asch, S. E. (1956). Studies of independence and conformity: I. A minority of one against a unanimous majority. *Psychological Monographs: General and Applied, 70*(9), 1–70.

157 **social comparison theory:** Festinger, L. (1954). A theory of social comparison processes. *Human Relations, 7*(2), 117–140.

158 **Diffusion of responsibility extends** Darley, J. M., & Latané, B. (1968). Bystander intervention in emergencies: Diffusion of responsibility. *Journal of Personality and Social Psychology, 8*(4), 377–383.

158 **"When only one bystander is present . . ."** Darley, J. M., & Latané, B. (1968). Bystander intervention in emergencies: Diffusion of responsibility. *Journal of Personality and Social Psychology, 8*(4), 377–383, p. 378.

158 **Geese will come** Kristof, N. D. (2008, July 31). A farm boy reflects. *The New York Times.*

and, Kristof, N. D. (2013, October 20). Are chicks brighter than babies? *The New York Times,* p. SR13.

158 **vervet monkeys** Cheney, D. L., & Seyfarth, R. M. (1990). *How monkeys see the world: Inside the mind of another species.* Chicago, IL: University of Chicago Press.

158 **meerkats stand guard** Santema, P., & Clutton-Brock, T. (2013). Meerkat helpers increase sentinel behaviour and bipedal vigilance in the presence of pups. *Animal Behavior, 85*(3), 655–661.

158 **Oxytocin—the same social-affiliative hormone** Madden, J. R., & Clutton-Brock, T. H. (2010). Experimental peripheral administration of oxytocin elevates a suite of cooperative behaviors in a wild social mammal. *Proceedings of the Royal Society B: Biological Sciences, 278*(1709), 1189–1194.

CHAPTER 5

160 **Ruth was a thirty-seven-year-old** This scenario is the only one not taken verbatim from the literature—it's a composite sketch of several frontal lobe patients for illustrative purposes to give the reader a flavor of the dysfunctions. The basic details are taken from Penfield, W. (1935). The frontal lobe in man: A clinical study of maximum removals. *Brain, 58*(1), 115–133.

160 **Ernie suddenly had lost the ability to properly evaluate future needs** Eslinger, P. J., & Damasio, A. R. (1985). Severe disturbance of higher cognition after bilateral frontal lobe ablation: Patient EVR. *Neurology, 35*(12), 1731. The names here have been changed for patient privacy.

161 **"I know what I want to draw, but I just don't do it. . . ."** Goel, V., & Grafman, J. (2000). Role of the right prefrontal cortex in ill-structured planning. *Cognitive Neuropsychology, 17*(5), 415–436, p. 423.

162 **the light waves themselves are colorless** Newton, I. (1995). *The Principia* (A. Motte, Trans.). New York, NY: Prometheus Books.

163 **After nightfall, time was kept** Lombardi, M. A. (2007, March 5). Why is a minute divided into 60 seconds, an hour into 60 minutes, yet there are only 24 hours in a day? *Scientific American.*

and, Masters, K. (2006, April 5). Why is a day divided into 24 hours? *Ask an astronomer.* Retrieved from http://curious.astro.cornell.edu/question.php?number=594

163 **Babylonians also used fixed duration** Wright, A. (2008). *Glut: Mastering information through the ages.* Ithaca, NY: Cornell University Press, p. 257.

163 **as did Hipparchus, the ancient Greek** North, J. D. (1975). Monasticism and the first mechanical clocks. In J. T. Fraser et al. (Eds.), *The study of time II.* New York, NY: Springer-Verlag.

164 **roughly 150,000 people who die** Centers for Disease Control and Prevention. (2014, February 13). Deaths and mortality. Retrieved from http://www.cdc.gov/nchs/fastats/deaths.htm

and, Central Intelligence Agency (2010). The world factbook. Washington, DC: U.S. Government Printing Office.

and, De Grey, A. D. N. J. (2007). Life span extension research and public debate: Societal considerations. *Studies in Ethics, Law, and Technology, 1*(1), 1941–6008.

164 **bad effects at older ages** Kirkwood, T. B. L., & Austad, S. N. (2000). Why do we age? *Nature, 408*(6809), 233–238.

164 **genetic variations that challenge survival** Kirkwood, T. B. L., & Austad, S. N. (2000). Why do we age? *Nature, 408*(6809), 233–238.

165 **maximum number of times** Shay, J. W., & Wright, W. E. (2000). Hayflick, his limit, and cellular ageing. *Nature Reviews Molecular Cell Biology, 1*(1), 72–76.

165 **60 to 100 beats per minute** Laskowski, E. R. (2009, September 29). What's a normal resting heart rate? Mayo Clinic. Retrieved from http://www.mayoclinic.com/health/heart-rate/AN01906

165 **Photographs are interesting because** I am grateful to David Crosby for this observation.

165 **once every 250 milliseconds** Roxin, A., Brunel, N., Hansel, D., Mongillo, G., & van Vreeswijk, C. (2011). On the distribution of firing rates in networks of cortical neurons. *The Journal of Neuroscience, 31*(45), 16217–16226.

166 **CEO of the brain** U.S. HHS (2013). Maturation of the Prefrontal Cortex. United States Department of Health and Human Services, Office of Population Affairs. Retrieved from http://www.hhs.gov/opa/familylife/tech_assistance/etraining/adolescent_brain/Development/prefrontal_cortex/

166 **connections between the prefrontal cortex** Knight, R. T., & Stuss, D. T. (2002). Prefrontal cortex: The present and the future. In D. T. Stuss & R. T. Knight (Eds.), *Principles of frontal lobe function* (pp. 573–598). New York, NY: Oxford University Press.

166 **something that most animals lack** Some nonhuman primates, notably chimps and monkeys, show an ability to delay gratification, and this is consistent with their developing, evolving prefrontal cortex.

and, Beran, M. J. (2013, May). Delay of gratification in nonhuman animals. *Psychological Science Agenda.* Retrieved from www.apa.org/science/about/psa/2013/05/nonhuman-animals.aspx

166 **humans until after age twenty** Beckman, M. (2004). Crime, culpability, and the adolescent brain. *Science, 305*(5684), 596–599.

and, Giedd, J. N., Blumenthal, J., Jeffries, N. O., Castellanos, F. X., Liu, H., Zijdenbos, A., . . . Rapoport, J. L. (1999). Brain development during childhood and adolescence: A longitudinal MRI study. *Nature Neuroscience, 2*(10), 861–863.

and, Sowell, E. R., Thompson, P. M., & Toga, A. W. (2004). Mapping changes in the human cortex throughout the span of life. *The Neuroscientist, 10*(4), 372–392.

and, Steinberg, L. (2004). Risk taking in adolescence: What changes, and why? *Annals of the New York Academy of Sciences, 1021*(1), 51–58.

166 **dysexecutive syndrome** Baddeley, A. D. (1986). *Working memory.* Oxford, UK: Clarendon Press.

166 **inhibiting the urge to imitate** Lhermitte, F. (1983). "Utilization behaviour" and its relation to lesions of the frontal lobes. *Brain, 106*(2), 237–255.

167 **revealing a failure in temporal control** Knight, R. T., & Grabowecky, M. (2000). Prefrontal cortex, time, and consciousness. In M. Gazzaniga (Ed.), *The new cognitive neurosciences* (pp. 1319–1337). Cambridge, MA: MIT Press.

167 **not aware of their deficit** Prigatano, G.P. (1991). Disturbances of self-awareness of deficit after traumatic brain injury. In G. P. Prigatano & D. L. Schacter (Eds.), *Awareness of deficit after brain injury: Clinical and theoretical issues* (pp. 111–126). New York, NY: Oxford University Press.

and, Stuss, D. T. (1991). Disturbances of self-awareness after frontal system damage. In G. P. Prigatano & D. L. Schacter (Eds.), *Awareness of deficit after brain injury: Clinical and theoretical issues* (pp. 63–83). New York, NY: Oxford University Press.

167 **resulting in a loss of creativity** Knight, R. T., & Stuss, D. T. (2002). Prefrontal cortex: The present and the future. In D. T. Stuss & R. T. Knight (Eds.), *Principles of frontal lobe function.* New York, NY: Oxford University Press.

167 **Alcohol interferes . . . by disrupting dopamine receptors** Trantham-Davidson, H., Burnett, E. J., Gass, J. T., Lopez, M. F., Mulholland, P. J., Centanni, S. W., . . . Chandler, L. J. (2014). Chronic alcohol disrupts dopamine receptor activity and the cognitive function of the medial prefrontal cortex. *The Journal of Neuroscience, 34*(10), 3706–3718.

167 **dopaminergic neurons in the frontal lobes** Courchesne, E., Mouton, P. R., Calhoun, M. E., Semendeferi, K., Ahrens-Barbeau, C., Hallet, M. J., . . . Pierce, K. (2011). Neuron number and size in prefrontal cortex of children with autism. *JAMA, 306*(18), 2001–2010.

168 **administration of L-dopa** Arnsten, A. F. T., & Dudley, A. G. (2005). Methylphenidate improves prefrontal cortical cognitive function through α2 adrenoceptor and dopamine D1 receptor actions: Relevance to therapeutic effects in Attention Deficit Hyperactivity Disorder. *Behavioral and Brain Functions, 1*(1), 2.

and, Owen, A. M., Sahakian, B. J., Hodges, J. R., Summers, B. A., Polkey, C. E., & Robbins, T. W. (1995). Dopamine-dependent frontostriatal planning deficits in early Parkinson's disease. *Neuropsychology, 9*(1), 126–140.

and, Tucha, L., Tucha, O., Sontag, T. A., Stasik, D., Laufkötter, R., & Lange, K. W. (2011). Differential effects of methylphenidate on problem solving in adults with ADHD. *Journal of Attention Disorders, 15*(2), 161–173.

168 **brain . . . consumes 20% of all the energy the body uses** Clarke, D. D., & Sokoloff, L. (1999). Circulation and energy metabolism of the brain: Substrates of cerebral metabolism. In G. J. Siegel, B. W. Agranoff, R. W. Albers, S. K. Fisher, & M. D. Uhler (Eds.), *Basic neurochemistry: Molecular, cellular and medical aspects* (6th ed.) (pp. 637–669). Philadelphia, PA: Lippincott-Raven.

168 **voltage output of a single resting neuron** The resting potential of a typical neuron is -70 mV, meaning that it has a negative charge, and the output of an iPod is positively charged.

168 **Playing music to the owl** Janata, P. (1997). Electrophysiological studies of auditory contexts. Dissertation Abstracts International: Section B: The Sciences and Engineering, University of Oregon.

168–69 **Chemicals are released . . . flow of information in the brain** Direct quote from Anderson, D. (2011). Your brain is more than a bag of chemicals. [Video] TedX CalTech.

169 **neurons . . . get that energy from glucose** Clarke, D. D., & Sokoloff, L. (1999). Circulation and energy metabolism of the brain: Substrates of cerebral metabolism. In G. J. Siegel, B. W. Agranoff, R. W. Albers, S. K. Fisher, & M. D. Uhler (Eds.), *Basic neurochemistry: Molecular, cellular and medical aspects* (6th ed.) (pp. 637–669). Philadelphia, PA: Lippincott-Raven.

and, Sokoloff, L., Reivich, M., Kennedy, C., Des Rosiers, M. H., Patlak, C. S., Pettigrew, K. E. A., . . . Shinohara, M. (1977). The [14C]deoxyglucose method for the measurement of local cerebral glucose utilization: Theory, procedure, and normal values in the conscious and anesthetized albino rat. *Journal of Neurochemistry, 28*(5), 897–916.

169 **except the testes** Himwich, H. E., & Nahum, L. H. (1929). The respiratory quotient of testicle. *American Journal of Physiology, 88*(4), 680–685.

and, Setchell, B. P., & Waites, G. M. H. (1964). Blood flow and the uptake of glucose and oxygen in the testis and epididymis of the ram. *Journal of Physiology, 171*(3), 411–425.

169 **eating or drinking glucose improves performance** Hoyland, A., Lawton, C. L., Dye, L. (2008). Acute effects of macronutrient manipulations on cognitive test performance in healthy young adults: A systematic research review. *Neuroscience & Biobehavioral Reviews, 32*(1), 72–85.

and, Riby, L. M., Law, A. S., McLaughlin, J., & Murray, J. (2011). Preliminary evidence that glucose ingestion facilitates prospective memory performance. *Nutrition Research, 31*(5), 370–377.

and, Scholey, A. B., Harper, S., & Kennedy, D. O. (2001). Cognitive demand and blood glucose. *Physiology & Behavior, 73*(4), 585–592.

169 **additional mental energy** Harvard Medical School. (2004, July.). Calories burned in thirty minutes for people of three different weights. *Harvard Heart Letter.* The number of calories depends on your weight—this is for a 150-pound person; add or subtract eight calories for each 25 pounds you add to or subtract from this.

169 **connecting neurons to one another** Harris, J. J., Jolivet, R., & Attwell, D. (2012). Synaptic energy use and supply. *Neuron, 75*(5), 762–777.

169 **a seamless thread of data coming in** Kastenbaum, S. (Producer). (2012, May 26). *Texting while walking a dangerous experiment in multitasking* [Audio podcast]. Retrieved from http://news.blogs.cnn.com/2012/05/26/texting-while-walking-a-dangerous-experiment-in-multitasking/

170 **". . . think in-depth about anything."** Quoted in Tuged, A. (2008, October 25). Multitasking can make you lose . . . um . . . focus. *The New York Times*, p. B7.

170 **brain's arousal system has a novelty bias** Tucker, D. M. (1987, May). Hemisphere specialization: A mechanism for unifying anterior and posterior brain regions. In D. Ottoson (Chair), *Duality and unity of the brain: Unified functioning and specialization of the hemispheres* (pp. 180–193). Symposium conducted at The Wenner-Gren Center, Stockholm, Sweden. New York, NY: Plenum Press.

170 **Humans will work just as hard** Nearly a direct quote from Gopnik, A. (2011, May 22). The great illusion. [Review of the book *Soul Dust* by N. Humphrey]. *The New York Times Book Review*, p. 19.

170 **trade-off between focus and creativity:** Some creative musicians who need to engage in repetitious tasks such as digital audio editing report that they take drugs

that enhance dopamine when they have editing or practicing to do, but would never dream of taking those drugs when writing or performing music.

171 **neurochemicals critical to paying attention** US National Library of Medicine. (2007, September). Genetics home reference: Genes, COMT. Retrieved from http://ghr.nlm.nih.gov/gene/COMT

171 **following instructions but are not especially creative** Colzato, L. S., Waszak, F., Nieuwenhuis, S., Posthuma, D., Hommel, B. (2010). The flexible mind is associated with the catechol-O-methyltransferase (COMT) Val158Met polymorphism: Evidence for a role of dopamine in the control of task-switching. *Neuropsychologia, 48*(9), 2764–2768.

and, He, Q., Xue, G., Chen, C., Lu, Z. L., Chen, C., Lei, X., . . . Bechara, A. (2012). COMT Val158Met polymorphism interacts with stressful life events and parental warmth to influence decision-making. *Scientific Reports, 2*(677).

172 **represented in the hippocampus** Eichenbaum, H. (2013). Memory on time. *Trends in Cognitive Sciences, 17*(2), 81–88.

173 **tons of vehicles, supplies, and personnel per day** Kennard, M. F. (1947, April 11). The Building of Mulberry Harbour. *The war illustrated, 10* (255), 771–772. London, UK: Amalgamated Press.

and, History Learning Site. (n.d.). The Mulberry Harbour. Retrieved from http://www.historylearningsite.co.uk

173 **(approximately 1.5 million cubic feet)** A standard of English timber equals 165 cubic feet. Urquhart, G. D. (1869). *Dues and charges on shipping in foreign ports: A manual of reference for the use of shipowners, shipbrokers, & shipmasters.* London, UK: George Philip and Son, p. 185.

and, Chest of Books. (n.d.). Petersburg standard of timber. Retrieved from http://chestofbooks.com/crafts/mechanics/Cyclopaedia/Petersburg-Standard-Of-Timber.html#.UYW9jt2Qc3I

173 **greatest engineering and military feats in human history** Kennard, M. F. (1947, April 11). The Building of Mulberry Harbour. *The war illustrated, 10* (255), 771–772. London, UK: Amalgamated Press.

175 **the metabolic costs of multitasking** Chevignard, M., Pillon, B., Pradat-Diehl, P., Taillefer, C., Rousseau, S., Le Bras, C., & Dubois, B. (2000). An ecological approach to planning dysfunction: Script execution. *Cortex, 36*(5), 649–669.

176 **adaptive strategies for living daily life** Goldberg, E. (2001). *The executive brain: Frontal lobes and the civilized mind.* New York, NY: Oxford University Press.

177 **a new rule without being prompted** Knight, R. T., & Stuss, D. T. (2002). Prefrontal cortex: The present and the future. In D. T. Stuss & R. T. Knight (Eds.), *Principles of frontal lobe function.* New York, NY: Oxford University Press.

177 **then they'll oscillate at a different frequency** Buschman, T. J., Denovellis, E. L., Diogo, C., Bullock, D., & Miller, E. K. (2012). Synchronous oscillatory neural ensembles for rules in the prefrontal cortex. *Neuron, 76*(4), 838–846.

177 **the environment that are competing for attention** Fallon, S. J., Williams-Gray, C. H., Barker, R. A., Owen, A. M., & Hampshire, A. (2013). Prefrontal dopamine levels determine the balance between cognitive stability and flexibility. *Cerebral Cortex, 23*(2), 361–369.

179 **". . . *We* take these for granted because we grew up with them."** Ferguson, J., personal communication. December 9, 2010.

179 **novels, and short stories** Gottschall, J. (2012). *The storytelling animal: How stories make us human.* New York, NY: Houghton Mifflin Harcourt Publishing Company.

and, Gottschall, J., & Wilson, D. S. (Eds.). (2005). *The literary animal: Evolution and the nature of narrative (rethinking theory).* Evanston, IL: Northwestern University Press.

180 **our brains to make them** Kurby, C. A., & Zacks, J. M. (2007). Segmentation in the perception and memory of events. *Trends in Cognitive Sciences, 12*(2), 72–79.

180 **modest number of meaningful units** Kurby, C. A., & Zacks, J. M. (2007). Segmentation in the perception and memory of events. *Trends in Cognitive Sciences, 12*(2), 72–79.

182–83 **Humor in single-panel cartoons:** Piraro, D., personal communication. March 8, 2014.

183 **become more strongly encoded in memory** Craik, F. I., & Lockhart, R. S. (1972). Levels of processing: A framework for memory research. *Journal of Verbal Learning and Verbal Behavior, 11*(6), 671–684.

183 **classrooms with great success** Crouch, C. H., & Mazur, E. (2001). Peer instruction: Ten years of experience and results. *American Journal of Physics, 69*(9), 970–977.

183 **become accessible to us for retrieval** This is nearly a direct quote from Kopasz, M., Loessl, B., Hornyak, M., Riemann, D., Nissen, C., Piosczyk, H., & Voderholzer, U. (2010). Sleep and memory in healthy children and adolescents—A critical review. *Sleep Medicine Reviews, 14*(3), 167–177.

184 **accomplished during distinct phases of sleep** Kopasz, M., Loessl, B., Hornyak, M., Riemann, D., Nissen, C., Piosczyk, H., & Voderholzer, U. (2010). Sleep and memory in healthy children and adolescents—A critical review. *Sleep Medicine Reviews, 14*(3), 167–177.

184 **outside world that we hold inside our heads** Diekelmann, S., & Born, J. (2010). The memory function of sleep. *Nature Reviews Neuroscience, 11*(2), 114–126.

and, Walker, M. P., & Stickgold, R. (2010). Overnight alchemy: Sleep-dependent memory evolution. *Nature Reviews Neuroscience, 11*(3), 218.

184 **confused with an actually occurring experience** McClelland, J. L., McNaughton, B. L., & O'Reilly, R. C. (1995). Why there are complementary learning systems in the hippocampus and neocortex: Insights from the successes and failures of connectionist models of learning and memory. *Psychological Review, 102*(3), 419–457.

184 **processing that occur during sleep** Walker, M. P., & Stickgold, R. (2010). Overnight alchemy: Sleep-dependent memory evolution. *Nature Reviews Neuroscience, 11*(3), 218.

184 **binds these together into a seamless whole** As Walker & Stickgold (2010) write: "Overnight unitization has been seen using a sequential finger-tapping motor-skill task in which subjects learn to type numerical sequences, such as 4-1-3-2-1-3-2-1-4. During initial learning, subjects appear to break the sequence into "chunks" (e.g., 413-21-3214), separated by brief pauses. But following a night of sleep, the sequence becomes unitized, and is typed without pauses (i.e., 413213214)."

This passage describes the prior work of: Kuriyama, K., Stickgold, R., & Walker, M. P. (2004). Sleep-dependent learning and motor-skill complexity. *Learning & Memory, 11*(6), 705–713.

184 **increase of ATP** Dworak, M., McCarley, R. W., Kim, T., Kalinchuk, A. V., & Basheer, R. (2010). Sleep and brain energy levels: ATP changes during sleep. *The Journal of Neuroscience, 30*(26), 9007–9016.

185 **equivalent period of being awake** Barrett, T. R., & Ekstrand, B. R. (1972). Effect of sleep on memory: III. Controlling for time-of-day effects. *Journal of Experimental Psychology, 96*(2), 321–327.

and, Fischer, S., Hallschmid, M., Elsner, A. L., & Born, J. (2002). Sleep forms memory for finger skills. *Proceedings of the National Academy of Sciences, 99*(18), 11987–11991.

and, Huber, R., Ghilardi, M. F., Massimini, M., & Tononi, G. (2004). Local sleep and learning. *Nature, 430*(6995), 78–81.

and, Jenkins, J. G., & Dallenbach, K. M. (1924). Obliviscence during sleep and waking. *American Journal of Psychology, 35*(4), 605–612.

and, Plihal, W., & Born, J. (1997). Effects of early and late nocturnal sleep on declarative and procedural memory. *Journal of Cognitive Neuroscience, 9(4),* 534–547.

and, Stickgold, R., James, L., & Hobson, J. A. (2000). Visual discrimination learning requires sleep after training. *Nature Neuroscience, 3*(12), 1237–1238.

and, Stickgold, R., Whidbee, D., Schirmer, B., Patel, V., & Hobson, J. A. (2000). Visual discrimination task improvement: A multi-step process occurring during sleep. *Journal of Cognitive Neuroscience, 12*(2), 246–254.

and, Walker, M., Brakefield, T., Morgan, A., Hobson, J. A., & Stickgold, R. (2002). Practice with sleep makes perfect: Sleep dependent motor skill learning. *Neuron, 35*(1), 205–211.

185 **performing it after one night's sleep** Allen, S. (2013). Memory stabilization and enhancement following music practice. *Psychology of Music.* Advance online publication. Retrieved from http://pom.sagepub.com

185 **equivalent amount of waking time** Wagner, U., Gais, S., Haider, H., Verleger, R., & Born, J. (2004). Sleep inspires insight. *Nature, 427*(6972), 352–355.

185 **you'll solve a problem requiring insight** Wagner, U., Gais, S., Haider, H., Verleger, R., & Born, J. (2004). Sleep inspires insight. *Nature, 427*(6972), 352–355.

185 **dreamed about abstract elements of the game** Stickgold, R., Malia, A., Maguire, D., Roddenberry, D., & O'Connor, M. (2000). Replaying the game: Hypnagogic images in normals and amnesiacs. *Science, 290*(5490), 350–353.

186 **dreams tend to be less elaborate** Siegel, J. (2006). The stuff dreams are made of: Anatomical substrates of REM sleep. *Nature Neuroscience, 9*(6), 721–722.

186 **increased levels of acetylcholine and cortisol** Hasselmo, M. E. (1999). Neuromodulation: Acetylcholine and memory consolidation. *Trends in Cognitive Sciences, 3*(9), 351–359.

186 **disparate brain regions during REM** Jones, M. W., & Wilson, M. A. (2005). Theta rhythms coordinate hippocampal-prefrontal interactions in a spatial memory task. *PLoS Biology, 3*(12), e402.

187 **bringing us from one state to the other** Lu, J., Sherman, D., Devor, M., Saper, C. B. (2006, June 1). A putative flip-flop switch for control of REM sleep. *Nature, 441,* 589–594.

187 **more later in the early morning hours** Domhoff, G. W. (2002). *The scientific study of dreams: Neural networks, cognitive development, and content analysis.* Washington, DC: APA Press.

187 **last 90 minutes of REM sleep in the morning** Stickgold, R. (2005). Sleep-dependent memory consolidation. *Nature, 437,* 1272–1278.

and, American Psychological Association. (n.d.). Why sleep is important and what happens when you don't get enough. Retrieved from http://www.apa.org/topics/sleep/why.aspx?item=11

188 **following two nights of good sleep** Stickgold, R., James, L., & Hobson, J. A. (2000). Visual discrimination learning requires sleep after training. *Nature Neuroscience, 3*(12), 1237–1238.

188 **fundamental property of neuronal metabolism** Domhoff, G. W. (2002). *The scientific study of dreams: Neural networks, cognitive development, and content analysis.* Washington, DC: APA Press.

and, Xie, L., Hongyi, K., Qiwu, X., Chen, M. J., Yonghong, L., Meenakshisundaram, T., . . . Nedergaard, M. (2013). Sleep drives metabolite clearance from the adult brain. *Science, 342*(6156), 373–377.

188 **that accumulate during waking thought** Xie, L., Hongyi, K., Qiwu, X., Chen, M. J., Yonghong, L., Meenakshisundaram, T., . . . Nedergaard, M. (2013). Sleep drives metabolite clearance from the adult brain. *Science, 342*(6156), 373–377.

189 **neurohormones are released to induce wakefulness** Van Dongen, H. P. A., & Dinges, D. P. (2000). Circadian rhythms in fatigue, alertness, and performance. In M. H. Kryger, T. Roth, & W. C. Dement (Eds.), *Principles and practice of sleep medicine* (3rd ed.) (pp. 391–399). Philadelphia, PA: W. B. Saunders.

and, Stenberg, D. (2007). Neuroanatomy and neurochemistry of sleep. *Cellular and Molecular Life Sciences, 64*(10), 1187–1204.

189 **performance for many days afterward** Krueger, J. M., Rector, D. M., Roy, S., Van Dongen, H. P. A., Belenky, G., & Panksepp, J. (2008). Sleep as a fundamental property of neuronal assemblies. *Nature Reviews Neuroscience, 9*(12), 910–919.

189 **three-point shooting each improved** Mah, C. D., Mah, K. E., Kezirian, E. J., & Dement, W. C. (2011). The effects of sleep extension on the athletic performance of collegiate basketball players. *Sleep, 34*(7), 943.

189 **second period of four or five hours of sleep** Ekirch, A. R. (2006). *At day's close: Night in times past.* New York, NY: W. W. Norton & Company.

and, Koslofsky, C. (2011). *Evening's empire: A history of the night in early modern Europe.* Cambridge, UK: Cambridge University Press.

and, Wehr (1992). In short photoperiods, human sleep is biphasic. *Journal of Sleep Research, 1*(2), 103–107.

189 **life satisfaction, efficiency, and performance** Chiang, Y-Y., Tsai, P-Y., Chen, P-C., Yang, M-H., Li, C-Y., Sung, F-C., & Chen, K-B. (2012). Sleep disorders and traffic accidents. *Epidemiology, 23*(4), 643–644.

and, United States Census Bureau. (n.d.). Transportation: Motor vehicle accidents and fatalities. Retrieved from http://www.census.gov/

190 **guidelines from research suggest the following** National Sleep Foundation. (n.d.). How much sleep do we really need? Retrieved from http://www.sleepfoundation.org/article/how-sleep-works/how-much-sleep-do-we-really-need

190 **what is indicated, and this appears to be hereditary** Hor, H., & Tafti, M. (2009). How much sleep do we need? *Science, 325*(5942), 825–826, p. 825.

190 **eight hours at a stretch** Van Dongen, H. P. A., & Dinges, D. P. (2000). Circadian rhythms in fatigue, alertness, and performance. In M. H. Kryger, T. Roth, & W. C. Dement (Eds.), *Principles and practice of sleep medicine* (3rd ed.) (pp. 391–399). Philadelphia, PA: W. B. Saunders.

191 **sleep deprivation a public health epidemic** Centers for Disease Control and Prevention. (n.d.). Insufficient sleep is a public health epidemic. Retrieved from http://www.cdc.gov/features/dssleep/index.html#References

191 **loss without adverse cognitive effects** This sentence is a direct quote from U.S. Institute of Medicine Committee on Sleep Medicine and Research. (2006). *Sleep disorders and sleep deprivation: An unmet public health problem.* Colton, H. R. & Altevogt, B. M. (Eds.) Washington, DC: The National Academies Press. Also available at http://www.ncbi.nlm.nih.gov/books/NBK19958/

See also, Dinges, D., Rogers, N., & Baynard, M. D. (2005). Chronic sleep deprivation. In M. H. Kryger, T. Roth, & W. C. Dement, (Eds.), *Principles and practice of sleep medicine* (4th ed.) (pp. 67–76). Philadelphia, PA: Elsevier/Saunders.

and, *Nightly news: Sleep deprivation costs companies billions* [Video file]. (2013, January 23). *NBC News.* Retrieved from http://www.nbcnews.com/

191 **shooting people on their own side** Kuruvilla, C. (2013, March 15). Captain of Air France plane that crashed into Atlantic Ocean killing everyone on board was running on one hour of sleep. *New York Daily News.*

and, Randall, D. K. (2012, August 3). Decoding the science of sleep. *The Wall Street Journal.*

and, U.S. Institute of Medicine Committee on Sleep Medicine and Research. (2006). *Sleep disorders and sleep deprivation: An unmet public health problem.* Colton, H. R. & Altevogt, B. M. (Eds.) Washington, DC: The National Academies Press. Also available at http://www.ncbi.nlm.nih.gov/books/NBK19958/

191 **some of the most well-known global disasters** Harrison, Y., & Horne, J. A. (2000). The impact of sleep deprivation on decision-making: A review. *Journal of Experimental Psychology: Applied, 6*(3), 236–249.

191 **the oil spill from the *Exxon Valdez*** U. S. National Transportation Safety Board. (1997). *Marine accident report: Grounding of the U. S. tankship Exxon Valdez on Bligh Reeff, Prince William Sound, near Valdez, Alaska.* NTSB Number MAR-90/04; PB90-916405. Washington, DC: U.S. Government Printing Office.

191 **the cruise ship *Star Princess*** U. S. National Transportation Safety Board (1997). *Marine accident report: Grounding of the Liberian passenger ship Star Princess on Poundstone Rock, Lynn Canal, Alaska.* NTSB Number MAR-97/02; PB97-916403. Washington, DC: U. S. Government Printing Office.

See also, Brown, D. B. (2007). Legal implications of obstructive sleep apnea. In C. A. Kushida (Ed.), *Obstructive sleep apnea: Diagnosis and treatment.* New York, NY: Informa Healthcare USA.

191 **the *Challenger* space shuttle** Presidential Commission on the Space Shuttle Challenger Accident (1986). Washington, DC: U. S. Government Printing Office.

191 **roughly the same as the annual revenue** CNN Money. (n.d.). Fortune global 500. Retrieved from http://money.cnn.com/

191 **obesity, stroke, and cancer** Randall, D. K. (2012, August 3). Decoding the science of sleep. *The Wall Street Journal.*

191–92 **". . . your life with your head on a pillow."** Randall, D. K. (2012). *Dreamland: Decoding the science of sleep.* New York, NY: W. W. Norton & Company.

192 **more effective than the prescription drug Ambien** Jacobs, G. D., Pace-Schott, E. F., Stickgold, R., & Otto, M. W. (2004). Cognitive behavior therapy and pharmacotherapy for insomnia: A randomized controlled trial and direct comparison. *Archives of Internal Medicine, 164*(17), 1888–1896.

192 **groggy we were upon waking up** Randall, D. K. (2012). *Dreamland: Decoding the science of sleep.* New York, NY: W. W. Norton & Company.

and, Randall, D. K. (2012, August 3). Decoding the science of sleep. *The Wall Street Journal.*

192 **such as orexin, cortisol, and adrenaline** Monti, J., Pandi-Perumal, S. R., Sinton, C. M., & Sinton, C. W. (Eds.). (2008). *Neurochemistry of sleep and wakefulness.* Cambridge, UK: Cambridge University Press.

and, Stenberg, D. (2007). Neuroanatomy and neurochemistry of sleep. *Cellular and Molecular Life Sciences, 64*(10), 1187–1204.

193 **counterproductive, though, causing sleep inertia** Mayo Clinic. (n.d.). Napping: Do's and don'ts for healthy adults. Retrieved from http://www.mayoclinic.com/health/napping/MY01383

193 **benefits of napping are well established** Nishida, M., Pearsall, J., Buckner, R. L., & Walker, M. P. (2009). REM sleep, prefrontal theta, and the consolidation of human emotional memory. *Cerebral Cortex 19*(5), 1158–1166.

193 **the more intellectual the work** Tucker, M. A., Hirota, Y., Wamsley, E. J., Lau, H., Chaklader, A., & Fishbein, W. (2006). A daytime nap containing solely non-REM sleep enhances declarative but not procedural memory. *Neurobiology of Learning & Memory, 86*(2), 241–247.

and, Wilson, J. K., Baran, B., Pace-Schott, E. F., Ivry, R. B., & Spencer, R. M. C. (2012). Sleep modulates word-pair learning but not motor sequence learning in healthy older adults. *Neurobiology of Aging, 33*(5), 991–1000.

193 **a nap can turn around negative emotions** Gujar, N., McDonald, S. A., Nishida, M., & Walker, M. P. (2011). A role for REM sleep in recalibrating the sensitivity of the human brain to specific emotions. *Cerebral Cortex, 21*(1), 115–123.

and, Mednick, S., Nakayama, K., & Stickgold, R. (2003). Sleep-dependent learning: A nap is as good as a night. *Nature Neuroscience, 6*(7), 697–698.

193 **disease, diabetes, stroke, and heart attacks** Markowitz, E. (2011, August 12). Should your employees take naps? *Inc.* Retrieved from http://www.inc.com/

and, Naska, A., Oikonomou, E., Tichopoulou, A., Psaltopoulou, T., & Tichopoulous, D. (2007). Siesta in healthy adults and coronary mortality in the general population. *JAMA Internal Medicine, 167*(3), 296–301.

and, Stein, R. (2007, February 13). Midday naps found to fend off heart disease. *The Washington Post.*

Note there is some controversy about this. First, the effect was shown to be statistically significant for men but not for women; this is probably a statistical artifact in that too few women died of heart disease to create an adequate control group.

A separate study showed that daily naps were associated with *increased* risk of myocardial infarction, and another that napping is associated with increased risks of mortality of all kinds, although these, too, are confounded with culture.

See, Campos, H., & Siles, X. (2000). Siesta and the risk of coronary heart disease: Results from a population-based, case-control study in Costa Rica. *International Journal of Epidemiology, 29*(3), 429–437.

and, Tanabe, N., Iso, H., Seki, N., Suzuki, H., Yatsuya, H., Toyoshima, H., & Tamakshi, A. (2010) Daytime napping and mortality, with a special reference to cardiovascular disease: The JACC study. *International Journal of Epidemiology, 39*(1), 233–243.

193 **many companies have dedicated nap rooms with cots** Markowitz, E. (2011, August 12). Should your employees take naps? *Inc.* Retrieved from http://www.inc.com/

194 **eastward gave up more than one run** Recht, L. D., Lew, R. A., & Schwartz, W. J. (1995). Baseball teams beaten by jet lag. *Nature, 377*(6550), 583.

194 **including reductions in muscle strength** Waterhouse, J., Reilly, T., Atkinson, G., & Edwards, B. (2007). Jet lag: Trends and coping strategies. *Lancet, 369*(9567), 1117–1129.

194 **Individuals over the age of sixty** Monk, T. (2005). Aging human circadian rhythms: Conventional wisdom may not always be right. *Journal of Biological Rhythms, 20*(4), 366–374.

and, Monk, T., Buysse, D., Carrier, J., & Kupfer, D. (2000). Inducing jet-lag in older people: Directional asymmetry. *Journal of Sleep Research, 9*(2), 101–116.

194 **what would be late afternoon** Burgess, H. J., Crowley, S. J., Gazda, C. J., Fogg, L. F., & Eastman, C. I. (2003). Preflight adjustment to eastward travel: 3 days of advancing sleep with and without morning bright light. *Journal of Biological Rhythms, 18*(4), 318–328.

195 **before bedtime can be effective** Suhner, A., Schlagenhauf, P., Johnson, R., Tschopp, A., & Steffen, R. (1998). Comparative study to determine the optimal melatonin dosage form for the alleviation of jet lag. *Chronobiology International, 15*(6), 655–666.

and, Waterhouse, J., Reilly, T., Atkinson, G., & Edwards, B. (2007). Jet lag: Trends and coping strategies. *Lancet, 369*(9567), 1117–1129.

195 **young people and pregnant women have been advised** Sanders, D., Chatuvedi, A., & Hordinsky, J. (1999). Melatonin: Aeromedical, toxicopharmacological, and analytical aspects. *Journal of Applied Toxicology, 23*(3), 159–167.

195 **produced as much melatonin as it can use** Eastman, C. I., & Burgess, H. J. (2009). How to travel the world without jet lag. *Sleep Medicine Clinics, 4*(2), 241–255.

195 **When We Procrastinate** Much of this section follows the order of presentation and ideas found in Steel, P., & Ferrari, J. (2013). Sex, education and procrastination: An epidemiological study of procrastinators' characteristics from a global sample. *European Journal of Personality, 27*(1), 51–58.

195 **very little patience, and he was easily bored** Eberts, J., personal communication. May 5, 2008, Magog, QC.

195 **Jake adopted a strict policy of "do it now."** Eberts, A., personal communication. November 26, 2013, Montreal, QC.

195 **Jake called it eating the frog** Eberts, A., personal communication. November 26, 2013, Montreal, QC.

"Eat a live frog" comes from a quote attributed to Mark Twain, "Eat a live frog first thing in the morning and nothing worse will happen to you the rest of the day."

196 **decision that would help us to reach our goals** Orellana-Damacela, L. E., Tindale, R. S., & Suárez-Balcázar, Y. (2000). Decisional and behavioral procrastination: How they relate to self-discrepancies. *Journal of Social Behavior & Personality, 15*(5), 225–238.

196 **so bad that treatment is no longer an option** Harlan, L. C., Bernstein, A. B., & Kessler, L. G. (1991). Cervical cancer screening: Who is not screened and why? *American Journal of Public Health, 81*(7), 885–890.

and, Jaberi, F. M., Parvizi, J., Haytmanek, C. T., Joshi, A., & Purtill, J. (2008). Procrastination of wound drainage and malnutrition affect the outcome of joint arthroplasty. *Clinical Orthopaedics and Related Research, 466*(6), 1368–1371.

and, Saposnik, G. (2009). Acute stroke management: Avoiding procrastination, the best way to optimize care delivery. *European Journal of Neurology, 16*(12), 1251–1252.

and, Steel, P., & Ferrari, J. (2013). Sex, education and procrastination: An epidemiological study of procrastinators' characteristics from a global sample. *European Journal of Personality, 27*(1), 51–58.

and, Worthley, D. L., Cole, S. R., Esterman, A., Mehaffey, S., Roosa, N. M., Smith, A., . . . Young, G. P. (2006). Screening for colorectal cancer by faecal occult blood test: Why people choose to refuse. *Internal Medicine Journal, 36*(9), 607–610.

196 **retirement savings plan until it's too late** Byrne, A., Blake, D., Cairns, A., & Dowd, K. (2006). There's no time like the present: The cost of delaying retirement saving. *Financial Services Review, 15*(3), 213–231.

and, Venti, S. (2006). Choice, behavior and retirement saving. In G. Clark, A. Munnell & M. Orszag (Eds.), *Oxford handbook of pensions and retirement income* (Vol. 1, pp. 21—30). New York, NY: Oxford University Press.

196 **graduate from college than men** Goldin, C., Katz, L. F., & Kuziemko, I. (2006). The homecoming of American college women: The reversal of the college gender gap. *The Journal of Economic Perspectives, 20*(4), 133–156.

and, Heckman, J. J., & LaFontaine, P. A. (2010). The American high school graduation rate: Trends and levels. *The Review of Economics and Statistics, 92*(2), 244–262.

and, Janosz, M., Archambault, I., Morizot, J., & Pagani, L. S. (2008). School engagement trajectories and their differential predictive relations to dropout. *Journal of Social Issues, 64*(1), 21–40.

196 **they are less likely to procrastinate** The correlations are extremely low and reach statistical significance because of the enormous *n* in these studies. The strongest of these correlations accounts for only 1% of the variance in procrastination behavior.

196 **shown to reduce the tendency to procrastinate** Kaplan, S., & Berman, M. G. (2010). Directed attention as a common resource for executive functioning and self-regulation. *Perspectives on Psychological Science, 5*(1), 43–57.

196 **but also with procrastination** Rentfrow, P., Gosling, S., & Potter, J. (2008). A theory of the emergence, persistence, and expression of geographic variation in psychological characteristics. *Perspectives on Psychological Science, 3*(5), 339–369.

197 **damage to this region of the brain** Freeman, W., & Watts, J. W. (1939). An interpretation of the functions of the frontal lobe: Based upon observations in forty-eight cases of prefrontal lobotomy. *The Yale Journal of Biology and Medicine, 11*(5), 527–539, p. 537.

and, Strub, R. L. (1989). Frontal lobe syndrome in a patient with bilateral globus pallidus lesions. *Archives of Neurology, 46*(9), 1024–1027.

197 **underlying factors lead us to procrastinate** Steel, P. (2007). The nature of procrastination: A meta-analytic and theoretical review of quintessential self-regulatory failure. *Psychological Bulletin, 133*(1), 65.

and, Steel, P. (2010). The procrastination equation: How to stop putting things off and start getting stuff done. New York, NY: HarperCollins.

198 **leads to an increase in procrastination** Steel constructs his equation as the inverse of the one I describe here, putting self-confidence and completion value in the numerator, with time-to-completion and distractibility in the denominator. This yields the *desirability* quotient for the task, which is inversely related to the likelihood of procrastination, that is:

$$\text{desirability} = \frac{\text{self-confidence} \times \text{value of completing task}}{\text{time to complete task} \times \text{distractibility}}$$

and it follows then that
likelihood of procrastination = 1/desirability.

With apologies to Steel, I've eliminated the extra step of flipping the proportion, for clarity of expression.

198 **feedback for completion of the task** This is based on equation 1 from, Steel, P., & König, C. J. (2006). Integrating theories of motivation. *Academy of Management Review, 31*(4), 889–913. Delay is more commonly expressed as T-t, the difference between the value of a reward *now* at time *T*, versus the value of that same reward *later* at time *t*.

199 **deficits, an inability to get started** Rabin, L. A., Fogel, J., & Nutter-Upham, K. E. (2011). Academic procrastination in college students: The role of self-reported executive function. *Journal of Clinical and Experimental Neuropsychology, 33*(3), 344–357.

199 **difficulties arise from a lack of planning** This is nearly a direct quote from Rabin, L. A., Fogel, J., & Nutter-Upham, K. E. (2011). Academic procrastination in college students: The role of self-reported executive function. *Journal of Clinical and Experimental Neuropsychology, 33*(3), 344–357.

199 **reducing this form of procrastination** Schouwenburg, H. C., & Lay, C. H. (1995). Trait procrastination and the Big Five factors of personality. *Personality and Individual Differences, 18*(4), 481–490.

200 **most of us would consider to be, well, *failures*** Plimpton, G. (1995). *The X factor: A quest for excellence.* New York, NY: W. W. Norton & Company.

200 **dorsolateral prefrontal cortex and the orbital cortex** Beer, J. S., John, O. P., Scabini, D., & Knight, R. T. (2006). Orbitofrontal cortex and social behavior:

Integrating self-monitoring and emotion-cognition interactions. *Journal of Cognitive Neuroscience, 18*(6), 871–879.

and, Luu, P., Collins, P., & Tucker, D. M. (2000). Mood, personality, and self-monitoring: Negative affect and emotionality in relation to frontal lobe mechanisms of error monitoring. *Journal of Experimental Psychology: General, 129*(1), 43–60, p. 43.

and, Passingham, R. E., Bengtsson, S. L., & Lau, H. C. (2010). Medial frontal cortex: From self-generated action to reflection on one's own performance. *Trends in Cognitive Sciences, 14*(1), 16–21.

201 **self-assessment that their ideas are not good enough** Limb, C. J., & Braun, A. R. (2008). Neural substrates of spontaneous musical performance: An fMRI study of jazz improvisation. *PLoS One, 3*(2), e1679.

201 **embarrassment or frustration** This is a direct quote from Freeman, W., & Watts, J. W. (1939). An interpretation of the functions of the frontal lobe: Based upon observations in forty-eight cases of prefrontal lobotomy. *The Yale Journal of Biology and Medicine, 11*(5), 527–539, p. 527.

201 **high-profile failures as successes** *Rolling Stone.* (n.d.). The many business failures of Donald Trump. Retrieved from http://www.rollingstone.com

201 **Trump Mortgage, four bankruptcies** *Donald Trump's companies filed for bankruptcy 4 times* [Video file]. (2011, April 21). *ABC News.* Retrieved from http://abcnews.go.com/Politics/donald-trump-filed-bankruptcy-times/story?id=13419250

201 **full-scale psychological disorders** Ronningstam, E. F. (2005). *Identifying and understanding the narcissistic personality.* New York, NY: Oxford University Press.

202 **What word can be joined to all** Jung-Beeman, M., Bowden, E. M., Haberman, J., Frymiare, J. L., Arambel-Liu, S., Greenblatt, R., . . . Kounios, J. (2004). Neural activity when people solve verbal problems with insight. *PLoS Biology, 2*(4), e97.

202 **The answer is** The word that unites these three is *apple.*

202 **"I need you to tell me that my life was worthwhile."** Friend, R., Lerner, G., & Foster, D. (Writers). (2012). *House: Holding on,* Season 8, Episode 22.

203 **less precise, they are better connected** Jung-Beeman, M. (2008). Quoted in J. Lehrer (2008, July 28). The eureka hunt. *The New Yorker,* 40–45.

203 **accompanied by a burst of gamma waves** Fleck, J. I., Green, D. L., Stevenson, J. L., Payne, L., Bowden, E. M., Jung-Beeman, M., & Kounios, J. (2008). The transliminal brain at rest: Baseline EEG, unusual experiences, and access to unconscious mental activity. *Cortex, 44*(10), 1353–1363.

203 **insights happen during warm showers** The relaxation phase is crucial. That's why so many insights happen during warm showers. This is from Jung-Beeman, M. (2008). Quoted in Lehrer J. (2008, July 28). The eureka hunt. *The New Yorker,* 40–45.

203 **amygdala, the brain's fear center** Bengtsson, S. L., Csíkszentmihályi, M., & Ullén, F. (2007). Cortical regions involved in the generation of musical structures during improvisation in pianists. *Journal of Cognitive Neuroscience, 19*(5), 830–842.

and, Ulrich, M., Keller, J., Hoenig, K., Waller, C., & Grön, G. (2014). Neural correlates of experimentally induced flow experiences. *NeuroImage, 86,* 194–202.

203 **the largest scales of the universe** In this section, I am paraphrasing and borrowing liberally from conversations with Csikszentmihalyi, and from our talks and public conversations at a symposium we both appeared at, hosted by the Department of Psychiatry, Stanford University, Stanford, CA, March 6, 2007.

204 **"It didn't feel like *I* was writing it. . . ."** Omaha, N. E., personal communication. September 15, 2010, and January, 1991. Parts of the latter conversation were published in Levitin, D. J. (1991). Rosanne Cash. *Recording-Engineering-Production, 22*(2), 18–19.

204 **"I opened my mouth to sing and . . ."** Huxley, P., personal communication. May 25, 2013, Washington, DC.

206 **they are modulated in . . . the striatum** Seamans, J. K., & Yang, C. R. (2004). The principal features and mechanisms of dopamine modulation in the prefrontal cortex. *Progress in Neurobiology, 74*(1), 1–58.

and, Ullén, F., de Manzano, Ö., Almeida, R., Magnusson, P. K. E., Pedersen, N. L., Nakamura, J., . . . Madison, G. (2012). Proneness for psychological flow in everyday life: Associations with personality and intelligence. *Personality and Individual Differences, 52*(2), 167–172.

206 **freedom to access stream-of-consciousness** Boulougouris, V., & Tsaltas, E. (2008). Serotonergic and dopaminergic modulation of attentional processes. *Progress in Brain Research, 172*, 517–542.

207 **this thinking disrupted the automatic application** Dietrich, A. (2004). Neurocognitive mechanisms underlying the experience of flow. *Consciousness and Cognition, 13*(4), 746–761.

208 **it's the price to pay for being creative** Young, N., personal communication. June, 1981, and April, 1984, Woodside, CA.

208 **the world to nourish his creativity** Wonder, S., personal communication. April, 1995, Burbank, CA. Parts of this conversation were published in Levitin, D. J. (1996). Conversation in the key of life: Stevie Wonder. *Grammy Magazine, 14*(3), 14–25.

208 **others to give him maximum freedom** Sting, personal communication. September 27, 2007, Barcelona, Spain.

209 **Procrastinators seldom do absolutely nothing** Perry, J. (2012). *The art of procrastination: A guide to effective dawdling, lollygagging and postponing.* New York, NY: Workman Publishing Company.

209 **scientific articles when an article was due** Tierney, J. (2013, January 15). This was supposed to be my column for New Year's Day. *The New York Times,* p. D3.

209 **Fish are seduced by** is nearly a direct quote from Kubey, R., & Csikszentmihalyi, M. (2002, February). Television addiction is no mere metaphor. *Scientific American, 48*–55.

210 **prefrontal cortex's central executive** Grafman, J. (1989). Plans, actions and mental sets: Managerial knowledge units in the frontal lobes. In E. Perecman (Ed.), *Integrating Theory and Practice in Clinical Neuropsychology* (pp. 93–138). Hillsdale, NJ: Erlbaum.

211 **what's the latest and loudest in your head** The Freelancers' Show (Producer). (2013, August 8). *The Freelancers' Show 073—Book club: Getting things done with David Allen* [Audio podcast]. Retrieved from http://www.freelancersshow.com/the-freelancers-show-073-book-club-getting-things-done-with-david-allen/

211 **chronic diseases and premature death** Warburton, D. E., Nicol, C. W., & Bredin, S. S. (2006). Health benefits of physical activity: The evidence. *Canadian Medical Association Journal, 174*(6), 801–809.

211 **fend off certain types of cancer** Friedenreich, C. M. (2001). Physical activity and cancer prevention from observational to intervention research. *Cancer Epidemiology Biomarkers & Prevention, 10*(4), 287–301.

and, Friedenreich, C. M., & Orenstein, M. R. (2002). Physical activity and cancer prevention: Etiologic evidence and biological mechanisms. *The Journal of Nutrition, 132*(11), 3456S–3464S.

211 **five days a week, will yield significant effects** Bassuk, S. S., Church, T. S., & Manson, J. E. (2013, August). Why exercise works magic. *Scientific American,* 74–79.

and, World Health Organization. (n.d.). Global recommendations on physical activity for health. Retrieved from http://www.who.int/dietphysicalactivity/factsheet_recommendations/en/

and, Erickson, K. I., Voss, M. W., Prakash, R. S., Basak, C., Szabo, A., Chaddock, L., . . . Kramer, A. F. (2011). Exercise training increases size of hippocampus and improves memory. *Proceedings of the National Academy of Sciences, 108*(7), 3017–3022.

211 **decline by increasing blood flow to the brain** Pereira A. C., Huddleston, D. E., Brickman, A. M., Sosunov, A. A., Hen, R., McKhann, G. M., . . . Small, S. M. (2007). An *in vivo* correlate of exercise-induced neurogenesis in the adult dentate gyrus. *Proceedings of the National Academy of Sciences, 104*(13), 5638–5643.

211 **increases in the size of the prefrontal cortex** Colcombe, S. J., Erickson, K. I., Scalf, P. E., Kim, J. S., Prakash, R., McAuley, E., . . . Kramer, A. F. (2006). Aerobic exercise training increases brain volume in aging humans. *The Journals of Gerontology Series A: Biological Sciences and Medical Sciences, 61*(11), 1166–1170.

and, Hillman, C. H., Erickson, K. I., & Kramer, A. F. (2008). Be smart, exercise your heart: Exercise effects on brain and cognition. *Nature Reviews Neuroscience, 9*(1), 58–65.

211 **memory, and critical thinking** Colcombe S. J., Kramer, A. F., Erickson, K. I., Scalf, P., McAuley, E. Cohen, N. J., . . . Elavsky, S. (2004). Cardiovascular fitness, cortical plasticity, and aging. *Proceedings of the National Academy of Sciences, 101*(9), 3316–3321.

213 **". . . only worth ten minutes of my time."** Lavin, D., personal communication. October 23, 2012.

213 **president of a $20 billion Fortune 100 company** This figure is in constant dollars; the company's revenues were $10 billion in 1988, and according to the U.S. Bureau of Labor Statistics, this is equivalent to $20 billion in 2013, the most recent year for which statistics are available.

United States Department of Labor Bureau of Labor Statistics. (n.d.). Databases, tables & calculators by subject, CPI inflation calculator. Retrieved from http://www.bls.gov/data/inflation_calculator.htm

213 **and his To Do list** Linda, personal communication. November 16, 2009.

215 **than when they were younger** Fraisse, P. (1963). *The psychology of time*. New York, NY: Harper & Row.

and, Walker, J. L. (1977). Time estimation and total subjective time. *Perceptual and Motor Skills, 44*(2), 527–532.

215 **ten-year-old than for a forty-year-old** Walker, J. L. (1977). Time estimation and total subjective time. *Perceptual and Motor Skills, 44*(2), 527-532.

The formula is $S = (A_1/A_2)^{1/2}$ where *S* equals the subjective duration, and *A* equals the age of the person in question.

215 **the actual speed of neural transmission slows** Block, R. A., Zakay, D., & Hancock, P. A. (1998). Human aging and duration judgments: A meta-analytic review. *Psychology and Aging, 13*(4), 584–596, p. 584.

and, McAuley, J. D., Jones, M. R., Holub, S., Johnston, H. M., & Miller, N. S. (2006). The time of our lives: Life span development of timing and event tracking. *Journal of Experimental Psychology: General, 135*(3), 348.

216 **such as spending time with family and friends** The two sentences that begin with *When time is perceived as open-ended* . . . are taken nearly verbatim from: Carstensen, L. L. (2006). The influence of a sense of time on human development. *Science, 312*(5782), 1913–1915.

216 **to view the world more like old people** Carstensen, L. L., & Fredrickson, B. L. (1998). Influence of HIV status and age on cognitive representations of others. *Health Psychology, 17*(6), 494–503, p. 494.

and, Fung, H. H., & Carstensen, L. L. (2006). Goals change when life's fragility is primed: Lessons learned from older adults, the September 11 attacks and SARS. *Social Cognition, 24*(3), 248–278.

216 **crêpes suzette or cassoulet de canard** Wansink, B., Kniffin, K. M., & Shimizu, M. (2012). Death row nutrition: Curious conclusions of last meals. *Appetite, 59*(3), 837–843.

216 **while younger adults show the opposite** Mather, M., & Carstensen, L. L. (2005). Aging and motivated cognition: The positivity effect in attention and memory. *Trends in Cognitive Sciences, 9*(10), 496–502.

217 **positivity bias is reflected in brain scans** Carstensen, L. L. (2006). The influence of a sense of time on human development. *Science, 312*(5782), 1913–1915.

217 **mental activity protects against Alzheimer's** Furst, A. J., Rabinovici, G. D., Rostomian, A. H., Steed, T., Alkalay, A., Racine, C., . . . Jagust, W. J. (2012). Cognition, glucose metabolism and amyloid burden in Alzheimer's disease. *Neurobiology of Aging, 33*(2), 215–225.

and, Jagust, W. J., & Mormino, E. C. (2011). Lifespan brain activity, β-amyloid, and Alzheimer's disease. *Trends in Cognitive Sciences, 15*(11), 520–526.

217 **". . . is probably more important."** "It has to do with lifelong patterns of behavior," says William Jagust, a neuroscientist at UC Berkeley. "We tend to focus on what people do at seventy-five in terms of dementia. But there is more evidence that what you do in your life, at forty or fifty, is probably more important."

Quoted in Grady, D. (2012, March 8). Exercising an aging brain. *The New York Times*, p. F6.

217 **life span is protective against Alzheimer's** Seeman, T. E., Miller-Martinez, D. M., Merkin, S. S., Lachman, M. E., Tun, P. A., & Karlamangla, A. S. (2011). Histories of social engagement and adult cognition: Midlife in the US study. *The Journals of Gerontology Series B: Psychological Sciences and Social Sciences, 66*(Suppl. 1), i141–i152.

218 **creativity combined with a measure of luck** Campbell, D. T. (1960). Blind variation and selective retentions in creative thought as in other knowledge processes. *Psychological Review, 67*(6), 380–400, p. 380.

CHAPTER 6

219 **"Nothing comes to my desk that is perfectly solvable"** Lewis, M. (2012, September 5). Barack Obama to Michael Lewis on a presidential loss of freedom: "You don't get used to it—at least, I don't." *Vanity Fair.*

220 **"I'm the one who has to choose . . ."** Wynn, S., personal communication. August 1, 2010.

222 **uncertainty about the best treatment** Gerstein, L. (M.D.), personal communication. April 9, 2013.

224 **probability of a baby being born a boy** The precise ratio of boys to girls is not as simple a question as it may seem. We need to specify whether we are interested only in live births; whether we're looking at hospital births only or all births; whether or not we're counting twins. Variations have been observed depending on these factors as well as the race of the parents, the country being considered, and many others. The ratio comes out to being very close to 50-50 but not exactly.

224 **90% chance** For the sake of completeness, there are rare cases where a statement like "There is a 90 percent chance I'm going to Susan's party" *is* actually based on a calculation. Say, for example, that my car is in the shop and it needs either a new fuel injector or a valve-and-ring overhaul. If it's just a fuel injector, they can have it ready for me by Friday—in time for me to take it to the party—but if it requires the overhaul, they need an extra week to pull the engine and get it to a machine shop. Now, my mechanic may have access to data from the automobile manufacturer that says that there is a 90% probability of fuel injector failure for cars with my mileage, and a 10% probability of needing the valve-and-ring overhaul. Here, my statement about attending Susan's party—normally an estimate of confidence, not a strict probability—is *tied* to an actual probability calculation, that of needing a new fuel injector. If I wanted to be completely accurate about the party, I'd say, "I'm hoping to go, but according to the mechanic, there's a 10 percent chance my car won't be ready, and then I won't go." This is cumbersome, but it makes clear that my probability statement is not an estimate, but rather, is tied to a calculated event.

224 **"There is a ten percent probability that a rogue nation . . ."** I'm being particularly optimistic with this 10% estimate. In 2006, Robert Gallucci, dean of the Georgetown University School of Foreign Service, estimated that "it is more likely than not that al-Qaeda or one of its affiliates will detonate a nuclear weapon in a U.S. city within the next five to ten years." The phrase "more likely than not" obviously means a greater than 50% chance. Quoted in Kittrie, O. F. (2007). Averting catastrophe: Why the nuclear nonproliferation treaty is losing its deterrence capacity and how to restore it. *Michigan Journal of International Law, 28*, 337–430, p. 342.

225 **the chance is 1 in 10,000** National Weather Service. (n.d.). How dangerous is lightning? Retrieved from http://www.lightningsafety.noaa.gov

225 **hit by lightning twice** (n.a.). (2011, May 2). How lucky can you get! Incredible story of how man survives being hit by lightning TWICE in remarkable CCTV footage. *Daily Mail.*

and, Campbell, K. (2000). *Guinness World Records 2001.* New York, NY: Guinness World Records Ltd., p. 36.

226 **Blank Airways just had their crash** I wrote this independently and then discovered that it closely mirrors a passage in the book by Hacking that I encountered only later. Hacking, I. (2001). *An introduction to probability and inductive logic.* New York, NY: Cambridge University Press, p. 31.

227 **each of which is equally likely** This is one of those cases where intuition—our gut—is engaging in faulty reasoning. The probability of getting ten heads in a row followed by one tail is exactly the same as the probability of getting ten heads in a row followed by one more head. Both sequences are extremely unlikely, but when you've already gotten those ten heads in a row, that eleventh outcome is still 50-50, and the toss can still go either way. Tails are not due. They don't need to appear in order to balance out the sequence.

227 **no one put down runs of seven heads or tails in a row** Hacking, I. (2001). *An introduction to probability and inductive logic.* New York, NY: Cambridge University Press, p. 31.

227 **14 flips are required to get three heads in a row** Ginsparg, P. (2005). How many coin flips on average does it take to get *n* consecutive heads? Retrieved from https://www.cs.cornell.edu/~ginsparg/physics/INFO295/mh.pdf

227 **in 100 flips, there's a greater than 99.9% chance** The probability of getting at least one run that's three heads or longer in *N* flips is

1–(1.236839844 / 1.087378025^(*N*+1))
Which for 100 flips is about 0.9997382.
Weisstein, E. W. (n.d.). Run. Retrieved from http://mathworld.wolfram.com/Run.html

227 **(all that is left are aces)** Mosteller, F., Rourke, R. E. K., & Thomas, G. B. (1961). *Probability and statistics.* Reading, MA: Addison-Wesley, p. 17.

228 **don't ignore the base rate** Gerstein, L. (M.D.), personal communication. April 9, 2013.

228 **850,000 doctors in the United States** Young, A., Chaudhry, H. J., Rhyne, J., & Dugan, M. (2011). A census of actively licensed physicians in the United States, 2010. *Journal of Medical Regulation, 96*(4), 10–20.

228 **only fifteen cabinet members** The White House. (n.d.). The cabinet. Retrieved from http://www.whitehouse.gov/administration/cabinet

There are sixteen cabinet members, counting the vice president.

228 **sixteen members of the 111th Congress were doctors** Manning, J. E. (2010). Membership of the 111th Congress: A Profile. Washington, DC: Congressional Research Service Publication https://www.senate.gov/CRSReports/crs-publish.cfm?pid=%260BL%29PL%3B%3D%0A_7-5700

230–31 **fourfold tables (also known as contingency tables)** Bishop, Y. M., Fienberg, S. E., & Holland, P. W. (1975). *Discrete multivariate analysis: Theory and practice.* Cambridge, MA: MIT Press.

and, Wickens, T. D. (1989). *Multiway contingency tables analysis for the social sciences.* Hillsdale, NJ: Lawrence Erlbaum Associates, Inc.

231 **a medication called chlorohydroxelene** I made this up. There is no medication called chlorohydroxelene. Any similarity between medications living or dead is coincidence.

234 **Unfortunately, these numbers are typical** The meds we're talking about here are for blurritis—I didn't mention anything about meds for the itchy back. In fact, there is a real condition in which you have an itch on your back just where you can't reach it—notalgia paresthetica—and it has no cure.

235 **assume a population of 120** You can choose any number you like here. I chose 120 because I knew it had to be divisible by 6 to retain whole numbers in the example. Whole numbers aren't necessary—you could start with a population of 100 and you'd end up with decimal places in the table, which is fine.

235 **green disease and 20 must have** This is solved with high school algebra. There is some number x that represents the number of people with the less common disease (the blue disease): $5x$ represents the more common disease (the green disease); $x + 5x$ has to equal the 120 that we designated would be our population for the purposes of this table. We set up the equation $x + 5x = 120$. Adding the two terms on the left gives us $6x = 120$. Dividing both sides of the equation by 6, to isolate the single x, gives us $x = 20$. Therefore, the number of people with the blue disease equals 20.

237 **come out ahead in the long run by paying parking tickets** My publisher told me I had to put in the following note: "I am not counseling anyone to break the law by parking illegally; I'm using this only to make a hypothetical point."

237 **$650 on parking tickets versus $1,040** We can add different outcomes for a total expected value. Suppose there is an urn full of paper money—$1, $5, and $20 bills. You're allowed to reach in and take one and you keep whatever you get. There are 65 $1 bills, 25 $5 bills and 10 $20 bills. What is the expected value of the game? Because the total number of bills adds up to 100 (65 + 25 + 10), it's easy to convert these into probabilities: There's a .65 chance of getting $1, a .25 chance of getting $5, and a .1 chance of getting $20. We multiply each probability by its payoff, and add them together:

$$\begin{array}{r} .65 \times \$1 = \$\ .65 \\ .25 \times \$5 = \$1.25 \\ \underline{.1 \times \$20 = \$2.00} \\ \$3.90 \end{array}$$

The expected value is therefore $3.90. Note that you can never actually get this exact amount of money. But this is the *average* amount you should expect to receive, and it helps to calculate how much you'd be willing to pay to play this game. The probabilities change slightly as the bills are sequentially drawn because fewer remain in the urn and you know which ones you've drawn already.

When you go to a carnival and pay to throw baseballs at milk bottles, or rings onto cones, you might be lured by the giant stuffed animals and other attractive prizes. The cost of playing the game is usually only a fraction of the value of the prize. But carnivals are in the business of making money and they've worked things out to favor "the house," the carnival or concession owner. The expected value of these games is always lower than the cost of playing it. Although a few people come out ahead, winning prizes that are greater in value than what they spend to play, in the long run the carnival makes a lot of money.

Casinos work the same way.

238 **your doctor is ill-equipped to walk through the statistics** I know this from having taught medical students for many years. In addition, most medical students fail to evaluate information sources as they are "ill equipped and unwilling" according to Thompson, N., Lewis, S., Brennan, P., & Robinson, J. (2010). Information literacy: Are final-year medical radiation science students on the pathway to success? *Journal of Allied Health, 39*(3), e83–e89. To be fair, medical training is so unbelievably detailed and intense, most students have little time for anything outside the prescribed curriculum—there is just an enormous amount to absorb in a relatively short time.

239 **"Doctors generate better knowledge of efficacy . . ."** Jones, D. S. (2012). *Broken hearts: The tangled history of cardiac care.* Baltimore, MD: The Johns Hopkins University Press.

239 **500,000 performed in the United States every year** University of Michigan Health System. (2013). Coronary artery bypass grafting (CABG). Retrieved from http://www.med.umich.edu/cardiac-surgery/patient/adult/adultcandt/cabg.shtml

239 **no survival benefit in most patients** Murphy, M. L., Hultgren, H. N., Detre, K., Thomsen, J., & Takaro, T. (1977). Treatment of chronic stable angina: A preliminary report of survival data of the randomized Veterans Administration Cooperative Study. *New England Journal of Medicine, 297*(12), 621–627.

239 **. . . they come to believe that it *does* work . . .** Jones, D. S. (2012). *Broken hearts: The tangled history of cardiac care.* Baltimore, MD: The Johns Hopkins University Press.

239 **Angioplasty went from zero to 100,000 procedures a year** Park, A. (2013, March–April). A cardiac conundrum: How gaps in medical knowledge affect matters of the heart. *Harvard Magazine,* 25–29.

239 **clinical trials show no survival benefit** Ellis, S. G., Mooney, M. R., George, B. S., Da Silva, E. E., Talley, J. D., Flanagan, W. H., & Topol, E. J. (1992). Randomized trial of late elective angioplasty versus conservative management for patients with residual stenoses after thrombolytic treatment of myocardial infarction. Treatment of Post-Thrombolytic Stenoses (TOPS) Study Group. *Circulation, 86*(5), 1400–1406.

and, Hueb, W., Lopes, N. H., Gersh, B. J., Soares, P., Machado, L. A., Jatene, F. B., . . . Ramires, J. A. (2007). Five-year follow-up of the Medicine, Angioplasty, or Surgery Study (MASS II): A randomized controlled clinical trial of 3 therapeutic strategies for multivessel coronary artery disease. *Circulation, 115*(9), 1082–1089.

and, Michels, K. B., & Yusuf, S. (1995). Does PTCA in acute myocardial infarction affect mortality and reinfarction rates? A quantitative overview (meta-analysis) of the randomized clinical trials. *Circulation, 91*(2), 476–485.

239 **extend life expectancy by even one day** Jones, D. S. (2012). *Broken hearts: The tangled history of cardiac care.* Baltimore, MD: The Johns Hopkins University Press.

239 **People given a choice** Engelmann, J. B., Capra, C. M., Noussair, C., & Berns, G. S. (2009). Expert financial advice neurobiologically "offloads" financial decision-making under risk. *PLoS One, 4*(3), e4957.

239 **hand over their decision to the expert** Hertz, N. (2013, October 20). Why we make bad decisions. *The New York Times,* p. SR6.

240 **prostate cancer treatments** I am borrowing liberally here from a piece I previously published. Levitin, D. J. (2011, October 9). Heal thyself. [Review of the book *Your*

medical mind: How to decide what is right for you by J. Groopman & P. Hartzband]. *The New York Times Sunday Book Review,* p. BR28.

240 **2.5 million men** Howlader, N., Noone, A. M., Krapcho, M., Neyman, N., Aminou, R., Waldron, W., . . . Cronin, K. A. (Eds.). SEER Cancer Statistics Review, 1975–2009 (Vintage 2009 Populations). Bethesda, MD: National Cancer Institute, based on November 2011 SEER data submission. Retrieved from http://seer.cancer.gov/archive/csr/1975_2009_pops09/

240 **3% of men will die** American Cancer Society. (2013). What are the key statistics about prostate cancer? Retrieved from http://www.cancer.org

240 **radical surgery to remove the prostate** National Cancer Institute. (2013). Prostate cancer treatment (PDQ®): Treatment option overview. Retrieved from http://www.cancer.gov

and, Scholz, M., & Blum, R. (2010). *Invasion of the prostate snatchers: No more unnecessary biopsies, radical treatment or loss of sexual potency.* New York, NY: Other Press, pp. 20–21.

240 **most men die *with* it** Groopman, J., & Hartzband, P. (2011). *Your medical mind: How to decide what is right for you.* New York, NY: Penguin, pp. 246–247.

and, Hessels, D., Verhaegh, G. W., Schalken, J. A., & Witjes, J. A. (2004). Applicability of biomarkers in the early diagnosis of prostate cancer. *Expert Review of Molecular Diagnostics, 4*(4), 513–526.

240 **what about the side effects?** Hugosson, J., Stranne, J., & Carlsson, S. V. (2011). Radical retropubic prostatectomy: A review of outcomes and side-effects. *Acta Oncologica, 50*(Suppl. 1), 92–97.

and, National Cancer Institute. (2014). Stage I prostate cancer treatment. Retrieved from http://www.cancer.gov

and, Prostate Doctor. (2011, June 4). Shortening of the penis after prostatectomy: Yes, it really happens [Web log message]. Retrieved from http://myprostatedoc.blogspot.com

and, Talcott, J. A., Rieker, P., Clark, J. A., Propert, K. J., Weeks, J. C., Beard, C. J., . . . Kantoff, P. W. (1998). Patient-reported symptoms after primary therapy for early prostate cancer: Results of a prospective cohort study. *Journal of Clinical Oncology, 16*(1), 275–283, p. 275.

and, Wilt, T. J., MacDonald R., Rutks, I., Shamliyan, T. A., Taylor, B. C., & Kane, R. L. (2008). Systematic review: Comparative effectiveness and harms of treatments for clinically localized prostate cancer. *Annals of Internal Medicine, 148*(6), 435–448.

240 **Forty-seven out of 48** Schröder, F. H., Hugosson, J., Roobol, M. J., Tammela, T., Ciatto, S., Nelen, V., . . . Auvinen, A. (2009). Screening and prostate cancer mortality in a randomized European study. *New England Journal of Medicine, 360*(13), 1320–1328.

241 **24 times more likely to be harmed** Kao, T. C., Cruess, D. F., Garner, D., Foley, J., Seay, T., Friedrichs, P., . . . Moul, J. W. (2000). Multicenter patient self-reporting questionnaire on impotence, incontinence and stricture after radical prostatectomy. *The Journal of Urology, 163*(3), 858–864.

and, Bates, T. S., Wright, M. P., & Gillatt, D.A. (1998). Prevalence and impact of incontinence and impotence following total prostatectomy assessed anonymously by the ICS-Male Questionnaire. *European Urology 33*(2), 165-169.

241 **20% regret their decision** Parker-Pope, T. (2008, August 27). Regrets after prostate surgery. *The New York Times.*

241 **"It's very hard to tell a surgeon . . ."** This quote comes from Pollock, A. (2013, May 8). New test improves assessment of prostate cancer risk, study says. *The New York Times,* p. B3.

241 **"Surgeons are taught . . ."** Kenet, B., personal communication. January 30, 2014, New York, NY.

243 **extend your life by one hour for every hour you exercise** Science Daily Health Behavior News Service. (2012). Exercise can extend your life by as much as five years. Retrieved from www.sciencedaily.com/releases/2012/12/121211082810.htm

243 **doesn't match a single person** Consider a statistic for the average number of hours per week that people spend watching television. In a small apartment building, maybe 4 people watch 1 hour a week, and 1 person watches 10 hours a week. To compute the average, we total the number of hours per week (1 + 1 + 1 + 1 + 10 = 14) and divide by the number of people (14/5) to get 2.8. No one in the apartment building watches 2.8 hours per week in this case, but it is the average.

I'm using the term *average* here interchangeably with the statistical concept of the "mean."

There are two other measures of central tendency, the median and the mode, and these are also called averages. The median is the midway point, the number at which half the observations are above and half are below. If we looked at weekly incomes in that same apartment building, and they were $500, $500, $600, $700, $800, the median is $600: Half the values are above and half are below. (By convention, when you have a bunch of ties as in the number of hours per week of TV watching, you still count up to the halfway point in the list and that number becomes the median; in the TV example, the median is 1). The other measure that is also called an average is the "mode," the value that occurs most often. In the hours per week of TV example, the mode is 1. In the weekly income, it is $500. Note that the mean, median, and mode can be different. They serve different functions. For examples of when each is useful, see Wheelan, C. (2013). *Naked statistics: Stripping the dread from the data.* New York, NY: W. W. Norton & Company.

245 **erectile dysfunction** Tuncel, A., Kirilmaz, U., Nalcacioglu, V., Aslan, Y., Polat, F., & Atan, A. (2008). The impact of transrectal prostate needle biopsy on sexuality in men and their female partners. *Urology, 71*(6), 1128–1131.

247 **". . . medical statistics are different from other statistics."** I hope that you, dear reader, will believe me when I say that medical statistics are *not* different from other statistics. The numbers in an equation don't know whether they're being used to describe cancer or faulty fuel injectors. I wish this one surgeon's reaction were an anomaly, but unfortunately, I've heard dozens of variations of this. I'm immensely grateful that surgeons are much better at surgery than they are at decision-making, but this just means all of us have to be more vigilant at the front end, deciding whether surgery is the best option in any given situation.

248 **both an art and a science** Edwards, A., Elwyn, G., & Mulley, A. (2002). Explaining risks: Turning numerical data into meaningful pictures. *BMJ, 324*(7341), 827–830.

250 **Diphtheria fell from 175,000 cases** National Immunization Program, CDC. (1999). Achievements in public health, 1900–1999 impact of vaccines universally

recommended for children—United States, 1990–1998. *Morbidity and Mortality Weekly Report, 48*(12), 243–248. Retrieved from http://www.cdc.gov/mmwr/preview/mmwrhtml/00056803.htm#00003753.htm

250 **World life expectancy since then has increased** Global life expectancy 10, 000 BCE–2003. (n.d.). Retrieved from http://cdn.singularityhub.com/wp-content/uploads/2013/09/life-expectancy-hockey-stick.png

250 **U.S. life expectancy** National Institutes of Health. (n.d.). U.S. life expectancy. Retrieved from http://www.nih.gov/about/impact/life_expectancy_graph.htm

250 **Infant, neonatal, and postneonatal mortality** Maternal and Child Health Bureau. (2013). Infant mortality. Retrieved from http://mchb.hrsa.gov/chusa13/perinatal-health-status-indicators/p/infant-mortality.html

250 **rates for childhood leukemia** Simone, J. V. (2003). Childhood leukemia—successes and challenges for survivors. *New England Journal of Medicine, 349*(7), 627–628.

251 **$60 billion business** Think yourself better. *The Economist.* (2011, May 19). The *New York Times* estimates it as a $32 billion business in the US.

and, O'Connor, A. (2013, December 21). Spike in harm to liver is tied to dietary aids. *The New York Times*, p. A1.

251 **Forty percent of Americans** Mayo Clinic Staff. (2011, October 20). Complementary and alternative medicine. Retrieved from http://www.mayoclinic.com/health/alternative-medicine/PN00001

251 **it is simply called *medicine*** I thank Ben Goldacre for this formulation.

252 **diluting a substance repeatedly** Ernst, E. (2002). A systematic review of systematic reviews of homeopathy. *British Journal of Clinical Pharmacology, 54*(6), 577–582.

and, Jonas, W. B., Kaptchuk, T. J., & Linde, K. (2003). A critical overview of homeopathy. *Annals of Internal Medicine, 138*(5), 393–399.

252 **According to homeopaths, the "vibrations"** Dancu, D. (1996). *Homeopathic vibrations: A guide for natural healing.* Longmont, CO: SunShine Press Publications.

and, Kratky, K. W. (2004). Homöopathie und Wasserstruktur: Ein physikalisches Modell [Homeopathy and structure of water: A physical model]. *Forschende Komplementärmedizin und Klassische Naturheilkunde [Research in Complementary and Classical Natural Medicine], 11*(1), 24–32.

and, Vithoulkas, G. (1980). *The science of homeopathy.* New York, NY: Grove Press.

252 **a very specific procedure** Goldacre, B. (2011, February 19). In case of overdose, consult a lifeguard. *The Guardian.*

and, Randi, J. [Rational Response Squad]. (2006, November 16). *James Randi explains homeopathy* [Video file]. Retrieved from http://www.youtube.com

252 **grain of rice in solar system:** Assume a grain of rice at $5 \times 1.4 \times 1.4$ mm, or a volume of 9.8 m^3. Convert to miles = 2.4×10^{-18}. Take for the size of our solar system the radius from the sun to one end of the Oort cloud, about 50 AUs or 4.65×10^{12} miles. Volume = $4/3\Pi r^3 = 4.21 \times 10^{38}$. One grain of rice in a sphere the volume of the solar system would be $(2.4 \times 10^{-18}) / (4.21 \times 1038) = 5.70 \times 10^{-57}$. To achieve a dilution of 1×101^{500} requires 1500/57 more dilutions, or 26 more times.

253 **Randi has offered $1 million** Solon, O. (2011, February 11). Sceptic offers $1 million for proof that homeopathy works. *Wired UK.*

253 **equivalent to placebo** Think yourself better. *The Economist.* (2011, May 19).

253 **multivitamins are not effective for anything** Ebbing, M., & Vollset, S. E. (2013). Long-term supplementation with multivitamins and minerals did not improve male US physicians' cardiovascular health or prolong their lives. *Evidence-Based Medicine, 18*(6), 218–219.

and, Guallar, E., Stranges, S., Mulrow, C., Appel, L. J., & Miller, E. R. (2013). Enough is enough: Stop wasting money on vitamin and mineral supplements. *Annals of Internal Medicine, 159*(12), 850–851.

and, Willig, A. (2014, January 19). Multivitamins are no use? *The Guardian.*

253 **Excess Vitamin D** Rattue, G. (2012, January 9). Can too much vitamin D harm cardiovascular health? Probably. *Medical News Today.*

253 **excess Vitamin B6** Sheehan, J. (n.d.). Can you take too much vitamin B6 & vitamin B12? Retrieved from http://healthyeating.sfgate.com/can-much-vitamin-b6-vitamin-b12-6060.html

253 **millions of Americans take Vitamin C** Marshall, C. W. (n.d.). *Vitamin C: Do high doses prevent colds?* Retrieved from http://www.quackwatch.com/01QuackeryRelatedTopics/DSH/colds.html

253 **echinacea when they feel a cold** Bauer, B. A. (n.d.). Will dietary supplements containing echinacea help me get over a cold faster? Retrieved from http://www.mayoclinic.com/health/echinacea/an01982

256 **"Every parent who has stayed up . . ."** Kahneman, D. (2011). *Thinking, fast and slow.* New York, NY: Farrar, Straus and Giroux.

256 **2,170 more people died** There exist conflicting statistics about this. Deonandan and Backwell (2011) found no difference in fatalities, but an increase in injuries. Blalock, Kadiyali, & Simon (2009) found an increase in fatalities of 982 for the last three months of 2001, but as many as 2,300 over the long term. The 9/11 effect appears to be continuing—hundreds more people die in highway accidents every September than the baseline for traffic accidents, due to fears that terrorists will strike again on or about the 9/11 anniversary (Hampson, 2011).

Gigerenzer (2006) writes: "An estimated 1,500 Americans died on the road in the attempt to avoid the fate of the passengers who were killed in the four fatal flights."

There is a very nicely argued article by Chapman & Harris (2002) about human failure to properly perceive risk, and to overreact to some forms of death and underreact to others. See also, Kenny (2011), and Sivac & Flannagan (2003).

Blalock, G., Kadiyali, V., & Simon, D. H. (2009). Driving fatalities after 9/11: A hidden cost of terrorism. *Applied Economics, 41*(14), 1717–1729.

and, Chapman, C. R., & Harris, A. W. (2002). A skeptical look at September 11th. *Skeptical Inquirer, 26*(5). Retrieved from http://www.csicop.org

and, Deonandan, R., & Backwell, A. (2011). Driving deaths and injuries post-9/11. *International Journal of General Medicine, 4*, 803–807.

and, Gigerenzer, G. (2006). Out of the frying pan into the fire: Behavioral reactions to terrorist attacks. *Risk Analysis, 26*(2), 347–351.

and, Hampson, R. (2011, September 5). After 9/11: 50 dates that quietly changed America. *USA Today.*

and, Kenny, C. (2011, November 18). Airport security is killing us. *Business Week.*

and, Sivak M., & Flannagan, M. (2003). Flying and driving after the September 11 attacks. *American Scientist, 91*(1), 6–8.

256 **ten million safe commercial flights** Snyder, B. (2012, January 9) An incredibly safe year for air travel. *CNN.* Retrieved from http://www.cnn.com

256 **"Terrorists can strike twice . . ."** Gaissmaier, W., & Gigerenzer, G. (2012). 9/11, Act II: A fine-grained analysis of regional variations in traffic fatalities in the aftermath of the terrorist attacks. *Psychological Science, 23*(12), 1449–1454.

256 **But they probably don't.** Kahneman, D. (2011). *Thinking, fast and slow.* New York, NY: Farrar, Straus and Giroux.

257 **accurate only 20% of the time** Christakis, N. A. (1999). *Death foretold: Prophecy and prognosis in medical care.* Chicago, IL: The University of Chicago Press.

257 **wrong for about 40%** Berner, E. S., & Graber, M. L., (2008). Overconfidence as a cause of diagnostic error in medicine. *American Journal of Medicine, 121*(5 Suppl.), S2–S23.

257 **70% of the companies** O'Connor, A. (2013, December 21). Spike in harm to liver is tied to dietary aids. *The New York Times*, p. A1.

258 **Christopher Herrera** O'Connor, A. (2013, December 21). Spike in harm to liver is tied to dietary aids. *The New York Times*, p. A1.

258 **He had suffered liver damage after using a green tea extract** This information is taken from O'Connor, A. (2013, December 22). Spike in harm to liver is tied to dietary aids. *The New York Times*, p. A1.

258 **plural of *anecdote* is not *data*** Sechrest, L., & Pitz, D. (1987). Commentary: Measuring the effectiveness of heart transplant programmes. *Journal of Chronic Diseases, 40*(Suppl. 1), 155S–158S.

259 **Steve Jobs . . . rejected surgery** Quora. (n.d). Why did Steve Jobs choose not to effectively treat his cancer? Retrieved from http://www.quora.com/Steve-Jobs/Why-did-Steve-Jobs-choose-not-to-effectively-treat-his-cancer

and, Walton, A. G. (2011, October 24). Steve Jobs' cancer treatment regrets. *Forbes.*

260 **(NIH) has set up a division** National Center for Complementary and Alternative Medicine (NCCAM). (n.d.). Retrieved from http://nccam.nih.gov/

260 **people who benefit from alternative therapies** See, for example, Garg, S. K., Croft, A. M., & Bager, P. (2014, January 20). Helminth therapy (worms) for induction of remission in inflammatory bowel disease. *Cochrane Database of Systematic Reviews,* (1), Art. No. CD009400. Retrieved from http://summaries.cochrane.org/CD009400/helminth-therapy-worms-for-induction-of-remission-in-inflammatory-bowel-disease

and, White, A. R., Rampes, H., Liu, J. P., Stead, L. F., & Campbell, J. (2014, January 23). Acupuncture and related interventions for smoking cessation. *Cochrane Database of Systematic Reviews,* (1), Art. No. CD000009. Retrieved from http://summaries.cochrane.org/CD000009/do-acupuncture-and-related-therapies-help-smokers-who-are-trying-to-quit

260 **150 people need to be treated with Vitamin D** Bjelakovic, G., Gluud, L., Nikolova, D., Whitfield, K., Wetterslev, J., Simonetti, R. G., . . . Gluud, C. (2014). Vitamin D supplementation for prevention of mortality in adults. *Cochrane Database of Systematic Reviews,* (1), Art. No. CD007470. Retrieved from http://summaries.cochrane.org/CD007470/vitamin-d-supplementation-for-prevention-of-mortality-in-adults#sthash.Z6rLxTiS.dpuf

260 **excess of Vitamin D to mortality** Durup, D., Jørgensen, H. L., Christensen, J., Schwarz, P., Heegaard, A. M., & Lind, B. (2012). A reverse J-shaped association of all-cause mortality with serum 25-hydroxyvitamin D in general practice: The CopD study. *The Journal of Clinical Endocrinology & Metabolism, 97*(8), 2644–2652.

and, Groopman, J., & Hartzband, P. (2011). *Your medical mind: How to decide what is right for you.* New York, NY: Penguin.

261 **four types of patients** I am borrowing liberally here from a piece I previously published. Levitin, D. J. (2011, October 9). Heal thyself. [Review of the book *Your medical mind: How to decide what is right for you* by J. Groopman & P. Hartzband]. *The New York Times Sunday Book Review,* p. BR28.

262 **prospect theory and expected utility** See, for example, Kahneman, D., & Tversky, A. (1979). Prospect theory: An analysis of decision under risk. *Econometrica, 47*(2), 263–292.

262 **Scenario D changes** Amos used to tell an elaborate story about a married man with two children who is taken captive by a rebel group of terrorists who force him to play a modified version of the game Russian roulette, in which various numbers of bullets are loaded into the revolver. The prisoner is allowed to pay his captors to remove one bullet from the gun. The dilemma is that he has to balance how much he values his life against the possibility of leaving his wife and children penniless. (We assume for the sake of the story that the captors are honorable and that they accurately tell him how many bullets are in the gun at the beginning of the game, and that they'll let him go after he plays the game once.)

a. How much would you pay to remove one bullet if there are six bullets in the gun, reducing the risk of dying from 6/6 to 5/6?
b. How much would you pay to remove one bullet if there are four bullets in the gun, reducing the risk of dying from 4/6 to 3/6?
c. How much would you pay to remove one bullet if there is only one bullet in the gun, reducing the risk of dying from 1/6 to 0?

Most of us would pay *any* amount of money in scenario C, to reduce the risk of dying to 0. And we might pay that much money for scenario A as well, showing the possibility effect. Scenario B somehow feels different than the other two. You're moving from one possibility to another possibility, not from certainty to possibility (scenario A) or from possibility to certainty (scenario C).

262 **Daniel Kahneman's *Thinking, Fast and Slow*** Kahneman, D. (2011). *Thinking, fast and slow.* New York, NY: Farrar, Straus and Giroux.

263 **even ridiculous manipulations** Kahneman, D., & Tversky, A. (1984). Choices, values, and frames. *American Psychologist, 39*(4), 341–350, p. 341.

263 **78 die by the end of five years** I've simplified these examples to focus on the critical factors. They are taken from Tversky, A., & Kahneman, D. (1986). Rational choice and the framing of decisions. *Journal of Business 59*(4 pt 2), S251–S278.

263 **better with pictures than with raw numbers** Ferrara, F., Pratt, D., & Robutti, O. (2006). The role and uses of technologies for the teaching of algebra and calculus. In A. Gutiérrez & P. Boero (Eds.), *Handbook of research on the psychology of*

mathematics education: Past, present and future (pp. 237–273). Boston, MA: Sense Publishers.

and, Tall, D. (1991). Intuition and rigour: The role of visualization in the calculus. In W. Zimmermann & S. Cunningham (Eds.), *Visualization in teaching and learning mathematics: A project* (pp. 105–119). Washington, DC: Mathematical Association of America.

264 **proportion of people in each category** Cates, C. (n.d.). Dr. Chris Cates' EBM website. Retrieved from http://www.nntonline.net/

265 **I asked a tire specialist about it** Crosswhite, R., personal communication. April 29, 2013, American Tire Depot, Sherman Oaks, CA.

See also, Montoya, R. (2011, November 18). How old—and dangerous—are your tires? Retrieved from http://www.edmunds.com

CHAPTER 7

268 **The ensuing government inquiry** Government of Quebec, Transports Quebec. (2007). *Commission of inquiry into the collapse of a portion of the de la Concorde overpass: Report.* Retrieved from http://www.cevc.gouv.qc.ca/UserFiles/File/Rapport/report_eng.pdf

268 **The history of shoddy construction** Tranquillus Suetonius, C. (1997). *Lives of the twelve Caesars* (H. M. Bird, Trans.). Hertfordshire, UK: Wordsworth Classics of World Literature.

269 **Up until the mid 1800s, businesses were primarily** Yates, J. (1989). *Control through communication: The rise of system in American management.* Baltimore, MD: The Johns Hopkins University Press. In this paragraph, I'm borrowing liberally, including close paraphrases of Yates's excellent discourse on pp. xv–xix.

There are a few exceptions. The Dutch East India Company, often cited as the first multinational company, had been around since 1602, and the Hudson's Bay Company was founded in 1670 and is still in business today.

Damodaran, A. (2009). The octopus: Valuing multi-business, multi-national companies. Retrieved from http://dx.doi.org/10.2139/ssrn.1609795

and, Lubinsky, P., Romero-Gonzalez, G. A., Heredia, S. M., & Zabel, S. (2011). Origins and patterns of vanilla cultivation in tropical America (1500–1900): No support for an independent domestication of vanilla in South America. In D. Havkin-Frenkel & F. Belanger (Eds.), *Handbook of vanilla science and technology* (p. 117). Oxford, UK: Blackwell Publishing.

and, Shorto, R. (2013). *Amsterdam: A history of the world's most liberal city.* New York, NY: Doubleday.

269 **The need for documentation and functional specialization** Parts of this passage are nearly direct quotes from Yates, J. (1989). *Control through communication: The rise of system in American management.* Baltimore, MD: The Johns Hopkins University Press, p. 1.

269 **No one was certain who** Yates (1989) gives a brief account of this and refers the reader to "Report on the collision of trains, near Chester," October 16, 1841, Western Railroad Clerk's File #74; in Western Railroad Collection, Case #1, Baker Library, Harvard Business School. Yates, J. (1989). *Control through communication: The rise of system in American management.* Baltimore, MD: The Johns Hopkins University Press.

269 **The railroad company investigators** In following the advice offered from these crash reports, railroads acknowledged the need for more formal and more structured communication. Managers began by identifying the items of information that were required—such as the speed of a given train, the time it left the station, how many cars it was pulling—in order to maximize efficiency (and thus profits), and minimize the possibility of accidents.

270 **or capacity of any single individual** "a continuing attempt to transcend dependence upon the skills, memory, or capacity of any single individual." This is a direct quote from Yates, p. 10, citing Jelinek, M. (1980). Toward systematic management: Alexander Hamilton Church. *Business History Review*, *54*(01), 63–79. Yates, J. (1989). *Control through communication: The rise of system in American management.* Baltimore, MD: The Johns Hopkins University Press.

270 **standardized ways of performing these duties** "a careful definition of duties and responsibilities coupled with standardized ways of performing these duties." This is a direct quote from Litterer, J. A. (1963). Systematic management: Design for organizational recoupling in American manufacturing firms. *Business History Review*, 37(4), 369–391, p. 389.

See also, Litterer, J. A. (1961). Systematic management: The search for order and integration. *Business History Review, 35* (4), 461–476.

270 **English efficiency engineer Alexander Hamilton Church** Jelinek, M. (1980). Toward systematic management: Alexander Hamilton Church. *Business History Review, 54*(1), 63–79, p. 69.

and, Litterer, J. A. (1961). Systematic management: The search for order and integration. *Business History Review, 35*(4), 461–476.

271 **reporting relationships among employees** Chandler, Jr., A. D. (1962). *Strategy and structure: Chapters in the history of the American industrial enterprise.* Cambridge, MA: MIT Press.

and, Kaliski, B. S. (2001). *Encyclopedia of business and finance.* New York, NY: Macmillan, p. 669.

271 **Network diagrams were first introduced** Moreno, J. L. (1943). Sociometry and the cultural order. *Sociometry 6*(3), 299–344.

and, Wasserman, S. (1994). *Social network analysis: Methods and applications* (Vol. 8). New York, NY: Cambridge University Press.

272 **Compare these two different org charts** Whitenton, K. (2013, November 10). Flat vs. deep web hierarchies. Nielsen Norman Group. Retrieved from http://www.nngroup.com/articles/flat-vs-deep-hierarchy/

272 **flat structure with decentralized control and communications** Dodson, J. R. (2006). Man-hunting, nexus topography, dark networks, and small worlds. *IO Sphere*, 7–10.

and, Heger, L., Jung, D., & Wong, W. H. (2012). Organizing for resistance: How group structure impacts the character of violence. *Terrorism and Political Violence*, *24*(5), 743–768.

and, Matusitz, J. (2011). Social network theory: A comparative analysis of the Jewish revolt in antiquity and the cyber terrorism incident over Kosovo. *Information Security Journal: A Global Perspective*, *20*(1), 34–44.

273 **coherence across different components of a project** Simon, H. A. (1957). *Administrative behavior: A study of decision-making processes in administrative organization.* New York, NY: Macmillan, p. 9.

273 **accountable for their decisions and their work product** Simon, H. A. (1957). *Administrative behavior: A study of decision-making processes in administrative organization.* New York, NY: Macmillan, p. 2.

273 **Fifty companies in the world** CNN Money. (n.d.). Top companies: Biggest employers. Retrieved from http://money.cnn.com/

and, Hess, A. E. M. (2013, August 22). The 10 largest employers in America. *USA Today.*

273 **Companies can be thought of as transactive** Wegner, D. M. (1987). Transactive memory: A contemporary analysis of the group mind. In B. Mullen & F. R. Goethals (Eds.), *Theories of group behavior* (pp. 185–208). New York, NY: Springer-Verlag.

274 **The vertical structure allows managers** This is almost a direct quote from Jones, G. R., Mills, A. J., Weatherbee, T. G., & Mills, J. H. (2006). *Organizational theory, design, and change* (Canadian ed.). Toronto, Canada: Prentice Hall, p. 150.

274 **Its corporate culture places a high value** Jones, G. R., Mills, A. J., Weatherbee, T. G., & Mills, J. H. (2006). *Organizational theory, design, and change* (Canadian ed.). Toronto, ON: Prentice Hall, p. 144.

274 **When Liz Claiborne was designing** Nearly a direct quote from Jones, G. R., Mills, A. J., Weatherbee, T. G., & Mills, J. H. (2006). *Organizational theory, design, and change* (Canadian ed.). Toronto, ON: Prentice Hall, p. 147.

274 **different structures work best for different companies** Andersen, J. A., & Jonsson, P. (2006). Does organization structure matter? On the relationship between the structure, functioning and effectiveness. *International Journal of Innovation and Technology Management, 3*(03), 237–263.

274 **rather, it increases the number of levels by a factor of 2** Blau, P. M. (1974). On the nature of organizations. *American Journal of Sociology, 82*(5). 1130–1132.

and, Delmastro, M. (2002). The determinants of the management hierarchy: Evidence from Italian plants. *International Journal of Industrial Organization, 20*(1), 119–137.

and, Graubner, M. (2006). *Task, firm size, and organizational structure in management consulting: An empirical analysis from a contingency perspective (Vol. 63).* Frankfurt, Germany: Deutscher Universitäts-Verlag.

275 **nine or ten levels in their hierarchy** Jones, G. R., Mills, A. J., Weatherbee, T. G., & Mills, J. H. (2006). *Organizational theory, design, and change* (Canadian ed.). Toronto, Canada: Prentice Hall, p. 146.

275 **number of hierarchical levels possible** Hill, C. W. L., & Jones, G. R. (2008). *Strategic management: An integrated approach* (8th ed.). New York, NY: Houghton Mifflin Company.

276 **A fire isn't put out by the fire chief** This section borrows liberally from Simon, H. A. (1957). *Administrative behavior: A study of decision-making processes in administrative organization* (2nd ed.). New York, NY: Macmillan, p. 2.

276 **including the insula and amygdala** Sanfey, A. G., Rilling, J. K., Aronson, J. A., Nystrom, L. E., & Cohen, J. D. (2003). The neural basis of economic decision-making in the ultimatum game. *Science, 300*(5626), 1755–1758.

277 **responsible for the fight-or-flight response** Basten, U., Biele, G., Heekeren, H. R., & Fiebach, C. J. (2010). How the brain integrates costs and benefits during decision-making. *Proceedings of the National Academy of Sciences, 107*(50), 21767–21772.

277 **we bring to decision-making is partly illusory** de Waal, F. B. M. (2008). How selfish an animal? The case of primate cooperation. In P. J. Zak (Ed.), *Moral markets: The critical role of values in the economy* (pp. *63–76).* Princeton, NJ: Princeton University Press, p. 63.

278 **"allowing subordinate and adjacent units . . ."** United States Department of the Army. (2011). *Unified land operations,* ADP3–0. Washington, DC: United States Department of the Army.

278 **". . . upon the province of a subordinate"** United States Department of the Army. (1923). *Field service regulations United States Army.* Washington, DC: Government Printing Office, p. 7.

278 **". . . The trust between all levels depends upon candor. . . ."** United States Department of the Army. (2012). *The army,* ADP 1. Washington, DC: United States Department of the Army, p. 2.

278 **". . . and a willingness to learn from mistakes. . . ."** United States Department of the Army. (2012). *The army,* ADP 1. Washington, DC: United States Department of the Army, pp. 2–4.

278 **". . . possible while keeping operations synchronized."** United States Department of the Army. (2012). *Mission command,* ADP 6–0. Washington, DC: United States Department of the Army, p. 8.

279 **trained, or experienced than the subordinate** Simon, H. A. (1957). *Administrative behavior: A study of decision-making processes in administrative organization* (2nd ed.). New York, NY: Macmillan, p. 236.

279 **can use it for making more important decisions** Nearly a direct quote from Simon, H. A. (1957). *Administrative behavior: A study of decision-making processes in administrative organization* (2nd ed.). New York, NY: Macmillan, p. 236.

279 **directly available to them and not to the superior** Nearly a direct quote from Simon, H. A. (1957). *Administrative behavior: A study of decision-making processes in administrative organization* (2nd ed.). New York, NY: Macmillan, p. 238.

279 **". . . knowledge they already have from the field."** McChrystal, S., personal communication. July 18, 2013.

280 **". . . decision themselves and be comfortable with it."** Wynn, S., personal communication. May 5, 2012, Las Vegas, NV.

280 **". . . do what he thought needed to be done."** Bloomberg, M., personal communication. July 20, 2013.

281 **wired into our brains, a product of evolution** Mikhail, J. (2007). Universal moral grammar: Theory, evidence and the future. *Trends in Cognitive Science, 11*(4), 143–152.

and, Petrinovich, L., O'Neill, P., & Jorgensen, M. (1993). An empirical study of moral intuitions: Toward an evolutionary ethics. *Journal of Personality and Social Psychology, 64*(3), 467–478, p. 467.

and, Wright, R. (1995). *The moral animal: Why we are, the way we are: The new science of evolutionary psychology* (First Vintage Books ed.). New York, NY: Random House Vintage Books.

281 **Even three-year-olds react to inequality** LoBue, V., Nishida, T., Chiong, C., DeLoache, J. S., & Haidt, J. (2011). When getting something good is bad: Even three-year-olds react to inequality. *Social Development, 20*(1), 154–170.

281 **". . . return from a campaign not only as good Soldiers . . ."** United States Department of the Army. (2012). *The army,* ADP 1. Washington, DC: United States Department of the Army, pp. 2-7.

281 **". . . effective and ethical application of combat power."** United States Department of the Army. (2012). *The army,* ADP 1. Washington, DC: United States Department of the Army, pp. 2-5.

282 **Making ethical or moral decisions** Salvador, R., & Folger, R. G. (2009). Business ethics and the brain. *Business Ethics Quarterly, 19*(1), 1–31.

282 **These two regions are also required** Harlow, J. M. (1848). Passage of an iron rod through the head. *Boston Medical and Surgical Journal, 39*(20), 389–393.

and, Moll, J., de Oliveira-Souza, R., Eslinger, P. J., Bramati, I. E., Mourão-Miranda, J., Andreiulo, P. A., & Pessoa, L. (2002). The neural correlates of moral sensitivity: A functional magnetic resonance imaging investigation of basic and moral emotions. *The Journal of Neuroscience, 22*(7), 2730–2736.

and, Spitzer, M., Fischbacher, U., Herrnberger, B., Grön, G., & Fehr, E. (2007). The neural signature of social norm compliance. *Neuron, 56*(1), 185–196.

282 **When damaged, they can lead to socially inappropriate** Salvador, R., & Folger, R. G. (2009). Business ethics and the brain. *Business Ethics Quarterly, 19*(1), 1–31.

282 **As long as the people in the video** King, J. A., Blair, R. J., Mitchell, D. G., Dolan, R. J., & Burgess, N. (2006). Doing the right thing: A common neural circuit for appropriate violent or compassionate behavior. *NeuroImage, 30*(3), 1069–1076.

and, Englander, Z. A., Haidt, J., & Morris, J. P. (2012). Neural basis of moral elevation demonstrated through inter-subject synchronization of cortical activity during free-viewing. *PloS One, 7*(6), e39384.

and, Cavanna, A. E., & Trimble, M. R. (2006). The precuneus: A review of its functional anatomy and behavioural correlates. *Brain, 129*(3), 564–583.

282 **The neuronal populations affected by this** Margulies, D. S., Vincent, J. L., Kelly, C., Lohmann, G., Uddin, L. Q., Biswal, B. B., . . . Petrides, M. (2009). Precuneus shares intrinsic functional architecture in humans and monkeys. *Proceedings of the National Academy of Sciences, 106*(47), 20069–20074.

and, de Waal, F. B. M., Leimgruber, K., & Greenberg, A. R. (2008). Giving is self-rewarding for monkeys. *Proceedings of the National Academy of Sciences, 105*(36), 13685–13689.

283 **If the experimenter gave a larger reward** van Wolkenten, M., Brosnan, S. F., & de Waal, F. B. M. (2007). Inequity responses of monkeys modified by effort. *Proceedings of the National Academy of Sciences, 104*(47), 18854–18859.

283 **Conceptions of leadership vary** Welch was CEO of GE and Kelleher of Southwest Airlines. The two men created very different corporate cultures. Welch was known for a time as Neutron Jack because of the ruthless way he would fire employees (emptying out the buildings but leaving them standing, in the way that a neutron bomb would). In one five-year period, he reduced the payroll by 25%. Kelleher created a climate of camaraderie and fun among his employees, and Southwest is consistently named one of the top five employers in the United States by *Fortune*.

283 **In a free society, an effective leader** United States Department of the Army. (2012). *Army leadership,* ADP 6–22. Washington, DC: United States Department of the Army, p. 1.

283 **A broader definition of leadership promoted** This incorporates a direct quote from Gardner, H. (2011). *Leading minds: An anatomy of leadership.* New York, NY: Basic Books.

284 **Leaders show greater integration of electrical** Harung, H. S., & Travis, F. (2012). Higher mind-brain development in successful leaders: Testing a unified theory of performance. *Cognitive Processing, 13*(2), 171–181.

and, Harung, H., Travis, F., Blank, W., & Heaton, D. (2009). Higher development, brain integration, and excellence in leadership. *Management Decision, 47*(6), 872-894.

284 **friendly luxury vehicle and a midsize** Tschampa, D., & Rosemain, M. (2013, January 24). BMW to build sports car with Toyota in deeper partnership. *Bloomberg News*

284 **"Toxic leaders consistently use . . ."** United States Department of the Army. (2012). *Army leadership,* ADP 6–22. Washington, DC: United States Department of the Army, p. 3.

285 **The latest version of their *Mission Command*** United States Department of the Army. (2012). *Mission command,* ADP 6–0. Washington, DC: United States Department of the Army, p. 2.

285 **Trust is gained or lost through everyday actions** Nearly a direct quote from United States Department of the Army. (2012). *Mission command,* ADP 6–0. Washington, DC: United States Department of the Army, p. 3.

286 **Having communicated a clear and concise** Direct quote from United States Department of the Army. (2012). *Mission command,* ADP 6–0. Washington, DC: United States Department of the Army, p. 4.

286 **". . . What's needed are more people who . . ."** Weisbord, M. R. (2004). *Productive workplace revisited: Dignity, meaning, and community in the 21st century.* San Francisco, CA: Jossey-Bass, p. xxi.

287 **Torelli and Scarlatti are credited with that** Symphony. (2003). In Randel, D. M. (Ed.), *The Harvard dictionary of music.* Cambridge, MA: The Belknap Press of Harvard University Press.

288 **exert the most influence on their lives** Rotter, J. B. (1954). *Social learning and clinical psychology.* Englewood Cliffs, NJ: Prentice Hall.

See also, Roark, M. H. (1978). *The relationship of perception of chance in finding jobs to locus of control and to job search variables on the part of human resource agency personnel* (Doctoral dissertation, Virginia Polytechnic University). Retrieved from Dissertation Abstracts International, *38*, 2070A. (University Microfilms No. 78-18558).

288 **as a group they perform better academically** Whyte, C. B. (1977). High-risk college freshman and locus of control. *The Humanist Educator, 16*(1), 2–5.

and, Whyte, C. B. (1978). Effective counseling methods for high-risk college freshmen. *Measurement and Evaluation in Guidance, 10*(4), 198–200.

See also, Altmann, H., & Arambasich, L. (1982). A study of locus of control with adult students. *Canadian Journal of Counselling and Psychotherapy, 16*(2), 97–101.

288 **who believe they can't respond better to larger-size models** Martin, B. A. S., Veer, E., & Pervan, S. J. (2007). Self-referencing and consumer evaluations of larger-sized female models: A weight locus of control perspective. *Marketing Letters 18*(3), 197–209.

288 **They are also more likely to believe that** Lefcourt, H. M. (1966). Internal versus external control of reinforcement: A review. *Psychological Bulletin, 65*(4), 206–220, p. 206.

and, Moore, S. M., & Ohtsuka, K. (1999). Beliefs about control over gambling among young people, and their relation to problem gambling. *Psychology of Addictive Behaviors, 13*(4), 339–347, p. 339.

and, Rotter, J. B. (1966). Generalized expectancies for internal versus external control of reinforcement. *Psychological Monographs: General and Applied, 80*(1), 1–28, p. 1.

289 **business owners whose shops were destroyed by hurricane Agnes** United States National Oceanic and Atmospheric Administration. (n.d.). Retrieved from http://www.noaa.gov/

289 **Those who were externals and who experienced** Anderson, C. R. (1977). Locus of control, coping behaviors, and performance in a stress setting: A longitudinal study. *Journal of Applied Psychology, 62*(4), 446–451.

289 **The locus-of-control construct is measurable** Spector (1986) advises, "The most widely used instrument to measure locus of control is Rotter's (1966) Internal-External (I-E) scale, which consists of 23 locus of control and six filler items in a forced-choice format."

Rotter, J. B. (1966). Generalized expectancies for internal versus external control of reinforcement. *Psychological Monographs: General and Applied, 80*(1), 1–28, p. 1.

289 **Employees who have an external locus** Spector, P. E. (1986). Perceived control by employees: A meta-analysis of studies concerning autonomy and participation at work. *Human Relations, 39*(11), 1005–1016.

290 **Higher managers tend to have** There is a literature on CEO locus of control, which the interested reader may wish to consult:

Boone, C., & De Brabander, B. (1993). Generalized vs. specific locus of control expectancies of chief executive officers. *Strategic Management Journal, 14*(8), 619–625.

and, Boone, C., De Brabander, B., & Witteloostuijn, A. (1996). CEO locus of control and small firm performance: An integrative framework and empirical test. *Journal of Management Studies, 33*(5), 667–700.

and, Miller, D., De Vries, M. F. R. K., & Toulouse, J-M. (1982). Top executive locus of control and its relationship to strategy-making, structure, and environment. *Academy of Management Journal, 25*(2), 237–253.

and, Nwachukwu, O. C. (2011). CEO locus of control, strategic planning, differentiation, and small business performance: A test of a path analytic model. *Journal of Applied Business Research (JABR), 11*(4), 9–14.

290 **Internals tend to be higher achievers** Benassi, V. A., Sweeney, P. D., & Dufour, C. L. (1988). Is there a relation between locus of control orientation and depression? *Journal of Abnormal Psychology, 97*(3), 357.

290 **Internals, as you might expect** Phares, E. J. (1976). *Locus of control in personality.* New York, NY: General Learning Press.

and, Wolk, S., & DuCette, J. (1974). Intentional performance and incidental learning as a function of personality and task dimensions. *Journal of Personality and Social Psychology, 29*(1), 90–101.

290 **Internals tend to exhibit less conformity than externals** Crowne, D. P., & Liverant, S. (1963). Conformity under varying conditions of commitment. *Journal of Abnormal and Social Psychology, 66*(6), 547–555.

290 **less attitude change after being exposed** Hjelle, L. A., & Clouser, R. (1970). Susceptibility to attitude change as a function of internal-external control. *Psychological Record, 20*(3), 305–310.

290 **Moreover, they're sensitive to reinforcement** Spector, P. E. (1982). Behavior in organizations as a function of employee's locus of control. *Psychological Bulletin, 91*(3), 482–497.

See also, Wang, Q., Bowling, N. A., & Eschleman, K. J. (2010). A meta-analytic examination of work and general locus of control. *Journal of Applied Psychology, 95*(4), 761-768, p. 761.

290 **scheduling, and organizational policy** Spector, P. E. (1982). Behavior in organizations as a function of employee's locus of control. *Psychological Bulletin, 91*(3), 482–497.

290 **". . . Externals, because of their greater compliance . . ."** Direct quote from Spector, P. E. (1982). Behavior in organizations as a function of employee's locus of control. *Psychological Bulletin, 91*(3), 482–497, p. 486.

290 **The combination of high autonomy** This, and the sentence that follows, are nearly direct quotes from p. 221 of Lonergan, J. M., & Maher, K. J. (2000). The relationship between job characteristics and workplace procrastination as moderated by locus of control. *Journal of Social Behavior & Personality, 15*(5), 213–224.

291 **The sandpaper salesman Richard G. Drew** Kelley, T., & Littman, J. (2005). *The ten faces of innovation: IDEO's strategies for defeating the devil's advocate & driving creativity throughout your organization*. New York, NY: Doubleday.

291 **external locus of control with more constrained jobs** Lonergan, J. M., & Maher, K. J. (2000). The relationship between job characteristics and workplace procrastination as moderated by locus of control. *Journal of Social Behavior & Personality, 15*(5), 213–224.

291 **By attributing shallow motives to employees** Epley, N. (2014). *Mindwise: How we understand what others think, believe, feel, and want.* New York, NY: Alfred A. Knopf.

291 **Take the GM auto plant in Fremont, California** Adler, P. S. (1993, January). Time-and-motion regained. *Harvard Business Review, 71*(1), 97–108.

and, Adler, P. S., & Cole, R. E. (1995). Designed for learning: A tale of two auto plants. *MIT Sloan Management Review 34*(3), 157–178.

and, Shook, J. (2010). How to change a culture: Lessons from NUMMI. *MIT Sloan Management Review, 51*(2), 42–51.

291 **Employees had no control over their jobs** This is nearly a direct quote from Epley, N. (2014). *Mindwise: How we understand what others think, believe, feel, and want.* New York, NY: Alfred A. Knopf.

292 **Sticking to a schedule helps** Currey, M. (2013). *Daily rituals: How great minds make time, find inspiration, and get to work.* London, UK: Picador.

292 **They're usually a waste of time** Cuban, M. (n. d.) Quoted in 15 ways to be more productive. *Inc.*

292–93 **Warren Buffett's datebook is nearly completely** Buffett, W. Quoted in Baer. D. (2013, June 11). Why some of the world's most productive people have empty schedules. *Lifehacker.* Retrieved from http://lifehacker.com/why-some-of-the-worlds-most-productive-people-have-emp-512473783

293 **Paper consumption has increased** *The Economist.* (2012, April 3). Daily chart: I'm a lumberjack.

293 **70 million tons of paper in a year** United States Environmental Protection Agency. (n.d.). Frequent questions: How much paper do we use in the United States each year? Retrieved from http://www.epa.gov/osw/conserve/materials/paper/faqs.htm#sources

293 **It would take six trees** *The Economist.* (2012, April 3). Daily chart: I'm a lumberjack.

293 **protocopier called the letter press** The modern office began taking shape in the 1870s. That decade saw the invention of the wire paper clip by the Gem company, of the stapler, and a few years later, the ballpoint pen, Burroughs adding machine, and rubber dating stamps. Yates, J. (1989). *Control through communication: The rise of system in American management.* Baltimore, MD: The Johns Hopkins University Press, p. 8.

Furthermore, Yates notes, "managers of large American railroads during the 1850s and 1860s invented nearly all of the basic techniques of modern accounting, refining financial accounting and inventing capital and cost accounting."

and, Chandler, A. D., Jr. (1977). *The visible hand: The managerial revolution in American business.* Cambridge, MA: Belknap Press of Harvard University Press, p. 109.

294 **Squirrels can locate hundreds of nuts** Jacobs, L. F., & Liman, E. R. (1991). Grey squirrels remember the locations of buried nuts. *Animal Behaviour, 41*(1), 103–110.

294 **The first big improvement** Lenning, M. A. (1920). *Filing methods: A text book on the filing of commercial and governmental records.* Philadelphia, PA: T. C. Davis & Sons.

295 **"... when large amounts of filing were done."** Yates, J. (1989). *Control through communication: The rise of system in American management.* Baltimore, MD: The Johns Hopkins University Press, p. 27.

296 **similar to the three-ring binders we now use** This consisted of two arched metal rings that could be opened and closed, and that were typically built inside of a horizontal drawer (these were often called Shannon files after a leading manufacturer of them).

296 **Vertical files that resemble the ones** Legacy of leadership: Edwin G. Seibels. (1999). Retrieved from http://www.knowitall.org/legacy/laureates/Edwin%20G.%20Seibels.html

296 **"A literate, book-buying Englishman ..."** Gleick, J. (2011). *The Information: A history, a theory, a flood.* New York, NY: Vintage, p. 58.

299 **"... The outside of the binder was clearly labeled ..."** Linda, personal communication. November 16, 2009.

300 **A third category of reference or archival papers** This is adapted from the Pendaflex School. Esselte.com.

302 **As long as they can put their hands** This information comes from interviews the author conducted with current and former White House staffers, including a former White House deputy chief of staff, all of whom requested anonymity because they were not authorized to speak on behalf of the White House.

303 **Mike Kelleher, the director of the Office of Correspondence** Kelleher, M. (2009, August 3). *Letters to the President* [Video file]. Retrieved from http://www.whitehouse.gov/blog/Letters-to-the-President

303 **produce an e-mail when requested** This information is based on interviews with three members of the White House staff, who requested anonymity because they were not authorized to speak on behalf of the administration.

304–5 **"These piles over here are from five years ago,"** Shepard, R., personal communication. February 18, 1998.

305 **"Yes, the desk was clean. . . ."** Kahneman, D., personal communication. December 12, 2012, New York, NY.

305 **Neat and organized are not necessarily the same thing** Allen, D. (2008). *Making it all work: Winning at the game of work and the business of life.* New York, NY: Penguin Books, p. 131.

306 **". . . switching from one task to another."** Citing an interview on the PBS Television program *Frontline.* Yardley, W. (2013, November 10). Clifford Nass, who warned of a data deluge, dies at 55. *The New York Times.*

306 **We all want to believe that we can do** This paragraph is nearly a direct quote from Konnikova, M. (2012, December 16). The power of concentration. *The New York Times,* p. SR8.

See also, Konnikova, M. (2013). *Mastermind: How to think like Sherlock Holmes.* New York, NY: Penguin Books.

306 **Many managers impose rules such as** PBS *Frontline.* (2010, February 2). Interview: Clifford Nass. Retrieved from http://www.pbs.org/wgbh/pages/frontline/digitalnation/interviews/nass.html

307 **As of this writing, there were thirteen hundred apps** Freierman, S. (2011, December 11). One million mobile apps, and counting at a fast pace. *The New York Times.*

and, Readwrite. (2013, January 7). Apple iOS App Store adding 20,000 apps a month, hits 40 billion downloads. Retrieved from http://readwrite.com/2013/01/07/apple-app-store-growing-by

307 **If you're in a stressful environment . . . Google puts Ping-Pong tables** John Kounios, quoted in Lehrer, J., (2008, July 28). The eureka hunt. *The New Yorker,* 40–45. Although there have been questions raised about Lehrer's scholarship, there is no evidence that the content and quotes in the article cited here are inacccurate. These two sentences are paraphrases of quotes from Lehrer's article.

See also: Lametti, D. (2012). Does the *New Yorker* give enough credit to its sources? Brow beat | Slate's culture blog. *Slate.* Retrieved from http://www.slate.com/

307 **installed a full gym at corporate headquarters** Somerville, H. (2013, May 12). Safeway CEO Steve Burd has legacy as a risk-taker. *San Jose Mercury News.*

307 **refueling time pays off for employers and for workers** *The Economist.* (2013, September 24). Working hours: Get a life.

and, Stanford University Department of Computer Science. (n.d.). The relationship between hours worked and productivity. Retrieved from http://www-cs-faculty.stanford.edu/~eroberts/cs181/projects/2004-05/crunchmode/econ-hours-productivity.html

307 **two hours of overtime to accomplish one hour of work** Mar, J. (2013, May 3). 60-hour work week decreases productivity: Study. Retrieved from http://www.canada.com/

307 **A ten-minute nap can be equivalent to an extra hour** Brooks, A., & Lack, L. (2006). A brief afternoon nap following nocturnal sleep restriction: Which nap duration is most recuperative? *Sleep, 29*(6), 831–840.

and, Hayashi, M., Motoyoshi, N., & Hori, T. (2005). Recuperative power of a short daytime nap with or without stage 2 sleep. *Sleep, 28*(7), 829–836.

and, Smith-Coggins, R., Howard, S. K., Mac, D. T., Wang, C., Kwan, S., Rosekind, M. R., . . . Gaba, D. M. (2006). Improving alertness and performance in emergency department physicians and nurses: The use of planned naps. *Annals of Emergency Medicine, 48*(5), 596–604.

308 **ratings from their supervisors improved** Schwartz, T. (2013, February 10). Relax! You'll be more productive. *The New York Times*, p. SR1.

308 **It is now well known that some** Crowley, S. (2013, November 11). Perks of the dot-com culture [Video file]. Retrieved from http://www.myfoxny.com/

308 **Deloitte encourages employees to donate** CNN Money. (2013). Fortune: 100 best companies to work for. Retrieved from http://money.cnn.com/

308 **simulated a military exercise** Streufert, S., Suedfeld, P., & Driver, M. J. (1965). Conceptual structure, information search, and information utilization. *Journal of Personality and Social Psychology, 2*(5), 736.

See also, Streufert, S., & Driver, M. J. (1965). Conceptual structure, information load and perceptual complexity. *Psychonomic Science 3*(1), 249–250.

309 **According to the theory of optimal information** Streufert, S., & Schroder, H. M. (1965). Conceptual structure, environmental complexity and task performance. *Journal of Experimental Research in Personality 1*(2), 132–137.

310 **consumers make poorer choices with more information** Jacoby, J. (1977). Information load and decision quality: Some contested issues. *Journal of Marketing Research, 14*(4), 569–573.

and, Jacoby, J., Speller, D. E., & Berning, C. K. (1974). Brand choice behavior as a function of information load: Replication and extension. *Journal of Consumer Research, 1*(1), 33–42.

and, Jacoby, J., Speller, D. E., & Kohn, C. A. (1974). Brand choice behavior as a function of information load. *Journal of Marketing Research, 11*(1), 63–69.

310 **the decision to purchase a home** Malhotra, N. K. (1982). Information load and consumer decision-making. *Journal of Consumer Research, 8*(4), 419–430.

311 **as how much, they make better decisions** Ariely, D. (2000). Controlling the information flow: Effects on consumers' decision-making and preferences. *Journal of Consumer Research, 27*(2), 233–248.

311 **information you don't care about and can't use** Kahneman, D., Slovic, P., & Tversky, A. (Eds.). (1982). *Judgment under uncertainty: Heuristics and biases.* Cambridge, UK: Cambridge University Press.

311 **developed information theory in the 1940s** Shannon, C. E. (1948). A mathematical theory of communication. *The Bell System Technical Journal, 27,* 379–423, 623–656.

See also, Cover, T. M., & Thomas, J. A. (2006). *Elements of information theory* (2nd ed.). New York, NY: Wiley-Interscience.

and, Hartley, R. V. L. (1928). Transmission of information. *The Bell System Technical Journal, 7*(3), 535–563.

Pierce, J. R. (1980) *An introduction to information theory: Symbols, signals, and noise.* New York, NY: Dover Publications.

311–12 **transmitted only 300–3300 hertz** Anderson, H., & Yull, S. (2002). *BTEC nationals—IT practioners tutor resource pack.* Oxford, UK: Newnes.

313 **The two additional facts that the grid** The bit calculation depends on how a programmer allocates the information to an algorithm. The three instructions might be

shape[square]
size[8]
coloration[alternate].
Or they could be
horizontal size[8]
vertical size[8]
coloration[alternate].

Either case requires 3 commands, and hence, in binary arithmetic, 2 bits (which leaves one bit to spare because 2^2 conveys 4 pieces of information).

313 **loaded chess board require a minimum of 64 pieces of information** Certain configurations could be described with less than 64 pieces of information, such as the starting configuration, which could be described in 32 pieces to represent each of the chess pieces, plus a 33rd instruction that said "all other squares are empty."

315 **Information theory can be applied** In mathematics (the branch of topology) and computer science, a completely downward hierarchical business org chart can be described as a special case of a directed acyclic graph (DAG). A DAG in which all supervision is downward is acyclic, meaning no person lower in the chart loops back up to supervise a higher-up on any occasion; indeed, this is the way in which most corporations function. However, an org chart that is drawn to represent not reporting structure but communication structure would naturally have loops representing when underlings report back up to their superiors.

See, for example, Bang-Jensen, J., & Gutin, G. (2007). *Digraphs: Theory, algorithms and applications.* Berlin, Germany: Springer-Verlag.

and, Christofides, N. (1975). *Graph theory: An algorithmic approach.* New York, NY: Academic Press.

and, Harary, F. (1994). *Graph theory.* Reading, MA: Addison-Wesley.

315 **completely and accurately specified in 2 bits** The org chart shown on page 315 can be conveyed in four computer instructions, or 2 bits:

Structure[standard tree]
Supervisees per supervisor[3]
Levels-like-this[4]
Supervisees per supervisor at last level[>=50, <=100]

316 **needs to be described individually** Kolmogorov, A. N. (1968). Three approaches to the quantitative definition of information. *International Journal of Computer Mathematics 2*(1–4), 157–168.

and, Kolmogorov, A. (1963). On tables of random numbers. *Sankhyā: The Indian Journal of Statistics, Series A 25*(4), 369–375.

317 **calculate the *degree of structure* (or organization)** This notion was first introduced to me in: Hellerman, L. (2006). Representations of living forms. *Biology and Philosophy, 21*(4), 537–552.

Hellerman used it to quantify the degree of organization in biological entities. For him, the principal feature of an organized system involved differentiability. That is, if the parts of an organism are differentiable, it can be said that it has greater organization. A unicellular organism has minimal organization.

He introduces a formula:

Let n_i denote the number of things in the *i*th part.
v denotes the value of the degree of structure in an information-theoretic sense
lg denotes the logarithm base 2
Then, $v(n1, n2, \ldots, nk) = n_1 lg(n/n_1) + n_2 lg(n/n_2) + \ldots + n_k lg(n/n_k)$

A flat structure with undifferentiated parts would have an organization value of 0.

Completely vertical and completely horizontal structure have the same amount of information because {0,8} = {8,0}. So there's a Pareto optimum for organization when the tree is well structured.

319 **Work flow charts can be similarly analyzed** Work flow chart taken from Cardoso, J. (2006). Approaches to compute workflow complexity. In F. Leymann, W. Reisig, S. R. Thatte, & W. van der Aalst (Eds.), *The role of business processes in service oriented architectures.* IBFI: Schloss Dagstuhl, Germany.

320 **To ensure you'll be able to locate important documents** Merrill, D. C., & Martin, J. A. (2010). *Getting organized in the Google era: How to get stuff out of your head, find it when you need it, and get it done right.* New York, NY: Crown Business.

320 **"When my assistant adds a new meeting . . ."** Merrill, D. C., & Martin, J. A. (2010). *Getting organized in the Google era: How to get stuff out of your head, find it when you need it, and get it done right.* New York, NY: Crown Business, p. 161.

321 **As of this writing, 90% of the world's data** Pinheiro, E., Weber, W-D., & Barroso, L. A. (2007). Failure trends in a large disk drive population. *Proceedings of the 5th USENIX Conference on File and Storage Technologies (FAST),* Mountain View, CA. Retrieved from http://static.googleusercontent.com/media/research.google.com/en//archive/disk_failures.pdf

321 **15 degrees Centigrade can double failure rates** Cole, G. (2000). Estimating drive reliability in desktop computers and consumer electronics systems. *Seagate Technology Paper TP-338.1.*

321 **Probabilities that a hard drive will fail** Schroeder & Gibson found failure rates in real installations of up to 13% per year. Application of the binomial theorem yields a 50% probability of at least one failure within five years.

Schroeder, B., & Gibson, G. A. (2007). Disk failures in the real world: What does an MTTF of 1,000,000 hours mean to you? *Proceedings of the 5th USENIX Conference on File and Storage Technologies (FAST),* Mountain View, CA. Retrieved from http://www.pdl.cmu.edu/ftp/Failure/failure-fast07.pdf

See also: He, Z., Yang, H., & Xie, M. (2012, October). Statistical modeling and analysis of hard disk drives (HDDs) failure. *Institute of Electrical and Electronics Engineers APMRC*, pp. 1–2.

321 **suffer a disk failure within two years** Vishwanath, K. V., & Nagappan, N. (2010). Characterizing cloud computing hardware reliability. In *Proceedings of the 1st ACM symposium on cloud computing.* New York, NY: ACM (pp. 193–204).

322 **". . . Scattered like confetti after New Year's Eve."** Boutin, P. (2013, December 12). An app that will never forget a file. *The New York Times*, p. B7.

CHAPTER 8

330–31 **This is according to no less an authority** Sanger, L. (2004, December 31). Why Wikipedia must jettison its anti-elitism. *Kuro5hin*. Retrieved from http://www.kuro5hin.org

To Wikipedia's credit, it contains an article titled "Criticism of Wikipedia," although that piece is, perhaps understandably, biased toward Wikipedia.

Criticism of Wikipedia. (n.d.). In *Wikipedia*. Retrieved March 19, 2014, from http://en.wikipedia.org/wiki/Criticism_of_Wikipedia

331 **Jimmy Wales has stated that experts** User: Jimbo Wales. (n.d.). In *Wikipedia*. Retrieved June 30, 2013, from http://en.wikipedia.org/wiki/User:Jimbo_Wales

333 **"Why would an expert bother contributing . . ."** Dharma. (December 30, 2004). Comment on Sanger, L. (2004, December 31). Why Wikipedia must jettison its anti-elitism [Online forum comment]. Retrieved from http://www.kuro5hin.org

334 **This all began with a *Star Trek* fanzine** Jenkins, H. (1992). *Textual poachers: Television fans and participatory culture.* New York, NY: Routledge.

and, Schulz, N. (n.d.). Fan fiction—TV viewers have it their way: Year in review 2001. In *Encyclopedia Britannica online.*

334 **When the music impresario Bill Graham** Graham, B., personal communication. October, 1983, San Francisco, CA.

335 **Of course, as detailed here, this free ethos for Wikipedia** With all these problems, you'd think that someone would start an online competitor to Wikipedia that uses professional editors and expert writers. Someone has—Larry Sanger—and it's called Citizendium. Unfortunately, it has not been able to catch up with Wikipedia and, sadly, appears to be floundering.

335 **The Smithsonian American Art Museum** Cohen, P. (2013, July 27). Museum welcomes Wikipedia editors. *The New York Times*, p. C1.

336 **As the *New Yorker* essayist** Gopnik, A. (2013, May). Commencement address at McGill University, Montreal, QC.

336 **Recall that being organized and conscientious** Friedman, H. S., Tucker, J. S., Schwartz, J. E., Martin, L. R., Tomlinson-Keasey, C., Wingard, D. L., & Criqui, M. H. (1995). Childhood conscientiousness and longevity: Health behaviors and cause of death. *Journal of Personality and Social Psychology, 68*(4), 696–703.

and, Friedman, H. S., Tucker, J. S., Tomlinson-Keasey, C., Schwartz, J. E., Wingard, D. L., & Criqui, M. H. (1993). Does childhood personality predict longevity? *Journal of Personality and Social Psychology, 65*(1), 176–185.

336 **more important trait than ever before** Goldberg, L. R., personal communication. May 13, 2013.

and, Gurven, M., von Rueden, C., Massenkoff, M., Kaplan, H., & Lero Vie, M. (2013). How universal is the Big Five? Testing the five-factor model of personality variation among forager-farmers in the Bolivian Amazon. *Journal of Personality and Social Psychology, 104*(2), 354–370.

337 **These difficulties arise for two reasons** Beckman, M. (2004). Crime, culpability, and the adolescent brain. *Science, 305*(5684), 596–599.

and, Giedd, J. N., Blumenthal, J., Jeffries, N. O., Castellanos, F. X., Liu, H., Zijdenbos, A., . . . Rapoport, J. L. (1999). Brain development during childhood and adolescence: A longitudinal MRI study. *Nature Neuroscience, 2*(10), 861–863.

and, Sowell, E. R., Thompson, P. M., & Toga, A. W. (2004). Mapping changes in the human cortex throughout the span of life. *The Neuroscientist, 10*(4), 372–392.

and, Steinberg, L. (2004). Risk taking in adolescence: What changes, and why? *Annals of the New York Academy of Sciences, 1021*(1), 51–58.

337 **"Eat the frog. Do that unpleasant thing . . ."** Eberts, A., personal communication. November 26, 2013, Montreal, QC.

339 **some of it deliberately planted** Keller, B. (2013, November 4). It's the golden age of news. *The New York Times*, p. A25. I'm sticking here very close to what Keller wrote: "The flood of social media was contaminated by misinformation (some of it deliberate) and filled with contradictions."

339 **"Social media isn't journalism . . ."** Keller, B. (2013, November 4). It's the golden age of news. *The New York Times*, p. A25. [Emphasis mine.]

339 **ideologically based biases in news reporting** Vallone, R. P., Ross, L., & Lepper, M. R. (1985). The hostile media phenomenon: Biased perception and perceptions of media bias in coverage of the Beirut Massacre. *Journal of Personality and Social Psychology, 49*(3), 577–585.

340 **Aristotle, Cicero, Josephus, and Plutarch for it** Murray, O. (1972). Herodotus and Hellenistic culture. *The Classical Quarterly, 22*(2), 200–213.

and, Sparks, K. L. (Ed.). (1998). *Ethnicity and identity in ancient Israel: Prolegomena to the study of ethnic sentiments and their expression in the Hebrew Bible*. Warsaw, IN: Eisenbrauns.

Although for an alternative view see Lateiner, D. (1989). *The historical method of Herodotus* (Vol. 23). Toronto, ON: University of Toronto Press.

340 **Biases come in many forms** Nelson, R. A. (2003). Tracking propaganda to the source: Tools for analyzing media bias. *Global Media Journal, 2*(3), Article 9.

341 **Librarians and other information specialists** Georgetown University. (2014). Evaluating Internet resources. Retrieved from http://www.library.georgetown.edu/tutorials/research-guides/evaluating-internet-content

and, University of California, Berkeley. (2012, August 5). Evaluating web pages: Techniques to apply and questions to ask. Retrieved from http://www.lib.berkeley.edu/TeachingLib/Guides/Internet/Evaluate.html

341 **(A guide prepared by NASA . . .)** NASA. (n.d.). Evaluating and validating information sources, including web sites. Retrieved from http://wiki.nasa.gov/federal-knowledge-management-working-group-kmwg/wiki/home/z-archives-legacy-content/federal-cio-council-where-technology-meets-human-creativity-2002/f-information-literacy/f-5-tutorial-evaluating-information/f-5c-tutorial-evaluating-and-validating-information-sources-including-web-sites/

341 **Is the page merely an opinion . . . exaggerated** Direct quote from University of California, Berkeley. (2012, August 5). Evaluating web pages: Techniques to apply and questions to ask. Retrieved from http://www.lib.berkeley.edu/TeachingLib/Guides/Internet/Evaluate.html

The nature of the Web is that anyone can copy an article from one website and paste it to another. A re-posted article may show up in search engines as new because it is new to that particular website, not because it is new-to-the-world. Information that is old and out of date can easily masquerade as information that is new. Dates are not always displayed prominently on websites, and so it is easy to stumble upon old, outdated news. You could be relying on statistics that are outdated, have been retracted, or that applied to a different year than the one you're interested in. Re-posters sometimes alter key information in the process; don't assume that content has been re-posted without alterations.

One tool to help identify an altered article is *the Wayback Machine* (named in a nod to Jay Ward's Peabody and Sherman cartoon from the 1950s and 1960s). The Wayback contains snapshots of the World Wide Web at different points in time. The archive isn't continuous—it takes snapshots at irregular intervals—but it can be helpful in conducting research and validating information to see what websites looked like in the past. www.http://webarchive.org. Related to the Wayback are services that alert you when the content of a web page changes, such as http://www.watchthatpage.com/.

What domain is the web page in? Like the Old West, there are good sides of town and sketchier sides. Official and authenticated government sites are granted special domains indicated by the extensions: .gov for the U.S. (federal, state, and local), .gc.ca for Canada, .gov.uk for the United Kingdom (central and local). Other official extensions include .mil (US military). Within the .gov domain in the United States, there are subdivisions. Each state has its own second-level or subdomain (e.g., .colorado.gov and .nebraska.gov), as do some cities (e.g., nyc.gov, burlingtonvt.gov) and public schools (the Westminster, California, school district is wsd.k12.ca.us; Dallas County public schools are dallascountytexas.us). To complicate matters, some official government sites use other domains, which makes it more difficult to authenticate them, such as Florida (www.StateOfFlorida.com), Broward County (www.broward.org), and the cities of Chicago (www.cityofchicago.org) and Madison (www.cityofmadison.com). In these cases, where you can't rely on the domain name to verify the site, there are other methods described below.

Recognized postsecondary institutions in the United States (colleges, universities, etc.) can apply for the .edu domain. *These are administered by a nonprofit organization named Educause, under an agreement with the U.S. Department of Commerce.* The system isn't perfect and a few diploma mills and other unsavory institutions have slipped through. See U.S. Department of Education. (n.d.). Diploma mills and accreditation—diploma mills. Retrieved from http://www2.ed.gov/students/prep/college/diplomamills/diploma-mills.html

The most well known domain is perhaps .com (for commercial), and the official sites for U.S. and some international corporations generally use it. It's an easy way to verify the identity of a site. If you want the manufacturer's information about a drug, Pfizer.com is a company site, Pfizer.info may or may not be. Look carefully at the URL. www.ChaseBank.verify.com and www.Microsoft.Software.com are not official websites of those companies just because the company name is in the URL—what counts is the name of the company *just before* the .com (in this case, verify.com and software.com are the web providers, not at all the same thing as Microsoft and Chase Bank).

Different countries have their own domains, and in many cases, these are used for any website originating within that country, public or private. [http://www.domainit.com/domains/country-domains.mhtml]. Some of these include .ch (Switzerland), .cn (China), .de (Germany), .fr (France), and .jp (Japan). These can be further subdivided, such as .ac.uk and .ac.jp for academic institutions, and the self-explanatory .judiciary.uk, .parliament.uk, and .police.uk.

What domain does the site come from and is it appropriate for the source? IRS.com and InternalRevenue.com are not official websites of the U.S. government because they don't have a .gov extension (even though the typeface of IRS.com looks very official). It is easy for crooks to make an official-looking web page.

It is easy to obtain information on the website's registered owner by going to networksolutions.com. For example, if you look up Ford.com, you'll get a readout that indicates the owner to be:

Ford Motor Company
20600 Rotunda Drive ECC Building
Dearborn MI 48121
US
dnsmgr@FORD.COM +1.3133903476 Fax: +1.3133905011

This appears to be the actual Ford Motor Company (you can verify their address using a search engine). (It is possible that hackers could take over Ford.com and fill it with false information. Common sense prevails; if the content seems odd, try contacting the company through conventional means, post your observation to a social networking site, or just wait—the company's own web technicians will usually be able to restore things in a matter of hours or days.)

Is it somebody's personal page or is it a professional organization? If a webpage is unfamiliar, acquaint yourself with the people behind it. Look for links that say "about us" or anything that will reveal the credentials, philosophy or political perspective of the organization that has responsibility for the site. There are issues here of both expertise and bias. Does the author possess the relevant credentials or expertise to be qualified to write on the topic? A religious organization opposing fracking may not have the technical expertise to discuss the environmental and engineering considerations; the Coffee Importers Association of America may not provide the best information about the health benefits of green tea. Hobbyists can be enthusiastic and even eloquent, but it doesn't mean that they are credible experts.

Do reputable pages link to this page? You can use Alexa.com to find out by pasting the URL you're interested into Alexa's search box, or by putting the URL into your search engine preceded by the word link: This will return pages that link to the URL you put in. You can also restrict this list by indicating sites that come from certain domains, such as .edu or .gov by using the phrase site:.edu. So for example, if you wanted to see only links from government sources to the website of the United States Fencing Association (www.usfa.org) you'd type: link:usfa.org site:.gov

341 **a fee in a parallel world of pseudoacademia** Kolata, G. (2013, April 8). Scientific articles accepted (personal checks, too). *The New York Times*, p. A1.

341 **"Most people don't know the journal universe. . . ."** Quoted in Kolata, G. (2013, April 8). Scientific articles accepted (personal checks, too). *The New York Times*, p. A1.

341 **predatory open-access journals** Beall, J. (2012). Predatory publishers are corrupting open access. *Nature*, *489*(7415), 179.

and, Scholarly Open Access. (n.d.). Beall's list: Potential, possible, or probably predatory scholarly open-access publishers. Retrieved from http://scholarlyoa.com/publishers/

342 **"Founded by pharmacists in 1995 . . ."** RxList. (2013, November 20). About RxList. Retrieved from http://www.rxlist.com/script/main/art.asp?articlekey=64467

342 **According to Alexa** This is only as of this writing, and Alexa's contents will no doubt have changed by the time this book is published. Alexa. (n.d.). How popular is rxlist.com? Retrieved from http://www.alexa.com/siteinfo/rxlist.com#trafficstats

342 **If you follow the link** rainbow05 (U14629301). (2010, October 26). Morphine/Butrans patches [Online forum comment]. Retrieved March 30, 2014, from http://www.bbc.co.uk/ouch/messageboards/NF2322273?thread=7841114

342 **A Google search of .gov sites** Search term used was *link:.rxlist.com site:.gov.*

342 **Among the first reported links** Graham, D. (1996, December). Scientific cybernauts: Tips for clinical medicine resources on the Internet. Retrieved from http://www.nih.gov/catalyst/back/96.11/cybernaut.html

347 **the money sits in an escrow account** FFreeThinker. (2012, May 23). *James Randi and the one million dollar paranormal challenge* [Video file]. Retrieved from http://www.youtube.com/watch?v=4Ja6ronAWsY

and, James Randi Educational Foundation. (2014). One million dollar paranormal challenge. Retrieved from http://www.randi.org/site/index.php/1m-challenge.html

and, The Skeptic's Dictionary. (2013, December 29). Randi $1,000,000 paranormal challenge. Retrieved from http://skepdic.com/randi.html

347 **"If psychic powers exist, they are impish . . ."** Ross, L., personal communication. February, 1991.

347 **with longer life span** Thomas, D. R. (2006). Vitamins in aging, health, and longevity. *Clinical Interventions in Aging*, *1*(1), 81–91.

347 **(As it happens, the evidence . . .)** Ebbing, M., & Vollset, S. E. (2013). Long-term supplementation with multivitamins and minerals did not improve male US physicians' cardiovascular health or prolong their lives. *Evidence Based Medicine*, *18*(6), 218–219.

347 **pirates is caused by global warming** Open letter to Kansas school board. Chart: Global average temperature vs. number of pirates. (n.d.). Retrieved from http://www.venganza.org/about/open-letter/

349 **90% of lung cancers occur among smokers** Centers for Disease Control and Prevention. (2013, November 21). Lung cancer. Retrieved from http://www.cdc.gov/cancer/lung/basic_info/risk_factors.htm

349 **toxic chemicals within the smoke-damaged** Centers for Disease Control and Prevention. (2013, November 21). Lung cancer. Retrieved from http://www.cdc.gov/cancer/lung/basic_info/risk_factors.htm

349 **prone to smoking** Eysenck, H. J. (1988). Personality, stress and cancer: Prediction and prophylaxis. *British Journal of Medical Psychology, 61*(1), 57–75.

and, Eysenck, H. J., Grossarth-Maticek, R., & Everitt, B. (1991). Personality, stress, smoking, and genetic predisposition as synergistic risk factors for cancer and coronary heart disease. *Integrative Physiological and Behavioral Science, 26*(4), 309–322.

350 **Denver suburbs than in other parts of the country** Fulton, J. P., Cobb, S., Preble, L., Leone, L., & Forman, E. (1980). Electrical wiring configurations and childhood leukemia in Rhode Island. *American Journal of Epidemiology, 111*(3), 292–296.

and, Savitz, D. A., Pearce, N. E., & Poole, C. (1989). Methodological issues in the epidemiology of electromagnetic fields and cancer. *Epidemiologic Reviews, 11*(1), 59–78.

and, Wertheimer, N., & Leeper, E. D. (1982). Adult cancer related to electrical wires near the home. *International Journal of Epidemiology, 11*(4), 345–355.

350 **Fish oil, rich in omega-3 fatty acids** Kris-Etherton, P. M., Harris, W. S., & Appel, L. J. (2002). AHA scientific statement: Fish consumption, fish oil, omega-3 fatty acids, and cardiovascular disease. *Circulation, 106*(21), 2747–2757.

350 **on the efficacy of fish oil** Kromhout, D., Yasuda, S., Geleijnse, J. M., & Shimokawa, H. (2012). Fish oil and omega-3 fatty acids in cardiovascular disease: Do they really work? *European Heart Journal, 33*(4), 436–443.

351 **In the summer of 2013, a study** Brasky, T. M., Darke, A. K., Song, X., Tangen, C. M., Goodman, P. J., Thompson, I. M., . . . Kristal, A. R. (2013). Plasma phospholipid fatty acids and prostate cancer risk in the SELECT trial. *Journal of the National Cancer Institute, 105*(15), 1132–1141.

351 **operates a website that sells omega-3 capsules** Dr. Hyman. (n.d.). Search results: Omega 3. Retrieved from http://store.drhyman.com/Store/Search?Terms=omega+3

351 **He voices concern about the way the blood** Hyman, M. (2013, July 26). Can fish oil cause prostate cancer? *Huffington Post.* Retrieved from http://www.huffingtonpost.com/dr-mark-hyman/omega-3s-prostate-cancer_b_3659735.html

352 **Incidentally, the American Heart Association** American Heart Association. (n.d.). Fish 101. Retrieved from http://www.heart.org/

352 **soy is preventive against prostate cancer** Yan, L., & Spitznagel, E. L. (2009). Soy consumption and prostate cancer risk in men: A revisit of a meta-analysis. *The American Journal of Clinical Nutrition 89*(4), 1155–1163.

352 **reduce prostate cancer recurrence** Bosland, M. C., Kato, I., Zeleniuch-Jacquotte, A., Schmoll, J., Rueter, E. E., Melamed, J., . . . Davies, J. A. (2013). Effect of soy protein isolate supplementation on biochemical recurrence of prostate cancer after radical prostatectomy. *JAMA, 310*(2), 170–178.

352 **And yet we then must make a certain choice** Another aspect of critical thinking asks, Is the information plausible?

In 1984, Fred Sanford, an unknown amateur songwriter from the Midwest, sued CBS Records, claiming that the Michael Jackson/Paul McCartney hit song "The Girl Is Mine" was stolen from him. How plausible is it that two of the most prolific and successful songwriters of our time would steal a song from someone else? Or that a completely unknown amateur songwriter with no track record could have written an internationally known hit single? How plausible is it that Michael Jackson could even have heard Sanford's version? Any one of these is implausible, and for all three to occur seems very unlikely. This doesn't prove that "The Girl Is Mine" wasn't plagiarized, but it's important to weigh the facts and consider their probabilities and likelihoods. Sanford lost his suit.

Plausibility depends on context. If a valuable—and highly insured—piece of jewelry goes missing from a person's home, her claim that "somebody must have stolen it" may seem implausible, especially if it turns out that she was deeply in debt, there is no sign of forced entry into the home, and the home security cameras don't show any unauthorized entry.

Conservative lawmakers were worried that unwed mothers were having babies just in order to claim the cash benefits available from the government. A newspaper article reported that a law was passed denying such benefits and that within six months of passage the birth rate dropped significantly. The claim itself is plausible—birthrates rise and drop all the time due to various factors—but the implication that the drop was due to the passage of the law is implausible, given that it takes nine months after conception to carry a baby to term.

353 **According to the NBA, Shaq is seven feet one inch** NBA. (n.d.). *Shaquille O'Neal.* Retrieved from http://stats.nba.com/playerProfile.html?PlayerID=406

The tallest NBA players in history were Manute Bol and Gheorghe Mureşan at seven feet seven inches.

Brown, D. H. (2007). *A basketball handbook.* Bloomington, IN: AuthorHouse, p. 20.

356 **For over a decade, when Google conducted** Carlson, N. (2009, November 5). Answers to 15 Google interview questions that will make you feel stupid. *Business Insider.*

and, Fateman, R., professor of Computer Science/EECS (retired), University of California at Berkeley, personal communication. January 13, 2013.

356 **How much does the Empire State Building weigh?** Carlson, N. (2009, November 5) Answers to 15 Google interview questions that will make you feel stupid. *Business Insider.*

and, Fateman, R., Professor of Computer Science/EECS (retired), University of California at Berkeley, personal communication. January 13, 2013.

361 **a cubic foot of wood is about 50 pounds** A cubic foot of maple wood actually weighs 44 pounds—well within an order of magnitude of this estimate. Reade Advanced Materials. (2006, January 11). Weight per cubic foot and specific gravity. Retrieved from http://www.reade.com/Particle_Briefings/spec_gra2.html

361 **that steel is about 10 times heavier than that** A cubic foot of steel weighs about 490 pounds. Reade Advanced Materials. (2006, January 11). Weight per cubic foot and specific gravity. Retrieved from http://www.reade.com/Particle_Briefings/spec_gra2.html

363 **estimate of the weight, and it comes in at 365,000 tons** esbnyc.com, the official site of the Empire State Building.

363 **". . . The weight of the building is the weight . . ."** Anonymous, personal communication. April 6, 2012.

364 **describes playing one session of this game** Ackerman, D. (2012). *One hundred names for love.* New York, NY: W. W. Norton & Company, pp. 82–83.

365 **"When you make a mistake say to yourself 'how interesting!' . . ."** Zander, B., personal communication. July 25, 2013.

365 **students must be taught to play an *active* role** American Library Association, Association of College & Research Librarians. (1989). *Presidential committee on information literacy: Final report.* Retrieved from www.ala.org/ala/mgrps/divs/acrl/publications/whitepapers/presidential.cfm

See also, Mackey, T. P., & Jacobson, T. E. (2011). Reframing information literacy as metaliteracy. *College & Research Libraries, 72*(1), 62–78.

366 **". . . 'Knowing' is the absence of alternatives of other beliefs."** Kahneman, D., personal communication. July 10, 2013, Stanford, CA.

367 **Eric Mazur in his book** *Peer Instruction* Mazur, E. (1996). *Peer instruction: A user's manual.* New York, NY: Pearson.

367 **Such rapidly presented events capture** This is a direct quote from Lillard, A. S., & Peterson, J. (2011). The immediate impact of different types of television on young children's executive function. *Pediatrics, 128*(4), 644–649. Retrieved from http://pediatrics.aappublications.org/content/early/2011/09/08/peds.2010-1919.full.pdf+html

368 **versus watching the slower-paced public television cartoon *Caillou*** Tanner, L. (2011, December 9). *SpongeBob SquarePants* causes attention problems: Study. *Huffington Post.* Retrieved from http://www.huffingtonpost.com/

368 **Second, *SpongeBob* is designed for six- to eleven-year-olds** This is pointed out by Nickelodeon spokesperson David Bittler, quoted in:

Tanner, L. (2011, December 9). *SpongeBob SquarePants* causes attention problems: Study. *Huffington Post.* Retrieved from http://www.huffingtonpost.com/

CHAPTER 9

370 **organization gives us the freedom to be a bit disorganized** Merrill, D. C., & Martin, J. A. (2011). *Getting organized in the Google era: How to stay efficient, productive (and sane) in an information-saturated world.* New York, NY: Random House.

371 **the U.S. Interstate Highway System** Office of Highway Policy Information (2011). *Table HM-20: Public Road Length—2010* (Report). U. S. Department of Transportation, Federal Highway Administration.

371 **Even numbers increase as they move from south to north** This is the opposite of the rule for the old U.S. highway system, and so is confusing for many people. A foundational principle of human interaction design is that if a standard exists, it should be used.

Norman, D. A. (2013). *The design of everyday things.* New York, NY: Basic Books.

372 **In New York State, I-87 is a principal north-south highway** This map is taken from Wikipedia and is in the public domain; http://en.wikipedia.org/wiki/Interstate_Highway_System#cite_note-hm20-2 Permission is explicitly granted by the creator, Stratosphere, for reuse. http://en.wikipedia.org/wiki/File:FHWA_Auxiliary_Route_Numbering_Diagram.svg

372 **The periodic table of the elements** The Periodic Table image is retrieved from http://0.tqn.com/d/chemistry/1/0/1/W/periodictable.jpg and tagged as "Public Domain—Free to Use" by Bing.

372 **Elements with similar physical properties** In the sixth and seventh row of the table, just to the right of Barium and Radium, the structure of the table breaks down. Rather than there being a single element in column 3, there are fifteen

elements squeezed in before Hafnium and Rutherfordium (respectively) in column 4. Moving down the table, atoms become larger and heavier. When they reach a certain minimum critical size and weight, the way that electron orbitals were being filled becomes less stable around Barium (atomic weight = 56) and so a new scheme for adding electrons, the f orbital, becomes necessary. In other words, the apparent discontinuities in the table occur as a function of the way the electron orbits are filled in this subset of elements. Classing them together in this way is further justified because these elements show a great deal of chemical similarities with one another. The sixth-row squeezed elements are called Lanthanides (rare earth metals) and those in the seventh row are called Actinides (radioactive metals).

I'm grateful to Dr. Mary Ann White for this explanation. White, M. A., personal communication. November 16, 2013.

374 **a familiar name with a new face** Remembering names is made difficult by the fact that unlike the limited set of names, there is an almost unlimited inventory of faces, and we don't have very good ways of describing and remembering them; memory for faces tends to be more holistic than feature based. If asked to describe a particular face, you might say, "She has an upturned nose, a dimple on her chin, and very thin eyebrows," but it's unlikely that you simply plucked this description from your memory; on the contrary, you probably pictured the face holistically and then tried to verbalize the features.

375 **if you meet a man named Adiel** The basic technique of remembering names you've never heard before goes back to the Greeks, who wrote extensively about memory—they had to, because a great deal of ancient knowledge was passed on orally.

375 **John Lennon recalled in an interview** Sheff, D. (2000). *All we are saying: The last major interview with John Lennon and Yoko Ono.* New York, NY: St. Martin's Press.

375 **in their dreams** James Watson. (2005, February). *James Watson: How we discovered DNA* [Video file]. Retrieved from http://www.ted.com/talks/james_watson_on_how_he_discovered_dna

and, Kaempffert, W. (Ed.). (1924). *A popular history of American invention* (Vol. 2). New York, NY: Scribner's Sons.

375 **The three books of *Thus Spake Zarathustra*** Cybulska, E. M. (2000). The madness of Nietzsche: A misdiagnosis of the millennium? *British Journal of Hospital Medicine, 61*(8), 571–575.

375 **"Every writer wonders where fictional ideas come from. . . ."** Robinson, M. (2013, November 17). The believer. Review of *A Prayer Journal* by F. O'Connor. *The New York Times Book Review*, p. 11.

376 **"*I* have not written this."** Hospers, J. (1985). Artistic creativity. *The Journal of Aesthetics and Art Criticism, 43*(3), 243–255.

376 **The central executive approach to problem solving** Claxton, G. (1999). *Hare brain, tortoise mind: How intelligence increases when you think less.* New York, NY: Harper Perennial.

and, Gediman, P., & Zaleski, J. (1999, January, 11). [Review of the book *Hare brain, tortoise mind: How intelligence increases when you think less* by Guy Claxton]. *Publisher's Weekly, 246*(2), p. 63.

376 **All bits are created equal** After writing this, I discovered the same phrase "all bits are created equal" in Gleick, J. (2011). *The information: A history, a theory, a flood.* New York, NY: Vintage.

376 **Information has thus become separated from meaning** Gleick writes "information is divorced from meaning." He cites the technology philosopher Lewis Mumford from 1970:

"Unfortunately, 'information retrieving,' however swift, is no substitute for discovering by direct personal inspection knowledge whose very existence one had possibly never been aware of, and following it at one's own pace through the further ramification of relevant literature."

Gleick, J. (2011). *The information: A history, a theory, a flood.* New York, NY: Vintage.

377 **"The medium does matter. . . ."** Carr, N. (2010). *The shallows: What the internet is doing to our brains.* New York, NY: W. W. Norton & Company.

377 **"too much information, and so much of it lost."** Gleick, J. (2011). *The information: A history, a theory, a flood.* New York, NY: Vintage.

380 **"The greatest scientists are artists as well"** Calaprice, A. (Ed.). (2000). *The expanded quotable Einstein.* Princeton, NJ: Princeton University Press, p. 245.

and, Root-Bernstein, M., & Root-Bernstein, R. (2010, March 31). Einstein on creative thinking: Music and the intuitive art of scientific imagination. *Psychology Today.*

380 **"When I arrived at Intel . . ."** Otellini, P., personal communication. July, 2013.

382 **a post on Reddit** Baez, J. (2013, September 29). Levels of excellence [Weblog]. Retrieved from http://johncarlosbaez.wordpress.com/2013/09/29/levels-of-excellence/

ACKNOWLEDGMENTS

I am grateful to my fiancée, Heather Bortfeld, for many thousands of hours of illuminating discussion and true companionship.

I thank everyone at the Wylie Agency, especially Sarah Chalfant and Rebecca Nagel, for helping me to externalize by letting me hand thousands of details over to them. Dawna Coleman and Karle-Philip Zamor of my laboratory at McGill, gracefully took care of thousands of other details, in many cases without my even knowing about them, and were instrumental in the completion of the book. Stephen Morrow, Stephanie Hitchcock, LeeAnn Pemberton, Daniel Lagin, Christine Ball, Amanda Walker, Diane Turbide, and Erin Kelly from Penguin were all incredibly helpful in bringing the manuscript to life.

For commenting on drafts, providing advice, and answering questions, I'm indebted to Mark Baldwin, Perry Cook, Jim Ferguson, Michael Gazzaniga, Lee Gerstein, Dan Gilbert, Lew Goldberg, Scott Grafton, Diane Halpern, Martin Hilbert, Daniel Kahneman, Jeffrey Kimball, Stephen Kosslyn, Lloyd Levitin, Shari Levitin, Sonia Levitin, Linda, Ed Littlefield Sr., Ed Littlefield Jr., Vinod Menon, Jeffrey Mogil, Regina Nuzzo, Jim O'Donnell, Michael Posner, Jason Rentfrow, Paul Simon, Malcolm Slaney, Stephen Stills, Tom Tombrello, and Steve Wynn. Additional helpful comments came from David Agus, MD, Gerry Altmann, Stephen Berens, MD, Melanie Dirks, Baerbel Knaüper, David Lavin, Eve-Marie Quintin, Tom Reis, Bradley Vines, and Renee Yan. For generously sharing their thoughts on organization, I'm grateful to José Cerda, Alexander Eberts, Stan

McChrystal, Paul Otellini, and Sting. A team of students in my lab helped to verify and format the end notes: Michael Chen, Caitlin Courchesne, Lian Francis, Yueyang Li, and Tyler Raycraft. Len Blum furnished a brilliant set of close edits.

Thanks to Joni Mitchell for letting me write part of the book in her backyard (and I've got to get myself back to the garden . . .) and to McGill University and the Minerva Schools at KGI for their encouragement and support during the writing of this book. In particular, Martin Grant, dean of science at McGill, and David Zuroff, chair of psychology at McGill, helped to create an enviable environment of productivity and intellectual stimulation.

INDEX

Note: Page numbers in *italics* indicate illustrations.

ILLUSTRATION CREDITS

Page vii © 2014 Daniel J. Levitin.

Page viii © 2014 Daniel J. Levitin.

Page 21 © 1990 by Roger N. Shepard, used with permission. Roger Shepard is the sole owner of the 1990 copyright for this image," Terror Subterra," which first appeared in his book *Mind Sights*, published in 1990 by W. H. Freeman and Company, New York.

Page 21 © 1990 by Roger N. Shepard, used with permission. Roger Shepard is the sole owner of the 1990 copyright for this image, "Terror Subterra," which first appeared in his book *Mind Sights*, published in 1990 by W. H. Freeman and Company, New York.

Page 42 Illustration by Dan Piraro © 2014. Used with permission.

Page 66 This image has been redrawn and is based on the one appearing in Labov, W. (1973). The boundaries of words and their meanings. New ways of analyzing variation in English, 1, 340–373.

Page 83 Picture of his and her key holders, available for purchase, from: http://www.keanmiles.com/key-holder.html and http://www.moderngent.com/j-me/his_hers_keyholders.php.

Page 182 © 2014 Dan Piraro. Used with permission.

Page 205 © 2014 Daniel J. Levitin.

Page 264 © 2002. This figure taken from Edwards, A., Elwyn, G., & Mulley, A. (2002). Explaining risks: Turning numerical data into meaningful pictures. *BMJ, 324*(7341), 827–830.

Used with permission.

Page 271 © 2014 Daniel J. Levitin.

Page 272 © 2014 Daniel J. Levitin.

Page 273 © 2014 Daniel J. Levitin.

Page 315 © 2014 Daniel J. Levitin.

Page 316 © 2014 Daniel J. Levitin.

Page 372 Illustration by Wikipedia user Stratosphere. Used by permission.

Page 373 Illustration by Wikipedia user DePiep. Used by permission.

Page 407 © 2014 Daniel J. Levitin.

Also by *New York Times* bestselling author
DANIEL J. LEVITIN

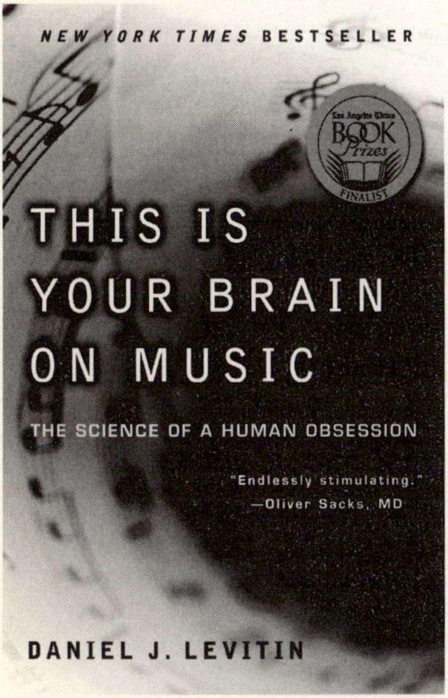

978-0-452-28852-2

978-0-452-29548-3

www.daniellevitin.com

PLUME